FIELDS OF

READING

MOTIVES FOR WRITING

Fifth Edition

FIELDS OF
READING

MOTIVES FOR WRITING

Fifth Edition

Nancy R. Comley
QUEENS COLLEGE, CUNY

David Hamilton
UNIVERSITY OF IOWA

Carl H. Klaus
UNIVERSITY OF IOWA

Robert Scholes
BROWN UNIVERSITY

Nancy Sommers
HARVARD UNIVERSITY

St. Martin's Press

NEW YORK

Sponsoring editor: Donna Erickson
Development editor: Kristin Bowen
Editorial assistant: Jason Noe
Manager, publishing services: Emily Berleth
Associate editor, publishing services: Meryl Gross
Project management: Books By Design, Inc.
Production supervisor: Joe Ford
Marketing manager: Karen Melton
Cover design: Patricia McFadden
Cover art: © Estate of Grant Wood/Licensed by VAGA, New York, NY.
Reynolds House, Museum of American Art, Winston-Salem, North
Carolina

Library of Congress Catalog Card Number: 97-65197

Manufactured in the United States of America.

3 2 1 0 9
f   e   d   c

For information, write:
St. Martin's Press, Inc.
175 Fifth Avenue
New York, NY 10010

ISBN: 0-312-15314-7

Acknowledgments

Maya Angelou. "Graduation." Excerpt from pages 164–180 in *I Know Why the Caged
Bird Sings* by Maya Angelou. Copyright © 1969 by Maya Angelou. Reprinted by permission of Random House, Inc.

Acknowledgments and copyrights are continued at the back of the book on
pages 741–745, which constitute an extension of the copyright page.

Contents

Contents

CONTENTS

CONTENTS

CONTENTS

Contents

CONTENTS

CONTENTS

Contents

Contents

Thematic Table of Contents

VALUES AND BELIEFS

CULTURES IN COLLISION AND CONTACT

RACE AND RACISM

THE EXPERIENCE OF WOMEN

INTERPRETING THE BODY

VIOLENCE AND WAR

LIFE AND DEATH

OBSERVING ANIMALS

UNDERSTANDING THE PHYSICAL WORLD

HUMAN PORTRAITS

TEACHING, LEARNING, AND SCHOOLING

HEALTH, DISEASE, AND MEDICINE

INTERPRETING THE PAST

THEMATIC TABLE OF CONTENTS

INTERPRETING CURRENT AFFAIRS AND CONTEMPORARY HUMAN EXPERIENCE

INTERPRETING THE ARTS AND POPULAR CULTURE

MYTHS AND RITUALS

Preface

Fields of Reading: Motives for Writing contains seventy-five readings from a broad range of academic and professional writing, organized around four main purposes for writing: Reflecting, Reporting, Explaining, and Arguing. In focusing on purposes, we give students and instructors the opportunity to explore the complex relationships among writers and readers that vary according to "what" and "why" people write and read. The new title for the fifth edition, *Fields of Reading: Motives for Writing,* more clearly identifies our goal of providing students with tools to establish and develop their own motives for writing throughout their college and professional lives.

HIGHLIGHTS

New Introduction to the Reading and Writing Process. The introduction explains and illustrates the interrelationship between reading and writing processes, primarily through an examination of a specially commissioned essay by Patricia Hampl. In "Reviewing Anne Frank," Hampl reflects on her own response to a particular writing assignment, a book review for the *New York Times.* In doing so, she both illustrates her own writing process and demonstrates that even accomplished writers struggle with some of the same challenges student writers face.

The introduction also includes a brief but important note for students on Acknowledging Your Sources. This section explains the purposes of documentation and offers various methods of meeting this basic obligation. We have also reprinted in this section Hampl's published review, "The Whole Anne Frank." These introductory materials, like the rest of the book, are meant to present reading and writing, not in abstract terms, but through discussion and examples that vividly demonstrate what is actually involved in each activity.

Flexible Organization. We have grouped the seventy-five selections into four broad rhetorical categories: Reflecting, Reporting, Explaining, and Arguing. These categories, we believe, represent essential kinds of reading and writing in virtually every academic or professional area. In every field, individuals consider past experience (reflecting), convey information (reporting), make sense of knowledge (explaining), and debate controversial ideas and issues (arguing). Within each of the four categories, we have grouped the selections by academic fields: Arts and Humanities, Social Sciences and Public Affairs, and Sciences and Technologies. We hope that this dual organization will assist instructors in discovering and assigning selections for a variety of classroom purposes.

New Selections. Twenty-seven of the seventy-five selections are new to the fifth edition. These new selections include pieces by a culturally varied array of writers, critics, and scholars who did not appear in the fourth edition, such as Amy Tan, William Gass, Evelyn Fox Keller, Douglas R. Hofstadter, Margaret Atwood, and William Least Heat-Moon. These new essays continue to provide students models of finely crafted writing from different fields.

New Thematic Connections. Adding new selections has also made it possible for us to provide nineteen new sets of thematically related pieces to support instructors who teach by theme. These sets feature new thematic clusters on Anne Frank, Interpreting the Body, Myths and Rituals, and Smoking. As a result, students will have numerous opportunities to read and consider different perspectives on a single issue or to explore a particular topic in depth. The updated Thematic Table of Contents makes it possible to teach any of the selections in terms of its themes or area of interest. Students are encouraged to pursue thematic relationships among the selections by responding to the special questions called Making Connections following each piece.

Extensive Critical Apparatus. Much of our critical apparatus focuses on the rhetorical concepts and techniques that apply to reading and writing across the curriculum as introduced in the preface, For Students. The detailed introductions to each of the four main sections, Reflecting, Reporting, Explaining, and Arguing (which are illustrated with passages from the anthologized readings) define the type of writing and discuss its use in differing fields and situations. The introductions also identify and explain the rhetorical methods used to achieve each type of writing's aims, for example, how description and narration are basic in reporting or how analogy, comparison and contrast, definition, and illustration are basic to explaining. All of the rhetorical aims and modes covered in the introductions are also referenced in the Rhetorical Index. The headnote for each piece identifies and, wherever necessary, explains the professional field of its author and the rhetorical context or source of its original publication. Likewise, the questions following each selection call for reading and writing that relate form and style to purpose, subject, and academic field.

ACKNOWLEDGMENTS

For their detailed reactions to the fourth edition of *Fields of Writing* and suggestions for improving the fifth edition, we are grateful to the following reviewers:

Glen Scott Allen, Towson State University; Michelle Bellavia, Southeastern Louisiana University; Mary Bly, University of California, Davis; Susan Callender, Sinclair Community College; Gail Caylor, Phoenix College; Al DeFazio, George Mason University; Michelle W. Dega, Boise State University; Debra M. Dove, James Madison University; Diane Dowdey, Sam Houston State University; Julia Ferganchick-Neufang, Murray State University; Louisa Franklin, Young Harris College; Stanley A. Galloway, Bridgewater College; Carol Peterson Haviland, California State University—San Bernadino; Lilith M. Haynes, Harvard University; Michael Hennessy, Southwest Texas State University; Petrina Jackson, Elgin Community College; Debra S. Knutson, Illinois State University; Jodi Labonte, University of New Hampshire; Dan Lackey, Boston University; Sohui Lee, Boston University; Susan Lowry, University of Wisconsin; Andrew S. McClure, University of New Mexico; Sara McLaughlin, Texas Tech University; David G. Miller, Mississippi College; Joseph R. Millichap, Western Kentucky University; Floyd Moos, College of the Canyons; Susan J. Norton, Boise State University; Shelby J. Pierce, Owens Community College; William Provost, University of Georgia; John Reiss, Western Kentucky University; Jerome Shea, University of New Mexico; Linda Stewart, University of New Hampshire; Marianna Torgovnick, Duke University; and Barbara Valdez, Boise State University.

N.R.C.
D.H.
C.H.K.
R.S.
N.S.

For Students

Fields of Reading: Motives for Writing, Fifth Edition, is intended to help you develop the abilities in reading and writing that you will need as you move from one course to another, one field of study to another, throughout your college career. In some senses, of course, all areas of study expect the same things of you—namely, close and careful reading as well as clear and exact writing, with an attentiveness above all to information and ideas. But the particular kinds of information, ideas, and concerns that distinguish each field of study also call for somewhat different reading and writing abilities. A book review for a literature course, for example, requires a different form and style from a lab report in physics. So we have tried to give you a sampling of the varied fields of writing you are likely to encounter in the academic world.

Most undergraduate schools are organized around some version of the traditional division of studies into "the humanities," "the social sciences," and "the sciences." The humanities generally include fields of learning that are thought of as having a cultural orientation, such as language, literature, history, philosophy, and religion. The social sciences, which include such fields as anthropology, economics, education, political science, psychology, and sociology, deal with social institutions and the behavior of their individual members. The sciences include fields of knowledge that are concerned with the natural and physical world, such as astronomy, botany, chemistry, physics, and zoology.

These traditional divisions of study are closely affiliated with applied areas of study and work that also exist in the professional world. The humanities, for example, are closely allied with the arts; the social sciences, with public affairs such as business and government; and the sciences, with technology. These divisions and clusterings of fields—Arts and Humanities, Social Sciences and Public Affairs, Sciences and Technologies—are so broadly applicable that we have used them as one of the organizing principles in our table of contents.

Like any set of categories, these divisions are a convenient, but by no means foolproof, system of classification. Although the system can help you to understand the academic world, it does not reflect the exact state of affairs in every specialized field at every college and university. Specialists in a particular field sometimes migrate from one area of learning to another, from the social sciences to the sciences, for example, according to the orientation of their research in a particular project. Or specialists from several fields may form an interdisciplinary area of research, such as environmental studies, which involves a wide range of academic disciplines—botany, chemistry, economics, philosophy, political science, and zoology. So, the writing that results from these projects often can be categorized in more than one broad area of learning.

The writing we have collected in *Fields of Reading* can be understood not only in terms of the area of learning that it represents, but also in terms of the particular purpose it is meant to achieve. Every piece of writing, of course, is the product of an author's personal and professional motives, so in a sense the purposes for writing are as varied and ultimately mysterious as are authors themselves. But setting aside the mysteries of human nature, it is possible to identify and define a set of different purposes for writing, which we refer to as Reflecting, Reporting, Explaining, and Arguing, one or another of which predominates in most academic and professional writing. So, we have used this set of purposes as the major organizing principle in our table of contents.

By Reflecting, we mean a kind of writing in which authors are concerned with recalling and thinking about their past experience, for personal experience is often an especially valuable source of knowledge and learning. By Reporting, we mean writing that is concerned primarily with conveying factual information about some particular aspect of the world, past or present. By Explaining, we mean writing that is concerned primarily with making sense of information or shedding light on a particular subject. By Arguing, we mean writing that is given to debating controversial explanations, values, or beliefs. Like our other categories, these are convenient, but not rigid, modes of classification. So, they need to be used tactfully, with an awareness that to some degree they are bound to overlap. Most pieces of explanation, for example, will at some point involve reporting, if only to convey the information or subject to be explained. And most pieces of argument will call for some explanation, if only to make clear the issues that are at odds with one another. But generally you will find one or another of these purposes to be dominant in any particular piece of writing.

We think that an awareness of these basic purposes can be especially helpful both in the process of reading and in the process of writing, no matter what academic or professional field is involved. So, we have introduced each section of our collection with an essay on Reflecting, Reporting, Explaining, or Arguing. In these essays, you will find detailed definitions and examples of each purpose, as well as explanations and illustrations of how to carry it out in differing fields and situations. Each selection is accompanied by a brief headnote, explanatory footnotes where necessary, and questions for you to think about in your reading and writing. In addition, each selection is also followed by questions to help you make connections among related readings in this collection.

Immediately following this preface, you will find an introduction to reading and writing. In the first section, we show an actual example of how one writer goes through the process of composing a piece of writing; in Reading and Rereading, we discuss various ways to read and understand the pieces in this book or any other material you might encounter in your studies; and in Acknowledging Sources, we explain various forms of documentation and why such acknowledgment is important in every field of study. This introduction, like the headnotes, questions, and sectional introductions, is meant to help you become a thoughtful and responsible reader and writer. The rest is up to your instructor, your classmates, and you.

Introduction: Why Write?

No matter what your field of study, you will need to read and write. Often you will need not just to read, but to read critically, not just to write, but to write clearly, sometimes with argumentative force. This book brings together many readings with those goals in mind. Among the readings you will find quite a few that discussion will only make richer. You should also find some that prompt you to write, perhaps even without an assignment. In putting this collection together, we have sought out readings that we have found provocative as readers and as teachers. Although we realize that a textbook is intended for the classroom and study, that hardly means it must be an enemy of pleasure. If you carry it with you on vacation or keep it by your bed, we will be pleased, of course, and not entirely shocked.

We assume that reading and writing are the daily concerns of your course, skills to be developed in interaction with your classmates and instructor rather than taught from a book's introduction. Nevertheless, in this introduction we wish to offer a few observations that readers and writers might well keep in mind. By emphasizing the situation of writers and writing, we will focus on what we take to be the deeper intention of your course. Along the way, however, we will touch frequently on reading, too, since no secure line can be drawn between them.

WRITING AS CONVERSATION

Scholars and professional writers take part in extended discussions, which we can think of as conversations. For example, suppose a new discovery is made about the prehistory of humankind, how ancient our species is, or when humans first migrated to the Americas. Any such discovery provokes discussion, modification, and dissent, all of which take place, back and forth, in the specialized publications of the field. Or suppose a less academic situation — a book review or a business report. In these examples as well, writing follows from much that has been said and written before, at the very least a book to be reviewed in the one case and a business situation with its own history — part oral, part written, and to some extent observable — in the other. Our motivation for writing often stems from wanting to join in a discussion about such matters and to offer understandings that are our own view of things.

In a short essay that follows, the writer Patricia Hampl reflects on how she once joined in such a discussion. Her essay is about writing a book review.

1

"Literature is a conversation," she says, and her review will play a part in one conversation. Quickly, therefore, Hampl conveys an image of herself as a reader. She has read the book under review. As she reveals in her essay, she has reviewed several other books before this one, and along the way, she has read numerous other reviews. How else would she know what a review is, much less have an idea of how to make hers in some way unusual?

In addition to hints about her reading, Hampl's essay allows us to consider her motivation to write. It is difficult to write well without motivation, and Hampl's motivation is complicated. She is moved by the book under review, a new edition of *The Diary of a Young Girl* by Anne Frank, and she wants to express that emotion. Our best writing usually follows from taking a personal interest in our topic, which Hampl has certainly done. But writing a review for a leading paper like the *New York Times* will also influence her standing in the literary community, which may play a part. Moreover, the *Times* will pay her for her work—no insignificant matter. Most of all, however, Hampl conveys a sense of urgency about the book. If money or standing were primary, she could have sought out other assignments rather than accepting this one.

For most student writers, the motivation for writing is normally a mixture of the same sorts of things: grades, class standing, and convictions about our subjects parallel the motivations Hampl brought to her work. Clearly, the last of these is the most important. When the first two are primary, the writer is simply doing a job. When the latter takes over, the writer becomes more of a presence in the writing and begins to express him- or herself.

So it is that when Hampl found herself caught up in the story of Anne Frank, she began with the following two, matter-of-fact paragraphs. The whole of her review can be found at the end of this introduction (p. 18).

> On Tuesday, March 28, 1944, Gerrit Bolkestein, Education Minister of the Dutch Government in exile, delivered a radio message from London urging his war-weary countrymen to collect "vast quantities of simple, everyday material," as part of the historical record of the Nazi occupation.
>
> "History cannot be written on the basis of official decisions and documents alone," he said. "If our descendants are to understand fully what we as a nation have had to endure and overcome during these years, then what we really need are ordinary documents—a diary, letters."

STORIES IN OUR WRITING

Straightforward as they may appear, these few sentences imply a story—stories within stories for that matter. Minister Bolkestein was aware that he was living through a significant historical moment. He foresaw composing a record of that moment that would stand as history, a history derived from a collection of "ordinary documents." He imagined future readers who would need to understand what the Dutch people had endured. Their understanding would be shaped by the stories such documents could offer. And as we will see, his words stimulated one writer, Anne Frank, to think of her diary differently.

But his words also played a role in the secondary story of Hampl's writing her review. In "Reviewing Anne Frank," the essay that follows, Hampl's story begins as she accepts the assignment to review the "Definitive Edition" of Anne Frank's *Diary*, a later, more complete edition than the one first published in 1947. Although Hampl's attitude toward reviewing books is positive and she thinks of it as a "pleasure" akin to the pleasure of reading, she found this assignment "daunting" as none other. She struggled to begin, and when she finally managed that, she launched herself by way of Bolkestein's remarks.

One story, then, signaled by the two short paragraphs above, is the opportunity Hampl seized to enter into a "conversation" when she agreed to review Anne Frank's book. Her agreement meant that she would participate in a larger public discussion. Every time you take up an essay assignment, you too are entering into a discussion of some sort. If we are speaking only to ourselves, it is unlikely that readers will sympathize with us much. If instead we discover a way to join in a conversation already begun, we are much more likely to be heard. Thus the importance of another story hinted at here, one having to do with the beginning Hampl found in Bolkestein's message. In those remarks she found a point of entrance that would lift her away from speaking to herself and make it much more likely that she would connect, through her writing, with us.

Let us turn now to Hampl and to her story.

REVIEWING ANNE FRANK
Patricia Hampl

Book reviewing is generally regarded as humble literary work, the bread-and-butter labor of the writing life, far removed from the expressive glories of poetry or fiction. At worst, reviewing is classed as hackwork. Not by me, though. For some reason, I have always harbored an idealistic, even a romantic, affection for reviewing. This romance may be rooted in the fact that my first published work, in my college newspaper when I was nineteen, was a book review—of a new book of poems called *Ariel* by someone named Sylvia Plath.

Although the job demands that a reviewer note the successes and failures in a book, reviewing has never struck me as having much to do with assigning scores or handing out demerits. The reviewer's job—and pleasure—is akin to any reader's. It is the pleasure of talk. Fundamentally, literature is a conversation, strangely intimate, conducted between writer and reader—countless writers, unknown readers. If nobody *talks* about books, if they are not discussed or somehow contended with, literature ceases to be a conversation, ceases to be dynamic. Most of all, it ceases to be intimate. It degenerates into the author's monologue or just a private mutter. Without the reader's response, a book would go silent, like a struck bell that gives no resonance. Reviews are the other half of a conversation that the author of a book begins. Without them, literature would be oddly mute in spite of all those words on all those pages.

But I have never had an assignment as daunting as the one given me to review the new "Definitive Edition" of Anne Frank's *Diary*. For many reasons, the *Diary* is a book like no other. For one thing, virtually every other book I have reviewed has just come off the press. A reviewer is usually a kind of first reader, an explorer describing a new book, like a new country, to the people who have yet to travel there. But who does not know about Anne Frank and her heartbreaking diary? It was first published almost fifty years ago and has been translated into virtually every language in the world that sustains a book culture. Most readers know this book, like very few others, from childhood, and they carry it into adulthood. Even if they haven't read it, people know the story and the essential personality of its extraordinary author. Besides the familiarity of the book, who on earth would claim to "review" Anne Frank? The book seems to defy the very enterprise of book reviewing. I suppose that the emotion ruling me as I approached my task was a paralyzing shyness: who was I to write about this beloved and historic icon of the Holocaust?

In the face of all this, my first act was to procrastinate as long as I could. I did everything to keep from writing the review. I was very good at this. I read the book slowly, I underlined passages that struck me, I took notes, jotting down lines from the *Diary*, some of them passages I remembered with surprising sharpness from girlhood when I had first read the book, some of them new to me. The more I felt the power of the book, the more hopeless I felt. I missed the first deadline and called my editor, begging for an extension. Granted! A reprieve.

Then I procrastinated some more. I developed a sudden urgency about 5 cleaning my oven and sorting out my sock drawer. I called friends, made lunch dates (I never go out to lunch when I'm working). I asked my friends what *they* thought about Anne Frank. I had a ferocious resistance to writing the review. I found yet another way to avoid writing that I could at least call "research": I dug up an essay about Anne Frank by the poet John Berryman, which I remembered having read or having heard about years before. I took notes on *that*.

I was genuinely fascinated, moved even, by the Berryman essay, "The Development of Anne Frank," which I saw from a note in the text had been written in 1967. I had been Berryman's student at the University of Minnesota that very year, taking two courses in "Humanities of the Western World" from him in a packed, overheated room with fifty or sixty other undergraduates. I found myself thinking about this great poet, my old teacher, about the fierce way he

4

had talked about literature, his uncanny ability to bring a roomful of under-graduates to tears just by reading aloud the farewell scene between Hector and Andromache in the *Iliad*. I thought with sorrow of his suicide only a few years after that, how he had jumped to his death from a bridge I walked across every day. I couldn't remember his ever saying anything about Anne Frank, but read-ing his essay about her all these years later brought him powerfully back to me, the force of his inquiring mind, his determination to understand what was at stake in her book. I still hadn't written a word.

But maybe at last my mind had wandered not away from the task at hand, but right into it. Though I ended up referring briefly to a remark in Berryman's essay when I wrote my own review (a kind of private homage to him), it wasn't so much what his essay said that began to unlock my own timidity. Rather, it was the tone I felt in his essay, a voice that was so poised on *trying to under-stand* that it had no room for the kind of hand-wringing and worry that I was indulging in myself.

Berryman began by telling how he had first come across Anne Frank's *Diary*—in 1952 when the first installment of the translated text appeared in *Commentary* magazine. "I read it with amazement," he says in his essay. He was so galvanized by the writing that, he says, "The next day, when I went to town to see my analyst, I stopped in the magazine's offices . . . to see if proofs of the *Diary's* continuation were available, and they were." Then, "like mil-lions of people later," he wrote, "I was bowled over with pity and horror and admiration for the astounding doomed little girl."

But he didn't stop with this emotional anchor. He demanded, right from the start, that he think as well as feel. "But what I *thought* was: a sane person. A sane person, in the twentieth century." I recognized that he had found the tip of his subject: how had such extraordinary sanity come to be developed in the crushing circumstances of Anne Frank's life? It wasn't necessary to know the details of Berryman's own tragic end to feel his urgency in searching for "a sane person in the twentieth century."

I liked the naturalness of this beginning, the casualness of his saying he was 10 "bowled over." I liked how, having established his feeling, he refused to dwell on it but pushed on to a thought. I could feel a mind at work—and more than that, I felt a story unfolding. He was writing a *story*, I suddenly thought, the story of his relation to this book. The *ideas* were like characters in the story that he kept looking at from one angle and then another, to make sense of them, to come to a conclusion, much the way a story must bring its characters to some resolving, if mysterious, finale.

Strangely enough, it was at this point (if I remember correctly) that I made my first mark on paper, my first stab at my own response to Anne Frank. I wrote the first three paragraphs of the review, more or less as they stand now, quite easily, as if there had been no procrastination, no moaning and groaning at all for several weeks of fretful nonwriting. After reading Berryman's essay, I knew what to do—at least for three paragraphs.

The connections between his essay and my review are not obvious. No one, reading his opening about being bowled over and then mine, which is a straightforward piece of historical information, would imagine that I had finally been nudged off the dime by Berryman's essay. His tone is personal and immediate. Mine is distanced (I don't make use of the first-person pronoun anywhere in my entire review) and rests its authority on certain historical facts I am able to present to the reader.

I got the hint about the Dutch education minister's clandestine radio message from the foreword to the "Definitive Edition," but I tracked down the exact quotation of the speech from another source at the library. If I wasn't going to allow myself the kind of authority and presence that Berryman had with the use of the personal pronoun, I needed to achieve that sense of immediacy another way. Direct quotation, I knew instinctively, would enliven this bit of historical information.

I tried to make Anne Frank's knowledge of the minister's radio message part of this story—as indeed it really was. I wanted the reader to see history happening as it happened for Anne Frank herself. That is why I began the review in a narrative, storylike way: "On Tuesday, March 28, 1944, Gerrit Bolkestein, Education Minister of the Dutch Government in exile, delivered a radio message from London . . ." To bolster the authority of this information in every way possible—and thereby bolster my own authority as the writer of the piece—I even checked at the library to find out what day of the week March 28 fell on in the year 1944 so that, casually, I could note that it was a Tuesday. I wanted to seduce the reader with the authority of simple facts. Words *are* small, but each one can count for a lot. And maybe I wasn't attempting to "seduce" my readers, but to assure them.

It is odd—even to me—that reading Berryman's very personal (though certainly highly intellectual and closely analytical) essay should have shown me the way into my own piece about Anne Frank. I had a number of constraints that hadn't hampered him. For one thing, I had much less space: my editor had allotted me a certain number of words and no more. Berryman had written an essay, a much more open form; I was writing a review.

Still, many reviewers rightly use the first-person voice, and Berryman certainly had won me over partly because of his very immediate presence in his own essay. So why did I steer away from that voice? I think I understood, after reading Berryman, the different task I had before me, especially given my space limitations and my audience in a newspaper. I wasn't coming upon Anne Frank's *Diary* as it came out in proofs for the first time. I was responding to a definitive edition of a book that has long been a classic of postwar literature. I did not need to present myself as having been moved by the *Diary*: History had provided several generations of such readers. But I benefited from the freedom of Berryman's prose, the genuineness of his inquiry. It was a model for me—not a model of style, but of intention.

6

Also, while I had been procrastinating by having lunch with my friends, one of my companions mentioned that there had been (and continues to be) an ugly and quite demented attempt to deny the authenticity of the *Diary*. Like many anti-Holocaust theories, this one tried to prove that while there might have been a little girl named Anne Frank who had died during the war of "natural causes" (or in some versions had not died but been "lost" or who was herself a fabrication), this child had never written a diary. *The Diary of a Young Girl*, these conspiracy theorists claimed, had been written by adults engaged in a "Jewish plot"—by Anne Frank's father (whose presence as the sole survivor of his murdered family this plot does not account for) or by others.

It was all quite mad, and like all such attempts to deny the truth of history, it was very disturbing and obviously fired by racial hatred. I wanted to be sure nothing I wrote could even remotely be used for such evil. The reason these allegations about the *Diary* had won any attention at all hinged on the fact that there were indeed several versions of Anne Frank's diaries. I studied the distinctions among the various texts carefully and attempted to present them briefly but clearly by making reference to the "Critical Edition," which had been published in 1986. I wanted to refute these very allegations, crazy and repugnant as they were, and to use my review, in part, to alert readers to false claims made in this regard.

Reading Berryman's essay had made me especially aware of the time that had passed between his first response to the book in 1952, hardly seven years after Anne Frank's death in Bergen-Belsen, and my reading of the 1995 "Definitive Edition" when she would have been sixty-six. I felt my task was to mediate time and history, at least in a modest way. I had to give readers some of the basic biographical information that for most readers, I knew would be unnecessary, but I also had to place the book in its public history.

With this in mind, I made reference at the end of the review to its age—fifty years old—and to Philip Roth's use of Anne Frank as a fictional character in his novel *The Ghost Writer*. I wanted to show how Anne Frank has entered our lives as a permanent presence, that to invoke her name is to invoke a person we know and who shall always be missing because her presence in her book has made her so alive it is "unthinkable and disorienting," as I say in my review, that she should have been snuffed out.

I remember feeling a kind of relief (not satisfaction, but the more unburdened feeling that the word *relief* suggests) when I stumbled on the word *disorienting*. I felt that this had something to do with the enduring grief and regret that mention of Anne Frank brings forward within us. I felt that my sense of being "disoriented" by her death was related to Berryman's relief in finding a "sane person in the twentieth century." We *should* be disoriented by such hellish hatred: I was writing my review, after all, as children were dying from similar sectarian hatred in Bosnia. I, too, needed to find a sane person in the twentieth century.

Finally, I wanted to remind people of the extraordinary person Anne Frank was, the splendid writer, the utterly natural girl-woman, and the gifted thinker. All my notes paid off, just as my luncheon with my friend had: I had many passages that I was able to use to present Anne Frank to readers not only as the icon of a murdered child, but as a strong and vital writer. I came away from my reading of the *Diary* convinced absolutely that had she lived, Anne Frank would have written many books and that we would know her not only as the author of her diary.

When I was a girl first reading the *Diary*, I had treasured it because of how Anne fought and contended with her mother, just as I did, how she battled to become a person—the very thing Berryman honored most in her, too. I *needed* Anne Frank then, not because she was the child who died and put a face on the six million murdered (I was not yet capable of taking in that historical fact), but because, like me, she was determined to live, to grow up to be herself and no one else. She was, simply, my friend. I don't think I was able to keep in mind that she was dead. I went to her *Diary* as she went to Kitty, for a friendship not to be found anywhere else but in books. As Anne Frank wrote to Kitty in a letter in her red plaid notebook, "Paper is more patient than people." It is the secret motto not only of a passionate teenager, but of any writer.

About two weeks after my review was published, I received a small white envelope, addressed in a careful hand in blue ink, forwarded to me from the *New York Times*, which had received it. There was no return address, but the envelope was postmarked New York. A fan letter, I thought with a brief flutter of vanity.

Inside was a single sheet, my name written again with the careful blue ink, and below that a crazy quilt of black headlines apparently photocopied from various articles in newspapers and periodicals. All of them claimed in their smudged, exclamatory way, to have evidence of the "Anne Frank Zionist Plot" or the "Frank Lies." The headlines were all broken off and crammed into one another; bits and pieces of the articles to which they belonged overlapped. There wasn't a complete sentence on the entire mashed and deranged page.

But there it was: the small insane mind responding spasmodically to the expansive sane person the poet John Berryman had been so relieved to discover, the same sane person so many girls recognize as their truest friend as they move into the uncharted territory of womanhood. I stood there holding that piece of paper (it literally felt *dirty*, perhaps because of the smudged typefaces, which looked like old-fashioned pornography), disoriented all over again.

And then I did the only thing possible: I burned it. Somehow it required burning, not just tossing out. I burned it in the kitchen sink and washed away the ashes. I still don't know what it will take to convince me of the world's capacity to hate life, that this dark instinct does exist. Anne Frank, I reminded myself, knew this hard truth as a child. And she refused to cave in to it even as she acknowledged it. I was glad I had acknowledged this when I quoted her: "I hear the approaching thunder that, one day, will destroy us too, I feel the suffering of millions." The conversation she began with Kitty, her imaginary correspondent to whom she addressed her diary, was founded on a discipline of compassion. Even in acknowledging her own likely death, she felt not only for herself, but felt "the suffering of millions."

This was the sane person who, Berryman says at the end of his essay, "remained able to weep with pity, in Auschwitz, for naked gypsy girls driven past to the crematory." She is the sane person we still seek at the end of the terrible twentieth century.

ENTERING THE CONVERSATION

Hampl's essay contains elements familiar to us all. She procrastinated. Daunted by the task, she found sock drawers to organize and sudden opportunities to lunch with friends. But she also read and reread the *Diary*, underlined useful passages, and thought ahead to her work.

One trustworthy motive for the writing to come was that Hampl cared deeply about this book, a "beloved and historic icon of the Holocaust" as she calls it. Hampl had known the *Diary* from childhood, and she assumed that this experience would be true for large numbers of her readers. Especially for women who grew up after World War II, *The Diary of a Young Girl* has gone beyond being an icon of the Holocaust and has succeeded as a poignant and persuasive account of growing up.

But Hampl's sense of the conversation before her is complicated. She not only knew and felt moved by the *Diary*, she knew and was "fascinated" by an essay on it written by a former teacher. Consequently, she felt as responsible to him as she did to Anne Frank. You can find this essay, John Berryman's "The Development of Anne Frank," later in this volume (p. 356).

Searching for a way to launch her own work, she not only immersed herself in the *Diary*, but read and reread Berryman's essay. In the end, it was not so much his specific ideas that shaped her response, as it was the example he set of pursuing an idea with conviction, of letting his ideas become, as she observes, "characters" in the story of John Berryman thinking about Anne Frank. The spur, though, that brought her first words to the page came from a hint she found in the foreword to the "Definitive Edition."

This is a crucial moment in Hampl's story of her writing because it underscores her resourcefulness. Bolkestein's plea is not quoted in that foreword; it is only mentioned. Hampl had to track it down and find the exact quotation in the library, but she does not explain how she decided to do so. How did it occur to her that remarks heard over the radio, and unknown to her so far, would make a strong opening for her review? Hampl says she "wanted the reader to see history happening as it happened for Anne Frank herself," but where did this approach, so different from Berryman's, come from? Hampl does not address this question directly, although she does observe that she

9

knew "instinctively" that "direct quotation . . . would enliven this bit of historical information."

We should take note of this moment because thoughts like these allow us to
find our own approach as we join a conversation. Whereas Berryman came to
his essay through a personal story (and, as Hampl also makes clear, through a
very personal concern for the nature of sanity and madness), Hampl begins
with historical information couched in direct quotation. Moreover, Hampl
went one canny step farther. Knowing the day of Bolkestein's address and finding the text of it, she decided to "bolster" her authority by providing the day of
the week on which March 28 fell in 1944. This extra, unexpected step, uncovering the telling detail that clinches a part of her story, is a hallmark of a strong
writer. It is the hallmark equally of the student who has gotten into her subject.
Hampl wished to "seduce" her readers "with the authority of simple facts." Accordingly, she made the effort to locate and verify more than we may have
thought was needed. Certainly, the day of the week is a detail we do not expect, which may be exactly why it attracts us.

In this example we can see how writing tends to be embedded in larger stories, and that most often, when we trace those stories, we find that they have
everything to do with our motivation to write. Here then is one more story, a
particularly telling one, that further shapes Hampl's review:

> In her diary the next day, Anne Frank mentions this broadcast,
> which she and her family heard on a clandestine radio in their Amster-
> dam hiding place. "Ten years after the war," she writes on March 29,
> "people would find it very amusing to read how we lived, what we ate
> and what we talked about as Jews in hiding."

Amusing, as Hampl is quick to observe, is hardly the word we would choose
now, but looking past the tragedy of Frank's situation, we can see how she, too,
was moved to contribute to a larger conversation and to think of herself less as
a young woman with a diary than as a writer. Consequently, as Hampl observes
in her review, Frank "immediately set about organizing the diary entries, giving
the residents of the 'Secret Annex' pseudonyms like characters in a novel, rearranging passages for better narrative effect."

As you may already know, Anne Frank began her diary when she was given
a small plaid notebook for her thirteenth birthday. Not long after, she took it
with her into hiding. Very quickly, Frank invented a necessary friend, Kitty,
who became her imagined reader. She began as almost all writers begin, in a
private world, taking notes, keeping a journal meant only for an intimate audience, writing "letters" to "dear Kitty." Although one can hardly imagine a more
intimate audience than a secret, imaginary playmate, no doubt over the two
years of her writing, Frank grew in confidence and prepared herself more or
less unconsciously for a larger audience. Thus we may conjecture that
Bolkestein's plea came at an appropriate time for her, precisely when she was
ready, even eager, to enlarge the world of her conversation. A more practiced

writer by then, Frank began to think more expansively. "I'd like to publish a book," she remarks. (You can trace more of this story in the excerpt "At Home, at School, in Hiding" from *The Diary of a Young Girl* beginning on p. 171.)

Two other strands of this conversation deserve notice. First, Berryman wrote in response to Saint Augustine, Sigmund Freud, and Bruno Bettelheim, whose "The Lesson of Anne Frank" begins on page 621. However much confidence Berryman expresses that his own thoughts matter and that he enjoys the freedom to record them, he was as aware as Hampl of how his own thinking had been stimulated and shaped by others. His indebtedness is not specific enough to require elaborate footnotes. Nevertheless, you can trace his thinking to these prior sources, and in one amusing footnote (p. 358), you can catch Berryman's reading of Bettelheim.

The final piece in this conversation is the letter Hampl received after her review was published. The sender, a fervent denier of Anne Frank, was also moved to write, or, let us say, to assemble a worded message. We will not agree that he or she entered into a conversation; still it is impossible to deny that for a moment one more opinion is heard. The voices that take part in a written conversation are often more varied than we might imagine; some are ugly.

REVIEWING THE WRITING PROCESS

Hampl's essay tells us a good deal about her writing process, one that is ongoing, acquiring clarity and focus in stages. Keeping in mind the significant steps of Hampl's process will help you prepare your own writing assignments. Note especially how revision happens by increments, and at all stages.

Getting Started and Overcoming Procrastination. Hampl approached her review in "a paralyzing shyness" and with an urge to procrastinate through a long period of reading and taking notes. Some of those notes would prove useful; some would not. At this early stage, Hampl did not discriminate among them. Her reading and note taking led instead to more procrastination by way of luncheon dates and conversation with friends, which in turn led finally to something that Hampl was willing to call research.

Exploring a Topic and Gathering Information. Another writer, John Berryman, a poet and scholar, and Hampl's former teacher, had also written about Anne Frank, so Hampl turned to his essay. She found herself fascinated by Berryman's work on their common subject. Suddenly Hampl had writing to react to, inspiring her to review her notes and distinguish the more valuable from the less. This was the first important step of her revising process: a general eagerness to write about the *Diary* was replaced by a more focused topic.

Finding a Beginning. As Hampl observes, her mind "had wandered not away from the task at hand, but right into it." She was drawn into "a story unfolding," that of Berryman's relation to the *Diary*. As Hampl recognized that

11

"he had found the tip of his subject," she discovered that his example had "nudged" her "off the dime," and soon she had her own opening paragraphs.

Doing Additional Research. Having taken the hint from the foreword to the "Definitive Edition," Hampl went to the library to track down the exact quotation she wanted. No longer following Berryman, she followed her own lead. Now she understood better that she did not share Berryman's perspective. Instead, she developed two different motivations for writing her review.

First, she stressed a "kinship" she felt with Anne Frank's experience of becoming a young woman. This Anne Frank, whom Hampl had taken from the first to be a friend, was also a fine writer, one who would have published more books had she lived. This conviction reinforced Hampl's desire to write. But she needed to offer reason for it, even if her conviction lies beyond absolute proof. She did so by describing Frank's power as a writer, her writerly authority on a subject she and Hampl share—becoming a woman and a person. This culminated in Hampl's recognizing "the motto of a writer" in one of Frank's remarks, "Paper is more patient than people."

These are good reasons for Hampl to find "kinship" with her subject. Thus they reinforce her second motivation, that she give no aid to deniers of the Holocaust, people whom Hampl is ready to call evil. Her commitment to that task inspired further library research. Hampl couldn't just deny the accusations swirling about; she needed to assemble evidence against them, so she "studied the distinctions among the various texts carefully and attempted to present them briefly but clearly."

Producing a First Draft. You may have noticed that Hampl does not talk about her first or second draft as such. Although *draft* is a word that Hampl does not use, she describes thinking about her topic and writing. She discovered ideas about what she needed to know and went to the library or elsewhere to find out. All the while she took notes, which later became explanations in her draft. Hampl does not say how many hours or days this took. But we get the sense from reading her essay that by writing, she explained her discoveries and her thinking to herself. When she had covered all that she felt compelled to say, she had a first draft.

Revising. Most writers today use word processors. Revision has never been easier; we can run through our writing again and again, making changes along the way without retyping the whole piece. However, with the use of word processors, writers leave less of a trail of their revisions than they once did, since the process is more continuous. In Hampl's essay, though, we can find several clues to her revision process.

First she tells us that after reading and thinking about Berryman she suddenly started to write and had her first three paragraphs all at once. Perhaps she touched them up a little but, nevertheless, those first paragraphs came quickly, and she was on her way. But what was the lag between that first start and the next? Where did the next impulse to proceed come from? Hampl's comment on Frank's word *amusing* is what follows in the review. Had a few minutes passed, a few hours, or a day before she wrote that next paragraph? As writers, we rarely set pen to paper, or our fingers to the keyboard, and just keep going. We write a bit, move back to the beginning, read through it all, and continue. Something in what we have written spurs the next thought. Whether or not we began with a list of topics, or an outline, or just with ideas in our head, as we write, our writing makes its own suggestions. All good writers learn to be alert to those suggestions.

Later Hampl says, "I remember feeling a kind of relief (not satisfaction, but the more unburdened feeling that the word *relief* suggests) when I stumbled on the word *disorienting*." Did Hampl find the word she wanted in the first act of writing that sentence, or did it occur afterward, on one of her later passes through her work? We cannot know for certain. But her own yoking of *stumbling* with *relief* is a fine shorthand for what we look for in revision: a sense of where a problem lies and a glimpse, however stumbling it may seem, of how we may deal with that. Stumbling in this case is a kind of lucky lurching ahead. It is a discovery, and a happy one, as Hampl's word *relief* suggests. Such discoveries are the rewards of revision. They come from paying close attention to our first drafts, from reading and rereading them.

Finally, returning to the first sentence of Hampl's review ("On Tuesday, March 28, 1944, Gerrit Bolkestein, Education Minister of the Dutch Government in exile, delivered a radio message . . ."), note that the detail she secured last she placed first. First the day of the week, then the date, then Bolkestein's name and title. Hampl tells us that she first found reference to the quotation, then looked up the exact quotation, then thought to make its date as exact as possible. In her writing, however, she inverted that order because she found the order as phrased above the most satisfying. That decision is another sign of Hampl's revising as she works. Revision is much more than catching errors of grammar and spelling; it is primarily our efforts, first to discover how to say things better, then equally to identify what else we need to find out.

Drawing Conclusions. The conclusions reached by Frank, by Berryman, and then by Hampl are never "the conclusion," wrapped up once and for all. A vital subject can always be extended; further refinements and angles can always be found. In other words, in principle, serious work always remains "under revision."

Some revisions prove indefensible, as Hampl records by reference to the letter she received. Holocaust deniers apparently wish to argue that if Anne Frank was indeed a real person, she died of "natural causes." Their vicious approach thrives on a mean-spirited insistence on narrow literalism, and accounts of Anne Frank's death hands them a crumb to work with.

For example, an Academy Award–winning feature documentary, *Anne Frank Remembered* (1996), includes interviews with Dutch survivors of the

Holocaust, several of whom knew Anne Frank. One survivor, Hanneli Goslar, speaks of meeting her at Bergen-Belsen and talking with her through a barbed wire fence. Another, Janny Brandes-Brilleslijper, the woman who first informed Otto Frank of his daughters' deaths only months after the end of the war, repeats that information for the camera, telling how the sisters died in misery of malnutrition and typhus, exposed to the cold in their bunks by the barracks door. Only the perverse would call their deaths "natural"—Anne and her sister Margot suffering the merciless conditions of Bergen-Belsen until they roll wasted from their bunks in their sleep—but Holocaust deniers do. They seize on illness as our normal understanding of "natural causes," ignore all other details about Bergen-Belsen, and insist that Anne Frank was simply sick.

Some arguments are best not joined, some conversations better refused than taken up. That is the choice Hampl makes, wisely it seems. Instead, she rids herself of the letter she received, for there is other, healthier work to do.

READING AND REREADING

If you have taken an interest in Patricia Hampl's story and in her example, you may have already done several things common to most writers. Having read her essay and this introduction's comments on it, you may have read Hampl's review or the excerpt from Frank's diary, or the essays by Berryman and Bettelheim. You may have gone to the library to look up related work or may have logged on to the Internet to see what you could find. No doubt you haven't taken in everything all at once. More than likely, you have gone back over some of this material and reread it.

As writers, we read and reread as we prepare to write. Anything in which we take a serious interest deserves rereading. Hampl's essay, for example, describes how she read slowly, underlined passages, jotted down lines, and took notes.

It is often useful to read things twice: skimming, or reading for an overview, then settling down to a thorough second reading. Sometimes our readings blend together, and they aren't always limited to two. We read and reread and go back to at least parts of a piece again if it is important, looking for details that we may not have caught earlier. Quite naturally, our understanding of a work becomes more subtle as we become familiar with its overall contours. Sometimes that first reading isn't really skimming, but it begins to feel like skimming as, on rereading, we notice more and more.

First Readings

To get an overall picture of a piece, begin by reading it through from beginning to end, primarily to get a sense of the author's subject, purpose, and main ideas. This initial reading will help you get acquainted with the piece as a whole. Don't get bogged down in details, but don't hesitate to note or underline important (or puzzling) words, phrases, sentences, ideas, or points that seem important and to which you may wish to return. Once you have completed your initial reading, jot down a few sentences about its main subject, purpose, points, and pertinent information.

Annotating

After you've got the gist of the piece, reread and annotate it more thoroughly. Annotations consist of explanatory notes. For example, if the piece contains words, names, titles of works, or other bits of information that you are unfamiliar with, consult dictionaries, encyclopedias, and other reference works, and make notes that you can refer to in the future.

Summarizing

If you are serious about a piece and want to test your understanding of it, one way is to write a summary. By definition, a summary will leave out much. Writing a summary requires you to discriminate the more important information from the less important information. Hampl doesn't summarize either the *Diary* or Berryman's essay completely, but she does offer partial summaries of both. These isolate what she finds of significance. The best way to see what a summary reveals is for several people to write summaries of the same text and to compare them.

Here, for example, is a summary of Hampl's essay.

> Hampl's intention is to reflect on and explain the process of writing a review of the "Definitive Edition" of Anne Frank's *Diary* for the *New York Times*. First, Hampl describes feeling paralyzed and resistant to starting her assignment. She also relates how after procrastinating, she discovered another writer's work on the subject, which helped her find inspiration for her own work. Finally, Hampl discusses her motivation to write the review, which was rooted in her desire to remind her audience of the extraordinary person Anne Frank was, and of what talent she had as a writer.

Outlining

Not all readers outline their reading, but it can be helpful. Like a summary, an outline asks you to decide what is important in something you've read. Unlike a summary, an outline also asks you to show how one important item relates to another. Often, we want to know both why and how a conclusion was reached. That conclusion will depend on evidence, and the relation of the claim to the supporting evidence can be shown in an outline.

An outline always identifies superior and subordinate items. Depending on how formal you wish to make it, those items can be labeled with letters and Roman numerals:

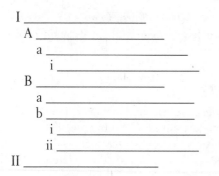

I _____
  A _____
    a _____
      i _____
  B _____
    a _____
    b _____
      i _____
      ii _____
II _____

One principle governs making any outline: superior items require subordinate items. The subordinate items are what we call support. You cannot make a claim without offering a reason. The more support you give your claims, the more willing readers will be to accept them. It's like building a firm foundation for a building. Arguments without this firm support will crumble.

In a very real sense, the lowercase letters and numerals are more important than the capital letters and capital Roman numerals. The smaller items hold the larger ones up. So if you want to think critically about an argument you have read, or if you want to avoid problems in arguments of your own, try making an outline. Be sure that the subordinate items go where they belong and that they provide secure support for your argument.

Toward the end of her essay, Hampl restates a claim that had been a strong motivation for her having written the review in the first place: "I wanted to remind people of the *extraordinary person* Anne Frank was, the *splendid writer*, the *utterly natural girl-woman*, and the *gifted thinker*." For Hampl, those last three terms add up to the first; they are what constitute an "extraordinary person," at least in this instance. Hence this outline:

  A. Extraordinary person
    a. Splendid writer
    b. Utterly natural girl-woman
    c. Gifted thinker

Now it is Hampl's responsibility to come through with evidence in support of *a, b,* and *c.* You could outline that evidence as *i, ii, iii,* and so on and arrange it beneath the lowercase letters.

ACKNOWLEDGING SOURCES

In most of the writing you will do, both during and after college, you will find yourself drawing on the ideas, information, and statements of others, interpreting this material, and combining it with your own experience, observation, and thought to generate new ideas of your own. Some of this material will come from your reading, some from lectures and class discussions, some from conversations and interviews. Our thinking does not take place in a vacuum, but is shaped by a wide array of influences and sources. In this introduction, we have seen Hampl refer to Berryman and to the Dutch minister of education, and we have mentioned that Berryman footnotes Bettelheim. Anne Frank's *Diary*, of course, has been openly acknowledged throughout and quoted several times. We have also cited a documentary film, specific information for which we found on the Internet. These are several instances of writers acknowledging their sources, specifically though still informally.

To acknowledge your intellectual debts is by no means a confession that your work is unoriginal or without merit. In fact, original work in every field invariably builds on the prior work of researchers and thinkers. Most pieces you find in this book, except for those that deal entirely with personal experience, include some kind of acknowledgment or reference to the ideas, information, or statements of others. By acknowledging their sources, the writers of these pieces implicitly establish what is new or special in their own way of thinking. The acknowledgment of sources also enables readers to verify the writer's claims and find material that they may wish to investigate in connection with their own research and writing. For a variety of important reasons, then, you should always make sure that you acknowledge the sources you have used in preparing a piece of writing.

To get some idea of the various ways in which sources can be acknowledged, note the ways different writers in this book handle this task. The different methods for acknowledging and citing sources are not just a question of differences among writers; different publications and disciplines have their own styles and standards. Within our collection, you will notice that some writers cite only the names of authors or interviewees or the titles of works from which they have gathered ideas or quoted statements. These citations are incorporated into the written discussion, as Hampl incorporates Berryman. You can see this technique used in Martin Luther King's "Pilgrimage to Nonviolence" (p. 90) and in the Associated Press's "Report of an Airplane Crash" (p. 284). Other writers use footnotes or endnotes in which they provide not only the names of authors or interviewees and the titles of works, but also dates of publication or of interviews and specific page references, as you can see by looking at Theodore R. Sizer's "What High School Is" (p. 325), Carol Gilligan's "Interviewing Adolescent Girls" (p. 409), Antonio R. Damasio's "Face Perception without Recognition" (p. 529), or Barbara Tuchman's "This Is the End of the World: The Black Death" (p. 219). Finally, instead of using footnotes, some writers provide author and page references in the text of their discussion and include more detailed publication data, such as titles and dates of publication, in a complete list of works cited at the end, as Monica M. Moore does in her "Nonverbal Courtship Patterns" (p. 469).

These various forms of acknowledgment are usually determined by the different purposes and audiences for which the pieces were written. Personal essays, newspaper reports, and magazine articles, which are written for a general audience, tend to rely on a more casual and shorthand form of acknowledgment, citing only the author or title of the source and placing that acknowledgment in the midst of the discussion. Work written for a more specialized audience, such as academic research papers and scholarly articles or books, tend to rely on more detailed and systematic forms of acknowledgment, using either footnotes or a combination of references in the text with a complete list of works cited at the end. These specialized forms vary somewhat from one field to another, but in general you will find that papers in the arts and humanities tend to follow the guidelines set down by the Modern Language Association (MLA) and that papers in the social sciences and sciences follow the system of the American Psychological Association (APA). The guidelines published by the MLA are used by writers in literature and languages as well as some other fields. For further reference, consult the *MLA Handbook for Writers of Research Papers*, 4th ed. (New York: The Modern Language Association of America, 1995). Guidelines for writers in the social sciences can be found in the manual by the APA, called *Publication Manual of the American Psychological Association*, 4th ed. (Washington, DC: American Psychological Association, 1994). Both manuals are also on-line. Their Internet addresses are <http://155.43.225.30/mla.htm> for the MLA and <http://155.43.225.30/apa/apa_index.htm> for the APA. (Note that these addresses may change.)

As you can see, making proper acknowledgment is both a matter of intellectual honesty and a social problem of many dimensions. Different groups will agree on and enforce their own standards. That goes for your writing course as well. For the moment, your college or university or perhaps your writing class is the ultimate authority for you. Therefore, don't hesitate to look to your instructor for guidance. Most instructors do have their own preferences, but they will all expect you to acknowledge your sources.

THE WHOLE ANNE FRANK
Patricia Hampl

On Tuesday, March 28, 1944, Gerrit Bolkestein, Education Minister of the Dutch Government in exile, delivered a radio message from London urging his war-weary countrymen to collect "vast quantities of simple, everyday material" as part of the historical record of the Nazi occupation.

"History cannot be written on the basis of official decisions and documents alone," he said. "If our descendants are to understand fully what we as a nation have had to endure and overcome during these years, then what we really need are ordinary documents—a diary, letters."

In her diary the next day, Anne Frank mentions this broadcast, which she and her family heard on a clandestine radio in their Amsterdam hiding place.

"Ten years after the war," she writes on March 29, "people would find it very amusing to read how we lived, what we ate and what we talked about as Jews in hiding."

The word "amusing" reads strangely now, chillingly. But her extraordinary commitment to the immediacy of individual experience in the face of crushing circumstance is precisely what has made Anne Frank's *Diary*—since the first edition of the book appeared in the Netherlands in 1947—the single most compelling personal account of the Holocaust (an account now augmented by this "Definitive Edition," published on the 50th anniversary of her death in Bergen-Belsen and containing entries not present in the earlier standard version).

Bolkestein's broadcast galvanized Anne Frank, or perhaps ignited an idea she already had: her diary, at first a private confidante, now struck her as a source for a book. "I'd like to publish a book called 'The Secret Annex,' " she writes on May 11, 1944. "It remains to be seen whether I'll succeed, but my diary can serve as the basis." She immediately set about organizing the diary entries, giving the residents of the "Secret Annex" pseudonyms like characters in a novel, rearranging passages for better narrative effect.

She was still engaged in this work when the hiding place was raided by the Gestapo on Aug. 4, 1944. Miep Gies, one of the office employees in the Frank spice and pectin firm who had been protecting the Jews hidden above the office, gathered all the diary notebooks and papers left in disarray by the Gestapo. She hid them in her desk for the rest of the war. After Anne's father, Otto Frank, returned to Amsterdam late in 1945, Miep Gies returned all the papers to him. He was the sole survivor of the eight people who had sheltered together for over two years in the annex.

Anne Frank had been keeping her diary since June 12, 1942, the day her parents gave her a red-and-white plaid notebook for her 13th birthday. Less than a month later the diary went with her into hiding.

From the first, she addressed the notebook as a trusted girlfriend: "I'll begin from the moment I got you, the moment I saw you lying on the table among my other birthday presents." A few days later this anonymous "you" becomes the imaginary "Kitty," and the entries turn into letters, giving the diary the intimacy and vivacity of a developing friendship. The growing relationship, of course, is with her own emerging self. As John Berryman said, the *Diary* has at its core a subject "even more mysterious and fundamental than St. Augustine's" in his classic "Confessions": namely, "the conversion of a child into a person."

Otto Frank, in preparing the first edition of the diary, was compelled, partly by his own sense of discretion and partly by the space limitations imposed on him by the original Dutch publisher, to limit the book. The restored entries, constituting, according to the publisher, 30 percent more material, do not alter our basic sense of Anne Frank, but they do give greater texture and nuance—and punch—to some of the hallmark concerns of the diary.

There are more searching passages about her erotic feelings and her urgent   10
curiosity about sexuality, more emphatic distancing from her dignified but apparently critical mother. None of these new entries, however, surpass the urgency shown in the standard version about the need to accomplish real work as a woman: "I can't imagine having to live like Mother, Mrs. van Daan and all the women who go about their work and are then forgotten," she writes on April 5, 1944. "I need to have something besides a husband and children to devote myself to! . . . I want to be useful or bring enjoyment to all people, even those I've never met. I want to go on living even after my death!"

The new material also includes sketches of short stories she was writing in the Secret Annex. The additions are not always whole entries or complete new letters to Kitty. Sometimes passages of only a few lines are set in a text already familiar. But the effect underscores the acuity of Anne Frank's eye, the keen relish of her descriptive powers. In one of her habitual reviews of the "inmates" of the annex, she regards the fussy dentist Dussel with the coolness of a practiced novelist: "One of my Sunday morning ordeals is having to lie in bed and look at Dussel's back when he's praying. . . . A praying Dussel is a terrible sight to behold."

Even her transports over her first kiss, with Peter van Daan, the son of the family sharing the Franks' hiding space, are subject to her mordant observation: "Oh, it was so wonderful. I could hardly talk, my pleasure was too intense; he caressed my cheek and arm, a bit clumsily." Only a born writer would snap that clear-eyed "a bit clumsily" into place, along with the body's first rhapsodic shiver of delight.

In 1986, a "Critical Edition" of the *Diary* was published that meticulously presented Anne's original diary (designated by its editors diary a), the version she was working on for her proposed book "The Secret Annex" (diary b), and the edition her father eventually published and which all the world has come to know (diary c). This monumental task included as well exhaustive scientific examination of the original documents to prove what should never have been questioned in the first place: that this is indeed the work of a girl named Anne Frank who lived and eventually died as she prophetically sensed she would: "I hear the approaching thunder that, one day, will destroy us too, I feel the suffering of millions."

The earlier "Critical Edition" is the book for research, but this "Definitive Edition," smoothly translated anew by Susan Massotty, is the reader's edition, unencumbered by notes, with only the barest afterword to conclude the story that Anne Frank was unable to finish herself.

The *Diary*, now 50 years old, remains astonishing and excruciating. It is a   15
work almost sick with terror and tension, even as it performs its miracle of lucidity. On Feb. 12, 1944, Anne Frank writes Kitty, "I feel as if I were about to explode. . . . I walk from one room to another, breathe through the crack in the window frame. . . . I think spring is inside me." The crack in the window frame was her purchase on the world: she put her nose to it and drew in life.

It is uncanny how, reading the *Diary*, one falls into escape fantasies for Anne Frank and the inhabitants of the Secret Annex. No wonder that in his 1979 novel "The Ghost Writer," Philip Roth sustains an entire section devoted to a detailed fabrication about how, after all, Anne Frank survived, how she came to America, how she lives among us still in disguise. It is unthinkable and disorienting to know that this life was crushed.

All that remains is this diary, evidence of her ferocious appetite for life. It gnaws at us still.

REFLECTING

Here in "Reflecting," as in other parts of this collection, you will encounter writing that touches on a wide range of topics—from a high school graduation in Arkansas to a sacred landmark in Oklahoma, from the structure of a grain of salt to the intricacies of memory. But you will also find that the writing in this particular section relies very heavily on personal experience. This personal element may strike you at first as being out of place in a college textbook. However, if you consider the matter just a bit, you will see that personal experience is a basic source of knowledge and understanding. Think for a moment about someone you have known for a long time or about a long-remembered event in your life; then think about what you have learned from being with that person or going through that event, and you will see that personal experience is, indeed, a valuable source of knowledge. You will probably also notice that in thinking about that person or event you rely very heavily on your remembrance of things past—on your memory of particular words or deeds or gestures or scenes that are especially important to you. Your memory, after all, is the storehouse of your personal knowledge, and whenever you look into this storehouse, you will invariably find an image or impression of your past experience. So, you should not be surprised to find the authors in this section looking into their own memories as they might look into a mirror. Ultimately, the activity of looking back is a hallmark of reflection because it involves writers in recalling and thinking about some aspect of their world in order to make sense of it for themselves and for others.

This essential quality of reflective writing can be seen in the following passage from George Orwell's "Shooting an Elephant":

> One day something happened which in a roundabout way was enlightening. It was a tiny incident in itself, but it gave me a better glimpse than I had had before of the real nature of imperialism—the real motives for which despotic governments act. Early one morning the sub-inspector at a police station the other end of the town rang me up on the phone and said that an elephant was ravaging the bazaar. Would I please come and do something about it? I did not know what I could do, but I wanted to see what was happening and I got on to a pony and started out.

23

This passage, which comes from the third paragraph of Orwell's essay, clearly presents him as being in a reflective frame of mind. In the opening sentence, for example, he looks back to a specific event from his personal experiences in Burma—to "one day" when "something happened." And in the midst of looking back, he also makes clear that this event is important to him because "in a roundabout way" it "was enlightening." Again, in the second sentence, he looks back not only to the event, "a tiny incident in itself," but also to the understanding that he gained from the event—"a better glimpse than I had had before of the real nature of imperialism—the real motives for which despotic governments act." Having announced the general significance of this event, he then returns to looking back at the event itself, to recalling the particular things that happened that day: the phone call informing him "that an elephant was ravaging the bazaar," the request that he "come and do something about it," and his decision to get "on to a pony" in order "to see what was happening."

This alternation between recalling things and commenting on their significance is typical not only of Orwell's piece, but of all the writing in this section. Sometimes, the alternation takes place within a single sentence, as in the opening of the previous passage. Sometimes, the alternation occurs between sentences or clusters of sentences, as in the following paragraph from Loren Eiseley's "The Bird and the Machine":

> I suppose their little bones have years ago been lost among the stones and winds of those high glacial pastures. I suppose their feathers blew eventually into the piles of tumbleweed beneath the straggling cattle fences and rotted there in the mountain snows, along with dead steers and all the other things that drift to an end in the corners of the wire. I do not quite know why I should be thinking of birds over the *New York Times* at breakfast, particularly the birds of my youth half a continent away. It is a funny thing what the brain will do with memories and how it will treasure them and finally bring them into odd juxtapositions with other things, as though it wanted to make a design, or get some meaning out of them, whether you want it or not, or even see it.

The first two sentences of this passage portray Eiseley as being in a contemplative mood, remembering some birds that he had evidently seen years ago in a high mountain pasture and wondering what became of them. But in the third sentence he is no longer wondering about the fate of the birds, so much as about the focus of his thoughts, about why he "should be thinking of birds over the *New York Times* at breakfast." His curiosity about the movement of his own mind then provokes him in the fourth sentence to reflect on the workings of the human brain, especially on "what the brain will do with memories." Though he ranges quite widely here and later in the piece, each image or idea that comes to his mind is occasioned either by a preceding memory or reflection or by some aspect of his immediate situation, such as his reading of the *Times*. His thoughts develop, then, by a process of association and suggestion, one thing leading to another. This linked sequence of memories, images, other bits of information, and ideas is typical of reflection. Reflective writing thus echoes the process that Eiseley attributes to the brain—calling upon memories, bringing them into "odd juxtapositions with other things," in order "to make a design, or get some meaning out of them."

The alternation between recalling and interpreting will vary from writer to writer, and from work to work, depending on the details of the experience and the author's reflective purpose. Nevertheless, every piece of reflective writing contains both kinds of material, for every reflective writer is concerned not only with sharing something memorable, but also with showing why it is memorable. And as it happens, most memorable experiences, images, or bits of information stick in our minds because they give us, as Orwell says, "a better glimpse than [we] had had before of the real nature of" someone, something, or some aspect of the world. So, as a reader of reflective writing, you should always be attentive not only to the details of an author's recollected experience, but also to the "glimpse" that it gives the author, and you, into the "real nature" of things. And in your own reflective writing, you should make sure that you convey both dimensions of your experience—both what happened and what the events enabled you to see.

THE RANGE OF REFLECTIVE WRITING

The range of reflective writing is in one sense limitless, for it necessarily includes the full range of things that make up our personal experience or the personal experience of anyone else in the world. Reflecting, in other words, may deal with anything that anyone has ever seen, heard, done, or thought about and considered memorable enough to write about. Though the range of reflective writing is extraordinarily broad, the subject of any particular piece is likely to be very specific, and as it happens, most pieces can be classified in terms of a few recurrent types of subject matter.

A single, memorable event is often the center of attention in reflective writing, as in Maya Angelou's "Graduation" or George Orwell's "Shooting an Elephant." In reflecting on this kind of subject, the author will usually provide not only a meticulous detailing of the event itself, but also some background information that serves as a context for making sense of the event. In "Graduation," for example, Angelou tells about all the pregraduation excitement in her home, at school, and around town before turning to the graduation ceremony itself. And in "Shooting an Elephant," Orwell gives an overall description of his life as a colonial officer in Burma before he turns to the story about shooting the elephant. The event, in turn, is of interest not only in itself, but also for what it reveals to the author (and the reader) about some significant aspect of experience. Thus for Angelou, graduation remains memorable because it helped her to see how African American people have been "sustained" by "Black known and unknown poets," and for Orwell, the shooting remains memorable because it helped him to see "the real nature of imperialism."

A notable person is a subject that often moves people to writing reflectively, as in N. Scott Momaday's "The Way to Rainy Mountain." In reflecting on a particular individual, writers may seek to discover and convey what they consider to be the most essential aspects of that person's character. They may survey a number of memorable incidents or images from the person's life. Momaday, for example, recalls not only the stories and legends that he heard from his grandmother, but also "the several postures that were peculiar to her" and her "long, rambling prayers."

Instead of concentrating on a particular person or event, reflective writing may center on a specific problem or significant issue in the past experience of an author, as in Frederick Douglass's "Learning to Read and Write" or Martin Luther King Jr.'s "Pilgrimage to Nonviolence." A piece with this kind of subject is likely to touch on a number of people and events, and to encompass a substantial period of time, in the process of recalling and reflecting on the problem with which it is concerned. Douglass, for example, covers seven years of his life in his piece about the problem of learning to read and write, and King recalls events and issues throughout his life that led him to espouse the principles of nonviolent resistance. In each case, the breadth of coverage serves to reveal the scope and complexity of the problem, as well as the author's special understanding of it.

As you can see from just this brief survey of possibilities, reflective writing may deal with a single event, several events, or a whole lifetime of events. It may be as restricted in its attention as a close-up or as all-encompassing as a wide-angle shot. But no matter how little, or how much, experience it takes into account, reflective writing is always decisively focused through the author's persistent attempt to make sense of the past, to push memory to the point of understanding the significance of experience.

METHODS OF REFLECTING

Your experience is unique, as is your memory, so in a sense you know the best methods to follow whenever you are of a mind to reflect on something that interests you. But once you have recalled something in detail and made sense of it for yourself, you are still faced with the problem of how to present it to readers in a way that will also make sense to them. Given the fact that your readers will probably not be familiar with your experience, you will need to be very careful in selecting and organizing your material so that you provide a clearly detailed account of it. By the same token, you will need to give special emphasis to aspects or elements of your experience that will enable readers to understand their significance. Usually, you will find that your choice of subject suggests a corresponding method of presenting it clearly and meaningfully to your readers.

If your reflections are focused on a single, circumscribed event, you will probably find it most appropriate to use a narrative presentation, telling your readers what happened in a relatively straightforward chronological order. Though you cover the event from beginning to end, your narrative should be carefully designed to emphasize the details that you consider most striking and significant. In "Shooting an Elephant," for example, Orwell devotes the largest segment in his piece to covering the very, very brief period of a few moments when he finds himself on the verge of having to shoot the elephant despite his strong desire not to do so. In fact, he devotes one-third of his essay to these few moments of inner conflict because they bring about one of his major insights—"that when the white man turns tyrant it is his own freedom that he destroys." So in telling about a memorable event of your own, you should deliberately pace your story to make it build toward some kind of climax or surprise or decisive incident, which in turn leads to a moment of insight for you (and your readers).

If your reflections are focused on a particular person, you will probably find it necessary to use both narrative and descriptive methods of presentation, telling about several events in order to make clear to readers the character and thought of the person in question. Though you rely heavily on narration, you will not be able to cover incidents in as much detail as if you were focusing on a single event. Instead, you will find it necessary to isolate only the most striking and significant details from each incident you choose to recall. Momaday, for instance, relates his grandmother's background by way of the history of the Kiowa. But to describe her individual character, he isolates particular details— her postures, her praying, her dress—that are carefully chosen to resonate with the "ancient awe" that Momaday says was "in her" and with which he regards her. So, too, in writing about an individual whom you have known, you should carefully select and arrange the details that you recall to make them convey a clear and compelling impression of that person's character.

If your reflections are focused on a particular problem or issue in your past experience, you will probably need to combine narrative, descriptive, and explanatory methods of presentation, bringing together your recollections of numerous events and persons to reveal the nature and significance of the problem. Although you will survey the problem chronologically from beginning to end, you will also need to organize your narrative so that it highlights the essential aspects, elements, or facets of the problem. For example, in "Pilgrimage to Nonviolence," King immediately focuses on the "new and sometimes complex doctrinal lands" through which he traveled. And from this point on, he recalls the various theological and philosophical ideas with which he struggled in formulating his belief in nonviolence. So in writing about a particular problem of your own, your recollections should be deliberately selected and organized to highlight your special understanding of the issue.

No matter what specific combination of methods you use in your reflective writing, you will probably find, as do most writers, that a striking recollection is the most effective way to interest your readers and that a significant observation about experience is the most rewarding means to send them on their way. In the following selections, you will get to see how a wide variety of writers use language to produce some very striking and significant pieces of reflection.

Arts and Humanities

GRADUATION

Maya Angelou

In her four volumes of autobiography, Maya Angelou (b. 1928) has written vividly of her struggles to achieve success as an actor, a dancer, a songwriter, a teacher, and a writer. An active worker in the civil rights movement in the 1960s, Angelou continues to focus much of her writing on racial issues. The following selection is from I Know Why the Caged Bird Sings *(1969), in which she writes, "I speak to the Black experience, but I am always talking about the human condition."*

The children in Stamps trembled visibly with anticipation.[1] Some adults were excited too, but to be certain the whole young population had come down with graduation epidemic. Large classes were graduating from both the grammar school and the high school. Even those who were years removed from their own day of glorious release were anxious to help with preparations as a kind of dry run. The junior students who were moving into the vacating classes' chairs were tradition-bound to show their talents for leadership and management. They strutted through the school and around the campus exerting pressure on the lower grades. Their authority was so new that occasionally if they pressed a little too hard it had to be overlooked. After all, next term was coming, and it never hurt a sixth grader to have a play sister in the eighth grade, or a tenth-year student to be able to call a twelfth grader Bubba. So all was endured in a spirit of shared understanding. But the graduating classes themselves were the nobility. Like travelers with exotic destinations on their minds, the graduates were remarkably forgetful. They came to school without their books, or tablets or even pencils. Volunteers fell over themselves to secure replacements for the missing equipment. When accepted, the willing workers might or might not be thanked, and it was of no importance to the pregradua-

---

[1]*Stamps:* a town in Arkansas. [Eds.]

tion rites. Even teachers were respectful of the now quiet and aging seniors, and tended to speak to them, if not as equals, as beings only slightly lower than themselves. After tests were returned and grades given, the student body, which acted like an extended family, knew who did well, who excelled, and what piteous ones had failed.

Unlike the white high school, Lafayette County Training School distinguished itself by having neither lawn, nor hedges, nor tennis court, nor climbing ivy. Its two buildings (main classrooms, the grade school and home economics) were set on a dirt hill with no fence to limit either its boundaries or those of bordering farms. There was a large expanse to the left of the school which was used alternately as a baseball diamond or basketball court. Rusty hoops on swaying poles represented the permanent recreational equipment, although bats and balls could be borrowed from the P.E. teacher if the borrower was qualified and if the diamond wasn't occupied.

Over this rocky area relieved by a few shady tall persimmon trees the graduating class walked. The girls often held hands and no longer bothered to speak to the lower students. There was a sadness about them, as if this old world was not their home and they were bound for higher ground. The boys, on the other hand, had become more friendly, more outgoing. A decided change from the closed attitude they projected while studying for finals. Now they seemed not ready to give up the old school, the familiar paths and classrooms. Only a small percentage would be continuing on to college—one of the South's A & M (agricultural and mechanical) schools, which trained Negro youths to be carpenters, farmers, handymen, masons, maids, cooks and baby nurses. Their future rode heavily on their shoulders, and blinded them to the collective joy that had pervaded the lives of the boys and girls in the grammar school graduating class.

Parents who could afford it had ordered new shoes and ready-made clothes for themselves from Sears and Roebuck or Montgomery Ward. They also engaged the best seamstresses to make the floating graduating dresses and to cut down secondhand pants which would be pressed to a military slickness for the important event.

Oh, it was important, all right. Whitefolks would attend the ceremony, and two or three would speak of God and home, and the Southern way of life, and Mrs. Parsons, the principal's wife, would play the graduation march while the lower-grade graduates paraded down the aisles and took their seats below the platform. The high school seniors would wait in empty classrooms to make their dramatic entrance.

In the Store I was the person of the moment. The birthday girl. The center. Bailey had graduated the year before,[2] although to do so he had had to forfeit all pleasures to make up for his time lost in Baton Rouge.

5

---

[2]*Bailey:* the author's brother. [Eds.]

My class was wearing butter-yellow piqué dresses, and Momma launched out on mine. She smocked the yoke into tiny crisscrossing puckers, then shirred the rest of the bodice. Her dark fingers ducked in and out of the lemony cloth as she embroidered raised daisies around the hem. Before she considered herself finished she had added a crocheted cuff on the puff sleeves, and a point crocheted collar.

I was going to be lovely. A walking model of all the various styles of fine hand sewing and it didn't worry me that I was only twelve years old and merely graduating from the eighth grade. Besides, many teachers in Arkansas Negro schools had only that diploma and were licensed to impart wisdom.

The days had become longer and more noticeable. The faded beige of former times had been replaced with strong and sure colors. I began to see my classmates' clothes, their skin tones, and the dust that waved off pussy willows. Clouds that lazed across the sky were objects of great concern to me. Their shiftier shapes might have held a message that in my new happiness and with a little bit of time I'd soon decipher. During that period I looked at the arch of heaven so religiously my neck kept a steady ache. I had taken to smiling more often, and my jaws hurt from the unaccustomed activity. Between the two physical sore spots, I suppose I could have been uncomfortable, but that was not the case. As a member of the winning team (the graduating class of 1940) I had outdistanced unpleasant sensations by miles. I was headed for the freedom of open fields.

Youth and social approval allied themselves with me and we trammeled   10
memories of slights and insults. The wind of our swift passage remodeled my features. Lost tears were pounded to mud and then to dust. Years of withdrawal were brushed aside and left behind, as hanging ropes of parasitic moss.

My work alone had awarded me a top place and I was going to be one of the first called in the graduating ceremonies. On the classroom blackboard, as well as on the bulletin board in the auditorium, there were blue stars and white stars and red stars. No absences, no tardinesses, and my academic work was among the best of the year. I could say the preamble to the Constitution even faster than Bailey. We timed ourselves often: "WethepeopleoftheUnitedStatesinordertoformamoreperfectunion. . . ." I had memorized the Presidents of the United States from Washington to Roosevelt in chronological as well as alphabetical order.

My hair pleased me too. Gradually the black mass had lengthened and thickened, so that it kept at last to its braided pattern, and I didn't have to yank my scalp off when I tried to comb it.

Louise and I had rehearsed the exercises until we tired out ourselves. Henry Reed was class valedictorian. He was a small, very black boy with hooded eyes, a long, broad nose and an oddly shaped head. I had admired him for years because each term he and I vied for the best grades in our class. Most often he bested me, but instead of being disappointed I was pleased that we shared top places between us. Like many Southern Black children, he lived with his grandmother, who was as strict as Momma and as kind as she knew how to be. He was courteous, respectful and soft-spoken to elders, but on the playground he chose to play the roughest games. I admired him. Anyone, I reckoned, sufficiently afraid or sufficiently dull could be polite. But to be able to operate at a top level with both adults and children was admirable.

His valedictory speech was entitled "To Be or Not to Be." The rigid tenth-grade teacher had helped him write it. He'd been working on the dramatic stresses for months.

The weeks until graduation were filled with heady activities. A group of small children were to be presented in a play about buttercups and daisies and bunny rabbits. They could be heard throughout the building practicing their hops and their little songs that sounded like silver bells. The older girls (non-graduates, of course) were assigned the task of making refreshments for the night's festivities. A tangy scent of ginger, cinnamon, nutmeg and chocolate wafted around the home economics building as the budding cooks made samples for themselves and their teachers.

In every corner of the workshop, axes and saws split fresh timber as the woodshop boys made sets and stage scenery. Only the graduates were left out of the general bustle. We were free to sit in the library at the back of the building or look in quite detachedly, naturally, on the measures being taken for our event.

Even the minister preached on graduation the Sunday before. His subject was, "Let your light so shine that men will see your good works and praise your Father, Who is in Heaven." Although the sermon was purported to be addressed to us, he used the occasion to speak to backsliders, gamblers and general ne'er-do-wells. But since he had called our names at the beginning of the service we were mollified.

Among Negroes the tradition was to give presents to children going only from one grade to another. How much more important this was when the person was graduating at the top of the class. Uncle Willie and Momma had sent away for a Mickey Mouse watch like Bailey's. Louise gave me four embroidered handkerchiefs. (I gave her crocheted doilies.) Mrs. Sneed, the minister's wife, made me an undershirt to wear for graduation, and nearly every customer gave me a nickel or maybe even a dime with the instruction "Keep on moving to higher ground," or some such encouragement.

Amazingly the great day finally dawned and I was out of bed before I knew it. I threw open the back door to see it more clearly, but Momma said, "Sister, come away from that door and put your robe on."

I hoped the memory of that morning would never leave me. Sunlight was itself young, and the day had none of the insistence maturity would bring it in a few hours. In my robe and barefoot in the backyard, under cover of going to see about my new beans, I gave myself up to the gentle warmth and thanked

God that no matter what evil I had done in my life He had allowed me to live to see this day. Somewhere in my fatalism I had expected to die, accidentally, and never have the chance to walk up the stairs in the auditorium and gracefully receive my hard-earned diploma. Out of God's merciful bosom I had won reprieve.

Bailey came out in his robe and gave me a box wrapped in Christmas paper. He said he had saved his money for months to pay for it. It felt like a box of chocolates, but I knew Bailey wouldn't save money to buy candy when we had all we could want under our noses.

He was as proud of the gift as I. It was a soft-leather-bound copy of a collection of poems by Edgar Allan Poe, or, as Bailey and I called him, "Eap." I turned to "Annabel Lee" and we walked up and down the garden rows, the cool dirt between our toes, reciting the beautifully sad lines.

Momma made a Sunday breakfast although it was only Friday. After we finished the blessing, I opened my eyes to find the watch on my plate. It was a dream of a day. Everything went smoothly and to my credit. I didn't have to be reminded or scolded for anything. Near evening I was too jittery to attend to chores, so Bailey volunteered to do all before his bath.

Days before, we had made a sign for the Store, and as we turned out the lights Momma hung the cardboard over the doorknob. It read clearly: CLOSED. GRADUATION.

My dress fitted perfectly and everyone said that I looked like a sunbeam in it. On the hill, going toward the school, Bailey walked behind with Uncle Willie, who muttered, "Go on, Ju." He wanted him to walk ahead with us because it embarrassed him to have to walk so slowly. Bailey said he'd let the ladies walk together, and the men would bring up the rear. We all laughed, nicely.

Little children dashed by out of the dark like fireflies. Their crepe-paper dresses and butterfly wings were not made for running and we heard more than one rip, dryly, and the regretful "uh uh" that followed.

The school blazed without gaiety. The windows seemed cold and unfriendly from the lower hill. A sense of ill-fated timing crept over me, and if Momma hadn't reached for my hand I would have drifted back to Bailey and Uncle Willie, and possibly beyond. She made a few slow jokes about my feet getting cold, and tugged me along to the now-strange building.

Around the front steps, assurance came back. There were my fellow "greats," the graduating class. Hair brushed back, legs oiled, new dresses and pressed pleats, fresh pocket handkerchiefs and little handbags, all homesewn. Oh, we were up to snuff, all right. I joined my comrades and didn't even see my family go in to find seats in the crowded auditorium.

The school band struck up a march and all classes filed in as had been rehearsed. We stood in front of our seats, as assigned, and on a signal from the choir director, we sat. No sooner had this been accomplished than the band started to play the national anthem. We rose again and sang the song, after which we recited the pledge of allegiance. We remained standing for a brief minute before the choir director and the principal signaled to us, rather desperately I thought, to take our seats. The command was so unusual that our carefully rehearsed and smooth-running machine was thrown off. For a full minute we fumbled for our chairs and bumped into each other awkwardly. Habits change or solidify under pressure, so in our state of nervous tension we had been ready to follow our usual assembly pattern: the American national anthem, then the pledge of allegiance, then the song every Black person I knew called the Negro National Anthem. All done in the same key, with the same passion and most often standing on the same foot.

Finding my seat at last, I was overcome with a presentiment of worse things 30 to come. Something unrehearsed, unplanned, was going to happen, and we were going to be made to look bad. I distinctly remember being explicit in the choice of pronoun. It was "we," the graduating class, the unit, that concerned me then.

The principal welcomed "parents and friends" and asked the Baptist minister to lead us in prayer. His invocation was brief and punchy, and for a second I thought we were getting on the high road to right action. When the principal came back to the dais, however, his voice had changed. Sounds always affected me profoundly and the principal's voice was one of my favorites. During assembly it melted and lowed weakly into the audience. It had not been in my plan to listen to him, but my curiosity was piqued and I straightened up to give him my attention.

He was talking about Booker T. Washington, our "late great leader," who said we can be as close as the fingers on the hand, etc. . . . Then he said a few vague things about friendship and the friendship of kindly people to those less fortunate than themselves. With that his voice nearly faded, thin, away. Like a river diminishing to a stream and then to a trickle. But he cleared his throat and said, "Our speaker tonight, who is also our friend, came from Texarkana to deliver the commencement address, but due to the irregularity of the train schedule, he's going to, as they say, 'speak and run.'" He said that we understood and wanted the man to know that we were most grateful for the time he was able to give us and then something about how we were willing always to adjust to another's program, and without more ado—"I give you Mr. Edward Donleavy."

Not one but two white men came through the door off-stage. The shorter one walked to the speaker's platform, and the tall one moved to the center seat and sat down. But that was our principal's seat, and already occupied. The dislodged gentleman bounced around for a long breath or two before the Baptist minister gave him his chair, then with more dignity than the situation deserved, the minister walked off the stage.

Donleavy looked at the audience once (on reflection, I'm sure that he wanted only to reassure himself that we were really there), adjusted his glasses and began to read from a sheaf of papers.

34

He was glad "to be here and to see the work going on just as it was in the   35 other schools."

At the first "Amen" from the audience I willed the offender to immediate death by choking on the word. But Amens and Yes, sir's began to fall around the room like rain through a ragged umbrella.

He told us of the wonderful changes we children in Stamps had in store. The Central School (naturally, the white school was Central) had already been granted improvements that would be in use in the fall. A well-known artist was coming from Little Rock to teach art to them. They were going to have the newest microscopes and chemistry equipment for their laboratory. Mr. Donleavy didn't leave us long in the dark over who made these improvements available to Central High. Nor were we to be ignored in the general betterment scheme he had in mind.

He said that he had pointed out to people at a very high level that one of the first-line football tacklers at Arkansas Agricultural and Mechanical College had graduated from good old Lafayette County Training School. Here fewer Amen's were heard. Those few that did break through lay dully in the air with the heaviness of habit.

He went on to praise us. He went on to say how he had bragged that "one of the best basketball players at Fisk sank his first ball right here at Lafayette County Training School."

The white kids were going to have a chance to become Galileos and   40 Madame Curies and Edisons and Gauguins, and our boys (the girls weren't even in on it) would try to be Jesse Owenses and Joe Louises.

Owens and the Brown Bomber were great heroes in our world, but what school official in the white-goddom of Little Rock had the right to decide that those two men must be our only heroes? Who decided that for Henry Reed to become a scientist he had to work like George Washington Carver, as a bootblack, to buy a lousy microscope? Bailey was obviously always going to be too small to be an athlete, so which concrete angel glued to what county seat had decided that if my brother wanted to become a lawyer he had to first pay penance for his skin by picking cotton and hoeing corn and studying correspondence books at night for twenty years?

The man's dead words fell like bricks around the auditorium and too many settled in my belly. Constrained by hard-learned manners I couldn't look behind me, but to my left and right the proud graduating class of 1940 had dropped their heads. Every girl in my row had found something new to do with her handkerchief. Some folded the tiny squares into love knots, some into triangles, but most were wadding them, then pressing them flat on their yellow laps.

On the dais, the ancient tragedy was being replayed. Professor Parsons sat, a sculptor's reject, rigid. His large, heavy body seemed devoid of will or willingness, and his eyes said he was no longer with us. The other teachers examined the flag (which was draped stage right) or their notes, or the windows which opened on our now-famous playing diamond.

Graduation, the hush-hush magic time of frills and gifts and congratulations and diplomas, was finished for me before my name was called. The accomplishment was nothing. The meticulous maps, drawn in three colors of ink, learning and spelling decasyllabic words, memorizing the whole of *The Rape of Lucrece*[3] — it was for nothing. Donleavy had exposed us.

We were maids and farmers, handymen and washerwomen, and anything   45
higher that we aspired to was farcical and presumptuous.

Then I wished that Gabriel Prosser and Nat Turner[4] had killed all white-folks in their beds and that Abraham Lincoln had been assassinated before the signing of the Emancipation Proclamation, and that Harriet Tubman[5] had been killed by that blow on her head and Christopher Columbus had drowned in the *Santa Maria*.

It was awful to be a Negro and have no control over my life. It was brutal to be young and already trained to sit quietly and listen to charges brought against my color with no chance of defense. We should all be dead. I thought I should like to see us all dead, one on top of the other. A pyramid of flesh with the whitefolks on the bottom, as the broad base, then the Indians with their silly tomahawks and teepees and wigwams and treaties, the Negroes with their mops and recipes and cotton sacks and spirituals sticking out of their mouths. The Dutch children should all stumble in their wooden shoes and break their necks. The French should choke to death on the Louisiana Purchase (1803) while silkworms ate all the Chinese with their stupid pigtails. As a species, we were an abomination. All of us.

Donleavy was running for election, and assured our parents that if he won we could count on having the only colored paved playing field in that part of Arkansas. Also—he never looked up to acknowledge the grunts of acceptance—also, we were bound to get some new equipment for the home economics building and the workshop.

He finished, and since there was no need to give any more than the most perfunctory thank-you's, he nodded to the men on the stage, and the tall white man who was never introduced joined him at the door. They left with the attitude that now they were off to something really important. (The graduation ceremonies at Lafayette County Training School had been a mere preliminary.)

The ugliness they left was palpable. An uninvited guest who wouldn't leave.   50
The choir was summoned and sang a modern arrangement of "Onward, Christian Soldiers," with new words pertaining to graduates seeking their place in

---

[3]*The Rape of Lucrece*: an 1,855-line narrative poem by William Shakespeare. [Eds.]

[4]*Gabriel Prosser and Nat Turner*: leaders of slave rebellions during the early 1800s in Virginia. [Eds.]

[5]*Harriet Tubman* (ca. 1820–1913): escaped slave who conducted others to freedom on the Underground Railroad and worked as an abolitionist. [Eds.]

the world. But it didn't work. Elouise, the daughter of the Baptist minister, recited "Invictus,"[6] and I could have cried at the impertinence of "I am the master of my fate, I am the captain of my soul."

My name had lost its ring of familiarity and I had to be nudged to go and receive my diploma. All my preparations had fled. I neither marched up to the stage like a conquering Amazon, nor did I look in the audience for Bailey's nod of approval. Marguerite Johnson, I heard the name again, my honors were read, there were noises in the audience of appreciation, and I took my place on the stage as rehearsed.

I thought about colors I hated: ecru, puce, lavender, beige and black.

There was shuffling and rustling around me, then Henry Reed was giving his valedictory address, "To Be or Not to Be." Hadn't he heard the whitefolks? We couldn't *be*, so the question was a waste of time. Henry's voice came out clear and strong. I feared to look at him. Hadn't he got the message? There was no "nobler in the mind" for Negroes because the world didn't think we had minds, and they let us know it. "Outrageous fortune"? Now, that was a joke. When the ceremony was over I had to tell Henry Reed some things. That is, if I still cared. Not "rub," Henry, "erase." "Ah, there's the erase." Us.

Henry had been a good student in elocution. His voice rose on tides of promise and fell on waves of warnings. The English teacher had helped him to create a sermon winging through Hamlet's soliloquy. To be a man, a doer, a builder, a leader, or to be a tool, an unfunny joke, a crusher of funky toadstools. I marveled that Henry could go through with the speech as if we had a choice.

I had been listening and silently rebutting each sentence with my eyes closed; then there was a hush, which in an audience warns that something unplanned is happening. I looked up and saw Henry Reed, the conservative, the proper, the A student, turn his back to the audience and turn to us (the proud graduating class of 1940) and sing, nearly speaking,

> "Lift ev'ry voice and sing
> Till earth and heaven ring
> Ring with the harmonies of Liberty . . ."

It was the poem written by James Weldon Johnson. It was the music composed by J. Rosamond Johnson. It was the Negro National Anthem. Out of habit we were singing it.

Our mothers and fathers stood in the dark hall and joined the hymn of encouragement. A kindergarten teacher led the small children onto the stage and the buttercups and daisies and bunny rabbits marked time and tried to follow:

---

[6]"*Invictus*": a poem by the nineteenth-century English poet William Ernest Henley. Its inspirational conclusion is quoted here. [Eds.]

"Stony the road we trod
Bitter the chastening rod
Felt in the days when hope, unborn, had died.
Yet with a steady beat
Have not our weary feet
Come to the place for which our fathers sighed?"

Each child I knew had learned that song with his ABC's and along with "Jesus Loves Me This I Know." But I personally had never heard it before. Never heard the words, despite the thousands of times I had sung them. Never thought they had anything to do with me.

On the other hand, the words of Patrick Henry had made such an impression on me that I had been able to stretch myself tall and trembling and say, "I know not what course others may take, but as for me, give me liberty or give me death."

And now I heard, really for the first time:

"We have come over a way that with tears
has been watered,
We have come, treading our path through
the blood of the slaughtered."

While echoes of the song shivered in the air, Henry Reed bowed his head, 60 said "Thank you," and returned to his place in the line. The tears that slipped down many faces were not wiped away in shame.

We were on top again. As always, again. We survived. The depths had been icy and dark, but now a bright sun spoke to our souls. I was no longer simply a member of the proud graduating class of 1940; I was a proud member of the wonderful, beautiful Negro race.

Oh, Black known and unknown poets, how often have your auctioned pains sustained us? Who will compute the only nights made less lonely by your songs, or the empty pots made less tragic by your tales?

If we were a people much given to revealing secrets, we might raise monuments and sacrifice to the memories of our poets, but slavery cured us of that weakness. It may be enough, however, to have it said that we survive in exact relationship to the dedication of our poets (include preachers, musicians and blues singers).

QUESTIONS

1. Why was graduation such an important event in Stamps, Arkansas? Note the rituals and preparations associated with this event. How do they compare with those accompanying your own junior high or high school graduation?

2. At the beginning of the graduation ceremony, Angelou was "overcome with a presentiment of worse things to come. Something unrehearsed, unplanned, was going to happen" (paragraph 30). What "unrehearsed, unplanned" event does occur? How does Angelou convey to the reader the meaning of this event?

3. Toward the end of the essay we are told, "I was no longer simply a member of the proud graduating class of 1940; I was a proud member of the wonderful, beautiful Negro race" (paragraph 61). How did the experience of the graduation change Angelou's way of thinking about herself and her people?

4. Understanding the structure of this essay is important for understanding the meaning of the essay. How does Angelou organize her material, and how does this organization reflect her purpose? Why do you think Angelou changes her point of view from third person in the first five paragraphs to first person in the rest of the essay?

5. Think of an event in your life that didn't turn out as you expected. What were your expectations of this event? What was the reality? Write an essay in which you show the significance of this event by contrasting how you planned for the event with how it actually turned out.

6. We have all had experiences that have changed the directions of our lives. These experiences may be momentous, such as moving from one country to another or losing a parent, or they may be experiences that did not loom so large at the time but that changed the way you thought about things, such as finding that your parents disapproved of your best friend because of her race. Recall such a turning point in your life, and present it so as to give the reader a sense of what your life was like before the event and how it changed after the event.

MAKING CONNECTIONS

1. The essays by Alice Walker (p. 40), Martin Luther King Jr. (p. 90), George Orwell (p. 104), and Loren Eiseley (p. 138) presented later in this section pinpoint formative moments in the life of the writer. Identify some of those moments, and compare one or more with Angelou's account of her graduation.

2. Compare the points of view taken by Angelou and Walker. How does the "presence" of the valedictorian in Angelou's essay influence the point of view she takes?

3. Two things link this essay with Orwell's "Shooting an Elephant" (p. 104): each essay turns on an unexpected event, and the reflections each event prompts have to do with political domination. Of course they are from dissimilar points of view. But Orwell, when he goes out to meet and shoot the elephant, finds himself forced before a native crowd, in somewhat the same way that Mr. Donleavy stands before Angelou's school. Write an essay in which you compare and contrast these two events.

BEAUTY
When the Other Dancer Is the Self
Alice Walker

Born in Eatonton, Georgia, in 1944, Alice Walker is the youngest of eight children. Her father was a sharecropper, and her mother was a maid. A graduate of Sarah Lawrence College, Walker has been an active worker for civil rights. She has been a fellow of the Radcliffe Institute, a contributing and consulting editor for Ms. magazine, and a teacher of literature and writing at a number of colleges and universities. She has published poetry, essays, short stories, and five novels: The Third Life of Grange Copeland *(1970),* Meridian *(1976),* The Color Purple *(1982), for which she won the Pulitzer Prize,* The Temple of My Familiar *(1989) and* Possessing the Secret of Joy *(1992). "Beauty: When the Other Dancer Is the Self" first appeared in Ms. magazine and later in a collection of essays,* In Search of Our Mothers' Gardens *(1983). When asked why she writes, Walker said, "I'm really paying homage to people I love, the people who are thought to be dumb and backward but who were the ones who first taught me to see beauty."*

It is a bright summer day in 1947. My father, a fat, funny man with beautiful eyes and a subversive wit, is trying to decide which of his eight children he will take with him to the county fair. My mother, of course, will not go. She is knocked out from getting most of us ready: I hold my neck stiff against the pressure of her knuckles as she hastily completes the braiding and then beribboning of my hair.

My father is the driver for the rich old white lady up the road. Her name is Miss Mey. She owns all the land for miles around, as well as the house in which we live. All I remember about her is that she once offered to pay my mother thirty-five cents for cleaning her house, raking up piles of her magnolia leaves, and washing her family's clothes, and that my mother—she of no money, eight children, and a chronic earache—refused it. But I do not think of this in 1947. I am two and a half years old. I want to go everywhere my daddy goes. I am excited at the prospect of riding in a car. Someone has told me fairs are fun. That there is room in the car for only three of us doesn't faze me at all. Whirling happily in my starchy frock, showing off my biscuit-polished patent-leather shoes and lavender socks, tossing my head in a way that makes my ribbons bounce, I stand, hands on hips, before my father. "Take me, Daddy," I say with assurance; "I'm the prettiest!"

Later, it does not surprise me to find myself in Miss Mey's shiny black car, sharing the back seat with the other lucky ones. Does not surprise me that I thoroughly enjoy the fair. At home that night I tell the unlucky ones all I can remember about the merry-go-round, the man who eats live chickens, and the teddy bears, until they say: that's enough, baby Alice. Shut up now, and go to sleep.

It is Easter Sunday, 1950. I am dressed in a green, flocked, scalloped-hem dress (handmade by my adoring sister, Ruth) that has its own smooth satin petticoat and tiny hot-pink roses tucked into each scallop. My shoes, new T-strap patent leather, again highly biscuit-polished. I am six years old and have learned one of the longest Easter speeches to be heard that day, totally unlike the speech I said when I was two: "Easter lilies / pure and white / blossom in / the morning light." When I rise to give my speech I do so on a great wave of love and pride and expectation. People in the church stop rustling their new crinolines. They seem to hold their breath. I can tell they admire my dress, but it is my spirit, bordering on sassiness (womanishness), they secretly applaud.

"That girl's a little *mess*," they whisper to each other, pleased.   5

Naturally I say my speech without stammer or pause, unlike those who stutter, stammer, or worst of all, forget. This is before the word "beautiful" exists in people's vocabulary, but "Oh, isn't she the *cutest* thing!" frequently floats my way. "And got so much sense!" they gratefully add . . . for which thoughtful addition I thank them to this day.

It was great fun being cute. But then, one day, it ended.

I am eight years old and a tomboy. I have a cowboy hat, cowboy boots, checkered shirt and pants, all red. My playmates are my brothers, two and four years older than I. Their colors are black and green, the only difference in the way we are dressed. On Saturday nights we all go to the picture show, even my mother; Westerns are her favorite kind of movie. Back home, "on the ranch," we pretend we are Tom Mix, Hopalong Cassidy, Lash LaRue (we've even named one of our dogs Lash LaRue); we chase each other for hours rustling cattle, being outlaws, delivering damsels from distress. Then my parents decide to buy my brothers guns. These are not "real" guns. They shoot "BBs," copper pellets my brothers say will kill birds. Because I am a girl, I do not get a gun. Instantly I am relegated to the position of Indian. Now there appears a great distance between us. They shoot and shoot at everything with their new guns. I try to keep up with my bow and arrows.

One day while I am standing on top of our makeshift "garage"—pieces of tin nailed across some poles—holding my bow and arrow and looking out toward the fields, I feel an incredible blow in my right eye. I look down just in time to see my brother lower his gun.

Both brothers rush to my side. My eye stings, and I cover it with my hand. "If you tell," they say, "we will get a whipping. You don't want that to happen, do you?" I do not. "Here is a piece of wire," says the older brother, picking it up from the roof; "say you stepped on one end of it and the other flew up and hit you." The pain is beginning to start. "Yes," I say. "Yes, I will say that is what happened." If I do not say this is what happened, I know my brothers will find ways to make me wish I had. But now I will say anything that gets me to my mother.

Confronted by our parents we stick to the lie agreed upon. They place me on a bench on the porch and I close my left eye while they examine the right. There is a tree growing from underneath the porch that climbs past the railing to the roof. It is the last thing my right eye sees. I watch as its trunk, its branches, and then its leaves are blotted out by the rising blood.

I am in shock. First there is intense fever, which my father tries to break using lily leaves bound around my head. Then there are chills: my mother tries to get me to eat soup. Eventually, I do not know how, my parents learn what has happened. A week after the "accident" they take me to see a doctor. "Why did you wait so long to come?" he asks, looking into my eye and shaking his head. "Eyes are sympathetic," he says. "If one is blind, the other will likely become blind too."

This comment of the doctor's terrifies me. But it is really how I look that bothers me most. Where the BB pellet struck there is a glob of whitish scar tissue, a hideous cataract, on my eye. Now when I stare at people—a favorite pastime, up to now—they will stare back. Not at the "cute" little girl, but at her scar. For six years I do not stare at anyone, because I do not raise my head.

Years later, in the throes of a mid-life crisis, I ask my mother and sister whether I changed after the "accident." "No," they say, puzzled. "What do you mean?"

What do I mean?

I am eight, and, for the first time, doing poorly in school, where I have been something of a whiz since I was four. We have just moved to the place where the "accident" occurred. We do not know any of the people around us because this is a different county. The only time I see the friends I knew is when we go back to our old church. The new school is the former state penitentiary. It is a large stone building, cold and drafty, crammed to overflowing with boisterous, ill-disciplined children. On the third floor there is a huge circular imprint of some partition that has been torn out.

"What used to be here?" I ask a sullen girl next to me on our way past it to lunch.

"The electric chair," says she.

At night I have nightmares about the electric chair, and about all the people reputedly "fried" in it. I am afraid of the school, where all the students seem to be budding criminals.

"What's the matter with your eye?" they ask, critically.   20

When I don't answer (I cannot decide whether it was an "accident" or not), they shove me, insist on a fight.

My brother, the one who created the story about the wire, comes to my rescue. But then brags so much about "protecting" me, I become sick.

After months of torture at the school, my parents decide to send me back to our old community, to my old school. I live with my grandparents and the teacher they board. But there is no room for Phoebe, my cat. By the time my grandparents decide there *is* room, and I ask for my cat, she cannot be found. Miss Yarborough, the boarding teacher, takes me under her wing, and begins to teach me to play the piano. But soon she marries an African—a "prince," she says—and is whisked away to his continent.

At my old school there is at least one teacher who loves me. She is the teacher who "knew me before I was born" and bought my first baby clothes. It is she who makes life bearable. It is her presence that finally helps me turn on the one child at the school who continually calls me "one-eyed bitch." One day I simply grab him by his coat and beat him until I am satisfied. It is my teacher who tells me my mother is ill.

My mother is lying in bed in the middle of the day, something I have never   25 seen. She is in too much pain to speak. She has an abscess in her ear. I stand looking down on her, knowing that if she dies, I cannot live. She is being treated with warm oils and hot bricks held against her cheek. Finally a doctor comes. But I must go back to my grandparents' house. The weeks pass but I am hardly aware of it. All I know is that my mother might die, my father is not so jolly, my brothers still have their guns, and I am the one sent away from home.

"You did not change," they say.

Did I imagine the anguish of never looking up?

I am twelve. When relatives come to visit I hide in my room. My cousin Brenda, just my age, whose father works in the post office and whose mother is a nurse, comes to find me. "Hello," she says. And then she asks, looking at my recent school picture, which I did not want taken, and on which the "glob," as I think of it, is clearly visible, "You still can't see out of that eye?"

"No," I say, and flop back on the bed over my book.

That night, as I do almost every night, I abuse my eye. I rant and rave at it,   30 in front of the mirror. I plead with it to clear up before morning. I tell it I hate and despise it. I do not pray for sight. I pray for beauty.

"You did not change," they say.

I am fourteen and baby-sitting for my brother Bill, who lives in Boston. He is my favorite brother and there is a strong bond between us. Understanding my feelings of shame and ugliness he and his wife take me to a local hospital, where the "glob" is removed by a doctor named O. Henry. There is still a small bluish crater where scar tissue was, but the ugly white stuff is gone. Almost immediately I become a different person from the girl who does not raise her head. Or so I think. Now that I've raised my head I win the boyfriend of my dreams. Now that I've raised my head I have plenty of friends. Now that I've raised my head classwork comes from my lips faultlessly as Easter speeches did, and I leave high school as valedictorian, most popular student, and *queen*, hardly believing my luck. Ironically, the girl who was voted most beautiful in our class (and was) was later shot twice through the chest by a male companion, using a "real" gun, while she was pregnant. But that's another story in itself. Or is it?

"You did not change," they say.

It is now thirty years since the "accident." A beautiful journalist comes to visit and to interview me. She is going to write a cover story for her magazine that focuses on my latest book. "Decide how you want to look on the cover," she says. "Glamorous, whatever."

Never mind "glamorous," it is the "whatever" that I hear. Suddenly all I can 35 think of is whether I will get enough sleep the night before the photography session: if I don't, my eye will be tired and wander, as blind eyes will.

At night in bed with my lover I think up reasons why I should not appear on the cover of a magazine. "My meanest critics will say I've sold out," I say. "My family will now realize I write scandalous books."

"But what's the real reason you don't want to do this?" he asks.

"Because in all probability," I say in a rush, "my eye won't be straight."

"It will be straight enough," he says. Then, "Besides, I thought you'd made your peace with that."

And I suddenly remember that I have. 40

I remember:

I am talking to my brother Jimmy, asking if he remembers anything unusual about the day I was shot. He does not know I consider that day the last time my father, with his sweet home remedy of cool lily leaves, chose me, and that I suffered and raged inside because of this. "Well," he says, "all I remember is standing by the side of the highway with Daddy, trying to flag down a car. A white man stopped, but when Daddy said he needed somebody to take his little girl to the doctor, he drove off."

I remember:

I am in the desert for the first time. I fall totally in love with it. I am so overwhelmed by its beauty, I confront for the first time, consciously, the meaning of the doctor's words years ago: "Eyes are sympathetic. If one is blind, the other will likely become blind too." I realize I have dashed about the world madly, looking at this, looking at that, storing up images against the fading of the light. *But I might have missed seeing the desert!* The shock of that possibility—and gratitude for over twenty-five years of sight—sends me literally to my knees. Poem after poem comes—which is perhaps how poets pray.

ON SIGHT

I am so thankful I have seen
The Desert
And the creatures in the desert
And the desert Itself.

The desert has its own moon
Which I have seen
With my own eye.

There is no flag on it.

Trees of the desert have arms
All of which are always up
That is because the moon is up
The sun is up
Also the sky
The stars
Clouds
None with flags.

If there *were* flags, I doubt
the trees would point.
Would you?

But mostly, I remember this: 45

I am twenty-seven, and my baby daughter is almost three. Since her birth I have worried about her discovery that her mother's eyes are different from other people's. Will she be embarrassed? I think. What will she say? Every day she watches a television program called "Big Blue Marble." It begins with a picture of the earth as it appears from the moon. It is bluish, a little battered-looking, but full of light, with whitish clouds swirling around it. Every time I see it I weep with love, as if it is a picture of Grandma's house. One day when I am putting Rebecca down for her nap, she suddenly focuses on my eye. Something inside me cringes, gets ready to try to protect myself. All children are cruel about physical differences, I know from experience, and that they don't always mean to be is another matter. I assume Rebecca will be the same.

But no-o-o-o. She studies my face intently as we stand, her inside and me outside her crib. She even holds my face maternally between her dimpled little hands. Then, looking every bit as serious and lawyerlike as her father, she says, as if it may just possibly have slipped my attention: "Mommy, there's a *world* in your eye." (As in, "Don't be alarmed, or do anything crazy.") And then, gently, but with great interest: "Mommy, where did you *get* that world in your eye?"

For the most part, the pain left then. (So what, if my brothers grew up to buy even more powerful pellet guns for their sons and to carry real guns themselves. So what, if a young "Morehouse man" once nearly fell off the steps of Trevor Arnett Library because he thought my eyes were blue.) Crying and laughing I ran to the bathroom, while Rebecca mumbled and sang herself off to sleep. Yes indeed, I realized, looking into the mirror. There *was* a world in my eye. And I saw that it was possible to love it: that in fact, for all it had taught me of shame and anger and inner vision, I *did* love it. Even to see it drifting out of orbit in boredom, or rolling up out of fatigue, not to mention floating back at attention in excitement (bearing witness, a friend has called it), deeply suitable to my personality, and even characteristic of me.

That night I dream I am dancing to Stevie Wonder's song "Always" (the name of the song is really "As," but I hear it as "Always"). As I dance, whirling and joyous, happier than I've ever been in my life, another bright-faced dancer joins me. We dance and kiss each other and hold each other through the night. The other dancer has obviously come through all right, as I have done. She is beautiful, whole and free. And she is also me.

QUESTIONS

1. Walker's essay moves forward in time through abrupt though steadily progressive descriptions of episodes. What effect on the reader does this structure produce? Why do you suppose Walker chose this form instead of providing transitions from one episode to the next?

2. Consider Walker's method of contrasting other people's memories with her own. What effect is created by the repetition of "You did not change"?

3. Consider Walker's choices of episodes or examples of beauty. How does each one work toward developing a definition of beauty?

4. In what ways does this essay play with the possible meanings of the familiar adage, "Beauty is in the eye of the beholder"?

5. One theme of this essay could be that of coming to terms with a disfigurement, an imagined loss of physical beauty. Recall an event (or accident) in your own life that changed your perception of yourself. Write a reflective narrative in which you use Walker's method of chronologically arranged episodes, including a reflection on the time before the change, as well as the change itself, and episodes from the time following. Like Walker, you may want to contrast (or compare) your memories with those of others.

6. Recall a memorable event that occurred a year or more ago. It might be an event in your family's life or a public event at which you and your friends were present. Write down your memories of the event, and then interview your family or friends and write down their recollections. Compare the various memories of the event. Come to some conclusion about the differences or similarities you find and perhaps about the selectivity of memory.

MAKING CONNECTIONS

Walker's daughter's exclamation, "Mommy, there's a *world* in your eye," is obviously a transcendent moment. It is also a metaphor. Other writers in this section could also be said to have a world in their eye. For example, Carl Sagan's description of how insight depends on a degree of restriction is closely related to Walker's theme (p. 132). Select another essay from this section, and show how Walker's reflections on her blind eye can help us understand the discoveries the writer of the other essay is making.

MIRRORS

Lucy Grealy

Lucy Grealy (b. 1963), an award-winning poet, attended the Iowa Writer's Workshop and was a fellow at the Bunting Institute of Radcliffe. At the age of nine, Grealy had cancer of the jaw, and the whole right side of her jaw was removed. In the following essay, which first appeared in Harper's *and which received the National Magazine Award, Grealy writes about the thirty operations she had in twenty years to try to reconstruct her face. In both this selection and her book,* Autobiography of a Face, *Grealy reflects on the overwhelming obsessions and perceptions of physical beauty that dominate our culture.*

There was a long period of time, almost a year, during which I never looked in a mirror. It wasn't easy; just as you only notice how often people eat on television when you yourself are on a diet, I'd never suspected just how omnipresent were our own images. I began as an amateur, avoiding merely mirrors, but by the end of the year I found myself with a professional knowledge of the reflected image, its numerous tricks and wiles, how it can spring up at any moment: a glass tabletop, a well-polished door handle, a darkened window, a pair of sunglasses, a restaurant's otherwise magnificent brass-plated coffee machine sitting innocently by the cash register.

I hadn't simply woken up one morning deciding not to look at myself as part of some personal experiment, as my friend Sally had attempted once before me: She'd lasted about three days before finally giving in to the need "to make sure I was still there." For Sally, not looking in the mirror meant enacting a conscious decision against a constant desire that, at the end of her three days, she still was at a loss to define as either solely habit or instinct. For me, however, the act of not looking was insidious. It was nihilistic, an insurgence too chaotic even to know if it was directed at the world or at myself.

At the time I was living alone in Scotland, surviving financially because of my eligibility for the dole, the vernacular for Britain's social security benefits. When I first arrived in Aberdeen I didn't know anyone, had no idea just how I was going to live, yet I went anyway because I'd met a plastic surgeon there who said he could help me. I had been living in London, working temp jobs. Before that I'd been in Berlin, and ostensibly had come to London only to earn money for a few weeks before returning to Germany. Exactly why I had this experience in London I don't know, but in my first week there I received more nasty comments about my face than I had in the past three years of living in

Iowa, New York, and Germany. These comments, all from men and all odi-ously sexual, hurt and disoriented me so much I didn't think twice about a friendly suggestion to go see a plastic surgeon. I'd already had more than a dozen operations in the States, yet my insurance ran out and so did my hope that any real difference could be made. Here, however, was a surgeon who had some new techniques, and here was a government willing to foot the bill: I didn't feel I could pass up yet another chance to "fix" my face, which I confusedly thought concurrent with "fixing" my self, my soul, my life.

Sixteen years earlier, when I was nine and living in America, I came home from school one day with a toothache. Several weeks and misdiagnoses later surgeons removed most of the right side of my jaw as part of an attempt to prevent the cancer they found there from spreading. No one properly explained the operation to me and I awoke in a cocoon of pain that prevented me from moving or speaking. Tubes ran in and out of my body and because I couldn't ask, I made up my own explanations for their existence.

Up until this time I'd been having a great time in the hospital. For starters it 5 was in "The City," a place of traffic and noise and dangers and, best of all, elevators. Never having been in an elevator before, I thrilled not just at the ride itself, but also at the game of nonchalance played out in front of the other elevator-savvy children who stepped on and off without thought.

Second, I was free from school. In theory a school existed on the third floor for children well enough to attend, but my friend Derek and I quickly discovered that the volunteer who came each day after lunch to pick us up was a sucker for a few well-timed groans, and once we learned to play straight man for each other there was little trouble getting out of it. We made sure the nurses kept thinking we had gone off to school, leaving us free for a few brief hours to wander the mazelike halls of the ancient hospital. A favorite spot was the emergency waiting room; they had good magazines and sometimes you got to see someone covered in blood come through the door. Derek tried to convince me that a certain intersection in the subbasement was an ideal place to watch for bodies heading toward the morgue, but the one time we did actually see one get wheeled by beneath its clichéd white sheet, we silently allowed each other to save face by suddenly deciding it was so much more fun to steal get-well cards from the gift shop than hang out in a cold basement. Once we stole the cards we sent them out randomly to other kids on the ward, signing them "Love and Kisses, Michael Jackson." Our theory was to watch them open up what they would think was a card from a famous star, but no one ever actually fell for it; by then we were well pegged as troublemakers.

There was something else going on too, something I didn't know how to articulate. Adults treated me in a mysterious manner. They asked me to do things: lie still for X rays, not cry for needles, things that, although not easy, never seemed equal to the praise I received in return. Reinforced to me again and again was how I was "a brave girl" for not crying, "a good girl" for not complaining, and soon I began defining myself this way, equating strength with silence.

Then the chemotherapy began. In the early seventies chemo was even cruder than it is now, the basic premise of it to poison the patient right up until the very brink of their own death. Up until this point I almost never cried, almost always received some sort of praise and attention in return for this, got what I considered the better part of the deal. But now, now it was like a practical joke that had gotten out of hand. Chemotherapy was a nightmare and I wanted it to stop, I didn't want to be brave any more. Yet I had so grown used to defining myself as "brave," i.e., silent, that even more terrifying was the thought of losing this sense of myself, certain that if I broke down this would be seen as despicable in the eyes of both my parents and doctors.

Mostly the task of taking me into the city for the injections fell upon my mother, though sometimes my father had to take me. Overwhelmed by the sight of the vomiting and weeping, my father developed the routine of "going to get the car," meaning that he left the office before the actual injection on the premise that then he could have the car ready and waiting when it was all over. Ashamed of my suffering, I felt relief when he was finally out of the room. When my mother was with me she stayed in the room, yet this only made the distance even more tangible, an almost palpable distance built on the intensity of our desperate longing to be anywhere else, anywhere at all. She explained that it was wrong to cry before the needle went in; afterward was one thing, but before, that was mere fear, and hadn't I already demonstrated my bravery earlier? Every week, every Friday, or "d-day" as we called it, for two and a half years I climbed up onto that too-big doctor's table and told myself not to cry, and every week I failed. The injections were really two large syringes, filled with chemicals so caustic to the vein that each had to be administered only very slowly. The whole process took about four minutes; I had to remain very still throughout it. Dry retching began in the first fifteen seconds, then the throb behind my eyes gave everything a yellow-green aura, and the bone-deep pain of alternating extreme hot and cold flashes made me tremble, yet still I had to sit motionless and not move my arm. No one spoke to me, not the doctor who was a paradigm of the cold-fish physician, not the nurse who told my mother I reacted much more violently than many of the other children, and not my mother, who, surely overwhelmed by the sight of her child's suffering, thought the best thing to do was remind me to be brave, to try and not cry. All the while I hated myself for having wept before the needle went in, convinced that the nurse and my mother were right, that I was "overdoing it," that the throwing up was psychosomatic, that my mother was angry with me for not being good or brave enough. So involved with controlling my guilt and shame, the problem of physical pain seemed easy by comparison.

Yet each week, usually two or three days after the injection, there came the first flicker of feeling better, the always forgotten and gratefully rediscovered understanding that simply to be well in my body was the greatest thing I could ask for. I thought other people felt this gratitude, this appreciation and physical joy all the time, and I felt cheated because I only was able to feel it once a week.

10

When you are only ten, which is when the chemotherapy began, two and a half years seems like your whole life, yet it did finally end. I remember the last day of chemotherapy very clearly for two reasons: one, because it was the only day on which I succeeded in not crying, and because later, in private, I cried harder than I had in years; I thought now I would no longer be "special," that without the arena of chemotherapy in which to prove myself no one would ever love me, that I would fade unnoticed into the background. This idea about not being different didn't last very long. Before I thought people stared because I was bald. I wore a hat constantly, but this fooled no one, least of all myself.

During this time my mother worked in a nursing home in a Hasidic community. Hasidism dictates that married women cover their hair, and most commonly this is done with a wig. My mother's friends were all too willing to donate their discarded wigs, and soon the house filled with wigs. I never wore one of them, they frightened me even when my mother insisted I looked better in one of the few that actually fit, yet we didn't know how to say no to the women who kept graciously offering their wigs. The cats enjoyed sleeping on them and the dogs playing with them, and we grew used to having to pick a wig up off a chair we wanted to sit in. It never struck us as odd until one day a visitor commented wryly as he cleared a chair for himself, and suddenly a great wave of shame overcame me. I had nightmares about wigs, felt a flush if I even heard the word, and one night I put myself out of my misery by getting up after everyone was asleep, gathering all the wigs except for one the dogs were fond of and might miss, and which they had chewed anyway into something other than a wig. I hid all the rest in an old chest where they weren't found for almost a year.

But my hair eventually grew in, and it didn't take long before I understood that I looked different for other reasons. People stared at me in stores, other children made fun of me to the point where I came to expect it constantly, wherever I went. School became a battleground, and I came home at the end of each day exhausted with the effort of keeping my body so tense and hard that I was sure anything would bounce off of it.

I was living in an extreme situation, and because I did not particularly care for the world I was in, I lived in others, and because the world I did live in was a dangerous one, I incorporated this danger into my private life. I saw movies about and envied Indians, imagined myself one. Walking down the streets I walked down through the forest, my body ready for any opportunity to fight or flee one of the big cats I knew stalked the area. Vietnam and Cambodia were other places I walked through frequently, daily even as I made my way down the school hall, knowing a landmine or a sniper might give themselves away at any moment with the subtle, soft metal clicks I'd read about in the books I took from the library. When faced with a landmine, a mere insult about my face seemed a frivolous thing.

In the early years, when I was still on the chemo, I lived in worse places 15 than Cambodia. Because I knew it was somehow inappropriate, I read only in secret Primo Levi, Elie Wiesel, every book by a survivor I could find by myself without resorting to asking the librarian for. Auschwitz, Birkenau: I felt the senseless blows of the Capos and somehow knew that because at any moment we might be called upon to live for a week on one loaf of bread and some water called soup, the peanut butter sandwich I found on my plate was nothing less than a miracle, an utter and sheer miracle capable of making me literally weep with joy.

I decided I wanted to become a "deep" person. I wasn't exactly sure what this would entail, but I believed that if I could just find the right philosophy, think the right thoughts, my suffering would end. To try to understand the world I was in, I undertook to find out what was "real," and quickly began seeing reality as existing in the lowest common denominator, that suffering was the one and only dependable thing. But rather than spend all of my time despairing, though certainly I did plenty of that, I developed a form of defensive egomania: I felt I was the only one walking about in the world who understood what was really important. I looked upon people complaining about the most mundane things—nothing on TV, traffic jams, the price of new clothes—and felt both joy because I knew how unimportant those things really were and unenlightened feelings of superiority because other people didn't. Because I lived a fantasy life in which I had to be thankful for each cold, blanketless night I survived on the cramped wooden bunks, chemotherapy—the nausea, pain, and deep despair it brought—was a breeze, a stroll through the country in comparison. I was often miserable, but I knew that to feel warm instead of cold was its own kind of joy, that to eat was a reenactment of the grace of some god whom I could only dimly define, and that simply to be alive was a rare, ephemeral miracle. It was like reliving The Fall a dozen times a day: I was given these moments of grace and insight, only to be invariably followed by a clumsy tumble into narcissism.

As I got older, as I became a teenager, I began to feel very isolated. My nonidentical twin sister started going out with boys, and I started, my most tragic mistake of all, to listen to and believe the taunts thrown at me daily by the very boys she and the other girls were interested in. I was a dog, a monster, the ugliest girl they had ever seen. Of all the remarks the most damaging wasn't even directed at me, but was really an insult to Jerry, a boy I never saw because every day, between fourth and fifth periods when I was cornered by this particular group, I was too ashamed to lift my eyes off the floor. "Hey, look, it's Jerry's girlfriend," they yelled when they saw me, and I felt such shame, knowing that this was the deepest insult they could throw at Jerry.

I became interested in horses and got a job at a run-down local stable. Having those horses to go to each day after school saved my life; I spent all of my time either with them or thinking about them. To keep myself thinking objectively I became an obsessive reader and an obsessive television watcher, anything to keep me away from the subjective. I convinced myself I was smarter than everyone else, that only I knew what mattered, what was important, but by the time I was sixteen this wasn't true, not by a long shot. Completely and utterly repressed, I was convinced that I never wanted a boyfriend, not ever, and wasn't it convenient for me, a blessing I even thought, that none would ever want me. I told myself I was free to concentrate on the "true reality" of life, whatever that was. My sister and her friends put on blue eye shadow, blow-dried their hair, and went to spend interminable hours in the local mall, and I looked down on them for this, knew they were misleading themselves and being overoccupied with the "mere surface" of living. I had thought like this when I was younger, but now it was different, now my philosophy was haunted by desires so frightening I was unable to even admit they existed.

It wasn't until I was in college that I finally allowed that maybe, just maybe, it might be nice to have a boyfriend. As a person I had, as they say, blossomed in college. I went to a small, liberal, predominantly female school and suddenly, after years of alienation in high school, discovered that there were other people I could enjoy talking to, people who thought me intelligent and talented. I was, however, still operating on the assumption that no one, not ever, would be physically attracted to me, and in a curious way this shaped my personality. I became forthright and honest and secure in the way only the truly self-confident are, those who do not expect to be rejected, and those like me, who do not even dare to ask and so also expect no rejection. I had come to know myself as a person, but it would be graduate school before I was literally, physically able to use my name and the word woman in the same sentence.

Throughout all of this I was undergoing reconstructive surgery in an attempt to rebuild my jaw. It started when I was fifteen, several years after the chemo ended. I had known for years I would have operations to fix my face, and sometimes at night I fantasized about how good my life would finally be then. One day I got a clue that maybe it would not be so easy. At fourteen I went first to an older plastic surgeon who explained the process of pedestals to me, and told me it would take ten years to fix my face. Ten years? Why even bother? I thought. I'll be ancient by then. I went to the library and looked up the pedestals he talked about. There were gruesome pictures of people with grotesque tubes of their own skin growing out of their bodies, tubes of skin that were harvested like some kind of crop and then rearranged in ways with results that did not look at all normal or acceptable to my eye. But then I met a younger surgeon, a man who was working on a new way of grafting that did not involve pedestals, and I became more hopeful and once again began awaiting the fixing of my face, of the day when I would be whole, content, loved.

Long-term plastic surgery is not like the movies. There is no one single operation that will change everything, and there is certainly no slow unwrapping of the gauze in order to view the final product. There is always swelling, sometimes grotesque, there are often bruises, and always there are scars. After each operation, too scared to simply go look in the mirror, I developed an oblique method comprised of several stages. First, I tried to catch my reflection in an overhead lamp: The roundness of the metal distorted my image just enough to

20

53

obscure details and give no true sense of size or proportion. Then I slowly worked my way up to looking at the reflection in someone's eyeglasses, and from there I went to walking as briskly as possible by a mirror, glancing only quickly. I repeated this as many times as it would take me, passing the mirror slightly more slowly each time until finally I was able to stand still and confront myself.

The theory behind most reconstructive surgery is to take large chunks of muscle, skin, and bone and slap them into the roughly appropriate place, then slowly begin to carve this mess into some sort of shape. It involves long, major operations, countless lesser ones, a lot of pain, and many, many years. And also, it does not always work. With my young surgeon in New York, who was becoming not so young with each passing year, I had two or three soft tissue grafts, two skin grafts, a bone graft, and some dozen other operations to "revise" my face, yet when I left graduate school at the age of twenty-five I was still more or less in the same position I had started in: a deep hole in the right side of my face and a rapidly shrinking left side and chin, a result of the radiation I'd had as a child and the stress placed upon it by the other operations. I was caught in a cycle of having a big operation, one that would force me to look monstrous from the swelling for many months, then have the subsequent revision operations that improved my looks tremendously, and then slowly, over the period of a few months or a year, watch the graft reabsorb back into my body, slowly shrink down an leave me with nothing but the scarred donor site the graft had originally come from.

I had little or no conception of how I appeared to other people. As a child, Halloween was my favorite holiday because I could put on a mask and walk among the blessed for a few brief, sweet hours. Such freedom I felt, walking down the street, my face hidden: Through the imperfect oval holes I could peer out at other faces, masked or painted or not, and see on those faces nothing but the normal faces of childhood looking back at me, faces I mistakenly thought were the faces everyone else but me saw all the time, faces that were simply curious and ready for fun, not the faces I usually braced myself for, the cruel, lonely, vicious ones I spent every day other than Halloween waiting to round each corner. As I breathed in the condensed, plastic air I somehow thought that I was breathing in normality, that his joy and weightlessness were what the world was comprised of, and it was only my face that kept me from it, my face that was my own mask, my own tangible barrier that kept me from knowing the true identity of the joy I was sure everyone but me lived with intimately. How could they not know it? not know that to be free of the fear of taunts and the burden of knowing no one would ever love you was all anyone could ever ask for? I was a pauper walking for a short while in the clothes of the prince, and when the day ended, I gave up my disguise with dismay.

I also came to love winter, when I could wrap the lower half of my face up in a scarf: I could speak to people and they would have no idea of who and what they were really speaking to. I developed the bad habits of letting my long hair hang in my face, and of always covering my chin and mouth with my hand, hoping it might be seen as a thoughtful, accidental gesture. My one concession to this came in college, when I cut my hair short, very short, in an attempt to stop hiding behind it. It was also an attempt, though I didn't see it as such at the time, to desex myself. I had long, blond hair, and I also had a thin figure. Sometimes, from a distance, men would see the thin blonde and whistle, something I dreaded more than anything else because I knew as they got closer their tone would inevitably change, they would stare openly or, worse, turn away quickly, and by cutting my hair I felt I might possibly avoid this, clear up any misconception anyone, however briefly, might have about my being attractive.

Once in college my patient friends repeated for me endlessly that most of it was in my mind, that, granted, I did not look like everyone else, but that didn't mean I looked bad. I am sure now that they were right some of the time. But with the constant surgery I was in a perpetual state of transfiguration. I rarely looked the same for more than six months at a time. So ashamed of my face, I was unable to even admit that this constant change affected me at all; I let everyone who wanted to know that it was only what was inside that mattered, that I had "grown used to" the surgery, that none of it bothered me at all. Just as I had done in childhood, I pretended nothing was wrong, and this was constantly mistaken by others for bravery. I spent a great deal of time looking in the mirror in private, positioning my head to show off my eyes and nose, which were not just normal, but quite pretty, as my still-patient friends told me often. But I could not bring myself to see them for more than a glimmer: I looked in the mirror and saw not the normal upper half of my face, but only the disfigured lower half. People still teased me. Not daily, not like when I was younger, but in ways that caused me more.pain than ever before. Children stared at me and I learned to cross the street to avoid them; this bothered me but not as much as the insults I got from men. They weren't thrown at me because I was disfigured, they were thrown at me because I was a disfigured woman.

They came from boys, sometimes men, and almost always a group of them. Only two or three times have I ever been teased by a single person, and I can think of only one time when I was ever teased by a woman. Had I been a man, would I have had to walk down the street while a group of young women followed and denigrated my sexual worth?

Not surprisingly, I viewed sex as my salvation. I was sure that if only I could get someone to sleep with me it would mean I wasn't ugly, that I was an attractive person, a lovable person. It would not be hard to guess where this line of reasoning led me, which was into the beds of a few manipulative men who liked themselves even less than they liked me, and I in turn left each short-term affair hating myself, obscenely sure that if only I had been prettier it would have worked, he would have loved me and it would have been like those other love affairs I was certain "normal" women had all the time. Gradually I became unable to say "I'm depressed," but could only say "I'm ugly," because the two had become inextricably linked in my mind. Into that universal lie, that sad equation of "if only" which we are all prey to, I was sure that if only I had a normal face, then I would be happy.

What our brains know is one thing, yet what our hearts know is another matter entirely, and when I met this new surgeon in Scotland, I offhandedly explained to my friends back home "why not, it's free, isn't it?" unable to admit that I believed in the fixability of life all over again.

Originally, it was planned I would have something called a tissue expander, followed by a bone graft. A tissue expander is a small balloon placed under the skin and then slowly blown up over the course of several months, the object being to stretch out the skin and create room and cover for the new bone. It is a bizarre, nightmarish thing to do to your face, yet I was hopeful about the end results and I was also able to spend the three months the expansion took in the hospital. I've always felt safe in hospitals: It's the one place I feel justified, sure of myself, free from the need to explain the way I look. For this reason the first tissue expander was bearable, just, and the bone graft that followed it was a success, it did not melt away like the previous ones.

However, the stress put upon my original remaining jaw from the surgery 30 instigated a period of deterioration of that bone, and it became apparent that I was going to need the same operation I'd just had on the right side done to the left. I remember my surgeon telling me this at an outpatient clinic. I planned to be traveling down to London that same night on an overnight train, and I barely made it to the station on time, I was in such a fumbling state of despair. I could not imagine doing it all over again, and just as I had done all my life, I was searching and searching through my intellect for a way to make it okay, make it bearable, for a way to do it. I lay awake all night on that train, feeling the tracks slip quickly and oddly erotic below me, when I remembered an afternoon from my three months in the hospital. Boredom was a big problem those long afternoons, the days punctuated and landmarked by meals and television programs. Waiting for the afternoon tea to come, wondering desperately how I could make time pass, it suddenly occurred to me I didn't have to make time pass, that it would do it of its own accord, that I simply had to relax and take no action. Lying on the train, remembering that, I realized I had no obligation to make my situation okay, that I didn't have to explain it, understand it, that I could invoke the idea of negative capability and just simply let it happen. By the time the train pulled into King's Cross Station, I felt able to bear it yet again, not entirely sure what other choice I had.

But there was an element I didn't yet know about. I returned to Scotland to set up a date to go in and have the tissue expander put in, and was told quite casually that I'd only be in the hospital three or four days. Wasn't I going to spend the whole expansion time in the hospital? I asked almost in a whisper. What's the point of that? You can just come in every day to the outpatient to have it expanded. Horrified by this, I was speechless. I would have to live and move about in the outside world with a giant balloon in my face? I can't remember what I did for the next few days before I went into the hospital, but I vaguely remember that these days involved a great deal of drinking alone in bars and at home.

I went in and had the operation and, just as they said, went home at the end of the week. The only thing I can truly say gave me any comfort during the months I lived with my tissue expander was my writing and Kafka. I started a novel and completely absorbed myself in it, writing for hours and hours every day. It was the only way I could walk down the street, to stand the stares I received, to think to myself "I'll bet none of them are writing a novel." It was that strange, old familiar form of egomania, directly related to my dismissive, conceited thoughts of adolescence. As for Kafka, who had always been one of my favorite writers even before the new fashion for him, he helped me in that I felt permission to feel alienated, and to have that alienation be okay, to make it bearable, noble even. In the way living in Cambodia helped me as a child, I walked the streets of my dark little Scottish city by the sea and knew without doubt that I was living in a story Kafka would have been proud to write.

This time period, however, was also the time I stopped looking in the mirror. I simply didn't want to know. Many times before in my life I have been repelled by the mirror, but the repulsion always took the form of a strange, obsessive attraction. Previously I spent many hours looking in the mirror, trying to see what it was that other people were seeing, a purpose I understand now was laughable, as I went to the mirror with an already clearly fixed, negative idea of what people saw. Once I even remember thinking how awful I looked in a mirror I was quickly passing in a shopping center, seeing perfectly all the flaws I knew were there, when I realized with a shock that I wasn't looking in a mirror, that I was looking through into a store at someone who had the same coat and haircut as me, someone who, when I looked closer, looked perfectly fine.

The one good thing about a tissue expander is that you look so bad with it in that no matter what you look like once it's finally removed, it has to be better. I had my bone graft and my fifth soft tissue graft and yes, even I had to admit I looked better. But I didn't look like me. Something was wrong: Was this the face I had waited through twenty years and almost thirty operations for? I somehow just couldn't make what I saw in the mirror correspond to the person I thought I was. I wasn't just that I felt ugly, I simply could not associate the image as belonging to me. My own image was the image of a stranger, and rather than try to understand this, I simply ignored it. I reverted quickly back to my tissue expander mode of not looking in the mirror, and quickly improved it to include not looking at any image of myself. I perfected the technique of brushing my teeth without a mirror, grew my hair in such a way that it would require only a quick simple brush, and wore clothes that were simply and easily put on, no complex layers or lines that might require even the most minor of visual adjustments.

On one level I understood that the image of my face was merely that, an image, a surface that was not directly related to any true, deep definition of the

35

self. But I also knew that it is only through image that we experience and make decisions about the everyday world, and I was not always able to gather the strength to prefer the deeper world over the shallower one. I looked for ways to relate the two, to find a bridge that would allow me access to both, anything no matter how tenuous, rather than ride out the constant swings between peace and anguish. The only direction I had to go in to achieve this was simply to strive for a state of awareness and self-honesty that sometimes, to this day, rewards me and sometimes exhausts me.

Our whole lives are dominated, though it is not always so clearly translatable, with the question "How do I look?" Take all the many nouns in our lives: car; house; job; family; love; friends; and substitute the personal pronoun—it is not that we are all so self-obsessed, it is that all things eventually relate back to ourselves, and it is our own sense of how we appear to the world by which we chart our lives, how we navigate our personalities that would otherwise be adrift in the ocean of other peoples' obsessions.

One particular afternoon I remember very lucidly, an afternoon, toward the end of my yearlong separation from the mirror. I was talking to someone, an attractive man as it happened, and we were having a wonderful, engaging conversation. For some reason it flickered across my mind to wonder what I looked like to him. What was he seeing when he saw me? So many times I've asked this of myself, and always the answer was a bad one, an ugly one. A warm, smart woman, yes, but still, an unattractive one. I sat there in the café and asked myself this old question and, startlingly, for the first time in my life I had no answer readily prepared. I had literally not looked in a mirror for so long that I quite simply had no clue as to what I looked like. I looked at the man as he spoke; my entire life I had been giving my negative image to people, handing it to them and watching the negative way it was reflected back to me. But now, because I had no idea what I was giving him, the only thing I had to judge by was what he was giving me, which, as reluctant as I was to admit it, was positive.

That afternoon in that café I had a moment of the freedom I had been practicing for behind my Halloween mask as a child. But where as a child I expected it to come as a result of gaining something, a new face, it came to me then as the result of shedding something, of shedding my image. I once thought that truth was an eternal, that once you understood something it was with you forever. I know now that this isn't so, that most truths are inherently unretainable, that we have to work hard all our lives to remember the most basic things. Society is no help; the images it gives us again and again want us only to believe that we can most be ourselves by looking like someone else, leaving our own faces behind to turn into ghosts that will inevitably resent us and haunt us. It is no mistake that in movies and literature the dead sometimes know they are dead only after they can no longer see themselves in the mirror. As I sat there feeling the warmth of the cup against my palm this small observation seemed like a great revelation to me, and I wanted to tell the man I was with about it, but he was involved in his own topic and I did not want to interrupt him, so instead I looked with curiosity over to the window behind him, its night-darkened glass reflecting the whole café, to see if I could recognize myself.

QUESTIONS

1. What did Grealy learn about herself from her yearlong separation from the mirror?

2. Why did Grealy think that "fixing" her face would "fix" herself, her soul, her life? What is the significance of the word *fix*?

3. One of the features of this essay that makes it so compelling is Grealy's command of details. Locate details that you believe are effective, and think about their function. Try to rewrite some of Grealy's sentences to remove the details. What is lost? How do details link the author and the reader?

4. Grealy tells us, "Most truths are inherently unretainable," and "we have to work hard all our lives to remember the most basic things" (paragraph 38). What truths does Grealy refer to?

5. How does Grealy use her personal experience as evidence so that her essay becomes a larger story with greater relevance to others?

6. Grealy writes about the freedom she feels as a result of accepting the truth about her face. Such freedom, as Grealy shows, is never easily achieved. Reflect on a struggle or conflict in your own life, and write a brief essay on the "truths" that have emerged from your struggle.

MAKING CONNECTIONS

1. Both Alice Walker (p. 40) and Lucy Grealy struggle to accept their bodies and their appearance. In what ways are their struggles similar? In what ways are they different? What does this struggle achieve for each writer?

2. Do you agree with the observation that Alice Walker loses sight in order to gain sight, and Lucy Grealy loses face in order to gain face?

LEARNING TO READ AND WRITE

Frederick Douglass

*Frederick Augustus Washington Bailey (1817–1895) was
born into slavery on the Eastern Shore of Maryland. His
mother was a black slave; his father, a white man. After his
escape from the South in 1838, he adopted the name of
Douglass and worked to free other slaves and later (after the
Civil War) to protect the rights of freed slaves. He was a
newspaper editor, a lecturer, United States minister to
Haiti, and the author of several books about his life and
times.* The Narrative of the Life of Frederick Douglass: An
American Slave *(1841), from which the following selection
has been taken, is his best-known work.*

I lived in Master Hugh's family about seven years. During this time, I succeeded in learning to read and write. In accomplishing this, I was compelled
to resort to various stratagems. I had no regular teacher. My mistress, who had
kindly commenced to instruct me, had, in compliance with the advice and direction of her husband, not only ceased to instruct, but had set her face against
my being instructed by any one else. It is due, however, to my mistress to say of
her, that she did not adopt this course of treatment immediately. She at first
lacked the depravity indispensable to shutting me up in mental darkness. It was
at least necessary for her to have some training in the exercise of irresponsible
power, to make her equal to the task of treating me as though I were a brute.

My mistress was, as I have said, a kind and tender-hearted woman; and in
the simplicity of her soul she commenced, when I first went to live with her, to
treat me as she supposed one human being ought to treat another. In entering
upon the duties of a slaveholder, she did not seem to perceive that I sustained
to her the relation of a mere chattel, and that for her to treat me as a human
being was not only wrong, but dangerously so. Slavery proved as injurious to
her as it did to me. When I went there, she was a pious, warm, and tender-
hearted woman. There was no sorrow or suffering for which she had not a tear.
She had bread for the hungry, clothes for the naked, and comfort for every
mourner that came within her reach. Slavery soon proved its ability to divest
her of these heavenly qualities. Under its influence, the tender heart became
stone, and the lamblike disposition gave way to one of tiger-like fierceness. The
first step in her downward course was in her ceasing to instruct me. She now
commenced to practise her husband's precepts. She finally became even more
violent in her opposition than her husband himself. She was not satisfied with
simply doing as well as he had commanded; she seemed anxious to do better.
Nothing seemed to make her more angry than to see me with a newspaper.

She seemed to think that here lay the danger. I have had her rush at me with a face made all up of fury, and snatch from me a newspaper, in a manner that fully revealed her apprehension. She was an apt woman; and a little experience soon demonstrated, to her satisfaction, that education and slavery were incompatible with each other.

From this time I was most narrowly watched. If I was in a separate room any considerable length of time, I was sure to be suspected of having a book, and was at once called to give an account of myself. All this, however, was too late. The first step had been taken. Mistress, in teaching me the alphabet, had given me the *inch*, and no precaution could prevent me from taking the *ell.*[1]

The plan which I adopted, and the one by which I was most successful, was that of making friends of all the little white boys whom I met in the street. As many of these as I could, I converted into teachers. With their kindly aid, obtained at different times and in different places, I finally succeeded in learning to read. When I was sent on errands, I always took my book with me, and by going one part of my errand quickly, I found time to get a lesson before my return. I used also to carry bread with me, enough of which was always in the house, and to which I was always welcome; for I was much better off in this regard than many of the poor white children in our neighborhood. This bread I used to bestow upon the hungry little urchins, who, in return, would give me that more valuable bread of knowledge. I am strongly tempted to give the names of two or three of those little boys, as a testimonial of the gratitude and affection I bear them; but prudence forbids;—not that it would injure me, but it might embarrass them; for it is almost an unpardonable offence to teach slaves to read in this Christian country. It is enough to say of the dear little fellows, that they lived on Philpot Street, very near Durgin and Bailey's ship-yard. I used to talk this matter of slavery over with them. I would sometimes say to them, I wished I could be as free as they would be when they got to be men. "You will be free as soon as you are twenty-one, *but I am a slave for life!* Have not I as good a right to be free as you have?" These words used to trouble them; they would express for me the liveliest sympathy, and console me with the hope that something would occur by which I might be free.

I was now about twelve years old, and the thought of being *a slave for life*   5 began to bear heavily upon my heart. Just about this time, I got hold of a book entitled "The Columbian Orator."[2] Every opportunity I got, I used to read this book. Among much of other interesting matter, I found in it a dialogue between a master and his slave. The slave was represented as having run away from his master three times. The dialogue represented the conversation which took place between them, when the slave was retaken the third time. In this dialogue, the whole argument in behalf of slavery was brought forward by the

---

[1]*ell:* a unit of measurement, no longer used, equal to 45 inches. [Eds.]

[2]*The Columbian Orator:* a popular schoolbook designed to introduce students to argument and rhetoric. [Eds.]

master, all of which was disposed of by the slave. The slave was made to say some very smart as well as impressive things in reply to his master—things which had the desired though unexpected effect; for the conversation resulted in the voluntary emancipation of the slave on the part of the master.

In the same book, I met with one of Sheridan's mighty speeches on and in behalf of Catholic emancipation.[3] These were choice documents to me. I read them over and over again with unabated interest. They gave tongue to interesting thoughts of my own soul, which had frequently flashed through my mind, and died away for want of utterance. The moral which I gained from the dialogue was the power of truth over the conscience of even a slaveholder. What I got from Sheridan was a bold denunciation of slavery, and a powerful vindication of human rights. The reading of these documents enabled me to utter my thoughts, and to meet the arguments brought forward to sustain slavery; but while they relieved me of one difficulty, they brought on another even more painful than the one of which I was relieved. The more I read, the more I was led to abhor and detest my enslavers. I could regard them in no other light than a band of successful robbers, who had left their homes, and gone to Africa, and stolen us from our homes, and in a strange land reduced us to slavery. I loathed them as being the meanest as well as the most wicked of men. As I read and contemplated the subject, behold! that very discontentment which Master Hugh had predicted would follow my learning to read had already come, to torment and sting my soul to unutterable anguish. As I writhed under it, I would at times feel that learning to read had been a curse rather than a blessing. It had given me a view of my wretched condition, without the remedy. It opened my eyes to the horrible pit, but to no ladder upon which to get out. In moments of agony, I envied my fellow-slaves for their stupidity. I have often wished myself a beast. I preferred the condition of the meanest reptile to my own. Any thing, no matter what, to get rid of thinking! It was this everlasting thinking of my condition that tormented me. There was no getting rid of it. It was pressed upon me by every object within sight or hearing, animate or inanimate. The silver trump of freedom had roused my soul to eternal wakefulness. Freedom now appeared, to disappear no more forever. It was heard in every sound, and seen in every thing. It was ever present to torment me with a sense of my wretched condition. I saw nothing without seeing it, I heard nothing without hearing it, and felt nothing without feeling it. It looked from every star, it smiled in every calm, breathed in every wind, and moved in every storm.

I often found myself regretting my own existence, and wishing myself dead; and but for the hope of being free, I have no doubt but that I should have killed myself, or done something for which I should have been killed. While in

---

[3]*Richard Brinsley Sheridan* (1751–1816): British dramatist, orator, and politician. Catholics were not allowed to vote in England until 1829. [Eds.]

this state of mind, I was eager to hear any one speak of slavery. I was a ready listener. Every little while, I could hear something about the abolitionists. It was some time before I found what the word meant. It was always used in such connections as to make it an interesting word to me. If a slave ran away and succeeded in getting clear, or if a slave killed his master, set fire to a barn, or did any thing very wrong in the mind of a slaveholder, it was spoken of as the fruit of *abolition*. Hearing the word in this connection very often, I set about learning what it meant. The dictionary afforded me little or no help. I found it was "the act of abolishing"; but then I did not know what was to be abolished. Here I was perplexed. I did not dare to ask any one about its meaning, for I was satisfied that it was something they wanted me to know very little about. After a patient waiting, I got one of our city papers, containing an account of the number of petitions from the north, praying for the abolition of slavery in the District of Columbia, and of the slave trade between the States. From this time I understood the words *abolition* and *abolitionist*, and always drew near when that word was spoken, expecting to hear something of importance to myself and fellow-slaves. The light broke in upon me by degrees. I went one day down on the wharf of Mr. Waters; and seeing two Irishmen unloading a scow of stone, I went, unasked, and helped them. When we had finished, one of them came to me and asked me if I were a slave. I told him I was. He asked, "Are ye a slave for life?" I told him that I was. The good Irishman seemed to be deeply affected by the statement. He said to the other that it was a pity so fine a little fellow as myself should be a slave for life. He said it was a shame to hold me. They both advised me to run away to the north; that I should find friends there, and that I should be free. I pretended not to be interested in what they said, and treated them as if I did not understand them; for I feared they might be treacherous. White men have been known to encourage slaves to escape, and then, to get the reward, catch them and return them to their masters. I was afraid that these seemingly good men might use me so; but I nevertheless remembered their advice, and from that time I resolved to run away. I looked forward to a time at which it would be safe for me to escape. I was too young to think of doing so immediately; besides, I wished to learn how to write, as I might have occasion to write my own pass. I consoled myself with the hope that I should one day find a good chance. Meanwhile, I would learn to write.

The idea as to how I might learn to write was suggested to me by being in Durgin and Bailey's ship-yard, and frequently seeing the ship carpenters, after hewing, and getting a piece of timber ready for use, write on the timber the name of that part of the ship for which it was intended. When a piece of timber was intended for the larboard side, it would be marked thus—"L." When a piece was for the starboard side, it would be marked thus—"S." A piece for the larboard side forward, would be marked thus—"L. F." When a piece was for starboard side forward, it would be marked thus—"S. F." For larboard aft, it would be marked thus—"L. A." For starboard aft, it would be marked thus—

"S. A." I soon learned the names of these letters, and for what they were intended when placed upon a piece of timber in the ship-yard. I immediately commenced copying them, and in a short time was able to make the four letters named. After that, when I met with any boy who I knew could write, I would tell him I could write as well as he. The next word would be, "I don't believe you. Let me see you try it." I would then make the letters which I had been so fortunate as to learn, and ask him to beat that. In this way I got a good many lessons in writing, which it is quite possible I should never have gotten in any other way. During this time, my copy-book was the board fence, brick wall, and pavement; my pen and ink was a lump of chalk. With these, I learned mainly how to write. I then commenced and continued copying the Italics in Webster's Spelling Book, until I could make them all without looking on the book. By this time, my little Master Thomas had gone to school, and learned how to write, and had written over a number of copy-books. These had been brought home, and shown to some of our near neighbors, and then laid aside. My mistress used to go to class meeting at the Wilk Street meetinghouse every Monday afternoon, and leave me to take care of the house. When left thus, I used to spend the time in writing in the spaces left in Master Thomas's copy-book, copying what he had written. I continued to do this until I could write a hand very similar to that of Master Thomas. Thus, after a long, tedious effort for years, I finally succeeded in learning how to write.

QUESTIONS

1. As its title proclaims, Douglass's book is a narrative, the story of his life. So, too, is this selection a narrative, the story of his learning to read and write. Identify the main events of this story, and list them in chronological order.

2. Douglass is reporting some of the events in his life in this selection, but certain events are not simply reported. Instead, they are described so that we may see, hear, and feel what was experienced by the people who were present during the event. Which events are described most fully in this narrative? How does Douglass seek to engage our interest and direct our feelings through such scenes?

3. In this episode from his life, as in his whole book, Douglass is engaged in evaluating an institution—slavery—and arguing a case against it. Can you locate the points in the text where reflecting gives way to argumentation? How does Douglass support his argument against slavery? What are the sources of his persuasiveness?

4. The situation of Irish Catholics is a subtheme in this essay. You can trace it by locating every mention of the Irish or of Catholicism in the text. How does this theme relate to African American slavery? Try to locate *The Columbian Orator* in your library, or find out more about who Sheridan was and why he had to argue on behalf of "Catholic emancipation" (paragraph 6).

5. A subnarrative in this text tells the story of Master Hugh's wife, the "mistress" of the household in which Douglass learned to read and write. Retell *her* story in your

own words. Consider how her story relates to Douglass's own story and how it relates to Douglass's larger argument about slavery.

6. Put yourself in the place of Master Hugh's wife, and retell all events in her words and from her point of view. To do so, you will have to decide both what she might have come to know about all these events and how she would feel about them. You will also have to decide when she is writing. Is she keeping a diary during this time (the early 1830s), or is she looking back from the perspective of later years? Has she been moved to write by reading Douglass's own book, which appeared in 1841? If so, how old would she be then, and what would she think about these past events? Would she be angry, bitter, repentant, embarrassed, indulgent, scornful, or what?

MAKING CONNECTIONS

1. What are the most common themes of the African American writers in this section (Angelou, Walker, and Douglass)? On what issues, when they write about writing, do they have the most in common with the authors represented here who are white?

2. For Maya Angelou (p. 29), Alice Walker (p. 40), and Frederick Douglass (p. 60), events of childhood and youth are particularly important. Compare how at least two of these writers viewed events when they were young, how they present their younger selves or viewpoints, and how they connect childhood experience to adult knowledge.

THE IGUANA

Isak Dinesen

Karen Dinesen (1885–1962) was a Danish woman who married a Swedish baron and went to Kenya in East Africa with him in 1914 to manage their coffee plantation. After their divorce she stayed in Kenya, managing the plantation until its failure in 1931. During this time she began to write in English (the language of whites in Kenya), taking the male first name of Isak. Her best-known books are Seven Gothic Tales *(1934), a volume of stories, and* Out of Africa *(1937), her reminiscences of Kenya. The following brief selection from the latter volume appeared in the section called "From an Immigrant's Notebook."*

In the Reserve I have sometimes come upon the Iguana, the big lizards,[1] as they were sunning themselves upon a flat stone in a river-bed. They are not pretty in shape, but nothing can be imagined more beautiful than their coloring. They shine like a heap of precious stones or like a pane cut out of an old church window. When, as you approach, they swish away, there is a flash of azure, green and purple over the stones, the color seems to be standing behind them in the air, like a comet's luminous tail.

Once I shot an Iguana. I thought that I should be able to make some pretty things from his skin. A strange thing happened then, that I have never afterwards forgotten. As I went up to him, where he was lying dead upon his stone, and actually while I was walking a few steps, he faded and grew pale, all color died out of him as in one long sigh, and by the time that I touched him he was grey and dull like a lump of concrete. It was the live impetuous blood pulsating within the animal, which had radiated out all that glow and splendor. Now that the flame was put out, and the soul had flown, the Iguana was as dead as a sandbag.

Often since I have, in some sort, shot an Iguana, and I have remembered the one of the Reserve. Up at Meru I saw a young Native girl with a bracelet on, a leather strap two inches wide, and embroidered all over with very small turquoise-colored beads which varied a little in color and played in green, light blue and ultramarine. It was an extraordinarily live thing; it seemed to draw breath on her arm, so that I wanted it for myself, and made Farah buy it from her.[2] No sooner had it come upon my own arm than it gave up the ghost. It was nothing now, a small, cheap, purchased article of finery. It had been the play of colors, the duet between the turquoise and the "nègre",—that quick,

---

[1] *the Reserve:* a game reserve in the Ngong Hills of Kenya, Africa. [Eds.]
[2] *Farah Aden:* Dinesen's Somali servant. [Eds.]

sweet, brownish black, like peat and black pottery, of the Native's skin,—that had created the life of the bracelet.

In the Zoological Museum of Pietermaritzburg, I have seen, in a stuffed deep-water fish in a showcase, the same combination of coloring, which there had survived death; it made me wonder what life can well be like, on the bottom of the sea, to send up something so live and airy. I stood in Meru and looked at my pale hand and at the dead bracelet, it was as if an injustice had been done to a noble thing, as if truth had been suppressed. So sad did it seem that I remembered the saying of the hero in a book that I had read as a child: "I have conquered them all, but I am standing amongst graves."

In a foreign country and with foreign species of life one should take measures to find out whether things will be keeping their value when dead. To the settlers of East Africa I give the advice: "For the sake of your own eyes and heart, shoot not the Iguana."

QUESTIONS

1. In this essay the act of shooting an iguana comes to stand as a type or model of other actions; it becomes a symbolic event. This is expressed explicitly at the beginning of paragraph 3: "Often since I have, *in some sort*, shot an Iguana" (italics added). How do the incidents described in paragraphs 3 and 4 help us to understand the full meaning of the symbolic action of shooting an iguana? Restate this meaning in your own words.

2. An argument that lurks beneath the surface of this meditative essay is made explicit in its last sentence. How do you understand that sentence and that argument?

3. The power of this essay grows from its effective representation—its ability to put us in the picture, to make us see and feel the events represented. Find a descriptive or comparative phrase that seems to you especially vivid, and explain why it is effective.

4. Dinesen uses three concrete examples in this selection. How are the three related? Why do you suppose she arranged them in the order in which she did?

5. In her meditation, Dinesen moves from lizard, to bracelet, to fish, and then uses these three specific, concrete instances to make the jump to generalizations about foreign species and foreign countries. Try this technique yourself. Find some incident in your own life that reminds you of other similar events, so that they can be brought together as being symbolic of a certain *kind* of event. To what broader point can you leap from these few recollected events?

MAKING CONNECTIONS

Consider the deaths and captivities of animals in this essay, in George Orwell's "Shooting an Elephant" (p. 104), and in Loren Eiseley's "The Bird and the Machine" (p. 138). Could Dinesen's final sentence and its implied argument be the theme of either of the other essays? Would it fit one better than the other? How would Orwell's or Eiseley's essay change if Dinesen's remark were to guide it?

DIALOGUES WITH THE DEAD

Christopher Clausen

*Christopher Clausen (b. 1942) is a professor of English at
The Pennsylvania State University. He is the author of* The
Place of Poetry: Two Centuries of an Art in Crisis *(1981),
named a "notable book of the year" by* The New York
Times Book Review, *and* My Life with President Kennedy
*(1994), a collection of historical and autobiographical es-
says about the effects of the 1960s on American culture. He
writes that "literature, poetry in particular, was once central
to our culture because readers took it seriously as an exploration of life, an attempt to grapple with the intellectual
and moral problems that beset human beings like themselves." His essays have appeared in* Kenyon Review, Sewa-
nee Review, *and* Children's Literature. *In the following
essay, which first appeared in* American Scholar, *Clausen
explores the relationship between the living and the dead.*

My great-grandmother's eighth pregnancy was a difficult one. After all, she
was nearly forty-eight years old when it began. Of her five living children (two
others having died in infancy), the two oldest, my grandfather and his sister
Marie, were already in their mid-teens. Contrary to what might have been expected, however, she carried the fetus to term and in the autumn of 1896 gave
birth to a healthy boy who would live through most of the following century.
Her own prognosis was not so fortunate. Never fully recovered from the birth
of her final child, after twenty-one months she knew she was dying. Moreover,
she knew only too well that her grief-stricken husband—"not a good provider,"
in the language of the day—would be hard-pressed to maintain an infant and
three other small children, whatever help the oldest son, now at work but eager
to enlist in the Spanish-American War, might provide. She was, like her husband, an immigrant. Her own family was far away.

Promise me, she said to her daughter Marie in German, *promise me that you
will keep the family together and raise your brother Charlie.* What could a late-
nineteenth-century girl say to such an appeal? Besides, she adored her mother.
Mama, she answered inevitably, *I promise.* In that world, that was how they did
things. What is more, they sometimes meant it. My great-aunt Marie kept the
family together, raised her brother Charlie, and, for good measure, helped raise
his children and grandchildren. She never married and lived to be ninety-
eight. When Charlie died a few years before she did, she felt reasonably
enough that life had become absurd and that it was high time to depart. Her

final wish was to be buried in the grave of her mother, to whom she had so spectacularly kept a promise made eighty-one years earlier, and with whom she had so long carried on a dialogue that furnished the pattern for an entire life. Near the end of 1979, the customs of the late twentieth century grudgingly yielded to the sentiments of the nineteenth, and the ancient grave was reopened for its second occupant.

The communication of the dead, according to T. S. Eliot, is tongued with fire beyond the language of the living. Death has freed them to tell us things they had no words for in life. Being dead, they presumably do not mind what shapes we impose on them. All the same, they have their revenge: by admitting their influence through dialogue with them, we impose lasting shapes and obligations on ourselves as well. The dead can strengthen and steady us; they can also drive us crazy. People in superstitious ages imagined ghosts to explain their sense of being haunted, of involuntarily carrying on transactions with those who had died. In more modern language, our conversations with the dead are the ultimate form of projection, in which we define ourselves most revealingly and recognize, consciously or not, our actual status in the world. Whether or not we choose to be buried in the same grave, there is after all that perfect bond of death between the generations.

According to Dr. Milton Helpern, former chief medical examiner of New York City, death is "the irreversible cessation of life. Death may be due to a wide variety of diseases and disorders, but in every case the underlying physiological cause is a breakdown in the body's oxygen cycle." Law, if not medicine, distinguishes rigorously between death from natural causes, accident, homicide, or suicide. So do the survivors; our dialogue with someone who has been murdered is quite different in tone and substance from our colloquy with one who died of heart disease. Much depends also on the age at death. Like cause of death, the age at which one's oxygen cycle breaks down communicates a definite view of the universe to the living. In contemporary America we hold far fewer dialogues with dead children than took place in centuries when infant mortality was a frequent guest in every family, and the death of someone who failed to live out a normal life span is a correspondingly more powerful cause of grief and bitterness. We tend to feel that such a person has been the victim of an outrage. In many ritualistic or traditional cultures, on the other hand, "to be a dead member of one's society is the individual's ultimate social status," according to John Middleton—*ultimate* meaning not only final but highest. Such societies find it easier, at least abstractly, to accept the inevitability of deaths at many ages and to maintain an equable dialogue with their vanished members, although that acceptance does not necessarily lessen either the grief or the extravagance of its expression.

"Must I remember?" the extravagantly grieving Hamlet asks himself reprovingly two months after the untimely death of his father. Memory of the dead is of course the beginning of dialogue with them, a dialogue usually commenced with the rituals of funeral and commitment to the earth. In Hamlet's case, as in many modern ones, the ritual has been foreshortened, with the predictable consequence that memory and dialogue acquire an unhealthy power over the survivors. This power is all the greater for being unanticipated. For we address the dead constantly if they were close to us; and if they had a powerful effect on us in life, they answer. Oh yes, they talk back, make demands, insist on undivided attention. Raise my family, share my grave—these are benign exigencies. Too often, the ghost demands revenge.

> Remember thee?
> Aye, thou poor ghost, whiles memory holds a seat
> In this distracted globe. Remember thee?
> Yea, from the table of my memory
> I'll wipe away all trivial fond records,
> All saws of books, all forms, all pressures past
> That youth and observation copied there,
> And thy commandment all alone shall live
> Within the book and volume of my brain,
> Unmixed with baser matter.

How to converse with a ghost who demands vengeance? To adopt its wishes as one's own is to become possessed, whether the ghost's name is Hamlet the elder, or Moses, or Mohammed; whether the essence of its demand is to kill the usurper or repossess the land he took. Share my grave. To deny the ghost, on the other hand, may involve such a renunciation of one's own identity as to be nearly impossible—and the ghost will still be there in any event, as dead as ever. Falling between two stools, as Hamlet did, may be the worst of all choices: as in the play, it may simply widen the power of the ghost to encompass other fates besides that of the individual possessed, leaving the family and the state in ruins and Horatio alone to tell the tale. But possession rarely involves much choice.

Hamlet, in the opinion of many critics, is a modern figure trapped in an archaic drama: a man not given to believing ghosts or committing bloody acts of revenge. That is his tragedy. The enlightened mind becomes genuinely unhinged when faced with such demands, or with such a demander. Ghosts, after all, are written into plays to entertain the groundlings, whose benighted state makes them more susceptible to haunting. Although groundlings still exist and ghosts are still created for them—television and Hollywood give ample recent instances—the dead, whether friendly or hateful, hold no dialogues with the truly modern mind. We have learned to outgrow all that. Life is for the living; the healthy mind looks to the future. We cremate the dead and scatter their ashes, dissolving not only the spirit but the material body itself into thin air. There is no grave to share. Nobody can haunt us.

"A ghost in search of vengeance," asks the ghostly narrator of Robertson Davies's novel *Murther & Walking Spirits*—"what is it to do in such a world as ours?"

The ghost, of course, was really Hamlet's unconscious speaking. Self-assertion and the desire for revenge, muddled up with Oedipal longings for his sexually accomplished mother, projected themselves quite naturally onto the image of the dead father, who then walked the stage as a ghost. Of course. The word *psychology* would not be invented for another two centuries. We know how to understand the character Hamlet and the play itself not just differently but better than any Elizabethan. In a sense, that is perfectly true. How important that sense may be is more debatable. In Shaw's *Saint Joan*, an indisputably modern play, the title character is informed that the voices of long-dead saints who talk to her are in fact the product of her imagination. "Of course," she answers unabashedly. "That is how the messages of God come to us." To take the ghost out of its shadowy existence in the world and enshrine it in the mind only increases its power, unless the implication is that understanding the true *locus* of the haunting somehow dispels it. Clearly it does no such thing. The dead whose final resting place is in our mind are no less potent than those who are assumed to keep an unquiet vigil in the world of space. Real ghosts could appear only at certain times and places, and they could be exorcised. Psychological ghosts, even of the friendly dead, have no such limitations. Once our dead are buried within us, they can stay there for as long as we live—longer insofar as the patterns they embody are passed on through us to others by way of upbringing or genetic inheritance. Ignoring them is no solution. The less we hold dialogue with them, the more unruly their effect on us becomes. We can never get away from a voice that lives inside us.

Sometimes the voices within are collective and historical rather than individual as are the ghosts of our private dead. My father-in-law was a career naval officer who served as a carrier pilot during World War II. Like a surprising number of American officers in that war, he was the grandson of a Confederate veteran and half-consciously saw his own war as a prolongation of his grandfather's, not in terms of the issues involved but rather as an opportunity to vindicate an honorable defeat by winning an even greater struggle eighty years later. Somehow the significance of the past could be changed by valor in the present, not exactly avenging a loss but perhaps removing the shame or sting of it. Although this particular way of looking at World War II was restricted to a small part of a single generation, the habit of seeing a current series of events in the light of the Civil War was not. Much of twentieth-century American history involves a dialogue with the ghosts of the Civil War, a conflict in which more Americans died than in all our other wars combined. If the Civil Rights movement had in some respects to defeat the ghosts of the Confederacy all over again, it also drew strength from the black heroes of Fort Wagner and many another battle a hundred years before. The ghost of Abraham Lincoln, the commander in chief, remains the most potent figure in American history, now reinforced by that of Martin Luther King Jr.

In the last year of his life, when his eyesight and many other things were failing, my father-in-law asked my wife to read him long stretches from Shelby

71

Foote's narrative history of the Civil War as a preparation for death. It was not that he had any wish to refight the war, still less that he expected Stonewall Jackson to meet him on the threshold of Valhalla with an entrance examination. He was a modern man with, for the most part, modern beliefs. No, it was rather that having (again like many Southern men of his generation) lived in the shadow of these events all his life, he wished to be as clear as possible about them before he died. There were lessons to be learned about living and dying; this seemed the best available way for him to learn them. What the dead had to say now was very different from what they had communicated forty or sixty years ago. One last long conversation with the ghosts, perhaps, and then he would be ready to join them. The Crater was the battle he liked to hear about most, but there was nothing bloodthirsty or sentimental in his reactions. Rather he was closing a circle that had begun when he first heard about Southern victories and defeats in childhood, preparing for death in a way that was appropriate to the life he had lived, like a cheerful stoic.

"Then with the knowledge of death as walking one side of me," wrote Walt Whitman in 1865, commemorating Lincoln and the dead of the Civil War,

> And the thought of death close-walking the other side of me,
> And I in the middle as with companions, and as holding the hands
>   of companions,
> I fled forth to the hiding receiving night that talks not . . .

Because he had so thoughtfully assimilated himself to the dead at the end of his life, and because, in the almost forgotten phrase, he was full of years, the ghost of my father-in-law is a quiet one, a familiar daily presence that inspires and does not disturb.

Early death is something else again. To die with manifest unfulfilled promise, to leave grieving parents behind, seems a violation of the natural order. These dead, if we were close to them, are the object not just of mourning but of shock and guilt, as though we should have been able to foresee and prevent. They speak of inconsolable loss, and a long time must pass before we can hear anything else they have to say.

The Boston cancer specialists thought they had cured my brother of lymphoma not once but twice. A political scientist of great talents, he had had a somewhat unlucky career, owing to the depressed academic job market of the seventies and, after he had gone into government, the change of administrations in 1981. But he had begun to work his way back, interrupted by chemotherapy and a marrow transplant, and had even managed to complete a book on nuclear proliferation in which many publishers expressed interest. A few days after he signed a contract for its publication, his doctor informed him that he had at most three months to live.

We drove up to visit him immediately. When we arrived he was in the hospital, but they discharged him after a few days. Perhaps there was hope—perhaps new therapies as yet untried—there are doctors and there are doctors. One of them was optimistic. My sister-in-law pretended to believe, but there was no hope, really, and my brother was full of bitterness. It was not *Why me?* It sounded more like *Why now?* Why not earlier or later? He was anxious for his family in a way that only someone with a deep capacity for happiness, a beloved eight-year-old son, and hardly any life insurance can be. That anxiety was the strongest note in everything he said.

It would be pointless to give details of the conversations we had with him then, or later by telephone. All of them were like conversations with someone who is already dead, who is looking back from the other side and seeing something quite different from the other people in the room. How does one discuss plans for the future of a widow and her son when her young husband is the most determined of the discussers? From a great distance he watched us sadly as we talked about mortgages, school fees, the raising of a child in which he would have no further living part to play. From whatever place he now inhabited, he pressed all the right questions, asked for and received all the right promises from everyone, unerringly noticed every feature of the situation that would soon face his survivors. Unwilling to die but perceiving no alternative, he expressed in his speech and actions an equal mixture of courage and anger. Eventually the anger faded, leaving only sorrow, courage, and deep concern for the two who needed him most.

"There must be wisdom with great Death," Tennyson wrote after the death of another young man: "The dead shall look me through and through." My brother unwillingly put his house in order, made such peace as he could, and died on an afternoon in early summer, the three months proving in the end to be thirty-eight days. At the funeral his father and two of his brothers were pallbearers, while his mother sat among the mourners, and I felt that whatever was in the casket was looking us through and through.

A depressing story, certainly, though far from a unique one in this or any other century. What kinds of dialogue will follow such a death? Of course it's too early to say. Like those of a true ghost, my brother's purposes must be fulfilled in the lives of others, in contrast to those of most people who live to what is thought to be a normal age. For the time being, he is an unquiet ghost who speaks only of loss and incompletion, who asks only about his wife and son and can be answered only with reassurances. Later on he will have other things to tell those who knew him, and they will speak to him less frantically. He was a much-loved person, not only by his family, and the value of his legacy—and consequently the richness of the dialogues in which he will participate while those who loved him are still alive—will be very great. The scope of those dialogues, like everything else in which the living take part, is unpredictable.

In a sense, any remembered dead person eventually says to us: *I lived in a different time, subject to different pressures, part of a story that has now, if not ended, at least reached a different stage, with different characters.* And later still, if anyone is around to hear: *Even if I had lived a normal life, I would be dead now.* Beyond that, is everything they tell us projection? Perhaps, in a way. If so, it is projection of a very special kind, in which by virtue of their being dead we find ourselves extended far beyond our everyday limits of understanding and learn things about ourselves and our world that no living person could tell us. In these strange dialogues, the dead do indeed look us through and through.

Many survivors of the Final Solution feel that they carry the dead within 20
them, an unbearable burden of guilt and remembrance. Here the conversation with the dead, who may include all the members of one's family, must surely reach the limits of possibility. Those who survived the atomic bombings of Hiroshima and Nagasaki tell a slightly different version: they sense that they carry death itself inside them. Perhaps such extreme calamities offer one reason that our time is so reluctant to be reminded of death as the common fate or of any claims that the dead might have on the living.

> They used to pour millet on graves or poppy seeds
> To feed the dead who would come disguised as birds.
> I put this book here for you, who once lived
> So that you should visit us no more,

Czeslaw Milosz wrote in the ruined Warsaw of 1945. If we pay them too much or too little attention, the dead can eat us up.

Even to us ordinary people, the dead speak all the time. Willingly or not, we conduct endless dialogues with them. People who live in periods with no widely accepted way of visualizing the status and influence of the dead will invent new ones or try to revive old ones; hence the widespread half-beliefs in reincarnation and New Age varieties of spiritualism. On a more everyday level, the husband who has lost a wife, the wife who has lost a husband, says, *How could you do this to me?* The other answers, *I had no choice. I would much rather have gone to the beach with you as we planned.* And sometimes, *You should get out more.* And even, *You should remarry, for your own sake and the sake of the children.* Often enough, we do what the dead tell us.

Finally, it is the dead who tell us who we are, not just as individuals (though that too) but as a species of animals that needs reminding. They tell us constantly that life is a rough place and nobody gets out of it alive. Or as Montaigne put it, "Live as long as you please, you will strike nothing off the time you will have to spend dead." Our dialogue with the dead is a conversation between equals. As late-twentieth-century people, we tend to find this familiar news morbid and tasteless, like a Victorian funeral. After all, we make a fetish of youth and health, the unbounded liberation of the self from all forms of oppression, which must surely include the freedom not to die if we so choose. The impersonal objectivity of death is an affront to everything we want to believe.

That reaction only increases the power of the ghosts whom we try so hard, and with so little success, to confine in the safe, invisible place we call the dead past. But the ghosts tell us, either kindly or cruelly depending mostly on our willingness to hear, that they actually represent our future. Share my grave whether you will or not. That irrefutable announcement, which they are now free to speak, is the beginning of all the other things we can learn from them, and if we pretend not to hear it, the rest of what they have to say will be unintelligible.

QUESTIONS

1. Clausen begins his essay by telling us a story about his great-grandmother and the promise she extracted from her daughter, Marie. Why do you think Clausen begins his essay with this story? What is the significance of Marie's promise? What does Clausen want us to understand about the promises we make to the living and to the dead?

2. Why does Clausen entitle his essay "Dialogues with the Dead"? What is the nature of the dialogue between the living and the dead? What are the ways in which the dead talk back, make demands, and insist on the undivided attention of the living?

3. Clausen offers his readers many different kinds of sources as evidence—anecdotes, poetry, and so forth. How do these various sources form a dialogue in this essay?

4. What does Clausen mean when he writes, "But the ghosts tell us, either kindly or cruelly depending mostly on our willingness to hear, that they actually represent our future" (paragraph 23)?

5. Clausen is interested in the emotional legacies that are buried within us and the ways in which patterns "are passed on . . . by way of upbringing or genetic inheritance" (paragraph 9). Reflect on your own life and the dialogues you have with your ancestors. What does this conversation sound like? What legacies and patterns have been passed on to you? Write an essay in which you reflect on your dialogues with the dead.

MAKING CONNECTIONS

Clausen suggests that the dead will eat us up if we pay too much or too little attention to them. Elisabeth Kübler-Ross in her essay "On the Fear of Death" (p. 421) suggests that we have significant lessons to learn from the dying. Kübler-Ross warns us that we might avoid thinking about death, but we do so at our own peril. What kind of dialogue can you imagine between Clausen and Kübler-Ross? Write an essay in which you create a conversation between these two essayists.

MOTHER TONGUE
Amy Tan

Born in 1952 in Oakland, California, Amy Tan is the daughter of immigrants who fled China's Cultural Revolution in the late 1940s. Her Chinese name, An-Mei, means "blessing from America." Tan has remarked that she once tried to distance herself from her ethnicity, but writing her first novel, The Joy Luck Club *(1989), helped her discover "how very Chinese I was." Known as a gifted storyteller, Tan has written two other novels,* The Kitchen God's Wife *(1991) and* The Hundred Secret Senses *(1995), as well as two children's books. The following essay, in which Tan reflects on her experience as a bilingual child speaking both Chinese and English, was originally published in the* Threepenny Review *in 1990.*

I am not a scholar of English or literature. I cannot give you much more than personal opinions on the English language and its variations in this country or others.

I am a writer. And by that definition, I am someone who has always loved language. I am fascinated by language in daily life. I spend a great deal of my time thinking about the power of language—the way it can evoke an emotion, a visual image, a complex idea, or a simple truth. Language is the tool of my trade. And I use them all—all the Englishes I grew up with.

Recently, I was made keenly aware of the different Englishes I do use. I was giving a talk to a large group of people, the same talk I had already given to half a dozen other groups. The nature of the talk was about my writing, my life, and my book *The Joy Luck Club*. The talk was going along well enough, until I remembered one major difference that made the whole talk sound wrong. My mother was in the room. And it was perhaps the first time she had heard me give a lengthy speech, using the kind of English I have never used with her. I was saying things like "The intersection of memory upon imagination" and "There is an aspect of my fiction that relates to thus-and-thus"—a speech filled with carefully wrought grammatical phrases, burdened, it suddenly seemed to me, with nominalized forms, past perfect tenses, conditional phrases, all the forms of standard English that I had learned in school and through books, the forms of English I did not use at home with my mother.

Just last week, I was walking down the street with my mother, and I again found myself conscious of the English I was using, the English I do use with her. We were talking about the price of new and used furniture and I heard myself saying this: "Not waste money that way." My husband was with us as well, and he didn't notice any switch in my English. And then I realized why. It's because over the twenty years we've been together I've often used that same kind of English with him, and sometimes he even uses it with me. It has become our language of intimacy, a different sort of English that relates to family talk, the language I grew up with.

So you'll have some idea of what this family talk I heard sounds like, I'll quote what my mother said during a recent conversation which I videotaped and then transcribed. During this conversation, my mother was talking about a political gangster in Shanghai who had the same last name as her family's, Du, and how the gangster in his early years wanted to be adopted by her family, which was rich by comparison. Later, the gangster became more powerful, far richer than my mother's family, and one day showed up at my mother's wedding to pay his respects. Here's what she said in part: 5

"Du Yusong having business like fruit stand. Like off the street kind. He is Du like Du Zong—but not Tsung-ming Island people. The local people call putong, the river east side, he belong to that side local people. That man want to ask Du Zong father take him in like become own family. Du Zong father wasn't look down on him, but didn't take seriously, until that man big like become a mafia. Now important person, very hard to inviting him. Chinese way, came only to show respect, don't stay for dinner. Respect for making big celebration, he shows up. Mean gives lots of respect. Chinese custom. Chinese social life that way. If too important won't have to stay too long. He come to my wedding. I didn't see, I heard it. I gone to boy's side, they have YMCA dinner. Chinese age I was nineteen."

You should know that my mother's expressive command of English belies how much she actually understands. She reads the *Forbes* report, listens to *Wall Street Week*, converses daily with her stockbroker, reads all of Shirley MacLaine's books with ease—all kinds of things I can't begin to understand. Yet some of my friends tell me they understand 50 percent of what my mother says. Some say they understand 80 to 90 percent. Some say they understand none of it, as if she were speaking pure Chinese. But to me, my mother's English is perfectly clear, perfectly natural. It's my mother tongue. Her language, as I hear it, is vivid, direct, full of observation and imagery. That was the language that helped shape the way I saw things, expressed things, made sense of the world.

Lately, I've been giving more thought to the kind of English my mother speaks. Like others, I have described it to people as "broken" or "fractured" English. But I wince when I say that. It has always bothered me that I can think of no way to describe it other than "broken," as if it were damaged and needed to be fixed, as if it lacked a certain wholeness and soundness. I've heard other terms used, "limited English," for example. But they seem just as bad, as if everything is limited, including people's perceptions of the limited English speaker.

I know this for a fact, because when I was growing up, my mother's "limited" English limited *my* perception of her. I was ashamed of her English. I believed that her English reflected the quality of what she had to say. That is, because she expressed them imperfectly her thoughts were imperfect. And I had plenty of empirical evidence to support me: the fact that people in department stores, at banks, and at restaurants did not take her seriously, did not give her good service, pretended not to understand her, or even acted as if they did not hear her.

My mother has long realized the limitations of her English as well. When I 10 was fifteen, she used to have me call people on the phone to pretend I was she. In this guise, I was forced to ask for information or even to complain and yell at people who had been rude to her. One time it was a call to her stockbroker in New York. She had cashed out her small portfolio and it just so happened we were going to go to New York the next week, our very first trip outside California. I had to get on the phone and say in an adolescent voice that was not very convincing, "This is Mrs. Tan."

And my mother was standing in the back whispering loudly, "Why he don't send me check, already two weeks late. So mad he lie to me, losing me money."

And then I said in perfect English, "Yes, I'm getting rather concerned. You had agreed to send the check two weeks ago, but it hasn't arrived."

Then she began to talk more loudly. "What he want, I come to New York tell him front of his boss, you cheating me?" And I was trying to calm her down, make her be quiet, while telling the stockbroker, "I can't tolerate any more excuses. If I don't receive the check immediately, I am going to have to speak to your manager when I'm in New York next week." And sure enough, the following week there we were in front of this astonished stockbroker, and I was sitting there red-faced and quiet, and my mother, the real Mrs. Tan, was shouting at his boss in her impeccable broken English.

We used a similar routine just five days ago, for a situation that was far less humorous. My mother had gone to the hospital for an appointment, to find out about a benign brain tumor a CAT scan had revealed a month ago. She said she had spoken very good English, her best English, no mistakes. Still, she said, the hospital did not apologize when they said they had lost the CAT scan and she had come for nothing. She said they did not seem to have any sympathy when she told them she was anxious to know the exact diagnosis, since her husband and son had both died of brain tumors. She said they would not give her any more information until the next time and she would have to make another appointment for that. So she said she would not leave until the doctor called her daughter. She wouldn't budge. And when the doctor finally called her daughter, me, who spoke in perfect English—lo and behold—we had assurances the CAT scan would be found, promises that a conference call on Monday would be held, and apologies for any suffering my mother had gone through for a most regrettable mistake.

I think my mother's English almost had an effect on limiting my possibili-   15
ties in life as well. Sociologists and linguists probably will tell you that a person's developing language skills are more influenced by peers. But I do think
that the language spoken in the family, especially in immigrant families which
are more insular, plays a large role in shaping the language of the child. And I
believe that it affected my results on achievement tests, IQ tests, and the SAT.
While my English skills were never judged as poor, compared to math, English
could not be considered my strong suit. In grade school I did moderately well,
getting perhaps B's, sometimes B-pluses, in English and scoring perhaps in the
sixtieth or seventieth percentile on achievement tests. But those scores were
not good enough to override the opinion that my true abilities lay in math and
science, because in those areas I achieved A's and scored in the ninetieth percentile or higher.

This was understandable. Math is precise; there is only one correct answer.
Whereas, for me at least, the answers on English tests were always a judgment
call, a matter of opinion and personal experience. Those tests were constructed
around items like fill-in-the-blank sentence completion, such as "Even though
Tom was_____, Mary thought he was_____." And the correct answer always seemed to be the most bland combinations of thoughts, for example,
"Even though Tom was shy, Mary thought he was charming," with the grammatical structure "even though" limiting the correct answer to some sort of semantic opposites, so you wouldn't get answers like "Even though Tom was
foolish. Mary thought he was ridiculous." Well, according to my mother, there
were very few limitations as to what Tom could have been and what Mary
might have thought of him. So I never did well on tests like that.

The same was true with word analogies, pairs of words in which you were
supposed to find some sort of logical, semantic relationship—for example,
"*Sunset* is to *nightfall* as_____ is to_____." And here you would be presented with a list of four possible pairs, one of which showed the same kind of
relationship: *red* is to *stoplight, bus* is to *arrival, chills* is to *fever, yawn* is to *boring*. Well, I could never think that way. I knew what the tests were asking, but I
could not block out of my mind the images already created by the first pair,
"*sunset* is to *nightfall*"—and I would see a burst of colors against a darkening
sky, the moon rising, the lowering of a curtain of stars. And all the other pairs
of words—*red, bus, stoplight, boring*—just threw up a mass of confusing images, making it impossible for me to sort out something as logical as saying: "A
sunset precedes nightfall" is the same as "a chill precedes a fever." The only
way I would have gotten that answer right would have been to imagine an associative situation, for example, my being disobedient and staying out past sunset, catching a chill at night, which turns into feverish pneumonia as punishment, which indeed did happen to me.

I have been thinking about all this lately, about my mother's English, about
achievement tests. Because lately I've been asked, as a writer, why there are not

more Asian Americans represented in American literature. Why are there few Asian Americans enrolled in creative writing programs? Why do so many Chinese students go into engineering? Well, these are broad sociological questions I can't begin to answer. But I have noticed in surveys—in fact, just last week—that Asian students, as a whole, always do significantly better on math achievement tests than in English. And this makes me think that there are other Asian American students whose English spoken in the home might also be described as "broken" or "limited." And perhaps they also have teachers who are steering them away from writing and into math and science, which is what happened to me.

Fortunately, I happen to be rebellious in nature and enjoy the challenge of disproving assumptions made about me. I became an English major my first year in college, after being enrolled as premed. I started writing nonfiction as a freelancer the week after I was told by my former boss that writing was my worst skill and I should hone my talents toward account management.

But it wasn't until 1985 that I finally began to write fiction. And at first I wrote using what I thought to be wittily crafted sentences, sentences that would finally prove I had mastery over the English language. Here's an example from the first draft of a story that later made its way into *The Joy Luck Club*, but without this line: "That was my mental quandary in its nascent state." A terrible line, which I can barely pronounce. 20

Fortunately, for reasons I won't get into today, I later decided I should envision a reader for the stories I would write. And the reader I decided upon was my mother, because these were stories about mothers. So with this reader in mind—and in fact she did read my early drafts—I began to write stories using all the Englishes I grew up with: the English I spoke to my mother, which for lack of a better term might be described as "simple"; the English she used with me, which for lack of a better term might be described as "broken"; my translation of her Chinese, which could certainly be described as "watered down"; and what I imagined to be her translation of her Chinese if she could speak in perfect English, her internal language, and for that I sought to preserve the essence, but neither an English nor a Chinese structure. I wanted to capture what language ability tests can never reveal: her intent, her passion, her imagery, the rhythms of her speech and the nature of her thoughts.

Apart from what any critic had to say about my writing, I knew I had succeeded where it counted when my mother finished reading my book and gave me her verdict: "So easy to read."

QUESTIONS

1. Why does Tan begin her essay with the disclaimer, "I am not a scholar of English or literature. I cannot give you much more than personal opinions on the English language and its variations in this country or others"? What advantage does this disclaimer offer Tan?

2. What are the different "Englishes" with which Tan grew up? Find an example of each "English." What did Tan need to learn about each?

3. Tan tells us that, as a writer, she cares about the way language "can evoke an emotion, a visual image, a complex idea, or a simple truth" (paragraph 2). Look closely at Tan's language. Find passages in her essay where her language is evocative. Where does Tan surprise you with her choice of words or her ability to use language to evoke emotion or imagery?

4. What did Tan learn about her "mother tongue"?

5. Think about your own mother tongue. In what ways does it reflect how you see and make sense of the world? What have you had to understand, accept, or reject about your mother tongue?

6. Tan writes that, "the language spoken in the family, especially in immigrant families . . . , plays a large role in shaping the language of the child" (paragraph 15). Write an essay in which you reflect on the role of language in your family.

MAKING CONNECTIONS

What kind of conversation can you imagine between Amy Tan and George Orwell, author of "Politics and the English Language" (p. 581)? How, for instance, would Tan respond to Orwell's claim that thought can corrupt language as much as language can corrupt thought?

Social Sciences and Public Affairs

THE DEATH OF THE PROFANE
A Commentary on the Genre of Legal Writing
Patricia J. Williams

Patricia J. Williams (b. 1951), a professor of law at Columbia University, is the great-great-granddaughter of a young female slave purchased at the age of eleven by a white lawyer who immediately impregnated her. In her book The Alchemy of Race and Rights *(1991), from which this selection is taken, Williams juxtaposes experiential accounts with sophisticated legal theories to expose the ideology underlying law in the United States. Williams, who has written widely on legal issues and race, challenges traditional legal thinking by questioning the ways in which such thinking represents racial identity. In the following essay, Williams reflects on the intersection of race, gender, class, and law.*

Buzzers are big in New York City. Favored particularly by smaller stores and boutiques, merchants throughout the city have installed them as screening devices to reduce the incidence of robbery: if the face at the door looks desirable, the buzzer is pressed and the door is unlocked. If the face is that of an undesirable, the door stays locked. Predictably, the issue of undesirability has revealed itself to be a racial determination. While controversial enough at first, even civil-rights organizations backed down eventually in the face of arguments that the buzzer system is a "necessary evil," that it is a "mere inconvenience" in comparison to the risks of being murdered, that suffering discrimination is not as bad as being assaulted, and that in any event it is not all blacks who are barred, just "17-year-old black males wearing running shoes and hooded sweat-shirts."[1]

The installation of these buzzers happened swiftly in New York; stores that had always had their doors wide open suddenly became exclusive or received people by appointment only. I discovered them and their meaning one Saturday in 1986. I was shopping in Soho and saw in a store window a sweater that I wanted to buy for my mother. I pressed my round brown face to the window and my finger to the buzzer, seeking admittance. A narrow-eyed, white teenager wearing running shoes and feasting on bubble gum glared out, evaluating me for signs that would pit me against the limits of his social understanding. After about five seconds, he mouthed "We're closed," and blew pink rubber at me. It was two Saturdays before Christmas, at one o'clock in the afternoon; there were several white people in the store who appeared to be shopping for things for *their* mothers.

I was enraged. At that moment I literally wanted to break all the windows of the store and *take* lots of sweaters for my mother. In the flicker of his judgmental gray eyes, that saleschild had transformed my brightly sentimental, joy-to-the-world, pre-Christmas spree to a shambles. He snuffed my sense of humanitarian catholicity, and there was nothing I could do to snuff his, without making a spectacle of myself.

I am still struck by the structure of power that drove me into such a blizzard of rage. There was almost nothing I could do, short of physically intruding upon him, that would humiliate him the way he humiliated me. No words, no gestures, no prejudices of my own would make a bit of difference to him; his refusal to let me into the store—it was Benetton's, whose colorfully punnish ad campaign is premised on wrapping every one of the world's peoples in its cottons and woolens—was an outward manifestation of his never having let someone like me into the realm of his reality. He had no compassion, no remorse, no reference to me; and no desire to acknowledge me even at the estranged level of arm's-length transactor. He saw me only as one who would take his money and therefore could not conceive that I was there to give him money.

In this weird ontological imbalance, I realized that buying something in that store was like bestowing a gift, the gift of my commerce, the lucre of my patronage. In the wake of my outrage, I wanted to take back the gift of appreciation that my peering in the window must have appeared to be. I wanted to take it back in the form of unappreciation, disrespect, defilement. I wanted to work so hard at wishing he could feel what I felt that he would never again mistake my hatred for some sort of plaintive wish to be included. I was quite willing to disenfranchise myself, in the heat of my need to revoke the flattery of

5

---

[1]"When 'By Appointment' Means Keep Out," *New York Times*, December 17, 1986, p. B1. Letter to the Editor from Michael Levin and Marguerita Levin, *New York Times*, January 11, 1987, p. E32.

my purchasing power. I was willing to boycott Benetton's, random white-owned businesses, and anyone who ever blew bubble gum in my face again.

My rage was admittedly diffuse, even self-destructive, but it was symmetrical. The perhaps loose-ended but utter propriety of that rage is no doubt lost not just to the young man who actually barred me, but to those who would appreciate my being barred only as an abstract precaution, who approve of those who would bar even as they deny that they would bar *me*.

The violence of my desire to burst into Benetton's is probably quite apparent. I often wonder if the violence, the exclusionary hatred, is equally apparent in the repeated public urgings that blacks understand the buzzer system by putting themselves in the shoes of white storeowners—that, in effect, blacks look into the mirror of frightened white faces for the reality of their undesirability; and that then blacks would "just as surely conclude that [they] would not let [themselves] in under similar circumstances."[2] (That some blacks might agree merely shows that some of us have learned too well the lessons of privatized intimacies of self-hatred and rationalized away the fullness of our public, participatory selves.)

On the same day I was barred from Benetton's, I went home and wrote the above impassioned account in my journal. On the day after that, I found I was still brooding, so I turned to a form of catharsis I have always found healing. I typed up as much of the story as I have just told, made a big poster of it, put a nice colorful border around it, and, after Benetton's was truly closed, stuck it to their big sweater-filled window. I exercised my first-amendment right to place my business with them right out in the street.

So that was the first telling of this story. The second telling came a few months later, for a symposium on Excluded Voices sponsored by a law review. I wrote an essay summing up my feelings about being excluded from Benetton's and analyzing "how the rhetoric of increased privatization, in response to racial issues, functions as the rationalizing agent of public unaccountability and, ultimately, irresponsibility." Weeks later, I received the first edit. From the first page to the last, my fury had been carefully cut out. My rushing, run-on-rage had been reduced to simple declarative sentences. The active personal had been inverted in favor of the passive impersonal. My words were different; they spoke to me upsidedown. I was afraid to read too much of it at a time—meanings rose up at me oddly, stolen and strange.

A week and a half later, I received the second edit. All reference to Benetton's had been deleted because, according to the editors and the faculty adviser, it was defamatory; they feared harassment and liability; they said printing it would be irresponsible. I called them and offered to supply a footnote attesting to this as my personal experience at one particular location and of a buzzer system not limited to Benetton's; the editors told me that they were not in the

10

---

[2]*New York Times*, January 11, 1987, p. E32.

habit of publishing things that were unverifiable. I could not but wonder, in this refusal even to let me file an affadavit, what it would take to make my experience verifiable. The testimony of an independent white bystander? (a requirement in fact imposed in U.S. Supreme Court holdings through the first part of the century[3]).

Two days *after* the piece was sent to press, I received copies of the final page proofs. All reference to my race had been eliminated because it was against "editorial policy" to permit descriptions of physiognomy. "I realize," wrote one editor, "that this was a very personal experience, but any reader will know what you must have looked like when standing at that window." In a telephone conversation to them, I ranted wildly about the significance of such an omission. "It's irrelevant," another editor explained in a voice gummy with soothing and patience; "It's nice and poetic," but it doesn't "advance the discussion of any principle. . . . This is a law review, after all." Frustrated, I accused him of censorship; calmly he assured me it was not. "This is just a matter of style," he said with firmness and finality.

Ultimately I did convince the editors that mention of my race was central to the whole sense of the subsequent text; that my story became one of extreme paranoia without the information that I am black; or that it became one in which the reader had to fill in the gap by assumption, presumption, prejudgment, or prejudice. What was most interesting to me in this experience was how the blind application of principles of neutrality, through the device of omission, acted either to make me look crazy or to make the reader participate in old habits of cultural bias.

That was the second telling of my story. The third telling came last April, when I was invited to participate in a law-school conference on Equality and Difference. I retold my sad tale of exclusion from Soho's most glitzy boutique, focusing in this version on the law-review editing process as a consequence of an ideology of style rooted in a social text of neutrality. I opined:

> Law and legal writing aspire to formalized, color-blind, liberal ideals. Neutrality is the standard for assuring these ideals; yet the adherence to it is often determined by reference to an aesthetic of uniformity, in which difference is simply omitted. For example, when segregation was eradicated from the American lexicon, its omission led many to actually believe that racism therefore no longer existed. Race-neutrality in law has become the presumed antidote for race bias in real life. With the entrenchment of the notion of race-neutrality came attacks on the concept of affirmative action and the rise of reverse discrimination suits. Blacks, for so many generations deprived of jobs based on the color of our skin, are now told that we ought to find it

---

[3]See generally *Blyew v. U.S.*, 80 U.S. 581 (1871), upholding a state's right to forbid blacks to testify against whites.

demeaning to be hired, based on the color of our skin. Such is the silliness of simplistic either-or inversions as remedies to complex problems.

What is truly demeaning in this era of double-speak-no-evil is going on interviews and not getting hired because someone doesn't think we'll be comfortable. It is demeaning not to get promoted because we're judged "too weak," then putting in a lot of energy the next time and getting fired because we're "too strong." It is demeaning to be told what we find demeaning. It is very demeaning to stand on street corners unemployed and begging. It is downright demeaning to have to explain why we haven't been employed for months and then watch the job go to someone who is "more experienced." It is outrageously demeaning that none of this can be called racism, even if it happens only to, or to large numbers of, black people; as long as it's done with a smile, a handshake and a shrug; as long as the phantom-word "race" is never used.

The image of race as a phantom-word came to me after I moved into my late godmother's home. In an attempt to make it my own, I cleared the bedroom for painting. The following morning the room asserted itself, came rushing and raging at me through the emptiness, exactly as it had been for twenty-five years. One day filled with profuse and overwhelming complexity, the next day filled with persistently recurring memories. The shape of the past came to haunt me, the shape of the emptiness confronted me each time I was about to enter the room. The force of its spirit still drifts like an odor throughout the house.

The power of that room, I have thought since, is very like the power of racism as status quo: it is deep, angry, eradicated from view, but strong enough to make everyone who enters the room walk around the bed that isn't there, avoiding the phantom as they did the substance, for fear of bodily harm. They do not even know they are avoiding; they defer to the unseen shapes of things with subtle responsiveness, guided by an impulsive awareness of nothingness, and the deep knowledge and denial of witchcraft at work.

The phantom room is to me symbolic of the emptiness of formal equal opportunity, particularly as propounded by President Reagan, the Reagan Civil Rights Commission and the Reagan Supreme Court. Blindly formalized constructions of equal opportunity are the creation of a space that is filled in by a meandering stream of unguided hopes, dreams, fantasies, fears, recollections. They are the presence of the past in imaginary, imagistic form—the phantom-roomed exile of our longing.

It is thus that I strongly believe in the efficacy of programs and paradigms like affirmative action. Blacks are the objects of a constitutional omission which has been incorporated into a theory of neutrality. It is thus that omission is really a form of expression, as oxymoronic as that sounds: racial omission is a literal part of original intent; it is the fixed, reiterated prophecy of the Founding Fathers. It is thus that affirmative action is an affirmation; the affirmative act of hiring—or hearing— blacks is a recognition of individuality that re-places blacks as a social statistic, that is profoundly interconnective to the fate of blacks and whites either as sub-groups or as one group. In this sense, affirmative action is as mystical and beyond-the-self as an initiation ceremony. It is an act of verification and of vision. It is an act of social as well as pro- fessional responsibility.

The following morning I opened the local newspaper, to find that the event of my speech had commanded two columns on the front page of the Metro section. I quote only the opening lines: "Affirmative action promotes prejudice by denying the status of women and blacks, instead of affirming them as its name suggests. So said New York City attorney Patricia Williams to an audi- ence Wednesday."[4]

I clipped out the article and put it in my journal. In the margin there is a note to myself: eventually, it says, I should try to pull all these threads together into yet another law-review article. The problem, of course, will be that in the hierarchy of law-review citation, the article in the newspaper will have more authoritative weight about me, as a so-called "primary resource," than I will have; it will take precedence over my own citation of the unverifiable testi- mony of my speech.

I have used the Benetton's story a lot, in speaking engagements at various schools. I tell it whenever I am too tired to whip up an original speech from scratch. Here are some of the questions I have been asked in the wake of its telling:

Am I not privileging a racial perspective, by considering only the black point of view? Don't I have an obligation to include the "salesman's side" of the story?

Am I not putting the salesman on trial and finding him guilty of racism without giving him a chance to respond to or cross-examine me?

Am I not using the store window as a "metaphorical fence" against the po- tential of his explanation in order to represent my side as "authentic"?

How can I be sure I'm right?

What makes my experience the real black one anyway?

Isn't it possible that another black person would disagree with my experi- ence? If so, doesn't that render my story too unempirical and subjective to pay any attention to?

---

[4]"Attorney Says Affirmative Action Denies Racism, Sexism," *Dominion Post* (Morgantown, West Virginia), April 8, 1988, p. B1.

Always a major objection is to my having put the poster on Benetton's window. As one law professor put it: "It's one thing to publish this in a law review, where no one can take it personally, but it's another thing altogether to put your own interpretation right out there, just like that, uncontested, I mean, with nothing to counter it."

QUESTIONS

1. Williams begins her essay with the simple sentence, "Buzzers are big in New York City." What does Williams want us to understand about the function of buzzers in our society? How does she use her personal experience as a meditation on racial identity? In what ways do you find her personal experience to be persuasive evidence?

2. Williams offers us three renditions of the same story. Summarize each rendition. What do we learn about Williams's experience from these different versions? What connections does she create between her different versions?

3. Reflect on the meaning of the title, "The Death of the Profane," and the subtitle, "A Commentary on the Genre of Legal Writing." What kind of commentary does Williams's essay offer her readers? What does Williams reveal about herself and her way of seeing the world of legal writing?

4. Imagine a conversation between Williams and the law professor who criticized her for putting the poster on Benetton's window. As you imagine such a conversation, decide what is at stake for both the professor and for Williams.

5. At the end of her essay, Williams offers us a number of questions she has been asked as she retells her Bennetton story. How would you respond to these various questions?

6. Using Williams's essay as a model, write three different versions of an experience you have had. Use these different versions to suggest an interpretation of the original story you tell.

MAKING CONNECTIONS

1. Select an idea about race or class that intrigues you in Williams's essay. How does this idea relate to a similar idea you find compelling in any of the other essays in "Reflecting"?

2. Williams is concerned with the questions of how an African American woman verifies and validates her own experience. What connections do you find between Williams's experience as an African American woman and the experience of Maya Angelou (p. 29) or Alice Walker (p. 40)?

PILGRIMAGE TO NONVIOLENCE
Martin Luther King Jr.

The son of a minister, Martin Luther King Jr. (1929–1968) was ordained a Baptist minister in his father's church in Atlanta, Georgia, at the age of eighteen. He sprang into prominence in 1955 when he called a citywide boycott of the segregated bus system in Montgomery, Alabama, and he continued to be the most prominent civil rights activist in America until his assassination on April 4, 1968. During those tumultuous years, he was jailed at least fourteen times and endured countless threats against his life, but he persevered in his fight against racial discrimination, using a synthesis of the nonviolent philosophy of Mahatma Gandhi and the Sermon on the Mount. The 1964 Nobel Peace Prize was only one of the many awards he received, and his several books are characterized as much by their eloquent prose style as by their moral fervor. "Pilgrimage to Nonviolence" originally appeared in the magazine Christian Century *and was revised and updated for a collection of his sermons,* Strength to Love *(1963), the source of the following text.*

In my senior year in theological seminary, I engaged in the exciting reading of various theological theories. Having been raised in a rather strict fundamentalist tradition, I was occasionally shocked when my intellectual journey carried me through new and sometimes complex doctrinal lands, but the pilgrimage was always stimulating, gave me a new appreciation for objective appraisal and critical analysis, and knocked me out of my dogmatic slumber.

Liberalism provided me with an intellectual satisfaction that I had never found in fundamentalism. I became so enamored of the insights of liberalism that I almost fell into the trap of accepting uncritically everything it encompassed. I was absolutely convinced of the natural goodness of man and the natural power of human reason.

I

A basic change in my thinking came when I began to question some of the theories that had been associated with so-called liberal theology. Of course, there are aspects of liberalism that I hope to cherish always: its devotion to the search for truth, its insistence on an open and analytical mind, and its refusal to abandon the best lights of reason. The contribution of liberalism to the philosophical-historical criticism of biblical literature has been of immeasurable value and should be defended with religious and scientific passion.

But I began to question the liberal doctrine of man. The more I observed the tragedies of history and man's shameful inclination to choose the low road, the more I came to see the depths and strength of sin. My reading of the works of Reinhold Niebuhr made me aware of the complexity of human motives and the reality of sin on every level of man's existence.[1] Moreover, I came to recognize the complexity of man's social involvement and the glaring reality of collective evil. I realized that liberalism had been all too sentimental concerning human nature and that it leaned toward a false idealism.

I also came to see the superficial optimism of liberalism concerning human nature overlooked the fact that reason is darkened by sin. The more I thought about human nature, the more I saw how our tragic inclination for sin encourages us to rationalize our actions. Liberalism failed to show that reason by itself is little more than an instrument to justify man's defensive ways of thinking. Reason, devoid of the purifying power of faith, can never free itself from distortions and rationalizations.

Although I rejected some aspects of liberalism, I never came to an all-out acceptance of neo-orthodoxy. While I saw neo-orthodoxy as a helpful corrective for a sentimental liberalism, I felt that it did not provide an adequate answer to basic questions. If liberalism was too optimistic concerning human nature, neo-orthodoxy was too pessimistic. Not only on the question of man, but also on other vital issues, the revolt of neo-orthodoxy went too far. In its attempt to preserve the transcendence of God, which had been neglected by an overstress of his immanence in liberalism, neo-orthodoxy went to the extreme of stressing a God who was hidden, unknown, and "wholly other." In its revolt against overemphasis on the power of reason in liberalism, neo-orthodoxy fell into a mood of antirationalism and semifundamentalism, stressing a narrow uncritical biblicism. This approach, I felt, was inadequate both for the church and for personal life.

So although liberalism left me unsatisfied on the question of the nature of man, I found no refuge in neo-orthodoxy. I am now convinced that the truth about man is found neither in liberalism nor in neo-orthodoxy. Each represents a partial truth. A large segment of Protestant liberalism defined man only in terms of his essential nature, his capacity for good; neo-orthodoxy tended to define man only in terms of his existential nature, his capacity for evil. An adequate understanding of man is found neither in the thesis of liberalism nor in

---

[1]*Reinhold Niebuhr* (1892–1971): American theologian, social activist, and noted writer on social and religious issues. [Eds.]

91

the antithesis of neo-orthodoxy, but in a synthesis which reconciles the truths of both.

During the intervening years I have gained a new appreciation for the philosophy of existentialism. My first contact with the philosophy came through my reading of Kierkegaard and Nietzsche.[2] Later I turned to a study of Jaspers, Heidegger, and Sartre.[3] These thinkers stimulated my thinking; while questioning each, I nevertheless learned a great deal through a study of them. When I finally engaged in a serious study of the writings of Paul Tillich,[4] I became convinced that existentialism, in spite of the fact that it had become all too fashionable, had grasped certain basic truths about man and his condition that could not be permanently overlooked.

An understanding of the "finite freedom" of man is one of the permanent contributions of existentialism, and its perception of the anxiety and conflict produced in man's personal and social life by the perilous and ambiguous structure of existence is especially meaningful for our time. A common denominator in atheistic or theistic existentialism is that man's existential situation is estranged from his essential nature. In their revolt against Hegel's essentialism,[5] all existentialists contend that the world is fragmented. History is a series of unreconciled conflicts, and man's existence is filled with anxiety and threatened with meaninglessness. While the ultimate Christian answer is not found in any of these existential assertions, there is much here by which the theologian may describe the true state of man's existence.

Although most of my formal study has been in systematic theology and philosophy, I have become more and more interested in social ethics. During my early teens I was deeply concerned by the problem of racial injustice. I considered segregation both rationally inexplicable and morally unjustifiable. I could never accept my having to sit in the back of a bus or in the segregated section of a train. The first time that I was seated behind a curtain in a dining car I felt as though the curtain had been dropped on my selfhood. I also learned that the inseparable twin of racial injustice is economic injustice. I saw how the systems of segregation exploited both the Negro and the poor whites. These early experiences made me deeply conscious of the varieties of injustice in our society.

10

---

[2]*Søren Kierkegaard* (1813–1855): Danish religious and aesthetic philosopher, concerned especially with the role of the individual; *Friedrich Nietzsche* (1844–1900): German philosopher and moralist looking for a heroic, creative rejuvenation of decadent Western civilization. [Eds.]

[3]*Karl Jaspers* (1883–1969): German philosopher; *Martin Heidegger* (1889–1976): German philosopher; *Jean-Paul Sartre* (1905–1980): French philosopher and novelist. All three were existentialists, concerned with the existence and responsibility of the individual in an unknowable universe. [Eds.]

[4]*Paul Tillich* (1886–1965): German-born American philosopher and theologian whose writings drew on psychology and existentialism. [Eds.]

[5]*Georg Friedrich Hegel* (1770–1831): German philosopher best known for his theory of the dialectic (thesis versus antithesis produces synthesis). [Eds.]

II

Not until I entered theological seminary, however, did I begin a serious intellectual quest for a method that would eliminate social evil. I was immediately influenced by the social gospel. In the early 1950s I read Walter Rauschenbusch's *Christianity and the Social Crisis*, a book which left an indelible imprint on my thinking. Of course, there were points at which I differed with Rauschenbusch. I felt that he was a victim of the nineteenth-century "cult of inevitable progress," which led him to an unwarranted optimism concerning human nature. Moreover, he came perilously close to identifying the Kingdom of God with a particular social and economic system, a temptation to which the church must never surrender. But in spite of these shortcomings, Rauschenbusch gave to American Protestantism a sense of social responsibility that it should never lose. The gospel at its best deals with the whole man, not only his soul but also his body, not only his spiritual well-being but also his material well-being. A religion that professes a concern for the souls of men and is not equally concerned about the slums that damn them, the economic conditions that strangle them, and the social conditions that cripple them, is a spiritually moribund religion.

After reading Rauschenbusch, I turned to a serious study of the social and ethical theories of the great philosophers. During this period I had almost despaired of the power of love to solve social problems. The turn-the-other-cheek and the love-your-enemies philosophies are valid, I felt, only when individuals are in conflict with other individuals; when racial groups and nations are in conflict, a more realistic approach is necessary.

Then I was introduced to the life and teachings of Mahatma Gandhi.[6] As I read his works I became deeply fascinated by his campaigns of nonviolent resistance. The whole Gandhian concept of *satyagraha* (*satya* is truth which equals love and *graha* is force; *satyagraha* thus means truth-force or love-force) was profoundly significant to me. As I delved deeper into the philosophy of Gandhi, my skepticism concerning the power of love gradually diminished, and I came to see for the first time that the Christian doctrine of love, operating through the Gandhian method of nonviolence, is one of the most potent weapons available to an oppressed people in their struggle for freedom. At that time, however, I acquired only an intellectual understanding and appreciation of the position, and I had no firm determination to organize it in a socially effective situation.

When I went to Montgomery, Alabama, as a pastor in 1954, I had not the slightest idea that I would later become involved in a crisis in which nonviolent resistance would be applicable. After I had lived in the community about a year, the bus boycott began. The Negro people of Montgomery, exhausted by

---

[6]*Mahatma Gandhi* (1869–1948): Hindu nationalist and spiritual leader. [Eds.]

the humiliating experience that they had constantly faced on the buses, expressed in a massive act of noncooperation their determination to be free. They came to see that it was ultimately more honorable to walk the streets in dignity than to ride the buses in humiliation. At the beginning of the protest, the people called on me to serve as their spokesman. In accepting this responsibility, my mind, consciously or unconsciously, was driven back to the Sermon on the Mount and the Gandhian method of nonviolent resistance. This principle became the guiding light of our movement. Christ furnished the spirit and motivation and Gandhi furnished the method.

The experience in Montgomery did more to clarify my thinking in regard to the question of nonviolence than all of the books that I had read. As the days unfolded, I became more and more convinced of the power of nonviolence. Nonviolence became more than a method to which I gave intellectual assent; it became a commitment to a way of life. Many issues I had not cleared up intellectually concerning nonviolence were now resolved within the sphere of practical action.   15

My privilege of traveling to India had a great impact on me personally, for it was invigorating to see firsthand the amazing results of a nonviolent struggle to achieve independence. The aftermath of hatred and bitterness that usually follows a violent campaign was found nowhere in India, and a mutual friendship, based on complete equality, existed between the Indian and British people within the Commonwealth.

I would not wish to give the impression that nonviolence will accomplish miracles overnight. Men are not easily moved from their mental ruts or purged of their prejudiced and irrational feelings. When the underprivileged demand freedom, the privileged at first react with bitterness and resistance. Even when the demands are couched in nonviolent terms, the initial response is substantially the same. I am sure that many of our white brothers in Montgomery and throughout the South are still bitter toward the Negro leaders, even though these leaders have sought to follow a way of love and nonviolence. But the nonviolent approach does something to the hearts and souls of those committed to it. It gives them new self-respect. It calls up resources of strength and courage that they did not know they had. Finally, it so stirs the conscience of the opponent that reconciliation becomes a reality.

III

More recently I have come to see the need for the method of nonviolence in international relations. Although I was not yet convinced of its efficacy in conflicts between nations, I felt that while war could never be a positive good, it could serve as a negative good by preventing the spread and growth of an evil force. War, horrible as it is, might be preferable to surrender to a totalitarian system. But I now believe that the potential destructiveness of modern weapons totally rules out the possibility of war ever again achieving a negative good. If we assume that mankind has a right to survive, then we must find an alternative to war and destruction. In our day of space vehicles and guided ballistic missiles, the choice is either nonviolence or nonexistence.

I am no doctrinaire pacifist, but I have tried to embrace a realistic pacifism which finds the pacifist position as the lesser evil in the circumstances. I do not claim to be free from the moral dilemmas that the Christian nonpacifist confronts, but I am convinced that the church cannot be silent while mankind faces the threat of nuclear annihilation. If the church is true to her mission, she must call for an end to the arms race.

Some of my personal sufferings over the last few years have also served to shape my thinking. I always hesitate to mention these experiences for fear of conveying the wrong impression. A person who constantly calls attention to his trials and sufferings is in danger of developing a martyr complex and impressing others that he is consciously seeking sympathy. It is possible for one to be self-centered in his self-sacrifice. So I am always reluctant to refer to my personal sacrifices. But I feel somewhat justified in mentioning them in this essay because of the influence they have had upon my thought.

Due to my involvement in the struggle for the freedom of my people, I have known very few quiet days in the last few years. I have been imprisoned in Alabama and Georgia jails twelve times. My home has been bombed twice. A day seldom passes that my family and I are not the recipients of threats of death. I have been the victim of a near-fatal stabbing. So in a real sense I have been battered by the storms of persecution. I must admit that at times I have felt that I could no longer bear such a heavy burden, and have been tempted to retreat to a more quiet and serene life. But every time such a temptation appeared, something came to strengthen and sustain my determination. I have learned now that the Master's burden is light precisely when we take his yoke upon us.

My personal trials have also taught me the value of unmerited suffering. As my sufferings mounted I soon realized that there were two ways in which I could respond to my situation — either to react with bitterness or seek to transform the suffering into a creative force. I decided to follow the latter course. Recognizing the necessity for suffering, I have tried to make of it a virtue, if only to save myself from bitterness, I have attempted to see my personal ordeals as an opportunity to transfigure myself and heal the people involved in the tragic situation which now obtains. I have lived these last few years with the conviction that unearned suffering is redemptive. There are some who still find the Cross a stumbling block, others consider it foolishness, but I am more convinced than ever before that it is the power of God unto social and individual salvation. So like the Apostle Paul I can now humbly, yet proudly, say, "I bear in my body the marks of the Lord Jesus."

The agonizing moments through which I have passed during the last few years have also drawn me closer to God. More than ever before I am convinced of the reality of a personal God. True, I have always believed in the per-

95

sonality of God. But in the past the idea of a personal God was little more than a metaphysical category that I found theologically and philosophically satisfying. Now it is a living reality that has been validated in the experiences of everyday life. God has been profoundly real to me in recent years. In the midst of outer dangers I have felt an inner calm. In the midst of lonely days and dreary nights I have heard an inner voice saying, "Lo, I will be with you." When the chains of fear and the manacles of frustration have all but stymied my efforts, I have felt the power of God transforming the fatigue of despair into the buoyancy of hope. I am convinced that the universe is under the control of a loving purpose, and that in the struggle for righteousness man has cosmic companionship. Behind the harsh appearances of the world there is a benign power. To say that this God is personal is not to make him a finite object beside other objects or attribute to him the limitations of human personality; it is to take what is finest and noblest in our consciousness and affirm its perfect existence in him. It is certainly true that human personality is limited, but personality as such involves no necessary limitations. It means simply self-consciousness and self-direction. So in the truest sense of the word, God is a living God. In him there is feeling and will, responsive to the deepest yearnings of the human heart: *this* God both evokes and answers prayer.

The past decade has been a most exciting one. In spite of the tensions and uncertainties of this period something profoundly meaningful is taking place. Old systems of exploitation and oppression are passing away; new systems of justice and equality are being born. In a real sense this is a great time to be alive. Therefore, I am not yet discouraged about the future. Granted that the easygoing optimism of yesterday is impossible. Granted that we face a world crisis which leaves us standing so often amid the surging murmur of life's restless sea. But every crisis has both its dangers and its opportunities. It can spell either salvation or doom. In a dark, confused world the Kingdom of God may yet reign in the hearts of men.

QUESTIONS

1. King found the extremes of liberalism on one hand and neo-orthodoxy on the other both unsatisfactory. Why?

2. Existentialism and Rauschenbusch's social gospel proved more useful to King than liberalism or neo-orthodoxy. How did these concepts help shape his outlook?

3. King is interested in religious and philosophical theories not for their own sake but for their usefulness in the social world. How do Gandhi's example and King's own experience in Montgomery (paragraphs 14, 15, and 17) illustrate this concern?

4. How did King's personal faith in God aid in his struggles and sufferings? Is his dream of a better society totally dependent on the existence of this "benign power" (paragraph 23)?

5. King's intellectual development is described as a pilgrimage from a simple fundamentalist attitude through conflicting theological and philosophical concepts to an intensified belief in a benign God and a commitment to international nonviolence. How is his final set of beliefs superior to his original one? Has he convinced you of the validity of his beliefs?

6. King writes for a general audience rather than one with theological and philosophical training. How successful is King at clarifying religious and philosophical concepts for the general reader? Point out examples that show how he treats such concepts.

7. Again and again King employs the classical rhetorical strategy of concession: the opposition's viewpoint is stated and partially accepted before King gives his own viewpoint. Locate two or three instances of this strategy, and explain how it aids a reader's understanding (if not acceptance) of King's views.

8. King's essay reflects on how he came to accept the method of nonviolence. Have you, over time, changed your thoughts or methods of approaching an issue or problem? Has someone you know well done this? If so, write an essay reflecting on the events central to this change and their significance.

9. King's hopes for a better world were expressed in the early 1960s. Based on your knowledge of history since then, write an essay in which you justify or disqualify King's guarded optimism.

MAKING CONNECTIONS

1. Like several other writers in this section, King reflects on a turning point in his life. Consider his essay in relation to two or three others, such as those by Maya Angelou (p. 29), Alice Walker (p. 40), George Orwell (p. 104), Zoë Tracy Hardy (p. 111), or Loren Eiseley (p. 138). Compare and contrast the ways these writers present their turning points. How does each present the crucial moment or event, and how does each show its meaning?

2. One way a writer convinces us is by the authority we sense in the person as he or she writes. What details in King's essay contribute to our sense of him as an authoritative person, a writer we are inclined to believe? What do you find of similar persuasiveness in the essays of Maya Angelou (p. 29), George Orwell (p. 104), Zoë Tracy Hardy (p. 111), or Patricia J. Williams (p. 83)?

THE WAY TO RAINY MOUNTAIN
N. Scott Momaday

N. Scott Momaday was born in Lawton, Oklahoma, in 1934. His father is a full-blooded Kiowa, and his mother is part Cherokee. After attending schools on Navajo, Apache, and Pueblo reservations, Momaday graduated from the University of New Mexico and earned his doctorate at Stanford University. He has published two collections of poetry, Angle of Geese and Other Poems *(1974) and* The Gourd Dancer *(1976), and a memoir,* The Names *(1976). In 1969 his novel* House Made of Dawn *won the Pulitzer Prize. When asked about his writing, Momaday said, "When I was growing up on the reservations of the Southwest, I saw people who were deeply involved in their traditional life, in the memories of their blood. They had, as far as I can see, a certain strength and beauty that I find missing in the modern world. I like to celebrate that involvement in my writing." The following essay appeared first in the* Reporter *magazine in 1967 and later as the introduction to* The Way to Rainy Mountain *(1969), a collection of Kiowa legends.*

A single knoll rises out of the plain in Oklahoma, north and west of the Wichita range. For my people, the Kiowas, it is an old landmark, and they gave it the name Rainy Mountain. The hardest weather in the world is there. Winter brings blizzards, hot tornadic winds arise in the spring, and in summer the prairie is an anvil's edge. The grass turns brittle and brown, and it cracks beneath your feet. There are green belts along the rivers and creeks, linear groves of hickory and pecan, willow and witch hazel. At a distance in July or August the steaming foliage seems almost to writhe in fire. Great green and yellow grasshoppers are everywhere in the tall grass, popping up like corn to sting the flesh, and tortoises crawl about on the red earth, going nowhere in the plenty of time. Loneliness is an aspect of the land. All things in the plain are isolate; there is no confusion of objects in the eye, but *one* hill or *one* tree or *one* man. To look upon that landscape in the early morning, with the sun at your back, is to lose the sense of proportion. Your imagination comes to life, and this, you think, is where Creation was begun.

I returned to Rainy Mountain in July. My grandmother had died in the spring, and I wanted to be at her grave. She had lived to be very old and at last infirm. Her only living daughter was with her when she died, and I was told that in death her face was that of a child.

I like to think of her as a child. When she was born, the Kiowas were living the last great moment of their history. For more than a hundred years they had controlled the open range from the Smoky Hill River to the Red, from the headwaters of the Canadian to the fork of the Arkansas and Cimarron. In alliance with the Comanches, they had ruled the whole of the Southern Plains. War was their sacred business, and they were the finest horsemen the world has ever known. But warfare for the Kiowas was pre-eminently a matter of disposition rather than of survival, and they never understood the grim, unrelenting advance of the U.S. Cavalry. When at last, divided and ill provisioned, they were driven onto the Staked Plains in the cold of autumn, they fell into panic. In Palo Duro Canyon they abandoned their crucial stores to pillage and had nothing then but their lives. In order to save themselves, they surrendered to the soldiers at Fort Sill and were imprisoned in the old stone corral that now stands as a military museum. My grandmother was spared the humiliation of those high gray walls by eight or ten years, but she must have known from birth the affliction of defeat, the dark brooding of old warriors.

Her name was Aho, and she belonged to the last culture to evolve in North America. Her forebears came down from the high country in western Montana nearly three centuries ago. They were a mountain people, a mysterious tribe of hunters whose language has never been classified in any major group. In the late seventeenth century they began a long migration to the south and east. It was a journey toward the dawn, and it led to a golden age. Along the way the Kiowas were befriended by the Crows, who gave them the culture and religion of the Plains. They acquired horses, and their ancient nomadic spirit was suddenly free of the ground. They acquired Tai-me, the sacred sun-dance doll, from that moment the object and symbol of their worship, and so shared in the divinity of the sun. Not least, they acquired the sense of destiny, therefore courage and pride. When they entered upon the Southern Plains they had been transformed. No longer were they slaves to the simple necessity of survival; they were a lordly and dangerous society of fighters and thieves, hunters and priests of the sun. According to their origin myth, they entered the world through a hollow log. From one point of view, their migration was the fruit of an old prophecy, for indeed they emerged from a sunless world.

Though my grandmother lived out her long life in the shadow of Rainy 5 Mountain, the immense landscape of the continental interior lay like memory in her blood. She could tell of the Crows, whom she had never seen, and of the Black Hills, where she had never been. I wanted to see in reality what she had seen more perfectly in the mind's eye, and drove fifteen hundred miles to begin my pilgrimage.

A dark mist lay over the Black Hills, and the land was like iron. At the top of a ridge I caught sight of Devil's Tower upthrust against the gray sky as if in the

birth of time the core of the earth had broken through its crust and the motion
of the world was begun. There are things in nature that engender an awful quiet
in the heart of man; Devil's Tower is one of them. Two centuries ago, because
of their need to explain it, the Kiowas made a legend at the base of the rock.
My grandmother said:

"Eight children were there at play, seven sisters and their brother. Suddenly
the boy was struck dumb; he trembled and began to run upon his hands and
feet. His fingers became claws, and his body was covered with fur. There was a
bear where the boy had been. The sisters were terrified; they ran, and the bear
after them. They came to the stump of a great tree, and the tree spoke to them.
It bade them climb upon it, and as they did so, it began to rise into the air.
The bear came to kill them, but they were just beyond its reach. It reared
against the tree and scored the bark all around with its claws. The seven sisters
were borne into the sky, and they became the stars of the Big Dipper." From
that moment, and so long as the legend lives, the Kiowas have kinsmen in the
night sky. Whatever they were in the mountains, they could be no more. However tenuous their well-being, however much they had suffered and would suffer again, they had found a way out of the wilderness.

My grandmother had a reverence for the sun, a holy regard that now is all
but gone out of mankind. There was a wariness in her, and an ancient awe.
She was a Christian in her later years, but she had come a long way about, and
she never forgot her birthright. As a child she had been to the sun dances; she
had taken part in that annual rite, and by it she had learned the restoration of
her people in the presence of Tai-me. She was about seven when the last
Kiowa sun dance was held in 1887 on the Washita River above Rainy Mountain Creek. The buffalo were gone. In order to consummate the ancient sacrifice—to impale the head of a buffalo bull upon the Tai-me tree—a delegation
of old men journeyed into Texas, there to beg and barter for an animal from
the Goodnight herd. She was ten when the Kiowas came together for the last
time as a living sun-dance culture. They could find no buffalo; they had to
hang an old hide from the sacred tree. Before the dance could begin, a company of soldiers rode out from Fort Sill under orders to disperse the tribe. Forbidden without cause the essential act of their faith, having seen the wild herds
slaughtered and left to rot upon the ground, the Kiowas backed away forever
from the tree. That was July 20, 1890, at the great bend of the Washita. My
grandmother was there. Without bitterness, and for as long as she lived, she
bore a vision of deicide.[1]

Now that I can have her only in memory, I see my grandmother in the several postures that were peculiar to her: standing at the wood stove on a winter
morning and turning meat in a great iron skillet; sitting at the south window,

---

[1]*deicide:* the killing of a deity or god. [Eds.]

bent above her beadwork, and afterwards, when her vision failed, looking down for a long time into the fold of her hands; going out upon a cane, very slowly as she did when the weight of age came upon her; praying. I remember her most often at prayer. She made long, rambling prayers out of suffering and hope, having seen many things. I was never sure that I had the right to hear, so exclusive were they of all mere custom and company. The last time I saw her she prayed standing by the side of the bed at night, naked to the waist, the light of a kerosene lamp moving upon her dark skin. Her long black hair, always drawn and braided in the day, lay upon her shoulders and against her breasts like a shawl. I do not speak Kiowa, and I never understood her prayers, but there was something inherently sad in the sound, some merest hesitation upon the syllables of sorrow. She began in a high and descending pitch, exhausting her breath to silence; then again and again—and always the same intensity of effort, of something that is, and is not, like urgency in the human voice. Transported so in the dancing light among the shadows of her room, she seemed beyond the reach of time. But that was illusion; I think I knew then that I should not see her again.

Houses are like sentinels in the plain, old keepers of the weather watch. 10 There, in a very little while, wood takes on the appearance of great age. All colors wear soon away in the wind and rain, and then the wood is burned gray and the grain appears and the nails turn red with rust. The window panes are black and opaque; you imagine there is nothing within, and indeed there are many ghosts, bones given up to the land. They stand here and there against the sky, and you approach them for a longer time than you expect. They belong in the distance; it is their domain.

Once there was a lot of sound in my grandmother's house, a lot of coming and going, feasting and talk. The summers there were full of excitement and reunion. The Kiowas are a summer people; they abide the cold and keep to themselves, but when the season turns and the land becomes warm and vital they cannot hold still; an old love of going returns upon them. The aged visitors who came to my grandmother's house when I was a child were made of lean and leather, and they bore themselves upright. They wore great black hats and bright ample shirts that shook in the wind. They rubbed fat upon their hair and wound their braids with strips of colored cloth. Some of them painted their faces and carried the scars of old and cherished enmities. They were an old council of warlords, come to remind and be reminded of who they were. Their wives and daughters served them well. The women might indulge themselves; gossip was at once the mark and compensation of their servitude. They made loud and elaborate talk among themselves, full of jest and gesture, fright and false alarm. They went abroad in fringed and flowered shawls, bright beadwork and German silver. They were at home in the kitchen, and they prepared meals that were banquets.

There were frequent prayer meetings, and nocturnal feasts. When I was a child I played with my cousins outside, where the lamplight fell upon the ground and the singing of the old people rose up around us and carried away into the darkness. There were a lot of good things to eat, a lot of laughter and surprise. And afterwards, when the quiet returned, I lay down with my grandmother and could hear the frogs away by the river and feel the motion of the air.

Now there is a funereal silence in the rooms, the endless wake of some final word. The walls have closed in upon my grandmother's house. When I returned to it in mourning, I saw for the first time in my life how small it was. It was late at night, and there was a white moon, nearly full. I sat for a long time on the stone steps by the kitchen door. From there I could see out across the land; I could see the long row of trees by the creek, the low light upon the rolling plains, and the stars of the Big Dipper. Once I looked at the moon and caught sight of a strange thing. A cricket had perched upon the handrail, only a few inches away. My line of vision was such that the creature filled the moon like a fossil. It had gone there, I thought, to live and die, for there, of all places, was its small definition made whole and eternal. A warm wind rose up and purled like the longing within me.

The next morning, I awoke at dawn and went out on the dirt road to Rainy Mountain. It was already hot, and the grasshoppers began to fill the air. Still, it was early in the morning, and birds sang out of the shadows. The long yellow grass on the mountain shone in the bright light, and a scissortail hied above the land. There, where it ought to be, at the end of a long and legendary way, was my grandmother's grave. She had at last succeeded to that holy ground. Here and there on the dark stones were ancestral names. Looking back once, I saw the mountain and came away.

QUESTIONS

1. What is this essay about? Explain whether it is a history of the Kiowas, a biography of Momaday's grandmother, or a narrative of his journey.

2. Trace the movement in time in this essay. How much takes place in the present, the recent past, the distant past, or legendary time? What effect does such movement create?

3. How much of the essay reports events, and how much of the essay represents a sense of place or of people through description of what Momaday sees and feels? Trace the pattern of reporting and representing, and consider Momaday's purpose in such an approach to his subject.

4. The first paragraph ends by drawing the reader into the writer's point of view: "Your imagination comes to life, and this, you think, is where Creation was begun." Given the description of the Oklahoma landscape that precedes this in the paragraph, how do you react to Momaday's summarizing statement? Why? What other passages in the essay evoke a sense of place?

5. Visit a place that has historical significance. It may be a place where you or members of your family lived in the past, or it may be a place of local or national historical

significance. Describe the place as it appears now, and report on events that took place there in the past. What, if any, evidence do you find in the present of those events that took place in the past?

6. If you have a grandparent or an older friend living nearby, ask this person about his or her history. What does this person remember about the past that is no longer in the present? Are there objects—pictures, clothing, medals, and so on—that can speak to you of your subject's past life? Reflect on the person's present life as well as on those events from the past that seem most memorable. Write an essay in which you represent your subject's life by concentrating on the place where he or she lives and the surrounding objects that help you to understand the past and present life.

MAKING CONNECTIONS

Compare Momaday's essay to Alice Walker's (p. 40), focusing on the way each essay moves through time. How do these essayists differ in their conception and representation of time, and how do those differences relate to their individual purposes as writers?

SHOOTING AN ELEPHANT
George Orwell

George Orwell (1903–1950) was the pen name of Eric Blair, the son of a British customs officer serving in Bengal, India. As a boy he was sent home to prestigious schools, where he learned to dislike the rich and powerful. After finishing school at Eton, he served as an officer of the British police in Burma, where he became disillusioned with imperialism. He later studied conditions among the urban poor and the coal miners of Wigan, a city in northwestern England, which strengthened his socialist beliefs. He was wounded in the Spanish civil war, defending the lost cause of the left against the fascists. Under the name Orwell, he wrote accounts of all of these experiences as well as the anti-Stalinist fable Animal Farm *and the novel* 1984. *In the following essay, first published in 1936, Orwell attacks the politics of imperialism.*

In Moulmein, in Lower Burma, I was hated by large numbers of people—the only time in my life that I have been important enough for this to happen to me. I was sub-divisional police officer of the town, and in an aimless, petty kind of way anti-European feeling was very bitter. No one had the guts to raise a riot, but if a European woman went through the bazaars alone somebody would probably spit betel juice over her dress. As a police officer I was an obvious target and was baited whenever it seemed safe to do so. When a nimble Burman tripped me up on the football field and the referee (another Burman) looked the other way, the crowd yelled with hideous laughter. This happened more than once. In the end the sneering yellow faces of young men that met me everywhere, the insults hooted after me when I was at a safe distance, got badly on my nerves. The young Buddhist priests were the worst of all. There were several thousands of them in the town and none of them seemed to have anything to do except stand on street corners and jeer at Europeans.

All this was perplexing and upsetting. For at that time I had already made up my mind that imperialism was an evil thing and the sooner I chucked up my job and got out of it the better. Theoretically—and secretly, of course—I was all for the Burmese and all against their oppressors, the British. As for the job I was doing, I hated it more bitterly than I can perhaps make clear. In a job like that you see the dirty work of Empire at close quarters. The wretched prisoners huddling in the stinking cages of the lock-ups, the grey, cowed faces of the long-term convicts, the scarred buttocks of the men who had been flogged

with bamboos—all these oppressed me with an intolerable sense of guil
could get nothing into perspective. I was young and ill-educated and I had had
to think out my problems in the utter silence that is imposed on every Englishman in the East. I did not even know that the British Empire is dying, still less
did I know that it is a great deal better than the younger empires that are going
to supplant it. All I knew was that I was stuck between my hatred of the empire
I served and my rage against the evil-spirited little beasts who tried to make my
job impossible. With one part of my mind I thought of the British Raj as an
unbreakable tyranny,[1] as something clamped down, in *saecula saeculorum*,[2]
upon the will of prostrate peoples; with another part I thought that the greatest
joy in the world would be to drive a bayonet into a Buddhist priest's guts. Feelings like these are the normal by-product of imperialism; ask any Anglo-Indian
official, if you can catch him off duty.

One day something happened which in a roundabout way was enlightening. It was a tiny incident in itself, but it gave me a better glimpse than I had
had before of the real nature of imperialism—the real motives for which
despotic governments act. Early one morning the sub-inspector at a police station the other end of the town rang me up on the phone and said that an elephant was ravaging the bazaar. Would I please come and do something about
it? I did not know what I could do, but I wanted to see what was happening
and I got on to a pony and started out. I took my rifle, an old .44 Winchester
and much too small to kill an elephant, but I thought the noise might be useful *in terrorem*.[3] Various Burmans stopped me on the way and told me about
the elephant's doings. It was not, of course, a wild elephant, but a tame one
which had gone "must."[4] It had been chained up, as tame elephants always are
when their attack of "must" is due, but on the previous night it had broken its
chain and escaped. Its mahout,[5] the only person who could manage it when it
was in that state, had set out in pursuit, but had taken the wrong direction and
was now twelve hours' journey away, and in the morning the elephant had suddenly reappeared in town. The Burmese population had no weapons and were
quite helpless against it. It had already destroyed somebody's bamboo hut,
killed a cow and raided some fruit-stalls and devoured the stock; also it had
met the municipal rubbish van and, when the driver jumped out and took to
his heels, had turned the van over and inflicted violences upon it.

The Burmese sub-inspector and some Indian constables were waiting for
me in the quarter where the elephant had been seen. It was a very poor quarter, a labyrinth of squalid bamboo huts, thatched with palm-leaf, winding all
over a steep hillside. I remember that it was a cloudy, stuffy morning at the be-

[1]*the British Raj:* the imperial government ruling British India and Burma. [Eds.]
[2]*saecula saeculorum:* forever and ever. [Eds.]
[3]*in terrorem:* for fright. [Eds.]
[4]*"must":* frenzied state of the bull elephant, due to sexual excitement. [Eds.]
[5]*mahout:* from Hindi, an elephant's keeper. [Eds.]

ginning of the rains. We began questioning the people as to where the elephant had gone and, as usual, failed to get any definite information. That is invariably the case in the East; a story always sounds clear enough at a distance, but the nearer you get to the scene of events the vaguer it becomes. Some of the people said that the elephant had gone in one direction, some said that he had gone in another, some professed not even to have heard of any elephant. I had almost made up my mind that the whole story was a pack of lies, when we heard yells a little distance away. There was a loud, scandalized cry of "Go away, child! Go away this instant!" and an old woman with a switch in her hand came round the corner of a hut, violently shooing away a crowd of naked children. Some more women followed, clicking their tongues and exclaiming; evidently there was something that the children ought not to have seen. I rounded the hut and saw a man's dead body sprawling in the mud. He was an Indian, a black Dravidian coolie,[6] almost naked, and he could not have been dead many minutes. The people said that the elephant had come suddenly upon him round the corner of the hut, caught him with its trunk, put its foot on his back and ground him into the earth. This was the rainy season and the ground was soft, and his face had scored a trench a foot deep and a couple of yards long. He was lying on his belly with arms crucified and head sharply twisted to one side. His face was coated with mud, the eyes wide open, the teeth bared and grinning with an expression of unendurable agony. (Never tell me, by the way, that the dead look peaceful. Most of the corpses I have seen looked devilish.) The friction of the great beast's foot had stripped the skin from his back as neatly as one skins a rabbit. As soon as I saw the dead man I sent an orderly to a friend's house nearby to borrow an elephant rifle. I had already sent back the pony, not wanting it to go mad with fright and throw me if it smelt the elephant.

The orderly came back in a few minutes with a rifle and five cartridges, and 5 meanwhile some Burmans had arrived and told us that the elephant was in the paddy fields below, only a few hundred yards away. As I started forward practically the whole population of the quarter flocked out of the houses and followed me. They had seen the rifle and were all shouting excitedly that I was going to shoot the elephant. They had not shown much interest in the elephant when he was merely ravaging their homes, but it was different now that he was to be shot. It was a bit of fun to them, as it would be to an English crowd; besides they wanted the meat. It made me vaguely uneasy. I had no intention of shooting the elephant—I had merely sent for the rifle to defend myself if necessary—and it is always unnerving to have a crowd following you. I marched down the hill, looking and feeling a fool, with the rifle over my shoulder and an ever-growing army of people jostling at my heels. At the bottom, when you got away from the huts, there was a metalled road and beyond that a

---

[6]*Dravidian coolie:* a *coolie* is an unskilled laborer; *Dravidian* refers to a large group from south and central India. [Eds.]

miry waste of paddy fields a thousand yards across, not yet ploughed bu
from the first rains and dotted with coarse grass. The elephant was standing
eight yards from the road, his left side towards us. He took not the slightest notice of the crowd's approach. He was tearing up bunches of grass, beating them
against his knees to clean them and stuffing them into his mouth.

I had halted on the road. As soon as I saw the elephant I knew with perfect
certainty that I ought not to shoot him. It is a serious matter to shoot a working
elephant—it is comparable to destroying a huge and costly piece of machin-
ery—and obviously one ought not to do it if it can possibly be avoided. And at
that distance, peacefully eating, the elephant looked no more dangerous than a
cow. I thought then and I think now that his attack of "must" was already passing off; in which case he would merely wander harmlessly about until the mahout came back and caught him. Moreover, I did not in the least want to shoot
him. I decided that I would watch him for a little while to make sure that he
did not turn savage again, and then go home.

But at that moment I glanced around at the crowd that had followed me. It
was an immense crowd, two thousand at the least and growing every minute. It
blocked the road for a long distance on either side. I looked at the sea of yellow
faces above the garish clothes—faces all happy and excited all over this bit of
fun, all certain that the elephant was going to be shot. They were watching me
as they would watch a conjurer about to perform a trick. They did not like me,
but with the magical rifle in my hands I was momentarily worth watching. And
suddenly I realized that I should have to shoot the elephant after all. The people expected it of me and I had got to do it; I could feel their two thousand
wills pressing me forward, irresistibly. And it was at this moment, as I stood
there with the rifle in my hands, that I first grasped the hollowness, the futility
of the white man's dominion in the East. Here was I, the white man with his
gun, standing in front of the unarmed native crowd—seemingly the leading
actor of the piece; but in reality I was only an absurd puppet pushed to and fro
by the will of those yellow faces behind. I perceived in this moment that when
the white man turns tyrant it is his own freedom that he destroys. He becomes
a sort of hollow, posing dummy, the conventionalized figure of a sahib. For it
is the condition of his rule that he shall spend his life in trying to impress the
"natives," and so in every crisis he has got to do what the "natives" expect of
him. He wears a mask, and his face grows to fit it. I had got to shoot the elephant. I had committed myself to doing it when I sent for the rifle. A sahib has
got to act like a sahib; he has got to appear resolute, to know his own mind
and do definite things. To come all that way, rifle in hand, with two thousand
people marching at my heels, and then to trail feebly away, having done
nothing—no, that was impossible. The crowd would laugh at me. And my
whole life, every white man's life in the East, was one long struggle not to be
laughed at.

But I did not want to shoot the elephant. I watched him beating his bunch
of grass against his knees, with that preoccupied grandmotherly air that ele-

phants have. It seemed to me that it would be murder to shoot him. At that age I was not squeamish about killing animals, but I had never shot an elephant and never wanted to. (Somehow it always seems worse to kill a *large* animal.) Besides, there was the beast's owner to be considered. Alive, the elephant was worth at least a hundred pounds; dead, he would only be worth the value of his tusks, five pounds, possibly. But I had got to act quickly. I turned to some experienced-looking Burmans who had been there when we arrived, and asked them how the elephant had been behaving. They all said the same thing: he took no notice of you if you left him alone, but he might charge if you went too close to him.

It was perfectly clear to me what I ought to do. I ought to walk up to within, say, twenty-five yards of the elephant and test his behavior. If he charged, I could shoot; if he took no notice of me, it would be safe to leave him until the mahout came back. But also I knew that I was going to do no such thing. I was a poor shot with a rifle and the ground was soft mud into which one would sink at every step. If the elephant charged and I missed him, I should have about as much chance as a toad under a steam-roller. But even then I was not thinking particularly of my own skin, only of the watchful yellow faces behind. For at the moment, with the crowd watching me, I was not afraid in the ordinary sense, as I would have been if I had been alone. A white man mustn't be frightened in front of "natives"; and so, in general, he isn't frightened. The sole thought in my mind was that if anything went wrong those two thousand Burmans would see me pursued, caught, trampled on and reduced to a grinning corpse like that Indian up the hill. And if that happened it was quite probable that some of them would laugh. That would never do. There was only one alternative. I shoved the cartridges into the magazine and lay down on the road to get a better aim.

The crowd grew very still, and a deep, low, happy sigh, as of people who see the theatre curtain go up at last, breathed from innumerable throats. They were going to have their bit of fun after all. The rifle was a beautiful German thing with cross-hair sights. I did not then know that in shooting an elephant one would shoot to cut an imaginary bar running from ear-hole to ear-hole. I ought, therefore, as the elephant was sideways on, to have aimed straight at his ear-hole; actually I aimed several inches in front of this, thinking the brain would be further forward. 10

When I pulled the trigger I did not hear the bang or feel the kick—one never does when a shot goes home—but I heard the devilish roar of glee that went up from the crowd. In that instant, in too short a time, one would have thought, even for the bullet to get there, a mysterious, terrible change had come over the elephant. He neither stirred nor fell, but every line of his body had altered. He looked suddenly stricken, shrunken, immensely old, as though the frightful impact of the bullet had paralyzed him without knocking him down. At last, after what seemed a long time—it might have been five seconds, I dare say—he sagged flabbily to his knees. His mouth slobbered. An enormous senility seemed to have settled upon him. One could have imagined hi[m?] sands of years old. I fired again into the same spot. At the second shot he did not collapse but climbed with desperate slowness to his feet and stood weakly upright, with legs sagging and head drooping. I fired a third time. That was the shot that did for him. You could see the agony of it jolt his whole body and knock the last remnant of strength from his legs. But in falling he seemed for a moment to rise, for as his hind legs collapsed beneath him he seemed to tower upward like a huge rock toppling, his trunk reaching skywards like a tree. He trumpeted, for the first and only time. And then down he came, his belly towards me, with a crash that seemed to shake the ground even where I lay.

I got up. The Burmans were already racing past me across the mud. It was obvious that the elephant would never rise again, but he was not dead. He was breathing very rhythmically with long rattling gasps, his great mound of a side painfully rising and falling. His mouth was wide open—I could see far down into caverns of pale pink throat. I waited for a long time for him to die, but his breathing did not weaken. Finally I fired my two remaining shots into the spot where I thought his heart must be. The thick blood welled out of him like red velvet, but still he did not die. His body did not even jerk when the shots hit him, the tortured breathing continued without a pause. He was dying, very slowly and in great agony, but in some world remote from me where not even a bullet could damage him further. I felt that I had got to put an end to that dreadful noise. It seemed dreadful to see the great beast lying there, powerless to move and yet powerless to die, and not even to be able to finish him. I sent back for my small rifle and poured shot after shot into his heart and down his throat. They seemed to make no impression. The tortured gasps continued as steadily as the ticking of a clock.

In the end I could not stand it any longer and went away. I heard later that it took him half an hour to die. Burmans were bringing dahs and baskets even before I left,[7] and I was told they had stripped his body almost to the bones by the afternoon.

Afterwards, of course, there were endless discussions about the shooting of the elephant. The owner was furious, but he was only an Indian and could do nothing. Besides, legally I had done the right thing, for a mad elephant has to be killed, like a mad dog, if its owner fails to control it. Among the Europeans opinion was divided. The older men said I was right, the younger men said it was a damn shame to shoot an elephant for killing a coolie, because an elephant was worth more than any damn Coringhee coolie. And afterwards I was very glad that the coolie had been killed; it put me legally in the right and it gave me a sufficient pretext for shooting the elephant. I often wondered whether any of the others grasped that I had done it solely to avoid looking a fool.

---

[7]*dahs:* butcher knives. [Eds.]

QUESTIONS

1. Describe Orwell's mixed feelings about serving as a police officer in Burma.

2. How do the natives "force" Orwell to shoot the elephant against his better judgment? How does he relate this personal episode to the larger problems of British imperialism?

3. What is Orwell's final reaction to his deed? How literally can we take his statement that he "was very glad that the coolie had been killed" (paragraph 14)?

4. From the opening sentence Orwell displays a remarkable candor concerning his feelings. How does this personal, candid tone add to or detract from the strength of the essay?

5. Orwell's recollection of shooting the elephant is shaped to support a specific point or thesis. Where does Orwell state this thesis? Is this placement effective?

6. In what ways does this essay read more like a short story than an expository essay? How effective is Orwell's use of narrative and personal experience?

7. Orwell often wrote with a political purpose, with a "desire to push the world in a certain direction, to alter other people's idea of the kind of society that they should strive after." To what extent does the "tiny incident" in this essay illuminate "the real nature of imperialism" (paragraph 3)? Does Orwell succeed in altering your idea of imperialism?

8. Using Orwell's essay as a model, write a reflection in which the narration of "a tiny incident" illuminates a larger social or political problem.

MAKING CONNECTIONS

The selections by Maya Angelou (p. 29), Zoë Tracy Hardy (p. 111), and Loren Eiseley (p. 138), in this section read somewhat like short stories, as does Orwell's essay. Compare the narrative designs of two of these writers, and discuss the usefulness of storytelling in reflective writing.

WHAT DID YOU DO
IN THE WAR, GRANDMA?
A Flashback to August, 1945

Zoë Tracy Hardy

Born in 1927 and raised in the Midwest, Zoë Tracy Hardy was one of millions of young women called "Rosie the Riveters" who worked in defense plants during World War II. Considered at first to be mere surrogates for male workers, these women soon were building bombers that their supervisors declared "equal in the construction [to] those turned out by experienced workmen in the plant's other departments," as a news feature at the time stated. After the eventful summer described in the following essay, Hardy finished college, married, and began teaching college English in Arizona, Guam, and Colorado. This essay first appeared in the August 1985 issue of Ms. *magazine—exactly forty years after the end of World War II.*

It was unseasonably cool that day in May, 1945, when I left my mother and father and kid brother in eastern Iowa and took the bus all the way to Omaha to help finish the war. I was 18, and had just completed my first year at the University of Iowa without distinction. The war in Europe had ended in April; the war against the Japanese still raged. I wanted to go where something *real* was being done to end this bitter war that had always been part of my adolescence.

I arrived in Omaha at midnight. The YWCA, where I promised my family I would get a room, was closed until 7 A.M., so I curled up in a cracked maroon leather chair in the crowded, smoky waiting room of the bus station.

In the morning I set off on foot for the YWCA, dragging a heavy suitcase and carrying my favorite hat trimmed in daisies in a large round hatbox. An hour of lugging and resting brought me to the Y, a great Victorian house of dark brick, where I paid two weeks in advance (most of my money) for board and a single room next to a bathroom that I would share with eight other girls. I surrendered my red and blue food-ration stamp books and my sugar coupons to the cook who would keep them as long as I stayed there.

I had eaten nothing but a wartime candy bar since breakfast at home the day before, but breakfast at the Y was already over. So, queasy and lightheaded, I went back out into the cold spring day to find my job. I set out for the downtown office of the Glenn L. Martin Company. It was at their plant

111

south of the city that thousands of workers, in around-the-clock shifts, built the famous B-29 bombers, the great Superfortresses, which the papers said would end the war.

I filled out an application and thought about the women welders and rivet-   5
ers and those who operated machine presses to help put the Superfortresses to-gether. I grew shakier by the minute, more and more certain I was unqualified for any job here.

My interview was short. The personnel man was unconcerned about my total lack of skills. If I passed the physical, I could have a job in the Reproduc-tion Department, where the blueprints were handled.

Upstairs in a gold-walled banquet room furnished with examination tables and hospital screens, a nurse sat me on a stool to draw a blood sample from my arm. I watched my blood rolling slowly into the needle. The gold walls wilted in the distance, and I slumped forward in a dead faint.

A grandfatherly doctor waved ammonia under my nose, and said if I would go to a café down the street and eat the complete 50-cent breakfast, I had the job.

The first week in the Reproduction Department, I learned to cut and fold enormous blueprints as they rolled from a machine that looked like a giant washing machine wringer. Then I was moved to a tall, metal contraption with a lurid light glowing from its interior. An ammonia guzzler, it spewed out smelly copies of specifications so hot my finger-tips burned when I touched them. I called it the dragon, and when I filled it with ammonia, the fumes re-minded me of gold walls dissolving before my eyes. I took all my breaks out-doors, even when it was raining.

My boss, Mr. Johnson,[1] was a sandy-haired man of about 40, who spoke   10
pleasantly when he came around to say hello and to check our work. Elsie, his secretary, a cool redhead, seldom spoke to any of us and spent most of her time in the darkroom developing negatives and reproducing photographs.

One of my coworkers in Reproduction was Mildred, a tall dishwater blond with a horsey, intelligent face. She was the first woman I'd ever met with an earthy unbridled tongue.

When I first arrived, Mildred warned me always to knock on the darkroom door before going in because Mr. Johnson and Elsie did a lot of screwing in there. I didn't believe her, I thought we were supposed to knock to give Elsie time to protect her negatives from the sudden light. "Besides," I said, "there isn't room to lie down in there." Mildred laughed until tears squeezed from the corners of her eyes. "You poor kid," she said. "Don't you *know* you don't have to lie down?"

---

[1] All names but the author's have been changed.

I was stunned. "But it's easier if you do," I protested, defensive about my sex education. My mother, somewhat ahead of her time, had always been explicit in her explanations, and I had read "Lecture 14," an idyllic description of love-making being passed around among freshman girls in every dormitory in the country.

"Sitting, standing, any quick way you can in time of war," Mildred winked wickedly. She was as virginal as I, but what she said reminded us of the steady dearth of any day-to-day presence of young men in our lives.

We were convinced that the war would be over by autumn. We were step- 15 ping up the napalm and incendiary bombing of the Japanese islands, the British were now coming to our aid in the Pacific, and the Japanese Navy was being reduced to nothing in some of the most spectacular sea battles in history.

Sometimes, after lunch, I went into the assembly areas to see how the skeletons of the B-29s were growing from our blueprints. At first there were enormous stark ribs surrounded by scaffolding two and three stories high. A few days later there was aluminum flesh over the ribs and wings sprouting from stubs on the fuselage. Women in overalls and turbans, safety glasses, and steel-toed shoes scrambled around the wings with riveting guns and welding torches, fitting fuel tanks in place. Instructions were shouted at them by hoarse, paunchy old men in hard hats. I cheered myself by thinking how we were pouring it on, a multitude of us together creating this great bird to end the war.

Away from the plant, however, optimism sometimes failed me. My room at the Y was bleak. I wrote letters to my unofficial fiancé and to other young men in the service who had been friends and classmates. Once in a while I attempted to study, thinking I would redeem my mediocre year at the university.

During those moments when I sensed real homesickness lying in wait, I would plan something to do with Betty and Celia, friends from high school, who had moved to Omaha "for the duration" and had jobs as secretaries for a large moving and storage company. Their small apartment was upstairs in an old frame house in Benson, a northwest suburb. Celia and Betty and I cooked, exchanged news from servicemen we all knew and talked about plans for the end of the war. Betty was engaged to her high school sweetheart, a soldier who had been wounded in Germany and who might be coming home soon. We guessed she would be the first one of us to be married, and we speculated, in the careful euphemisms of "well-brought-up girls," about her impending introduction to sex.

By the first of July, work and the pace of life had lost momentum. The war news seemed to repeat itself without advancing, as day after day battles were fought around jungly Pacific islands that all seemed identical and unreal.

At the plant, I was moved from the dragon to a desk job, a promotion of 20 sorts. I sat on a high stool in a cubicle of pigeonholed cabinets and filed blueprints, specs, and deviations in the proper holes. While I was working, I saw no one and couldn't talk to anybody.

In mid-July Betty got married. Counsel from our elders was always to wait—wait until things settle down after the war. Harold, still recuperating from shrapnel wounds, asked Betty not to wait.

Celia and I attended the ceremony on a sizzling afternoon in a musty Presbyterian church. Harold was very serious, gaunt-faced and thin in his loose-hanging Army uniform. Betty, a fair-skinned, blue-eyed brunet in a white street dress, looked pale and solemn. After the short ceremony, they left the church in a borrowed car. Someone had given them enough gasoline stamps for a honeymoon trip to a far-off cabin on the shore of a piney Minnesota lake.

Celia and I speculated on Betty's introduction to lovemaking. I had "Lecture 14" in mind and hoped she would like lovemaking, especially way off in Minnesota, far from the sweltering city and the war. Celia thought it didn't matter much whether a girl liked it or not, as long as other important parts of marriage got off to a good start.

That weekend Celia and I took a walk in a park and watched a grandfather carefully pump a seesaw up and down for his small grandson. We saw a short, middle-aged sailor walking with a sad-faced young woman who towered over him. "A whore," Celia said, "Probably one of those from the Hotel Bianca." Celia had been in Omaha longer than I and knew more of its secrets.

I wanted, right then, to see someone young and male and healthy cross the grass under the trees, someone without wounds and without a cap, someone with thick disheveled hair that hadn't been militarily peeled down to the green skin on the back of his skull. Someone wearing tennis shorts to show strong, hair-matted legs, and a shirt with an open neck and short sleeves revealing smooth, hard muscles and tanned skin. Someone who would pull me out of this gloom with a wide spontaneous smile as he passed.

In the next few days, the tempo of the summer changed subtly. From friends stationed in the Pacific, I began to get letters free from rectangular holes where military censors had snipped out "sensitive" words. Our Navy was getting ready to surround the Japanese islands with a starvation blockade, and our B-29s had bombed the industrial heart of the country. We were dropping leaflets warning the Japanese people that we would incinerate hundreds of thousands of them by firebombing 11 of their major cities. Rumors rippled through the plant back in Omaha. The Japanese Empire would collapse in a matter of weeks, at most.

One Friday night, with Celia's help, I moved out of the Y to Celia's apartment in Benson. We moved by streetcar. Celia carried my towels and my full laundry bag in big rolls, one under each arm, and wore my straw picture hat with the daisies, which bobbled wildly on top of her head. My hatbox was crammed with extra underwear and the war letters I was determined to save. When we climbed aboard the front end of the streetcar, I dropped the hatbox, spilled an armload of books down the aisle, and banged my suitcase into the knees of an elderly man who was trying to help me retrieve them.

We began to laugh, at everything, at nothing, and were still laughing when we hauled everything off the car and down one block to the apartment, the daisies all the while wheeling recklessly on Celia's head.

It was a good move. Summer nights were cooler near the country, and so quiet I could hear the crickets. The other upstairs apartment was occupied by Celia's older sister, Andrea, and her husband, Bob, who hadn't been drafted.

Late in July, an unusual thing happened at the plant. Mr. Johnson asked us   30
to work double shifts for a few days. The situation was urgent, he said, and he wanted 100 percent cooperation from the Reproduction Department, even if it meant coming to work when we felt sick or postponing something that was personally important to us.

The next morning no one from the day shift was missing, and the place was full of people from the graveyard shift. Some of the time I worked in my cubicle counting out special blueprints and deviations. The rest of the time I helped the crews sweating over the blueprint machine cut out prints that contained odd lines and numbers that I had never seen before. Their shapes were different, too, and there was no place for them in the numbered pigeonholes of my cubicle. Some prints were small, about four inches square. Mildred said they were so cute she might tuck one in her shoe and smuggle it home as a souvenir even if it meant going to the federal pen if she got caught.

During those days I learned to nap on streetcars. I had to get up at 4:30, bolt down breakfast, and catch the first car to rumble out of the darkness at 5:15. The double shift wasn't over until 11:30, so I got home about one in the morning.

The frenzy at the plant ended as suddenly as it had begun. Dazed with fatigue, I slept through most of a weekend and hoped we had pushed ourselves to some limit that would lift us over the last hump of the war.

On Monday the familiar single shift was not quite the same. We didn't know what we had done, but an undercurrent of anticipation ran through the department because of those double shifts—and the news. The papers told of factories that were already gearing up to turn out refrigerators, radios, and automobiles instead of bombs and planes.

In Reproduction, the pace began to slacken. Five hundred thirty-six B-29s,   35
planes we had put together on the Nebraska prairie, had firebombed the principal islands of the Japanese Empire: Hokkaido, Honshu, Kyushu, Shikoku. We had reduced to ashes more than 15 square miles of the heart of Tokyo. The battered and burned Japanese were so near defeat that there couldn't be much left for us to do. With surprising enthusiasm, I began to plan for my return to college.

Going home on the streetcar the first Tuesday afternoon in August, I heard about a puzzling new weapon. Some excited people at the end of the car were jabbering about it, saying the Japanese would be forced to surrender in a matter of hours.

When I got home, Andrea, her round bespectacled face flushed, met me at the head of the stairs. "Oh, come and listen to the radio—it's a new bomb— it's almost over!"

I sat down in her living room and listened. There was news, then music, then expanded news. Over and over the newscaster reported that the United States had unlocked a secret of the universe and unleashed a cosmic force— from splitting atoms of uranium—on the industrial seaport of Hiroshima. Most of the city had been leveled to the ground, and many of its inhabitants disinte- grated to dust in an instant by a single bomb. "Our scientists have changed the history of the world," the newscaster said. He sounded as if he could not be- lieve it himself.

We ate dinner from our laps and continued to listen as the news pounded on for an hour, then two, then three. I tried, at last, to *think* about it. In high school physics we had already learned that scientists were close to splitting an atom. We imagined that a cupful of the tremendous energy from such a phenomenon might run a car back and forth across the entire country dozens of times. I could visualize that. But I could not imagine how such energy put into a small bomb would cause the kind of destruction described on the radio.

About nine, I walked over to McCollum's grocery store to buy an evening   40 paper. The headline said we had harnessed atomic power. I skimmed through a front page story. Science had ushered us into a strange new world, and Presi- dent Truman had made two things clear: the bomb had created a monster that could wipe out civilization; and some protection against this monster would have to be found before its secret could be given to the world.

Back out in the dark street, I hesitated. For the first time I could remember, I felt a rush of terror at being out in the night alone.

When I got back to the apartment, I made a pot of coffee and sat down at the kitchen table to read the rest of the paper. President Truman had said: "The force from which the sun draws its power has been loosed against those who brought war to the Far East. . . . If they do not now accept our terms they may expect a rain of ruin from the air the like of which has never been seen on this earth." New and more powerful bombs were now being developed.

I read everything, looking for some speculation from someone about how we were going to live in this new world. There was nothing. About midnight Andrea knocked on my open door to get my attention. She stood there a mo- ment in her nightgown and curlers looking at me rather oddly. She asked if I was all right.

I said yes, just trying to soak it all in.

Gently she told me I had better go to bed and think about how soon the war   45 would be over.

The next day Reproduction was nearly demolished by the spirit of celebra- tion. The *Enola Gay*, the plane that had dropped the bomb, was one of ours.

By Thursday morning the United States had dropped a second atomic bomb, an even bigger one, on an industrial city, Nagasaki, and the Russians had declared war on Japan.

At the end of the day, Mr. Johnson asked us to listen to the radio for announcements about when to return to work, then shook hands all around. "You've all done more than you know to help win the war," he said.

We said tentative good-byes. I went home and over to McCollum's for an evening paper. An Army Strategic Air Forces expert said that there was no comparison between the fire caused by the atomic bomb and that of a normal conflagration. And there were other stories about radiation, like X-rays, that might cripple and poison living things for hours, weeks, maybe years, until they died.

I went to bed late and had nightmares full of flames and strange dry gale winds. The next noon I got up, exhausted, and called Mildred. She said they were still saying not to report to work until further notice. "It's gonna bore our tails off," she moaned. "I don't know how long we can sit around here just playing hearts." I could hear girls laughing in the background.

"Mildred," I blurted anxiously, "do you think we should have done this thing?"

"Why not? Better us than somebody else, kid."

I reminded her that we knew the Japanese were finished weeks ago and asked her if it wasn't sort of like kicking a dead horse—brutally.

"Look," she said. "The war is really over even if the bigwigs haven't said so yet. What more do you want?"

The evening paper finally offered a glimmer of relief. One large headline said that serious questions about the morality of *Americans* using such a weapon were being raised by some civilians of note and some churchmen. I went to bed early and lay listening to the crickets and thinking about everyone coming home—unofficial fiancés, husbands, fathers, brothers—all filling the empty spaces between kids and women and old men, putting a balance in our lives we hadn't known in years.

Yet the bomb haunted me. I was still awake when the windowpanes lightened up at daybreak.

It was all over on August 14, 1945. Unconditional surrender.

For hours at a time, the bomb's importance receded in the excitement of that day. Streetcar bells clanged up and down the streets; we heard sirens, whistles, church bells. A newscaster described downtown Omaha as a free-for-all. Perfect strangers were hugging each other in the streets; some were dancing. Churches had thrown open their doors, and people were streaming in and out, offering prayers of thanksgiving. Taverns were giving away free drinks.

Andrew wanted us to have a little whiskey, even though we were under age, because there would never be another day like this as long as we lived. I hated

117

the first taste of it, but as we chattered away, inventing wild, gratifying futures, I welcomed the muffler it wrapped around the ugliness of the bomb.

In the morning Mildred called to say our jobs were over and that we should report to the plant to turn in our badges and get final paychecks. She had just talked to Mr. Johnson, who told her that those funny blueprints we had made during double shift had something to do with the bomb.

"Well, honey," she said, "I don't understand atomic energy, but old jazzy   60
Johnson said we had to work like that to get the *Enola Gay* and the *thing* to go together."

I held my breath, waiting for Mildred to say she was kidding, as usual. Ordinary 19- and 20-year-old girls were not, not in the United States of America, required to work night and day to help launch scientific monsters that would catapult us all into a precarious "strange new world"—forever. But I knew in my bones that Mildred, forthright arrow-straight Mildred, was only telling me what I had already, unwillingly, guessed.

After a long silence she said, "Well, kid, give me your address in Iowa, and I'll send you a Christmas card for auld lang syne."

I wanted to cry as we exchanged addresses. I liked Mildred. I hated the gap that I now sensed would always be between me and people like her.

"It's been nice talking dirty to you all summer," she said.

"Thanks." I hung up, slipped down the stairs, and walked past the streetcar   65
line out into the country.

The whole countryside was sundrenched, fragrant with sweet clover and newly mown alfalfa. I leaned against a fence post and tried to think.

The President had said we had unleashed the great secret of the universe in this way, to shorten the war and save American lives. Our commitment to defeat the Japanese was always clear to me. They had attacked us first. But we had already firebombed much of the Japanese Empire to char. That seemed decisive enough, and terrible enough.

If he had asked me whether I would work very hard to help bring this horror into being, knowing it would shorten the war but put the world into jeopardy for all time, how would I have answered?

I would have said, "No. With all due respect, Sir, how could such a thing make a just end to our just cause?"

But the question had never been asked of us. And I stood now, in the warm   70
sun, gripping a splintery fence post, outraged by our final insignificance—all of us who had worked together in absolute trust to end the war.

An old cow stood near the fence switching her tail. I looked at her great, uncomprehending brown eyes and began to sob.

After a while I walked back to the apartment, mentally packing my suitcase and tying up my hatbox of war letters. I knew it was going to be very hard, from now on, for the whole world to take care of itself.

I wanted very much to go home.

QUESTIONS

1. How does Hardy's attitude toward the war change in the course of this essay? What event causes her to reevaluate her attitude?

2. Describe Hardy's feelings about the introduction of atomic power into her world. Are they optimistic or pessimistic?

3. "You've all done more than you know to help win the war," Hardy's boss tells her (paragraph 47). How does she react to the fact that she was not informed by the authorities of the purpose of her work? How does her reaction differ from that of her coworker Mildred?

4. As Hardy's attitude toward war changes, her attitude toward sex changes as well. Trace this change in attitude; what connection, if any, do you see between the two?

5. Is this essay merely a personal reminiscence, or does the author have a larger purpose? Explain what you think her purpose is.

6. This essay was published more than ten years ago and forty years after the events it describes. Are Hardy's fears and speculations (on atomic power, on the authority of the government, on sex) dated in any way, or are they still relevant today? Explain your answer.

7. Have you, like Hardy, ever wondered about the larger social implications of any job that you've held or that a friend or parent holds? Write an essay like Hardy's reflecting on that job and describing how your attitude changed as you placed the job in a larger context.

MAKING CONNECTIONS

Could Hardy's essay be described as a "pilgrimage" to a particular intellectual or political position, somewhat like Martin Luther King Jr.'s "Pilgrimage to Nonviolence" (p. 90)? How fair would that retitling be to Hardy's essay? What aspects of pilgrimage do you find in it?

Sciences and Technologies

A MASK ON THE FACE OF DEATH
Richard Selzer

Richard Selzer (b. 1928) is the son of a general practitioner father and a singer mother, both of whom wanted their son to follow in their footsteps. At ten he began sneaking into his father's office to look at his medical textbooks, where he discovered "the rich alliterative language of medicine — words such as cerebellum which, when said aloud, melt in the mouth and drip from the end of the tongue like choco- late." After his father's death he decided to become a doctor and was for many years a professor of surgery at Yale Med- ical School. Only after working as a doctor for many decades did he begin to write. About the similarities be- tween surgery and writing he says, "In surgery, it is the body that is being opened up and put back together. In writing it is the whole world that is taken in for repairs, then put back in working order piece by piece." His articles have appeared in Vanity Fair, Harper's, Esquire, *and the* New York Times Magazine. *His books include a volume of short stories,* Rituals of Surgery *(1974), a collection of autobio- graphical essays,* Mortal Lessons *(1976), an autobiography,* Down from Troy *(1992), and a collection of autobiograph- ical and fictional pieces,* Raising the Dead *(1994). This essay appeared in* Life *in 1988.*

It is ten o'clock at night as we drive up to the Copacabana, a dilapidated brothel on the rue Dessalines in the red-light district of Port-au-Prince. My guide is a young Haitian, Jean-Bernard. Ten years before, J-B tells me, at the age of fourteen, "like every good Haitian boy" he had been brought here by his older cousins for his *rite de passage.* From the car to the entrance, we are ac- costed by a half dozen men and women for sex. We enter, go down a long hall that breaks upon a cavernous room with a stone floor. The cubicles of the prostitutes, I am told, are in an attached wing of the building. Save for a red-purple glow from small lights on the walls, the place is unlit. Dark shapes float by, each with a blindingly white stripe of teeth. Latin music is blaring. We take seats at the table farthest from the door. Just outside, there is the rhythmic lapping of the Caribbean Sea. About twenty men are seated at the tables or lean against the walls. Brightly dressed women, singly or in twos or threes, stroll about, now and then exchanging banter with the men. It is as though we have been deposited in act two of Bizet's *Carmen*. If this place isn't Lillas Pastia's tavern, what is it?

Within minutes, three light-skinned young women arrive at our table. They are very beautiful and young and lively. Let them be Carmen, Mercedes and Frasquita.

"I want the old one," says Frasquita, ruffling my hair. The women laugh uproariously.

"Don't bother looking any further," says Mercedes. "We are the prettiest ones."

"We only want to talk," I tell her.   5

"Aaah, aaah," she crows. "*Massissi.* You are *massissi.*" It is the contemptuous Creole term for homosexual. If we want only to talk, we must be gay. Mercedes and Carmen are slender, each weighing one hundred pounds or less. Frasquita is tall and hefty. They are dressed for work: red taffeta, purple chiffon and black sequins. Among them a thousand gold bracelets and earrings multiply every speck of light. Their bare shoulders are like animated lamps gleaming in the shadowy room. Since there is as yet no business, the women agree to sit with us. J-B orders beer and cigarettes. We pay each woman $10.

"Where are you from?" I begin.

"We are Dominican."

"Do you miss your country?"

"Oh, yes, we do." Six eyes go muzzy with longing. "Our country is the most   10
beautiful in the world. No country is like the Dominican. And it doesn't stink like this one."

"Then why don't you work there? Why come to Haiti?"

"Santo Domingo has too many whores. All beautiful, like us. All light-skinned. The Haitian men like to sleep with light women."

"Why is that?"

"Because always, the whites have all the power and the money. The black men can imagine they do, too, when they have us in bed."

Eleven o'clock. I looked around the room that is still sparsely peopled with   15
men.

"It isn't getting any busier," I say. Frasquita glances over her shoulder. Her eyes drill the darkness.

"It is still early," she says.

"Could it be that the men are afraid of getting sick?" Frasquita is offended.

"Sick! They do not get sick from us. We are healthy, strong. Every week we go for a checkup. Besides, we know how to tell if we are getting sick."

"I mean sick with AIDS." The word sets off a hurricane of taffeta, chiffon and gold jewelry. They are all gesticulation and fury. It is Carmen who speaks. 20

"AIDS!" Her lips curl about the syllable. "There is no such thing. It is a false disease invented by the American government to take advantage of the poor countries. The American President hates poor people, so now he makes up AIDS to take away the little we have." The others nod vehemently.

"*Mira, mon cher.* Look, my dear," Carmen continues. "One day the police came here. Believe me, they are worse than the *tonton macoutes* with their submachine guns. They rounded up one hundred and five of us and they took our blood. That was a year ago. None of us have died, you see? We are all still here. *Mira,* we sleep with all the men and we are not sick."

"But aren't there some of you who have lost weight and have diarrhea?"

"One or two, maybe. But they don't eat. That is why they are weak."

"Only the men die," says Mercedes. "They stop eating, so they die. It is hard 25 to kill a woman."

"Do you eat well?"

"Oh, yes, don't worry, we do. We eat like poor people, but we eat." There is a sudden scream from Frasquita. She points to a large rat that has emerged from beneath our table.

"My God!" she exclaims. "It is big like a pig." They burst into laughter. For a moment the women fall silent. There is only the restlessness of their many bracelets. I give them each another $10.

"Are many of the men here bisexual?"

"Too many. They do it for money. Afterward, they come to us." Carmen 30 lights a cigarette and looks down at the small lace handkerchief she has been folding and unfolding with immense precision on the table. All at once she turns it over as though it were the ace of spades.

"*Mira, blanc* . . . look, white man," she says in a voice suddenly full of foreboding. Her skin seems to darken to coincide with the tone of her voice.

"*Mira,* soon many Dominican women will die in Haiti!"

"Die of what?"

She shrugs. "It is what they do to us."

"Carmen," I say, "if you knew that you had AIDS, that your blood was bad, 35 would you still sleep with men?" Abruptly, she throws back her head and laughs. It is the same laughter with which Frasquita had greeted the rat at our feet. She stands and the others follow.

"*Méchant!* You wicked man," she says. Then, with terrible solemnity, "You don't know anything."

"But you are killing the Haitian men," I say.

"As for that," she says, "everyone is killing everyone else." All at once, I want to know everything about these three—their childhood, their dreams, what they do in the afternoon, what they eat for lunch.

"Don't leave," I say. "Stay a little more." Again, I reach for my wallet. But they are gone, taking all the light in the room with them—Mercedes and Carmen to sit at another table where three men have been waiting. Frasquita is strolling about the room. Now and then, as if captured by the music, she breaks into a few dance steps, snapping her fingers, singing to herself.

Midnight. And the Copacabana is filling up. Now it is like any other seedy nightclub where men and women go hunting. We get up to leave. In the center a couple are dancing a *méringue*. He is the most graceful dancer I have ever watched; she, the most voluptuous. Together they seem to be riding the back of the music as it gallops to a precisely sexual beat. Closer up, I see that the man is short of breath, sweating. All at once, he collapses into a chair. The woman bends over him, coaxing, teasing, but he is through. A young man with a long polished stick blocks my way.

"I come with you?" he asks. "Very good time. You say yes? Ten dollars? Five?"

I have been invited by Dr. Jean William Pape to attend the AIDS clinic of which he is the director. Nothing from the outside of the low whitewashed structure would suggest it as a medical facility. Inside, it is divided into many small cubicles and a labyrinth of corridors. At nine A.M. the hallways are already full of emaciated silent men and women, some sitting on the few benches, the rest leaning against the walls. The only sounds are subdued moans of discomfort interspersed with coughs. How they eat us with their eyes as we pass.

The room where Pape and I work is perhaps ten feet by ten. It contains a desk, two chairs and a narrow wooden table that is covered with a sheet that will not be changed during the day. The patients are called in one at a time, asked how they feel and whether there is any change in their symptoms, then examined on the table. If the patient is new to the clinic, he or she is questioned about sexual activities.

A twenty-seven-year-old man whose given name is Miracle enters. He is wobbly, panting, like a groggy boxer who has let down his arms and is waiting for the last punch. He is neatly dressed and wears, despite the heat, a heavy woolen cap. When he removes it, I see that his hair is thin, dull reddish and straight. It is one of the signs of AIDS in Haiti, Pape tells me. The man's skin is covered with a dry itchy rash. Throughout the interview and examination he scratches himself slowly, absentmindedly. The rash is called prurigo. It is another symptom of AIDS in Haiti. This man has had diarrhea for six months. The laboratory reports that the diarrhea is due to an organism called cryptosporidium, for which there is no treatment. The telltale rattling of the tuberculous moisture in his chest is audible without a stethoscope. He is like a leaky cistern that bubbles and froths. And, clearly, exhausted.

"Where do you live?" I ask.

"Kenscoff." A village in the hills above Port-au-Prince.

"How did you come here today?"

"I came on the *tap-tap*." It is the name given to the small buses that swarm the city, each one extravagantly decorated with religious slogans, icons, flowers, animals, all painted in psychedelic colors. I have never seen a *tap-tap* that was not covered with passengers as well, riding outside and hanging on. The vehicles are little masterpieces of contagion, if not of AIDS then of the multitude of germs which Haitian flesh is heir to. Miracle is given a prescription for a supply of Sera, which is something like Gatorade, and told to return in a month.

"*Mangé kou bêf*," says the doctor in farewell. "Eat like an ox." What can he mean? The man has no food or money to buy any. Even had he food, he has not the appetite to eat or the ability to retain it. To each departing patient the doctor will say the same words—"*Mangé kou bêf*." I see that it is his way of offering a hopeful goodbye.

"Will he live until his next appointment?" I ask.

"No." Miracle leaves to catch the *tap-tap* for Kenscoff.

Next is a woman of twenty-six who enters holding her right hand to her forehead in a kind of permanent salute. In fact, she is shielding her eye from view. This is her third visit to the clinic. I see that she is still quite well nourished.

"Now, you'll see something beautiful, tremendous," the doctor says. Once seated upon the table, she is told to lower her hand. When she does, I see that her right eye and its eyelid are replaced by a huge fungating ulcerated tumor, a side product of her AIDS. As she turns her head, the cluster of lymph glands in her neck to which the tumor has spread is thrown into relief. Two years ago she received a blood transfusion at a time when the country's main blood bank was grossly contaminated with AIDS. It has since been closed down. The only blood available in Haiti is a small supply procured from the Red Cross.

"Can you give me medicine?" the woman wails.

"No."

"Can you cut it away?"

"No."

"Is there radiation therapy?" I ask.

"No."

"Chemotherapy?" The doctor looks at me in what some might call weary amusement. I see that there is nothing to do. She has come here because there is nowhere else to go.

"What will she do?"

"Tomorrow or the next day or the day after that she will climb up into the mountains to seek relief from the *houngan*, the voodoo priest, just as her slave ancestors did two hundred years ago."

Then comes a frail man in his thirties, with a strangely spiritualized face, like a child's. Pus runs from one ear onto his cheek, where it has dried and caked. He has trouble remembering, he tells us. In fact, he seems confused. It is from toxoplasmosis of the brain, an effect of his AIDS. This man is bisexual. Two years ago he engaged in oral sex with foreign men for money. As I palpate the swollen glands of his neck, a mosquito flies between our faces. I swat at it,

125

miss. Just before coming to Haiti I had read that the AIDS virus had been isolated from a certain mosquito. The doctor senses my thought.

"Not to worry," he says. "So far as we know there has never been a case transmitted by insects."

"Yes," I say. "I see." 65

And so it goes until the last, the thirty-sixth AIDS patient has been seen. At the end of the day I am invited to wash my hands before leaving. I go down a long hall to a sink. I turn on the faucets but there is no water.

"But what about *you?*" I ask the doctor. "You are at great personal risk here—the tuberculosis, the other infections, no water to wash . . ." He shrugs, smiles faintly and lifts his hands palm upward.

We are driving up a serpiginous steep road into the barren mountains above Port-au-Prince. Even in the bright sunshine the countryside has the bloodless color of exhaustion and indifference. Our destination is the Baptist Mission Hospital, where many cases of AIDS have been reported. Along the road there are slow straggles of schoolchildren in blue uniforms who stretch out their hands as we pass and call out, "Give me something." Already a crowd of outpatients has gathered at the entrance to the mission compound. A tour of the premises reveals that in contrast to the aridity outside the gates, this is an enclave of productivity, lush with fruit trees and poinsettia.

The hospital is clean and smells of creosote. Of the forty beds, less than a third are occupied. In one male ward of twelve beds, there are two patients. The chief physician tells us that last year he saw ten cases of AIDS each week. Lately the number has decreased to four or five.

"Why is that?" we want to know. 70

"Because we do not admit them to the hospital, so they have learned not to come here."

"Why don't you admit them?"

"Because we would have nothing but AIDS here then. So we send them away."

"But I see that you have very few patients in bed."

"That is also true." 75

"Where do the AIDS patients go?"

"Some go to the clinic in Port-au-Prince or the general hospital in the city. Others go home to die or to the voodoo priest."

"Do the people with AIDS know what they have before they come here?"

"Oh, yes, they know very well, and they know there is nothing to be done for them."

Outside, the crowd of people is dispersing toward the gate. The clinic has 80 been canceled for the day. No one knows why. We are conducted to the office of the reigning American pastor. He is a tall, handsome Midwesterner with an ecclesiastical smile.

"It is voodoo that is the devil here." He warms to his subject. "It is a demonic religion, a cancer on Haiti. Voodoo is worse than AIDS. And it is one of the reasons for the epidemic. Did you know that in order for a man to become a *houngan*[1] he must perform anal sodomy on another man? No, of course you didn't. And it doesn't stop there. The *houngans* tell the men that in order to appease the spirits they too must do the same thing. So you have ritualized homosexuality. That's what is spreading the AIDS." The pastor tells us of a nun who witnessed two acts of sodomy in a provincial hospital where she came upon a man sexually assaulting a houseboy and another man mounting a male patient in his bed.

"Fornication," he says. "It is Sodom and Gomorrah all over again, so what can you expect from these people?" Outside his office we are shown a cage of terrified, cowering monkeys to whom he coos affectionately. It is clear that he loves them. At the car, we shake hands.

"By the way," the pastor says, "what is your religion? Perhaps I am a kinsman?"

"While I am in Haiti," I tell him, "it will be voodoo or it will be nothing at all."

Abruptly, the smile breaks. It is as though a crack had suddenly appeared in   85
the face of an idol.

From the mission we go to the general hospital. In the heart of Port-au-Prince, it is the exact antithesis of the immaculate facility we have just left—filthy, crowded, hectic and staffed entirely by young interns and residents. Though it is associated with a medical school, I do not see any members of the faculty. We are shown around by Jocelyne, a young intern in a scrub suit. Each bed in three large wards is occupied. On the floor about the beds, hunkered in the posture of the innocent poor, are family members of the patients. In the corridor that constitutes the emergency room, someone lies on a stretcher receiving an intravenous infusion. She is hardly more than a cadaver.

"Where are the doctors in charge?" I ask Jocelyne. She looks at me questioningly.

"We are in charge."

"I mean your teachers, the faculty."

"They do not come here."   90

"What is wrong with that woman?"

"She has had diarrhea for three months. Now she is dehydrated." I ask the woman to open her mouth. Her throat is covered with the white plaques of thrush, a fungus infection associated with AIDS.

"How many AIDS patients do you see here?"

---

[1]*houngan:* a Voodoo priest. [Eds.]

"Three or four a day. We send them home. Sometimes the families abandon them, then we must admit them to the hospital. Every day, then, a relative comes to see if the patient has died. They want to take the body. That is important to them. But they know very well that AIDS is contagious and they are afraid to keep them at home. Even so, once or twice a week the truck comes to take away the bodies. Many are children. They are buried in mass graves."

"Where do the wealthy patients go?"   95

"There is a private hospital called Canapé Vert. Or else they go to Miami. Most of them, rich and poor, do not go to the hospital. Most are never diagnosed."

"How do you know these people have AIDS?"

"We don't know sometimes. The blood test is inaccurate. There are many false positives and false negatives. Fifteen percent of those with the disease have negative blood tests. We go by their infections—tuberculosis, diarrhea, fungi, herpes, skin rashes. It is not hard to tell."

"Do they know what they have?"

"Yes. They understand at once and they are prepared to die."   100

"Do the patients know how AIDS is transmitted?"

"They know, but they do not like to talk about it. It is taboo. Their memories do not seem to reach back to the true origins of their disaster. It is understandable, is it not?"

"Whatever you write, don't hurt us any more than we have already been hurt." It is a young Haitian journalist with whom I am drinking a rum punch. He means that any further linkage of AIDS and Haiti in the media would complete the economic destruction of the country. The damage was done early in the epidemic when the Centers for Disease Control in Atlanta added Haitians to the three other high-risk groups—hemophiliacs, intravenous drug users and homosexual and bisexual men. In fact, Haitians are no more susceptible to AIDS than anyone else. Although the CDC removed Haitians from special scrutiny in 1985, the lucrative tourism on which so much of the country's economy was based was crippled. Along with tourism went much of the foreign business investment. Worst of all was the injury to the national pride. Suddenly Haiti was indicted as the source of AIDS in the western hemisphere.

What caused the misunderstanding was the discovery of a large number of Haitian men living in Miami with AIDS antibodies in their blood. They denied absolutely they were homosexuals. But the CDC investigators did not know that homosexuality is the strongest taboo in Haiti and that no man would ever admit to it. Bisexuality, however, is not uncommon. Many married men and heterosexually oriented males will occasionally seek out other men for sex. Further, many, if not most, Haitian men visit female prostitutes from time to time. It is not difficult to see that once the virus was set loose in Haiti, the spread would be swift through both genders.

Exactly how the virus of AIDS arrived is not known. Could it have been 105 brought home by the Cuban soldiers stationed in Angola and thence to Haiti, about fifty miles away? Could it have been passed on by the thousands of Haitians living in exile in Zaire, who later returned home or immigrated to the United States? Could it have come from the American and Canadian homosexual tourists, and, yes, even some U.S. diplomats who have traveled to the island to have sex with impoverished Haitian men all too willing to sell themselves to feed their families? Throughout the international gay community Haiti was known as a good place to go for sex.

On a private tip from an official at the Ministry of Tourism, J-B and I drive to a town some fifty miles from Port-au-Prince. The hotel is owned by two Frenchmen who are out of the country, one of the staff tells us. He is a man of about thirty and clearly he is desperately ill. Tottering, short of breath, he shows us about the empty hotel. The furnishings are opulent and extreme— tiger skins on the wall, a live leopard in the garden, a bedroom containing a giant bathtub with gold faucets. Is it the heat of the day or the heat of my imagination that makes these walls echo with the painful cries of pederasty?

The hotel where we are staying is in Pétionville, the fashionable suburb of Port-au-Prince. It is the height of the season but there are no tourists, only a dozen or so French and American businessmen. The swimming pool is used once or twice a day by a single person. Otherwise, the water remains undisturbed until dusk, when the fruit bats come down to drink in midswoop. The hotel keeper is an American. He is eager to set me straight on Haiti.

"What did and should attract foreign investment is a combination of reliable weather, an honest and friendly populace, low wages and multilingual managers."

"What spoiled it?"

"Political instability and a bad American press about AIDS." He pauses, 110 then adds: "To which I hope you won't be contributing."

"What about just telling the truth?" I suggest.

"Look," he says, "there is no more danger of catching AIDS in Haiti than in New York or Santo Domingo. It is not where you are but what you do that counts." Agreeing, I ask if he had any idea that much of the tourism in Haiti during the past few decades was based on sex.

"No idea whatsoever. It was only recently that we discovered that that was the case."

"How is it that you hoteliers, restaurant owners and the Ministry of Tourism did not know what *tout* Haiti knew?"

"Look. All I know is that this is a middle-class, family-oriented hotel. We 115 don't allow guests to bring women, or for that matter men, into their rooms. If they did, we'd ask them to leave immediately."

At five A.M. the next day the telephone rings in my room. A Creole-accented male voice.

"Is the lady still with you, sir?"

"There is no lady here."

"In your room, sir, the lady I allowed to go up with a package?"

"There is no lady here, I tell you."   120

At seven A.M. I stop at the front desk. The clerk is a young man.

"Was it you who called my room at five o'clock?"

"Sorry," he says with a smile. "It was a mistake, sir. I meant to ring the room next door to yours." Still smiling, he holds up his shushing finger.

Next to Dr. Pape, director of the AIDS clinic, Bernard Liautaud, a dermatologist, is the most knowledgeable Haitian physician on the subject of the epidemic. Together, the two men have published a dozen articles on AIDS in international medical journals. In our meeting they present me with statistics:

- There are more than one thousand documented cases of AIDS in Haiti, and as many as one hundred thousand carriers of the virus.
- Eighty-seven percent of AIDS is now transmitted heterosexually. While it is true that the virus was introduced via the bisexual community, that route has decreased to 10 percent or less.
- Sixty percent of the wives or husbands of AIDS patients tested positive for the antibody.
- Fifty percent of the prostitutes tested in the Port-au-Prince area are infected.
- Eighty percent of the men with AIDS have had contact with prostitutes.
- The projected number of active cases in four years is ten thousand. (Since my last visit, the Haitian Medical Association broke its silence on the epidemic by warning that one million of the country's six million people could be carriers by 1992.)

The two doctors have more to tell. "The crossing over of the plague from   125
the homosexual to the heterosexual community will follow in the United States within two years. This, despite the hesitation to say so by those who fear to sow panic among your population. In Haiti, because bisexuality is more common, there was an early crossover into the general population. The trend, inevitably, is the same in the two countries."

"What is there to do, then?"

"Only education, just as in America. But here the Haitians reject the use of condoms. Only the men who are too sick to have sex are celibate."

"What is to be the end of it?"

"When enough heterosexuals of the middle and upper classes die, perhaps there will be the panic necessary for the people to change their sexual lifestyles."

This evening I leave Haiti. For two weeks I have fastened myself to this lovely fragile land like an ear pressed to the ground. It is a country to break a traveler's heart. It occurs to me that I have not seen a single jogger. Such a public expenditure of energy while everywhere else strength is ebbing—it would be obscene. In my final hours, I go to the Cathédrale of Sainte Trinité, the inner walls of which are covered with murals by Haiti's most renowned artists. Here are all the familiar Bible stories depicted in naïveté and piety, and all in such an <u>exuberance</u> of color as to tax the capacity of the retina to receive it, as though all the vitality of Haiti had been turned to paint and brushed upon these walls. How to explain this efflorescence at a time when all else is <u>lassitude</u> and <u>inertia</u>? Perhaps one day the plague will be rendered in poetry, music, painting, but not now. Not now.

QUESTIONS

1. Summarize the scene at the Copacabana. Which details are memorable? Why does Selzer spend so much time with Carmen, Mercedes, and Frasquita? Why are their attitudes toward AIDS so important?

2. Selzer writes at great length about his visit to the AIDS clinic directed by Dr. Jean William Pape. What does Selzer learn from observing patients at this clinic? What does Selzer learn about AIDS from the doctor at work?

3. A young Haitian journalist tells Selzer, "Whatever you write, don't hurt us any more than we have already been hurt" (paragraph 103). What is the significance of this request? After reading Selzer's essay, do you think Selzer has honored this request?

4. In the final paragraph of the essay, Selzer writes, "For two weeks I have fastened myself to this lovely fragile land like an ear pressed to the ground. It is a country to break a traveler's heart." What has Selzer learned about the politics of AIDS from his journey to Haiti?

5. Look at the various scenes and vignettes Selzer offers his readers. How does he connect these different scenes? How does this structure succeed in presenting his reflections?

6. What have you learned about the politics of AIDS from reading Selzer's essay? Write an essay reflecting on Selzer's essay.

7. Selzer offers his reflections as a way of justifying his strong feelings about AIDS. In other words, his reflections become a kind of argument. How would you make a more objective argument for his position?

MAKING CONNECTIONS

Selzer and Loren Eiseley (p. 138) write about subjects that technically are not "scientific." What commonalities or connections can you find among their questions, approaches, or methods?

CAN WE KNOW THE UNIVERSE?
Reflections on a Grain of Salt

Carl Sagan

Carl Sagan (1934–1996) was renowned both as a scientist and a writer. For his work with the National Aeronautics and Space Administration's Mariner, Viking, *and* Voyager *expeditions, he was awarded NASA's Medals for Exceptional Scientific Achievement and for Distinguished Public Service. Sagan produced the* Cosmos *television series for public television and received the Peabody Award in 1981. For his book,* The Dragons of Eden *(1977), he received the Pulitzer Prize in literature. Among his later works are* Comet *(1985),* Contact *(1985), a novel (with Ann Druyan),* Shadows of Forgotten Ancestors *(1992), and* Billions and Billions: Thoughts on Life and Death at the Brink of the Millennium *(1997). The following selection is from* Broca's Brain: Reflections on the Romance of Science *(1979).*

Nothing is rich but the inexhaustible wealth
of nature. She shows us only surfaces,
but she is a million fathoms deep.

Ralph Waldo Emerson

Science is a way of thinking much more than it is a body of knowledge. Its goal is to find out how the world works, to seek what regularities there may be, to penetrate to the connections of things—from subnuclear particles, which may be the constituents of all matter, to living organisms, the human social community, and thence to the cosmos as a whole. Our intuition is by no means an infallible guide. Our perceptions may be distorted by training and prejudice or merely because of the limitations of our sense organs, which, of course, perceive directly but a small fraction of the phenomena of the world. Even so straightforward a question as whether in the absence of friction a pound of lead falls faster than a gram of fluff was answered incorrectly by Aristotle and almost everyone else before the time of Galileo. Science is based on experiment, on a willingness to challenge old dogma, on an openness to see the universe as it really is. Accordingly, science sometimes requires courage—at the very least the courage to question the conventional wisdom.

Beyond this the main trick of science is to *really* think of something: the shape of clouds and their occasional sharp bottom edges at the same altitude everywhere in the sky; the formation of a dewdrop on a leaf; the origin of a name or a word—Shakespeare, say, or "philanthropic"; the reason for human social customs—the incest taboo, for example; how it is that a lens in sunlight can make paper burn; how a "walking stick" got to look so much like a twig; why the Moon seems to follow us as we walk; what prevents us from digging a hole down to the center of the Earth; what the definition is of "down" on a spherical Earth; how it is possible for the body to convert yesterday's lunch into today's muscle and sinew; or how far is up—does the universe go on forever, or if it does not, is there any meaning to the question of what lies on the other side? Some of these questions are pretty easy. Others, especially the last, are mysteries to which no one even today knows the answer. They are natural questions to ask. Every culture has posed such questions in one way or another. Almost always the proposed answers are in the nature of "Just So Stories," attempted explanations divorced from experiment, or even from careful comparative observations.

But the scientific cast of mind examines the world critically as if many alternative worlds might exist, as if other things might be here which are not. Then we are forced to ask why what we see is present and not something else. Why are the Sun and the Moon and the planets spheres? Why not pyramids, or cubes, or dodecahedra? Why not irregular, jumbly shapes? Why so symmetrical, worlds? If you spend any time spinning hypotheses, checking to see whether they make sense, whether they conform to what else we know, thinking of tests you can pose to substantiate or deflate your hypotheses, you will find yourself doing science. And as you come to practice this habit of thought more and more you will get better and better at it. To penetrate into the heart of the thing—even a little thing, a blade of grass, as Walt Whitman said—is to experience a kind of exhilaration that, it may be, only human beings of all the beings on this planet can feel. We are an intelligent species and the use of our intelligence quite properly gives us pleasure. In this respect the brain is like a muscle. When we think well, we feel good. Understanding is a kind of ecstasy.

But to what extent can we *really* know the universe around us? Sometimes this question is posed by people who hope the answer will be in the negative, who are fearful of a universe in which everything might one day be known. And sometimes we hear pronouncements from scientists who confidently state that everything worth knowing will soon be known—or even is already known—and who paint pictures of a Dionysian or Polynesian age in which the zest for intellectual discovery has withered, to be replaced by a kind of subdued languor, the lotus eaters drinking fermented coconut milk or some other mild hallucinogen. In addition to maligning both the Polynesians, who were intrepid explorers (and whose brief respite in paradise is now sadly ending), as well as the inducements to intellectual discovery provided by some hallucinogens, this contention turns out to be trivially mistaken.

Let us approach a much more modest question: not whether we can know the universe or the Milky Way Galaxy or a star or a world. Can we know, ultimately and in detail, a grain of salt? Consider one microgram of table salt, a speck just barely large enough for someone with keen eyesight to make out without a microscope. In that grain of salt there are about 10^{16} sodium and chlorine atoms. This is a 1 followed by 16 zeros, 10 million billion atoms. If we wish to know a grain of salt, we must know at least the three-dimensional positions of each of these atoms. (In fact, there is much more to be known—for example, the nature of the forces between the atoms—but we are making only a modest calculation.) Now, is this number more or less than the number of things which the brain can know?

How much *can* the brain know? There are perhaps 10^{11} neurons in the brain, the circuit elements and switches that are responsible in their electrical and chemical activity for the functioning of our minds. A typical brain neuron has perhaps a thousand little wires, called dendrites, which connect it with its fellows. If, as seems likely, every bit of information in the brain corresponds to one of these connections, the total number of things knowable by the brain is no more than 10^{14}, one hundred trillion. But this number is only one percent of the number of atoms in our speck of salt.

So in this sense the universe is intractable, astonishingly immune to any human attempt at full knowledge. We cannot on this level understand a grain of salt, much less the universe.

But let us look more deeply at our microgram of salt. Salt happens to be a crystal in which, except for defects in the structure of the crystal lattice, the position of every sodium and chlorine atom is predetermined. If we could shrink ourselves into this crystalline world, we could see rank upon rank of atoms in an ordered array, a regularly alternating structure—sodium, chlorine, sodium, chlorine, specifying the sheet of atoms we are standing on and all the sheets above us and below us. An absolutely pure crystal of salt could have the position of every atom specified by something like 10 bits of information.[1] This would not strain the information-carrying capacity of the brain.

If the universe had natural laws that governed its behavior to the same degree of regularity that determines a crystal of salt, then, of course, the universe would be knowable. Even if there were many such laws, each of considerable complexity, human beings might have the capacity to understand them all. Even if such knowledge exceeded the information-carrying capacity of the brain, we might store the additional information outside our bodies—in books, for example, or in computer memories—and still, in some sense, know the universe.

Human beings are, understandably, highly motivated to find regularities, natural laws. The search for rules, the only possible way to understand such a vast and

10

---

[1] Chlorine is a deadly poison gas employed on European battlefields in World War I. Sodium is a corrosive metal which burns upon contact with water. Together they make a placid and unpoisonous material, table salt. Why each of these substances has the properties it does is a subject called chemistry, which requires more than 10 bits of information to understand.

complex universe, is called science. The universe forces those who live in it to understand it. Those creatures who find everyday experience a muddled jumble of events with no predictability, no regularity, are in grave peril. The universe belongs to those who, at least to some degree, have figured it out.

It is an astonishing fact that there *are* laws of nature, rules that summarize conveniently—not just qualitatively but quantitatively—how the world works. We might imagine a universe in which there are no such laws, in which the 10^{80} elementary particles that make up a universe like our own behave with utter and uncompromising abandon. To understand such a universe we would need a brain at least as massive as the universe. It seems unlikely that such a universe could have life and intelligence, because beings and brains require some degree of internal stability and order. But even if in a much more random universe there were such beings with an intelligence much greater than our own, there could not be much knowledge, passion or joy.

Fortunately for us, we live in a universe that has at least important parts that are knowable. Our common-sense experience and our evolutionary history have prepared us to understand something of the workaday world. When we go into other realms, however, common sense and ordinary intuition turn out to be highly unreliable guides. It is stunning that as we go close to the speed of light our mass increases indefinitely, we shrink toward zero thickness in the direction of motion, and time for us comes as near to stopping as we would like. Many people think that this is silly, and every week or two I get a letter from someone who complains to me about it. But it is a virtually certain consequence not just of experiment but also of Albert Einstein's brilliant analysis of space and time called the Special Theory of Relativity. It does not matter that these effects seem unreasonable to us. We are not in the habit of traveling close to the speed of light. The testimony of our common sense is suspect at high velocities.

Or consider an isolated molecule composed of two atoms shaped something like a dumbbell—a molecule of salt, it might be. Such a molecule rotates about an axis through the line connecting the two atoms. But in the world of quantum mechanics, the realm of the very small, not all orientations of our dumbbell molecule are possible. It might be that the molecule could be oriented in a horizontal position, say, or in a vertical position, but not at many angles in between. Some rotational positions are forbidden. Forbidden by what? By the laws of nature. The universe is built in such a way as to limit, or quantize, rotation. We do not experience this directly in everyday life; we would find it startling as well as awkward in sitting-up exercises, to find arms outstretched from the sides or pointed up to the skies permitted but many intermediate positions forbidden. We do not live in the world of the small, on the scale of 10^{-13} centimeters, in the realm where there are twelve zeros between the decimal place and the one. Our common-sense intuitions do not count. What does count is experiment—in this case observations from the far infrared spectra of molecules. They show molecular rotation to be quantized.

The idea that the world places restrictions on what humans might do is frustrating. Why *shouldn't* we be able to have intermediate rotational positions? Why *can't* we travel faster than the speed of light? But so far as we can tell, this is the way the universe is constructed. Such prohibitions not only press us toward a little humility; they also make the world more knowable. Every restriction corresponds to a law of nature, a regularization of the universe. The more restrictions there are on what matter and energy can do, the more knowledge human beings can attain. Whether in some sense the universe is ultimately knowable depends not only on how many natural laws there are that encompass widely divergent phenomena, but also on whether we have the openness and the intellectual capacity to understand such laws. Our formulations of the regularities of nature are surely dependent on how the brain is built, but also, and to a significant degree, on how the universe is built.

For myself, I like a universe that includes much that is unknown and, at the same time, much that is knowable. A universe in which everything is known would be static and dull, as boring as the heaven of some weakminded theologians. A universe that is unknowable is no fit place for a thinking being. The ideal universe for us is one very much like the universe we inhabit. And I would guess that this is not really much of a coincidence.

15

QUESTIONS

1. How are *science* and *scientific thinking* defined in the first three paragraphs? What is Sagan's purpose in defining these terms? What does this tell you about Sagan's conception of his audience?

2. Sagan's mode of reflection might be considered less personal than others in this section in that he is reflecting on an idea rather than on an event in his life. How does Sagan keep the tone from becoming abstract? What elements of the personal are present in this essay?

3. Sagan cites scientists who believe that "everything worth knowing will soon be known" (paragraph 4). How does the evidence in this essay challenge that assumption?

4. We might consider paragraph 15 to be Sagan's most personal statement in his reflections on the universe: he likes "a universe that includes much that is unknown and, at the same time, much that is knowable." Why is this balance important to Sagan? Do you agree with his closing statements?

5. Consider the statement, "The more restrictions there are on what matter and energy can do, the more knowledge human beings can attain" (paragraph 14). Describe an example in your own experience (or another's) when you learned that rules or laws were helpful in ensuring your personal freedom.

6. In paragraph 3 Sagan concludes, "Understanding is a kind of ecstasy." Describe a time in your life when you understood something for the first time; when, as they say, the light went on in your head, shining on a difficult problem, and bringing about a realization. Could your feelings at the time be considered ecstatic, or did you experience some other emotion?

7. What sort of universe would you consider ideal? What would you like to know about the universe that is now unknown to you? Explain.

MAKING CONNECTIONS

1. A number of the writers in this section offer their reflections in order to justify a belief or a strong feeling about a subject. In other words, their reflections become a kind of argument. Isak Dinesen (p. 66), Martin Luther King Jr. (p. 90), George Orwell (p. 104), and Zoë Tracy Hardy (p. 111) come to mind as well as Sagan. How convincing is the argument in each case? How has the writer used purely personal responses to make a persuasive case? How would you go about developing a more objective argument for one of their positions? What would be the difference in effect?

2. Does Sagan's concern for "passion" and "joy" (paragraph 11) surprise you? Where else, especially in the writings by scientists in this section, do you find evidence of the same concerns? Citing several examples from essayists you have read, write an essay on the role of passion and joy in the work of scientists and other writers.

THE BIRD AND THE MACHINE
Loren Eiseley

Loren Eiseley (1907–1977) rode the rails as a young hobo before he finished college, went to graduate school at the University of Pennsylvania, and began a distinguished career as an anthropologist, archaeologist, essayist, and poet. Through his writing, Eiseley made the ideas and findings of anthropology comprehensible to the public. He found significance in small incidents—the flights of birds, the web of a spider, and the chance encounter with a young fox. Eiseley once wrote that animals understand their roles, but that man, "bereft of instinct, must search continually for meanings." This essay is taken from his collection, The Immense Journey *(1957).*

I suppose their little bones have years ago been lost among the stones and winds of those high glacial pastures. I suppose their feathers blew eventually into the piles of tumbleweed beneath the straggling cattle fences and rotted there in the mountain snows, along with dead steers and all the other things that drift to an end in the corners of the wire. I do not quite know why I should be thinking of birds over the *New York Times* at breakfast, particularly the birds of my youth half a continent away. It is a funny thing what the brain will do with memories and how it will treasure them and finally bring them into odd juxtapositions with other things, as though it wanted to make a design, or get some meaning out of them, whether you want it or not, or even see it.

It used to seem marvelous to me, but I read now that there are machines that can do these things in a small way, machines that can crawl about like animals, and that it may not be long now until they do more things—maybe even make themselves—I saw that piece in the *Times* just now. And then they will, maybe—well, who knows—but you read about it more and more with no one making any protest, and already they can add better than we and reach up and hear things through the dark and finger the guns over the night sky.

This is the new world that I read about at breakfast. This is the world that confronts me in my biological books and journals, until there are times when I sit quietly in my chair and try to hear the little purr of the cogs in my head and the tubes flaring and dying as the messages go through them and the circuits snap shut or open. This is the great age, make no mistake about it; the robot has been born somewhat appropriately along with the atom bomb, and the brain they say now is just another type of more complicated feedback system. The engineers have its basic principles worked out; it's mechanical, you know;

nothing to get superstitious about; and man can always improve on nature once he gets the idea. Well, he's got it all right and that's why, I guess, that I sit here in my chair, with the article crunched in my hand, remembering those two birds and that blue mountain sunlight. There is another magazine article on my desk that reads "Machines Are Getting Smarter Every Day." I don't deny it, but I'll still stick with the birds. It's life I believe in, not machines.

Maybe you don't believe there is any difference. A skeleton is all joints and pulleys, I'll admit. And when man was in his simpler stages of machine building in the eighteenth century, he quickly saw the resemblances. "What," wrote Hobbes, "is the heart but a spring, and the nerves but so many strings, and the joints but so many wheels, giving motion to the whole body?" Tinkering about in their shops it was inevitable in the end that men would see the world as a huge machine "subdivided into an infinite number of lesser machines."

The idea took on with a vengeance. Little automatons toured the country— 5 dolls controlled by clockwork. Clocks described as little worlds were taken on tours by their designers. They were made up of moving figures, shifting scenes and other remarkable devices. The life of the cell was unknown. Man, whether he was conceived as possessing a soul or not, moved and jerked about like these tiny puppets. A human being thought of himself in terms of his own tools and implements. He had been fashioned like the puppets he produced and was only a more clever model made by a greater designer.

Then in the nineteenth century, the cell was discovered, and the single machine in its turn was found to be the product of millions of infinitesimal machines—the cells. Now, finally, the cell itself dissolves away into an abstract chemical machine—and that into some intangible, inexpressible flow of energy. The secret seems to lurk all about, the wheels get smaller and smaller, and they turn more rapidly, but when you try to seize it the life is gone—and so, by popular definition, some would say that life was never there in the first place. The wheels and the cogs are the secret and we can make them better in time—machines that will run faster and more accurately than real mice to real cheese.

I have no doubt it can be done, though a mouse harvesting seeds on an autumn thistle is to me a fine sight and more complicated, I think, in his multiform activity, than a machine "mouse" running a maze. Also, I like to think of the possible shape of the future brooding in mice, just as it brooded once in a rather ordinary mousy insectivore who became a man. It leaves a nice fine indeterminate sense of wonder that even an electronic brain hasn't got, because you know perfectly well that if the electronic brain changes, it will be because of something man has done to it. But what man will do to himself he doesn't really know. A certain scale of time and a ghostly intangible thing called change are ticking in him. Powers and potentialities like the oak in the seed, or a red and awful ruin. Either way, it's impressive; and the mouse has it, too. Or those birds, I'll never forget those birds—yet before I measured their significance, I learned the lesson of time first of all. I was young then and left alone in a great desert—part of an expedition that had scattered its men over several hundred miles in order to carry on research more effectively. I learned there that time is a series of planes existing superficially in the same universe. The tempo is a human illusion, a subjective clock ticking in our own kind of protoplasm.

As the long months passed, I began to live on the slower planes and to observe more readily what passed for life there. I sauntered, I passed more and more slowly up and down the canyons in the dry baking heat of midsummer. I slumbered for long hours in the shade of huge brown boulders that had gathered in tilted companies out on the flats. I had forgotten the world of men and the world had forgotten me. Now and then I found a skull in the canyons, and these justified my remaining there. I took a serene cold interest in these discoveries. I had come, like many a naturalist before me, to view life with a wary and subdued attention. I had grown to take pleasure in the divested bone.

I sat once on a high ridge that fell away before me into a waste of sand dunes. I sat through hours of a long afternoon. Finally, as I glanced beside my boot an indistinct configuration caught my eye. It was a coiled rattlesnake, a big one. How long he had sat with me I do not know. I had not frightened him. We were both locked in the sleep-walking tempo of the earlier world, baking in the same high air and sunshine. Perhaps he had been there when I came. He slept on as I left, his coils, so ill discerned by me, dissolving once more among the stones and gravel from which I had barely made him out.

Another time I got on a higher ridge, among some tough little wind-warped pines half covered over with sand in a basin-like depression that caught everything carried by the air up to those heights. There were a few thin bones of birds, some cracked shells of indeterminable age, and the knotty fingers of pine roots bulged out of shape from their long and agonizing grasp upon the crevices of the rock. I lay under the pines in the sparse shade and went to sleep once more.

It grew cold finally, for autumn was in the air by then, and the few things that lived thereabouts were sinking down into an even chillier scale of time. In the moments between sleeping and waking I saw the roots about me and slowly, slowly, a foot in what seemed many centuries, I moved my sleep-stiffened hands over the scaling bark and lifted my numbed face after the vanishing sun. I was a great awkward thing of knots and aching limbs, trapped up there in some long, patient endurance that involved the necessity of putting living fingers into rock and by slow, aching expansion bursting those rocks asunder. I suppose, so thin and slow was the time of my pulse by then, that I might have stayed on to drift still deeper into the lower cadences of the frost, or the crystalline life that glitters in pebbles, or shines in a snowflake, or dreams in the meteoric iron between the worlds.

It was a dim descent, but time was present in it. Somewhere far down in that scale the notion struck me that one might come the other way. Not many months thereafter I joined some colleagues heading higher into a remote windy tableland where huge bones were reputed to protrude like boulders from the turf. I had drowsed with reptiles and moved with the century-long pulse of trees; now, lethargically, I was climbing back up some invisible ladder of quickening hours. There had been talk of birds in connection with my duties. Birds are intense, fast-living creatures—reptiles, I suppose one might say, that have escaped out of the heavy sleep of time, transformed fairy creatures dancing over sunlit meadows. It is a youthful fancy, no doubt, but because of something that happened up there among the escarpments of that range, it remains with me a lifelong impression. I can never bear to see a bird imprisoned.

We came into that valley through the trailing mists of a spring night. It was a place that looked as though it might never have known the foot of man, but our scouts had been ahead of us and we knew all about the abandoned cabin of stone that lay far up on one hillside. It had been built in the land rush of the last century and then lost to the cattlemen again as the marginal soils failed to take to the plow.

There were spots like this all over that country. Lost graves marked by unlettered stones and old corroding rim-fire cartridge cases lying where somebody had made a stand among the boulders that rimmed the valley. They are all that remain of the range wars; the men are under the stones now. I could see our cavalcade winding in and out through the mist below us: torches, the reflection of the truck lights on our collecting tins, and the far-off bumping of a loose dinosaur thigh bone in the bottom of a trailer. I stood on a rock a moment looking down and thinking what it cost in money and equipment to capture the past.

We had, in addition, instructions to lay hands on the present. The word had come through to get them alive—birds, reptiles, anything. A zoo somewhere abroad needed restocking. It was one of those reciprocal matters in which science involves itself. Maybe our museum needed a stray ostrich egg and this was the payoff. Anyhow, my job was to help capture some birds and that was why I was there before the trucks.

The cabin had not been occupied for years. We intended to clean it out and live in it, but there were holes in the roof and the birds had come in and were roosting in the rafters. You could depend on it in a place like this where everything blew away, and even a bird needed some place out of the weather and away from coyotes. A cabin going back to nature in a wild place draws them till they come in, listening at the eaves, I imagine, pecking softly among the shingles till they find a hole and then suddenly the place is theirs and man is forgotten.

Sometimes of late years I find myself thinking the most beautiful sight in the world might be the birds taking over New York after the last man has run away to the hills. I will never live to see it, of course, but I know just how it will sound because I've lived up high and I know the sort of watch birds keep on us. I've listened to sparrows tapping tentatively on the outside of air conditioners when they thought no one was listening, and I know how other birds test the vibrations that come up to them through the television aerials.

"Is he gone?" they ask, and the vibrations come up from below, "Not yet, not yet."

Well, to come back, I got the door open softly and I had the spotlight all ready to turn on and blind whatever birds there were so they couldn't see to get out through the roof. I had a short piece of ladder to put against the far wall where there was a shelf on which I expected to make the biggest haul. I had all the information I needed just like any skilled assassin. I pushed the door open, the hinges squeaking only a little. A bird or two stirred—I could hear them— but nothing flew and there was a faint starlight through the holes in the roof.

I padded across the floor, got the ladder up and the light ready, and slith-   20
ered up the ladder till my head and arms were over the shelf. Everything was dark as pitch except for the starlight at the little place back of the shelf near the eaves. With the light to blind them, they'd never make it. I had them. I reached my arm carefully over in order to be ready to seize whatever was there and I put the flash on the edge of the shelf where it would stand by itself when I turned it on. That way I'd be able to use both hands.

Everything worked perfectly except for one detail—I didn't know what kind of birds were there. I never thought about it at all, and it wouldn't have mattered if I had. My orders were to get something interesting. I snapped on the flash and sure enough there was a great beating and feathers flying, but instead of my having them, they, or rather he, had me. He had my hand, that is, and for a small hawk not much bigger than my fist he was doing all right. I heard him give one short metallic cry when the light went on and my hand descended on the bird beside him; after that he was busy with his claws and his beak was sunk in my thumb. In the struggle I knocked the lamp over on the shelf, and his mate got her sight back and whisked neatly through the hole in the roof and off among the stars outside. It all happened in fifteen seconds and you might think I would have fallen down the ladder, but no, I had a professional assassin's reputation to keep up, and the bird, of course, made the mistake of thinking the hand was the enemy and not the eyes behind it. He chewed my thumb up pretty effectively and lacerated my hand with his claws, but in the end I got him, having two hands to work with.

He was a sparrow hawk and a fine young male in the prime of life. I was sorry not to catch the pair of them, but as I dripped blood and folded his wings carefully, holding him by the back so that he couldn't strike again, I had to admit the two of them might have been more than I could have handled under the circumstances. The little fellow had saved his mate by diverting me, and that was that. He was born to it, and made no outcry now, resting in my hand hopelessly, but peering toward me in the shadows behind the lamp with a fierce, almost indifferent glance. He neither gave nor expected mercy and something out of the high air passed from him to me, stirring a faint embarrassment.

I quit looking into that eye and managed to get my huge carcass with its fist full of prey back down the ladder. I put the bird in a box too small to allow him to injure himself by struggle and walked out to welcome the arriving trucks. It had been a long day, and camp still to make in the darkness. In the morning that bird would be just another episode. He would go back with the bones in the truck to a small cage in a city where he would spend the rest of his life. And a good thing, too. I sucked my aching thumb and spat out some blood. An assassin has to get used to these things. I had a professional reputation to keep up.

In the morning, with the change that comes on suddenly in that high country, the mist that had hovered below us in the valley was gone. The sky was a deep blue, and one could see for miles over the high outcroppings of stone. I was up early and brought the box in which the little hawk was imprisoned out onto the grass where I was building a cage. A wind as cool as a mountain spring ran over the grass and stirred my hair. It was a fine day to be alive. I looked up and all around and at the hole in the cabin roof out of which the other little hawk had fled. There was no sign of her anywhere that I could see.

"Probably in the next county by now," I thought cynically, but before beginning work I decided I'd have a look at my last night's capture. 25

Secretively, I looked again all around the camp and up and down and opened the box. I got him right out in my hand with his wings folded properly and I was careful not to startle him. He lay limp in my grasp and I could feel his heart pound under the feathers but he only looked beyond me and up.

I saw him look that last look away beyond me into a sky so full of light that I could not follow his gaze. The little breeze flowed over me again, and nearby a mountain aspen shook all its tiny leaves. I suppose I must have had an idea then of what I was going to do, but I never let it come up into consciousness. I just reached over and laid the hawk on the grass.

He lay there a long minute without hope, unmoving, his eyes still fixed on that blue vault above him. It must have been that he was already so far away in heart that he never felt the release from my hand. He never even stood. He just lay with his breast against the grass.

In the next second after that long minute he was gone. Like a flicker of light, he had vanished with my eyes full on him, but without actually seeing even a premonitory wing beat. He was gone straight into that towering emptiness of light and crystal that my eyes could scarcely bear to penetrate. For another long moment there was silence. I could not see him. The light was too intense. Then from far up somewhere a cry came ringing down.

I was young then and had seen little of the world, but when I heard that cry 30 my heart turned over. It was not the cry of the hawk I had captured; for, by shifting my position against the sun, I was now seeing further up. Straight out of the sun's eye, where she must have been soaring restlessly above us for untold hours, hurtled his mate. And from far up, ringing from peak to peak of the summits over us, came a cry of such unutterable and ecstatic joy that it sounds down across the years and tingles among the cups on my quiet breakfast table.

I saw them both now. He was rising fast to meet her. They met in a great soaring gyre that turned to a whirling circle and a dance of wings. Once more, just once, their two voices, joined in a harsh wild medley of question and response, struck and echoed the pinnacles of the valley. Then they were gone forever somewhere into those upper regions beyond the eyes of men.

I am older now, and sleep less, and have seen most of what there is to see and am not very much impressed any more, I suppose, by anything. "What Next in the Attributes of Machines?" my morning headline runs. "It Might Be the Power to Reproduce Themselves."

I lay the paper down and across my mind a phrase floats insinuatingly: "It does not seem that there is anything in the construction, constituents, or behavior of the human being which it is essentially impossible for science to duplicate and synthesize. On the other hand . . ."

All over the city the cogs in the hard, bright mechanisms have begun to turn. Figures move through computers, names are spelled out, a thoughtful machine selects the fingerprints of a wanted criminal from an array of thousands. In the laboratory an electronic mouse runs swiftly through a maze toward the cheese it can neither taste nor enjoy. On the second run it does better than a living mouse.

"On the other hand . . ." Ah, my mind takes up, on the other hand the machine does not bleed, ache, hang for hours in the empty sky in a torment of hope to learn the fate of another machine, nor does it cry out with joy nor dance in the air with the fierce passion of a bird. Far off, over a distance greater than space, that remote cry from the heart of heaven makes a faint buzzing among my breakfast dishes and passes on and away. 35

QUESTIONS

1. According to Eiseley, what is the difference between birds and machines?

2. Why does Eiseley tell the story about his experience as a young anthropologist exploring life in the American desert? How does this story relate to the rest of the essay?

3. Trace the associative movement of Eiseley's mind. How does one thought suggest another? How does this movement help illustrate his point?

4. Eiseley projects himself from the beginning as someone remembering and reflecting on his experience. How did the meditative process of this essay, with its various twists and turns of thought, affect you as a reader?

5. Eiseley writes, "It is a funny thing what the brain will do with memories and how it will treasure them and finally bring them into odd juxtapositions with other things, as though it wanted to make a design, or get some meaning out of them, whether you want it or not, or even see it" (paragraph 1). Begin reflecting on some important memories from your past, and see where these reflections take you. As your mind wanders be-

tween past and present, see if any kind of design or meaning emerges for you. See what associations you can shape into an essay of your own.

MAKING CONNECTIONS

Consider the titles of the essays by Carl Sagan, "Can We Know the Universe? Reflections on a Grain of Salt" (p. 132), and Alice Walker, "Beauty: When the Other Dancer Is the Self" (p. 40), in relation to this essay by Eiseley. Would either of those titles be appropriate here? In the second case, "Beauty" might indicate the sparrow hawk, and the "Other Dancer" might be the author. Would that work? Write a commentary on Eiseley's essay supposing that one of the other titles (and the themes it suggests) applies to this essay as well.

HOW MEMORY SPEAKS

John Kotre

*Born in Evanston, Illinois, in 1940, John Kotre received his
doctorate in 1970 and is presently a professor of psychology
at the University of Michigan, Dearborn. Kotre has written
more than fifteen articles and reviews for professional journals and popular magazines, including* America *and*
Commonweal. *He has published several books on memory
autobiographical subjects, including* Outliving the Self:
Generativity and the Interpretation of Lives *(1984),* White
Gloves: How We Create Ourselves through Memory
(1995), and with his wife, Elizabeth Hall, he coauthored
Seasons of Life: Our Dramatic Journey from Birth to
Death *(1990). This essay appeared in a wide-ranging sci-
ence onthology,* Mysteries of Life and the Universe: New
Essays from America's Finest Writers on Science *(1992).*

It's a great puzzle, this memory of ours. A scene we experience for a moment—and only once—remains clear in our minds for a lifetime, yet we forget
the looks of things we see and touch almost every day. Once, when I recorded
the life story of a young woman, she spoke of a glance that never left her. She
was recalling the birth of her first child: "I remember taking him to my
mom—my mom had not seen him—and I'll never forget the look. It—she—
just crushed me. She looked at him as if to say, 'Is that him?'"

There are moments, good as well as bad, that none of us will ever forget.
But there are plenty of ordinary objects and events for which our memory is a
blur at best. How much, for example, can you remember about a penny? A lot,
you say? Well, try drawing one—now.

It ought to be easy, but it isn't. When you get stuck, compare what you've
drawn with an actual penny. On the "heads" side, did you have Lincoln facing
toward the right, where the year 19– appears? Did you have In God We Trust
written across the top and Liberty on the left? For "tails," did you draw a building in the middle (it's the Lincoln Memorial), and did you write United States
of America across the top, E. Pluribus Unum just below that, and One Cent
across the bottom?

The difference between a mother's momentary glance and the details of a
penny is, of course, the meaning of each. In a study by psychologists Raymond
Nickerson and Marilyn Jager Adams, only 20 percent of the subjects recalled
even half of a penny's 8 features correctly. But one subject got everything right.
He happened to be an <u>avid</u> coin collector; he could picture pennies in minute

detail because they had a special place in the story of his life. They were part of what researchers are now calling *autobiographical memory*.

Autobiographical memory is memory for the events and feelings that go into the story of a life. For many years, clinical psychologists, psychiatrists, and social workers have dealt with this kind of memory. It's the stuff of which "insight" therapies and "talking" cures are made. I have worked with autobiographical memory, too, but in a different context. I have recorded the stories of people's lives and put them—or parts of them—into books, audio programs, and on one occasion a public television series called "Seasons of Life." And I've wondered again and again about the mystery of memory, about mental pictures from long ago that warm the face of one storyteller, moisten the eyes of another, and bring the "shakes" to a third. Are these memories photographic or even remotely accurate? And, accurate or not, what do they mean? What do the memories speak of, and how do they speak?

Thankfully, a new breed of memory researchers ventured forth from the laboratory in the late 1970s in pursuit of "ecological validity." Abandoning research on nonsense syllables and word lists—on memories of a few minutes' duration—they began to investigate such real-world phenomena as legal testimony, diaries, and recollections of historical events. Elsewhere in psychology there grew a new interest in narrative forms of thought. Taken together, these approaches are helping us decipher the special language of autobiographical memory, helping us understand the stories we tell ourselves about ourselves, the stories we'll eventually pass on to our successors.

WHAT PART OF OUR LIVES DO WE REMEMBER BEST?

A man I interviewed some years ago—I'll call him Chris Vitullo—had a vivid, 70-year-old memory of two coins. Chris looked like a clean-shaven Santa Claus. He had neatly trimmed white hair, a red nose, a thick torso that rested on sturdy legs, and a hoarse Sicilian accent. The coins he remembered weren't pennies, and Chris would have had a hard time recalling the features of each. But they did have an important place in the story of his life.

Chris spent his first four years in Sicily while his father was working in America. But the day came when his father rejoined his family. "I'm getting the goose pimple now," Chris said as he relived the experience of meeting him for the first time. His mother had told him what to do. "I kissed his hand, and I asked him to bless me. '*Mi benedica, Padre.*' Naturally, my dad, he picked me up and he put me in his chest, and then he put two fingers in his vest pocket and he got a couple big coins, silver coins. They were dollars, and he gave them to me. Just think how tickled I was, huh? Oh, boy! The first time I met him, he gave me two coins made out of silver, two silver dollars."

This is one of a host of memories that Chris produced from his childhood, adolescent, and young-adult years. The sheer number of memories raises an interesting question about autobiographical memory: what part of our lives do we

remember best? We can't possibly recall everything that happened to us—
every hour of every day of every year. When we think of our life as a whole, to
what stages do our thoughts instinctively turn?

Chris Vitullo's thoughts turned to his beginnings. He spoke of the tales his   10
mother told him as a child, of his apprenticeship at the age of 7 to an old barber named Antonino, of his voyage, alone, to America when he was 13. Leaving his mother and father on the dock, "I had a lump in my throat as big as a
fist." He remembered everything about the trip: the strange languages and the
strange foods, the way the boat listed so that Chris could see the ocean on one
side but not on the other. Then someone spotted the Statute of Liberty. "*La
liberta! Viva la liberta!*" From New York, Chris took a two-day train trip to
Saint Louis, got off at the wrong station, and then, with an incredible bit of
luck, walked straight to the front door of his sister's home. All these events
Chris recounted in great detail. Several years after arriving in Saint Louis, he
moved to Detroit and opened a barbershop with a friend. His father and
mother came from Sicily to arrange his marriage to a girl named Gloria, and
by the age of 21 the course of Chris's adult life had been set.

Chris was full of energy as he described these events. But once he came to
his marriage to Gloria, his narrative slowed to a crawl. "When we got married,"
he said, "we were very happy after that, with an exception that whatever comes
along, you have to take, sickness or otherwise. We lived together forty-five
years, Gloria and me. Yeah, we lived together forty-five years. We had a lot of
good times together and a lot of bad times together. We worked, we paid our
bills honorably, and we dressed well. We bought a house, we paid for the
house, we had a little bit of money, whatever God provided, but we did it all in
a good faith and honestly, and we arrived to the point that probably if God
wouldn't want Gloria to pass away, maybe Gloria and I, we would be together
today. But that's the way it goes in life, and we have to take what's coming
to us."

There it was: after hours on his first 21 years, a minute or two on his next
45. In subsequent interviews I was able to learn more about Chris's marriage to
Gloria and her death 10 years prior to my first interview, but it took a lot of
questioning and checking. Chris wasn't resistant to speaking of this time; it was
just that his memory had condensed nearly half a century into a single whole,
with much of the detail forgotten. What Chris remembered best—and with the
greatest joy—were the years of his life from 6 to 21.

There are quicker ways to pinpoint the years the stand out in most of our
minds than gathering individual life histories. One of the simplest goes back
over a hundred years to Sir Francis Galton, who is best known for his innova-
tions in statistical analysis and his obsession with measuring psychological
traits. Galton's memory technique is akin to Freudian free association. Subjects
are given a cue word—*window*, for example. They then report a memory that
the word triggers. After several dozen cues are presented, subjects go back and
date each remembered incident as closely as possible. You can try it yourself.

Common cue words are *avenue, box, coin, flower, game, mountain, picture, storm, ticket,* and *yard.*

When memories are dated in this fashion and averaged across a number of subjects, an interesting pattern emerges: People in the second half of life do not apportion their memories the way people in the first half do. Memory researcher David Rubin has pieced together the results of half a dozen studies and found that in response to cue words, 20-year-olds produce a high proportion of very recent memories and relatively few from the distant past. Thirty-year-olds aren't much different, once you allow for the fact that they are looking back on an additional decade of life. In general, the responses of both age groups fit the normal forgetting curve. This curve looks like a slope for expert skiers. Most of our memories are of recent events—particularly those of the last few days. Then there is a rapid decline in <u>retention</u> until a point is reached at which forgetting becomes more gradual: we've lost most of what we're going to lose. At this point, the forgetting curve turns into a gentle slope that carries us back to the beginning of life.

But not to the very beginning. When you're dealing with autobiographical memory, the normal forgetting curve runs into a drop-off that wipes out recollections of our earliest years. People vary a great deal, but most say their first memory of life comes from when they were 3 or 4. (Women generally report an earlier date for their first memory than do men; the average difference is several months.) In our first 3 years, our brain isn't mature enough, nor is language developed enough, to enable us to store episodes in memory. The darkness covering these years is known as infantile amnesia.

All age groups experience the drop-off of infantile amnesia. But only in the second half of life does something else happen. Responding to the same cue words as younger people, subjects in their 50s and 70s (the only other age groups for which data are available) report a disproportionate number of memories from the early years, especially the second and third decades of life. This bonus of memories forms an extra hill at the bottom of the forgetting slope, just before the drop-off of infantile amnesia. Rubin calls the hill *reminiscence,* something over and above normal remembering. We'll return later to the question of what it means.

The cue word method for dating autobiographical memories may seem a bit artificial, and a lot depends on how you set up the experiment, but I have found that the results fit a surprising number of life-story tellers. My experience has been that the hill begins even before the second decade of life, around the age of 6, when a string of continuous episodes—not just isolated fragments— can first be found in adults' memories.

At 76, Chris Vitullo fit the basic profile of 70-year-olds, though his excess of memories came from the second decade of his life rather than the second and the third. Remarkably, his pattern was quite close to that of another 76-year-old—a woman who had lost a good deal of her memory and who, in the words of Mark Twain, could remember anything "whether it happened or not."

Recording her story, I had little idea which of her memories were fact and which were fantasy. Yet the temporal location of her recollections fit the pattern of forgetting slope, reminiscence hill, and infantile drop-off. A phenomenon that persists even when you're dealing with fantasy makes you wonder what autobiographical memory is up to. Let's see what's going on.

A KEEPER OF ARCHIVES

Not that long ago, many psychologists thought of memory as a library that stored every experience we ever had, something like a video recorder that was always on. Freud's views on the repressed unconscious contributed to this model of memory; a lesser-known influence was the work of Montreal brain surgeon Wilder Penfield. In the 1940s, Penfield treated patients with severe seizures by removing damaged tissue from the outer layer of the brain, known as the *cortex*. While doing so, he was able to map certain areas of the cortex by seeing what body parts moved when those areas were electrically stimulated. Since the brain has no pain receptors, his patients were able to remain awake during the procedure. Occasionally they reported hearing things in response to stimulation, things like a mother calling a little boy. Penfield had a hunch that he was activating long-forgotten memories. They had always been there, in the brain, but inaccessible until touched by his electrode.

Hypnotists were also encountering fascinating experiences when they took [20] people on age regressions. Under hypnosis, subjects were told that they were 3 or 4 years old; they started to talk like children and produce vivid memories of events they had apparently long since forgotten. Therapists saw in hypnosis a way of uncovering details of trauma in a client's past; criminal investigators saw a way to heighten the awareness of detail in witnesses. In 1949, Robert True published in *Science* magazine a study in which he took hypnotized volunteers back to Christmases and birthday parties at ages 4, 7, and 10. He then asked them what day of the week it was. The results were astonishing: 82 percent of the answers were correct. Had subjects simply been guessing, only 1 in 7 answers would have been right. Hypnosis appeared to be doing the same thing as Penfield's electrodes—finding the light switch in the darkest regions of the library of memory.

If you ask ordinary people what they think memory is like, most will reply with a version of the library model. At least, that's what psychologists who have done the studies have found out. People may picture memory as a storage chest or a tape recorder or a computer, but their basic belief is that everything—even the appearance of a penny—is *in there*, somehow, somewhere. The trick is finding it all. The vivid memories in which we have such confidence are simply the photographs that haven't faded with time.

In this view, memory is like a keeper of archives, a fastidious librarian who tries to keep original materials in pristine form. That, after all, is the ideal of memory. We are proudest of recollections that go back a long time and remain as fresh as on the day they were first filed away.

But the picture of autobiographical memory as a careful keeper of archives hasn't held up under recent scrutiny. When psychologists Elizabeth and Geoffrey Loftus examined the flashbacks of Penfield's patients more closely, many turned out to be fabrications. The patients recalled being in places they had never even visited, for example. And when researchers in hypnosis were unable to replicate True's age-regression results, it was discovered that he had not asked subjects, "What day of the week is it?" but rather, "Is it Sunday?," "Is it Monday?," and so on, and that he himself had known the correct answer when asking the question. That tiny detail made all the difference: it takes only the merest vocal inflection, even unintended, to communicate the right answer to a subject. What True had demonstrated was not the power of memory but the power of suggestion.

In the early 1970s, Elizabeth Loftus demonstrated the power of suggestion in the memories of nonhypnotized subjects. College students in her experiment watched a brief film in which a few seconds were devoted to a traffic accident. Afterward, some of the subjects were asked to estimate how fast the cars in the film were going when they "hit" each other. Others were asked to estimate the speeds when the cars "smashed" into each other. Both groups saw the same film, but the "smashed" group gave higher estimates of speed than the "hit" group. A week later, both groups were asked if they had seen any broken glass. More members of the "smashed" group, and more of those who had given high estimates of speed, said yes. Actually, there had been no broken glass in the film. Subsequent research has convinced Loftus that leading questions can change the mental picture of rememberers; they now *see* broken glass, or a white vehicle, or a stop sign, or a barn, or whatever has been suggested. Loftus believes that two kinds of information go into a memory. The first is the original perception of the event; the second is information supplied after the event. With time the two become blended into one "memory."

The word that's used for this blending is *reconstruction*. Memories don't sit inertly on the shelves of a library; they undergo constant revision. Think back to one of your earliest memories of life—a move to a new house, the birth of a baby brother or sister, a birthday party, an accident, whatever it might be. Do you see yourself in the memory? Many people do, and it's more evidence of the reconstructive nature of memory: when you originally experienced the remembered event, you weren't outside of your body looking at yourself. Several studies have shown that the older a memory is, the more likely it is to be rebuilt with an out-of-body observer.

If autobiographical memory is reconstructive, it turns out that the brain, our organ of memory, is no different—even in a physical sense. Today we know what Penfield didn't, that in the course of brain development there is a continual weeding out of nerve cells and even of connections between cells. During the first half of the prenatal period, all the nerve cells that a brain will ever possess have already been born. At that point begins a massive die-off, which slows down but continues throughout the life span. Something similar happens with *synapses*, the connections that carry messages from one nerve cell to another. Their number reaches a peak around the age of 2 and diminishes after that. We know, too, that branches on nerve cells grow in complexity when one's environment is stimulating; if the environment is impoverished, branches fail to develop. In short, the brain revises itself over and over in the course of a lifetime. It's far from a static keeper of archives.

A MAKER OF MYTH

One way of seeing how autobiographical memory reconstructs the past is by comparing a memory when it first enters the mind with the same memory years later. In 1972, psychologist Marigold Linton set herself precisely that task. Every day she wrote down on cards brief descriptions of at least 2 events from her day, 1 event per card. After a while she began giving herself monthly tests. Could she remember an event well enough to date it? At the end of six years, Linton wrote in her article "Transformations of Memory in Everyday Life," she had recorded over 5,500 events and was spending 6 to 12 hours on her monthly tests. After 12 years, she had learned a great deal about autobiographical memory.

In one way, her memory functioned very much like a library, storing recent events on shelves marked New Books—things that happened last week or last month. Linton was able to retrieve these memories with a simple chronological search. But after a year or so, events were moved to the main stacks of her memory, organized now in terms of their content—as things done with friends, for example, or things done in connection with work. Except for major landmarks, *when* faded as a retrieval cue; in comparison, *what* grew stronger. You yourself can probably remember what you did this past summer; but you would have a hard time recalling the events of three or four summers ago—unless you thought of them, say, as vacations or projects or episodes in a faltering relationship.

The fading of *when* is important because it leads us to autobiographical memory's real interest: the creation of a myth about the self. A *myth*, in the sense that I'm using the term, is not a falsehood but a comprehensive view of reality. It's a story that speaks to the heart as well as the mind, seeking to generate conviction about what it thinks is true. We think of myths as belonging to a culture—to a group. But there are also personal myths. When a myth is personal, it seeks to generate conviction about the self—about who "I" am.

One way memory makes myth is by deciding what an episode means and therefore where it belongs in the library. Interestingly, once the decision has been made, we no longer need to remember similar episodes. In her self-study, Linton was surprised to discover how much she had forgotten because events had lost their distinctiveness. She remembered a new class she taught but not

30

all the times she had taught an old one, a match with a new racquet partner but not all her matches with a former one. What remained in her memory were unique events, the first times, but not all the subsequent times. Most libraries are interested in duplicates, but most memories are not. Duplicates contribute nothing to meaning.

Starting with the 4th year of her testing, Linton began to notice something else. A few of the cards that were supposed to jog her memory not only failed to do so but made absolutely no sense. She simply could not understand what she had once written. "I could hear my voice describe fragments from my own life that were somehow completely meaningless." The problem wasn't in the original writing. The events, rather, connected with no pattern that had developed in her life. They hadn't led anywhere, didn't fit anywhere. They were orphans in an autobiographical memory system fashioning generic memories of *what* events mean.

Psychologists have all sorts of names for generic memories: scripts, schemas, MOPs (memory organization packets), and TOPs (thematic organization points), to list just a few. No matter what generic memories are called, the idea is that we create them from the specifics of everyday life and arrange them in a kind of hierarchy. At the top of the hierarchy is a self, a person who says, "This is me, and this is how I got to be the way I am." Listen again to Chris Vitullo's generic memory of 45 years with Gloria: "We had a lot of good times together and a lot of bad times together. . . . We had a little bit of money, whatever God provided, but we did it all in a good faith and honestly, and we arrived to the point that probably if God wouldn't want Gloria to pass away, maybe Gloria and I, we would be together today." Meaning is present in a myth of God's action, but nearly all the events that yield the meaning are absent. The condensation that has taken place is one of the ways autobiographical memory makes a long story short.

Generic memories have powerful effects. They can lead to the phenomenon known as *déjà vu*. You walk into a restaurant and have a strange feeling you've been there before. But you know you haven't. You've probably activated a generic memory—a "script" for entering restaurants. Studies have shown that generic memories can alter the recollection of specific details. A professor delivering a lecture may never point to information on the blackboard, for example, but many students will "remember" that she did. Pointing to the blackboard is part of the standard script for lectures.

These effects of generic memories are failures to meet the ideal of memory, to preserve the past in its original form. But something else is going on: the making of myth. Myth making is illustrated in a now-famous study of memory. In June of 1973, John Dean testified before the Senate committee investigating the Watergate cover-up about a meeting he had had with then-President Nixon nine months before, on September 15, 1972. Dean prefaced his testimony by saying that he believed he had an excellent memory. After hearing him testify, the press began to call him "a human tape recorder." When it was later revealed that an actual tape recorder had been recording during the meeting about which Dean testified, an experiment of nature was created. Ulric Neisser, whose *Memory Observed* opened up the ecological approach to memory, compared the transcript of Dean's testimony with the transcript of the actual tape-recorded meeting. He found rampant reconstruction. In a literal sense—who sat where, who said what—Dean's testimony wasn't even close to being accurate. But in the sense of what the meeting meant in the larger scheme of things, it was all true. Nixon had the knowledge Dean attributed to him; there was a cover-up. In Dean's mind, a single event—his meeting with the president—symbolized a pattern of repeated events. The symbol was so compelling that Dean "remembered" specifics that never took place on the occasion in question.

Dean's memory was inaccurate but true. It had decided on meaning and was making myth. Neisser's comparison showed that Dean inserted into his memory something he yearned for at the meeting but never received—an opening compliment from the president. In memory, Dean gave himself the benefit of hindsight, reversing a prediction that had proved to be wrong. And in his recollections he saw himself as more central to ongoing events than he really was. "What his testimony really describes," wrote Neisser in conclusion, "is not the September 15 meeting itself but his fantasy of it: the meeting as it should have been, so to speak. . . . By June, this fantasy had become the way Dean 'remembered' the meeting." 35

Autobiographical memory is interested in specific events, but only insofar as they contribute to meaning. Ultimately, meaning will arise in a comprehensive story of the self, a story replete with wishes and prophecies, a story that puts the self at center stage. By day, autobiographical memory may be a keeper of archives, but by night it's a maker of myth.

THE MOST IMPORTANT MYTH

As a psychologist, I've always been interested in dreams. Terrifying, comforting, amusing—no matter what their mood, they have such a sense of immediacy that it's often a jolt to leave them for the world of waking "reality." And the wisdom one sees in them . . . There are dreams from long ago that I never want to lose the memory of, so I repeat them to myself and to the most important person in my life. Sometimes I wonder if I could tell the story of my inner journey by touching on the dreams that came at the turning points, dreams that are mythic landmarks along the way.

But over the years I've discovered bits and pieces of mental life that are even more fascinating than dreams. They are fragments from our earliest years, the shards of remembrance that come just before the drop-off of infantile amnesia. What's the earliest thing in life you can remember? I've had an 11-year-old tell me it was a "dippy" dress her mother made her wear—and a profound sense of embarrassment. A strong young man of 20 said it was being in the hospital, where he fearfully awaited a shot from a nurse. An energetic woman in her 50s told me she remembered being bored and restless in a baby carriage; she wanted to escape the confinement. And a man in his 60s recalled that when he was 18 months old he walked to the edge of the front porch, only to be grabbed and pulled back by his mother. I've collected hundreds and hundreds of first memories, and, unlike dreams, they are all experienced as veridical—as the work of a keeper of archives. There are no "special effects" in them (what Freud called *dream-work*), no flying through the air, no objects changing before your eyes, no gross distortions that say this is only fantasy. That's why older people are so proud of the age and clarity of a mental picture that goes back 60, 70, or 80 years, a picture they can prove they were not just told about.

When researchers John Kihlstrom and Judith Harakiewicz collected first memories from 314 high-school and college students, they found that most memories fell into the categories of trauma (a childhood accident, for example), transition (such as a move to a new home or the birth of a sibling), and trivia (such as sitting on the beach playing in the sand). But clinicians following in the tradition of neo-Freudian Alfred Adler approach early memories in quite a different way. In Adler's words, a person's first memory is "his subjective starting point, the beginning of the autobiography he has made for himself." Our earliest memory is our most important myth, the one that says, "This is how 'I' began."

A woman of 44 who told me of a lifelong fear of displeasing other people 40 knew exactly what her earliest memory was. As a toddler, she had stood behind a glass door and watched an angry mother walk out on her. "I can still see the sidewalk that she walked down, and the cracks in the sidewalk," she said. "That had a real lasting effect on me. It was like, 'You do what I say or I'll leave you.'" It has taken this woman many years to realize that her life does not have to end in the same mythic place where it began. She doesn't have to be afraid of people walking out if she fails to do their bidding.

The subjective starting points established by our first memories are like the creation stories that humans have always told about the origins of the earth. In some of these stories, the earth developed from a mother who sacrificed herself so that we might live off the nourishment of her body. In others, our world came from the intercourse of Father Sky and Mother Earth, or from a cosmic egg, or from a turtle rising like an island from the sea, or from the Word of a purposeful deity. The myths differ, but they have something in common. They represent people's efforts to say what their identity is, where they belong, and how they ought to live. "This is who we are," the creation stories say, "because this is how we began." In a similar way, the individual self—knowing how its story is coming out—selects its earliest memories to say, "This is who I am because this is how I began." The self says, for example, "I have always been afraid of displeasing others 'because' my mother walked away from me when I was three."

There are other "firsts" that serve the same mythic function as our earliest memories, establishing how themes in our stories and aspects of our selves develop. For instance, research has shown that far more alcoholics than nonalcoholics remember their first drink and remember it as one of life's most significant episodes. The memory of that drink is a "first time" that stands for other times. It's a creation story that underwrites a present identity: "I am an alcoholic."

Most of life's significant firsts (such as your first day of school, your first date, the first time you made love, your first job, the first home of your own—even the look on your mother's face when she first saw your baby) usually occur during the period that will eventually form the hill of reminiscence. These are the years of expansion in a life, the period when we try out new roles, make mistakes, and gradually shape our identities. By the age of 30 most of us have made the choices that count, and by the age of 50 we are beginning to see their long-range consequences. Why does a reminiscence hill appear in the second half of life? Because the maker of myth is turning its attention to our origins. Knowing how our story is coming out, it's setting up a beginning that will explain the ending.

There is variation in all of this, of course, variation in the contents of our memories, variation in the years that we remember best. But the variation speaks to who we are. And there's more to the mystery of memory than the stories of individuals. There's the collective remembering that goes on in families, tribes, and nations—with the same tension between the keeper of archives and the maker of myth. What is memory like when it goes beyond mere *auto*biography—when we tell our children stories of our parents and grandparents? Another great puzzle lies in that question, another great story in the answer.

QUESTIONS

1. Kotre begins his essay with this sentence: "It's a great puzzle, this memory of ours." According to Kotre, what is the puzzle of memory?

2. Kotre tells us that most people think of memory as a library. Others picture memory as a storage chest, a tape recorder, or a computer. What do these various images of memory tell us about "how memory speaks"? What image or model have you constructed to explain the workings of memory?

3. Kotre offers us a paradox when he explains that memories might be "inaccurate but true" (paragraph 35). Explain this paradox. What does the case of John Dean illustrate? Can you offer some examples of memories that might be "inaccurate but true"?

4. Kotre covers a lot of ground in his essay. What techniques does he use as a writer to keep his readers' attention? What techniques does he use to make his ideas accessible and memorable?

5. Kotre writes, "Our earliest memory is our most important myth, the one that says, 'This is how "I" began'" (paragraph 39). What, according to Kotre, is the function of our first memory? Why do individuals need creation myths?

6. Kotre suggests that there are plenty of ordinary objects for which our memory is a blur. Think of an object that is part of your daily life, and write a one-page description of it. After writing, take a close look at the object. What details did you forget? What do you see now that your memory didn't see?

7. Kotre's essay makes us think about the stories we tell ourselves about ourselves. Write an essay in which you retell one of your favorite stories about yourself, and then reflect on the significance of this story. How has this story helped you explain who you are?

MAKING CONNECTIONS

Kotre writes, "Memories don't sit inertly on the shelves of a library; they undergo constant revision" (paragraph 25). Imagine a conversation between Kotre and any one of the following writers: Alice Walker (p. 40), Lucy Grealy (p. 48), Patricia J. Williams (p. 83), or George Orwell (p. 104). How would Kotre explain to the writer you have selected the ways in which memory speaks? How might that writer respond to Kotre's suggestion about memories being "inaccurate but true"?

FROM WORKING SCIENTIST TO FEMINIST CRITIC

Evelyn Fox Keller

Born in New York City in 1936, Evelyn Fox Keller has been a compelling voice in tracing the exclusion of women from science and exploring the link between masculinity, rationality, and scientific research. Currently a professor of history and philosophy of science at the Massachusetts Institute of Technology, Keller has written widely on issues of gender and science, often speculating on what science might be like if it were gender-free. Her work includes Refiguring Life: Metaphors of Twentieth-Century Biology *(1996) and* Reflections on Gender and Science *(1988). The following essay is taken from Keller's book* Secrets of Life, Secrets of Death: Essays on Language, Gender, and Science *(1992).*

I begin with three vignettes, all drawn from memory.

1965. In my first few years out of graduate school, I held quite conventional beliefs about science. I believed not only in the possibility of clear and certain knowledge of the world, but also in the uniquely privileged access to this knowledge provided by science in general, and by physics in particular. I believed in the accessibility of an underlying (and unifying) "truth" about the world we live in, and I believed that the laws of physics gave us the closest possible approximation of this truth. In short, I was well trained in both the traditional realist worldviews assumed by virtually all scientists and in the conventional epistemological ordering of the sciences. I had, after all, been trained, first, by theoretical physicists, and later, by molecular biologists. This is not to say that I lived my life according to the teachings of physics (or molecular biology), only that when it came to questions about what "really is," I knew where, and how, to look. Although I had serious conflicts about my own ability to be part of this venture, I fully accepted science, and scientists, as arbiters of truth. Physics (and physicists) were, of course, the highest arbiters.

Somewhere around this time, I came across the proceedings of the first major conference held in the United States on "Women and the Scientific Professions" (Mattfield and Van Aiken 1965)—a subject of inevitable interest to me. I recall reading in those proceedings an argument for more women in science, made by both Erik Erikson and Bruno Bettelheim, based on the invaluable contributions a "specifically female genius" could make to science.

Although earlier in their contributions both Erikson and Bettelheim had each made a number of eminently reasonable observations and recommendations, I flew to these concluding remarks as if waiting for them, indeed forgetting everything else they had said. From the vantage point I then occupied, my reaction was predictable: To put it quite bluntly, I laughed. Laws of nature are universal—how could they possibly depend on the sex of their discoverers? Obviously, I snickered, these psychoanalysts know little enough about science (and by implication, about truth).

1969. I was living in a suburban California house and found myself with time to think seriously about my own mounting conflicts (as well as those of virtually all my female cohorts) about being a scientist. I had taken a leave to accompany my husband on his sabbatical, remaining at home to care for our two small children. Weekly, I would talk to the colleague I had left back in New York and hear his growing enthusiasm as he reported the spectacular successes he was having in presenting our joint work. In between, I would try to understand why my own enthusiasm was not only not growing, but actually diminishing. How I went about seeking such an understanding is worth noting: What I did was to go to the library to gather data about the fate of women scientists in general—more truthfully, to document my own growing disenchantment (even in the face of manifest success) as part of a more general phenomenon reflecting an underlying misfit between women and science. And I wrote to Erik Erikson for further comment on the alarming (yet somehow satisfying) attrition data I was collecting. In short, only a few years after ridiculing his thoughts on the subject, I was ready to at least entertain if not embrace an argument about women in, or out of, science based on "women's nature." Not once during that entire year did it occur to me that at least part of my disenchantment might be related to the fact that I was in fact not sharing in the *kudos* my colleague was reaping for our joint work.

1974. I had not dropped out of science, but I had moved into interdisciplinary, undergraduate teaching. And I had just finished teaching my first women's studies course when I received an invitation to give a series of "Distinguished Lectures" on my work in mathematical biology at the University of Maryland. It was a great honor, and I wanted to do it, but I had a problem. In my women's studies course, I had yielded to the pressure of my students and colleagues to talk openly about what it had been like, as a woman, to become a scientist. In other words, I had been persuaded to publicly air the exceedingly painful story of the struggle that had actually been—a story I had previously only talked about in private, if at all. The effect of doing this was that I actually came to *see* that story as public, that is, of political significance, rather than as simply private, of merely personal significance. As a result, the prospect of continuing to present myself as a disembodied scientist, of talking about my work

159

as if it had been done in a vacuum, as if the fact of my being a woman was entirely irrelevant, had come to feel actually dishonest.

I resolved the conflict by deciding to present in my last lecture a demographic model of women in science—an excuse to devote the bulk of that lecture to a review of the many barriers that worked against the survival of women as scientists, and to a discussion of possible solutions. I concluded my review with the observation that perhaps the most important barrier to success for women in science derived from the pervasive belief in the intrinsic masculinity of scientific thought. Where, I asked, does such a belief come from? What is it doing in science, reputedly the most objective, neutral, and abstract endeavor we know? And what consequences does that belief have for the actual doing of science?

In 1974 "women in science" was not a proper subject for academic or scientific discussion; I was aware of violating professional protocol. Having given the lecture—having "carried it off"—I felt profoundly liberated. I had passed an essential milestone.

Although I did not know it then, and wouldn't recognize it for another two years, this lecture marked the beginning of my work as a feminist critic of science. In it I raised three of the central questions that were to mark my research and writing over the next decade. I can now see that, with the concluding remarks of that lecture, I had also completed the basic shift in mind-set that made it possible to begin such a venture. Even though my views about gender, science, knowledge, and truth were to evolve considerably over the years to come, I had already made the two most essential steps: I had shifted attention from the question of male and female nature to that of *beliefs about* male and female nature, that is, to gender ideology. And I had admitted the possibility that such beliefs could affect science itself.

In hindsight, these two moves may seem simple enough, but when I reflect on my own history, as well as that of other women scientists, I can see that they were not. Indeed, from my earlier vantage point, they were unthinkable. In that mind-set, there was room neither for a distinction between sexual identity and beliefs about sexual identity (not even for the prior distinction between sex and gender upon which it depends), nor for the possibility that beliefs could affect science—a possibility that requires a distinction analogous to that between sex and gender, only now between nature and science. I was, of course, able to accommodate a distinction between belief and reality, but only in the sense of "false" beliefs—that is, mere illusion, or mere prejudice; "true" beliefs I took to be synonymous with the "real."

It seems to me that in that mind-set, beliefs per se were not seen as having 10 any real force—neither the force to shape the development of men and women, nor the force to shape the development of science. Some people may "misperceive" nature, human or otherwise, but properly seen, men and women simply *are*, faithful reflections of male and female biology—just as science simply *is*, a faithful reflection of nature. Gravity has (or is) a force, DNA has force, but beliefs do not. In other words, as scientists, we are trained to see the locus of real force in the world as physical, not mental.

There is of course a sense in which they are right: Beliefs per se cannot exert force on the world. But the people who carry such beliefs can. Furthermore, the language in which their beliefs are encoded has the force to shape what others—as men, as women, and as scientists—think, believe, and, in turn, actually do. It may have taken the lens of feminist theory to reveal the popular association of science, objectivity, and masculinity as a statement about the social rather than natural (or biological) world, referring not to the bodily and mental capacities of individual men and women, but to a collective consciousness; that is, as a set of beliefs given existence by language rather than by bodies, and by that language, granted the force to shape what individual men and women might (or might not) do. But to see how such culturally laden language could contribute to the shaping of science takes a different kind of lens. That requires, first and foremost, a recognition of the social character (and force) of the enterprise we call "science," a recognition quite separable from—and in fact, historically independent of—the insights of contemporary feminism.

QUESTIONS

1. Keller offers us three vignettes, as she tells us at the beginning of the essay, "all drawn from memory." Summarize each vignette. What do we learn from each of them? What overarching idea connects these separate moments in her life?

2. What does Keller mean by the phrase "culturally laden language" of science (paragraph 11)? What examples does she offer?

3. Keller is both reflecting and arguing in this essay. How does she use her reflections to form the basis of her arguments? Identify passages in her essay where you see the move from reflecting to arguing.

4. Keller suggests that the language of science has led us to focus on some questions while ignoring others. Why, according to the author, has this happened? What questions have been ignored?

5. Using your own experience as a source of information, reflect on the ways in which you have been taught science. Your reflections might include the ways you have or have not been encouraged to take science courses or pursue a career in science. Do you think your experience would have been different if you were of the opposite sex?

6. Using Keller's essay as a model, offer your readers three vignettes from different times in your life to show us some change of belief or way of seeing or understanding. Keller illustrates, through her vignettes, her movement from "working scientist to feminist critic." What might your vignettes illustrate? Like Keller, your larger purpose of rendering these vignettes could be to argue a position.

MAKING CONNECTIONS

1. Keller writes, "I begin with three vignettes, all drawn from memory." Why does she remember these moments in time? Using John Kotre's essay, "How Memory Speaks" (p. 146), as a frame for your analysis, analyze the myth of creation Keller is constructing.

2. Keller shows us some part of her journey from "working scientist to feminist critic." Compare what Keller learns about science to what Patricia J. Williams learns about law (p. 83). What links their journeys?

REPORTING

Here in "Reporting" you will find writing that reflects a wide array of academic and professional situations—a naturalist describing the tool-using behavior of chimpanzees, a brain surgeon detailing the progress of a delicate operation, a historian telling about the plague that swept through medieval Europe, a travel writer describing life at a major international airport. Informative writing is basic to every field of endeavor, and the writers in this section seek to fulfill that basic need by reporting material drawn from various sources—a data recorder, a voice recorder, a telescope, articles, books, public records, and firsthand observation. Working from such varied sources, these writers aim to provide detailed and reliable accounts of things—to give the background of a case, to convey the look and smell and feel of a place, to describe the appearance and behavior of people, to tell the story of recent or ancient events.

Though reporting depends on a careful gathering of information, it is by no means a mechanical and routine activity that consists simply of getting some facts and writing them up. Newspaper editors and criminal investigators often say that they want "just the facts," but they know that somehow the facts are substantially shaped by the point of view of the person who is gathering and reporting them. By point of view, we mean both the physical and the mental standpoints from which a person observes or investigates something. Each of us, after all, stands at a particular point in space and time, as well as in thought and feeling, whenever we look at any subject. And where we stand in relation to the subject will determine the particular aspects of it that we perceive and bring out in an account.

The influence that point of view exerts on reporting can be seen in the following passage from an article about an airline crash that took place outside of Washington, D.C., on December 1, 1974:

> According to the National Transportation Safety Board, today's was the first fatal crash by an airliner approaching Dulles, which opened in 1962.
>
> A T.W.A. spokesman said 85 passengers and a crew of seven were aboard the flight, which originated in Indianapolis. He said 46 persons got on at Columbus.

The plane crashed about one and one-half miles from an underground complex that reportedly is designed to serve as a headquarters for high government officials in the event of nuclear war. A Federal spokesman acknowledged only that the facility was operated by the little known Office of Preparedness, whose responsibilities, he said, include "continuity of government in a time of national disaster."

This report by the Associated Press (AP) was evidently written by someone who had ready access to a number of sources, for virtually every bit of information in this excerpt comes from a different agency or "spokesman." In fact, the AP report as a whole refers not only to the three sources that are explicitly identified in this passage—namely, the National Transportation Safety Board, a "T.W.A. spokesman," and a "Federal spokesman"—but also to twelve others, including a county medical examiner, a telephone worker, a state police officer, a T.W.A. ground maintenance employee, and the Dulles control tower. Drawing on these sources, the writer of this report is able not only to cover the vital statistics—such as the origin of the flight, the number of people aboard, and the location of the crash—but also to give a vividly detailed impression of the weather, the scarred landscape, and the scattered wreckage at and around the scene of the crash. The writer also reveals some fascinating details about the "underground complex" near the site of the crash. As you read through this piece, however, you will discover that it reports very little about the events leading up to the crash or about the circumstances that caused it. The anonymous writer was evidently not in a position either to track the plane before the crash or to speculate about the cause of the crash only hours after it had taken place.

An extensive investigation of the crash was carried out by the National Transportation Safety Board (NTSB), a federal agency that is charged with tracing the causes of airline accidents. Almost one year later, the Board issued an elaborately detailed, forty-two-page report of its findings, a segment of which is reprinted in our collection. If you look at this segment of the NTSB "Aircraft Accident Report," you will see that it grew out of a completely different point of view from the one that produced the AP report. The NTSB report, for example, does not make any reference to the "secret government installation" that is highlighted in the AP report; nor does it contain any vividly descriptive passages, like those in the AP report, about the weather, the scarred landscape, or the scattered wreckage at the site of the crash; nor does it even mention some of the sources who figure prominently in the AP report. Conversely, some matters that are barely touched on in the AP report are extensively covered in the NTSB report. In particular, the NTSB report provides a detailed "History of the Flight," which includes summaries of cockpit conversation and navigational information at key points during the flight and excerpts of the conversation that took place among members of the flight crew during the last five minutes of the flight. And the NTSB report provides detailed information about some topics that are not mentioned at all in the AP report.

Given such striking differences in the emphases of these two pieces, you might wonder which one offers a more accurate report of the crash. Actually, both are true to the crash within the limits of their points of view on it. The AP report, for example, concentrates on the scene at the site of the crash, drawing material from a number of firsthand observers, and this standpoint brings into focus the appalling spectacle that must have been visible on the mountainside where the crash took place. The NTSB report, by contrast, views the crash within a much broader context that takes into account not only a detailed history of the flight itself, but also the complex system of navigational rules and procedures that were in effect at the time of the flight. And this perspective enables the NTSB to reveal that the mountainside crash resulted in part from serious "inadequacies and lack of clarity in the air traffic control procedures." Thus each point of view affords a special angle on the crash, obscuring some aspects of it, revealing others. And these are only two of many standpoints from which the crash might have been seen and reported. Imagine, for example, how the crash might have been viewed by workers who scoured the mountainside for remains of the passengers, by specialists who identified their remains, by relatives and friends of the victims, or by crews and passengers aboard other flights into Dulles that day.

Once you try to imagine the various perspectives from which anything can be observed or investigated, you will see that no one person can possibly uncover everything there is to know about something. For this reason, above all, point of view is an important aspect of reporting to be kept in mind by both readers and writers. As a reader of reportorial writing, you should always attempt to identify the point of view from which the information was gathered to help yourself assess the special strengths and weaknesses in the reporting that arise from that point of view. By the same token, in your own reporting you should carefully decide on the point of view that you already have or plan to use in observing or gathering information about something. Once you begin to pay deliberate attention to point of view, you will come to see that it is closely related to the various purposes for which people gather and report information in writing.

THE RANGE OF REPORTORIAL WRITING

The purpose of reporting is in one sense straightforward and self-evident, particularly when it is defined in terms of its commonly accepted value to readers. Whether it involves a firsthand account of some recent happening or the documented record of a long-past sequence of events, reportorial writing informs readers about the various subjects that may interest them but that they cannot possibly observe or investigate on their own. You may never get to see chimpanzees in their native African habitats, but you can get a glimpse of their behavior through the firsthand account of Jane van Lawick-Goodall. So, too, you will probably never have occasion to make your way through the many public records and personal reports of the bubonic plague that beset Europe in the mid-fourteenth century, but you can get a synoptic view of the plague from Barbara Tuchman's account, which is based on a thorough investigation of those sources. Reporting expands the range of its readers' perceptions and knowledge beyond the limits of their own immediate experience. From the outlook of readers, then, the function of reporting does seem to be very clear-cut.

But if we shift our focus and look at reporting in terms of the purposes to which it is evidently put by writers, it often turns out to serve a more complex function than might at first be supposed. An example of this complexity can be seen in the following passage from van Lawick-Goodall's account:

> Suddenly I stopped, for I saw a slight movement in the long grass about sixty yards away. Quickly focusing my binoculars I saw that it was a single chimpanzee, and just then he turned in my direction. I recognized David Graybeard.
>
> Cautiously I moved around so that I could see what he was doing. He was squatting beside the red earth mound of a termite nest, and as I watched I saw him carefully push a long grass stem down into a hole in the mound. After a moment he withdrew it and picked something from the end with his mouth.

This passage seems on the whole to be a very neutral bit of scientific reporting that details van Lawick-Goodall's observation of a particular chimpanzee probing for food in a termite nest. The only unusual aspect of the report is her naming of the creature, which has the unscientific effect of personifying the animal. Otherwise, she is careful in the opening part of the description to establish the physical point of view from which she observed the chimpanzee. And at the end of the passage she is equally careful not to identify or even conjecture about "something" beyond her range of detailed vision. As it turns out, however, this passage is a record not only of her observations but also of a pivotal moment in the story of how she came to make an important discovery about chimpanzees—that they are tool users—and thus how she came to regard their behavior as being much closer to that of human beings than had previously been supposed. So, she climaxes her previous description of the chimpanzee with this sentence:

> I was too far away to make out what he was eating, but it was obvious that he was actually using a grass stem as a tool.

Here as elsewhere, then, her reporting is thoughtfully worded and structured to make a strong case for her ideas about chimpanzee and human behavior. Thus, she evidently intends her report to be both informative and persuasive.

A different set of purposes can be seen in yet another firsthand account— this time of a medical patient, as observed by his doctor, Richard Selzer:

> From the doorway of Room 542 the man in the bed seems deeply tanned. Blue eyes and close-cropped white hair give him the appearance of vigor and good health. But I know that his skin is not brown from the sun. It is rusted, rather, in the last stage of containing the vile repose within. And the blue eyes are frosted, looking inward like the windows of a snowbound cottage. This man is blind. This man is also legless—the right leg missing from midthigh down, the left from just below the knee. It gives him the look of a bonsai, roots and branches pruned into the dwarfed facsimile of a great tree.

In this passage, Selzer seeks to describe both the seemingly healthy visual appearance of the patient and his decaying physical condition. Thus he begins by reporting visual details, such as the "deeply tanned" skin as well as the "blue eyes and close-cropped white hair," that convey "the appearance of vigor and good health." Then in the sentences that follow, Selzer relies heavily on figurative language, on a striking sequence of metaphors and similes, each of which reverses the initial impression so as to convey the drastically impaired condition of the patient. The patient's skin turns out to be "rusted," his eyes "frosted," and his body like "the dwarfed facsimile of a great tree." Yet it is also clear from these and other bits of figurative language in the passage that Selzer is not only trying to convey the dire physical condition of his patient, but also to suggest his own intense personal feelings about him. Clearly, he intends his report to be provocative as well as informative.

As is apparent from just this handful of selections, writers invariably seem to use reporting for a combination of purposes—not only to provide information, but also to convey their attitudes, beliefs, or ideas about it and to influence the views of their readers. This joining of purposes is hardly surprising, given the factors involved in any decision to report on something. After all, whenever we make a report, we do so presumably because we believe that the subject of our report is important enough for others to be told about it. And presumably we believe the subject to be important because of what we have come to know and think about it. So, when we are faced with deciding what information to report and how to report it, we inevitably base our decisions on these ideas. At every point in the process of planning and writing a report, we act on the basis of our particular motives and priorities for conveying information about the subject. And how could we do otherwise? How else could van Lawick-Goodall have decided what information to report out of all she must have observed during her first few months in Africa? How else could Selzer have decided what to emphasize out of all the information that he must have gathered from the time he first met his patient until the time of the patient's death? Without specific purposes to control our reporting, our records of events would be as long as the events themselves.

Reporting, as you can see, necessarily serves a widely varied range of purposes—as varied as the writers and their subjects. Thus, whenever you read a piece of reportorial writing, you should always try to discover for yourself what appear to be its guiding purposes by examining its structure, its phrasing, and its wording, much as we have earlier in this discussion. And once you have identified the purpose, you should then consider how it has influenced the selection, arrangement, and weighting of information in the report. When you turn to doing your own writing, you should be equally careful in determining your purposes for reporting as well as in organizing your report so as to put the information in a form that is true to what you know and think about the subject.

METHODS OF REPORTING

In planning a piece of reportorial writing, you should be sure to keep in mind not only your ideas about the subject, but also the needs of your readers. Given that most of your readers will probably not be familiar with your information, you should be very careful in selecting and organizing it to provide a clear and orderly report. Usually, you will find that the nature of your information suggests a corresponding method of presenting it most clearly and conveniently to your readers.

If the information concerns a single, detailed event or covers a set of events spread over time, the most effective method probably is narration—in the form of storytelling—in a more or less chronological order. This is the basic form that van Lawick-Goodall uses, and it proves to be a very clear and persuasive form for gradually unfolding her discovery about the behavior of chimpanzees. If the information concerns a particular place or scene or spectacle, the most convenient method is description—presenting your information in a clear-cut spatial order to help your reader visualize both the overall scene and its important details. This is the method that Selzer uses not only in describing his patient's condition, but also in detailing the patient's posture and his hospital room. If the information is meant to provide a synoptic body of knowledge about a particular subject, the clearest form will be a topical summation, using a set of categories appropriate to the subject at hand. This is the basic form used in the NTSB report, which takes us through a comprehensive survey of material about the airline crash, methodically organized under clearly defined headings: "History of the Flight," "Meteorological Information," "Aids to Navigation," and so on.

Although narration, description, topical summation, and other forms of reporting are often treated separately for purposes of convenience in identifying each of them, they usually end up working in combination with one another. Narratives, after all, involve not only events but also people and places, so it is natural that they include descriptive passages. Similarly, descriptions of places frequently entail stories about events taking place in them, so it is not surprising that they include bits of narration. And given the synoptic nature of topical summations, they are likely to involve both descriptive and narrative elements.

In writing, as in most other activities, form should follow function, rather than being forced to fit arbitrary rules of behavior.

Once you have settled on a basic form, you should then devise a way of managing your information within that form—of selecting, arranging, and proportioning it—to achieve your purposes most effectively. To carry out this task, you will need to review all of the material you have gathered with an eye to determining what you consider to be the most important information to report. Some bits or kinds of information inevitably will strike you as more significant than others, and these are the ones that you should feature in your report. Likewise, you will probably find that some information is simply not important enough even to be mentioned. Van Lawick-Goodall, for example, produces a striking account of her first few months in Africa because she focuses primarily on her observation of chimpanzees, subordinating all the other material she reports to her discoveries about their behavior. Thus, only on a couple of occasions does she include observations about the behavior of animals other than chimpanzees—in particular about the timidities of a bushbuck and a leopard. And she only includes these observations to point up by contrast the distinctively sociable behavior of chimpanzees. For much the same reasons, she proportions her coverage of the several chimpanzee episodes she reports to give the greatest amount of detail to the one that provides the most compelling indication of their advanced intelligence—namely, the final episode, which shows the chimpanzees to be tool users and makers, a behavior previously attributed only to human beings.

To help achieve your purposes, you should also give special thought to deciding on the perspective from which you present your information to the reader. Do you want to present the material in the first or third person? Do you want to be present in the piece, as are van Lawick-Goodall and Selzer? Or do you want to be invisible, as are the authors of the AP and NTSB reports? To some extent, of course, your answer to these questions will depend on whether you gathered the information through your own firsthand observations and want to convey your firsthand reactions to your observations, as van Lawick-Goodall and Selzer do in their pieces. But just to show that there are no hard-and-fast rules on this score, you might look at "A Delicate Operation" by Roy C. Selby Jr. You will notice at once that although Selby must have written this piece on the basis of firsthand experience, he tells the story in the third person, removing himself almost completely from it except for such distant-sounding references to himself as "the surgeon." Clearly, Selby is important to the information in this report, yet he evidently decided to de-emphasize himself in writing the report. Ultimately, then, the nature of a report is substantially determined not only by *what* a writer gathers from various sources, but also by *how* a writer presents the information.

In the reports that follow in this section, you will have an opportunity to see various ways of presenting things in writing. In later sections, you will see how reporting combines with other kinds of writing—explaining and arguing.

Arts and Humanities

AT HOME, AT SCHOOL, IN HIDING

Anne Frank

Anne Frank (1929–1945) was born in Germany and lived there until 1933, when her family moved to Holland to avoid the anti-Jewish laws and other anti-Jewish conditions that were then taking hold in Nazi Germany. But the oppressiveness of those conditions spread to Holland after the Nazi occupation in the summer of 1940, as Frank reports in the following excerpt from her dairy. She started her diary on June 12, 1942, and continued keeping it until August 1, 1944. Three days after the last entry, the Frank family and a few employees who had been hiding from the Nazis with them since July 1942 were arrested and taken to a concentration camp in Auschwitz, Poland. In October 1944, Anne and her sister, Margot, were moved to a concentration camp at Bergen-Belsen, Germany, where Anne died of typhoid fever in late February or early March 1945, a month or so before the camp was liberated by British troops. Her father, Otto Frank, was the only member of the family to survive the Holocaust, and in 1947 he produced a condensed version of the diary, which had been hidden for safekeeping by two of his secretaries. The following excerpt is from the "Definitive Edition," published in 1995, which includes all of the material that Anne Frank had imagined herself using in "a novel" or some other kind of account about "how we lived, what we ate and what we talked about as Jews in hiding." Her thoughts about making her story known came to mind after she heard a radio broadcast in March 1944 about a planned postwar collection of diaries and letters dealing with the war.

SATURDAY, JUNE 20, 1942

Writing in a diary is a really strange experience for someone like me. Not only because I've never written anything before, but also because it seems to me that later on neither I nor anyone else will be interested in the musings of a thirteen-year-old schoolgirl. Oh well, it doesn't matter. I feel like writing, and I have an even greater need to get all kinds of things off my chest.

"Paper has more patience than people." I thought of this saying on one of those days when I was feeling a little depressed and was sitting at home with my chin in my hands, bored and listless, wondering whether to stay in or go out. I finally stayed where I was, brooding. Yes, paper *does* have more patience, and since I'm not planning to let anyone else read this stiff-backed notebook grandly referred to as a "diary," unless I should ever find a real friend, it probably won't make a bit of difference.

Now I'm back to the point that prompted me to keep a diary in the first place: I don't have a friend.

Let me put it more clearly, since no one will believe that a thirteen-year-old girl is completely alone in the world. And I'm not. I have loving parents and a sixteen-year-old sister, and there are about thirty people I can call friends. I have a throng of admirers who can't keep their adoring eyes off me and who sometimes have to resort to using a broken pocket mirror to try and catch a glimpse of me in the classroom. I have a family, loving aunts and a good home. No, on the surface I seem to have everything, except my one true friend. All I think about when I'm with friends is having a good time. I can't bring myself to talk about anything but ordinary everyday things. We don't seem to be able to get any closer, and that's the problem. Maybe it's my fault that we don't confide in each other. In any case, that's just how things are, and unfortunately they're not liable to change. This is why I've started the diary.

To enhance the image of this long-awaited friend in my imagination, I don't   5
want to jot down the facts in this diary the way most people would do, but I want the diary to be my friend, and I'm going to call this friend *Kitty*.

Since no one would understand a word of my stories to Kitty if I were to plunge right in, I'd better provide a brief sketch of my life, much as I dislike doing so.

My father, the most adorable father I've ever seen, didn't marry my mother until he was thirty-six and she was twenty-five. My sister Margot was born in Frankfurt am Main in Germany in 1926. I was born on June 12, 1929. I lived in Frankfurt until I was four. Because we're Jewish, my father immigrated to Holland in 1933, when he became the Managing Director of the Dutch Opekta Company, which manufactures products used in making jam. My mother, Edith Holländer Frank, went with him to Holland in September, while Margot and I were sent to Aachen to stay with our grandmother. Margot went to Holland in December, and I followed in February, when I was plunked down on the table as a birthday present for Margot.

I started right away at the Montessori nursery school. I stayed there until I was six, at which time I started first grade. In sixth grade my teacher was Mrs. Kuperus, the principal. At the end of the year we were both in tears as we said a heartbreaking farewell, because I'd been accepted at the Jewish Lyceum, where Margot also went to school.

Our lives were not without anxiety, since our relatives in Germany were suffering under Hitler's anti-Jewish laws. After the pogroms[1] in 1938 my two uncles (my mother's brothers) fled Germany, finding safe refuge in North America. My elderly grandmother came to live with us. She was seventy-three years old at the time.

After May 1940 the good times were few and far between: first there was the war, then the capitulation and then the arrival of the Germans, which is when the trouble started for the Jews. Our freedom was severely restricted by a series of anti-Jewish decrees: Jews were required to wear a yellow star; Jews were required to turn in their bicycles; Jews were forbidden to use streetcars; Jews were forbidden to ride in cars, even their own; Jews were required to do their shopping between 3 and 5 P.M.; Jews were required to frequent only Jewish-owned barbershops and beauty parlors; Jews were forbidden to be out on the streets between 8 P.M. and 6 A.M.; Jews were forbidden to attend theaters, movies or any other forms of entertainment; Jews were forbidden to use swimming pools, tennis courts, hockey fields or any other athletic fields; Jews were forbidden to go rowing; Jews were forbidden to take part in any athletic activity in public; Jews were forbidden to sit in their gardens or those of their friends after 8 P.M.; Jews were forbidden to visit Christians in their homes; Jews were required to attend Jewish schools, etc. You couldn't do this and you couldn't do that, but life went on. Jacque always said to me, "I don't dare do anything anymore, 'cause I'm afraid it's not allowed."

In the summer of 1941 Grandma got sick and had to have an operation, so my birthday passed with little celebration. In the summer of 1940 we didn't do much for my birthday either, since the fighting had just ended in Holland. Grandma died in January 1942. No one knows how often *I* think of her and still love her. This birthday celebration in 1942 was intended to make up for the others, and Grandma's candle was lit along with the rest.

The four of us are still doing well, and that brings me to the present date of June 20, 1942, and the solemn dedication of my diary.

SATURDAY, JUNE 20, 1942

Dearest Kitty!

Let me get started right away; it's nice and quiet now. Father and Mother are out and Margot has gone to play Ping-Pong with some other young people

---

[1]*pogroms:* organized massacres of Jewish people. [Eds.]

at her friend Trees's. I've been playing a lot of Ping-Pong myself lately. So much that five of us girls have formed a club. It's called "The Little Dipper Minus Two." A really silly name, but it's based on a mistake. We wanted to give our club a special name; and because there were five of us, we came up with the idea of the Little Dipper. We thought it consisted of five stars, but we turned out to be wrong. It has seven, like the Big Dipper, which explains the "Minus Two." Ilse Wagner has a Ping-Pong set, and the Wagners let us play in their big dining room whenever we want. Since we five Ping-Pong players like ice cream, especially in the summer, and since you get hot playing Ping-Pong, our games usually end with a visit to the nearest ice-cream parlor that allows Jews: either Oasis or Delphi. We've long since stopped hunting around for our purses or money—most of the time it's so busy in Oasis that we manage to find a few generous young men of our acquaintance or an admirer to offer us more ice cream than we could eat in a week.

You're probably a little surprised to hear me talking about admirers at such a tender age. Unfortunately, or not, as the case may be, this vice seems to be rampant at our school. As soon as a boy asks if he can bicycle home with me and we get to talking, nine times out of ten I can be sure he'll become enamored on the spot and won't let me out of his sight for a second. His ardor eventually cools, especially since I ignore his passionate glances and pedal blithely on my way. If it gets so bad that they start rambling on about "asking Father's permission," I swerve slightly on my bike, my schoolbag falls, and the young man feels obliged to get off his bike and hand me the bag, by which time I've switched the conversation to another topic. These are the most innocent types. Of course, there are those who blow you kisses or try to take hold of your arm, but they're definitely knocking on the wrong door. I get off my bike and either refuse to make further use of their company or act as if I'm insulted and tell them in no uncertain terms to go on home without me.

There you are. We've now laid the basis for our friendship. Until tomorrow.   15

Yours, Anne

SUNDAY, JUNE 21, 1942

Dearest Kitty,

Our entire class is quaking in its boots. The reason, of course, is the upcoming meeting in which the teachers decide who'll be promoted to the next grade and who'll be kept back. Half the class is making bets. G. Z. and I laugh ourselves sick at the two boys behind us, C. N. and Jacques Kocernoot, who have staked their entire vacation savings on their bet. From morning to night, it's "You're going to pass," "No, I'm not," "Yes, you are," "No, I'm not." Even G.'s pleading glances and my angry outbursts can't calm them down. If you ask me, there are so many dummies that about a quarter of the class should be kept back, but teachers are the most unpredictable creatures on earth. Maybe this time they'll be unpredictable in the right direction for a change.

I'm not so worried about my girlfriends and myself. We'll make it. The only subject I'm not sure about is math. Anyway, all we can do is wait. Until then, we keep telling each other not to lose heart.

I get along pretty well with all my teachers. There are nine of them, seven men and two women. Mr. Keesing, the old fogey who teaches math, was mad at me for the longest time because I talked so much. After several warnings, he assigned me extra homework. An essay on the subject "A Chatterbox." A chatterbox, what can you write about that? I'd worry about that later, I decided. I jotted down the assignment in my notebook, tucked it in my bag and tried to keep quiet.

That evening, after I'd finished the rest of my homework, the note about the essay caught my eye. I began thinking about the subject while chewing the tip of my fountain pen. Anyone could ramble on and leave big spaces between the words, but the trick was to come up with convincing arguments to prove the necessity of talking. I thought and thought, and suddenly I had an idea. I wrote the three pages Mr. Keesing had assigned me and was satisfied. I argued that talking is a female trait and that I would do my best to keep it under control, but that I would never be able to break myself of the habit, since my mother talked as much as I did, if not more, and that there's not much you can do about inherited traits.

Mr. Keesing had a good laugh at my arguments, but when I proceeded to   20
talk my way through the next class, he assigned me a second essay. This time it was supposed to be on "An Incorrigible Chatterbox." I handed it in, and Mr. Keesing had nothing to complain about for two whole classes. However, during the third class he'd finally had enough. "Anne Frank, as punishment for talking in class, write an essay entitled "'Quack, Quack, Quack,' Said Mistress Chatterback.'"

The class roared. I had to laugh too, though I'd nearly exhausted my ingenuity on the topic of chatterboxes. It was time to come up with something else, something original. My friend Sanne, who's good at poetry, offered to help me write the essay from beginning to end in verse. I jumped for joy. Keesing was trying to play a joke on me with this ridiculous subject, but I'd make sure the joke was on him.

I finished my poem, and it was beautiful! It was about a mother duck and a father swan with three baby ducklings who were bitten to death by the father because they quacked too much. Luckily, Keesing took the joke the right way. He read the poem to the class, adding his own comments, and to several other classes as well. Since then I've been allowed to talk and haven't been assigned any extra homework. On the contrary, Keesing's always making jokes these days.

Yours, Anne

. . .

Wednesday, July 1, 1942

Dearest Kitty,

Until today I honestly couldn't find the time to write you. I was with friends all day Thursday, we had company on Friday, and that's how it went until today.

Hello and I have gotten to know each other very well this past week, and he's told me a lot about his life. He comes from Gelsenkirchen and is living with his grandparents. His parents are in Belgium, but there's no way he can get there. Hello used to have a girlfriend named Ursula. I know her too. She's perfectly sweet and perfectly boring. Ever since he met me, Hello has realized that he's been falling asleep at Ursul's side. So I'm kind of a pep tonic. You never know what you're good for!

Jacque spent Saturday night here. Sunday afternoon she was at Hanneli's, and I was bored stiff.

Hello was supposed to come over that evening, but he called around six. I answered the phone, and he said, "This is Helmuth Silberberg. May I please speak to Anne?"

"Oh, Hello. This is Anne."

"Oh, hi, Anne. How are you?"

"Fine, thanks."

"I just wanted to say I'm sorry but I can't come tonight, though I would like to have a word with you. Is it all right if I come by and pick you up in about ten minutes?"

"Yes, that's fine. Bye-bye!"

"Okay, I'll be right over. Bye-bye!"

I hung up, quickly changed my clothes and fixed my hair. I was so nervous I leaned out the window to watch for him. He finally showed up. Miracle of miracles, I didn't rush down the stairs, but waited quietly until he rang the bell. I went down to open the door, and he got right to the point.

"Anne, my grandmother thinks you're too young for me to be seeing you on a regular basis. She says I should be going to the Lowenbachs', but you probably know that I'm not going out with Ursul anymore."

"No, I didn't know. What happened? Did you two have a fight?"

"No, nothing like that. I told Ursul that we weren't suited to each other and so it was better for us not to go together anymore, but that she was welcome at my house and I hoped I would be welcome at hers. Actually, I thought Ursul was hanging around with another boy, and I treated her as if she were. But that wasn't true. And then my uncle said I should apologize to her, but of course I didn't feel like it, and that's why I broke up with her. But that was just one of the reasons.

"Now my grandmother wants me to see Ursul and not you, but I don't agree and I'm not going to. Sometimes old people have really old-fashioned ideas, but that doesn't mean I have to go along with them. I need my grandparents, but in a certain sense they need me too. From now on I'll be free on Wednesday evenings. You see, my grandparents made me sign up for a wood-carving class, but actually I go to a club organized by the Zionists.[2] My grandparents don't want me to go, because they're anti-Zionists. I'm not a fanatic Zionist, but it interests me. Anyway, it's been such a mess lately that I'm planning to quit. So next Wednesday will be my last meeting. That means I can see you Wednesday evening, Saturday afternoon, Saturday evening, Sunday afternoon and maybe even more."

"But if your grandparents don't want you to, you shouldn't go behind their backs."

"All's fair in love and war."

Just then we passed Blankevoort's Bookstore and there was Peter Schiff with   40 two other boys; it was the first time he'd said hello to me in ages, and it really made me feel good.

Monday evening Hello came over to meet Father and Mother. I had bought a cake and some candy, and we had tea and cookies, the works, but neither Hello nor I felt like sitting stiffly on our chairs. So we went out for a walk, and he didn't deliver me to my door until ten past eight. Father was furious. He said it was very wrong of me not to get home on time. I had to promise to be home by ten to eight in the future. I've been asked to Hello's on Saturday.

Wilma told me that one night when Hello was at her house, she asked him, "Who do you like best, Ursul or Anne?"

He said, "It's none of your business."

But as he was leaving (they hadn't talked to each other the rest of the evening), he said, "Well, I like Anne better, but don't tell anyone. Bye!" And whoosh . . . he was out the door.

In everything he says or does, I can see that Hello is in love with me, and   45 it's kind of nice for a change. Margot would say that Hello is eminently suitable. I think so too, but he's more than that. Mother is also full of praise: "A good-looking boy. Nice and polite." I'm glad he's so popular with everyone. Except with my girlfriends. He thinks they're very childish, and he's right about that. Jacque still teases me about him, but I'm not in love with him. Not really. It's all right for me to have boys as friends. Nobody minds.

Mother is always asking me who I'm going to marry when I grow up, but I bet she'll never guess it's Peter, because I talked her out of that idea myself, without batting an eyelash. I love Peter as I've never loved anyone, and I tell myself he's only going around with all those other girls to hide his feelings for me. Maybe he thinks Hello and I are in love with each other, which we're not. He's just a friend, or as Mother puts it, a beau.

Yours, Anne

. . .

---

[2]*Zionists:* belonging to the international movement to establish a Jewish state in modern-day Israel. [Eds.]

WEDNESDAY, JULY 8, 1942

Dearest Kitty,

It seems like years since Sunday morning. So much has happened it's as if the whole world had suddenly turned upside down. But as you can see, Kitty, I'm still alive, and that's the main thing, Father says. I'm alive all right, but don't ask where or how. You probably don't understand a word I'm saying today, so I'll begin by telling you what happened Sunday afternoon.

At three o'clock (Hello had left but was supposed to come back later), the doorbell rang. I didn't hear it, since I was out on the balcony, lazily reading in the sun. A little while later Margot appeared in the kitchen doorway looking very agitated. "Father has received a call-up notice from the SS,"[3] she whispered. "Mother has gone to see Mr. van Daan" (Mr. van Daan is Father's business partner and a good friend.)

I was stunned. A call-up: everyone knows what that means. Visions of concentration camps and lonely cells raced through my head. How could we let Father go to such a fate? "Of course he's not going," declared Margot as we waited for Mother in the living room. "Mother's gone to Mr. van Daan to ask whether we can move to our hiding place tomorrow. The van Daans are going with us. There will be seven of us altogether." Silence. We couldn't speak. The thought of Father off visiting someone in the Jewish Hospital and completely unaware of what was happening, the long wait for Mother, the heat, the suspense—all this reduced us to silence.

Suddenly the doorbell rang again. "That's Hello," I said.

"Don't open the door!" exclaimed Margot to stop me. But it wasn't necessary, since we heard Mother and Mr. van Daan downstairs talking to Hello, and then the two of them came inside and shut the door behind them. Every time the bell rang, either Margot or I had to tiptoe downstairs to see if it was Father, and we didn't let anyone else in. Margot and I were sent from the room, as Mr. van Daan wanted to talk to Mother alone.

When she and I were sitting in our bedroom, Margot told me that the call-up was not for Father, but for her. At this second shock, I began to cry. Margot is sixteen—apparently they want to send girls her age away on their own. But thank goodness she won't be going; Mother had said so herself, which must be what Father had meant when he talked to me about our going into hiding. Hiding . . . where would we hide? In the city? In the country? In a house? In a shack? When, where, how . . . ? These were questions I wasn't allowed to ask, but they still kept running through my mind.

Margot and I started packing our most important belongings into a schoolbag. The first thing I stuck in was this diary, and then curlers, handkerchiefs, schoolbooks, a comb and some old letters. Preoccupied by the thought of

50

---

[3]SS: Nazi police in charge of intelligence and elimination of those thought "undesirable." [Eds.]

going into hiding, I stuck the craziest things in the bag, but I'm not sorry. Memories mean more to me than dresses.

Father finally came home around five o'clock, and we called Mr. Kleiman to ask if he could come by that evening. Mr. van Daan left and went to get Miep. Miep arrived and promised to return later that night, taking with her a bag full of shoes, dresses, jackets, underwear and stockings. After that it was quiet in our apartment; none of us felt like eating. It was still hot, and everything was very strange.

We had rented our big upstairs room to a Mr. Goldschmidt, a divorced man 55 in his thirties, who apparently had nothing to do that evening, since despite all our polite hints he hung around until ten o'clock.

Miep and Jan Gies came at eleven. Miep, who's worked for Father's company since 1933, has become a close friend, and so has her husband Jan. Once again, shoes, stockings, books and underwear disappeared into Miep's bag and Jan's deep pockets. At eleven-thirty they too disappeared.

I was exhausted, and even though I knew it'd be my last night in my own bed, I fell asleep right away and didn't wake up until Mother called me at five-thirty the next morning. Fortunately, it wasn't as hot as Sunday; a warm rain fell throughout the day. The four of us were wrapped in so many layers of clothes it looked as if we were going off to spend the night in a refrigerator, and all that just so we could take more clothes with us. No Jew in our situation would dare leave the house with a suitcase full of clothes. I was wearing two undershirts, three pairs of underpants, a dress, and over that a skirt, a jacket, a raincoat, two pairs of stockings, heavy shoes, a cap, a scarf and lots more. I was suffocating even before we left the house, but no one bothered to ask me how I felt.

Margot stuffed her schoolbag with schoolbooks, went to get her bicycle and, with Miep leading the way, rode off into the great unknown. At any rate, that's how I thought of it, since I still didn't know where our hiding place was.

At seven-thirty we too closed the door behind us; Moortje, my cat, was the only living creature I said good-bye to. According to a note we left for Mr. Goldschmidt, she was to be taken to the neighbors, who would give her a good home.

The stripped beds, the breakfast things on the table, the pound of meat for 60 the cat in the kitchen—all of these created the impression that we'd left in a hurry. But we weren't interested in impressions. We just wanted to get out of there, to get away and reach our destination in safety. Nothing else mattered.

More tomorrow.

Yours, Anne

QUESTIONS

1. In the first entry for June 20, Frank writes at length about wanting her diary to be a very special kind of friend. What kind of friend does she have in mind? How would

179

you characterize Frank's friendship with Kitty as it develops over the several entries included in this excerpt?

2. How are your impressions of the friendship (and of Frank) affected by the fact that she sometimes goes several days without writing anything in her diary?

3. What kind of person does Frank appear to be from the information she reports and the stories she tells about her family? About anti-Jewish decrees? About her boyfriends? About her experiences at school?

4. What kind of person does Frank appear to be from the thoughts and feelings she expresses about these different aspects of her life? Does she come across differently (or similarly) when she is writing about these different aspects of her life?

5. In what respects does Frank's life as a thirteen-year-old seem most different from yours when you were thirteen? In what respects does it seem most similar to yours when you were that age? In what ways do you identify with Frank? In what ways do you find her experience so different as to greatly distance you from her?

6. Given what you discover about Frank's day-to-day life with her friends and at school, what do you consider to be the most important similarities and differences between young adolescent life then and now?

7. Compare and contrast the anti-Jewish decrees that Frank reports with racist decrees that you have read about in South Africa, the United States, and other countries around the world.

8. Keep a diary for several weeks in which you try to make a detailed report of the different aspects of your life in a form that you might be willing to share not only with a close friend (real or imaginary), but also with a large body of readers.

MAKING CONNECTIONS

1. Read Bruno Bettelheim's "The Ignored Lesson of Anne Frank" (p. 621), and then write a piece in which you speculate on how Frank might respond to Bettelheim's critique of her family's mode of life during the Nazi occupation.

2. Read Carol Gilligan's "Interviewing Adolescent Girls" (p. 409), and then write a piece considering the similarities or differences between Frank and the young adolescents that Gilligan describes in her study.

HATSUYO NAKAMURA

John Hersey

John Hersey (1914–1993) was born in Tientsin, China, where his father was a YMCA secretary and his mother a missionary. After graduating from Yale in 1936, Hersey was a war correspondent in China and Japan. When the United States entered World War II, Hersey covered the war in the South Pacific, the Mediterranean, and Moscow. In 1945, he won the Pulitzer Prize for his novel, A Bell for Adano. *In 1946,* Hiroshima, *a report about the effects of the atomic bomb on the lives of six people, was widely acclaimed. Almost forty years later, Hersey went back to Japan to find those six people to see what their lives had been like. Their stories form the final chapter of the 1985 edition of* Hiroshima. *The selection presented here first appeared in the* New Yorker, *as did the first edition of* Hiroshima. *A prolific writer of fiction and nonfiction, Hersey believes that "journalism allows its readers to witness history; fiction gives its readers an opportunity to live it."*

In August, 1946, a year after the bombing of Hiroshima, Hatsuyo Nakamura was weak and destitute. Her husband, a tailor, had been taken into the Army and had been killed at Singapore on the day of the city's capture, February 15, 1942. She lost her mother, a brother, and a sister to the atomic bomb. Her son and two daughters—ten, eight, and five years old—were buried in rubble when the blast of the bomb flung her house down. In a frenzy, she dug them out alive. A month after the bombing, she came down with radiation sickness; she lost most of her hair and lay in bed for weeks with a high fever in the house of her sister-in-law in the suburb of Kabe, worrying all the time about how to support her children. She was too poor to go to a doctor. Gradually, the worst of the symptoms abated, but she remained feeble; the slightest exertion wore her out.

She was near the end of her resources. Fleeing from her house through the fires on the day of the bombing, she had saved nothing but a rucksack of emergency clothing, a blanket, an umbrella, and a suitcase of things she had stored in her air-raid shelter; she had much earlier evacuated a few kimonos to Kabe in fear of a bombing. Around the time her hair started to grow in again, her brother-in-law went back to the ruins of her house and recovered her late husband's Sankoku sewing machine, which needed repairs. And though she had lost the certificates of a few bonds and other meager wartime savings, she had

181

luckily copied off their numbers before the bombing and taken the record to Kabe, so she was eventually able to cash them in. This money enabled her to rent for fifty yen a month—the equivalent then of less than fifteen cents—a small wooden shack built by a carpenter in the Nobori-cho neighborhood, near the site of her former home. In this way, she could free herself from the charity of her in-laws and begin a courageous struggle, which would last for many years, to keep her children and herself alive.

The hut had a dirt floor and was dark inside, but it was a home of sorts. Raking back some rubble next to it, she planted a garden. From the debris of collapsed houses she scavenged cooking utensils and a few dishes. She had the Sankoku fixed and began to take in some sewing, and from time to time she did cleaning and laundry and washed dishes for neighbors who were somewhat better off than she was. But she got so tired that she had to take two days' rest for every three days she worked, and if she was obliged for some reason to work for a whole week she then had to rest for three or four days. She soon ran through her savings and was forced to sell her best kimono.

At that precarious time, she fell ill. Her belly began to swell up, and she had diarrhea and so much pain she could no longer work at all. A doctor who lived nearby came to see her and told her she had roundworm, and he said, incorrectly, "If it bites your intestine, you'll die." In those days, there was a shortage of chemical fertilizers in Japan, so farmers were using night soil, and as a consequence many people began to harbor parasites, which were not fatal in themselves but were seriously debilitating to those who had had radiation sickness. The doctor treated Nakamura-san (as he would have addressed her) with santonin, a somewhat dangerous medicine derived from certain varieties of artemisia.[1] To pay the doctor, she was forced to sell her last valuable possession, her husband's sewing machine. She came to think of that as marking the lowest and saddest moment of her whole life.

In referring to those who went through the Hiroshima and Nagasaki bombings, the Japanese tended to shy away from the term "survivors," because in its focus on being alive it might suggest some slight to the sacred dead. The class of people to which Nakamura-san belonged came, therefore, to be called by a more neutral name, "hibakusha"—literally, "explosion-affected persons." For more than a decade after the bombings, the hibakusha lived in an economic limbo, apparently because the Japanese government did not want to find itself saddled with anything like moral responsibility for heinous acts of the victorious United States. Although it soon became clear that many hibakusha suffered consequences of their exposure to the bombs which were quite different in nature and degree from those of survivors even of the ghastly fire bombings in Tokyo and elsewhere, the government made no special provision for their

5

---

[1]*artemisia:* a genus of herbs and shrubs, including sagebrush and wormwood, distinguished by strong-smelling foliage. [Eds.]

relief—until, ironically, after the storm of rage that swept across Japan when the twenty-three crewmen of a fishing vessel, the Lucky Dragon No. 5, and its cargo of tuna were irradiated by the American test of a hydrogen bomb at Bikini in 1954. It took three years even then for a relief law for the hibakusha to pass the Diet.

Though Nakamura-san could not know it, she thus had a bleak period ahead of her. In Hiroshima, the early postwar years were, besides, a time, especially painful for poor people like her, of disorder, hunger, greed, thievery, black markets. Non-hibakusha employers developed a prejudice against the survivors as word got around that they were prone to all sorts of ailments, and that even those like Nakamura-san, who were not cruelly maimed and had not developed any serious overt symptoms, were unreliable workers, since most of them seemed to suffer, as she did, from the mysterious but real malaise that came to be known as one kind of lasting "A-bomb sickness": a nagging weakness and weariness, dizziness now and then, digestive troubles, all aggravated by a feeling of oppression, a sense of doom, for it was said that unspeakable diseases might at any time plant nasty flowers in their bodies, and even in those of their descendants.

As Nakamura-san struggled to get from day to day, she had no time for attitudinizing about the bomb or anything else. She was sustained, curiously, by a kind of passivity, summed up in a phrase she herself sometimes used—"*Shikata ga-nai*," meaning, loosely, "It can't be helped." She was not religious, but she lived in a culture long colored by the Buddhist belief that resignation might lead to clear vision; she had shared with other citizens a deep feeling of powerlessness in the face of a state authority that had been divinely strong ever since the Meiji Restoration, in 1868; and the hell she had witnessed and the terrible aftermath unfolding around her reached so far beyond human understanding that it was impossible to think of them as the work of resentable human beings, such as the pilot of the Enola Gay, or President Truman, or the scientists who had made the bomb[2]—or even, nearer at hand, the Japanese militarists who had helped to bring on the war. The bombing almost seemed a natural disaster—one that it had simply been her bad luck, her fate (which must be accepted), to suffer.

When she had been wormed and felt slightly better, she made an arrangement to deliver bread for a baker named Takahashi, whose bakery was in Nobori-cho. On days when she had the strength to do it, she would take orders for bread from retail shops in her neighborhood, and the next morning she would pick up the requisite number of loaves and carry them in baskets and boxes through the streets to the stores. It was exhausting work, for which she earned the equivalent of about fifty cents a day. She had to take frequent rest days.

---

[2]*Enola Gay*: the airplane that dropped the atomic bomb on Hiroshima; *Harry S. Truman* (1884–1972): president of the United States who made the decision to drop the bomb. [Eds.]

After some time, when she was feeling a bit stronger, she took up another kind of peddling. She would get up in the dark and trundle a borrowed two-wheeled pushcart for two hours across the city to a section called Eba, at the mouth of one of the seven estuarial rivers that branch from the Ota River through Hiroshima. There, at daylight, fishermen would cast their leaded skirt-like nets for sardines, and she would help them to gather up the catch when they hauled it in. Then she would push the cart back to Nobori-cho and sell the fish for them from door to door. She earned just enough for food.

A couple of years later, she found work that was better suited to her need for occasional rest, because within certain limits she could do it on her own time. This was a job of collecting money for deliveries of the Hiroshima paper, the *Chugoku Shimbun*, which most people in the city read. She had to cover a big territory, and often her clients were not at home or pleaded that they couldn't pay just then, so she would have to go back again and again. She earned the equivalent of about twenty dollars a month at this job. Every day, her will power and her weariness seemed to fight to an uneasy draw.

In 1951, after years of this drudgery, it was Nakamura-san's good luck, her fate (which must be accepted), to become eligible to move into a better house. Two years earlier, a Quaker professor of dendrology from the University of Washington named Floyd W. Schmoe, driven, apparently, by deep urges for expiation and reconciliation, had come to Hiroshima, assembled a team of carpenters, and, with his own hands and theirs, begun building a series of Japanese-style houses for victims of the bomb; in all, his team eventually built twenty-one. It was to one of these houses that Nakamura-san had the good fortune to be assigned. The Japanese measure their houses by multiples of the area of the floor-covering *tsubo* mat, a little less than four square yards, and the Dr. Shum-o houses, as the Hiroshimans called them, had two rooms of six mats each. This was a big step up for the Nakamuras. This home was redolent of new wood and clean matting. The rent, payable to the city government, was the equivalent of about a dollar a month.

Despite the family's poverty, the children seemed to be growing normally. Yaeko and Myeko, the two daughters, were anemic, but all three had so far escaped any of the more serious complications that so many young hibakusha were suffering. Yaeko, now fourteen, and Myeko, eleven, were in middle school. The boy, Toshio, ready to enter high school, was going to have to earn money to attend it, so he took up delivering papers to the places from which his mother was collecting. These were some distance from their Dr. Shum-o house, and they had to commute at odd hours by streetcar.

The old hut in Nobori-cho stood empty for a time, and, while continuing with her newspaper collections, Nakamura-san converted it into a small street shop for children, selling sweet potatoes, which she roasted, and *dagashi*, or little candies and rice cakes, and cheap toys, which she bought from a wholesaler.

All along, she had been collecting for papers from a small company, Suyama Chemical, that made mothballs sold under the trade name Paragen. A friend of hers worked there, and one day she suggested to Nakamura-san that she join the company, helping wrap the product in its packages. The owner, Nakamura-san learned, was a compassionate man, who did not share the bias of many employers against hibakusha; he had several on his staff of twenty women wrappers. Nakamura-san objected that she couldn't work more than a few days at a time; the friend persuaded her that Suyama would understand that.

So she began. Dressed in company uniforms, the women stood, somewhat 15 bent over, on either side of a couple of conveyor belts, working as fast as possible to wrap two kinds of Paragen in cellophane. Paragen had a dizzying odor, and at first it made one's eyes smart. Its substance, powdered paradichlorobenzene, had been compressed into lozenge-shaped mothballs and into larger spheres, the size of small oranges, to be hung in Japanese-style toilets, where their rank pseudomedicinal smell would offset the unpleasantness of non-flushing facilities.

Nakamura-san was paid, as a beginner, a hundred and seventy yen—then less than fifty cents—a day. At first, the work was confusing, terribly tiring, and a bit sickening. Her boss worried about her paleness. She had to take many days off. But little by little she became used to the factory. She made friends. There was a family atmosphere. She got raises. In the two ten-minute breaks, morning and afternoon, when the moving belt stopped, there was a birdsong of gossip and laughter, in which she joined. It appeared that all along there had been, deep in her temperament, a core of cheerfulness, which must have fueled her long fight against A-bomb lassitude, something warmer and more vivifying than mere submission, than saying "*Shikata ga-nai.*" The other women took to her; she was constantly doing them small favors. They began calling her, affectionately, *Oba-san*—roughly, "Auntie."

She worked at Suyama for thirteen years. Though her energy still paid its dues, from time to time, to the A-bomb syndrome, the searing experiences of that day in 1945 seemed gradually to be receding from the front of her mind.

The Lucky Dragon No. 5 episode took place the year after Nakamura-san started working for Suyama Chemical. In the ensuing fever of outrage in the country, the provision of adequate medical care for the victims of the Hiroshima and Nagasaki bombs finally became a political issue. Almost every year since 1946, on the anniversary of the Hiroshima bombing, a Peace Memorial Meeting had been held in a park that the city planners had set aside, during the city's rebuilding, as a center of remembrance, and on August 6, 1955, delegates from all over the world gathered there for the first World Conference Against Atomic and Hydrogen Bombs. On its second day, a number of hibakusha tearfully testified to the government's neglect of their plight. Japanese political parties took up the cause, and in 1957 the Diet at last passed the

A-Bomb Victims Medical Care Law. This law and its subsequent modifications defined four classes of people who would be eligible for support: those who had been in the city limits on the day of the bombing; those who had entered an area within two kilometers of the hypocenter in the first fourteen days after it; those who had come into physical contact with bomb victims, in administering first aid or in disposing of their bodies; and those who had been embryos in the wombs of women in any of the first three categories. These hibakusha were entitled to receive so-called health books, which would entitle them to free medical treatment. Later revisions of the law provided for monthly allowances to victims suffering from various aftereffects.

Like a great many hibakusha, Nakamura-san had kept away from all the agitation, and, in fact, also like many other survivors, she did not even bother to get a health book for a couple of years after they were issued. She had been too poor to keep going to doctors, so she had got into the habit of coping alone, as best she could, with her physical difficulties. Besides, she shared with some other survivors a suspicion of ulterior motives on the part of the political-minded people who took part in the annual ceremonies and conferences.

Nakamura-san's son, Toshio, right after his graduation from high school,   20
went to work for the bus division of the Japanese National Railways. He was in the administrative offices, working first on timetables, later in accounting. When he was in his midtwenties, a marriage was arranged for him, through a relative who knew the bride's family. He built an addition to the Dr. Shum-o house, moved in, and began to contribute to his mother's support. He made her a present of a new sewing machine.

Yaeko, the older daughter, left Hiroshima when she was fifteen, right after graduating from middle school, to help an ailing aunt who ran a *ryo-kan*, a Japanese-style inn. There, in due course, she fell in love with a man who ate at the inn's restaurant, and she made a love marriage.

After graduating from high school, Myeko, the most susceptible of the three children to the A-bomb syndrome, eventually became an expert typist and took up instructing at typing schools. In time, a marriage was arranged for her.

Like their mother, all three children avoided pro-hibakusha and antinuclear agitation.

In 1966, Nakamura-san, having reached the age of fifty-five, retired from Suyama Chemical. At the end, she was being paid thirty thousand yen, or about eighty-five dollars, a month. Her children were no longer dependent on her, and Toshio was ready to take on a son's responsibility for his aging mother. She felt at home in her body now; she rested when she needed to, and she had no worries about the cost of medical care, for she had finally picked up Health Book No. 1023993. It was time for her to enjoy life. For her pleasure in being able to give gifts, she took up embroidery and the dressing of traditional *kimekomi* dolls, which are supposed to bring good luck. Wearing a bright kimono, she went once a week to dance at the Study Group of Japanese Folk

Music. In set movements, with expressive gestures, her hands now and then tucking up the long folds of the kimono sleeves, and with head held high, she danced, moving as if floating, with thirty agreeable women to a song of celebration of entrance into a house:

> May your family flourish
> For a thousand generations,
> For eight thousand generations.

A year or so after Nakamura-san retired, she was invited by an organization called the Bereaved Families' Association to take a train trip with about a hundred other war widows to visit the Yasukuni Shrine, in Tokyo. This holy place, established in 1869, was dedicated to the spirits of all the Japanese who had died in wars against foreign powers, and could be thought roughly analogous, in terms of its symbolism for the nation, to the Arlington National Cemetery—with the difference that souls, not bodies, were hallowed there. The shrine was considered by many Japanese to be a focus of a still smoldering Japanese militarism, but Nakamura-san, who had never seen her husband's ashes and had held on to a belief that he would return to her someday, was oblivious of all that. She found the visit baffling. Besides the Hiroshima hundred, there were huge crowds of women from other cities on the shrine grounds. It was impossible for her to summon up a sense of her dead husband's presence, and she returned home in an uneasy state of mind.

Japan was booming. Things were still rather tight for the Nakamuras, and Toshio had to work very long hours, but the old days of bitter struggle began to seem remote. In 1975, one of the laws providing support to the hibakusha was revised, and Nakamura-san began to receive a so-called health-protection allowance of six thousand yen, then about twenty dollars, a month; this would gradually be increased to more than twice that amount. She also received a pension, toward which she had contributed at Suyama, of twenty thousand yen, or about sixty-five dollars, a month; and for several years she had been receiving a war widow's pension of another twenty thousand yen a month. With the economic upswing, prices had, of course, risen steeply (in a few years Tokyo would become the most expensive city in the world), but Toshio managed to buy a small Mitsubishi car, and occasionally he got up before dawn and rode a train for two hours to play golf with business associates. Yaeko's husband ran a shop for sales and service of air-conditioners and heaters, and Myeko's husband ran a newsstand and candy shop near the railroad station.

In May each year, around the time of the Emperor's birthday, when the trees along broad Peace Boulevard were at their feathery best and banked azaleas were everywhere in bloom, Hiroshima celebrated a flower festival. Entertainment booths lined the boulevard, and there were long parades, with floats and bands and thousands of marchers. This year, Nakamura-san danced with the women of the folk-dance association, six dancers in each of sixty rows.

They danced to "Oiwai-Ondo," a song of happiness, lifting their arms in gestures of joy and clapping in rhythms of threes:

> Green pine trees, cranes and turtles . . .
> You must tell a story of your hard times
> And laugh twice.

The bombing had been four decades ago. How far away it seemed!

The sun blazed that day. The measured steps and the constant lifting of the arms for hours at a time were tiring. In midafternoon, Nakamura-san suddenly felt woozy. The next thing she knew, she was being lifted, to her great embarrassment and in spite of begging to be let alone, into an ambulance. At the hospital, she said she was fine; all she wanted was to go home. She was allowed to leave.

QUESTIONS

1. What does Hatsuyo Nakamura's story tell us about the larger group of atomic-bomb survivors?

2. Why do you think Hersey chose Hatsuyo Nakamura as a subject to report on? How is she presented to us? How are we meant to feel about her?

3. In composing his article, Hersey presumably interviewed Nakamura and reports from her point of view. At what points does he augment her story? For example, look at paragraph 5. What material in the article probably comes from Nakamura? What material probably comes from other sources?

4. How has Hersey arranged his material? He has covered forty years of Hatsuyo Nakamura's life in twenty-six paragraphs. Make a list of the events he chose to report. At what points does he condense large blocks of time?

5. Interview a relative or someone you know who participated in World War II or in some other war, such as Vietnam. How did the war change that person's life? What events does he or she consider most important in the intervening years?

6. No doubt every person then in Hiroshima remembers the day of the bombing just as Americans of certain ages remember days of critical national events—the attack on Pearl Harbor, the Kennedy and King assassinations, the space shuttle disaster, and so on. Interview several people about one such day, finding out where they were when they first learned of the event, how they reacted, what long-term impact they felt, and how they view that day now. Use the information from your interviews to write a report.

MAKING CONNECTIONS

1. Imagine an encounter between Hatsuyo Nakamura and either Zoë Tracy Hardy ("What Did You Do in the War, Grandma?," p. 111), or William L. Laurence ("Atomic Bombing of Nagasaki Told by Flight Member," p. 230). What might these people say to one another? Write the dialogue for a possible conversation between them.

2. One characteristic of reports is to be tentative or even oblique in drawing conclusions. Compare Hersey's report to one by Pico Iyer (p. 249), Roy C. Selby Jr. (p. 280), or Richard Selzer (p. 276), all presented in this section, and assess their differing methods of coming to a conclusion. What would you say the points are of the two reports you chose to compare?

THE LONG GOOD-BYE
Mother's Day in Federal Prison

Amanda Coyne

*Amanda Coyne (b. 1966) was born in Colorado and subse-
quently migrated with her family from Alaska to ten other
states as her father's "relentless pursuit of better employment" led him to hold such titles as fry cook, janitor, librarian, college professor, magazine editor, and presidential
speechwriter. Coyne describes her own life as having thus
far been "similarly kinetic and varied." "Between traveling,
experimenting with religion, countercultural lifestyles, and
writing," she has been employed as a waitress, nursing
home assistant, teacher, public relations associate, and public policy analyst. Coyne is currently pursuing a master's degree in nonfiction writing at the University of Iowa, where
she received her undergraduate degree in English. The following essay, which appeared in* Harper's *(May 1997), is
her first publication.*

You can spot the convict-moms here in the visiting room by the way they
hold and touch their children and by the single flower that is perched in front
of them—a rose, a tulip, a daffodil. Many of these mothers have untied the
bow that attaches the flower to its silver-and-red cellophane wrapper and are
using one of the many empty soda cans at hand as a vase. They sit proudly before their flower-in-a-Coke-can, amid Hershey bar wrappers, half-eaten Ding
Dongs, and empty paper coffee cups. Occasionally, a mother will pick up her
present and bring it to her nose when one of the bearers of the single flower—
her child—asks if she likes it. And the mother will respond the way that mothers always have and always will respond when presented with a gift on this day.
"Oh, I just love it. It's perfect. I'll put it in the middle of my Bible." Or, "I'll
put it on my desk, right next to your school picture." And always: "It's the best
one here."

But most of what is being smelled today is the children themselves. While
the other adults are plunking coins into the vending machines, the mothers
take deep whiffs from the backs of their children's necks, or kiss and smell the
backs of their knees, or take off their shoes and tickle their feet and then pull
them close to their noses. They hold them tight and take in their own second
scent—the scent assuring them that these are still their children and that they
still belong to them.

The visitors are allowed to bring in pockets full of coins, and today that Mother's Day flower, and I know from previous visits to my older sister here at the Federal Prison Camp for women in Pekin, Illinois, that there is always an aberrant urge to gather immediately around the vending machines. The sandwiches are stale, the coffee weak, the candy bars the ones we always pass up in a convenience store. But after we hand the children over to their mothers, we gravitate toward those machines. Like milling in the kitchen at a party. We all do it, and nobody knows why. Polite conversation ensues around the microwave while the popcorn is popping and the processed-chicken sandwiches are being heated. We ask one another where we are from, how long a drive we had. An occasional whistle through the teeth, a shake of the head. "My, my, long way from home, huh?" "Staying at the Super 8 right up the road. Not a bad place." "Stayed at the Econo Lodge last time. Wasn't a good place at all." Never asking the questions we really want to ask: "What's she in for?" "How much time's she got left?" You never ask in the waiting room of a doctor's office either. Eventually, all of us—fathers, mothers, sisters, brothers, a few boyfriends, and very few husbands—return to the queen of the day, sitting at a fold-out table loaded with snacks, prepared for five or so hours of attempted normal conversation.

Most of the inmates are elaborately dressed, many in prison-crafted dresses and sweaters in bright blues and pinks. They wear meticulously applied makeup in corresponding hues, and their hair is replete with loops and curls—hair that only women with the time have the time for. Some of the better seamstresses have crocheted vests and purses to match their outfits. Although the world outside would never accuse these women of making haute-couture fashion statements, the fathers and the sons and the boyfriends and the very few husbands think they look beautiful, and they tell them so repeatedly. And I can imagine the hours spent preparing for this visit—hours of needles and hooks clicking over brightly colored yards of yarn. The hours of discussing, dissecting, and bragging about these visitors—especially the men. Hours spent in the other world behind the door where we're not allowed, sharing lipsticks and mascaras, and unraveling the occasional hair-tangled hot roller, and the brushing out and lifting and teasing . . . and the giggles that abruptly change into tears without warning—things that define any female-only world. Even, or especially, if that world is a female federal prison camp.

While my sister Jennifer is with her son in the playroom, an inmate's 5
mother comes over to introduce herself to my younger sister, Charity, my brother, John, and me. She tells us about visiting her daughter in a higher-security prison before she was transferred here. The woman looks old and tired, and her shoulders sag under the weight of her recently acquired bitterness.

"Pit of fire," she says, shaking her head. "Like a pit of fire straight from hell. Never seen anything like it. Like something out of an old movie about prisons." Her voice is getting louder and she looks at each of us with pleading eyes.

"My *daughter* was there. Don't even get me started on that place. Women die there."

John and Charity and I silently exchange glances.

"My daughter would come to the visiting room with a black eye and I'd think, 'All she did was sit in the car while her boyfriend ran into the house.' She didn't even touch the stuff. Never even handled it."

She continues to stare at us, each in turn. "Ten years. That boyfriend talked and he got three years. She didn't know anything. Had nothing to tell them. They gave her ten years. They called it conspiracy. Conspiracy? Aren't there real criminals out there?" She asks this with hands outstretched, waiting for an answer that none of us can give her.

The woman's daughter, the conspirator, is chasing her son through the maze of chairs and tables and through the other children. She's a twenty-four-year-old blonde, whom I'll call Stephanie, with Dorothy Hamill hair and matching dimples. She looks like any girl you might see in any shopping mall in middle America. She catches her chocolate-brown son and tickles him, and they laugh and trip and fall together onto the floor and laugh harder.

Had it not been for that wait in the car, this scene would be taking place at home, in a duplex Stephanie would rent while trying to finish her two-year degree in dental hygiene or respiratory therapy at the local community college. The duplex would be spotless, with a blown-up picture of her and her son over the couch and ceramic unicorns and horses occupying the shelves of the entertainment center. She would make sure that her son went to school every day with stylishly floppy pants, scrubbed teeth, and a good breakfast in his belly. Because of their difference in skin color, there would be occasional tension—caused by the strange looks from strangers, teachers, other mothers, and the bullies on the playground, who would chant after they knocked him down, "Your Momma's white, your Momma's white." But if she were home, their weekends and evenings would be spent together transcending those looks and healing those bruises. Now, however, their time is spent eating visiting-room junk food and his school days are spent fighting the boys in the playground who chant, "Your Momma's in prison, your Momma's in prison."

He will be ten when his mother is released, the same age my nephew will be when his mother is let out. But Jennifer, my sister, was able to spend the first five years of Toby's life with him. Stephanie had Ellie after she was incarcerated. They let her hold him for eighteen hours, then sent her back to prison. She has done the "tour," and her son is a well-traveled six-year-old. He has spent weekends visiting his mother in prisons in Kentucky, Texas, Connecticut (the Pit of Fire), and now at last here, the camp—minimum security, Pekin, Illinois.

Ellie looks older than his age. But his shoulders do not droop like his grandmother's. On the contrary, his bitterness lifts them and his chin higher than a child's should be, and the childlike, wide-eyed curiosity has been replaced by defiance. You can see his emerging hostility as he and his mother play together. She tells him to pick up the toy that he threw, say, or to put the deck of cards away. His face turns sullen, but she persists. She takes him by the shoulders and looks him in the eye, and he uses one of his hands to swat at her. She grabs the hand and he swats with the other. Eventually, she pulls him toward her and smells the top of his head, and she picks up the cards or the toy herself. After all, it is Mother's Day and she sees him so rarely. But her acquiescence makes him angrier, and he stalks out of the playroom with his shoulders thrown back.

Toby, my brother and sister and I assure one another, will not have these resentments. He is better taken care of than most. He is living with relatives in Wisconsin. Good, solid, middle-class, churchgoing relatives. And when he visits us, his aunts and his uncle, we take him out for adventures where we walk down the alley of a city and pretend that we are being chased by the "bad guys." We buy him fast food, and his uncle, John, keeps him up well past his bedtime enthralling him with stories of the monkeys he met in India. A perfect mix, we try to convince one another. Until we take him to see his mother and on the drive back he asks the question that most confuses him, and no doubt all the other children who spend much of their lives in prison visiting rooms: "Is my Mommy a bad guy?" It is the question that most seriously disorders his five-year-old need to clearly separate right from wrong. And because our own need is perhaps just as great, it is the question that haunts us as well.

Now, however, the answer is relatively simple. In a few years, it won't be. In a few years we will have to explain mandatory minimums, and the war on drugs, and the murky conspiracy laws, and the enormous amount of money and time that federal agents pump into imprisoning low-level drug dealers and those who happen to be their friends and their lovers. In a few years he might have the reasoning skills to ask why so many armed robbers and rapists and child-molesters and, indeed, murderers are punished less severely than his mother. When he is older, we will somehow have to explain to him the difference between federal crimes, which don't allow for parole, and state crimes, which do. We will have to explain that his mother was taken from him for five years not because she was a drug dealer but because she made four phone calls for someone she loved.

But we also know it is vitally important that we explain all this without betraying our bitterness. We understand the danger of abstract anger, of being disillusioned with your country, and, most of all, we do not want him to inherit that legacy. We would still like him to be raised as we were, with the idea that we live in the best country in the world with the best legal system in the world—a legal system carefully designed to be immune to political mood swings and public hysteria; a system that promises to fit the punishment to the crime. We want him to be a good citizen. We want him to have absolute faith that he lives in a fair country, a country that watches over and protects its most vulnerable citizens: its women and children.

So for now we simply say, "Toby, your mother isn't bad, she just did a bad thing. Like when you put rocks in the lawn mower's gas tank. You weren't bad then, you just did a bad thing."

Once, after being given this weak explanation, he said, "I wish I could have done something really bad, like my Mommy. So I could go to prison too and be with her."

We notice a circle forming on one side of the visiting room. A little boy stands in its center. He is perhaps nine years old, sporting a burnt-orange three-piece suit and pompadour hair. He stands with his legs slightly apart, eyes half-shut, and sways back and forth, flashing his cuffs and snapping his fingers while singing:

> . . . Doesn't like crap games with barons and earls.
> Won't go to Harlem in ermine and pearls.
> Won't dish the dirt with the rest of the girls.
> That's why the lady is a tramp.

He has a beautiful voice and it sounds vaguely familiar. One of the visitors   20
informs me excitedly that the boy is the youngest Frank Sinatra impersonator and that he has been on television even. The boy finishes his performance and the room breaks into applause. He takes a sweeping bow, claps his miniature hands together, and points both little index fingers at the audience. "More. Later. Folks." He spins on his heels and returns to the table where his mother awaits him, proudly glowing. "Don't mess with the hair, Mom," we overhear. "That little boy's slick," my brother says with true admiration.

Sitting a few tables down from the youngest Frank Sinatra is a table of Mexican-Americans. The young ones are in white dresses or button-down oxfords with matching ties. They form a strange formal contrast to the rest of the rowdy group. They sit silently, solemnly listening to the white-haired woman, who holds one of the table's two roses. I walk past and listen to the grandmother lecture her family. She speaks of values, of getting up early every day, of going to work. She looks at one of the young boys and points a finger at him. "School is the most important thing. *Nada mas importante.* You get up and you go to school and you study, and you can make lots of money. You can be big. You can be huge. Study, study, study."

The young boy nods his head. "Yes, *abuelita.* Yes, *abuelita,*" he says.

The owner of the other flower is holding one of the group's three infants. She has him spread before her. She coos and kisses his toes and nuzzles his stomach.

When I ask Jennifer about them, she tells me that it is a "mother and daughter combo." There are a few of them here, these combos, and I notice that they have the largest number of visitors and that the older inmate, the grandmother, inevitably sits at the head of the table. Even here, it seems, the hierarchical family structure remains intact. One could take a picture, replace the fast-food wrappers with chicken and potatoes, and these families could be at any restaurant in the country, could be sitting at any dining room table, paying homage on this day to the one who brought them into the world.

Back at our table, a black-haired, Middle Eastern woman dressed in loose   25
cottons and cloth shoes is whispering to my brother with a sense of urgency
that makes me look toward my sister Charity with questioning eyes and a tilt of
my head. Charity simply shrugs and resumes her conversation with a nineteen-
year-old ex–New York University student—another conspirator. Eight years.

Prison, it seems, has done little to squelch the teenager's rebellious nature. She
has recently been released from solitary confinement. She wears new retro-
bellbottom jeans and black shoes with big clunky heels. Her hair is short, clipped
perfectly ragged and dyed white—all except the roots, which are a stylish black.
She has beautiful pale skin and beautiful red lips. She looks like any midwestern
coed trying to escape her origins by claiming New York's East Village as home.
She steals the bleach from the laundry room, I learn later, in order to maintain that
fashionable white hue. But stealing the bleach is not what landed her in the hole.
She committed the inexcusable act of defacing federal property. She took one of
her government-issue T-shirts and wrote in permanent black magic marker, "I
have been in your system. I have examined your system." And when she turned
around it read, "I find it very much in need of repair."

But Charity has more important things to discuss with the girl than re-
belling against the system. They are talking fashion. They talk prints versus
plains, spring shoes, and spring dresses. Charity informs the girl that sling-back,
high-heeled sandals and pastels are all the rage. She makes a disgusted face
and says, "Damn! Pinks and blues wash me out. I hate pastels. I don't *have* any
pastels."

This fashion blip seems to be putting the girl into a deep depression. And so
Charity, attempting to lighten up the conversation, puts her nose toward the
girl's neck.

"New Armani scent, Gio," my sister announces.

The girl perks up. She nods her head. She calls one of the other inmates   30
over.

Charity performs the same ritual: "Coco Chanel." And again: "Paris, Yves
St. Laurent."

The line gets longer, and the girls talk excitedly to one another. It seems
that Charity's uncanny talent for divining brand-name perfumes is perhaps
nowhere on earth more appreciated than here with these sensory-starved inmates.

As Charity continues to smell necks and call out names, I turn back to my
brother and find that the woman who was speaking to him so intensely has
gone. He stares pensively at the concrete wall ahead of him.

"What did she want?" I ask.

"She heard I was a sculptor. She wants me to make a bust, presented in her   35
name, for Qaddafi."

"A bust of what?"

"Of Qaddafi. She's from Libya. She was a freedom fighter. Her kids are
farmed out to strangers here—foster homes. It's Qaddafi's twenty-eighth an-

195

niversary as dictator in September. She knows him. He's mad at her now, but she thinks that he'll get over it and get her kids back to Libya if she gives him a present."

"Obsession. Calvin Klein," I hear my sister pronounce. The girls cheer in unison.

I get up and search for the girl. I want to ask her about her crime. I look in the book room only to find the four-foot Frank Sinatra crooning "Somewhere over the Rainbow" to a group of spellbound children.

I ask Ponytail, one of the female guards, where the woman went. "Rule," 40 she informs me. "Cannot be in the visiting room if no visitor is present. Should not have been here. Had to go back to unit one." I have spoken to Ponytail a few times while visiting my sister and have yet to hear her use a possessive pronoun, a contraction, or a conjunction.

According to Jennifer, Ponytail has wanted to be a prison guard since she was a little girl. She is one of the few female guards here and she has been here the longest, mainly because the male guards are continuously being fired for "indiscretions" with the inmates. But Ponytail doesn't mess around. She is also the toughest guard here, particularly in regard to the federal rules governing exposed skin. She is disgusted by any portion of the leg showing above the required eight-inch shorts length. In summer, they say, she is constantly whipping out her measuring tape and writing up those who are even a fraction of an inch off.

Last summer posed a particular problem for Ponytail, though. It seems that the shorts sold in the commissary were only seven inches from crotch to seam. And because they were commissary-issued, Ponytail couldn't censor them. So, of course, all the women put away their own shorts in favor of the commissary's. The disturbed Ponytail—a condition that eventually, according to one of the girls, developed into a low-grade depression. "She walked around with that sad old tape in her hands all summer, throwing it from one hand to the other and looking at our legs. After a while, not one of us could get her even to crack a smile—not that she's a big smiler, but you can get those corners to turn sometimes. Then she started looking downright sad, you know real depressed like."

Ponytail makes sure that the girls get proper medical care. Also none of the male guards will mess with them when she's around. But even if those things weren't true, the girls would be fond of Ponytail. She is in a way just another woman in the system, and perhaps no other group of women realizes the absolute necessity for female solidarity. These inmates know with absolute certainty what women on the outside only suspect—that men still hold ultimate power over their bodies, their property, and their freedom.

So as a token of this solidarity, they all agreed to slip off their federal shorts and put on their own. Ponytail perked up, the measuring tape appeared again with a vengeance, and quite a few of the shorts owners spent much of their free time that summer cleaning out toilet bowls and wiping the scuffs off the gym floor.

    It's now 3:00. Visiting ends at 3:30. The kids are getting cranky, and the adults 45 are both exhausted and wired from too many hours of conversation, too much coffee and candy. The fathers, mothers, sisters, brothers, and the few boyfriends, and the very few husbands are beginning to show signs of gathering the trash. The mothers of the infants are giving their heads one last whiff before tucking them and their paraphernalia into their respective carrying cases. The visitors meander toward the door, leaving the older children with their mothers for one last word. But the mothers never say what they want to say to their children. They say things like, "Do well in school," "Be nice to your sister," "Be good for Aunt Betty, or Grandma." They don't say, "I'm sorry I'm sorry I'm sorry. I love you more than anything else in the world and I think about you every minute and I worry about you with a pain that shoots straight to my heart, a pain so great I think I will just burst when I think of you alone, without me. I'm sorry."

We are standing in front of the double glass doors that lead to the outside world. My older sister holds her son, rocking him gently. They are both crying. We give her a look and she puts him down. Charity and I grasp each of his small hands, and the four of us walk through the doors. As we're walking out, my brother sings one of his banana songs to Toby.

"Take me out to the—" and Toby yells out, "Banana store!"

"Buy me some—"

"Bananas!!"

"I don't care if I ever come back. For it's root, root, root for the—" 50

"Monkey team!"

I turn back and see a line of women standing behind the glass wall. Some of them are crying, but many simply stare with dazed eyes. Stephanie is holding both of her son's hands in hers and speaking urgently to him. He is struggling, and his head is twisting violently back and forth. He frees one of his hands from her grasp, balls up his fist, and punches her in the face. Then he walks with purpose through the glass doors and out the exit. I look back at her. She is still in a crouched position. She stares, unblinking, through those doors. Her hands have left her face and are hanging on either side of her. I look away, but before I do, I see drops of blood drip from her nose, down her chin, and onto the shiny marble floor.

QUESTIONS

    1. How would you describe Coyne's point of view in this piece? Detached or involved? Insider or outsider? How does her point of view affect your perception of the federal prison for women that she writes about in this piece?

2. Why do you suppose that Coyne focuses on Mother's Day at the prison? What kinds of details is she able to report that might not be observable on most other days at the prison? What kinds of details are likely to be missing (or obscured) on such a day as this?

3. Given the fact that Coyne has come to visit her sister Jennifer, why do you suppose she tells so little about Jennifer compared to what she reports about the other prisoners, particularly Stephanie and the nineteen-year-old ex–New York University student? By the same token, why do you suppose that Coyne tells so much about Stephanie's child, Ellie, and the young Frank Sinatra impersonator, but so little by comparison about Jennifer's child, Toby?

4. What do you infer from the special attention that Coyne gives to reporting on the actions of her sister Charity and the guard Ponytail?

5. Given the selection and arrangement of descriptive detail about the various people who figure in this account, what do you consider to be Coyne's major purposes in writing this piece?

6. Compare and contrast Coyne's piece on women's prisons and female prisoners to one or two other stories you can find on this subject in newspapers, magazines, or on the Internet.

7. Spend a few hours investigating a prison in your community, and write a report highlighting the details that you think are most important in revealing the quality of life in that prison.

MAKING CONNECTIONS

1. Compare and contrast the way that worlds collide in the visiting room of the women's prison with the collisions that Pico Iyer describes taking place in the Los Angeles International Airport (p. 249).

2. Using the material that Coyne provides in her essay, write a report about the prison in the style of William Least Heat-Moon (p. 199).

PANCAKES AND SCRIPTURE CAKE
William Least Heat-Moon

William Least Heat-Moon is the pen name of William Trogdon, who was born in Kansas City, Missouri, in 1939. He studied at the University of Missouri, where he received an undergraduate degree in journalism and a doctorate in English. The youngest child of a part-Osage father and a mother of English-Irish ancestry, Trogdon based his pen name on a Native American name (Heat-Moon) that his father had created for himself during a lengthy career in the Boy Scouts. Having first used the name during his own days in the scouts, Trogdon, a former college English teacher, resurrected it in the process of writing Blue Highways: A Journey into America *(1982). In this extensive travelogue, Heat-Moon offers detailed descriptions of the people he met and the small towns he observed during a thirteen-thousand-mile trip that he took, in a van called Ghost Dancing, down the back roads (the blue highways) of the United States. The following piece about a college he visited in Clinton, Mississippi, is an excerpt from* Blue Highways. *Heat-Moon's preoccupation with small, forgotten places is also reflected in his second book,* PrairyErth (A Deep Map) *(1991), which focuses on Chase County, Kansas, as an emblem of the tallgrass prairie and the prairie life that once existed in that part of the country.*

A century and a half ago, the founders of Mississippi College hoped the school would become the state university. But that didn't work out, so they gave it to the Presbyterians; that didn't work out either, and the Presbyterians gave it back. The Baptists had a go at it, and the college got on in its own quiet way, eventually turning out three governors. Actually, all the changing around may have made little difference. A student told me that everyone in town was a Baptist anyway, even the Presbyterians.

I was eating breakfast in the cafeteria. A crewcut student wearing mesh step-in casuals sat down to a tall stack of pancakes. He was a methodical fellow. After a prayer running almost a minute, he pulled from his briefcase a Bible, reading stand, clips to hold the book open, a green felt-tip, a pink, and yellow; next came a squeeze-bottle of liquid margarine, a bottle of Log Cabin syrup wrapped in plastic, a linen napkin, and one of those little lemony wet-wipes.

The whole business looked like the old circus act where twelve men get out of a car the size of a trashcan.

A woman with a butter-almond smile sat down across from me. Her hair, fresh from the curling wand, dropped in loose coils the color of polished pecan, and her breasts, casting shadows to her waist, pressed full against a glossy dress that looked wet. A golden cross swung gently between, and high on her long throat was a small PISCES amulet. Her dark, musky scent brought to mind the swamp. We nodded and she said in soft Mississippian. "You were very interested in Jerry's pancakes."

"It was the briefcase. I thought he was going to pull out a Water-Pik and the Ark of the Covenant next."

"He's a nice boy. His parameters just aren't yours." She couldn't have sur- 5 prised me more had she said floccinaucinihilipilification. "The bottom line is always parameters no matter what the input."

"Let me make a crazy guess. You're in computer programming."

"I'm in business, but my brother is a computer programmer in Jackson. He's got me interested in it. He plays with the computer after hours. Made up his Christmas cards on an IBM three-sixty-one-fifty-eight last year and did his own wedding invitations two years ago. But we're channelized different. I want to use the computer to enrich spiritual life. Maybe put prayers on a computer like that company in California that programs them. For two dollars, they run your prayer through twice a day for a week. They send up ten thousand a month."

"What if God doesn't know Fortran?"

"Come on, you! People are critical, but they don't ridicule prayer wheels or rosaries and those are just prayer machines."

"Does God get a printout?" 10

"Quit it! You get the printout. Suitable for framing. Quit smiling!"

"Sorry, but you said they send the prayers 'up,' and I just wondered what kind of hard copy we're dealing with here."

"You're a fuddydud! It's all just modalities. The prayer still has to come from a heart. Japanese write prayers on slips of paper and tie them to branches so the wind sort of distributes them. Same thing—people just trying to maximize the prayer function."

"You're a Pisces?"

"Would a Sagittarius wear a Pisces necklace?" 15

"How can you believe in astrology and wear a cross?"

"What a fuddydud! Who made the stars? Astrology's just another modality too." She took a computer card from her notebook. "I've got to get to class, but here's one more modality. In India, people pray when they eat— like each chew is a prayer. Try it sometime. Even grumpy fuddyduds like it."

She handed me the card and hurried off. Here it is, word for word:

SCRIPTURE CAKE

2 cups Proverbs 30:33	1 cup Genesis 43:11
3½ cups Exodus 29:2	6 Isaiah 10:14
3 cups Jeremiah 6:20	2 tbsp I Corinthians 5:6
2 cups I Samuel 30:12	1 tbsp I Samuel 14:25
2 cups Nahum 3:12	Season with I Kings 10:10
½ cup Judges 4:19	Follow Leviticus 24:5

SERVE WITH LOVE . . . SALLY

QUESTIONS

1. What do you make of the fact that Heat-Moon begins this brief report with a capsule history of Mississippi College but never says anything more about the college itself? What impressions do you get of the college from this paragraph? What impressions do you get of it from the descriptions and dialogue that follow in paragraphs 2 to 18?

2. Consider Heat-Moon's description of the crewcut student and his behavior in paragraph 2. How is your response to the student affected by the description of the woman in paragraph 3? Why do you suppose that Heat-Moon offers such different kinds of detail in each case—about the student's actions, about the woman's looks?

3. What initial impressions do you get of the woman from Heat-Moon's description of her in paragraph 3? What other impressions do you get of the woman from her conversation with Heat-Moon?

4. What initial impressions do you get of Heat-Moon himself from the descriptions he offers of the student and the woman in paragraphs 2 and 3? What other impressions do you get of Heat-Moon from the questions he asks the woman later?

5. Why do you think the woman keeps referring to Heat-Moon as a "fuddydud"? Do you agree with this description of him?

6. Consult the Bible to get an exact idea of the ingredients that go into the making of Sally's "Scripture cake." Based on your reading of those passages, what do you think is the basic message of this recipe? Why does Heat-Moon end this episode with the recipe and no commentary of his own?

7. Based on his selection and arrangement of descriptive details and dialogue, what is Heat-Moon trying to convey in this report?

8. Visit your school's cafeteria or a small restaurant you've never been in before, and spend some time observing, overhearing, and possibly conversing with some customers or people you don't know. Then write a brief piece, focusing on only two or three people, in which the descriptive details and the dialogue you report create a distinct impression of the people, yourself, and the restaurant or college without any explanatory or judgmental commentary of your own.

MAKING CONNECTIONS

1. Imagine how the woman in this piece might react to Charity and the ex–New York University student in Amanda Coyne's "The Long Good-bye" (p. 190). Also consider how Charity and the NYU student might respond to the woman in this piece. Then write a brief imaginary conversation for the three of them.

2. How do you suppose Abigail Witherspoon (p. 203) might react to the students that Heat-Moon describes in this selection?

THIS PEN FOR HIRE
On Grinding Out Papers
for College Students
Abigail Witherspoon

Abigail Witherspoon is the pseudonym of an American woman (or perhaps a man) who lives in Canada and ghostwrites academic papers on a wide variety of subjects, primarily in the humanities and social sciences. The author has withheld personal information and has changed the name of the company she works for and the names of everyone mentioned in the piece for fear of being fired or deported. But from evidence within the piece, it appears that Witherspoon attended undergraduate school during the early 1980s, majoring in history at a Canadian university located in a city large enough to contain "three or four smaller schools a few minutes' drive away." "After some years at home in the States," the author returned to that Canadian city and, for lack of work and money, obtained the job that is chronicled in the following journal.

I am an academic call girl. I write college kids' papers for a living. Term papers, book reports, senior theses, take-home exams. My "specialties": art history and sociology, international relations and comparative literature, English, psychology, "communications," Western philosophy (ancient and contemporary), structural anthropology, film history, evolutionary biology, waste management and disposal, media studies, and pre-Confederation Canadian history. I throw around allusions to Caspar Weinberger and Alger Hiss, Sacco and Vanzetti, Haldeman and Ehrlichman, Joel Steinberg and Baby M. The teaching assistants eat it up. I can do simple English or advanced jargon. Like other types of prostitutes, I am, professionally, very accommodating.

I used to tell myself I'd do this work only for a month or two, until I found something else. But the official unemployment rate in this large Canadian city where I live is almost 10 percent, and even if it were easy to find a job, I'm American, and therefore legally prohibited from receiving a paycheck. So each day I walk up the stairs of a rotting old industrial building to an office with a sign on the window: TAILORMADE ESSAYS, WRITING AND RESEARCH. The owner, whom I'll call Matthew, claims that he started the business for ghostwriters, speechwriters, and closet biographers, and only gradually moved into academic work as a sideline. But even Grace, the oldest surviving writer on

Tailormade's staff, can't remember anybody ever writing much other than homework for students at one university or another.

This is a good city for Tailormade. Next door is the city's university and its tens of thousands of students, a school that was once somewhat better when not all of its computer-registered classes numbered in the hundreds. Orders come in from Vancouver, Calgary, Winnipeg. There are plenty of essay services in the States, of course; they advertise in campus newspapers and the back pages of music magazines. Some of the big ones have toll-free phone numbers. They're sprinkled all over: California, Florida, New Jersey. But we still get American business too. Orders come in here from Michigan, Vermont, Pennsylvania; from Illinois, Wisconsin, upstate New York, sometimes California; from Harvard, Cornell, and Brown. They come in from teachers' colleges, from people calling themselves "gifted students" (usually teenagers at boarding schools), and, once in a while, from the snazzy places some of our customers apparently vacation with their divorced dads, like Paris.

Matthew runs the business with his wife, Sylvia. Or maybe she is his ex-wife, nobody's exactly sure. When you call Tailormade—it's now in the phone book—you hear Sylvia say that Tailormade is Canada's foremost essay service; that our very qualified writers handle most academic subjects; and that we are fast, efficient, and completely confidential. Sylvia speaks loudly and slowly and clearly, especially to Asian customers. She is convinced that everyone who phones the office will be Asian, just as she's convinced that all Asians drive white Mercedes or black BMWs with cellular phones in them. From my personal experience, I find the Asian customers at least more likely to have done the assigned reading.

Matthew and Sylvia are oddly complementary. Matthew, gentle and fumbly, 5 calls out mechanically, "Thank you, sir, ma'am, come again" after each departing back slinking down the hall. Sylvia asks the Chinese customers loudly, "SIMPLE ENGLISH?" She tells the uncertain, "Well, don't show up here till you know what you want," and demands of the dissatisfied, "Whaddya mean you didn't like it? You ordered it, din'cha?"

This afternoon, October 10, I'm here to hand in a paper and fight it out with the other writers for more assignments. Some of us are legal, some aren't. Some have mortgages and cars, some don't. All of us are hungry. The office is jammed, since it's almost time for midterms. Tailormade does a brisk business from October to May, except for January. The chairs are full of customers studiously filling out order forms. You can always tell who is a student and who is a writer. The students are dressed elegantly and with precision; the writers wear ripped concert T-shirts or stained denim jackets with white undershirts peeking out. The students wear mousse and hair gel and nail polish and Tony Lama western boots and Tourneau watches and just the right amount of makeup. They smell of Escape, Polo for men, and gum. The writers smell of sweat, house pets, and crushed cigarettes. Four of the other writers are lolling in their chairs and fidgeting; work usually isn't assigned until all the order forms have been filled out, unless somebody requests a topic difficult to fill. Then Matthew will call out like an auctioneer: "Root Causes of the Ukrainian Famine? Second year? Anyone? Grace?" or "J. S. Mill's Brand of Humane Utilitarianism? Third year? Henry, that for you?" as some customer hovers in front of the desk, eyes straight ahead. Someone else in the room might idly remark that he or she took that course back in freshman year and it was a "gut" or a "real bird."

I suspect that each of us in the Tailormade stable of hacks sorts out the customers differently: into liberal-arts students and business students; into those that at least do the reading and those that don't bother; into those that have trouble writing academic English and those that just don't care about school; into those that do their assignments in other subjects and those that farm every last one of them out to us; into the struggling and inept versus the rich, lazy, and stupid. But for Matthew and Sylvia, the clientele are divisible, even before cash versus credit card, or paid-up versus owing, into Asian customers and non-Asian ones. There's been an influx of wealthy immigrants from Hong Kong in recent years, fleeing annexation. Matthew and Sylvia seem to resent their presence and, particularly, their money. Yet they know that it's precisely this pool of customers—who have limited written English language skills but possess education, sophistication, ambition, cash, and parents leaning hard on them for good grades—that keeps the business going.

When I hand in my twelve pages on "The Role of Market Factors in the Development of the Eighteenth-Century Fur Trade," Matthew tells me, "This lady's been patiently waiting without complaining." I must be very late. Turning to the client, he picks up one of my sheets and waves it. "At least it's a nice bib," he points out to her. "Look at that." Although I wasn't provided with any books for this essay, I managed to supply an extensive bibliography. I can't remember what I put on it.

I'm still waiting for an assignment. In fact, all the writers are still waiting. We often wait at the bar around the corner; Tailormade has its own table there, permanently reserved. But we all have to get ourselves to the office eventually to pick up assignments. Grace, the oldest writer and by now, probably, the best, sits sorrowfully by the window, her long gray hair falling into her lap and her head jammed into her turtleneck, on her thin face a look of permanent tragedy. Grace gets up at three in the morning to work; she never forgets a name, a fact, or an assignment; she has a deep, strange love for Japanese history and in ten years here has probably hatched enough pages and research for several doctoral dissertations in that field. Elliott, another writer, reclines near the door, his little dog asleep under his chair. He uses the dog as an icebreaker with the clients, especially young women. He is six and a half feet tall and from somewhere far up in the lunar landscape of northern Ontario. He has a huge head of blond hair down to his eyes and pants as tight as a rock star's. Elliott is the business writer. He specializes in finance, investment, management, and economics. He lives out of a suitcase; he and the little dog, perhaps practicing fiscal restraint, seem to stay with one of a series of girlfriends. When the relationship comes to an end, Elliott and the little dog wind up back in the office, where they sleep in the fax room and Elliott cranks out essays on his laptop. Henry and Russell, two other writers, twist around, changing position, the way travelers do when they're trying to nap on airport lounge chairs. They both look a little like El Greco saints, although perhaps it just seems that way to me because lately I've been doing a lot of art history papers. They both have long skinny legs, long thin white nervous twiddling hands, long thin faces with two weeks' worth of unintentional beard. Henry points out how good Russell looks, and we all agree. Russell is forty. He has a new girlfriend half his age who has, he says, provided a spiritual reawakening. Before he met her, Russell drank so much and held it so badly that he had the distinction of being the only staff member to be banned from the bar around the corner for life. Henry, by contrast, looks terrible. He's always sick, emaciated, coughing, but he invariably manages to meet his deadlines, to make his page quotas, and to show up on time. We used to have another writer on staff, older even than Russell or Grace, who smoked a pipe, nodded a lot, and never said anything. He was a professor who'd been fired from some school, we were never really sure where. Eventually, he went AWOL and started an essay-writing service of his own. He's now Tailormade's main competition. The only other competitors, apparently, worked out of a hot-dog stand parked next to a campus bookstore. Nobody knows whether they're open anymore.

In general, there is a furtiveness about the way we writers talk to one another, the way we socialize. In the office, we're a little like people who know each other from A.A. meetings or rough trade bars encountering each other on a Monday morning at the photocopy machine. It's not because we're competing for work. It's not even because some of us are illegal and everyone else knows it. It is, if anything, collective embarrassment. We know a lot more than Matthew and Sylvia do. They sit dumbly as we bullshit with the clients about their subjects and assignments ("Ah, introductory psychology! The evolution of psychotherapy is a fascinating topic . . . ever read a guy called Russell Jacoby?") in order to impress them and get them to ask for us. This must be the equivalent of the harlots' competitive bordello promenade. But we work for Matthew and Sylvia. They have the sense to pit us against each other, and it works. We can correct their pronunciation of "Goethe" and they don't care. They know it makes no difference. I suspect they have never been farther away than Niagara Falls; neither of them may have even finished high school. It doesn't matter. The laugh's on us, of course: they own the business. 10

OCTOBER 12, 1994.   A tall gangly kid comes in for a twenty-page senior history essay about the ancient local jail. It involves research among primary sources in the provincial archives, and I spend a week there, going page by page through the faded brown script of the warden's prison logbooks of the

1830s. Agitators are being executed for "high treason" or "banished from the realm," which, I assume, means being deported. Once in a while there's a seductive joy to a project. You forget that you've undertaken it for money, that it isn't yours.

Most of the time, though, all I think about is the number of pages done, the number to go. Tailormade charges twenty dollars Canadian a page for first- and second-year course assignments, twenty-two a page for third- and fourth-year assignments, twenty-four for "technical, scientific, and advanced" topics. "Technical, scientific, and advanced" can mean nuclear physics, as it does in September when there is no business. Or it can mean anything Matthew and Sylvia want it to, as it does in March. Most major spring-term essays are due when final exams begin, in April, and so in March kids are practically lined up in the office taking numbers and spilling out into the hall. The writers get half, in cash: ten and eleven bucks a page; twelve for the technical, scientific, and advanced.

There's one other charge: if the client doesn't bring in her or his own books, except in September and January, she or he is "dinged," charged an extra two dollars a page for research. When the writers get an assignment, we ask if there are books. If there are, it saves us time, but we have to lug them home, and often they're the wrong books. If there are no books, we have to go to the libraries and research the paper ourselves. "Client wants twelve pages on clinical social work intervention," Matthew and Sylvia might tell us. "She has a reading list but no books. I think we can ding her." "He wants a book report on something called *Gravity's Rainbow?* Doesn't have the book, though. I'm gonna ding him."

OCTOBER 13.   I am assigned a paper on the French philosopher Michel Foucault. The client has been dinged; I have to find some books. Foucault's *Discipline and Punish* and *Madness and Civilization* are hot properties in the public library system. They are not to be found anywhere. Perhaps this is because professors think Foucault is a hot property, too; he's all over everyone's syllabus.

I warn the client about this in the office. "If you don't find anything by the guy, call me," he says. He gives me his home phone number. "Only, *please* don't say you're from the essay service. Say you're ... a classmate of mine." I promise to be discreet. Most of the clients get scared when you call them at home; most never give out their numbers. I don't blame them.

It was different, though, when I was a university student in the early 1980s. I wasn't aware of anyone who bought his or her homework anywhere, although it must have happened. It was about that time that Tailormade was putting up signs on the telephone poles outside the university's main classroom buildings. It advertised just outside the huge central library as well as outside the libraries of three or four smaller schools a few minutes' drive away. This burst of entrepreneurial confidence almost led to the service's undoing. In a spectacular

207

cooperative sting operation among the security departments of the various schools, the office was raided. This event has become a sort of fearsome myth at Tailormade, discussed not unlike the way Syrians might occasionally mention the Israeli raid on Entebbe. Matthew and Sylvia were hauled off to court and a dozen or so clients were thrown out of their respective universities. Matthew and Sylvia, however, must have hired the right lawyer: they were allowed to reopen, provided that they stayed away from campuses and that they stamped every page of every essay TAILORMADE ESSAY SERVICE: FOR RESEARCH PURPOSES ONLY. Now the clients take the stamped essays home, retype them, and print them out on high-end laser printers much better than ours. If the client is obnoxious, complains, or is considered a whiner, each typewritten page will be stamped in the middle. If the client is steady and has good credit, each page will be stamped in the margin so that the stamp can be whited out and the pages photocopied.

By the time Tailormade reopened, I had moved back to this country after some years at home in the States. I had no money and no prospects of a legal job. I came in, handed Matthew a résumé, spent a couple of weeks on probationary trial, and then began a serious career as a hack. "What are your specialties?" Matthew had asked me. I told him I'd majored in history and political science as an undergraduate. Over time, as my financial situation grew worse, my "specialties" grew to include everything except math, accounting, economics, and the hard sciences.

OCTOBER 23.   Three weeks ago I was assigned an essay on the establishment and growth of political action committees among the Christian right. I am earnest about this one; I actually overprepare. I want to document, with carefully muted horror, the world of Paul Laxalt and direct mail, the arm-twisting of members of Congress on the school prayer issue. My contempt for the client was mixed with pity: he knew not how much he was missing. Only afterward do I realize that after doing an essay I take seriously, I still expect, as in college, to get something back with a mark on it, as a reward or at least as an acknowledgment. I hear nothing, of course. I feel oddly let down. I'm certain it got the client an A. Today, the same client stops in to order something else and helpfully points out what he thinks I could have done to improve the essay I'd written for him.

OCTOBER 25.   This summer, a woman wanted me to write about how aboriginal peoples' systems of law and justice were better developed than those of conquering colonials. I took books with titles like *The Treaties of Canada with the Indians of Manitoba and the North-West Territories, 1880* to the beach. After finishing the client's reading material, I still had no idea what aboriginal peoples thought about law or anything else; she had given me only books about the conquering colonials. So the paper went on, for twenty-odd pages, about the conquering colonials. Now she wants me to rewrite it. The time I will spend on this second version waters my pay down to about a dollar an hour.

NOVEMBER 8.   I will not go into any of the university's libraries. I will not 20 risk running into anyone I know, anyone who might think I'm one of those perpetual graduate students who never finished their dissertations and drift pathetically around university libraries like the undead, frightening the undergraduates. It would be as bad to be thought one of these lifelong grad students as to be suspected of being what I am. So I use the public libraries, usually the one closest to my apartment, on my street corner. It's a community library, with three wonderful librarians, three daily newspapers, and remarkably few books. If I haven't been given the books already, if the client has been dinged and I have to do research on my own, I come here. I have my favorite chair. The librarians assume I am a "mature" and "continuing" community college student, and make kind chitchat with me.

Sometimes, when I can't find any of the sources listed in the library's computer and don't have time to go to a real library, I use books barely appropriate for the essay: books for "young adults," which means twelve-year-olds, or books I have lying around my apartment—like Jane Jacob's *The Death and Life of Great American Cities*, H. D. F. Kitto's *The Greeks*, Eduardo Galeano's *Open Veins of Latin America*, Roy Medvedev's book on Stalin or T. H. White's on John Kennedy, books by J. K. Galbraith, Lewis Mumford, Christopher Lasch, Erich Fromm. Books somewhere between the classic and the old chestnut; terrific books, yet with no relation to the topic at hand. But they're good for the odd quote and name-drop, and they can pad a bibliography. Sometimes I can't get away with this, though, and then I have no choice but to go back to an actual place of research, like the archives.

The archives are, in fact, a difficult place for me. They are full of oak tables, clicking laptops, whirring microfiche readers, and self-assured middle-aged men working with pretty young women whose hair is pinned up in nineteenth-century styles. Perhaps some of them are lovers, but certainly all of them are graduate students with their profs. I, by contrast, am a virtual student, a simulacrum.

NOVEMBER 16.   I have also been pulling at least one or two all-nighters a week for three weeks now. They're very much like the all-nighters I did as an undergraduate. I eat licorice nibs for energy and drink molehill coffee for caffeine. You make molehill coffee by pouring an entire half cup of coffee grounds, the finer the better, in a number 4 paper filter, one filter per cup. At midnight the razzy voice of Tom Waits is temporarily replaced by the BBC news hour. It would be great to be able to speak just like the BBC newscaster. Somebody hyphen-Jones. If I sounded like that I'm sure I would be able to get credit, somehow, for writing about the birth of the Carolingian Renaissance, or the displacement of the samurai in Tokugawa times, or the inadequacies of the Treaty of Versailles.

I know by experience that if I start writing at midnight I can time my output: first page by the BBC's second news summary, second page by the financial news on the half hour, third page finished by the time they read the rugby scores. Except that the first page, the one with the thesis paragraph in it, is the hardest to write, and it clocks in at well over fifteen minutes.

At two-thirty I hit a wall. The molehill coffee still hasn't kicked in yet, or else it did and I didn't notice, and now it's worn off, or else I've just built up a fatal tolerance to the stuff, like a crack addict. I begin to fall asleep in my chair, even with my headphones on. I turn up the music and blast it through the headphones. This works for the time being. I plug along. I can't really remember what I said in my thesis paragraph, but I am not going to worry about it. The client wants fifteen pages, and when I find myself on the fourteenth I'll read the thing over and brace myself, if I have to, for a bow-out. Bow-outs, like legal fine print, allow you to dart gracefully out of the large ambitious thesis statement you've started the essay with: "The topic of bird evolution is an enormous one; I have been able to touch on just one or two interesting controversies within it." "Space does not permit a detailed discussion of all the internal contradictions within Sri Lanka's postcolonial history." And so on. Nine and a half pages down. Five and a half to go. I can still barely remember what I said in my thesis statement. I can barely remember what this paper is *about*. I want to put my head down for a minute on the keyboard, but God only knows what it would end up typing.

NOVEMBER 18.   Things are picking up for Christmas vacation; everything, it seems, is due December 5 or December 15. The essay order form asks, "Subject & Level," "Topic," "No. of Pages," "Footnotes," "Bibliography," and then a couple of lines marked "Additional Information," by far the most common of which is "Simple English." As the year rolls on, we hacks will all, out of annoyance, laziness, or just boredom, start unsimplifying this simple English; by April it will approach the mega-watt vocabulary and tortured syntax of the Frankfurt School. But people hand these papers in and don't get caught, people who have difficulty speaking complete sentences in English; perhaps this is because classes and even tutorials are so big they never have to speak. But in December we're all still on pretty good behavior, simple instead of spiteful. I've just handed in an assignment in "Simple English," a paper titled "Mozart's Friendship with Joseph and Johann Michael Haydn and Its Impact on Mozart's Chamber Music." It reads, in part:

> Mozart was undeniably original. He was never derivative. That was part of his genius. So were the Haydn brothers. All of them were totally unique.

The little library on my corner didn't have much on Mozart or the Haydn brothers. As a result, one of the items in my bibliography is a child's book with a cardboard pop-up of a doughy-looking little Mozart, in a funky pigtail and knee breeches, standing proudly beside a harpischord.

NOVEMBER 22.   I'm assigned an overnight rush essay on the causes of the English Civil War. It may sound perverse, but I love rush essays. We get paid a dollar more a page (two for technical, scientific, and advanced), and if it's lousy we can always say, "Well, you wanted it in a hurry." Although I majored in history, I never took any courses on the English Civil War; I figured, wrongly, that Shakespeare's histories would take care of that. Now I find myself reading the books I took out from the little corner library, not for quotes, or to form an opinion on the roots, germination, feeding, and watering of the war, but just to find out what the hell went on. I find out enough to write five pages. It takes me all night.

NOVEMBER 23.   I am handing in something entitled "Sri Lanka: A Study in Ethnic Division and Caste Co-optation," which Sylvia assigned me, over the phone, a week ago. "The girl says to tell you that *she's* Sri Lankan." Last year I wrote a senior sociology thesis on "The Italian-Canadian Family: Bedrock of Tradition or Agent of Change?" With that one I heard, "The girl says to tell you that *she's* Italian." I wanted to ask Sylvia if the client knew I wasn't, but I was afraid she'd interpret that as meaning I didn't want the work and she'd give it to someone else.

DECEMBER 2.   Occasionally there is an assignment the writers fight for. 30 This week somebody—not me—gets to take home *Fanny Hill* and *Lady Chatterley's Lover*, and get paid for it. I guess some kids really, *really* hate to read.

DECEMBER 5.   A bad assignment: unnecessarily obscure, pedantic, pointless. Certain courses seem to consist of teaching kids the use of jargon as though it were a substitute for writing or thinking well. Often there is an implied pressure to agree with the assigned book. And many are simply impossible to understand; I often take home a textbook or a sheaf of photocopies for an assignment and see, next to a phrase such as "responsible acceptance of the control dimension," long strings of tiny Chinese characters in ballpoint pen. No wonder the students find the assignments incomprehensible; they are incomprehensible to me.

DECEMBER 8.   I hand in a paper on Machiavelli. "How'd it go?" asked the client, a boy in a leather bomber jacket reading John Grisham. I begin to go on about how great one of the books was, a revisionist biography called *Machiavelli in Hell*. I am hoping, with my scholarly enthusiasm, to make the client feel particularly stupid. "It's an amazing book," I tell him. "It makes a case for

211

Machiavelli actually being kind of a liberal humanist instead of the cynical guy everybody always thinks he was—amazing." "That's good," the kid says. "I'm glad you're enjoying yourself on my tab. Did you answer the essay question the way you were supposed to?"

DECEMBER 16.   Every so often clients come in with an opinion they want us to replicate. The freshman sociology and political science essays are already starting to rain in: a deluge of "Show why immigrants are a dead weight on the economy and take jobs away from us"; "Show why most social programs will become too expensive for an aging population"; "Show why gun control can be interpreted as an infringement on civil rights"; "Show the Pacific Rim's single-handed assault on North American economies." I ignore them. I write, depending on my mood, about the INS's unequal criteria for refugee status, or the movie *Roger and Me*, or the NRA's political clout. For instance, there is today's assignment: to describe Locke's influence, as an Enlightenment figure, on our own time. I think this is baloney. I talk about how the postwar military-industrial complex proves that God really did give the world, whatever Locke thought, to the covetous and contentious instead of to the industrious and the rational. No one's ever complained about finding my opinion in a paper instead of their own. Now I realize this isn't because I've persuaded anybody of anything. It's just laziness: there are some customers who actually retype their stamped essays without bothering to read them.

DECEMBER 27.   During Christmas vacation, friends of mine invite me to a party. Some people will be there whom we know from college; they are in the process of becoming successful, even making it big. It will be important to project confidence, the illusion of fulfilling my abandoned early promise. "What do I say," I ask my friends, "when somebody asks me what I do for a living?"

"Tell them you're a writer." 35

My friend Lisa sticks by me loyally all evening. When people ask me, "What is it you do?" Lisa answers for me quickly: "She's a writer."

"Oh, what is it you write?"

"*Essays*," I say, spitefully, drunkenly. Lisa thinks fast.

"Articles," she says. "She writes articles, on Sri Lanka, and Machiavelli, and the English Civil War."

"Isn't *that* interesting," they say, leaving us for the guacamole. 40

JANUARY 10, 1995.   School has been back in session for a week now. The only work that is in are essays from the education students. I hate these assignments. I have trouble manipulating the self-encapsulated second language in which teaching students seem compelled to write. But it's after Christmas, and I'm broke. Education assignments all involve writing up our customers' encounters in their "practicum." Teaching students work several times a week as assistant teachers in grade school classrooms; instead of getting paid for this work, they pay tuition for it. Unfortunately, these expensive practice sessions don't seem to go well. My first such assignment was to write "reflections" on a "lesson plan" for a seventh-grade English class. The teaching student had given me some notes, and I had to translate these into the pedagogical jargon used in her textbooks. The idea seems to be that you have to say, as obscurely as possible, what you did with your seventh-grade kids and what you think about what you did:

> Preliminary Lesson Formulations: My objectives were to integrate lesson content with methodology to expand students' receptiveness and responsiveness to the material and to one another by teaching them how to disagree with one another in a constructive way. The class will draw up a T-chart covering "Disagreeing in an Agreeable Way," roughly in the manner of Bennett et al. Check for understanding. When the students discuss this, they are encouraged to listen to one another's language carefully and "correct" it if the wording is unhelpful, negative, or destructive. I shared my objectives with the class by asking them to read a fable and then divide into pairs and decide together what the moral was. Clearly, this is the "Think-Pair-Share" technique, as detailed in Bennett et al. The three strategies in use, then, are: 1) pair and sharing; 2) group discussion of the fable with mind-mapping; 3) group discussion of ways of disagreement. The teacher, modeling, divides the board in two with a line.

"Pair and share" seemed to mean "find a partner." I had no idea what "mind-mapping" or a "T-chart" was supposed to be. And come to think of it, after reading the fable, I had no idea what the moral was.

JANUARY 18.   Somebody is applying to the graduate program in family therapy at some university somewhere and wants us to write the application. "She's my friend," said the young woman sitting across from Matthew at the desk. "She wants to start her own private practice as a therapist, right? So she can buy a house, right? And if you're a psychiatrist you have to go all the way through med school, right? So she's given me some notes for you about her here—she only needs one credit for her B.A. in psychology, and she volunteered at a shelter one summer. She wants you to tell them all that. Maybe make up some other things."

"See," Matthew tells me after she leaves. "If you ever go to one of those therapists, that's something you should think about."

JANUARY 20.   When I first started this work, friends of mine would try to comfort me by telling me it would teach me to write better. Actually, academic prostitution, just like any other kind, seems to bring with it diseases, afflictions, vices, and bad habits. There is, for instance, the art of pretending you've read a book you haven't. It's just like every speed-reading course ever offered by the

45

Learning Annex: read the introduction, where the writer outlines what he's going to say, and the conclusion, where he repeats what he's said.

> In his book *The Technological Society*, Jacques Ellul begins by defining the technical simply as the search for efficiency. He claims, however, that technique itself is subdivided into three categories: the social, the organizational, and the economic.

This is all on the book's *first four pages*. Sometimes—often—I find myself eating up as much space as possible. There are several ways to do this. One is to reproduce lengthy, paragraph-long quotes in full; another is to ramble on about your own apparently passionate opinion on something. Or you start talking about the United States and what a handbasket it's going to hell in. This is equally useful, for different reasons, on either side of the border. You can ask rhetorical questions to obsessive excess. ("Can Ellul present the technical in such a reductionist way? Can he really define technique in such a way? And is it really valid to distinguish between the social and the organizational?" etc.) And there's always the art of name-dropping as a way to fill pages and convince the teaching assistant that your client has read *something*, even if it wasn't what was on the syllabus.

> Certainly, as writers from Eduardo Galeano to Andre Gunder Frank to Noam Chomsky to Philip Agee to Allan Frankovich to Ernesto Laclau document, the CIA has long propped up the United Fruit Company.

At least you can make the client feel stupid. It's the third week of January, my apartment is cold, and I am bitter.

FEBRUARY 8.   I'm learning, as the environmentalists tell us, to reuse and recycle. It's easier when I adapt a paper, with minor changes, on the same topic for different classes, or when I use the same paper for the same class again the following year. I've never worried much about a recycled essay being recognized: the pay for teaching assistants is low enough, and the burnout rate high enough, that the odds are substantially against the same person reading and grading papers for the same course two years in a row. Some topics just seem to beg for recycling: freshmen are forever being asked to mull over the roles of determinism, hubris, and moral responsibility in the Oedipus cycle; sociology and philosophy majors, the ethics of abortion. There are essays on shantytowns in developing countries, export-oriented economies in developing countries, structural adjustment in developing countries, and one only has to make the obvious case that the three are interrelated to be able to extend the possibilities for parts of essays in any of those three categories to resurface magically within another. Other essays can be recycled with just a little tinkering to surmount minor differences in topic or in emphasis: for instance, "Italian Fascists in North America," to which "The Italian-Canadian Family" lends itself nicely;

"Taboo-Breaking in Racine and Ford," which re-emerges, after minor cosmetic surgery, as "Master-Slave Relationships in Ford and Racine: What They Tell Us About Lust, Fate, and Obligation." And so on.

FEBRUARY 15. I'm sitting on the floor with a pile of old magazines, cutting out pictures of Oreo cookies and Wendy's burgers. This is Andy's essay. It's not an essay, actually, it's a food bingo chart. I have to find a large sheet of cardboard, divide it into squares, and glue on pictures of what is recognizably food. Andy is another education student: he wants to teach junior kindergarten, and his assignment is, apparently, to teach the little tots where food comes from, or what it is, or that advertising is a vital component of each of the four basic food groups, or something. I come into Tailormade with food bingo under my arm. I've gotten some strange looks on the subway. It nets me twenty-five bucks.

MARCH 7. I was supposed to turn in an essay today, one I don't have. I fell asleep at the keyboard last night and accidentally slept through the whole night, headphones and all.

MARCH 16. There's a regular customer whose course load would be appro- 50 priate for the résumé of a U.N. secretary general. She's taking several courses on developing economies, including one referred to by other clients in the same class as "Third World Women." And one on the history of black Americans from Reconstruction to the present. I wrote her a twenty-five-page history of the early years of the civil-rights movement. She was sitting in the office when I handed it in. "Interesting course, isn't it?" she asked. She requested me again. I wrote her a paper on Costa Rica, one on dowry murders in India, one on the black leader W. E. B. Du Bois. "It's a great course, isn't it?" she asked me when she got the paper on dowry murders. "He seems like a fascinating guy," she said the day she collected W. E. B. Du Bois. "Somebody told me he wound up in *Ghana.*" Today I take a shortcut across the university campus on my way to the essay service and see her with a group of other students. I make a direct beeline for her and I smile. I watch her blanch, look around, try to decide whether to pretend not to know me, decide that maybe that isn't a good idea. She gives me a stricken look and a big toothy grin.

MARCH 26. One day I'm given five pages on the Treaty of Versailles. Last year at the same time, I was assigned a paper on the same topic. A memorable paper. Two days after I turned it in, there was a camera crew outside. It turned out to be the local cable station for kids, doing an "exposé" on cheating. We taped it when it came on. It featured kids sitting in shadow, faces obscured, *60 Minutes* style.

"There she is, the little rat," Sylvia glowered at the time. The pretty young fake client handed my paper to some professor sitting behind a desk and asked, "What do you think about this? Is it better or worse than what you would normally get? Would you assume that it was a real paper or one that had been bought?"

"Well . . . it's a *credible* paper," said the professor. "I mean, one wouldn't think it was . . . *synthetic* unless one had reason to."

"What kind of grade would you give it?"

"Oh, I'd give it . . . a B minus."   55

"Please." I was really offended. Elliott comforted me. "Well, he has to say that. Now that he knows it's ours, he can't admit it's an A paper even if he wants to."

We all sat tight and waited for every professor within fifty miles to call us, threatening death. But professors don't watch cable shows for teenagers; neither do ambitious young teaching assistants. Instead, the show turned out to be a free advertising bonanza. Soon the phone rang off the hook with kids calling up and asking, "You mean, like, you can write my term paper for me if I pay you?"

APRIL 16.   Today, working on a paper, I was reminded that there *are* good professors. They're the ones who either convince the kids the course content is inherently interesting and get them to work hard on the assignments or who figure out ways to make the assignments, at least, creative events to enjoy. But students with shaky language skills falter at surprises, even good ones; lazy students farm the assignments out no matter what they are. Such assignments are oddly comforting for me: I can almost pretend the two of us are talking over the clients' heads. When I'm alone in my room, in front of the computer and between the headphones, it's hard not to want to write something good for myself and maybe even for the imaginary absentee professor or appreciative T.A., something that will last. But when I'm standing in the crowded Tailormade office, next to someone elegant and young and in eight hundred bucks' worth of calfskin leather, someone who not only has never heard of John Stuart Mill and never read Othello but doesn't even know he hasn't, doesn't even mind that he hasn't, and doesn't even care that he hasn't, the urge to make something that will last somehow vanishes.

APRIL 28.   The semester is almost at an end. Exams have started; the essays have all been handed in. Elliott and Russell begin their summer jobs as bike couriers. Henry, like me, is illegal; but he confides to me that he's had enough. "You can only do so much of this," he says. I know, I tell him. I know.

QUESTIONS

1. Rather than providing a straightforward description or topically organized report on her job and working conditions, Witherspoon presents her material in the form of a journal. How were your impressions of the job, the students, and Witherspoon affected by this form of presentation?

2. Witherspoon's first entry, for October 10, is much longer than the others, and its date is not revealed until the sixth paragraph. What kind of information does Witherspoon provide before the date? What kind of information is revealed after the date? Examine the following entries to see if you can find any recurrent (or predominant) types of information or methods of reporting and organizing information.

3. By the end of the first entry, what reactions do you have to Tailormade? To its owners? To the ghostwriters? To the students? As the journal unfolds from October through April, how do your reactions change, if at all, to Tailormade, its owners, the ghostwriters, and the students?

4. What were your initial impressions of Witherspoon and her job? How did your impressions of her change, if at all, over the course of the selection?

5. As the journal unfolds, what do you discover about Witherspoon's attitudes toward the job, her employers, her fellow ghostwriters, and the students? Given your overall impressions of her, how reliable a reporter do you consider her to be?

6. What do you consider to be Witherspoon's main purposes in writing this piece?

7. Using this selection as your primary source of information, write a brief (one- to two-page) report about the academic ghostwriting business. What do you think is lost— and what gained—by turning Witherspoon's journal into a condensed and differently organized report?

8. Spend a few weeks keeping a daily (or every-other-day) journal that focuses on an assignment you have to do for one of your courses. Write up your journal in a way that might help make it not only informative, but also interesting for others to read. Before you begin this project, take a few minutes to consider what kinds of detail you plan to include and your reasons for doing so. Also consider how you might organize your entries and how long they might run. Once you've finished the project, consider how closely you stuck to your original plans and what caused you to change them (if you changed your plans in any significant ways).

MAKING CONNECTIONS

1. Imagine a conversation between the students who patronize Tailormade, the students whom William Least Heat-Moon describes in "Pancakes and Scripture Cake" (p. 199), and the ex–New York University student whom Amanda Coyne tells about in "The Long Good-bye" (p. 190). What do you suppose they might say to one another? Try writing a few lines of dialogue to suggest what their conversation might be like.

2. Compare and contrast the worlds that collide (and the ways they collide) at Los Angeles International Airport, as described by Pico Iyer (p. 249), with the worlds that collide in the waiting room of Tailormade, as described by Witherspoon.

Social Sciences and Public Affairs

"THIS IS THE END OF THE WORLD"
The Black Death

Barbara Tuchman

For more than twenty-five years, Barbara Wertheim Tuch-man (1912–1989) wrote books on historical subjects, rang-ing over the centuries from the Middle Ages to World War II. Her combination of careful research and lively writing enabled her to produce books like The Guns of August *(1962),* A Distant Mirror *(1978), and* The March of Folly: From Troy to Vietnam *(1984), which pleased not only the general public, but many professional historians as well. She twice won the Pulitzer Prize.* A Distant Mirror, *from which the following selection has been taken, was on the* New York Times *best-seller list for more than nine months. Her final book,* The First Salute *(1988), is notable for the presence of Tuchman's characteristic scholarship and wit.*

In October 1347, two months after the fall of Calais, Genoese trading ships put into the harbor of Messina in Sicily with dead and dying men at the oars. The ships had come from the Black Sea port of Caffa (now Feodosiya) in the Crimea, where the Genoese maintained a trading post. The diseased sailors showed strange black swellings about the size of an egg or an apple in the armpits and groin. The swellings oozed blood and pus and were followed by spreading boils and black blotches on the skin from internal bleeding. The sick suffered severe pain and died quickly within five days of the first symptoms. As the disease spread, other symptoms of continuous fever and spitting of blood appeared instead of the swellings or buboes. These victims coughed and sweated heavily and died even more quickly, within three days or less, sometimes in 24 hours. In both types everything that issued from the body—breath, sweat, blood from the buboes and lungs, bloody urine, and blood-blackened excrement—smelled foul. Depression and despair accompanied the physical symptoms, and before the end "death is seen seated on the face."

The disease was bubonic plague, present in two forms: one that infected the bloodstream, causing the buboes and internal bleeding, and was spread by contact; and a second, more virulent pneumonic type that infected the lungs and was spread by respiratory infection. The presence of both at once caused the high mortality and speed of contagion. So lethal was the disease that cases were known of persons going to bed well and dying before they woke, of doctors catching the illness at a bedside and dying before the patient. So rapidly did it spread from one to another that to a French physician, Simon de Covino, it seemed as if one sick person "could infect the whole world." The malignity of the pestilence appeared more terrible because its victims knew no prevention and no remedy.

The physical suffering of the disease and its aspects of evil mystery were expressed in a strange Welsh lament which saw "death coming into our midst like black smoke, a plague which cuts off the young, a rootless phantom which has no mercy for fair countenance. Woe is me of the shilling in the armpit! It is seething, terrible . . . a head that gives pain and causes a loud cry . . . a painful angry knob . . . Great is its seething like a burning cinder . . . a grievous thing of ashy color." Its eruption is ugly like the "seeds of black peas, broken fragments of brittle sea-coal . . . the early ornaments of black death, cinders of the peelings of the cockle weed, a mixed multitude, a black plague like halfpence, like berries. . . ."

Rumors of a terrible plague supposedly arising in China and spreading through Tartary (Central Asia) to India and Persia, Mesopotamia, Syria, Egypt, and all of Asia Minor had reached Europe in 1346. They told of a death toll so devastating that all of India was said to be depopulated, whole territories covered by dead bodies, other areas with no one left alive. As added up by Pope Clement VI at Avignon, the total of reported dead reached 23,840,000. In the absence of a concept of contagion, no serious alarm was felt in Europe until the trading ships brought their black burden of pestilence into Messina while other infected ships from the Levant carried it to Genoa and Venice.

By January 1348 it penetrated France via Marseille, and North Africa via Tunis. Shipborne along coasts and navigable rivers, it spread westward from Marseille through the ports of Languedoc to Spain and northward up the Rhône to Avignon, where it arrived in March. It reached Narbonne, Montpellier, Carcassonne, and Toulouse between February and May, and at the same time in Italy spread to Rome and Florence and their hinterlands. Between June and August it reached Bordeaux, Lyon, and Paris, spread to Burgundy and Normandy, and crossed the Channel from Normandy into southern England. From Italy during the same summer it crossed the Alps into Switzerland and reached eastward to Hungary.

In a given area the plague accomplished its kill within four to six months and then faded, except in the larger cities, where, rooting into the close-quartered population, it abated during the winter, only to reappear in spring and rage for another six months.

In 1349 it resumed in Paris, spread to Picardy, Flanders, and the Low Countries, and from England to Scotland and Ireland as well as to Norway, where a ghost ship with a cargo of wool and a dead crew drifted offshore until it ran aground near Bergen. From there the plague passed into Sweden, Denmark, Prussia, Iceland, and as far as Greenland. Leaving a strange pocket of immunity in Bohemia, and Russia unattacked until 1351, it had passed from most of Europe by mid-1350. Although the mortality rate was erratic, ranging from one fifth in some places to nine tenths or almost total elimination in others, the overall estimate of modern demographers has settled—for the area extending from India to Iceland—around the same figure expressed in Froissart's casual words: "a third of the world died." His estimate, the common one at the time, was not an inspired guess but a borrowing of St. John's figure for mortality from plague in Revelation, the favorite guide to human affairs of the Middle Ages.

A third of Europe would have meant about 20 million deaths. No one knows in truth how many died. Contemporary reports were an awed impression, not an accurate count. In crowded Avignon, it was said, 400 died daily; 7,000 houses emptied by death were shut up; a single graveyard received 11,000 corpses in six weeks; half the city's inhabitants reportedly died, including 9 cardinals or one third of the total, and 70 lesser prelates. Watching the endlessly passing death carts, chroniclers let normal exaggeration take wings and put the Avignon death toll at 62,000 and even at 120,000, although the city's total population was probably less than 50,000.

When graveyards filled up, bodies at Avignon were thrown into the Rhône until mass burial pits were dug for dumping the corpses. In London in such pits corpses piled up in layers until they overflowed. Everywhere reports speak of the sick dying too fast for the living to bury. Corpses were dragged out of homes and left in front of doorways. Morning light revealed new piles of bodies. In Florence the dead were gathered up by the Compagnia della Misericordia—founded in 1244 to care for the sick—whose members wore red robes and hoods masking the face except for the eyes. When their efforts failed, the dead lay putrid in the streets for days at a time. When no coffins were to be had, the bodies were laid on boards, two or three at once, to be carried to graveyards or common pits. Families dumped their own relatives into the pits, or buried them so hastily and thinly "that dogs dragged them forth and devoured their bodies."

Amid accumulating death and fear of contagion, people died without last rites and were buried without prayers, a prospect that terrified the last hours of the stricken. A bishop in England gave permission to laymen to make confession to each other as was done by the Apostles, "or if no man is present then

221

even to a woman," and if no priest could be found to administer extreme unction, "then faith must suffice." Clement VI found it necessary to grant remissions of sin to all who died of the plague because so many were unattended by priests. "And no bells tolled," wrote a chronicler of Siena, "and nobody wept no matter what his loss because almost everyone expected death. . . . And people said and believed, 'This is the end of the world.'"

In Paris, where the plague lasted through 1349, the reported death rate was 800 a day, in Pisa 500, in Vienna 500 to 600. The total dead in Paris numbered 50,000 or half the population. Florence, weakened by the famine of 1347, lost three to four fifths of its citizens, Venice two thirds, Hamburg and Bremen, though smaller in size, about the same proportion. Cities, as centers of transportation, were more likely to be affected than villages, although once a village was infected, its death rate was equally high. At Givry, a prosperous village in Burgundy of 1,200 to 1,500 people, the parish register records 615 deaths in the space of fourteen weeks, compared to an average of thirty deaths a year in the previous decade. In three villages of Cambridgeshire, manorial records show a death rate of 47 percent, 57 percent, and in one case 70 percent. When the last survivors, too few to carry on, moved away, a deserted village sank back into the wilderness and disappeared from the map altogether, leaving only a grass-covered ghostly outline to show where mortals once had lived.

In enclosed places such as monasteries and prisons, the infection of one person usually meant that of all, as happened in the Franciscan convents of Carcassonne and Marseille, where every inmate without exception died. Of the 140 Dominicans at Montpellier only seven survived. Petrarch's brother Gherardo, member of a Carthusian monastery, buried the prior and 34 fellow monks one by one, sometimes three a day, until he was left alone with his dog and fled to look for a place that would take him in. Watching every comrade die, men in such places could not but wonder whether the strange peril that filled the air had not been sent to exterminate the human race. In Kilkenny, Ireland, Brother John Clyn of the Friars Minor, another monk left alone among dead men, kept a record of what had happened lest "things which should be remembered perish with time and vanish from the memory of those who come after us." Sensing "the whole world, as it were, placed within the grasp of the Evil One," and waiting for death to visit him too, he wrote, "I leave parchment to continue this work, if perchance any man survive and any of the race of Adam escape this pestilence and carry on the work which I have begun." Brother John, as noted by another hand, died of the pestilence, but he foiled oblivion.

The largest cities of Europe, with populations of about 100,000, were Paris and Florence, Venice and Genoa. At the next level, with more than 50,000, were Ghent and Bruges in Flanders, Milan, Bologna, Rome, Naples, and Palermo, and Cologne. London hovered below 50,000, the only city in England except York with more than 10,000. At the level of 20,000 to 50,000 were Bordeaux, Toulouse, Montpellier, Marseille, and Lyon in France, Barcelona, Seville, and Toledo in Spain, Siena, Pisa, and other secondary cities in Italy, and the Hanseatic trading cities of the Empire. The plague raged through them all, killing anywhere from one third to two thirds of their inhabitants. Italy, with a total population of 10 to 11 million, probably suffered the heaviest toll. Following the Florentine bankruptcies, the crop failures and workers' riots of 1346–47, the revolt of Cola di Rienzi that plunged Rome into anarchy, the plague came as the peak of successive calamities. As if the world were indeed in the grasp of the Evil One, its first appearance on the European mainland in January 1348 coincided with a fearsome earthquake that carved a path of wreckage from Naples up to Venice. Houses collapsed, church towers toppled, villages were crushed, and the destruction reached as far as Germany and Greece. Emotional response, dulled by horrors, underwent a kind of atrophy epitomized by the chronicler who wrote, "And in these days was burying without sorrowe and wedding without friendschippe."

In Siena, where more than half the inhabitants died of the plague, work was abandoned on the great cathedral, planned to be the largest in the world, and never resumed, owing to loss of workers and master masons and "the melancholy and grief" of the survivors. The cathedral's truncated transept still stands in permanent witness to the sweep of death's scythe. Agnolo di Tura, a chronicler of Siena, recorded the fear of contagion that froze every other instinct. "Father abandoned child, wife husband, one brother another," he wrote, "for this plague seemed to strike through the breath and sight. And so they died. And no one could be found to bury the dead for money or friendship. . . . And I, Agnolo di Tura, called the Fat, buried my five children with my own hands, and so did many others likewise."

There were many to echo his account of inhumanity and few to balance it, for the plague was not the kind of calamity that inspired mutual help. Its loathsomeness and deadliness did not herd people together in mutual distress, but only prompted their desire to escape each other. "Magistrates and notaries refused to come and make the wills of the dying," reported a Franciscan friar of Piazza in Sicily; what was worse, "even the priests did not come to hear their confessions." A clerk of the Archbishop of Canterbury reported the same of English priests who "turned away from the care of their benefices from fear of death." Cases of parents deserting children and children their parents were reported across Europe from Scotland to Russia. The calamity chilled the hearts of men, wrote Boccaccio in his famous account of the plague in Florence that serves as introduction to the *Decameron*. "One man shunned another . . . kinsfolk held aloof, brother was forsaken by brother, oftentimes husband by wife; nay, what is more, and scarcely to be believed, fathers and mothers were found to abandon their own children to their fate, untended, unvisited as if they had been strangers." Exaggeration and literary pessimism were common in the 14th

15

223

century, but the Pope's physician, Guy de Chauliac, was a sober, careful observer who reported the same phenomenon: "A father did not visit his son, nor the son his father. Charity was dead."

Yet not entirely. In Paris, according to the chronicler Jean de Venette, the nuns of the Hotel Dieu or municipal hospital, "having no fear of death, tended the sick with all sweetness and humility." New nuns repeatedly took the places of those who died, until the majority "many times renewed by death now rest in peace with Christ as we may piously believe."

When the plague entered northern France in July 1348, it settled first in Normandy and, checked by winter, gave Picardy a deceptive interim until the next summer. Either in mourning or warning, black flags were flown from church towers of the worst-stricken villages of Normandy. "And in that time," wrote a monk of the abbey of Fourcarment, "the mortality was so great among the people of Normandy that those of Picardy mocked them." The same unneighborly reaction was reported of the Scots, separated by a winter's immunity from the English. Delighted to hear of the disease that was scourging the "southrons," they gathered forces for an invasion, "laughing at their enemies." Before they could move, the savage mortality fell upon them too, scattering some in death and the rest in panic to spread the infection as they fled.

In Picardy in the summer of 1349 the pestilence penetrated the castle of Coucy to kill Enguerrand's mother,[1] Catherine, and her new husband. Whether her nine-year-old son escaped by chance or was perhaps living elsewhere with one of his guardians is unrecorded. In nearby Amiens, tannery workers, responding quickly to losses in the labor force, combined to bargain for higher wages. In another place villagers were seen dancing to drums and trumpets, and on being asked the reason, answered that, seeing their neighbors die day by day while their village remained immune, they believed that they could keep the plague from entering "by the jollity that is in us. That is why we dance." Further north in Tournai on the border of Flanders, Gilles li Muisis, Abbot of St. Martin's, kept one of the epidemic's most vivid accounts. The passing bells rang all day and all night, he recorded, because sextons were anxious to obtain their fees while they could. Filled with the sound of mourning, the city became oppressed by fear, so that the authorities forbade the tolling of bells and the wearing of black and restricted funeral services to two mourners. The silencing of funeral bells and of criers' announcements of deaths was ordained by most cities. Siena imposed a fine on the wearing of mourning clothes by all except widows.

Flight was the chief recourse of those who could afford it or arrange it. The rich fled to their country places like Boccaccio's young patricians of Florence, who settled in a pastoral palace "removed on every side from the roads" with

---

[1]*Enguerrand de Coucy:* a French nobleman. Tuchman follows his life as a way of unifying her study of the fourteenth century. [Eds.]

"wells of cool water and vaults of rare wines." The urban poor died in their burrows, "and only the stench of their bodies informed neighbors of their deaths." That the poor were more heavily afflicted than the rich was clearly remarked at the time, in the north as in the south. A Scottish chronicler, John of Fordun, stated flatly that the pest "attacked especially the meaner sort and common people—seldom the magnates." Simon de Covino of Montpellier made the same observation. He ascribed it to the misery and want and hard lives that made the poor more susceptible, which was half the truth. Close contact and lack of sanitation was the unrecognized other half. It was noticed too that the young died in greater proportion than the old; Simon de Covino compared the disappearance of youth to the withering of flowers in the fields.

In the countryside peasants dropped dead on the roads, in the fields, in their houses. Survivors in growing helplessness fell into apathy, leaving ripe wheat uncut and livestock untended. Oxen and asses, sheep and goats, pigs and chickens ran wild and they too, according to local reports, succumbed to the pest. English sheep, bearers of the precious wool, died throughout the country. The chronicler Henry Knighton, canon of Leicester Abbey, reported 5,000 dead in one field alone, "their bodies so corrupted by the plague that neither beast nor bird would touch them," and spreading an appalling stench. In the Austrian Alps wolves came down to prey upon sheep and then, "as if alarmed by some invisible warning, turned and fled back into the wilderness." In remote Dalmatia bolder wolves descended upon a plague-stricken city and attacked human survivors. For want of herdsmen, cattle strayed from place to place and died in hedgerows and ditches. Dogs and cats fell like the rest.

The dearth of labor held a fearful prospect because the 14th century lived close to the annual harvest both for food and for next year's seed. "So few servants and laborers were left," wrote Knighton, "that no one knew where to turn for help." The sense of a vanishing future created a kind of dementia of despair. A Bavarian chronicler of Neuberg on the Danube recorded that "Men and women . . . wandered around as if mad" and let their cattle stray "because no one had any inclination to concern themselves about the future." Fields went uncultivated, spring seed unsown. Second growth with nature's awful energy crept back over cleared land, dikes crumbled, salt water reinvaded and soured the lowlands. With so few hands remaining to restore the work of centuries, people felt, in Walsingham's words, that "the world could never again regain its former prosperity."

Though the death rate was higher among the anonymous poor, the known and the great died too. King Alfonso XI of Castile was the only reigning monarch killed by the pest, but his neighbor King Pedro of Aragon lost his wife, Queen Leonora, his daughter Marie, and a niece in the space of six months. John Cantacuzene, Emperor of Byzantium, lost his son. In France the lame Queen Jeanne and her daughter-in-law Bonne de Luxemburg, wife of the Dauphin, both died in 1349 in the same phase that took the life of Enguerrand's mother. Jeanne, Queen of Navarre, daughter of Louis X, was another

225

victim. Edward III's second daughter, Joanna, who was on her way to marry Pedro, the heir of Castile, died in Bordeaux. Women appear to have been more vulnerable than men, perhaps because, being more housebound, they were more exposed to fleas. Boccaccio's mistress Fiammetta, illegitimate daughter of the King of Naples, died, as did Laura, the beloved—whether real or fictional—of Petrarch. Reaching out to us in the future, Petrarch cried, "Oh happy posterity who will not experience such abysmal woe and will look upon our testimony as a fable."

In Florence Giovanni Villani, the great historian of his time, died at 68 in the midst of an unfinished sentence: "... *e dure questo pistolenza fino a* ... (in the midst of this pestilence there came to an end ...)." Siena's master painters, the brothers Ambrogio and Pietro Lorenzetti, whose names never appear after 1348, presumably perished in the plague, as did Andrea Pisano, architect and sculptor of Florence. William of Ockham and the English mystic Richard Rolle of Hampole both disappear from mention after 1349. Francisco Datini, merchant of Prato, lost both his parents and two siblings. Curious sweeps of mortality afflicted certain bodies of merchants in London. All eight wardens of the Company of Cutters, all six wardens of the Hatters, and four wardens of the Goldsmiths died before July 1350. Sir John Pulteney, master draper and four times Mayor of London, was a victim, likewise Sir John Montgomery, Governor of Calais.

Among the clergy and doctors the mortality was naturally high because of the nature of their professions. Out of 24 physicians in Venice, 20 were said to have lost their lives in the plague, although, according to another account, some were believed to have fled or to have shut themselves up in their houses. At Montpellier, site of the leading medieval medical school, the physician Simon de Covino reported that, despite the great number of doctors, "hardly one of them escaped." In Avignon, Guy de Chauliac confessed that he performed his medical visits only because he dared not stay away for fear of infamy, but "I was in continual fear." He claimed to have contracted the disease but to have cured himself by his own treatment; if so, he was one of the few who recovered.

Clerical mortality varied with rank. Although the one-third toll of cardinals reflects the same proportion as the whole, this was probably due to their concentration in Avignon. In England, in strange and almost sinister procession, the Archbishop of Canterbury, John Stratford, died in August 1348, his appointed successor died in May 1349, and the next appointee three months later, all three within a year. Despite such weird vagaries, prelates in general managed to sustain a higher survival rate than the lesser clergy. Among bishops the deaths have been estimated at about one in twenty. The loss of priests, even if many avoided their fearful duty of attending the dying, was about the same as among the population as a whole.

Government officials, whose loss contributed to the general chaos, found, on the whole, no special shelter. In Siena four of the nine members of the governing oligarchy died, in France one third of the royal notaries, in Bristol 15 out of the 52 members of the Town Council or almost one third. Tax-collecting obviously suffered, with the result that Philip VI was unable to collect more than a fraction of the subsidy granted him by the Estates in the winter of 1347–48.

Lawlessness and debauchery accompanied the plague as they had during the great plague of Athens of 430 B.C., when according to Thucydides, men grew bold in the indulgence of pleasure: "For seeing how the rich died in a moment and those who had nothing immediately inherited their property, they reflected that life and riches were alike transitory and they resolved to enjoy themselves while they could." Human behavior is timeless. When St. John had his vision of plague in Revelation, he knew from some experience or race memory that those who survived "repented not of the work of their hands. . . . Neither repented they of their murders, nor of their sorceries, nor of their fornication, nor of their thefts."

NOTES[2]

1. "death is seen seated": Simon de Covino, q. Campbell, 80.
2. "could infect the whole world": q. Gasquet, 41.
3. Welsh lament: q. Ziegler, 190.
9. "dogs dragged them forth": Agnolo di Tura, q. Ziegler, 58.
10. "or if no man is present": Bishop of Bath and Wells, q. Ziegler, 125. "No Bells Tolled": Agnolo di Tura, q. Schevill, *Siena*, 211. The same observation was made by Gabriel de Muisis, notary of Piacenza, q. Crawfurd, 113.
11. Givry parish register: Renouard, 111. three villages of Cambridgeshire: Saltmarsh.
12. Petrarch's brother: Bishop, 273. Brother John Clyn: q. Ziegler, 195.
13. "And in these days": q. Deaux, 143, citing only "an old northern chronicle."
14. Agnolo Di Tura, "Father abandoned child": q. Ziegler, 58.
15. "Magistrates and notaries": q. Deaux, 49. English Priests Turned Away: Ziegler, 261. Parents Deserting Children: Hecker, 30. Guy De Chauliac, "A Father": q. Gasquet, 50–51.
16. nuns of the Hotel Dieu: *Chron. Jean de Venette*, 49.
17. Picards and Scots mock mortality of neighbors: Gasquet, 53, and Ziegler, 198.
18. Catherine de Coucy: *L'Art de vérifier*, 237. Amiens Tanners: Gasquet, 57. "By the Jollity That Is in Us": *Grandes Chrôns.*, VI, 486–87.
19. John of Fordun: q. Ziegler, 199. Simon de Covino on the poor: Gasquet, 42. on youth: Cazelles, *Peste*.
20. Knighton on sheep: q. Ziegler, 175. Wolves of Austria and Dalmatia: ibid., 84, 111. dogs and cats: Muisis, q. Gasquet, 44, 61.

---

[2]Tuchman does not use numbered footnotes, but at the back of her book she identifies the source of every quotation or citation. The works cited follow in a bibliography. Although Tuchman's notes are labeled by page number, the numbers here refer to the paragraphs in which the sources are mentioned. [Eds.]

21. Bavarian chronicler of Neuberg: q. Ziegler, 84. Walsingham, "the world could never": Denifle, 273.

22. "Oh happy posterity": q. Ziegler, 45.

23. Giovanni Villani, "*e dure questo*": q. Snell, 334.

24. physicians of Venice: Campbell, 98. Simon de Covino: ibid., 31. Guy de Chauliac, "I was in continual fear": q. Thompson *Ec. and Soc.*, 379.

27. Thucydides: q. Crawfurd, 30–31.

BIBLIOGRAPHY

L'Art de vérifier les dates des faits historiques, par un Religieux de la Congregation de St.-Maur, vol. XII. Paris, 1818.

Bishop, Morris. *Petrarch and His World.* Indiana University Press, 1963.

Campbell, Anna M. *The Black Death and Men of Learning.* Columbia University Press, 1931.

Cazelles, Raymond. "*La Peste de 1348–49 en Langue d'oil: épidémie prolitarienne et enfantine.*" *Bull philologique et historique,* 1962, pp. 293–305.

Chronicle of Jean de Venette. Trans. Jean Birdsall. Ed. Richard A. Newhall. Columbia University Press, 1853.

Crawfurd, Raymond. *Plague and Pestilence in Literature and Art.* Oxford, 1914.

Deaux, George. *The Black Death,* 1347. London, 1969.

Denifle, Henri. *La Dèsolation des églises, monastères et hopitaux en France pendant la guerre de cent ans,* vol. I. Paris, 1899.

Gasquet, Francis Aidan, Abbot. *The Black Death of 1348 and 1349,* 2nd ed. London, 1908.

Grandes Chroniques de France, vol. VI (to 1380). Ed. Paulin Paris. Paris, 1838.

Hecker, J. F. C. *The Epidemics of the Middle Ages.* London, 1844.

Renouard, Yves. "*La Peste noirs de 1348–50.*" *Rev. de Paris,* March, 1950.

Saltmarsh, John. "Plague and Economic Decline in England in the Later Middle Ages," *Cambridge Historical Journal,* vol. VII, no. 1, 1941.

Schevill, Ferdinand. *Siena: The History of a Medieval Commune.* New York, 1909.

Snell, Frederick. *The Fourteenth Century.* Edinburgh, 1899.

Thompson, James Westfall. *Economic and Social History of Europe in the Later Middle Ages.* New York, 1931.

Ziegler, Philip. *The Black Death.* New York, 1969. (The best modern study.)

QUESTIONS

1. Try to imagine yourself in Tuchman's position. If you were assigned the task of reporting on the black plague in Europe, how would you go about it? What problems would you expect to encounter in the research and in the composition of your report?

2. The notes and bibliography reveal a broad scholarly base: Tuchman's research was clearly prodigious. But so were the problems of organization after the research had been done. Tuchman had to find a way to present her information to readers that would be clear and interesting. How has she solved her problem? What overall patterns of organization do you find in this selection? Can you mark off subsections with topics of their own?

3. How does Tuchman organize her paragraphs? Consider paragraph 20, for example. What is the topic? What are the subtopics? Why does the paragraph begin and end as it does? Consider paragraph 22. How does the first sentence serve as a transition from the previous paragraph? How is the rest of the paragraph ordered? Does the next paragraph start a new topic or continue developing the topic announced at the beginning of paragraph 22?

4. Many paragraphs end with direct quotations. Examine some of these. What do they have in common? Why do you suppose Tuchman closes so many paragraphs in this way?

5. Much of this essay is devoted to the reporting of facts and figures. This could be supremely dull, but Tuchman is an expert at avoiding dullness. How does she help the reader see and feel the awfulness of the plague? Locate specific examples in the text, and discuss their effectiveness.

6. Examine Tuchman's list of sources, and explain how she has used them. Does she quote directly from each source, or does she paraphrase it? Does she use a source to illustrate a point, as evidence for argument, or in some other way? Describe Tuchman's general method of using sources.

7. Taking Tuchman as a model, write a report on some other catastrophe, blending factual reporting with description of what it was like to be there. This will require both careful research and artful selection and arrangement of the fruits of that research.

8. Using Tuchman's notes to A *Distant Mirror* as a reference guide, find out more about some specific place or event mentioned by Tuchman. Write a report of your findings.

MAKING CONNECTIONS

1. Compare this account of the black death to the writings by Farley Mowat (p. 237) or Jane van Lawick-Goodall (p. 241), included in this section. Make your comparison in terms of the points of view established and sustained in the reports you compare. What is Tuchman's point of view toward her subject?

2. Using the terms of our introduction to this section, would you say that Tuchman's basic method of reporting is narrative, that it emphasizes spatial order, or that it makes a topical summation of categories appropriate to its subject? How does her handling of sources compare to the National Transportation Safety Board's report on an airplane crash (p. 284)?

ATOMIC BOMBING OF NAGASAKI TOLD BY FLIGHT MEMBER

William L. Laurence

William L. Laurence (1888–1997) was born in Lithuania and came to the United States in 1905. He studied at Harvard and the Boston University Law School. His main interest, however, had always been in science, and after working at the New York World *for five years, Laurence went to the* New York Times *as a science reporter. During World War II, Laurence was the only reporter to know about the top-secret testing of the atomic bomb. On August 9, 1945, he was permitted to fly with the mission to drop the second atomic bomb on Nagasaki. Three days earlier, more than one hundred thousand people had been killed in the Hiroshima bombing. Laurence won the Pulitzer Prize for this account of the bombing of Nagasaki. The article appeared in the* New York Times *on September 9, 1945.*

With the atomic-bomb mission to Japan, August 9 (Delayed)—We are on our way to bomb the mainland of Japan. Our flying contingent consists of three specially designed B-29 Superforts, and two of these carry no bombs. But our lead plane is on its way with another atomic bomb, the second in three days, concentrating in its active substance an explosive energy equivalent to twenty thousand and, under favorable conditions, forty thousand tons of TNT.

We have several chosen targets. One of these is the great industrial and shipping center of Nagasaki, on the western shore of Kyushu, one of the main islands of the Japanese homeland.

I watched the assembly of this man-made meteor during the past two days and was among the small group of scientists and Army and Navy representatives privileged to be present at the ritual of its loading in the Superfort last night, against a background of threatening black skies torn open at intervals by great lightning flashes.

It is a thing of beauty to behold, this "gadget." Into its design went millions of man-hours of what is without doubt the most concentrated intellectual effort in history. Never before had so much brain power been focused on a single problem.

This atomic bomb is different from the bomb used three days ago with such 5 devastating results on Hiroshima.

I saw the atomic substance before it was placed inside the bomb. By itself it is not at all dangerous to handle. It is only under certain conditions, produced

230

in the bomb assembly, that it can be made to yield up its energy, and even then it gives only a small fraction of its total contents—a fraction, however, large enough to produce the greatest explosion on earth.

The briefing at midnight revealed the extreme care and the tremendous amount of preparation that had been made to take care of every detail of the mission, to make certain that the atomic bomb fully served the purpose for which it was intended. Each target in turn was shown in detailed maps and in aerial photographs. Every detail of the course was rehearsed—navigation, altitude, weather, where to land in emergencies. It came out that the Navy had rescue craft, known as Dumbos and Superdumbos, stationed at various strategic points in the vicinity of the targets, ready to rescue the fliers in case they were forced to bail out.

The briefing period ended with a moving prayer by the chaplain. We then proceeded to the mess hall for the traditional early-morning breakfast before departure on a bombing mission.

A convoy of trucks took us to the supply building for the special equipment carried on combat missions. This included the Mae West,[1] a parachute, a lifeboat, an oxygen mask, a flak suit, and a survival vest. We still had a few hours before take-off time, but we all went to the flying field and stood around in little groups or sat in jeeps talking rather casually about our mission to the Empire, as the Japanese home islands are known hereabouts.

In command of our mission is Major Charles W. Sweeney, twenty-five, of 124 Hamilton Avenue, North Quincy, Massachusetts. His flagship, carrying the atomic bomb, is named *The Great Artiste*, but the name does not appear on the body of the great silver ship, with its unusually long, four-bladed, orange-tipped propellers. Instead, it carries the number 77, and someone remarks that it was "Red" Grange's winning number on the gridiron.

We took off at 3:50 this morning and headed northwest on a straight line for the Empire. The night was cloudy and threatening, with only a few stars here and there breaking through the overcast. The weather report had predicted storms ahead part of the way but clear sailing for the final and climactic stages of our odyssey.

We were about an hour away from our base when the storm broke. Our great ship took some heavy dips through the abysmal darkness around us, but it took these dips much more gracefully than a large commercial air liner, producing a sensation more in the nature of a glide than a "bump," like a great ocean liner riding the waves except that in this case the air waves were much higher and the rhythmic tempo of the glide was much faster.

I noticed a strange eerie light coming through the window high above the navigator's cabin, and as I peered through the dark all around us I saw a startling phenomenon. The whirling giant propellers had somehow become great

10

---

[1]*Mae West:* an inflatable life jacket named for the actor. [Eds.]

luminous disks of blue flame. The same luminous blue flame appeared on the plexiglass windows in the nose of the ship, and on the tips of the giant wings. It looked as though we were riding the whirlwind through space on a chariot of blue fire.

It was, I surmised, a surcharge of static electricity that had accumulated on the tips of the propellers and on the di-electric material of the plastic windows. One's thoughts dwelt anxiously on the precious cargo in the invisible ship ahead of us. Was there any likelihood of danger that this heavy electric tension in the atmosphere all about us might set it off?

I expressed my fears to Captain Bock, who seems nonchalant and unper- 15
turbed at the controls. He quickly reassured me.

"It is a familiar phenomenon seen often on ships. I have seen it many times on bombing missions. It is known as St. Elmo's fire."

On we went through the night. We soon rode out the storm and our ship was once again sailing on a smooth course straight ahead, on a direct line to the Empire.

Our altimeter showed that we were traveling through space at a height of seventeen thousand feet. The thermometer registered an outside temperature of thirty-three degrees below zero Centigrade, about thirty below Fahrenheit. Inside our pressurized cabin the temperature was that of a comfortable air-conditioned room and a pressure corresponding to an altitude of eight thousand feet. Captain Bock cautioned me, however, to keep my oxygen mask handy in case of emergency. This, he explained, might mean either something going wrong with the pressure equipment inside the ship or a hole through the cabin by flak.

The first signs of dawn came shortly after five o'clock. Sergeant Curry, of Hoopeston, Illinois, who had been listening steadily on his earphones for radio reports, while maintaining a strict radio silence himself, greeted it by rising to his feet and gazing out the window.

"It's good to see the day," he told me. "I get a feeling of claustrophobia 20
hemmed in this cabin at night."

He is a typical American youth, looking even younger than his twenty years. It takes no mind reader to read his thoughts.

"It's a long way from Hoopeston," I find myself remarking.

"Yep," he replies, as he busies himself decoding a message from outer space.

"Think this atomic bomb will end the war?" he asks hopefully.

"There is a very good chance that this one may do the trick," I assured him, 25
"but if not, then the next one or two surely will. Its power is such that no nation can stand up against it very long." This was not my own view. I had heard it expressed all around a few hours earlier, before we took off. To anyone who had seen this manmade fireball in action, as I had less than a month ago in the desert of New Mexico, this view did not sound overoptimistic.

By 5:50 it was really light outside. We had lost our lead ship, but Lieutenant Godfrey, our navigator, informs me that we had arranged for that contingency.

We have an assembly point in the sky above the little island of Yakushima, southeast of Kyushu, at 9:10. We are to circle there and wait for the rest of our formation.

Our genial bombardier, Lieutenant Levy, comes over to invite me to take his front-row seat in the transparent nose of the ship, and I accept eagerly. From that vantage point in space, seventeen thousand feet above the Pacific, one gets a view of hundreds of miles on all sides, horizontally and vertically. At that height the vast ocean below and the sky above seem to merge into one great sphere.

I was on the inside of that firmament, riding above the giant mountains of white cumulus clouds, letting myself be suspended in infinite space. One hears the whirl of the motors behind one, but it soon becomes insignificant against the immensity all around and is before long swallowed by it. There comes a point where space also swallows time and one lives through eternal moments filled with an oppressive loneliness, as though all life had suddenly vanished from the earth and you are the only one left, a lone survivor traveling endlessly through interplanetary space.

My mind soon returns to the mission I am on. Somewhere beyond these vast mountains of white clouds ahead of me there lies Japan, the land of our enemy. In about four hours from now one of its cities, making weapons of war for use against us, will be wiped off the map by the greatest weapon ever made by man: In one tenth of a millionth of a second, a fraction of time immeasurable by any clock, a whirlwind from the skies will pulverize thousands of its buildings and tens of thousands of its inhabitants.

But at this moment no one yet knows which one of the several cities chosen as targets is to be annihilated. The final choice lies with destiny. The winds over Japan will make the decision. If they carry heavy clouds over our primary target, the city will be saved, at least for the time being. None of its inhabitants will ever know that the wind of a benevolent destiny had passed over their heads. But that same wind will doom another city.

Our weather planes ahead of us are on their way to find out where the wind blows. Half an hour before target time we will know what the winds have decided.

Does one feel any pity or compassion for the poor devils about to die? Not when one thinks of Pearl Harbor and of the Death March on Bataan.[2]

Captain Bock informs me that we are about to start our climb to bombing altitude.

He manipulates a few knobs on his control panel to the right of him, and I alternately watch the white clouds and ocean below me and the altimeter on the bombardier's panel. We reached our altitude at nine o'clock. We were

---

[2]*Pearl Harbor:* on December 7, 1941, a surprise bombing attack by the Japanese on this United States naval base in Hawaii caused the death of 1,177 people and prompted the United States to enter World War II; *Death March on Bataan:* physically weakened American and Filipino defenders of the Bataan peninsula were forced by their Japanese captors to march ninety miles under brutal conditions to a prisoner-of-war camp in Manila. Many did not survive. [Eds.]

233

then over Japanese waters, close to their mainland. Lieutenant Godfrey motioned to me to look through his radar scope. Before me was the outline of our assembly point. We shall soon meet our lead ship and proceed to the final stage of our journey.

We reached Yakushima at 9:12 and there, about four thousand feet ahead of 35
us, was *The Great Artiste* with its precious load. I saw Lieutenant Godfrey and Sergeant Curry strap on their parachutes and I decided to do likewise.

We started circling. We saw little towns on the coastline, heedless of our presence. We kept on circling, waiting for the third ship in our formation.

It was 9:56 when we began heading for the coastline. Our weather scouts had sent us code messages, deciphered by Sergeant Curry, informing us that both the primary target as well as the secondary were clearly visible.

The winds of destiny seemed to favor certain Japanese cities that must remain nameless. We circled about them again and again and found no opening in the thick umbrella of clouds that covered them. Destiny chose Nagasaki as the ultimate target.

We had been circling for some time when we noticed black puffs of smoke coming through the white clouds directly at us. There were fifteen bursts of flak in rapid succession, all too low. Captain Bock changed his course. There soon followed eight more bursts of flak, right up to our altitude, but by this time they were too far to the left.

We flew southward down the channel and at 11:33 crossed the coastline 40
and headed straight for Nagasaki, about one hundred miles to the west. Here again we circled until we found an opening in the clouds. It was 12:01 and the goal of our mission had arrived.

We heard the prearranged signal on our radio, put on our arc welder's glasses, and watched tensely the maneuverings of the strike ship about half a mile in front of us.

"There she goes!" someone said.

Out of the belly of *The Great Artiste* what looked like a black object went downward.

Captain Bock swung to get out of range; but even though we were turning away in the opposite direction, and despite the fact that it was broad daylight in our cabin, all of us became aware of a giant flash that broke through the dark barrier of our arc welder's lenses and flooded our cabin with intense light.

We removed our glasses after the first flash, but the light still lingered on, a 45
bluish-green light that illuminated the entire sky all around. A tremendous blast wave struck our ship and made it tremble from nose to tail. This was followed by four more blasts in rapid succession, each resounding like the boom of cannon fire hitting our plane from all directions.

Observers in the tail of our ship saw a giant ball of fire rise as though from the bowels of the earth, belching forth enormous white smoke rings. Next they saw a giant pillar of purple fire, ten thousand feet high, shooting skyward with enormous speed.

By the time our ship had made another turn in the direction of the atomic explosion the pillar of purple fire had reached the level of our altitude. Only about forty-five seconds had passed. Awe-struck, we watched it shoot upward like a meteor coming from the earth instead of from outer space, becoming ever more alive as it climbed skyward through the white clouds. It was no longer smoke, or dust, or even a cloud of fire. It was a living thing, a new species of being, born right before our incredulous eyes.

At one stage of its evolution, covering millions of years in terms of seconds, the entity assumed the form of a giant square totem pole, with its base about three miles long, tapering off to about a mile at the top. Its bottom was brown, its center was amber, its top white. But it was a living totem pole, carved with many grotesque masks grimacing at the earth.

Then, just when it appeared as though the thing had settled down into a state of permanence, there came shooting out of the top a giant mushroom that increased the height of the pillar to a total of forty-five thousand feet. The mushroom top was even more alive than the pillar, seething and boiling in a white fury of creamy foam, sizzling upward and then descending earthward, a thousand Old Faithful geysers rolled into one.

It kept struggling in an elemental fury, like a creature in the act of breaking 50 the bonds that held it down. In a few seconds it had freed itself from its gigantic stem and floated upward with tremendous speed, its momentum carrying it into the stratosphere to a height of about sixty thousand feet.

But no sooner did this happen when another mushroom, smaller in size than the first one, began emerging out of the pillar. It was as though the decapitated monster was growing a new head.

As the first mushroom floated off into the blue it changed its shape into a flowerlike form, its giant petals curving downward, creamy white outside, rose-colored inside. It still retained that shape when we last gazed at it from a distance of about two hundred miles. The boiling pillar of many colors could also be seen at that distance, a giant mountain of jumbled rainbows, in travail. Much living substance had gone into those rainbows. The quivering top of the pillar was protruding to a great height through the white clouds, giving the appearance of a monstrous prehistoric creature with a ruff around its neck, a fleecy ruff extending in all directions, as far as the eye could see.

QUESTIONS

1. What do we learn about the crew members on the mission? Why has Laurence bothered to tell us about them?

2. Laurence's description of the bomb as "a thing of beauty" (paragraph 4) suggests that this eyewitness report is not wholly objective. What is Laurence's moral stance on this mission?

3. Consider Laurence's arrangement of time in his narrative. What effect do you think he wishes to create by switching back and forth between past and present tense?

4. Consider Laurence's description of the blast and its resulting cloud (paragraphs 44 through 52). His challenge as a writer is to help his readers see this strange and awesome thing. What familiar images does he use to represent this unfamiliar sight? What do those images say—especially the last one—about Laurence's feelings as he watched the cloud transform itself?

5. Write an eyewitness report on an event that you consider important. Present the preparations or actions leading up to the event, and include information about others involved. What imagery can you use to describe the glorious, funny, or chaotic event itself?

6. For a report on the basis for Laurence's attitude toward the bombings of Hiroshima and Nagasaki, look at as many newspapers as you can for August 6 through 10 in 1945. Be sure to look at the editorial pages as well as the front pages. If possible, you might also interview relatives and friends who are old enough to remember the war or who might have fought in it. What attitudes toward the bomb and its use were expressed then? How do these compare or contrast with Laurence's attitude?

MAKING CONNECTIONS

1. Describe the differences in point of view taken toward this cataclysmic event by Laurence, John Hersey (p. 181), and Zoë Tracy Hardy (p. 111). How does each writer respond to this unparalleled story? Which responses do you find most unusual, most believable, most sympathetic? Why?

2. Imagine a meeting today between Laurence and Hatsuyo Nakamura from John Hersey's piece (p. 181). What might they say to one another? How might Laurence reflect today on his feelings more than fifty years ago? Imagine this meeting, and write a report of it. Or, if you prefer, substitute Zoë Tracy Hardy (p. 111) for Hatsuyo Nakamura.

OBSERVING WOLVES

Farley Mowat

*Farley Mowat was born in Ontario, Canada, in 1921 and
finished college at the University of Toronto in 1949, after
wartime service and two years living in the Arctic. He makes
his living as a writer rather than a scientist, but he works in
the same areas covered by anthropologists and zoologists.
Often he writes more as a partisan of indigenous peoples
and animals than as an "objective" scientist, and his work
has reached a wide audience. He has written engagingly
about the strange animals he grew up with in* Born Naked
(1995) and about wolves in Never Cry Wolf *(1963), from
which the following selection is taken.*

During the next several weeks I put my decision into effect with the thoroughness for which I have always been noted. I went completely to the wolves.
To begin with I set up a den of my own as near to the wolves as I could conveniently get without disturbing the even tenor of their lives too much. After all,
I *was* a stranger, and an unwolflike one, so I did not feel I should go too far too
fast.

Abandoning Mike's cabin (with considerable relief, since as the days warmed
up so did the smell) I took a tiny tent and set it up on the shore of the bay immediately opposite to the den esker.[1] I kept my camping gear to the barest
minimum—a small primus stove, a stew pot, a teakettle, and a sleeping bag
were the essentials. I took no weapons of any kind, although there were times
when I regretted this omission, even if only fleetingly. The big telescope was
set up in the mouth of the tent in such a way that I could observe the den by
day or night without even getting out of my sleeping bag.

During the first few days of my sojourn with the wolves I stayed inside the
tent except for brief and necessary visits to the out-of-doors which I always undertook when the wolves were not in sight. The point of this personal conceal-
ment was to allow the animals to get used to the tent and to accept it as only
another bump on a very bumpy piece of terrain. Later, when the mosquito
population reached full flowering, I stayed in the tent practically all of the time
unless there was a strong wind blowing, for the most bloodthirsty beasts in the
Arctic are not wolves, but the insatiable mosquitoes.

My precautions against disturbing the wolves were superfluous. It had required a week for me to get their measure, but they must have taken mine at

---

[1]*esker:* a long, narrow deposit of gravel and sand left by a stream flowing from a glacier. [Eds.]

our first meeting; and, while there was nothing overtly disdainful in their evident assessment of me, they managed to ignore my presence, and indeed my very existence, with a thoroughness which was somehow disconcerting.

Quite by accident I had pitched my tent within ten yards of one of the major paths used by the wolves when they were going to, or coming from, their hunting grounds to the westward; and only a few hours after I had taken up residence one of the wolves came back from a trip and discovered me and my tent. He was at the end of a hard night's work and was clearly tired and anxious to go home to bed. He came over a small rise fifty yards from me with his head down, his eyes half-closed, and a preoccupied air about him. Far from being the preternaturally alert and suspicious beast of fiction, this wolf was so self-engrossed that he came straight on to within fifteen yards of me, and might have gone right past the tent without seeing it at all, had I not banged my elbow against the teakettle, making a resounding clank. The wolf's head came up and his eyes opened wide, but he did not stop or falter in his pace. One brief, sidelong glance was all he vouchsafed to me as he continued on his way.

It was true that I wanted to be inconspicuous, but I felt uncomfortable at being so totally ignored. Nevertheless, during the two weeks which followed, one or more wolves used the track past my tent almost every night—and never, except on one memorable occasion, did they evince the slightest interest in me.

By the time this happened I had learned a good deal about my wolfish neighbors, and one of the facts which had emerged was that they were not nomadic roamers, as is almost universally believed, but were settled beasts and the possessors of a large permanent estate with very definite boundaries.

The territory owned by my wolf family comprised more than a hundred square miles, bounded on one side by a river but otherwise not delimited by geographical features. Nevertheless there *were* boundaries, clearly indicated in wolfish fashion.

Anyone who has observed a dog doing his neighborhood rounds and leaving his personal mark on each convenient post will have already guessed how the wolves marked out *their* property. Once a week, more or less, the clan made the rounds of the family lands and freshened up the boundary markers—a sort of lupine beating of the bounds. This careful attention to property rights was perhaps made necessary by the presence of two other wolf families whose lands abutted on ours, although I never discovered any evidence of bickering or disagreements between the owners of the various adjoining estates. I suspect, therefore, that it was more of a ritual activity.

In any event, once I had become aware of the strong feeling of property rights which existed amongst the wolves, I decided to use this knowledge to make them at least recognize my existence. One evening, after they had gone off for their regular nightly hunt, I staked out a property claim of my own, embracing perhaps three acres, with the tent at the middle, and *including a hundred-yard-long section of the wolves' path.*

Staking the land turned out to be rather more difficult than I had anticipated. In order to ensure that my claim would not be overlooked, I felt obliged
to make a property mark on stones, clumps of moss, and patches of vegetation
at intervals of not more than fifteen feet around the circumference of my
claim. This took most of the night and required frequent returns to the tent to
consume copious quantities of tea; but before dawn brought the hunters home
the task was done, and I retired, somewhat exhausted, to observe results.

I had not long to wait. At 0814 hours, according to my wolf log, the leading
male of the clan appeared over the ridge behind me, padding homeward with
his usual air of preoccupation. As usual he did not deign to glance at the tent;
but when he reached the point where my property line intersected the trail, he
stopped as abruptly as if he had run into an invisible wall. He was only fifty
yards from me and with my binoculars I could see his expression very clearly.

His attitude of fatigue vanished and was replaced by a look of bewilderment.
Cautiously he extended his nose and sniffed at one of my marked bushes. He
did not seem to know what to make of it or what to do about it. After a minute
of complete indecision he backed away a few yards and sat down. And then, finally, he looked directly at the tent and at me. It was a long, thoughtful, considering sort of look.

Having achieved my object—that of forcing at least one of the wolves to
take cognizance of my existence—I now began to wonder if, in my ignorance,
I had transgressed some unknown wolf law of major importance and would
have to pay for my temerity. I found myself regretting the absence of a weapon
as the look I was getting became longer, yet more thoughtful, and still more
intent.

I began to grow decidedly fidgety, for I dislike staring matches, and in this   15
particular case I was up against a master, whose yellow glare seemed to become more baleful as I attempted to stare him down.

The situation was becoming intolerable. In an effort to break the impasse I
loudly cleared my throat and turned my back on the wolf (for a tenth of a second) to indicate as clearly as possible that I found his continued scrutiny impo-
lite, if not actually offensive.

He appeared to take the hint. Getting to his feet he had another sniff at my
marker, and then he seemed to make up his mind. Briskly, and with an air of
decision, he turned his attention away from me and began a systematic tour of
the area I had staked out as my own. As he came to each boundary marker he
sniffed it once or twice, then carefully placed *his* mark on the outside of each
clump of grass or stone. As I watched I saw where I, in my ignorance, had
erred. He made his mark with such economy that he was able to complete the
entire circuit without having to reload once, or, to change the simile slightly,
he did it all on one tank of fuel.

The task completed—and it had taken him no longer than fifteen minutes—he rejoined the path at the point where it left my property and trotted off
towards his home—leaving me with a good deal to occupy my thoughts.

QUESTIONS

1. What did you know about wolves before reading this piece? What was the most surprising—or amusing—information you acquired from reading about Mowat's experience?

2. Write a paragraph summarizing the information about wolves that you can infer from this selection.

3. How would you describe the narrator of this piece? What does he tell us about himself, and how do his actions describe him?

4. Mowat concludes by saying that he was left "with a good deal to occupy my thoughts" (paragraph 18). What, do you suppose, were those thoughts?

5. Find a more objective, "scientific" account of wolves. Which of Mowat's observations are substantiated there?

6. Rewrite the main events in this piece from the wolf's point of view.

7. Observe the actions of a dog or cat as it roams your neighborhood. Write an objective report of the animal's actions. Conclude with your reactions to the animal's behavior and, if pertinent, the animal's reactions to your behavior.

MAKING CONNECTIONS

1. Several of the essays in this section deal with the intricacies of placing humans in relation to specific animals and not only observing but sometimes interfering with their lives. Consider the essays by Jane van Lawick-Goodall (p. 241) and Loren Eiseley (p. 138) as well as this one by Mowat. Then, choosing two essays, compare the degrees of intervention taken by the writers and how that intervention affects the stories they tell.

2. Compare and contrast the similarities and differences in procedure of Mowat's study of wolves and Jane van Lawick-Goodall's study of chimpanzees (p. 241).

FIRST OBSERVATIONS
Jane van Lawick-Goodall

Jane van Lawick-Goodall (b. 1934), British student of animal behavior, began her work as an assistant to Louis Leakey, an anthropologist and paleontologist who has studied human origins. In 1960, with his help, she settled in Tanzania, East Africa, in the Gombe Stream Game Reserve to investigate the behavior of chimpanzees in their natural habitat. Her discoveries have been widely published in professional journals and in a number of books for more general audiences, including Through a Window: My Thirty Years with the Chimpanzees of Gombe *(1990). The selection reprinted here is taken from* In the Shadow of Man *(1971), a popular work in which she is careful to report her own behavior as well as that of her chimpanzee subjects.*

For about a month I spent most of each day either on the Peak or overlooking Mlinda Valley where the chimps, before or after stuffing themselves with figs, ate large quantities of small purple fruits that tasted, like so many of their foods, as bitter and astringent as sloes or crab apples. Piece by piece, I began to form my first somewhat crude picture of chimpanzee life.

The impression that I had gained when I watched the chimps at the msulula tree of temporary, constantly changing associations of individuals within the community was substantiated. Most often I saw small groups of four to eight moving about together. Sometimes I saw one or two chimpanzees leave such a group and wander off on their own or join up with a different association. On other occasions I watched two or three small groups joining to form a larger one.

Often, as one group crossed the grassy ridge separating the Kasekela Valley from the fig trees on the home valley, the male chimpanzee, or chimpanzees, of the party would break into a run, sometimes moving in an upright position, sometimes dragging a fallen branch, sometimes stamping or slapping the hard earth. These charging displays were always accompanied by loud pant-hoots and afterward the chimpanzee frequently would swing up into a tree overlooking the valley he was about to enter and sit quietly, peering down and obviously listening for a response from below. If there were chimps feeding in the fig trees they nearly always hooted back, as though in answer. Then the new arrivals would hurry down the steep slope and, with more calling and screaming, the two groups would meet in the fig trees. When groups of females and youngsters with no males present joined other feeding chimpanzees, usually there was none of this excitement; the newcomers merely climbed up into the trees, greeted some of those already there, and began to stuff themselves with figs.

While many details of their social behavior were hidden from me by the foliage, I did get occasional fascinating glimpses. I saw one female, newly arrived in a group, hurry up to a big male and hold her hand toward him. Almost regally he reached out, clasped her hand in his, drew it toward him, and kissed it with his lips. I saw two adult males embrace each other in greeting. I saw youngsters having wild games through the treetops, chasing around after each other or jumping again and again, one after the other, from a branch to a springy bough below. I watched small infants dangling happily by themselves for minutes on end, patting at their toes with one hand, rotating gently from side to side. Once two tiny infants pulled on opposite ends of a twig in a gentle tug-of-war. Often, during the heat of midday or after a long spell of feeding, I saw two or more adults grooming each other, carefully looking through the hair of their companions.

At that time of year the chimps usually went to bed late, making their nests   5 when it was too dark to see properly through binoculars, but sometimes they nested earlier and I could watch them from the Peak. I found that every individual, except for infants who slept with their mothers, made his own nest each night. Generally this took about three minutes: the chimp chose a firm foundation such as an upright fork or crotch, or two horizontal branches. Then he reached out and bent over smaller branches onto this foundation, keeping each one in place with his feet. Finally he tucked in the small leafy twigs growing around the rim of his nest and lay down. Quite often a chimp sat up after a few minutes and picked a handful of leafy twigs, which he put under his head or some other part of his body before settling down again for the night. One young female I watched went on and on bending down branches until she had constructed a huge mound of greenery on which she finally curled up.

I climbed up into some of the nests after the chimpanzees had left them. Most of them were built in trees that for me were almost impossible to climb. I found that there was quite complicated interweaving of the branches in some of them. I found, too, that the nests were fouled with dung; and later, when I was able to get closer to the chimps, I saw how they were always careful to defecate and urinate over the edge of their nests, even in the middle of the night.

During that month I really came to know the country well, for I often went on expeditions from the Peak, sometimes to examine nests, more frequently to collect specimens of the chimpanzees' food plants, which Bernard Verdcourt had kindly offered to identify for me. Soon I could find my way around the sheer ravines and up and down the steep slopes of three valleys—the home valley, the Pocket, and Mlinda Valley—as well as a taxi driver finds his way about in the main streets and byways of London. It is a period I remember vividly, not only because I was beginning to accomplish something at last, but also because of the delight I felt in being completely by myself. For those who love to be alone with nature I need add nothing further; for those who do not, no words of mine could ever convey, even in part, the almost mystical awareness of beauty and eternity that accompanies certain treasured moments. And, though the beauty was always there, those moments came upon me unaware: when I was watching the pale flush preceding dawn; or looking up through the rustling leaves of some giant forest tree into the greens and browns and black shadows that occasionally ensnared a bright fleck of the blue sky; or when I stood, as darkness fell, with one hand on the still-warm trunk of a tree and looked at the sparkling of an early moon on the never still, sighing water of the lake.

One day, when I was sitting by the trickle of water in Buffalo Wood, pausing for a moment in the coolness before returning from a scramble in Mlinda Valley, I saw a female bushbuck moving slowly along the nearly dry streambed. Occasionally she paused to pick off some plant and crunch it. I kept absolutely still, and she was not aware of my presence until she was little more than ten yards away. Suddenly she tensed and stood staring at me, one small forefoot raised. Because I did not move, she did not know what I was—only that my outline was somehow strange. I saw her velvet nostrils dilate as she sniffed the air, but I was downwind and her nose gave her no answer. Slowly she came closer, and closer—one step at a time, her neck craned forward—always poised for instant flight. I can still scarcely believe that her nose actually touched my knee; yet if I close my eyes I can feel again, in imagination, the warmth of her breath and the silken impact of her skin. Unexpectedly I blinked and she was gone in a flash, bounding away with loud barks of alarm until the vegetation hid her completely from my view.

It was rather different when, as I was sitting on the Peak, I saw a leopard coming toward me, his tail held up straight. He was at a slightly lower level than I, and obviously had no idea I was there. Ever since arrival in Africa I had had an ingrained, illogical fear of leopards. Already, while working at the Gombe, I had several times nearly turned back when, crawling through some thick undergrowth, I had suddenly smelled the rank smell of cat. I had forced myself on, telling myself that my fear was foolish, that only wounded leopards charged humans with savage ferocity.

On this occasion, though, the leopard went out of sight as it started to climb up the hill—the hill on the peak of which I sat. I quickly hastened to climb a tree, but halfway there I realized that leopards can climb trees. So I uttered a sort of halfhearted squawk. The leopard, my logical mind told me, would be just as frightened of me if he knew I was there. Sure enough, there was a thudding of startled feet and then silence. I returned to the Peak, but the feeling of unseen eyes watching me was too much. I decided to watch for the chimps in Mlinda Valley. And, when I returned to the Peak several hours later, there, on the very rock which had been my seat, was a neat pile of leopard dung. He

10

must have watched me go and then, very carefully, examined the place where such a frightening creature had been and tried to exterminate my alien scent with his own.

As the weeks went by the chimpanzees became less and less afraid. Quite often when I was on one of my food-collecting expeditions I came across chimpanzees unexpectedly, and after a time I found that some of them would tolerate my presence provided they were in fairly thick forest and I sat still and did not try to move closer than sixty to eighty yards. And so, during my second month of watching from the Peak, when I saw a group settle down to feed I sometimes moved closer and was thus able to make more detailed observations.

It was at this time that I began to recognize a number of different individuals. As soon as I was sure of knowing a chimpanzee if I saw it again, I named it. Some scientists feel that animals should be labeled by numbers—that to name them is anthropomorphic—but I have always been interested in the *differences* between individuals, and a name is not only more individual than a number but also far easier to remember. Most names were simply those which, for some reason or other, seemed to suit the individuals to whom I attached them. A few chimps were named because some facial expression or mannerism reminded me of human acquaintances.

The easiest individual to recognize was old Mr. McGregor. The crown of his head, his neck, and his shoulders were almost entirely devoid of hair, but a slight frill remained around his head rather like a monk's tonsure. He was an old male—perhaps between thirty and forty years of age (the longevity record of a captive chimp is forty-seven years). During the early months of my acquaintance with him, Mr. McGregor was somewhat belligerent. If I accidentally came across him at close quarters he would threaten me with an upward and backward jerk of his head and a shaking of branches before climbing down and vanishing from my sight. He reminded me, for some reason, of Beatrix Potter's old gardener in *The Tale of Peter Rabbit*.

Ancient Flo with her deformed, bulbous nose and ragged ears was equally easy to recognize. Her youngest offspring at that time were two-year-old Fifi, who still rode everywhere on her mother's back, and her juvenile son, Figan, who was always to be seen wandering around with his mother and little sister. He was then about six years old; it was approximately a year before he would attain puberty. Flo often traveled with another old mother, Olly. Olly's long face was also distinctive; the fluff of hair on the back of her head—though no other feature—reminded me of my aunt, Olwen. Olly, like Flo, was accompanied by two children, a daughter younger than Fifi, and an adolescent son about a year older than Figan.

Then there was William, who, I am certain, must have been Olly's blood brother. I never saw any special signs of friendship between them, but their faces were amazingly alike. They both had long upper lips that wobbled when they suddenly turned their heads. William had the added distinction of several thin, deeply etched scar marks running down his upper lip from his nose.

Two of the other chimpanzees I knew well by sight at that time were David Graybeard and Goliath. Like David and Goliath in the Bible, these two individuals were closely associated in my mind because they were very often together. Goliath, even in those days of his prime, was not a giant, but he had a splendid physique and the springy movements of an athlete. He probably weighed about one hundred pounds. David Graybeard was less afraid of me from the start than were any of the other chimps. I was always pleased when I picked out his handsome face and well-marked silvery beard in a chimpanzee group, for with David to calm the others, I had a better chance of approaching to observe them more closely.

Before the end of my trial period in the field I made two really exciting discoveries—discoveries that made the previous months of frustration well worth while. And for both of them I had David Graybeard to thank.

One day I arrived on the Peak and found a small group of chimps just below me in the upper branches of a thick tree. As I watched I saw that one of them was holding a pink-looking object from which he was from time to time pulling pieces with his teeth. There was a female and a youngster and they were both reaching out toward the male, their hands actually touching his mouth. Presently the female picked up a piece of the pink thing and put it to her mouth: it was at this moment that I realized the chimps were eating meat.

After each bite of meat the male picked off some leaves with his lips and chewed them with the flesh. Often, when he had chewed for several minutes on this leafy wad, he spat out the remains into the waiting hands of the female. Suddenly he dropped a small piece of meat, and like a flash the youngster swung after it to the ground. Even as he reached to pick it up the undergrowth exploded and an adult bushpig charged toward him. Screaming, the juvenile leaped back into the tree. The pig remained in the open, snorting and moving backward and forward. Soon I made out the shapes of three small striped piglets. Obviously the chimps were eating a baby pig. The size was right and later, when I realized that the male was David Graybeard, I moved closer and saw that he was indeed eating piglet.

For three hours I watched the chimps feeding. David occasionally let the female bite pieces from the carcass and once he actually detached a small piece of flesh and placed it in her outstretched hand. When he finally climbed down there was still meat left on the carcass; he carried it away in one hand, followed by the others. [20]

Of course I was not sure, then, that David Graybeard had caught the pig for himself, but even so, it was tremendously exciting to know that these chimpanzees actually ate meat. Previously scientists had believed that although these apes might occasionally supplement their diet with a few insects or small rodents and the like they were primarily vegetarians and fruit eaters. No one had suspected that they might hunt larger mammals.

It was within two weeks of this observation that I saw something that excited me even more. By then it was October and the short rains had begun. The blackened slopes were softened by feathery new grass shoots and in some places the ground was carpeted by a variety of flowers. The Chimpanzees' Spring, I called it. I had had a frustrating morning, tramping up and down three valleys with never a sign or sound of a chimpanzee. Hauling myself up the steep slope of Mlinda Valley I headed for the Peak, not only weary but soaking wet from crawling through dense undergrowth. Suddenly I stopped, for I saw a slight movement in the long grass about sixty yards away. Quickly focusing my binoculars I saw that it was a single chimpanzee, and just then he turned in my direction. I recognized David Graybeard.

Cautiously I moved around so that I could see what he was doing. He was squatting beside the red earth mound of a termite nest, and as I watched I saw him carefully push a long grass stem down into a hole in the mound. After a moment he withdrew it and picked something from the end with his mouth. I was too far away to make out what he was eating, but it was obvious that he was actually using a grass stem as a tool.

I knew that on two occasions casual observers in West Africa had seen chimpanzees using objects as tools: one had broken open palm-nut kernels by using a rock as a hammer, and a group of chimps had been observed pushing sticks into an underground bees' nest and licking off the honey. Somehow I had never dreamed of seeing anything so exciting myself.

For an hour David feasted at the termite mound and then he wandered slowly away. When I was sure he had gone I went over to examine the mound. I found a few crushed insects strewn about, and a swarm of worker termites sealing the entrances of the nest passages into which David had obviously been poking his stems. I picked up one of his discarded tools and carefully pushed it into a hole myself. Immediately I felt the pull of several termites as they seized the grass, and when I pulled it out there were a number of worker termites and a few soldiers, with big red heads, clinging on with their mandibles. There they remained, sticking out at right angles to the stem with their legs waving in the air.

Before I left I trampled down some of the tall dry grass and constructed a rough hide—just a few palm fonds leaned up against the low branch of a tree and tied together at the top. I planned to wait there the next day. But it was another week before I was able to watch a chimpanzee "fishing" for termites again. Twice chimps arrived, but each time they saw me and moved off immediately. Once a swarm of fertile winged termites—the princes and princesses, as they are called—flew off on their nuptial flight, their huge white wings fluttering frantically as they carried the insects higher and higher. Later I realized that it is at this time of year, during the short rains, when the worker termites extend the passages of the nest to the surface, preparing for these emigrations. Several such swarms emerge between October and January. It is principally during these months that the chimpanzees feed on termites.

On the eighth day of my watch David Graybeard arrived again, together with Goliath, and the pair worked there for two hours. I could see much better: I observed how they scratched open the sealed-over passage entrances with a thumb or forefinger. I watched how they bit the end off their tools when they became bent, or used the other end, or discarded them in favor of new ones. Goliath once moved at least fifteen yards from the heap to select a firm-looking piece of vine, and both males often picked three or four stems while they were collecting tools, and put the spares beside them on the ground until they wanted them.

Most exciting of all, on several occasions they picked small leafy twigs and prepared them for use by stripping off the leaves. This was the first recorded example of a wild animal not merely *using* an object as a tool, but actually modifying an object and thus showing the crude beginnings of tool*making*.

Previously man had been regarded as the only tool-making animal. Indeed, one of the clauses commonly accepted in the definition of man was that he was a creature who "made tools to a regular and set pattern." The chimpanzees, obviously, had not made tools to any set pattern. Nevertheless, my early observations of their primitive toolmaking abilities convinced a number of scientists that it was necessary to redefine man in a more complex manner than before. Or else, as Louis Leakey put it, we should by definition have to accept the chimpanzee as Man.

QUESTIONS

1. This essay is an example, principally, of reporting; that is, it is a gathering of facts by a clearheaded, unbiased observer. Identify passages in the essay in which this kind of reporting clearly takes place.

2. Although van Lawick-Goodall, in the main, is a neutral observer of chimpanzee behavior, that neutrality is in fact impossible in any absolute sense. It is clear that she writes, for example, with an eye always on comparisons of chimpanzee and human behavior. Make a list of words, just from paragraphs 3 and 4, that reveal that particular bias.

3. Describe how van Lawick-Goodall's comparison of chimpanzee with human behavior becomes increasingly prominent in the course of her essay.

4. Paraphrase the last discovery van Lawick-Goodall reports toward the end of her essay. What, exactly, was her contribution to science in this instance? What other activities, described earlier in the piece, make that discovery understandable, perhaps even unsurprising once we come to it?

5. What do you make of the choice outlined in paragraph 29? Which choice do you suppose the scientists made? Why?

6. Van Lawick-Goodall's scientific work resembles that of an anthropologist in that she goes into the field to observe the behavior of another social group. Even from this short piece we can learn a good deal about the practices and the way of life of such a worker in the field. Describe van Lawick-Goodall's life in the field as best you can, making whatever inferences you can from this single essay.

7. Amplify your description of van Lawick-Goodall's life in the field, done for question 6, by reading whatever articles you can find that tell more about her and about her work.

8. Place yourself somewhere and observe behavior more or less as van Lawick-Goodall does. You might observe wildlife—pigeons, sparrows, crows, squirrels, or whatever is available—or you might observe some aspect of human behavior. If you choose the latter, look for behavior that is unfamiliar to you, such as that of children at play, of workers on the job, or of members of a social group very different from your own. Write a report detailing your observations.

9. After you have completed question 8, write a second, shorter report in which you comment on the nature of your task as an observer. Was it difficult to watch? Was it difficult to decide what was meaningful behavior? Did you influence what you saw so that you could not be confident that the behavior was representative? Looking back on your experience as a field worker, what else seems questionable to you now?

10. One of the tools that van Lawick-Goodall lacks in her writing is the ability to interview relevant parties. Don't you imagine she would have liked to interview Mr. McGregor, Goliath, or David Graybeard? Imagine her doing so. What questions would she be likely to ask? What would you like to know from one of those individuals were you able to interview him? Write out the interview that you can imagine.

MAKING CONNECTIONS

1. Both van Lawick-Goodall and Farley Mowat (p. 237) study a specific kind of animal in its natural habitat. How are their procedures similar? How are they different? What kinds of refinement do they venture in their studies as they proceed? How do their procedures influence both their findings and their presentation of those findings?

2. Compare and contrast van Lawick-Goodall's account of observing the chimpanzees with Pico Iyer's observations of human beings at the Los Angeles International Airport (p. 249). To what extent are both writers ethnographers, studying and describing behavior in a specific society?

WHERE WORLDS COLLIDE
In Los Angeles International Airport, the Future Touches Down
Pico Iyer

Pico Iyer, a travel writer with a special interest in the hybrid cultures of East and West, was born in Oxford, England, in 1957 and immigrated to the United States in 1966. Educated at Eton, Oxford, and Harvard, he has turned his traveling and his cultural curiosity to account as an essayist for Time *magazine and a contributing editor at* Conde Nast Traveler. *Iyer is best known for his wide-ranging, vividly detailed collections of travel pieces,* Video Night in Kathmandu and Other Reports from the Not-So-Far East *(1988) and* Falling Off the Map: Some Lonely Places of the World *(1993), and* Tropical Classical: Essays from Several Directions *(1997). His interest in travel writing has also led him to produce an evocative novel,* Cuba and the Night *(1995), about contemporary life in Havana. The selection reprinted here was originally published in* Harper's *(August 1995).*

They come out, blinking, into the bleached, forgetful sunshine, in Dodgers caps and Rodeo Drive T-shirts, with the maps their cousins have drawn for them and the images they've brought over from *Cops* and *Terminator 2;* they come out, dazed, disoriented, heads still partly in the clouds, bodies still several time zones—or centuries—away, and they step into the Promised Land.

In front of them is a Van Stop, a Bus Stop, a Courtesy Tram Stop, and a Shuttle Bus Stop (the shuttles themselves tracing circuits A, B, and C). At the Shuttle Bus Stop, they see the All American Shuttle, the Apollo Shuttle, Celebrity Airport Livery, the Great American Stageline, the Movie Shuttle, the Transport, Ride-4-You, and forty-two other magic buses waiting to whisk them everywhere from Bakersfield to Disneyland. They see Koreans piling into the Taeguk Airport Shuttle and the Seoul Shuttle, which will take them to Koreatown without their ever feeling they've left home; they see newcomers from the Middle East disappearing under the Arabic script of the Sahara Shuttle. They see fast-talking, finger-snapping, palm-slapping jive artists straight from their TV screens shouting incomprehensible slogans about deals, destinations, and drugs. Over there is a block-long white limo, a Lincoln Continental, and, over there, a black Chevy Blazer with Mexican stickers all over its windows, being towed. They have arrived in the Land of Opportunity, and the opportunities are swirling dizzily, promiscuously, around them.

They have already braved the ranks of Asian officials, the criminal-looking security men in jackets that say "Elsinore Airport Services," the men shaking tins that say "Helping America's Hopeless." They have already seen the tilting mugs that say "California: a new slant on life" and the portable fruit machines in the gift shop. They have already, perhaps, visited the rest room where someone has written, "Yes on Proposition 187. Mexicans go home," the snack bar where a slice of pizza costs $3.19 (18 quetzals, they think in horror, or 35,000 dong), and the sign that urges them to try the Cockatoo Inn Grand Hotel. The latest arrivals at Los Angeles International Airport are ready now to claim their new lives.

Above them in the terminal, voices are repeating, over and over, in Japanese, Spanish, and unintelligible English, "Maintain visual contact with your personal property at all times." Out on the sidewalk, a man's voice and a woman's voice are alternating an unending refrain: "The white zone is for loading and unloading of passengers only. No parking." There are "Do Not Cross" yellow lines cordoning off parts of the sidewalk and "Wells Fargo Alarm Services" stickers on the windows; there are "Aviation Safeguard" signs on the baggage carts and "Beware of Solicitors" signs on the columns; there are even special phones "To Report Trouble." More male and female voices are intoning, continuously, "Do not leave your car unattended" and "Unattended cars are subject to immediate tow-away." There are no military planes on the tarmac here, the newcomers notice, no khaki soldiers in fatigues, no instructions not to take photographs, as at home; but there are civilian restrictions every bit as strict as in many a police state.

"This Terminal Is in a Medfly Quarantine Area," says the sign between the   5 terminals. "Stop the Spread of Medfly!" If, by chance, the new Americans have to enter a parking lot on their way out, they will be faced with "Cars left over 30 days may be impounded at Owner's Expense" and "Do not enter without a ticket." It will cost them $16 if they lose their parking ticket, they read, and $56 if they park in the wrong zone. Around them is an unending cacophony of antitheft devices, sirens, beepers, and car-door openers; lights are flashing everywhere, and the man who fines them $16 for losing their parking ticket has the tribal scars of Tigre across his forehead.

The blue skies and palm trees they saw on TV are scarcely visible from here: just an undifferentiated smoggy haze, billboards advertising Nissan and Panasonic and Canon, and beyond those an endlessly receding mess of gray streets. Overhead, they can see the all-too-familiar signs of Hilton and Hyatt and Holiday Inn; in the distance, a sea of tract houses, mini-malls, and highrises. The City of Angels awaits them.

It is a commonplace nowadays to say that cities look more and more like airports, cross-cultural spaces that are a gathering of tribes and races and variegated tongues; and it has always been true that airports are in many ways like miniature cities, whole, self-sufficient communities, with their own chapels and museums and gymnasiums. Not only have airports colored our speech (teaching us about being upgraded, bumped, and put on standby, coaching us in the ways of fly-by-night operations, holding patterns, and the Mile High Club); they have also taught us their own rules, their own codes, their own customs. We eat and sleep and shower in airports; we pray and weep and kiss there. Some people stay for days at a time in these perfectly convenient, hermetically sealed, climate-controlled duty-free zones, which offer a kind of caesura from the obligations of daily life.

Airports are also, of course, the new epicenters and paradigms of our dawning post-national age—not just the bus terminals of the global village but the prototypes, in some sense, for our polyglot, multicolored, user-friendly future. And in their very universality—like the mall, the motel, or the McDonald's outlet—they advance the notion of a future in which all the world's a multi-culture. If you believe that more and more of the world is a kind of mongrel hybrid in which many cities (Sydney, Toronto, Singapore) are simply suburbs of a single universal order, then Los Angeles's LAX, London's Heathrow, and Hong Kong's Kai Tak are merely stages on some great global Circle Line, shut-tling variations on a common global theme. Mass travel has made L.A. con-tiguous to Seoul and adjacent to São Paulo, and has made all of them now feel a little like bedroom communities for Tokyo.

And as with most social trends, especially the ones involving tomorrow, what is true of the world is doubly true of America, and what is doubly true of America is quadruply true of Los Angeles. L.A., legendarily, has more Thais than any city but Bangkok, more Koreans than any city but Seoul, more El Sal-vadorans than any city outside of San Salvador, more Druze than anywhere but Beirut; it is, at the very least, the easternmost outpost of Asia and the northern-most province of Mexico. When I stopped at a Traveler's Aid desk at LAX recently, I was told I could request help in Khamu, Mien, Tigrinya, Tajiki, Pashto, Dari, Pangasinan, Pampangan, Waray-Waray, Bambara, Twi, and Bicolano (as well, of course, as French, German, and eleven languages from India). LAX is as clear an image as exists today of the world we are about to enter, and of the world that's entering us.

For me, though, LAX has always had a more personal resonance: it was in   10
LAX that I arrived myself as a new immigrant, in 1966; and from the time I was in the fourth grade, it was to LAX that I would go three times a year, as an "unaccompanied minor," to fly to school in London—and to LAX that I re-turned three times a year for my holidays. Sometimes it seems as if I have spent half my life in LAX. For me, it is the site of my liberation (from school, from the Old World, from home) and the place where I came to design my own new future.

Often when I have set off from L.A. to some distant place—Havana, say, or Hanoi, or Pyongyana—I have felt that the multicultural drama on display in

251

LAX, the interaction of exoticism and familiarity, was just as bizarre as anything I would find when I arrived at my foreign destination. The airport is an Amy Tan novel, a short story by Bharati Mukherjee, a Henry James sketch set to an MTV beat; it is a cross-generational saga about Chang Hsieng meeting his daughter Cindy and finding that she's wearing a nose ring now and is shacked up with a surfer from Berlin. The very best kind of airport reading to be found in LAX these days is the triple-decker melodrama being played out all around one—a complex tragicomedy of love and war and exile, about people fleeing centuries-old rivalries and thirteenth-century mullahs and stepping out into a fresh, forgetful, born-again city that is rewriting its script every moment.

Not long ago I went to spend a week in LAX. I haunted the airport by day and by night, I joined the gloomy drinkers listening to air-control-tower instructions on earphones at the Proud Bird bar. I listened each morning to Airport Radio (530 AM), and I slept each night at the Airport Sheraton or the Airport Hilton. I lived off cellophaned crackers and Styrofoam cups of tea, browsed for hours among Best Actor statuettes and Beverly Hills magnets, and tried to see what kinds of America the city presents to the new Americans, who are remaking America each day.

It is almost too easy to say that LAX is a perfect metaphor for L.A., a flat, spaced-out desert kind of place, highly automotive, not deeply hospitable, with little reading matter and no organizing principle. (There are eight satellites without a center here, many international arrivals are shunted out into the bleak basement of Terminal 2, and there is no airline that serves to dominate LAX as Pan Am once did JFK.) Whereas "SIN" is a famously ironical airline code for Singapore, cathedral of puritanical rectitude, "LAX" has always seemed perilously well chosen for a city whose main industries were traditionally thought to be laxity and relaxation. LAX is at once a vacuum waiting to be colonized and a joyless theme park—Tomorrowland, Adventureland, and Fantasyland all at once.

The postcards on sale here (made in Korea) dutifully call the airport "one of the busiest and most beautiful air facilities in the world," and it is certainly true that LAX, with thirty thousand international arrivals each day—roughly the same number of tourists that have visited the Himalayan country of Bhutan in its entire history—is not uncrowded. But bigger is less and less related to better: in a recent survey of travel facilities, *Business Traveller* placed LAX among the five worst airports in the world for customs, luggage retrieval, and passport processing.

LAX is, in fact, a surprisingly shabby and hollowed-out kind of place, certainly not adorned with the amenities one might expect of the world's strongest and richest power. When you come out into the Arrivals area in the International Terminal, you will find exactly one tiny snack bar, which serves nine items; of them, five are identified as Cheese Dog, Chili Dog, Chili Cheese

Dog, Nachos with Cheese, and Chili Cheese Nachos. There is a large panel on the wall offering rental-car services and hotels, and the newly deplaned American dreamer can choose between the Cadillac Hotel, the Banana Bungalow (which offers a Basketball Court, "Free Toast," "Free Bed Sheets," and "Free Movies and Parties"), and the Backpacker's Paradise (with "Free Afternoon Tea and Crumpets" and "Free Evening Party Including Food and Champagne").

Around one in the terminal is a swirl of priests rattling cans, Iranians in suits brandishing pictures of torture victims, and Japanese girls in Goofy hats. "I'm looking for something called Clearasil," a distinguished-looking Indian man diffidently tells a cashier. "Clearasil?" shouts the girl. "For your face?"

Upstairs, in the Terrace Restaurant, passengers are gulping down "Dutch Chocolate" and "Japanese Coffee" while students translate back and forth between English and American, explaining that "soliciting" loses something of its cachet when you go across the Atlantic. A fat man is nuzzling the neck of his outrageously pretty Filipina companion, and a few Brits are staring doubtfully at the sign that assures them that seafood is "cheerfully served at your table!" Only in America, they are doubtless thinking. A man goes from table to table, plunking down on each one a key chain attached to a globe. As soon as an unsuspecting customer picks one up, touched by the largesse of the New World and convinced now that there *is* such a thing as a free lunch in America, the man appears again, flashes a sign that says "I Am a Deaf," and requests a dollar for the gift.

At a bank of phones, a saffron-robed monk gingerly inserts a credit card, while schoolkids page Jesse Jackson at the nearest "white courtesy telephone." One notable feature of the modern airport is that it is wired, with a vengeance: even in a tiny, two-urinal men's room, I found two telephones on offer; LAX bars rent out cellular phones; and in the Arrivals area, as you come out into the land of plenty, you face a bank of forty-six phones of every kind, with screens and buttons and translations, from which newcomers are calling direct to Bangalore or Baghdad. Airports are places for connections of all kinds and *loci classici*, perhaps for a world ruled by IDD and MCI, DOS and JAL.

Yet for all these grounding reminders of the world outside, everywhere I went in the airport I felt myself in an odd kind of twilight zone of consciousness, that weightless limbo of a world in which people are between lives and between selves, almost sleepwalking, not really sure of who or where they are. Light-headed from the trips they've taken, ears popping and eyes about to do so, under a potent foreign influence, people are at the far edge of themselves in airports, ready to break down or through. You see strangers pouring out their life stories to strangers here, or making new life stories with other strangers. Everything is at once intensified and slightly unreal. One L.A. psychiatrist advises shy women to practice their flirting here, and religious groups circle in the hope of catching unattached souls.

Airports, which often have a kind of perpetual morning-after feeling (the   20
end of the holiday, the end of the affair), are places where everyone is ruled by
the clock, but all the clocks show different times. These days, after all, we fly
not only into yesterday or this morning when we go across the world but into
different decades, often, of the world's life and our own: in ten or fifteen hours,
we are taken back into the twelfth century or into worlds we haven't seen since
childhood. And in the process we are subjected to transitions more jolting than
any imagined by Oscar Wilde or Sigmund Freud: if the average individual
today sees as many images in a day as a Victorian saw in a lifetime, the average
person today also has to negotiate switches between continents inconceivable
only fifty years ago. Frequent fliers like Ted Turner have actually become ill
from touching down and taking off so often; but, in less diagnosable ways, all
of us are being asked to handle difficult suspensions of the laws of Nature and
Society when moving between competing worlds.

This helps to compound the strange statelessness of airports, where all bets
are off and all laws are annulled—modern equivalents, perhaps, to the hundred yards of no-man's-land between two frontier crossings. In airports we are
often in dreamy, floating, out-of-body states, as ready to be claimed as that suitcase on Carousel C. Even I, not traveling, didn't know sometimes if I was
awake or asleep in LAX, as I heard an announcer intone, "John Cheever, John
Cheever, please contact a Northwest representative in the Baggage Claim area.
John Cheever, please contact a service representative at the Northwest Baggage
Claim area."

As I started to sink into this odd, amphibious, bipolar state, I could begin to
see why a place like LAX is a particular zone of fear, more terrifying to many
people than anywhere but the dentist's office. Though dying in a plane is, notoriously, twenty times less likely than dying in a car, every single airline crash
is front-page news and so dramatic—not a single death but three hundred—
that airports are for many people killing grounds. Their runways are associated
in the mind's (televisual) eye with hostages and hijackings; with bodies on the
tarmac or antiterrorist squads storming the plane.

That general sense of unsettledness is doubtless intensified by all the people
in uniform in LAX. There are ten different security agencies working the Tom
Bradley Terminal alone, and the streets outside are jam-packed with Airport
Police cars, FBI men, and black-clad airport policemen on bicycles. All of
them do as much, I suspect, to instill fear as to still it. "People are scared here,"
a gloomy Pakistani security guard told me, "because undercover are working.
Police are working. You could be undercover, I could be undercover. Who
knows?"

And just as L.A. is a province of the future in part because so many people
take it to be the future, so it is a danger zone precisely because it is imagined
to be dangerous. In Osaka's new $16 billion airport recently, I cross-examined
the Skynet computer (in the Departures area) about what to expect when arriving at LAX or any other foreign airport. "Guard against theft in the arrival

hall," it told me (and, presumably, even warier Japanese). "A thief is waiting for a chance to take advantage of you." Elsewhere it added, "Do not dress too touristy," and, "Be on your guard when approached by a group of suspicious-looking children, such as girls wearing bright-colored shirts and scarves." True to such dark prognostications, the side doors of the Airport Sheraton at LAX are locked every day from 8:00 P.M. to 6:00 A.M., and you cannot even activate the elevators without a room key. "Be extra careful in parking garages and stair-wells," the hotel advises visitors. "Always try to use the main entrance to your hotel, particularly late in the evening. Never answer your hotel room door without verifying who is there."

One reason airports enjoy such central status in our imaginations is that they play such a large part in forming our first (which is sometimes our last) impression of a place; this is the reason that poor countries often throw all their resources into making their airports sleek, with beautifully landscaped roads leading out of them into town. L.A., by contrast, has the bareness of arrogance, or simple inhospitality. Usually what you see as you approach the city is a grim penitential haze through which is visible nothing but rows of gray build-ings, a few dun-hued warehouses, and ribbons of dirty freeway: a no-colored blur without even the comforting lapis ornaments of the swimming pools that dot New York or Johannesburg. (Ideally, in fact, one should enter L.A. by night, when the whole city pulses like an electric grid of lights—or the back of a transistor radio, in Thomas Pynchon's inspired metaphor. While I was staying in LAX, Jackie Collins actually told *Los Angeles* magazine that "Flying in [to LAX] at night is just an orgasmic thrill.") You land, with a bump, on a mess of gray runways with no signs of welcome, a hangar that says "T ans W rld Air-lines," another broken sign that announces "Tom Bradl y International Ai port," and an air-control tower under scaffolding.

The first thing that greeted me on a recent arrival was a row of Asians sitting on the floor of the terminal, under a sign that told them of a $25,000 fine for bringing in the wrong kinds of food. As I passed through endless corridors, I was faced with almost nothing except long escalators (a surprisingly high per-centage of the accidents recorded at airports comes from escalators, bewilder-ing to newcomers) and bare hallways. The other surprise, for many of my fel-low travelers, no doubt, was that almost no one we saw looked like Robert Redford or Julia Roberts or, indeed, like anyone belonging to the race we'd been celebrating in our in-flight movies. As we passed into the huge, bare as-sembly hall that is the Customs and Immigration Center here, I was directed into one of the chaotic lines by a Noriko and formally admitted to the country by a C. Chen. The man waiting to transfer my baggage (as a beagle sniffed around us in a coat that said "Agriculture's Beagle Brigade" on one side and "Protecting American Agriculture" on the other) was named Yoji Yosaka. And the first sign I saw, when I stepped into America, was a big board being waved by the "Executive Sedan Service" for one "Mr. T. Ego."

25

For many immigrants, in fact, LAX is quietly offering them a view of their own near futures: the woman at the Host Coffee Shop is themselves, in a sense, two years from now, and the man sweeping up the refuse is the American dream in practice. The staff at the airport seems to be made up almost entirely of recent immigrants: on my very first afternoon there, I was served by a Hoa, an Ephraim, and a Glinda; the wait-people at a coffee shop in Terminal 5 were called Ignacio, Ever, Aura, and Erick. Even at the Airport Sheraton (where the employees all wear nameplates), I was checked in by Viera (from "Bratislavia") and ran into Hasmik and Yovik (from Ethiopia), Faye (from Vietnam), Ingrid (from Guatemala City), Khrystyne (from Long Beach, by way of Phnom Penh, I think), and Moe (from West L.A., she said). Many of the bright-eyed dreamers who arrive at LAX so full of hope never actually leave the place.

The deeper drama of any airport is that it features a kind of interaction almost unique in our lives, wherein many of us do not know whom we are going to meet or whom others are going to meet in us. You see people standing at the barriers outside the Customs area looking into their pasts, while wide-open newcomers drift out, searching for their futures. Lovers do not know if they will see the same person who kissed them good-bye a month ago; grandparents wonder what the baby they last saw twenty years ago will look like now.

In L.A. all of this has an added charge, because unlike many cities, it is not a hub but a terminus: a place where people come to arrive. Thus many of the meetings you witness are between the haves and the hope-to-haves, between those who are affecting a new ease in their new home and those who are here in search of that ease. Both parties, especially if they are un-American by birth, are eager to stress their Americanness or their fitness for America; and both, as they look at each other's made-up self, see themselves either before or after a stay in L.A.'s theater of transformation. And so they stream in, wearing running shoes or cowboy hats or 49ers jackets, anxious to make a good first impression; and the people who wait for them, under a halfhearted mural of Desertland, are often American enough not to try to look the part. Juan and Esperanza both have ponytails now, and Kimmie is wearing a Harley-Davidson cap backwards and necking with a Japanese guy; the uncle from Delhi arrives to find that Rajiv not only has grown darker but has lost weight, so that he looks more like a peasant from back home than ever.

And the newcomers pour in in astonishing numbers. A typical Sunday 30 evening, in a single hour, sees flights arriving from England, Taiwan, the Philippines, Indonesia, Mexico, Austria, Germany, Spain, Costa Rica, and Guatemala; and each new group colors and transforms the airport: an explosion of tropical shades from Hawaiian Air, a rash of blue blazers and white shirts around the early flight from Tokyo. Red-haired Thais bearing pirated Schwarzenegger videos, lonely Africans in Aerial Assault sneakers, farmers from changeless Confucian cultures peering into the smiles of a Prozac city, children whose parents can't pronounce their names. Many of them are returning, like Odysseus, with the spoils of war: young brides from Luzon, business cards from Shanghai, boxes of macadamia nuts from Oahu. And for many of them the whole wild carnival will feature sights they have never seen before: Japanese look anxiously at the first El Salvadorans they've ever seen, and El Salvadorans ogle sleek girls from Bangkok in thigh-high boots. All of them, moreover, may not be pleased to realize that the America they've dreamed of is, in fact, a land of tacos and pita and pad thai—full, indeed, of the very Third World cultures that other Third Worlders look down upon.

One day over lunch I asked my Ethiopian waitress about her life here. She liked it well enough, she said, but still she missed her home. And yet, she added, she couldn't go back. "Why not?" I asked, still smiling. "Because they killed my family," she said. "Two years back. They killed my father. They killed my brother." "They," I realized, referred to the Tigreans—many of them working just down the corridor in other parts of the hotel. So, too, Tibetans who have finally managed to flee their Chinese-occupied homeland arrive at LAX to find Chinese faces everywhere; those who fled the Sandinistas find themselves standing next to Sandinistas fleeing their successors. And all these people from ancient cultures find themselves in a country as amnesiac as the morning, where World War II is just a rumor and the Gulf War a distant memory. Their pasts are escaped, yes, but by the same token they are unlikely to be honored.

It is dangerously tempting to start formulating socioeconomic principles in the midst of LAX: people from rich countries (Germany and Japan, say) travel light, if only because they are sure that they can return any time; those from poor countries come with their whole lives in cardboard boxes imperfectly tied with string. People from poor countries are often met by huge crowds—for them each arrival is a special occasion—and stagger through customs with string bags and Gold Digger apple crates, their addresses handwritten on them in pencil; the Okinawan honeymooners, by contrast, in the color-coordinated outfits they will change every day, somehow have packed all their needs into a tiny case.

If airports have some of the excitement of bars, because so many people are composing (and decomposing) selves there, they also have some of the sadness of bars, the poignancy of people sitting unclaimed while everyone around them has paired off. A pretty girl dressed in next to nothing sits alone in an empty Baggage Claim area, waiting for a date who never comes; a Vietnamese man, lost, tells an official that he has friends in Orange County who can help him, but when the friends are contacted, they say they know no one from Vietnam. I hear of a woman who got off and asked for "San Mateo," only to learn that she was meant to disembark in San Francisco; and a woman from Nigeria who came out expecting to see her husband in Monroe, Louisiana, only to learn that someone in Lagos had mistaken "La." on her itinerary for "L.A."

The greetings I saw in the Arrivals area were much more tentative than I had expected, less passionate—as ritualized in their way as the kisses placed on

Bob Barker's cheek—and much of that may be because so many people are meeting strangers, even if they are meeting people they once knew. Places like LAX—places like L.A.—perpetuate the sense that everyone is a stranger in our new floating world. I spent one afternoon in the airport with a Californian blonde, and I saw her complimented on her English by a sweet Korean woman and asked by an Iranian if she was Indian. Airports have some of the unsteady brashness of singles bars, where no one knows quite what is expected of them. "Mike, is that you?" "Oh, I didn't recognize you." "I'd have known you anywhere." "It's so kind of you to come and pick me up." And already at a loss, a young Japanese girl and a broad, lonely-looking man head off toward the parking lot, not knowing, in any sense, who is going to be in the driver's seat.

The driving takes place, of course, in what many of the newcomers, primed   35
by video screenings of *L.A. Law* and *Speed*, regard as the ultimate heart of darkness, a place at least as forbidding and dangerous as Africa must have seemed to the Victorians. They have heard about how America is the murder capital of the world; they have seen Rodney King get pummeled by L.A.'s finest; they know of the city as the site of drive-by shootings and freeway snipers, of riots and celebrity murders. The "homeless" and the "tempest-tost" that the Statue of Liberty invites are arriving, increasingly, in a city that is itself famous for its homeless population and its fires, floods, and earthquakes.

In that context, the ideal symbol of LAX is, perhaps, the great object that for thirty years has been the distinctive image of the place: the ugly white quadruped that sits in the middle of the airport like a beached white whale or a jet-age beetle, featuring a 360-degree circular restaurant that does not revolve and an observation deck from which the main view is of twenty-three thousand parking places. The Theme Building, at 201 World Way, is a sad image of a future that never arrived, a monument to Kennedy-era idealism and the thrusting modernity of the American empire when it was in its prime; it now has the poignancy of an abandoned present with its price tag stuck to it. When you go there (and almost nobody does) you are greeted by photos of Saturn's rings and Jupiter and its moons, by a plaque laid down by L.B.J. and a whole set of symbols from the time when NASA was shooting for the heavens. Now the "landmark" building, with its "gourmet-type restaurant," looks like a relic from a time long past, when it must have looked like the face of the future.

Upstairs, a few desperately merry waiters are serving nonalcoholic drinks and cheeseburgers to sallow diners who look as if they've arrived at the end of the world; on the tarmac outside, speedbirds inch ahead like cars in a traffic jam. "Hello All the New People of LAX—Welcome," says the graffiti on the elevator.

The Theme Restaurant comes to us from an era when L.A. was leading the world. Nowadays, of course, L.A. is being formed and reformed and led by the world around it. And as I got ready to leave LAX, I could not help but feel that the Theme Building stands, more and more, for a city left behind by our accelerating planet. LAX, I was coming to realize, was a good deal scruffier than the airports even of Bangkok or Jakarta, more chaotic, more suggestive of Third World lawlessness. And the city around it is no more golden than Seoul, no more sunny than Taipei, and no more laid-back than Moscow. Beverly Hills, after all, is largely speaking Farsi now. Hollywood Boulevard is sleazier than 42nd Street. And Malibu is falling into the sea.

Yet just as I was about to give up on L.A. as yesterday's piece of modernity, I got on the shuttle bus that moves between the terminals in a never-ending loop. The seats next to me were taken by two rough-looking dudes from nearby South Central, who were riding the free buses and helping people on and off with their cases (acting, I presumed, on the safe assumption that the Japanese, say, new to the country and bewildered, had been warned beforehand to tip often and handsomely for every service they received). In between terminals, as a terrified-looking Miss Kudo and her friend guarded their luggage, en route from Nagoya to Las Vegas, the two gold-plated sharks talked about the Raiders' last game and the Lakers' next season. Then one of them, without warning, announced, "The bottom line is the spirit is with you. When you work out, you chill out and, like, you meditate in your spirit. You know what I mean? Meditation is recreation. Learn math, follow your path. That's all I do, man, that's all I live for: learnin' about God, learnin' about Jesus. I am *possessed* by that spirit. You know, I used to have all these problems, with the flute and all, but when I heard about God, I learned about the body, the mind, and the flesh. People forget, they don't know, that the Bible isn't talkin' about the flesh, it's talkin' about the spirit. And I was reborn again in the spirit."

His friend nodded. "When you recreate, you meditate. Recreation is a spiritually uplifting experience." 40

"Yeah. When you do that, you allow the spirit to breathe."

"Because you're gettin' into the physical world. You're lettin' the spirit flow. You're helpin' the secretion of the endorphins in the brain."

Nearby, the Soldiers of the Cross of Christ Church stood by the escalators, taking donations, and a man in a dog collar approached another stranger.

I watched the hustlers allowing the spirit to breathe, I heard the Hare Krishna devotees plying their wares. I spotted some Farrakhan flunkies collecting a dollar for a copy of their newspaper, *The Final Call*—redemption and corruption all around us in the air—and I thought: welcome to America, Miss Kudo, welcome to L.A.

QUESTIONS

1. What do you think Iyer means by his main title? By his subtitle? In what sense is he writing about the collision of worlds rather than a single world? In what respect is he writing about the future rather than the present?

2. Notice how strangely this piece begins, with a vague pronoun (*They*) and an equally vague verb (*come out*). Who is Iyer referring to? Where are they coming from?

Why do you think he writes about "they" and "them" at such length without ever explicitly identifying them in detail?

3. In paragraph 12, Iyer says that he spent a week at the Los Angeles International Airport. What evidence can you find in the essay of his having carried out such a lengthy and in-depth observation of the airport? Why do you suppose he doesn't offer a day-by-day, increasingly more in-depth report of his airport observations? How would you describe or classify the organization of his piece?

4. Though this piece is about a specific place, Iyer never describes the airport building, or its physical layout, or its surrounding landscape and runways. What aspects of the place or its inhabitants does he describe in sufficient detail for you to visualize them in your mind's eye?

5. Aside from the physical details of the airport, what other aspects of it is Iyer concerned with in this piece? In other words, what are his purposes for writing this detailed report about LAX?

6. Spend a couple of days at an airport, railroad station, or bus terminal near your hometown or college. Then writ an essay reporting what you have discovered about that place, the people you observed there, the worlds that seem to collide in that place, and the significance for you of those collisions.

7. Consider your college campus as a place "where worlds collide." Then write an essay reporting and interpreting some of the collisions you've observed there.

MAKING CONNECTIONS

1. Compare Iyer's method of observing and reporting human behavior at the airport with Farley Mowat's or Jane van Lawick-Goodall's method of observing and reporting animal behavior in the wild (pp. 237 and 241).

2. Iyer's essay on worlds colliding at the airport and Marc Shell's essay on "Babel in America" (p. 445) are both concerned with manifestations of cultural diversity in the United States. In what respects do they offer overlapping or reinforcing information and interpretations? In what respects might they disagree or diverge from each other?

Sciences and Technologies

LOVE CANAL AND
THE POISONING OF AMERICA
Michael Brown

Michael Brown (b. 1952) is a freelance writer interested in environmental issues. His investigations into the dumping of toxic waste, which have appeared in newspaper and magazine articles, have won him three Pulitzer Prize nominations and a special award from the Environmental Protection Agency. He has authored several books including The Toxic Cloud: Poisoning of America's Air *(1988) and* Laying Waste: The Poisoning of America by Toxic Chemicals *(1980), from which this essay is taken.*

Niagara Falls is a city of unmatched natural beauty; it is also a tired industrial workhorse, beaten often and with a hard hand. A magnificent river—a strait, really—connecting Lake Erie to Lake Ontario flows hurriedly north, at a pace of a half-million tons a minute, widening into a smooth expanse near the city before breaking into whitecaps and taking its famous 186-foot plunge. Then it cascades through a gorge of overhung shale and limestone to rapids higher and swifter than anywhere else on the continent.

The falls attract long lines of newlyweds and other tourists. At the same time, the river provides cheap electricity for industry; a good stretch of its shore is now filled with the spiraled pipes of distilleries, and the odors of chlorine and sulfides hang in the air.

Many who live in the city of Niagara Falls work in chemical plants, the largest of which is owned by the Hooker Chemical Company, a subsidiary of Occidental Petroleum since the 1960s. Timothy Schroeder did not. He was a cement technician by trade, dealing with the factories only if they needed a pathway poured, or a small foundation set. Tim and his wife, Karen, lived in a ranch-style home with a brick and wood exterior at 460 99th Street. One of the Schroeder's most cherished purchases was a Fiberglas pool, built into the ground and enclosed by a red-wood fence.

261

Karen looked from a back window one morning in October 1974, noting with distress that the pool had suddenly risen two feet above the ground. She called Tim to tell him about it. Karen then had no way of knowing that this was the first sign of what would prove to be a punishing family and economic tragedy.

Mrs. Schroeder believed that the cause of the uplift was the unusual groundwater flow of the area. Twenty-one years before, an abandoned hydro-electric canal directly behind their house had been backfilled with industrial rubble. The underground breaches created by this disturbance, aided by the marshland nature of the region's surficial layer, collected large volumes of rain-fall and undermined the back yard. The Schroeders allowed the pool to remain in its precarious position until the following summer and then pulled it from the ground, intending to pour a new pool, cast in cement. This they were unable to do, for the gaping excavation immediately filled with what Karen called "chemical water," rancid liquids of yellow and orchid and blue. These same chemicals had mixed with the groundwater and flooded the entire yard, attacking the redwood posts with such a caustic bite that one day the fence simply collapsed. When the chemicals receded in the dry weather, they left the gardens and shrubs withered and scorched, as if by a brush fire.

How the chemicals got there was no mystery. In the late 1930s, or perhaps early 1940s, the Hooker Company, whose many processes included the manu-facture of pesticides, plasticizers, and caustic soda, began using the abandoned canal as a dump for at least 20,000 tons of waste residues—"still-bottoms," in the language of the trade.

Karen Schroeder's parents had been the first to experience problems with the canal's seepage. In 1959, her mother, Aileen Voorhees, encountered a strange black sludge bleeding through the basement walls. For the next twenty years, she and her husband, Edwin, tried various methods of halting the irritat-ing intrusion, pasting the cinder-block wall with sealants and even constructing a gutter along the walls to intercept the inflow. Nothing could stop the chemi-cal smell from permeating the entire household, and neighborhood calls to the city for help were fruitless. One day, when Edwin punched a hole in the wall to see what was happening, quantities of black liquid poured from the block. The cinder blocks were full of the stuff.

More ominous than the Voorhees basement was an event that occurred at 11:12 P.M. on November 21, 1968, when Karen Schroeder gave birth to her third child, a seven-pound girl named Sheri. No sense of elation filled the de-livery room. The child was born with a heart that beat irregularly and had a hole in it, bone blockages of the nose, partial deafness, deformed ear exteriors, and a cleft palate. Within two years, the Schroeders realized Sheri was also mentally retarded. When her teeth came in, a double row of them appeared on her lower jaw. And she developed an enlarged liver.

The Schroeders considered these health problems, as well as illnesses among their other children, as acts of capricious genes—a vicious quirk of nature. Like Mrs. Schroeder's parents, they were concerned that the chemicals were devaluing their property. The crab apple tree and evergreens in the back were dead, and even the oak in front of the home was sick; one year, the leaves had fallen off on Father's Day.

The canal had been dug with much fanfare in the late nineteenth century 10 by a flamboyant entrepreneur named William T. Love, who wanted to construct an industrial city with ready access to water power, and major markets. The setting for Love's dream was to be a navigable power channel that would extend seven miles from the Upper Niagara before falling two hundred feet, circumventing the treacherous falls and at the same time providing cheap power. A city would be constructed near the point where the canal fed back into the river, and he promised it would accommodate half a million people.

So taken with his imagination were the state's leaders that they gave Love a free hand to condemn as much property as he liked, and to divert whatever amounts of water. Love's dream, however, proved grander than his resources, and he was eventually forced to abandon the project after a mile-long trench, ten to forty feet deep and generally twenty yards wide, had been scoured perpendicular to the Niagara River. Eventually, the trench was purchased by Hooker.

Few of those who, in 1977, lived in the numerous houses that had sprung up by the site were aware that the large and barren field behind them was a burial ground for toxic waste. Both the Niagara County Health Department and the city said it was a nuisance condition, but not a serious danger to the people. Officials of the Hooker Company refused comment, claiming only that they had no records of the chemical burials and that the problem was not their responsibility. Indeed, Hooker had deeded the land to the Niagara Falls Board of Education in 1953, for a token $1. With it the company issued no detailed warnings of the chemicals, only a brief paragraph in the quitclaim document that disclaimed company liability for any injuries or deaths which might occur at the site.

Though Hooker was undoubtedly relieved to rid itself of the contaminated land, the company was so vague about the hazards involved that one might have thought the wastes would cause harm only if touched, because they irritated the skin; otherwise, they were not of great concern. In reality, as the company must have known, the dangers of these wastes far exceeded those of acids or alkalines or inert salts. We now know that the drums Hooker had dumped in the canal contained a veritable witch's brew—compounds of truly remarkable toxicity. There were solvents that attacked the heart and liver, and residues from pesticides so dangerous that their commercial sale was shortly thereafter restricted outright by the government; some of them were already suspected of causing cancer.

Yet Hooker gave no hint of that. When the board of education, which wanted the parcel for a new school, approached Hooker, B. Kaussen, at the time Hooker's executive vice president, said in a letter to the board: "Our officers have carefully considered your request. We are very conscious of the need for new elementary schools and realize that the sites must be carefully selected. We will be willing to donate the entire strip of property which we own between Colvin Boulevard and Frontier Avenue to be used for the erection of a school at a location to be determined. . . ."

The board built the school and playground at the canal's midsection. Construction progressed despite the contractor's hitting a drainage trench that gave off a strong chemical odor and the discovery of a waste pit nearby. Instead of halting the work, the authorities simply moved the school eighty feet away. Young families began to settle in increasing numbers alongside the dump, many of them having been told that the field was to be a park and recreation area for their children.

Children found the "playground" interesting, but at times painful. They sneezed, and their eyes teared. In the days when the dumping was still in progress, they swam at the opposite end of the canal, occasionally arriving home with hard pimples all over their bodies. Hooker knew children were playing on its spoils. In 1958, three children were burned by exposed residues on the canal's surface, much of which, according to residents, had been covered with nothing more than fly ash and loose dirt. Because it wished to avoid legal repercussions, the company chose not to issue a public warning of the dangers it knew were there, nor to have its chemists explain to the people that their homes would have been better placed elsewhere.

The Love Canal was simply unfit as a container for hazardous substances, poor even by the standards of the day, and now, in 1977, local authorities were belatedly finding that out. Several years of heavy snowfall and rain had filled the sparingly covered channel like a bathtub. The contents were overflowing at a frightening rate.

The city of Niagara Falls, I was assured, was planning a remedial drainage program to halt in some measure the chemical migration off the site. But no sense of urgency had been attached to the plan, and it was stalled in red tape. No one could agree on who should pay the bill—the city, Hooker, or the board of education—and engineers seemed confused over what exactly needed to be done.

Niagara Falls City Manager Donald O'Hara persisted in his view that, however displeasing to the eyes and nose, the Love Canal was not a crisis matter, mainly a question of aesthetics. O'Hara reminded me that Dr. Francis Clifford, county health commissioner, supported that opinion.

With the city, the board, and Hooker unwilling to commit themselves to a remedy, conditions degenerated in the area between 97th and 99th streets, until, by early 1978, the land was a quagmire of sludge that oozed from the canal's every pore. Melting snow drained the surface soot onto the private yards, while on the dump itself the ground had softened to the point of collapse, exposing the crushed tops of barrels. Beneath the surface, masses of sludge were finding their way out at a quickening rate, constantly forming

15

20

springs of contaminated liquid. The Schroeder back yard, once featured in a local newspaper for its beauty, had reached the point where it was unfit even to walk upon. Of course, the Schroeders could not leave. No one would think of buying the property. They still owed on their mortgage and, with Tim's salary, could not afford to maintain the house while they moved into a safer setting. They and their four children were stuck.

Apprehension about large costs was not the only reason the city was reluctant to help the Schroeders and the one hundred or so other families whose properties abutted the covered trench. The city may also have feared distressing Hooker. To an economically depressed area, the company provided desperately needed employment—as many as 3000 blue-collar jobs and a substantial number of tax dollars. Hooker was speaking of building a $17 million headquarters in downtown Niagara Falls. So anxious were city officials to receive the new building that they and the state granted the company highly lucrative tax and loan incentives, and made available to the firm a prime parcel of property near the most popular tourist park on the American side.

City Manager O'Hara and other authorities were aware of the nature of Hooker's chemicals. In fact, in the privacy of his office, O'Hara, after receiving a report on the chemical tests at the canal, had informed the people at Hooker that it was an extremely serious problem. Even earlier, in 1976, the New York State Department of Environmental Conservation had been made aware that dangerous compounds were present in the basement sump pump of at least one 97th Street home, and soon after, its own testing had revealed that highly injurious halogenated hydrocarbons were flowing from the canal into adjoining sewers. Among them were the notorious PCBs; quantities as low as one part PCBs to a million parts normal water were enough to create serious environmental concerns; in the sewers of Niagara Falls, the quantities of halogenated compounds were thousands of times higher. The other materials tracked, in sump pumps or sewers, were just as toxic as PCBs, or more so. Prime among the more hazardous ones was residue from hexachlorocyclopentadiene, or C-56, which was deployed as an intermediate in the manufacture of several pesticides. In certain dosages, the chemical could damage every organ in the body.

While the mere presence of C-56 should have been cause for alarm, government remained inactive. Not until early 1978—a full eighteen months after C-56 was first detected—was testing conducted in basements along 97th and 99th streets to see if the chemicals had vaporized off the sump pumps and walls and were present in the household air.

While the basement tests were in progress, the rains of spring arrived at the canal, further worsening the situation. Heavier fumes rose above the barrels. More than before, the residents were suffering from headaches, respiratory discomforts, and skin ailments. Many of them felt constantly fatigued and irritable, and the children had reddened eyes. In the Schroeder home, Tim developed a rash along the backs of his legs. Karen could not rid herself of throbbing pains in her head. Their daughter, Laurie, seemed to be losing some of her hair.

The EPA test revealed that benzene, a known cause of cancer in humans, had been readily detected in the household air up and down the streets. A widely used solvent, benzene was known in chronic-exposure cases to cause headaches, fatigue, loss of weight, and dizziness followed by pallor, nosebleeds, and damage to the bone marrow.

No public announcement was made of the benzene hazard. Instead, officials appeared to shield the finding until they could agree among themselves on how to present it.

Dr. Clifford, the county health commissioner, seemed unconcerned by the detection of benzene in the air. His health department refused to conduct a formal study of the people's health, despite the air-monitoring results. For this reason, and because of the resistance growing among the local authorities, I went to the southern end of 99th Street to take an informal health survey of my own. I arranged a meeting with six neighbors, all of them instructed beforehand to list the illnesses they were aware of on their block, with names and ages specified for presentation at the session.

The residents' list was startling. Though unafflicted before they moved there, many people were now plagued with ear infections, nervous disorders, rashes, and headaches. One young man, James Gizzarelli, said he had missed four months of work owing to breathing troubles. His wife was suffering epileptic-like seizures which her doctor was unable to explain. Meanwhile, freshly applied paint was inexplicably peeling from the exterior of their house. Pets too were suffering, most seriously if they had been penned in the back yards nearest to the canal, constantly breathing air that smelled like mothballs and weedkiller. They lost their fur, exhibited skin lesions, and, while still quite young, developed internal tumors. A great many cases of cancer were reported among the women, along with much deafness. On both 97th and 99th streets, traffic signs warned passing motorists to watch for deaf children playing near the road.

Evidence continued to mount that a large group of people, perhaps all of the one hundred families immediately by the canal, perhaps many more, were in imminent danger. While watching television, while gardening or doing a wash, in their sleeping hours, they were inhaling a mixture of damaging chemicals. Their hours of exposure were far longer than those of a chemical factory worker, and they wore no respirators or goggles. Nor could they simply open a door and escape. Helplessness and despair were the main responses to the blackened craters and scattered cinders behind their back yards.

But public officials often characterized the residents as hypochondriacs. Every agent of government had been called on the phone or sent pleas for help, but none offered aid.

Commissioner Clifford expressed irritation at my printed reports of illness, and disagreement began to surface in the newsroom on how the stories should be printed. "There's a high rate of cancer among my friends," Dr. Clifford argued. "It doesn't mean anything."

Yet as interest in the small community increased, further revelations shook the neighborhood. In addition to benzene, eighty or more other compounds were found in the makeshift dump, ten of them potential carcinogens. The physiological effects they could cause were profound and diverse. At least fourteen of them could impact on the brain and central nervous system. Two of them, carbon tetrachloride and chlorobenzene, could readily cause narcotic and anesthetic consequences. Many others were known to cause headaches, seizures, loss of hair, anemia, or skin rashes. Together, the compounds were capable of inflicting innumerable illnesses, and no one knew what new concoctions were being formulated by their mixture underground.

Edwin and Aileen Voorhees had the most to be concerned about. When a state biophysicist analyzed the air content of their basement, he determined that the safe exposure time there was less than 2.4 minutes—the toxicity in the basement was thousands of times the acceptable limit for twenty-four-hour-breathing. This did not mean they would necessarily become permanently ill, but their chances of contracting cancer, for example, had been measurably increased. In July, I visited Mrs. Voorhees for further discussion of her problems, and as we sat in the kitchen, drinking coffee, the industrial odors were apparent. Aileen, usually chipper and feisty, was visibly anxious. She stared down at the table, talking only in a lowered voice. Everything now looked different to her. The home she and Edwin had built had become their jail cell. Their yard was but a pathway through which toxicants entered the cellar walls. The field out back, that proposed "park," seemed destined to be the ruin of their lives.

On July 14 I received a call from the state health department with some shocking news. A preliminary review showed that women living at the southern end had suffered a high rate of miscarriages and had given birth to an abnormally high number of children with birth defects. In one age group, 35.3 percent had records of spontaneous abortions. That was far in excess of the norm. The odds against it happening by chance were 250 to one. These tallies, it was stressed, were "conservative" figures. Four children in one small section of the neighborhood had documentable birth defects, club feet, retardation, and deafness. Those who lived there the longest suffered the highest rates.

The data on miscarriages and birth defects, coupled with the other accounts of illness, finally pushed the state's bureaucracy into motion. A meeting was scheduled for August 2, at which time the state health commissioner, Dr. Robert Whalen, would formally address the issue. The day before the meeting, Dr. Nicholas Vianna, a state epidemiologist, told me that the residents were also incurring some degree of liver damage. Blood analyses had shown hepatitislike symptoms in enzyme levels. Dozens if not hundreds of people, apparently, had been adversely affected.

In Albany, on August 2, Dr. Whalen read a lengthy statement in which he urged that pregnant women and children under two years of age leave the southern end of the dump site immediately. He declared the Love Canal an official emergency, citing it as a "great and imminent peril to the health of the general public."

When Commissioner Whalen's words hit 97th and 99th streets, by way of one of the largest banner headlines in the Niagara *Gazette's* 125-year history, dozens of people massed on the streets, shouting into bullhorns and microphones to voice frustrations that had been accumulating for months. Many of them vowed a tax strike because their homes were rendered unmarketable and unsafe. They attacked their government for ignoring their welfare. A man of high authority, a physician with a title, had confirmed that their lives were in danger. Most wanted to leave the neighborhood immediately.

Terror and anger roiled together, exacerbated by Dr. Whalen's failure to provide a government-funded evacuation plan. His words were only a recommendation: individual families had to choose whether to risk their health and remain, or abandon their houses and, in so doing, write off a lifetime of work and savings.

On August 3, Dr. Whalen decided he should speak to the people. He arrived with Dr. David Axelrod, a deputy who had directed the state's investigation, and Thomas Frey, a key aide to Governor Hugh Carey.

At a public meeting, held in the 99th Street School auditorium, Frey was 40 given the grueling task of controlling the crowd of 500 angry and frightened people. In an attempt to calm them, he announced that a meeting between the state and the White House had been scheduled for the following week. The state would propose that Love Canal be classified a national disaster, thereby freeing federal funds. For now, however, he could promise no more. Neither could Dr. Whalen and his staff of experts. All they could say was what was already known: twenty-five organic compounds, some of them capable of causing cancer, were in their homes, and because young children were especially prone to toxic effects, they should be moved to another area.

Dr. Whalen's order had applied only to those living at the canal's southern end, on its immediate periphery. But families living across the street from the dump site, or at the northern portion, where the chemicals were not so visible at the surface, reported afflictions remarkably similar to those suffered by families whose yards abutted the southern end. Serious respiratory problems, nervous disorders, and rectal bleeding were reported by many who were not covered by the order.

Throughout the following day, residents posted signs of protest on their front fences or porch posts. "Love Canal Kills," they said, or "Give Me Liberty, I've Got Death." Emotionally exhausted and uncertain about their future, men stayed home from work, congregating on the streets or comforting their wives. By this time the board of education had announced it was closing the 99th Street School for the following year, because of its proximity to the exposed toxicants. Still, no public relief was provided for the residents.

Another meeting was held that evening, at a firehall on 102nd Street. It was unruly, but the people, who had called the session in an effort to organize themselves, managed to form an alliance, the Love Canal Homeowners Association, and to elect as president Lois Gibbs, a pretty, twenty-seven-year-old woman with jet-black hair who proved remarkably adept at dealing with experienced politicians and at keeping the matter in the news. After Mrs. Gibbs' election, Congressman John LaFalce entered the hall and announced, to wild applause, that the Federal Disaster Assistance Administration would be represented the next morning, and that the state's two senators, Daniel Patrick Moynihan and Jacob Javits, were working with him in an attempt to get funds from Congress.

With the Love Canal story now attracting attention from the national media, the Governor's office announced that Hugh Carey would be at the 99th Street School on August 7 to address the people. Decisions were being made in Albany and Washington. Hours before the Governor's arrival, a sudden burst of "urgent" reports from Washington came across the newswires. President Jimmy Carter had officially declared the Hooker dump site a national emergency.

Hugh Carey was applauded on his arrival. The Governor announced that the state, through its Urban Development Corporation, planned to purchase, at fair market value, those homes rendered uninhabitable by the marauding chemicals. He spared no promises. "You will not have to make mortgage payments on homes you don't want or cannot occupy. Don't worry about the banks. The state will take care of them." By the standards of Niagara Falls, where the real estate market was depressed, the houses were in the middle-class range, worth from $20,000 to $40,000 apiece. The state would assess each house and purchase it, and also pay the costs of moving, temporary housing during the transition period, and special items not covered by the usual real estate assessment, such as installation of telephones.

First in a trickle and then, by September, in droves, the families gathered their belongings and carted them away. Moving vans crowded 97th and 99th streets. Linesmen went from house to house disconnecting the telephones and electrical wires, while carpenters pounded plywood over the windows to keep vandals away. By the following spring, 237 families were gone; 170 of them had moved into new houses. In time the state erected around a six-block residential area a green chain-link fence, eight feet in height, clearly demarcating the contamination zone.

In October 1978, the long-awaited remedial drainage program began at the south end. Trees were uprooted, fences and garages torn down, and swimming pools removed from the area. So great were residents' apprehensions that dangerous fumes would be released over the surrounding area that the state, at a cost of $500,000, placed seventy-five buses at emergency evacuation pickup

269

spots during the months of work, in the event that outlying homes had to be vacated quickly because of an explosion. The plan was to construct drain tiles around the channel's periphery, where the back yards had been located, in order to divert leakage to seventeen-foot-deep wet wells from which contaminated groundwater could be drawn and treated by filtration through activated carbon. (Removing the chemicals themselves would have been financially prohibitive, perhaps costing as much as $100 million—and even then the materials would have to be buried elsewhere.) After the trenching was complete, and the sewers installed, the canal was to be covered by a sloping mound of clay and planted with grass. One day, city officials hoped, the wasteland would become a park.

In spite of the corrective measures and the enormous effort by the state health department, which took thousands of blood samples from past and current residents and made uncounted analyses of soil, water, and air, the full range of the effects remained unknown. In neighborhoods immediately outside the official "zone of contamination," more than 500 families were left near the desolate setting, their health still in jeopardy. The state announced it would buy no more homes.

The first public indication that chemical contamination had probably reached streets to the east and west of 97th and 99th streets, and to the north and south as well, came on August 11, 1978, when sump-pump samples I had taken from 100th and 101st streets, analyzed in a laboratory, showed the trace presence of a number of chemicals found in the canal itself, including lindane, a restricted pesticide that had been suspected of causing cancer in laboratory animals. While probing 100th Street, I knocked on the door of Patricia Pino, thirty-four, a blond divorcee with a young son and daughter. I had noticed that some of the leaves on a large tree in front of her house exhibited a black oiliness much like that on the trees and shrubs of 99th Street; she was located near what had been a drainage swale.

After I had extracted a jar of sediment from her sump pump for the analysis, 50 we conversed about her family situation and what the trauma now unfolding meant to them. Ms. Pino was extremely depressed and embittered. Both of her children had what appeared to be slight liver abnormalities, and her son had been plagued with "non-specific" allergies, teary eyes, sinus trouble, which improved markedly when he was sent away from home. Patricia told of times, during the heat of summer, when fumes were readily noticeable in her basement and sometimes even upstairs. She herself had been treated for a possibly cancerous condition of her cervix. But, like others, her family was now trapped.

On September 24, 1978, I obtained a state memorandum that said chemical infiltration of the outer regions was significant indeed. The letter, sent from the state laboratories to the U.S. Environmental Protection Agency, said, "Preliminary analysis of soil samples demonstrates extensive migration of potentially toxic materials outside the immediate canal area." There it was, in the state's own words. Not long afterward, the state medical investigator, Dr. Nicholas Vianna, reported indications that residents from 93rd to 103rd streets might also have incurred liver damage.

On October 4, a young boy, John Allen Kenny, who lived quite a distance north of the evacuation zone, died. The fatality was due to the failure of another organ that can be readily affected by toxicants, the kidney. Naturally, suspicions were raised that his death was in some way related to a creek that still flowed behind his house and carried, near an outfall, the odor of chlorinated compounds. Because the creek served as a catch basin for a portion of the Love Canal, the state studied an autopsy of the boy. No conclusions were reached. John Allen's parents, Norman, a chemist, and Luella, a medical research assistant, were unsatisfied with the state's investigation, which they felt was "superficial." Luella said, "He played in the creek all the time. There had been restrictions on the older boys, but he was the youngest and played with them when they were old enough to go to the creek. We let him do what the other boys did. He died of nephrosis. Proteins were passing through his urine. Well, in reading the literature, we discovered that chemicals can trigger this. There was no evidence of infection, which there should have been, and there was damage to his thymus and brain. He also had nosebleeds and headaches, and dry heaves. So our feeling is that chemicals probably triggered it."

The likelihood that water-carried chemicals had escaped from the canal's deteriorating bounds and were causing problems quite a distance from the site was not lost upon the Love Canal Homeowners Association and its president, Lois Gibbs, who was attempting to have additional families relocated. Because she lived on 101st Street, she was one of those left behind, with no means of moving despite persistent medical difficulties in her six-year-old son, Michael, who had been operated on twice for urethral strictures. [Mrs. Gibbs's husband, a worker at a chemical plant, brought home only $150 a week, she told me, and when they subtracted from that the $90 a week for food and other necessities, clothing costs for their two children, $125 a month for mortgage payments and taxes, utility and phone expenses, and medical bills, they had hardly enough cash to buy gas and cigarettes, let alone vacate their house.]

Assisted by two other stranded residents, Marie Pozniak and Grace Mc-Coulf, and with the professional analysis of a Buffalo scientist named Beverly Paigen, Lois Gibbs mapped out the swale and creekbed areas, many of them long ago filled, and set about interviewing the numerous people who lived on or near formerly wet ground. The survey indicated that these people were suffering from an abnormal number of kidney and bladder aggravations and problems of the reproductive system. In a report to the state, Dr. Paigen claimed to have found, in 245 homes outside the evacuation zone, thirty-four miscarriages, eighteen birth defects, nineteen nervous breakdowns, ten cases of epilepsy, and high rates of hyperactivity and suicide.

In their roundabout way, the state health experts, after an elaborate investigation, confirmed some of the homeowners' worst fears. On February 8, 1979, 55

271

Dr. David Axelrod, who by then had been appointed health commissioner, and whose excellence as a scientist was widely acknowledged, issued a new order that officially extended the health emergency of the previous August, citing high incidences of birth deformities and miscarriages in the areas where creeks and swales had once flowed, or where swamps had been. With that, the state offered to evacuate temporarily those families with pregnant women or children under the age of two from the outer areas of contamination, up to 103rd Street. But no additional homes would be purchased; nor was another large-scale evacuation, temporary or otherwise, under consideration. Those who left under the new plan would have to return when their children passed the age limit.

Twenty-three families accepted the state's offer. Another seven families, ineligible under the plan but of adequate financial means to do so, simply left their homes and took the huge loss of investment. Soon boarded windows speckled the outlying neighborhoods.

The previous November and December, not long after the evacuation of 97th and 99th streets, I became interested in the possibility that Hooker might have buried in the Love Canal waste residues from the manufacture of what is known as 2,4,5-trichlorophenol. My curiosity was keen because I knew that this substance, which Hooker produced for the manufacture of the antibacterial agent hexachlorophene, and which was also used to make defoliants such as Agent Orange, the herbicide employed in Vietnam, carries with it an unwanted by-product technically called 2,3,7,8-tetrachlorodibenzo-para-dioxin, or tetra dioxin. The potency of dioxin of this isomer is nearly beyond imagination. Although its toxicological effects are not fully known, the few experts on the subject estimate that if three ounces were evenly distributed and subsequently ingested among a million people, or perhaps more than that, all of them would die. It compares in toxicity to the botulinum toxin. On skin contact, dioxin causes a disfiguration called "chloracne," which begins as pimples, lesions, and cysts, but can lead to calamitous internal damage. Some scientists suspect that dioxin causes cancer, perhaps even malignancies that occur, in galloping fashion, within a short time of contact. At least two (some estimates went as high as eleven) pounds of dioxin were dispersed over Seveso, Italy, in 1976, after an explosion of a trichlorophenol plant: dead animals littered the streets, and more than 300 acres of land were immediately evacuated. In Vietnam, the spraying of Agent Orange, because of the dioxin contaminant, was banned in 1970, when the first effects on human beings began to surface, including dioxin's powerful teratogenic, or fetus-deforming, effects.

I posed two questions concerning trichlorophenol: Were wastes from the process buried in the canal? If so, what were the quantities?

On November 8, before Hooker answered my queries, I learned that, indeed, trichlorophenol had been found in liquids pumped from the remedial drain ditches. No dioxin had been found yet, and some officials, ever wary of more emotionalism among the people, argued that, because the compound was not soluble in water, there was little chance it had migrated off-site. Officials at Newco Chemical Waste Systems, a local waste disposal firm, at the same time claimed that if dioxin had been there, it had probably been photolytically destroyed. Its half-life, they contended, was just a few short years.

I knew from Whiteside, however, that in every known case, waste from 60 2,4,5-trichlorophenol carried dioxin with it. I also knew that dioxin *could* become soluble in groundwater and migrate into the neighborhood upon mixing with solvents such as benzene. Moreover, because it had been buried, sunlight would not break it down.

On Friday, November 10, I called Hooker again to urge that they answer my questions. Their spokesman, Bruce Davis, came to the phone and, in a controlled tone, gave me the answer: His firm had indeed buried trichlorophenol in the canal—200 tons of it.

Immediately I called Whiteside. His voice took on an urgent tone. According to his calculation, if 200 tons of trichlorophenol were there, in all likelihood they were accompanied by 130 pounds of tetra dioxin, an amount equaling the estimated total content of dioxin in the thousands of tons of Agent Orange rained upon Vietnamese jungles. The seriousness of the crisis had deepened, for now the Love Canal was not only a dump for highly dangerous solvents and pesticides; it was also the broken container for one of the most toxic substances ever synthesized by man.

I reckoned that the main danger was to those working on the remedial project, digging in the trenches. The literature on dioxin indicated that, even in quantities at times too small to detect, the substance possessed vicious characteristics. In one case, workers in a trichlorophenol plant had developed chloracne, although the substance could not be traced on the equipment with which they worked. The mere tracking of minuscule amounts of dioxin on a pedestrian's shoes in Seveso led to major concerns, and, according to Whiteside, a plant in Amsterdam, upon being found contaminated with dioxin, had been "dismantled, brick by brick, and the material embedded in concrete, loaded at a specially constructed dock, on ships, and dumped at sea, in deep water near the Azores." Workers in trichlorophenol plants had died of cancer or severe liver damage, or had suffered emotional and sexual disturbances.

Less than a month after the first suspicions arose, on the evening of December 9, I received a call from Dr. Axelrod. "We found it. The dioxin. In a drainage trench behind 97th Street. It was in the part-per-trillion range."

The state remained firm in its plans to continue the construction, and, de- 65 spite the ominous new findings, no further evacuations were announced. During the next several weeks, small incidents of vandalism occurred along 97th and 99th streets. Tacks were spread on the road, causing numerous flat tires on the trucks. Signs of protest were hung in the school. Meetings of the Love Canal Homeowners Association became more vociferous. Christmas was near, and in the association's office at the 99th Street School, a holiday tree was decorated with bulbs arranged to spell "DIOXIN."

The Love Canal people chanted and cursed at meetings with the state officials, cried on the telephone, burned an effigy of the health commissioner,
traveled to Albany with a makeshift child's coffin, threatened to hold officials
hostage, sent letters and telegrams to the White House, held days of mourning
and nights of prayer. On Mother's Day this year, they marched down the industrial corridor and waved signs denouncing Hooker, which had issued not so
much as a statement of remorse. But no happy ending was in store for them.
The federal government was clearly not planning to come to their rescue, and
the state felt it had already done more than its share. City Hall was silent and
remains silent today. Some residents still hoped that, miraculously, an agency
of government would move them. All of them watched with anxiety as each
newborn came to the neighborhood, and they looked at their bodies for signs
of cancer.

One hundred and thirty families from the Love Canal area began leaving
their homes last August and September, seeking temporary refuge in local
hotel rooms under a relocation plan funded by the state which had been implemented after fumes became so strong, during remedial trenching operations, that the United Way abandoned a care center it had opened in the
neighborhood.

As soon as remedial construction is complete, the people will probably be
forced to return home, as the state will no longer pay for their lodging. Some
have threatened to barricade themselves in the hotels. Some have mentioned
violence. Anne Hillis of 102nd Street, who told reporters her first child had
been born so badly decomposed that doctors could not determine its sex, was
so bitter that she threw table knives and a soda can at the state's on-site co-
ordinator.

In October, Governor Carey announced that the state probably would buy
an additional 200 to 240 homes, at an expense of some $5 million. In the
meantime, lawyers have prepared lawsuits totaling about $2.65 billion and
have sought court action for permanent relocation. Even if the latter action is
successful, and they are allowed to move, the residents' plight will not necessarily have ended. The psychological scars are bound to remain among them
and their children, along with the knowledge that, because they have already
been exposed, they may never fully escape the Love Canal's insidious grasp.

QUESTIONS

1. What caused the poisoning of Love Canal? Why did it take so long for both local
and state officials to acknowledge the seriousness of the condition of Love Canal?

2. What kind of information does Brown provide to document the tragedy of Love
Canal? What role did he play in uncovering this information?

3. Consider the introduction to this article. Why did Brown choose to tell the story
of the Schroeder family in the opening paragraphs?

4. The power of this essay has much to do with the overwhelming tragedy and horror it relates. Find passages in the essay that you feel are especially effective. Explain how Brown creates this effect on the reader.

5. In this essay, Brown relies primarily on the factual data he has collected to tell the story of Love Canal. Compare this writer's approach with that found in newspapers featuring sensational headlines. Analyze one of the headlined stories. How much factual evidence is present? How would such a newspaper's treatment of the story of the Schroeder family differ from Brown's treatment?

6. Environmental calamities such as Love Canal or Three Mile Island have become a permanent part of our lives. The Environmental Protection Agency reports that in most communities the groundwater has become so laced with toxic chemicals that it is no longer safe to drink. Investigate some aspect of the environment in your community such as the water supply or the quality of the air. Write a report based on your investigation.

MAKING CONNECTIONS

Compare Brown's position as a reporter with Barbara Tuchman's in "'This Is the End of the World'" (p. 219). What similarities and differences can you find in the ways that Brown and Tuchman have gathered their information? In their organization and presentation of that information? In the points of view that they have taken toward the disasters they write about? On the basis of these comparisons, what do you think is the most effective way to present stories of large-scale human disasters and similarly provocative subject matter?

THE DISCUS THROWER
Richard Selzer

Richard Selzer (b. 1928) is a surgeon who has written widely, publishing articles in popular magazines as well as occasional short fiction. (See earlier biographical note, page 121, for additional details.) In the essay reprinted here, which first appeared in Harper's *magazine in 1977, Selzer reports on the visits he made to one of his patients.*

I spy on my patients. Ought not a doctor to observe his patients by any means and from any stance, that he might the more fully assemble evidence? So I stand in the doorways of hospital rooms and gaze. Oh, it is not all that furtive an act. Those in bed need only look up to discover me. But they never do.

From the doorway of Room 542 the man in the bed seems deeply tanned. Blue eyes and close-cropped white hair give him the appearance of vigor and good health. But I know that his skin is not brown from the sun. It is rusted, rather, in the last stage of containing the vile repose within. And the blue eyes are frosted, looking inward like the windows of a snowbound cottage. This man is blind. This man is also legless—the right leg missing from midthigh down, the left from just below the knee. It gives him the look of a bonsai, roots and branches pruned into the dwarfed facsimile of a great tree.

Propped on pillows, he cups his right thigh in both hands. Now and then he shakes his head as though acknowledging the intensity of his suffering. In all of this he makes no sound. Is he mute as well as blind?

The room in which he dwells is empty of all possessions—no get-well cards, small, private caches of food, day-old flowers, slippers, all the usual kickshaws of the sickroom. There is only the bed, a chair, a nightstand, and a tray on wheels that can be swung across his lap for meals.

"What time is it?" he asks. 5

"Three o'clock."

"Morning or afternoon?"

"Afternoon."

He is silent. There is nothing else he wants to know.

"How are you?" I say. 10

"Who is it?" he asks.

"It's the doctor. How do you feel?"

He does not answer right away.

"Feel?" he says.

"I hope you feel better," I say. 15

I press the button at the side of the bed.

"Down you go," I say.

"Yes, down," he says.

He falls back upon the bed awkwardly. His stumps, unweighted by legs and feet, rise in the air, presenting themselves. I unwrap the bandages from the stumps, and begin to cut away the black scabs and the dead, glazed fat with scissors and forceps. A shard of white bone comes loose. I pick it away. I wash the wounds with disinfectant and redress the stumps. All this while, he does not speak. What is he thinking behind those lids that do not blink? Is he remembering a time when he was whole? Does he dream of feet? Of when his body was not a rotting log?

He lies solid and inert. In spite of everything, he remains impressive, as   20
though he were a sailor standing athwart a slanting deck.

"Anything more I can do for you?" I ask.

For a long moment he is silent.

"Yes," he says at last and without the least irony. "You can bring me a pair of shoes."

In the corridor, the head nurse is waiting for me.

"We have to do something about him," she says. "Every morning he orders   25
scrambled eggs for breakfast, and, instead of eating them, he picks up the plate and throws it against the wall."

"Throws his plate?"

"Nasty. That's what he is. No wonder his family doesn't come to visit. They probably can't stand him any more than we can."

She is waiting for me to do something.

"Well?"

"We'll see," I say.   30

The next morning I am waiting in the corridor when the kitchen delivers his breakfast. I watch the aide place the tray on the stand and swing it across his lap. She presses the button to raise the head of the bed. Then she leaves.

In time the man reaches to find the rim of the tray, then on to find the dome of the covered dish. He lifts off the cover and places it on the stand. He fingers across the plate until he probes the eggs. He lifts the plate in both hands, sets it on the palm of his right hand, centers it, balances it. He hefts it up and down slightly, getting the feel of it. Abruptly, he draws back his right arm as far as he can.

There is the crack of the plate breaking against the wall at the foot of his bed and the small wet sound of the scrambled eggs dropping to the floor.

And then he laughs. It is a sound you have never heard. It is something new under the sun. It could cure cancer.

Out in the corridor, the eyes of the head nurse narrow.   35

"Laughed, did he?"

She writes something down on her clipboard.

277

A second aide arrives, brings a second breakfast tray, puts it on the nightstand, out of his reach. She looks over at me shaking her head and making her mouth go. I see that we are to be accomplices.

"I've got to feed you," she says to the man.

"Oh, no you don't," the man says. 40

"Oh, yes I do," the aide says, "after the way you just did. Nurse says so."

"Get me my shoes," the man says.

"Here's oatmeal," the aide says. "Open." And she touches the spoon to his lower lip.

"I ordered scrambled eggs," says the man.

"That's right," the aide says. 45

I step forward.

"Is there anything I can do?" I say.

"Who are you?" the man asks.

In the evening I go once more to that ward to make my rounds. The head nurse reports to me that Room 542 is deceased. She has discovered this quite by accident, she says. No, there had been no sound. Nothing. It's a blessing, she says.

I go into his room, a spy looking for secrets. He is still there in his bed. His 50 face is relaxed, grave, dignified. After a while, I turn to leave. My gaze sweeps the wall at the foot of the bed, and I see the place where it has been repeatedly washed, where the wall looks very clean and very white.

QUESTIONS

1. Why does Selzer say, "I spy on my patients" (paragraph 1)? Don't doctors usually look in on their patients? What effect does Selzer hope to achieve by starting with such a statement?

2. Selzer uses the present tense throughout this piece. Would the past tense be just as effective? Explain your answer.

3. Selzer writes in the first person. Why might he have decided to make himself prominent in the report in this way? How would his report have come across if it had been written in the third person rather than the first person?

4. How would you describe this doctor's attitude toward his patient? How would you describe the nurse's attitude toward the patient? How does the narrator manage to characterize himself in one way and the nurse in another?

5. Is the title, "The Discus Thrower," appropriate for this piece? In a slightly revised version, the title was changed to "Four Appointments with the Discus Thrower." Is this a better title?

6. What do you think Selzer's purpose was in writing this essay? Did he simply wish to shock us, or is there a message in this piece for the medical profession or for those of us who fear illness and death?

7. The essay reports on four visits to the patient by Selzer. Write a shorter version reporting on two or more visits by the head nurse. How would she react to the patient's request for shoes? How might her point of view explain some of her reactions?

8. For many of us, knowledge of hospitals is limited, perhaps to television shows in which the hospital functions as a backdrop for the romances of its staff. Write a short essay in which you present your conception of what a hospital is and in which you consider how Selzer's essay either made you revise that conception or reaffirmed what you know through experience.

MAKING CONNECTIONS

Selzer and Roy C. Selby Jr. (p. 280) write of human subjects. Farley Mowat (p. 237) and Jane van Lawick-Goodall (p. 241) write of animals. Does this choice of subject seem to affect the distance the writer maintains, achieves, or overcomes in offering his or her report? Do you find any common denominators here? How do you account for them?

A DELICATE OPERATION

Roy C. Selby Jr.

*Roy C. Selby Jr. (b. 1930) graduated from Louisiana State
University and the University of Arkansas Medical School,
where he specialized in neurology and neurosurgery. He is
the author of numerous professional articles on neurosurgery and is now retired from practice. "A Delicate Operation," which first appeared in* Harper's *magazine in 1975,
reports for a more general audience the details of a difficult
brain operation.*

In the autumn of 1973 a woman in her early fifties noticed, upon closing
one eye while reading, that she was unable to see clearly. Her eyesight grew
slowly worse. Changing her eyeglasses did not help. She saw an ophthalmologist, who found that her vision was seriously impaired in both eyes. She then
saw a neurologist, who confirmed the finding and obtained X rays of the skull
and an EMI scan—a photograph of the patient's head. The latter revealed a
tumor growing between the optic nerves at the base of the brain. The woman
was admitted to the hospital by a neurosurgeon.

Further diagnosis, based on angiography, a detailed X-ray study of the circulatory system, showed the tumor to be about two inches in diameter and supplied by many small blood vessels. It rested beneath the brain, just above the
pituitary gland, stretching the optic nerves to either side and intimately close to
the major blood vessels supplying the brain. Removing it would pose many
technical problems. Probably benign and slow-growing, it may have been
present for several years. If left alone it would continue to grow and produce
blindness and might become impossible to remove completely. Removing it,
however, might not improve the patient's vision and could make it worse. A
major blood vessel could be damaged, causing a stroke. Damage to the under-
surface of the brain could cause impairment of memory and changes in mood
and personality. The hypothalamus, a most important structure of the brain,
could be injured, causing coma, high fever, bleeding from the stomach, and
death.

The neurosurgeon met with the patient and her husband and discussed the
various possibilities. The common decision was to operate.

The patient's hair was shampooed for two nights before surgery. She was
given a cortisonelike drug to reduce the risk of damage to the brain during
surgery. Five units of blood were cross-matched, as a contingency against hem-
orrhage. At 1:00 P.M. the operation began. After the patient was anesthetized
her hair was completely clipped and shaved from the scalp. Her head was

prepped with an organic iodine solution for ten minutes. Drapes were placed over her, leaving exposed only the forehead and crown of the skull. All the routine instruments were brought up—the electrocautery used to coagulate areas of bleeding, bipolar coagulation forceps to arrest bleeding from individual blood vessels without damaging adjacent tissues, and small suction tubes to remove blood and cerebrospinal fluid from the head, thus giving the surgeon a better view of the tumor and surrounding areas.

A curved incision was made behind the hairline so it would be concealed when the hair grew back. It extended almost from ear to ear. Plastic clips were applied to the cut edges of the scalp to arrest bleeding. The scalp was folded back to the level of the eyebrows. Incisions were made in the muscle of the right temple, and three sets of holes were drilled near the temple and the top of the head because the tumor had to be approached from directly in front. The drill, powered by nitrogen, was replaced with a fluted steel blade, and the holes were connected. The incised piece of skull was pried loose and held out of the way by a large sponge.

Beneath the bone is a yellowish leatherlike membrane, the dura, that surrounds the brain. Down the middle of the head the dura carries a large vein, but in the area near the nose the vein is small. At that point the vein and dura were cut, and clips made of tantalum, a hard metal, were applied to arrest and prevent bleeding. Sutures were put into the dura and tied to the scalp to keep the dura open and retracted. A malleable silver retractor, resembling the blade of a butter knife, was inserted between the brain and skull. The anesthesiologist began to administer a drug to relax the brain by removing some of its water, making it easier for the surgeon to manipulate the retractor, hold the brain back, and see the tumor. The nerve tracts for smell were cut on both sides to provide additional room. The tumor was seen approximately two-and-one-half inches behind the base of the nose. It was pink in color. On touching it, it proved to be very fibrous and tough. A special retractor was attached to the skull, enabling the other retractor blades to be held automatically and freeing the surgeon's hands. With further displacement of the frontal lobes of the brain, the tumor could be seen better, but no normal structures—the carotid arteries, their branches, and the optic nerves—were visible. The tumor obscured them.

A surgical microscope was placed above the wound. The surgeon had selected the lenses and focal length prior to the operation. Looking through the microscope, he could see some of the small vessels supplying the tumor and he coagulated them. He incised the tumor to attempt to remove its core and thus collapse it, but the substance of the tumor was too firm to be removed in this fashion. He then began to slowly dissect the tumor from the adjacent brain tissue and from where he believed the normal structures to be.

Using small squares of cotton, he began to separate the tumor from very loose fibrous bands connecting it to the brain and to the right side of the part of the skull where the pituitary gland lies. The right optic nerve and carotid artery came into view, both displaced considerably to the right. The optic nerve had a normal appearance. He protected these structures with cotton compresses placed between them and the tumor. He began to raise the tumor from the skull and slowly to reach the point of its origin and attachment—just in front of the pituitary gland and medial to the left optic nerve, which still could not be seen. The small blood vessels entering the tumor were cauterized. The upper portion of the tumor was gradually separated from the brain, and the branches of the carotid arteries and the branches to the tumor were coagulated. The tumor was slowly and gently lifted from its bed, and for the first time the left carotid artery and optic nerve could be seen. Part of the tumor adhered to this nerve. The bulk of the tumor was amputated, leaving a small bit attached to the nerve. Very slowly and carefully the tumor fragment was resected.

The tumor now removed, a most impressive sight came into view—the pituitary gland and its stalk of attachment to the hypothalamus, the hypothalamus itself, and the brainstem, which conveys nerve impulses between the body and the brain. As far as could be determined, no damage had been done to these structures or other vital centers, but the left optic nerve, from chronic pressure of the tumor, appeared gray and thin. Probably it would not completely recover its function.

After making certain there was no bleeding, the surgeon closed the wounds   10 and placed wire mesh over the holes in the skull to prevent dimpling of the scalp over the points that had been drilled. A gauze dressing was applied to the patient's head. She was awakened and sent to the recovery room.

Even with the microscope, damage might still have occurred to the cerebral cortex and hypothalamus. It would require at least a day to be reasonably certain there was none, and about seventy-two hours to monitor for the major postoperative dangers—swelling of the brain and blood clots forming over the surface of the brain. The surgeon explained this to the patient's husband, and both of them waited anxiously. The operation had required seven hours. A glass of orange juice had given the surgeon some additional energy during the closure of the wound. Though exhausted, he could not fall asleep until after two in the morning, momentarily expecting a call from the nurse in the intensive care unit announcing deterioration of the patient's condition.

At 8:00 A.M. the surgeon saw the patient in the intensive care unit. She was alert, oriented, and showed no sign of additional damage to the optic nerves or the brain. She appeared to be in better shape than the surgeon or her husband.

QUESTIONS

1. Why did Selby decide to operate? What could have happened if the patient chose not to have the operation? What effect does knowing this information have on the reader?

2. Although the essay is probably based on Selby's experience, it is reported in the third person. What effect does this have on the information reported? How would the report have come across if it had been written in the first person?

3. Selby uses different methods of reporting to create the drama of "A Delicate Operation." At what point in the essay does he provide background information? How much of the essay reports events before, during, and after the operation? At what points does the writer explain terms and procedures for the reader?

4. Which passages in this essay do you find especially powerful? How did Selby create this effect?

5. Write a report of a procedure with which you are familiar. Select a procedure that calls for some expertise or sensitivity or a combination of these because there is the chance that something could go wrong. Proceed step-by-step, giving the reader as much information as necessary to understand and follow the procedure. At appropriate points, also include the problems you face. Suggestions are trimming a Christmas tree, carrying out a chemistry experiment, getting a child off to school, or preparing a gourmet meal.

MAKING CONNECTIONS

1. Compare Selby's essay with Richard Selzer's "The Discus Thrower" (p. 276). Whereas Selby writes in the third person, Selzer uses the first. How do those choices affect the resulting essays?

2. Rewrite several paragraphs of Selby's and Selzer's essays, changing the first piece from third person to first person and the other from first to third. How do these changes alter the nature of the information presented and the effect of each report?

TWO REPORTS
OF AN AIRPLANE CRASH

The Associated Press and
The National Transportation Safety Board

The crash of a TWA jetliner on its way into Dulles Interna-
tional Airport outside Washington, D.C., was the lead story
in the New York Times *on December 2, 1974. Almost*
a year later, the National Transportation Safety Board
(NTSB) reported the results of its investigation into the
causes of that crash. The work of the NTSB, which is also
responsible for investigating rail, highway, marine, and
pipeline accidents, has contributed significantly to the low
rate of airline accidents in this country. Presented here are
the newspaper article and the first part of the NTSB report,
which reviews the accident itself, as examples of two differ-
ent approaches to the reporting of the same event.

BY THE ASSOCIATED PRESS

Upperville, Va., Dec. 1—

A Trans World Airlines 727, battling a driving rainstorm, slammed into a wooded slope near a secret government installation today, killing all 92 persons aboard. It was the worst air disaster of the year in the United States.

Capt. William Carvello of the state police declared "there are no survivors" after rescue workers had combed for hours through the wreckage on Mount Weather, a foothill of the Blue Ridge Mountains.

The plane, Flight 514, was bound for Washington from Columbus, Ohio, and was approaching Dulles International Airport when the tower lost radar contact at 11:10 A.M.

The crash site was about five miles north of Upperville, a tiny community in the tip of the state and about 20 miles northwest of Dulles.

First on Dulles Approach

According to the National Transportation Safety Board, today's was the first   5
fatal crash by an airliner approaching Dulles, which opened in 1962.

A T.W.A. spokesman said 85 passengers and a crew of seven were aboard the flight, which originated in Indianapolis. He said 46 persons got on at Columbus.

The plane crashed about one and one-half miles from an underground complex that reportedly is designed to serve as a headquarters for high government officials in the event of nuclear war. A Federal spokesman acknowledged only that the facility was operated by the little known Office of Preparedness, whose responsibilities, he said, include "continuity of government in a time of national disaster."

All of Mount Weather, a peak of about 2000 feet, is owned by the Federal Government. One official confirmed that several government employees were at work at the building complex, and helped in search and rescue efforts.

The airlines released a list of the victims' names tonight after relatives had been notified. The remains were taken to a makeshift morgue at the Bluemont Community Center, five miles from the site. Rescue operations were halted at 8:15 P.M. because of fog, high winds, and rain.

Dr. George Hocker, Loudoun County medical examiner, said the plane hit   10
just below the summit and cut a swath 60 to 70 yards wide and about a quarter of a mile long.

"There were just chunks of metal and total destruction," he said.

The police initially sealed off an area within a five-mile radius of the site to all but law enforcement and rescue officials. A reporter who viewed the wreckage several hours later said that much of it was still burning and the largest piece of metal he could find measured only 5 by 10 feet.

The Federal Aviation Administration said there were no unusual communications from the plane before the crash, "just routine flight conversation."

The flight had been scheduled to land at National Airport near Washington at 10:23 A.M. but was diverted to Dulles, a larger facility about 20 miles west of the capital, because of high winds.

When the Dulles tower lost radar contact 37 minutes later, it notified the   15
local authorities to begin a search. Captain Carvello said two state troopers found the wreckage almost immediately.

Apparently no one on the ground was hit by the crash nor were any buildings. But a worker for the Chesapeake and Potomac Telephone Company said the wreckage had severed the main underground phone line into the secret government installation. It was restored after two-and-a-half hours.

According to Federal aviation experts examining the wreckage, the airliner broke down through the treetops and its underbelly was apparently ripped off by a 10-foot-high rock ledge at the end of a secondary road.

Visibility on the ground was only about 100 feet, with snow flurries mixed with rain and some fog. The Dulles tower said that at the proper altitude, visibility would have been up to five miles, despite the rain.

John Reed, chairman of the National Transportation Safety Board, said "it was impossible to say" what the cause of the crash was, outside of "an obviously premature descent." He said his team of accident investigators was still searching for the cockpit voice recorder and the aircraft's technical data recorder.

Mr. Reed said it was hoped that when these instruments were recovered, 20 they would provide a clue to the fateful last minutes.

Bill Smith, a member of the Marshall, Va. Rescue Squad, said the plane hit "well below" the peak and there was "quite a bit of fire" at the site. He said the plane devastated about 700 to 800 yards of the mountain's surface.

Vance Berry of Bluemont, who said he lived about three miles from the scene, walked to it about an hour after the crash.

"There was nothing left but what looked like a bunch of crumpled up tinfoil," he said. "You couldn't tell it had been a plane. What was left of the fuselage was burning fiercely with a blue flame, even in the rain. For 100 yards the tops of the trees had been cut off."

Mr. Berry added, "The weather was fierce—winds up to 50 miles per hour, raining and foggy. I'd say the visibility was about 100 or 150 yards."

Richard Eastman, a ground maintenance employee of T.W.A., said after 25 viewing the wreckage, "If you didn't know it was an airplane you could never guess it. The parts of the plane were scattered all over the area. There's no tail or wing that you could make out."

In Washington, relatives and friends of the victims waited in despair at private lounges at National and Dulles Airports for news from the crash site.

Carl Zwisler, a lawyer who said he believed his parents were on the plane, said Senator Birch Bayh, Democrat of Indiana, who had planned to take the plane back to Indianapolis, came into the lounge "and was very comforting."

"He was very helpful," Mr. Zwisler said. "He gave us his number and offered to try to help us any way he could."

T.W.A. said the seven crew members included three pilots, all based in Los Angeles, three stewardesses from Chicago and one from Kansas City.

AIRCRAFT ACCIDENT REPORT BY THE NATIONAL TRANSPORTATION SAFETY BOARD

At 1110 e.s.t.,[1] December 1, 1974, Trans World Airlines, Inc., Flight 514, a Boeing 727-231, N54328, crashed 25 nautical miles northwest of Dulles International Airport, Washington, D.C. The accident occurred while the flight was descending for a VOR/DME approach to runway 12 at Dulles during instrument meteorological conditions.[2] The 92 occupants—85 passengers and 7 crewmembers—were killed and the aircraft was destroyed.

---

[1] All times are eastern standard times expressed on a twenty-four-hour clock. [Eds.]

[2] VOR: very high frequency omnidirectional radio range, a radio navigation aid supplying bearing information; DME: distance measuring equipment, a radio navigation aid that provides distance information. VOR/DME is basic equipment used for an instrument landing in bad weather. [Eds.]

The National Transportation Safety Board determines that the probable cause of the accident was the crew's decision to descend to 1,800 feet before the aircraft had reached the approach segment where that minimum altitude applied. The crew's decision to descend was a result of inadequacies and lack of clarity in the air traffic control procedures which led to a misunderstanding on the part of the pilots and of the controllers regarding each other's responsibilities during operations in terminal areas under instrument meteorological conditions. Nevertheless, the examination of the plan view of the approach chart should have disclosed to the captain that a minimum altitude of 1,800 feet was not a safe altitude.

Contributing factors were:

(1) The failure of the FAA to take timely action to resolve the confusion and misinterpretation of air traffic terminology although the Agency had been aware of the problem for several years;

(2) The issuance of the approach clearance when the flight was 44 miles from the airport on an unpublished route without clearly defined minimum altitudes; and

(3) Inadequate depiction of altitude restrictions on the profile view of the approach chart for the VOR/DME approach to runway 12 at Dulles International Airport.

1. Investigation

1.1 *History of the Flight*

Trans World Airlines, Inc., Flight 514 was a regularly scheduled flight from Indianapolis, Indiana, to Washington, D.C., with an intermediate stop at Columbus, Ohio. There were 85 passengers and 7 crewmembers aboard the aircraft when it departed Columbus.

The flight was dispatched by TWA's dispatch office in New York through the operations office in Indianapolis. The captain received a dispatch package which included en route and destination weather information. The flight operated under a computer-stored instrument flight rules (IFR) flight plan.

Flight 514 departed Indianapolis at 0853 e.s.t. and arrived in Columbus at 0932. The crew obtained weather and aircraft load information. The flight departed Columbus at 1024, 11 minutes late.

At 1036, the Cleveland Air Route Traffic Control Center (ARTCC) informed the crew of Flight 514 that no landings were being made at Washington National Airport because of high crosswinds, and that flights destined for that airport were either being held or being diverted to Dulles International Airport.

At 1038, the captain of Flight 514 communicated with the dispatcher in New York and advised him of the information he had received. The dispatcher, with the captain's concurrence, subsequently amended Flight 514's release to allow the flight to proceed to Dulles.

At 1042, Cleveland ARTCC cleared Flight 514 to Dulles Airport via the Front Royal VOR, and to maintain flight level (FL) 290.[3] At 1043, the controller cleared the flight to descend to FL 230 and to cross a point 40 miles west of Front Royal at that altitude. Control of the flight was then transferred to the Washington ARTCC and communications were established with that facility at 1048.

During the period between receipt of the amended flight release and the transfer of control of Washington ARTCC, the flightcrew discussed the instrument approach to runway 12, the navigational aids, and the runways at Dulles, and the captain turned the flight controls over to the first officer.   10

When radio communications were established with Washington ARTCC, the controller affirmed that he knew the flight was proceeding to Dulles. Following this contact, the cockpit voice recorder (CVR) indicated that the crew discussed the various routings they might receive to conduct a VOR/DME approach to runway 12 at Dulles. They considered the possibilities of proceeding via Front Royal VOR, via Martinsburg VOR, or proceeding on a "straight-in" clearance.

At 1051, the Washington ARTCC controller requested the flight's heading. After being told that the flight was on a heading of 100°, the controller cleared the crew to change to a heading of 090°, to intercept the 300° radial of the Armel VOR, to cross a point 25 miles northwest of Armel to maintain 8,000 feet,[4] and ". . . the 300° radial will be for a VOR approach to runway 12 at Dulles." He gave the crew an altimeter setting of 29.74 for Dulles.[5] The crew acknowledged this clearance. The CVR recording indicated that the Armel VOR was then tuned on a navigational receiver. The pilots again discussed the VOR/DME approach to runway 12 at Dulles.

At 1055, the landing preliminary checklist was read by the flight engineer and the other crewmembers responded to the calls. A reference speed of 127 kn was calculated and set on the airspeed indicator reference pointers. The altimeters were set at 29.74.

At 1057, the crew again discussed items on the instrument approach chart including the Round Hill intersection, the final approach fix, the visual approach slope indicator and runway lights, and the airport diagram.

At 1059, the captain commented that the flight was descending from 11,000   15
feet to 8,000 feet. He then asked the controller if there were any weather obstructions between the flight and the airport. The controller replied that he did

---

[3] Altitude reference used above 18,000 feet m.s.l., using an altimeter setting of 29.92. [Eds.]

[4] All altitudes and elevations are expressed in feet above mean sea level unless otherwise noted. [Eds.]

[5] *altimeter:* an instrument that shows the altitude of the airplane with respect to a fixed level, such as sea level. [Eds.]

not see any significant weather along the route. The captain replied that the crew also did not see any weather on the aircraft weather radar. The CVR recording indicated that the captain then turned on the anti-icing system.

At 1101, the controller cleared the flight to descend to and maintain 7,000 feet and to contact Dulles approach control. Twenty-six seconds later, the captain initiated a conversation with Dulles approach control and reported that the aircraft was descending from 10,000 feet to maintain 7,000 feet. He also reported having received the information "Charlie" transmitted on the ATIS broadcast.[6]

The controller replied with a clearance to proceed inbound to Armel and to expect a VOR/DME approach to runway 12. The controller then informed the crew that ATIS information Delta was current and read the data to them. The crew determined that the difference between information Charlie and Delta was the altimeter setting which was given in Delta as 29.70. There was no information on the CVR to indicate that the pilots reset their altimeters from 29.74.

At 1104, the flight reported it was level at 7,000 feet. Five seconds after receiving that report, the controller said, "TWA 514, you're cleared for a VOR/DME approach to runway 12." This clearance was acknowledged by the captain. The CVR recorded the sound of the landing gear warning horn followed by a comment from the captain that "Eighteen hundred is the bottom." The first officer then said, "Start down." The flight engineer said, "We're out here quite a ways. I better turn the heat down."

At 1105:06, the captain reviewed the field elevation, the minimum descent altitude, and the final approach fix and discussed the reason that no time to the missed approach point was published. At 1106:15, the first officer commented that, "I hate the altitude jumping around." Then he commented that the instrument panel was bouncing around. At 1106:15, the captain said, "We have a discrepancy in our VOR's, a little but not much." He continued, "Fly yours, not mine." At 1106:27, the captain discussed the last reported ceiling and minimum descent altitude. He concluded, ". . . should break out."

At 1106:42, the first officer said, "Gives you a headache after a while, watching this jumping around like that." At 1107:27, he said, ". . . you can feel that wind down here now." A few seconds later, the captain said, "You know, according to this dumb sheet it says thirty-four hundred to Round Hill—is our minimum altitude." The flight engineer then asked where the captain saw that and the captain replied, "Well, here. Round Hill is eleven and a half DME." The first officer said, "Well, but—" and the captain replied, "When he clears you, that means you can go to your—" An unidentified voice said, "Initial approach," and another unidentified voice said, "Yeah!" Then the captain said "Initial approach altitude." The flight engineer then said, "We're out a—

20

---

[6]*ATIS*—Automatic Terminal Information Service. [Eds.]

twenty-eight for eighteen." An unidentified voice said, "Right," and someone said, "One to go."

At 1108:14, the flight engineer said, "Dark in here," and the first officer stated, "And bumpy too." At 1108:25, the sound of an altitude alert horn was recorded. The captain said, "I had ground contact a minute ago," and the first officer replied, "Yeah, I did too." At 1108:29, the first officer said, "* power on this #."[7] The captain said "Yeah—you got a high sink rate." The first officer replied, "Yeah." An unidentified voice said, "We're going uphill," and the flight engineer replied, "We're right there, we're on course." Two voices responded, "Yeah!" The captain then said, "You ought to see ground outside in just a minute.—Hang in there boy." The flight engineer said, "We're getting seasick."

At 1108:57, the altitude alert sounded. Then the first officer said, "Boy, it was—wanted to go right down through there, man," to which an unidentified voice replied, "Yeah!" Then the first officer said, "Must have had a # of a downdraft."

At 1109:14, the radio altimeter warning horn sounded and stopped. The first officer said, "Boy!" At 1109:20, the captain said, "Get some power on." The radio altimeter warning horn sounded again and stopped. At 1109:22, the sound of impact was recorded.

At 1109:54, the approach controller called Flight 514 and said, "TWA 514, say your altitude." There was no response to this or subsequent calls.

The controller subsequently testified that he noticed on the radarscope that the flight's altitude was about 2,000 feet just before he called them.

The flight data recorder (FDR) readout indicated that after the aircraft left 7,000 feet, the descent was continuous with little rate variation until the indicated altitude was about 1,750 feet. The altitude increased about 150 feet over a 15-second period and then decreased about 200 feet during a 20-second period. The recorded altitude remained about 1,750 feet until impact.

During that same portion of the flight, the indicated airspeed varied from 240 kn to 230 kn until the altitude trace leveled off about 1,750 feet after which the airspeed decreased and fluctuated between 222 kn to 248 kn. Some of the fluctuations occurred within short time spans while others were within longer spans.

The heading trace showed little variation during the latter portion of the flight. As the aircraft left 7,000 feet, the heading changed from an indication of 112° to about 120° in about 2.5 minutes. The heading did not vary more than 2° to 4° from that indication until impact.

As the aircraft left 7,000 feet, the vertical acceleration (g) trace was smooth with little fluctuation. After 40 seconds, the g trace activity increased to about ± 0.1 g. This continued for about 1 minute and then increased in amplitude to

[7]*Indicates unintelligible word(s); # indicates nonpertinent word(s).

about ± 0.2 g for about 70 seconds. At this point there was a blank in the g trace. When the trace reappeared, it was still active, with variations in indicated g ranging from ± 0.2 to 0.5 g, until impact.

The accident occurred on the west slope of Mount Weather, Virginia, about 25 nmi from Dulles, at an elevation of about 1,670 feet. The latitude was 39° 04.6°N and the longitude was 77° 52.9°W.

1.2 Injuries to Persons

Injuries	Crew	Passengers	Others
Fatal	7	85	0
Nonfatal	0	0	0
None	0	0	

1.3 Damage to Aircraft

The aircraft was destroyed.

1.4 Other Damage

Power and communications lines were damaged.

1.5 Crew Information

The flightcrew was qualified and certificated in accordance with the existing FAA requirements. The captain was qualified to operate into Dulles under the provisions of 14 CFR 121.443.

1.6 Aircraft Information

The aircraft was certified and maintained in accordance with FAA-approved procedures. The aircraft weight and balance were calculated to be within limits at takeoff and at the time of the accident. The aircraft was serviced with Jet A fuel, and there were 29,700 pounds of fuel aboard when the flight departed Columbus. There were about 19,300 pounds of fuel aboard at impact.

1.7 Meteorological Information

The weather in the area where the accident occurred was characterized by low clouds, rain mixed with occasional wet snow, and strong, gusty easterly winds. A complex low-pressure system extended from western Kentucky to southeastern Virginia and the eastern Carolinas with small low centers located in western Kentucky and south-central Virginia. An occluded front extended from the Kentucky low through North Carolina into the Virginia low.[8] A warm front extended northeastward from the Virginia low into the Atlantic, while a cold front extended from the same low to the Virginia coast, then southward into the Atlantic. A large area of low cloudiness and precipitation extended from the mid-Atlantic states to the Great Lakes, and southward to Tennessee. High gusty winds extended from the Middle Atlantic States to the Great Lakes.

The aviation weather observations taken at Washington National Airport between 0853 and 1054 reported scattered clouds at 700 feet, overcast at 1,200 feet, and visibility of 5 or more miles with very light to light rain. The winds were blowing from 70°, and the velocity varied from 25 to 28 kn with gusts of 35 kn reported at 0853, 44 kn reported at 0953, and 49 kn reported at 1054.

The aviation weather observations taken at Dulles International Airport between 0858 and 1055 reported an overcast at 900 feet with visibility varying from 3 to 7 miles in light rain. The winds were from: 080° at 20 kn gusting to 32 kn reported at 0858; 090° at 26 kn, gusting to 40 kn reported at 0955; and, 080° at 25 kn, gusting to 36 kn, reported at 1055.

The 1131 radar weather observation from Patuxent, Maryland, showed a large area of weather echoes which included the accident area. One-tenth of the area was covered with thunderstorms which were producing moderate rain showers, and five-tenths of the area was covered with moderate rain. The thunderstorm cells were moving from 170° at 45 kn. The maximum cloud tops were at 24,000 feet between Charlottesville, Virginia, and the accident site.

There were three SIGMETS[9] in effect at the time of the accident. They recommended caution due to "... moderate to severe mixed icing in clouds and precipitation above the freezing level" and embedded thunderstorms with tops near 40,000 feet. The cells were moving northeastward at 25 to 30 kn.

Although there were numerous pilot reports of weather conditions in the area around Washington, none was received from pilots flying in the area where the accident occurred.

Ground witnesses in the accident area stated that, at about the time of the accident, the local weather was characterized by low ceilings with visibilities ranging from 50 to 100 feet at the crash site. The wind was estimated at 40 mph with stronger gusts. There was a steady drizzle in the accident area.

At the request of the Safety Board, the National Weather Service (NWS) studied the possibility of pressure changes in the accident area which could have contributed to the cause of the accident. Based on the observed wind direction and velocity at Dulles at 1025 (43 kn), the NWS calculated that a pressure drop of 0.4 millibars, equivalent to 0.012 in. Hg., could have occurred if

---

[8]*occluded front:* the front formed when a warm front is overtaken by a cold front and the warm air is forced upward from the surface of the earth. [Eds.]

[9]*SIGMETS:* advisory warnings of weather severe enough to be potentially hazardous to all aircraft. They are broadcast on navigation aid voice frequencies and by flight service stations. They are also transmitted on the Service A weather teletype circuits. [Eds.]

the wind conditions in the accident area were the same as the winds at Dulles.[10] This pressure change could result in an aircraft altimeter reading 13 feet higher than the actual altitude of the aircraft. They further calculated that if the wind velocity was 60 kn, the resulting pressure change could be 3.2 millibars (0.094 in. Hg.) causing an altimeter reading 95 feet higher than the actual altitude. A wind velocity of 80 kn could result in an altitude indication 218 feet higher than the aircraft altitude.

The accident occurred in clouds and during the hours of daylight.

1.8 *Aids to Navigation*

The navigational aids in use for the VOR/DME approach to runway 12 at Dulles included the Martinsburg, Front Royal, Linden, and Armel VOR's. These navigational aids were flightchecked after the accident and were operating within the prescribed tolerances. The distance measuring function of Armel had been inoperative about 2 hours before the accident, but it was operating without reported malfunction shortly before and after the accident.

Automated radar terminal system equipment (ARTS III) was used by the approach controller to observe and control the traffic. The ARTS III is a system which automatically processes the transponder beacon return from all transponder-equipped aircraft.[11] The computed data are selectively presented on a data block next to each aircraft's updated position on the air traffic controller's radar display. The information provided on the video display is aircraft identification, groundspeed in knots, and, when the transponder of the aircraft being tracked has Mode C capability, pressure altitude in 100-foot increments. The aircraft's transponder has this capability. The position accuracy of these data is limited to about $1/4°$ in azimuth and $1/16$ nmi in range.[12] Altitude is presented with a tolerance of ± 100 feet.

The controller's radarscopes are equipped with video maps which depict various terrain features, the position of navigational aids, and other pertinent data. In this case, the video map did not display the Round Hill intersection which is the intermediate approach fix for this approach, nor did it display the high terrain northwest of that fix. The updated video maps depicting the Round Hill intersection had been ordered but had not been received at the time of the accident.

There was no current letter of agreement between Dulles Approach Control and the adjacent ARTCC's regarding the use of the Armel VOR/DME approach to runway 12 at Dulles.

---

[10]*Hg.:* mercury, used to measure atmospheric changes and thus changes in altitude. [Eds.]

[11]*transponder:* a radio transmitter-receiver. [Eds.]

[12]*azimuth:* the horizontal direction of a celestial point from a terrestrial point; *range:* a line of bearing defined by a radio range. [Eds.]

1.9 *Communications*

No air-to-ground radio communication difficulties were reported.

1.10 *Aerodrome and Ground Facilities*

Dulles International Airport is equipped with three primary runways: 12/30, 1L/19R, and 1R/19L. The north-south runways (1L/19R and 1R/19L) are 11,500 feet long and 12/30 (runway 12) is 10,000 feet long. There are provisions for ILS approaches to the north-south runways. Runway 12 is served by a VOR/DME approach. In addition, a surveillance radar approach is available to all runways. Runway 12 is equipped with high intensity runway lights but not with approach lights. There is a visual approach slope indicator (VASI) installed on the left side of the runway.

1.11 *Flight Recorders*

N54328 was equipped with Lockheed Aircraft Service Model 109-D flight data recorder, serial No. 117, and a Fairchild Model A-100 cockpit voice recorder, serial No. 1123. Both recorders were installed in a nonpressurized area aft of the pressure bulkhead. 50

The flight data recorder parameter traces were clearly recorded. There were no recorder malfunctions. A readout was made of the last 15 minutes 25 seconds of the flight. There was a small gap in the vertical acceleration trace shown on the data graph at time 13 minutes 30 seconds because of foil damage which obliterated the trace.

The cockpit voice recorder remained intact and the recording was clear. A composite flight track was prepared by correlating the recorder data.

1.12 *Wreckage*

The wreckage was contained within an area about 900 feet long and 200 feet wide. The evidence of first impact was trees whose tops were cut off about 70 feet above the ground. The elevation at the base of the trees was 1,605 feet. The wreckage path was oriented along a line 118° magnetic. Calculations indicated that the left wing went down about 6° as the aircraft passed through the trees and the aircraft was descending at an angle of about 1°. After about 500 feet of travel through the trees, the aircraft struck a rock outcropping at an elevation of about 1,675 feet. Numerous heavy components of the aircraft were thrown forward of the outcropping.

The wing flaps, wing leading edge devices, and the landing gears were retracted. The condition of the flight control system could not be determined because of impact and fire damage. No evidence was found of preimpact structural failure or control system malfunction.

All three engines separated from the aircraft and were damaged.

The major rotating compressor components were bent or broken in a direction opposite to normal rotation. There was no evidence found of preimpact engine fire or malfunction.

Most of the instruments on the pilots' instrument panels were destroyed, as were most of the aircraft navigational and flight instrument systems' components. Among those that were recovered and from which useful information could be obtained were the first officer's DME indicator which read 12 miles; the first officer's course deviation indicator which showed a selected course of 123°; and the first officer's altimeter, set at 29.70 in. Hg., with an internal indication of 1,818 feet. The first officer's flight director indicator showed the altitude marker at "0" feet, and the pitch display showed 5° aircraft noseup. An airspeed indicator was recovered with the reference pointer set at 123 kn; and a radio altimeter was found which indicated 10 feet. One distance measuring equipment interrogator unit was recovered; it showed a mileage indication of 12 miles and was tuned to a channel paired with 115.3 MHz., the frequency of the Front Royal VOR.[13]

1.13 *Medical and Pathological Information*

All of the occupants of the aircraft died of traumatic injuries. Post-mortem examinations and toxicological and histological analyses were conducted on all flight crewmembers. No evidence of disease was found and the analyses were negative. The medical histories of the flight crewmembers disclosed no evidence of abnormal conditions.

1.14 *Fire*

No evidence of in-flight fire was found. Scattered intense ground fires occurred throughout the wreckage area. Local fire departments were notified of the location of the wreckage about 1145 and about 150 fire and rescue personnel responded with six pumpers and several rescue vehicles.

1.15 *Survival Aspects*

This was not a survivable accident.

---

[13]*MHz.*: megahertz, a unit of frequency equal to one million hertz, or cycles per second. [Eds.]

QUESTIONS

1. What information is present in the Associated Press article but missing in the NTSB report? What does the NTSB report include that the newspaper account does not?

2. What does this difference in information tell you about the writers' conceptions of audience and purpose? Look back at the first two paragraphs of each report. How do these two openings reflect these conceptions?

3. The editors had to go to a library reference room to look up terms not explained by the writers of the NTSB report. Choose a term from the report that is not glossed or that is not explained clearly. Then find the best source in your library that explains the term better than the editors (or the NTSB) did.

4. Using the NTSB report, write an article for the *New York Times* in which you summarize the information in the report. Be sure to provide a headline.

5. Select an event familiar to you, and write a report about it aimed at a general audience that will need key terms explained. You might choose an event such as participating in a bicycle race or tour, entering a pet in a show, participating in a band concert or a wrestling match, preparing a special meal, or building a doghouse. Give your report to a classmate for comments on any areas that may need revision for clarity.

MAKING CONNECTIONS

Compare and contrast the in-flight recording of information that appears in the National Transportation Safety Board report with William L. Laurence's in-flight reporting of the atomic bombing of Nagasaki (p. 230). What similarities and differences can you find in the kind of information they report? In the organization and presentation of the information? In their styles of reporting?

REDUCTIO EXPANSIOQUE AD ABSURDUM

Douglas R. Hofstadter

Douglas R. Hofstadter (b. 1945) is professor of cognitive science and computer science at Indiana University, where he directs the Center for Research on Concepts and Cognition. He is known for his sophisticated ideas about creativity, analogical thought, artificial intelligence, and the nature of the mind—ideas that he has developed in several books, most notably Metamagical Themas: Questing for the Essence of Mind and Pattern *(1985),* Gödel, Escher, Bach: An Eternal Golden Braid *(1979), and* Fluid Concepts and Creative Analogies: Computer Models of the Fundamental Mechanisms of Thought *(1995). As an online review put it, this work has attracted attention for its "unorthodox vision of the mind in which perception at an abstract level is the key: perception of situations, of patterns, of patterns among patterns." Most recently he published* Le ton beau de Marot: In Praise of the Music of Language *(1997), both a celebration of the five-hundredth birthday of French poet Clément Marot and a far-flung treatise connecting translation with computer models of the mind, with analogy making, with the relationship between words and concepts, and with language in general. The following selection appeared in the collection* Mysteries of Life and the Universe: New Essays from America's Finest Writers on Science *(1994).*

In memory of Kees Boeke, author of Cosmic View

I. REDUCTIO

Scale One

She swung around the bend—a little too fast, she knew, but she needed to get there quickly. Her headlights bounced across the snow, revealing corrugated mounds several feet high at the road's edge, lining the fields. She stepped on the accelerator again and gunned the car down a straight stretch. Ahead she saw a haystack and realized another bend was coming. Timing it carefully, she put on the brakes and careened around the bend to the left, al-

297

most but not quite skidding out of control. Risky? She knew it was, yet it was exhilarating at the same time—living at the edge of the abyss, tempting fate.

Her headlights' glare caught something—something moving—something darting ahead. What's that? She slammed on the brakes. There was a loud noise as a deer smashed into her car's front end, bumper then hood then windshield, all in a fraction of a second, all blindingly fast, leaving her windshield a shattered web of white with a large hole on it where the antlers and then the head had pierced. The car was still going forty miles an hour when the deer's antlers entered her skull.

Scale Two

A piece of antler horn was movingly slowly through the air, first left, then right, then bobbing up and down a bit. A suddenly loud-growing roar was accompanied by a freezing-in-place of the bit of horn. Only half a second later, there was an enormously loud sound and the piece of horn jerked wildly. Suddenly it was being dragged along at forty miles an hour and in a strange path.

The piece of horn bounced down and slid across a cold, painted metal surface and in a tenth of a second encountered a thick sheet of glass. By itself, it would just have glanced off the glass, but it was part of a much larger piece of horn that was attached to a large massive object that was also being propelled in a strange, violent path toward the glass. So the horn, when it hit the glass, exerted much force on the sheet, and in a thousandth of a second, the sheet yielded and then cracked, with glassy splinters moving away in several directions at once from the hole the horn was opening up, while a little farther away, rays of white were shooting through the glass and forming an intricate, dense, crisscrossing web of fracture lines. The end of the piece of horn was now quite blunted, but it continued to move in approximately the same trajectory, as it was still attached to the larger body behind it, close on its heels, moving toward the glass, where it would soon open up a much larger gaping hole.

The horn fragment was now in open air, not too many inches from a sus- 5
pended mirror. It was moving at about thirty-five miles an hour relative to the mirror, having been slightly slowed down by the collision with the glass. Now it quickly crossed a one-foot stretch of empty space, and then encountered a piece of softer material—a light-colored, warm membrane, which it instantaneously pierced. This membrane covered a heavier piece of bone a quarter of an inch thick, which offered as much resistance as the glass had. It was moving toward the mirror at about five miles an hour, so the horn entered the bone at nearly forty miles an hour. Again the large mass behind it impelled it forward and the bone gave way, splintering and cracking audibly.

Beyond the bone there was a very soft mass of sticky substance much warmer than the outside air. The piece of horn moved swiftly into that substance, which was so viscous that it soon impeded the horn's further motion after a couple of inches. The horn came to rest lodged in a hunk of red, oozing, spongy matter, warm and pulsing.

Scale Three

A packet of neurons was firing away rhythmically, receiving and sending pulses every few milliseconds. Its many thousands of neurons were all engaged in a collective mode, like birds in a flock, so that when one altered its activity, all the others were quickly affected and a ripple would pass through the many neurons, putting the team into a slightly different collective mode. Every eight milliseconds, roughly, the periodic pulsing of this particular mode took place. As regular as an oscilloscope trace of a slowly changing sound, the pattern repeated. Each cycle was just barely distinguishable from the preceding one—an adiabatically changing pattern.

Then an anomalous pulse train came in from another team of neurons that didn't usually communicate with this team. Its pulses were a little faster than normal, and they had an imperative quality to them. The pulse pattern was thus disrupted from its slowly drifting, adiabatically shifting periodic firing pattern, and it made a rather abrupt transition into a different mode.

In this mode it carried out about a dozen complete cycles when another disruptive event took place: several hundred of its neurons were severed from the main body (which contained around eight thousand neurons altogether), and no more influence from them was felt. Thus the firing pattern was again altered and became less periodic, for the usual stabilizing effect of the closed system was gone. The pulsing was a little irregular but continued for many thousands of periods longer. Then it slowly ebbed, and there was a gradual cessation of firing.

Scale Four

A retinal cell was firing away quite intensely. Its job was to respond to a brightness gradient oriented at about sixty degrees from the horizontal, relative to the straight-ahead gaze of the eye to which it belonged (although it knew nothing of eyes or their gazes). The cell was firing fairly rapidly because there was, in fact, just such a brightness gradient, a fairly strong one, at forty degrees, which was close enough to sixty degrees to induce a pretty strong firing rate.

A few milliseconds passed, and the intensity gradient shifted to the next cell. At the first cell, then, the intensity became zero and so the cell slowed up in its firing. A few more milliseconds passed, and then there was a new intensity gradient, this one at about fifty degrees from the horizontal. The cell obediently switched back to a high firing rate—slightly higher than before, in fact. It stayed this way for many thousands of cycles. In fact, it was an unusually constant stimulus, for generally such stimuli changed within a small fraction of a second. But this one just stayed at exactly the same spot for so many cycles that cellular fatigue set in and the cell fired less intensely.

The cell continued to fire sporadically but began to have less and less fuel to supply its energy for firing. Usually fuel was delivered regularly, allowing firing to go ahead without any trouble. But now, for some reason, fuel supplies were diminishing, and, like the clicks of a winding-down music box, each individual pulse threatened to be the very last one, and yet the next always just barely managed to occur.

And then one time it didn't. There wasn't enough energy to make it go one more time. The cell stopped firing altogether.

Scale Five

A ribosome was clicking away, codon by codon, down a very long strand of messenger RNA. This strand was exactly like the other strand that the ribosome had run down a while earlier, but it didn't know that. It simply chugged along, and codon by codon snapped a transfer-RNA molecule into place and fastened an amino acid onto a growing polypeptide chain.

Click-click-click-click . . . Over and over, repetitive work. This ribosome was inside a mitochondrion, inside a retinal cell, inside a—but that is hardly the point. It was doing its job. It had plenty of ATP floating nearby to power the reactions that snapped off the amino acids from the strangely shaped tRNAs. The ATP molecules were small and floated near the ribosome, where they were automatically attracted whenever tRNAs entered a certain channel and were guided into a special narrow chamber deep within the ribosome.

Usually the density of ATP molecules was such that several thousand of them clustered around the ribosome. Right now, however, there were only a couple of thousand, and so the ribosome's progress was slightly retarded. Consequently, this particular copy of this familiar enzyme came off the assembly line in about twice the time it usually took. As the protein grew, new ATPs floated into the vicinity of the ribosome to take the place of ones that had been used. However, there were slightly fewer, even, to replace the used ones, and the ribosome consequently worked a little more slowly. Still, it chugged smoothly down the irregularly winding strand of messenger RNA.

As the ATPs got sparser, the ribosome slowed down. After a while, there were too few ATPs around to make the ribosome really work. Every once in a while it clicked down one more codon, but eventually it stopped.

Scale Six

An electron was circling a phosphorus nucleus, fairly far out and therefore in a fairly classical orbit. It was an easily detachable electron and was attracted by ions of all sorts when they passed nearby. This kind of electron was sure to be pulled away from the phosphorus nucleus within a very short amount of time—at least statistics would have predicted so up till now—for all the other analogous electrons had been snatched away from their nuclei quickly.

But somehow, the proper ions were simply not passing by at the right distance. The phosphorus atom was not getting linked up with the proper partners. So this particular electron, instead of do-si-do-ing its way from one atom to another, continued to cycle rhythmically and periodically around its mother nucleus.

II. EXPANSIO

Scale One

The funeral was Friday morning, and her whole bridge club turned up to 20 mourn the loss of their friend who had been so eager to join them that snowy Wednesday night in Oskaloosa. The minister uttered a moving prayer to the Lord, offering thanks for the time on earth that her soul had enjoyed, comfortingly reminding the gathered sorrowful ones that her soul had gone on to a place of peace and rest and joy. Amen.

Scale Zero

The Earth continued to spin and to revolve about the Sun. It did so many, many times in a row. After a few million such rotations, it was a bit closer in to the Sun than before, although not much. It was a little hotter, on average, partly because it was a little closer and partly because the Sun was burning its fuel differently.

After a while the Sun ballooned and its gases swallowed up the Earth and expanded far beyond it.

By this time the galaxy had rotated six times and was approaching another galaxy. Twenty rotations later, the two galaxies interpenetrated, and for a while they passed through each other like two ghosts or two ripples in water. A few million stars were destroyed, but most were unperturbed. Then after about two more rotations, the two galaxies came apart and went their separate ways.

POSTSCRIPT: Kees Boeke was a Dutch schoolteacher with a deep sense of wonder about the universe. In an attempt to share this sense with others, he wrote a classic little book called *Cosmic View: The Universe in Forty Jumps*. The book is based on a simple but powerful idea. It consists of two series of pictures: the first, beginning with a little girl sitting in a chair, zooms out over and over again, first revealing her schoolyard, then her town, then all of Holland, all of Europe, eventually engulfing the earth, the Solar System, the Galaxy, and so on to the murky edge of the known universe. A second series, starting again with the little girl, zooms inward, focusing first on a mosquito sitting on her hand, then on a nearby crystal of salt, a skin cell, a molecule, an atom, and eventually reaching the even murkier domain of elementary particles. Each of the forty jumps either increases or reduces the linear scale by an exact factor of ten, so both progressions are very smooth. The pictures are carefully drawn and clearly annotated, resulting in a book that does a wonderful job of imparting a sense of profound humility and awe for the many-tiered and mysterious universe we inhabit. Boeke's *Cosmic View* inspired a short film bearing the same name, as well as several other books, most notably *Powers of Ten*, by Philip and Phylis Morrison and Charles and Ray Eames.

QUESTIONS

1. Though the title of this piece is in Latin, you can probably figure it out by checking your college dictionary, either under *ad absurdum* or *reductio ad absurdum*. Once you have discovered the meaning of this well-known rhetorical term, speculate about what Hofstadter might have meant by altering the phrase with the addition of *Expansioque*.

2. Since this piece clearly concerns a fatal automobile accident and its aftermath, why not call it "Accident Report/Coroner's Report"? In what respects do you think it is similar to such reports? In what ways does it differ from them?

3. How would you describe the organization and development of the piece within the "Reductio" section? Why do you suppose Hofstadter refers to his subsections as "Scale One," "Scale Two," and so on? Why not just number them or refer to them as "Part One" and so on?

4. What patterns can you find repeated in each of the subsections of "Reductio"? In what respects does the "scale" change as Hofstadter moves from one subsection to the next? In what respects does the content change? In what respects does the point of view change?

5. Compare and contrast the "Reductio" and "Expansio" sections in terms of length, content, organization, development, patterns, and point of view.

6. How is your understanding of the piece affected by the biographical note about Kees Boeke that appears at the end?

7. What do you consider to be the real purposes of Hofstadter's report? In other words, what do you think Hofstadter is actually writing about here, and what is he trying to convey about it?

8. Think of an incident you've observed or read about recently, and write a report of it using Hofstadter's method in the "Reductio" section. Then write another section based on his method in "Expansio."

MAKING CONNECTIONS

Compare and contrast Hofstadter's report of this accident with the National Transportation Safety Board's report of the airplane accident (p. 284). To what extent might the numerical subsections of the NTSB report be considered similar to the "Scale" subsections of Hofstadter's report? What patterns, if any, can you find repeated in the numerical subsections of the NTSB report?

EXPLAINING

Here in "Explaining," you will find writing by specialists from a wide range of fields seeking to account for matters as various as the color of the sky, the origin of the universe, the content of urban legends, and the art of Georgia O'Keeffe. Explanation is an essential kind of writing in every academic field and profession. Facts, after all, do not speak for themselves, nor do figures add up on their own. To make sense of a subject, we need to see it in terms of something that is related to it—the color of the sky in terms of light-waves from the sun, the content of urban legends in terms of the immediate circumstances in which they are told. To understand a subject, in other words, we must examine it in terms of some relevant context that will shed light on its origin and development, its nature and design, its elements and functions, its causes and effects, or its meaning and significance. For this reason, you will repeatedly find the writers in this section drawing on specific bodies of knowledge and systems of interpretation to explain the problems and subjects that they address.

This essential element of explaining can be seen in connection with the following passage from James Jeans's "Why the Sky Is Blue":

> We know that sunlight is a blend of lights of many colors—as we can prove for ourselves by passing it through a prism, or even through a jug of water, or as Nature demonstrates to us when she passes it through the raindrops of a summer shower and produces a rainbow. We also know that light consists of waves, and that the different colors of light are produced by waves of different lengths, red light by long waves and blue light by short waves. The mixture of waves which constitutes sunlight has to struggle through the obstacles it meets in the atmosphere, just as the mixture of waves at the seaside has to struggle past the columns of the pier. And these obstacles treat the light-waves much as the columns of the pier treat the sea-waves. The long waves which constitute red light are hardly affected, but the short waves which constitute blue light are scattered in all directions.
>
> Thus, the different constituents of sunlight are treated in different ways as they struggle through the earth's atmosphere. A wave of blue light may be scattered by a dust particle, and turned out of its course. After a time a second dust particle again turns it out of its course, and

303

so on, until finally it enters our eyes by a path as zigzag as that of a flash of lightning. Consequently the blue waves of the sunlight enter our eyes from all directions. And that is why the sky looks blue.

Jeans's purpose here is to explain why the sky looks blue, and as you can see from the opening sentence of the passage, he systematically establishes an explanatory context by setting forth directly relevant information about the nature and properties of sunlight, light, and light-waves. That is, he approaches the explanatory problem in terms of knowledge drawn from his specialized fields of astronomy and physics. With this knowledge in hand, he then proceeds to show how "the different constituents of sunlight are treated in different ways as they struggle through the earth's atmosphere." In this way, he develops his explanation according to the analytic framework one would expect of an astronomer and physicist, concerning himself with the interaction of the atmosphere and lightwaves. Having formulated a cause-and-effect analysis demonstrating that blue light is scattered "in all directions," Jeans is able to conclude that "the blue waves of the sunlight enter our eyes from all directions. And that is why the sky looks blue." Thus, the particular body of information that Jeans draws on from astronomy and physics makes it possible for him to offer a knowledgeable, systematic, and instructive explanation.

To appreciate how significant an explanatory context can be, you need only consider how knowledge from other fields might influence an understanding of why the sky looks blue. A zoologist specializing in optics, for example, might note the importance of the retinal organs known as cones, which in animals are thought to be the mechanism primarily responsible for the reception of color. Given this crucial bit of information, a zoologist might observe that the sky looks blue to human beings because their eyes are equipped with cones, whereas it does not look blue to animals lacking cones, such as guinea pigs, owls, and armadillos. An anthropologist, in turn, might think it worth noting that coastal and island cultures, given their maritime environments, tend to develop unusually rich vocabularies for describing how the sea looks and how the sky looks. Thus, an anthropologist might conclude that members of maritime cultures are likely to be especially discerning about the colors of the sea and sky.

Our hypothetical zoologist and anthropologist would both differ from Jeans in their explanatory approaches to the blue sky. Whereas Jeans approached it in terms of accounting for the source and prevalence of blue color, a zoologist and an anthropologist might take the color for granted and seek instead to account for the human ability to perceive the color or the propensity of some cultures to be especially discriminating in their perception of it. Their differing approaches would result from their differing fields of study. Each academic area, after all, involves a distinctive body of knowledge, a distinctive array of interests, and a distinctive set of methods for making sense of the subjects that fall within its field of interest. Thus it follows that each area is likely to approach problems from different angles and arrive at different kinds of explanations. It follows, too, that no area can lay claim to the ultimate truth about things. But, as the case of the blue sky illustrates, each field does have a special angle on the truth, particularly about subjects that fall within its area of specialization. A zoologist and an anthropologist could be as valid and as enlightening in this case as astronomer-physicist Jeans. In a broader sense, you can see from the case of the blue sky that in trying to explain a particular subject or problem one always has to look at it or approach it from a particular angle or a combination of viewpoints and that any particular approach brings a corresponding body of knowledge to bear on an understanding of the subject. Relevant knowledge, quite simply, is the most essential element of explaining.

But knowledge alone is not sufficient to produce intelligible and effective explanation. Jeans's explanation, for example, depends not only on a body of information about the properties and movement of light and lightwaves but also, as you will see, on the form and style in which the information is presented. To develop your ability to explain, then, you will need to develop a resourcefulness in putting your knowledge to use. One way to do that is to familiarize yourself with some of the many different forms that explanatory writing can take in different academic and professional situations.

THE RANGE OF EXPLANATORY WRITING

Explanatory writing serves a wide range of academic, professional, and public purposes. Rules and regulations, guidelines and instructions—all these are familiar examples of explanation in the service of telling people how to carry on many of the practical and public activities of their lives. Textbooks, such as the one you are reading right now, as well as popularized presentations of highly specialized research or theory are common examples of explanatory writing in the service of helping people understand a particular body of information and ideas. Scholarly research papers, government documents, and other highly technical presentations of data and analysis, though less familiar to the general reader, are important kinds of explanation that advance knowledge and informed decision making.

To serve the differing needs of such varied purposes and audiences, explanatory writing necessarily incorporates various styles of presentation. Jeans's piece about the sky, for example, comes from a book intended as an introduction to astronomy. Thus, he writes in a style that depends on a vocabulary accessible to most readers. And to make sure that beginners will understand the important concepts in his explanation, Jeans repeatedly illustrates his discussion with analogies and references to familiar experiences. In fact, if you look at the whole of Jeans's piece, you will see that he establishes his analogy of light-waves to sea-waves at the very beginning of his discussion and then systematically uses it to organize and clarify the rest of his explanation.

305

By contrast, the scientific paper by Antonio R. Damasio, "Face Perception without Recognition," is written for a highly specialized audience of researchers, as you can tell immediately from the abstract that precedes it as well as from its highly technical language and scholarly reference notes. Thus, Damasio does not structure his explanation in terms of a familiar analogy but instead uses a highly methodological format for reviewing research on a particular problem. According to this format, his review begins with a definition of the research topic and a summary of established knowledge, then moves into a detailed discussion of research on issues about which there has been "considerable controversy," and finally concludes with a look at some "new developments" in the study of the problem. In each of these sections of his review, Damasio refers to specific pieces of published research, which he enumerates and documents at the end of his article. Thus, the review of research not only provides readers with an explanatory overview of investigation, but also tells them where to look for more detailed information on the subject.

For yet another variation in the format and style of explanatory writing, we need only look at Oliver Sacks's "The Man Who Mistook His Wife for a Hat." Here Sacks is offering the results of a case study, which entails the close observation of an individual subject over time. Because the subject of a case study is by definition unique, the study cannot be replicated by other researchers. A case study, therefore, must be written up in sufficient detail not only to document the observer's understanding of the subject, but also to enable other researchers to draw their own conclusions about the subject. You will find that Sacks provides an extensively detailed description, history, and analysis of Dr. P.'s behavior. You will also find that Sacks writes on the whole in a standard rather than specialized style, as befits an audience of generally educated readers.

We need only look at the following passage from the first paragraph of Joan Didion's essay, "Georgia O'Keeffe," to see that style and format do not always adhere to audience and purpose exactly as we might expect:

> I recall an August afternoon in Chicago in 1973 when I took my daughter, then seven, to see what Georgia O'Keeffe had done with where she had been. One of the vast O'Keeffe "Sky Above Clouds" canvases floated over the back stairs in the Chicago Art Institute that day, dominating what seemed to be several stories of empty light, and my daughter looked at it once, ran to the landing, and kept on looking. "Who drew it," she whispered after a while. I told her. "I need to talk to her," she said finally.

Judging from the plain style as well as the personal aspects of the story that Didion tells about her daughter's reaction to O'Keeffe's painting, you might think that this piece belongs in "Reflecting" rather than here in "Explaining." But if you read the whole of Didion's essay, you will discover that it is a highly informed piece in which she tells some surprising stories about O'Keeffe in

306

order to identify and explain what she perceives to be the most distinctive elements and qualities in O'Keeffe's work. Didion organizes her material and tells her stories in a way that is often quite surprising, yet also quite appropriate to what she considers to be most distinctive about O'Keeffe.

As you can see from our brief discussion of just this handful of selections, explanation is a widely varied form of writing, involving as it does in every case a delicate mix of adjustments to the audience, purpose, specialized field, and subject matter. As a reader of explanation, you will have to be very flexible in your approach, always willing to make your way through unfamiliar territory on the way to a clear understanding of the subject being discussed, or perhaps to a clear recognition that understanding may be beyond the scope of your knowledge in a particular field. As a writer, you will have to be equally flexible in your choice of language and your selection and arrangement of material so as to put your knowledge and understanding in a form that not only satisfies you, but also fulfills the complex set of conditions to which your explanation is addressed.

METHODS OF EXPLAINING

In planning a piece of explanatory writing, you should begin by reviewing your material with an eye to selecting an overall approach to use. You should aim to develop an approach that is adjusted to all the conditions of your explanatory situation. Some methods, you will find, are inescapable, no matter what your subject, audience, or purpose. Every piece of explanation requires that ideas be clarified and demonstrated through *illustration*—that is, through the citing of specific examples, as you can see from the earlier passage by Jeans and in the following excerpt from Sacks's essay on Dr. P., the musician:

> He saw all right, but what did he see? I opened out a copy of the *National Geographic Magazine* and asked him to describe some pictures in it.
>
> His responses here were very curious. His eyes would dart from one thing to another, picking up tiny features, individual features, as they had done with my face. A striking brightness, a color, a shape would arrest his attention and elicit comment—but in no case did he get the scene-as-a-whole. He failed to see the whole, seeing only details, which he spotted like blips on a radar screen. He never entered into relation with the picture as a whole—never faced, so to speak, *its* physiognomy. He had no sense whatever of a landscape or scene.
>
> I showed him the cover, an unbroken expanse of Sahara dunes.
>
> "What do you see here?" I asked.
>
> "I see a river," he said. "And a little guest-house with its terrace on the water. People are dining out on the terrace. I see colored parasols here and there." He was looking, if it was "looking," right off the cover into mid-air and confabulating nonexistent features, as if the absence

of features in the actual picture had driven him to imagine the river and the terrace and the colored parasols.

I must have looked aghast, but he seemed to think he had done rather well. There was a hint of a smile on his face. He also appeared to have decided that the examination was over and started to look around for his hat. He reached out his hand and took hold of his wife's head, tried to lift it off, to put it on. He had apparently mistaken his wife for a hat! His wife looked as if she was used to such things.

Sacks's obligation to illustrate and demonstrate Dr. P.'s unusual symptoms leads him here, as elsewhere in his piece, to turn to a detailed *description* and *narration* of Dr. P.'s actions. So it is that reporting constitutes an essential element of explaining—and not only for reasons of clarity, but also for purposes of reliability and credibility. If an explanation cannot be illustrated or can be only weakly documented, it is likely to be much less reliable and therefore much less credible to readers than one that can be amply and vividly detailed.

Some methods, while not required in every case, are often so important in certain pieces of explanation that they should be kept in mind. An essay that depends on the use of special terms or concepts almost certainly will call for *definitions* to ensure that the reader understands them exactly as the writer intends them to be understood. In "Urban Legends: 'The Boyfriend's Death,'" for example, Jan Harold Brunvand begins his study by carefully defining urban legends as a subclass of folklore and by defining in turn what is entailed in the study of folklore.

In his essay about Dr. P., Sacks proceeds in a different way. He presents the case of Dr. P., who is suffering from visual agnosia, by trying to replicate for the reader his own process of uncovering the mystery lying behind Dr. P.'s unusual behavior. He shows, through description and dialogue with Dr. P. and his wife, the remarkable things Dr. P. can do—demonstrate his extraordinary musical ability, for example—and the ordinary things he cannot do, such as recognize the faces of his wife and friends. At the end of this descriptive section, Sacks reveals the pathological cause of Dr. P.'s visual agnosia. But that is insufficient explanation for Sacks. He then goes on to ask how Dr. P.'s inability to make cognitive judgments should be interpreted. He talks about the limitations of neurological and psychological explanations of what appear to be neuropsychological disorders when those sciences overlook "the judgmental, the particular, the personal" and rely on the "abstract and computational" alone. In so doing, Sacks defines the limits of cognitive neurology and psychology, suggesting that they, too, may suffer from "an agnosia essentially similar to Dr. P's." Definition, in other words, can be carried out in a variety of ways—by citing examples, by identifying essential qualities or characteristics, by offering synonyms, by making distinctions.

Other methods of explanation, while not necessarily imperative, can be very effective in a broad range of explanatory situations. If you are trying to explain the character, design, elements, or nature of something, you will often do best to *compare and contrast* it with something to which it is logically and self-evidently related. Comparison calls attention to similarities; contrast focuses on differences. Together, the methods work to clarify and emphasize important points by playing related subjects against each other. In his study of urban legends, for example, Brunvand attempts to shed light on the complex circumstances that influence the content of such folktales by comparing and contrasting several versions of the same legendary story. This method enables him to show that popular urban legends, such as "The Boyfriend's Death," retain a basically unvarying situation and plot as they travel from one storyteller and locale to another, but that specific details are altered by individual storytellers to make them fit the circumstances of a particular audience. Like Brunvand's piece, some examples of comparison and contrast rely on a strategic balancing of similarities and differences. Other pieces depend largely on a sustained contrast. And still other pieces might work primarily in terms of comparison. By the same token, you should make sure that whenever you use comparison and contrast, your attention to similarities and differences is adjusted to the needs of your explanatory situation.

A special form of comparison, namely *analogy*, can also be useful in many explanatory situations. Analogies help readers understand difficult or unfamiliar ideas by putting them in tangible and familiar terms. In "Why the Sky Is Blue," for example, Jeans's analogy of lightwaves to seawaves enables us to visualize a process that we could not otherwise see. And in "Times and Distances, Large and Small," Francis Crick discusses a variety of analogies that scientists have used to help people grasp measurements of space and time that are either so vast or so diminutive as to be otherwise quite difficult to comprehend. As useful as analogies are, however, they rely at last on drawing particular resemblances between things that are otherwise unlike. Seawaves, after all, are not lightwaves, and the dimensions of the universe are not the same as anything within the range of ordinary human experience. Whenever you develop an analogy, you should be careful in applying it to your explanatory situation to make sure that the analogy fits and that it does not involve misleading implications.

Some explanatory methods are especially suited to a particular kind of situation. If you are trying to show how to do something or how something works or how something was done, you will find it best to use a method known as *process analysis*. In analyzing a process, your aim is to make it clear to a reader by providing a narrative breakdown and presentation of it step-by-step, by identifying and describing each step or stage in the process, by showing how each step leads to the next, and by explaining how the process as a whole leads to its final result. Jeans's piece, for example, analyzes the process by which lightwaves from the sun make their way through the earth's atmosphere and determine human perception of the color of the sky.

A method related to process analysis is *causal analysis*. As the term suggests, this type of analysis seeks to get at the causes of things, particularly causes that are sufficiently complex as to be open to various lines of explanation. Usually, then, a causal analysis involves a careful investigation that works backward from something difficult to account for through an examination of various causes that might account for the situation. Sometimes, however, an analysis might work forward from a particular cause to the various effects it has produced; Carol Gilligan uses this method in "Interviewing Adolescent Girls" when she shows that the problems of adolescent girls are problems of connection, of "drowning" in "the sea of Western [largely male] culture." Because no two things can be identically accounted for, no set method exists for carrying out a causal analysis. Keep in mind, however, a few cautionary procedures. You should review other possible causes and other related circumstances before attempting to assert the priority of one cause or set of causes over another, and you should present enough evidence to demonstrate the reliability of your explanation. By doing so, you will avoid the temptation to oversimplify things.

As you can probably tell by now, almost any piece of writing that aims to make sense of something will invariably have to combine several methods of explanation. This should come as no surprise if you stop to think about the way people usually explain even the simplest things in their day-to-day conversations with each other. Just ask someone, for example, to give you directions for getting from one place to another, and you will probably find that the person gives you both an overview of where the place is situated and a step-by-step set of movements to follow and places to look for, as well as brief descriptions of the most prominent guideposts along the way, and possibly even a review of the original directions, together with a brief remark or two about misleading spots to avoid. By the same token, whenever people try to explain something in writing, they want to help readers get from one place to another in a particular subject matter. Thus, in the midst of giving a process analysis or causal analysis, a writer might feel compelled to illustrate this point or define that term or offer a telling analogy.

In the several pieces that make up this section, you will see how writers in different fields combine various methods of explaining things. And in the next section, you will see how explaining also contributes to arguing.

Arts and Humanities

GEORGIA O'KEEFFE
Joan Didion

Joan Didion was born in Sacramento, California, in 1934 and graduated with a bachelor's degree in English from the University of California at Berkeley in 1956. Until the publication of her first novel, Run River, *in 1963, she worked as an associate feature editor for* Vogue *magazine. Since then she has written four more novels,* Play It As It Lays *(1971),* A Book of Common Prayer *(1977),* Democracy *(1984), and* The Last Thing He Wanted *(1997) as well as five books of essays,* Slouching towards Bethlehem *(1969),* The White Album *(1982),* Salvador *(1983),* Miami *(1987), and* After Henry *(1993). As an essayist, she has shown herself to be a trenchant observer and interpreter of American society. The following essay on Georgia O'Keeffe, a major American painter, is taken from* The White Album.

"Where I was born and where and how I have lived is unimportant," Georgia O'Keeffe told us in the book of paintings and words published in her ninetieth year on earth. She seemed to be advising us to forget the beautiful face in the Stieglitz[1] photographs. She appeared to be dismissing the rather condescending romance that had attached to her by then, the romance of extreme good looks and advanced age and deliberate isolation. "It is what I have done with where I have been that should be of interest." I recall an August afternoon in Chicago in 1973 when I took my daughter, then seven, to see what Georgia O'Keeffe had done with where she had been. One of the vast O'Keeffe "Sky Above Clouds" canvases floated over the back stairs in the Chicago Art Institute that day, dominating what seemed to be several stories of empty light, and my daughter looked at it once, ran to the landing, and kept

---

[1]*Alfred Stieglitz* (1864–1946): photographer and husband of O'Keeffe. [Eds.]

on looking. "Who drew it," she whispered after a while. I told her. "I need to talk to her," she said finally.

My daughter was making, that day in Chicago, an entirely unconscious but quite basic assumption about people and the work they do. She was assuming that the glory she saw in the work reflected a glory in its maker, that the painting was the painter as the poem is the poet, that every choice one made alone—every word chosen or rejected, every brush stroke laid or not laid down—betrayed one's character. *Style is character.* It seemed to me that afternoon that I had rarely seen so instinctive an application of this familiar principle, and I recall being pleased not only that my daughter responded to style as character but that it was Georgia O'Keeffe's particular style to which she responded: this was a hard woman who had imposed her 192 square feet of clouds on Chicago.

"Hardness" has not been in our century a quality much admired in women, nor in the past twenty years has it even been in official favor for men. When hardness surfaces in the very old we tend to transform it into "crustiness" or eccentricity, some tonic pepperiness to be indulged at a distance. On the evidence of her work and what she has said about it, Georgia O'Keeffe is neither "crusty" nor eccentric. She is simply hard, a straight shooter, a woman clean of received wisdom and open to what she sees. This is a woman who could early on dismiss most of her contemporaries as "dreamy," and would later single out one she liked as "a very poor painter." (And then add, apparently by way of softening the judgment: "I guess he wasn't a painter at all. He had no courage and I believe that to create one's own world in any of the arts takes courage.") This is a woman who in 1939 could advise her admirers that they were missing her point, that their appreciation of her famous flowers was merely sentimental. "When I paint a red hill," she observed coolly in the catalog for an exhibition that year, "you say it is too bad that I don't always paint flowers. A flower touches almost everyone's heart. A red hill doesn't touch everyone's heart." This is a woman who could describe the genesis of one of her most well-known paintings—the "Cow's Skull: Red, White and Blue" owned by the Metropolitan—as an act of quite deliberate and derisive orneriness. "I thought of the city men I had been seeing in the East," she wrote. "They talked so often of writing the Great American Novel—the Great American Play—the Great American Poetry. . . . So as I was painting my cow's head on blue I thought to myself, 'I'll make it an American painting. They will not think it great with the red stripes down the sides—Red, White and Blue—but they will notice it.'"

The city men. The men. They. The words crop up again and again as this astonishingly aggressive woman tells us what was on her mind when she was making her astonishingly aggressive paintings. It was those city men who stood accused of sentimentalizing her flowers: "I made you take time to look at what I saw and when you took time to really notice my flower you hung all your associations with flowers on my flower and you write about my flower as if I think and see what you think and see—and I don't." *And I don't.* Imagine those words spoken, and the sound you hear is *don't tread on me.* "The men" believed it impossible to paint New York, so Georgia O'Keeffe painted New York. "The men" didn't think much of her bright color, so she made it brighter. The men yearned toward Europe so she went to Texas, and then New Mexico. The men talked about Cézanne, "long involved remarks about the 'plastic quality' of his form and color," and took one another's long involved remarks, in the view of his angelic rattlesnake in their midst, altogether too seriously. "I can paint one of those dismal-colored paintings like the men," the woman who regarded herself always as an outsider remembers thinking one day in 1922, and she did: a painting of a shed "all low-toned and dreary with the tree beside the door." She called this act of rancor "The Shanty" and hung it in her next show. "The men seemed to approve of it," she reported fifty-four years later, her contempt undimmed. "They seemed to think that maybe I was beginning to paint. That was my only low-toned dismal-colored painting."

Some women fight and others do not. Like so many successful guerrillas in   5 the war between the sexes, Georgia O'Keeffe seems to have been equipped early with an immutable sense of who she was and a fairly clear understanding that she would be required to prove it. On the surface her upbringing was conventional. She was a child on the Wisconsin prairie who played with china dolls and painted watercolors with cloudy skies because sunlight was too hard to paint and with her brother and sisters, listened every night to her mother read stories of the Wild West, of Texas, of Kit Carson and Billy the Kid. She told adults that she wanted to be an artist and was embarrassed when they asked what kind of artist she wanted to be: she had no idea "what kind." She had no idea what artists did. She had never seen a picture that interested her, other than a pen-and-ink Maid of Athens in one of her mother's books, some Mother Goose illustrations printed on cloth, a tablet cover that showed a little girl with pink roses, and the painting of Arabs on horseback that hung in her grandmother's parlor. At thirteen, in a Dominican convent, she was mortified when the sister corrected her drawing. At Chatham Episcopal Institute in Virginia she painted lilacs and sneaked time alone to walk out to where she could see the line of the Blue Ridge Mountains on the horizon. At the Art Institute in Chicago she was shocked by the presence of live models and wanted to abandon anatomy lessons. At the Art Students League in New York one of her fellow students advised her that, since he would be a great painter and she would end up teaching painting in a girls' school, any work of hers was less important than modeling for him. Another painted over her work to show her how the Impressionists did trees. She had not before heard how the Impressionists did trees and she did not much care.

At twenty-four she left all those opinions behind and went for the first time to live in Texas, where there were no trees to paint and no one to tell her how not to paint them. In Texas there was only the horizon she craved. In Texas she had her sister Claudia with her for a while, and in the late afternoons they

313

would walk away from town and toward the horizon and watch the evening star come out. "The evening star fascinated me," she wrote. "It was in some way very exciting to me. My sister had a gun, and as we walked she would throw bottles into the air and shoot as many as she could before they hit the ground. I had nothing but to walk into nowhere and the wide sunset space with the star. Ten watercolors were made from that star." In a way one's interest is compelled as much by the sister Claudia with the gun as by the painter Georgia with the star, but only the painter left us this shining record. Ten watercolors were made from that star.

QUESTIONS

1. Didion's first paragraph brings together two kinds of material: research and personal experience. Didion quotes from two sources, a ninety-year-old woman and a seven-year-old child. The result is that we encounter three "I"s in the first paragraph—all female—and we also encounter a mixture of the personal and the impersonal. What is the effect of all this? How did you react to this mixture of research and personal experience? What connections can you make among the three "I"s?

2. Paragraph 3 opens with the word *hardness*. Comment on the importance of this word to Didion's essay. What does this concept add to her mixture of research and personal experience? What would the essay be like without this concept?

3. Extend your study of O'Keeffe by locating a book in the library that reproduces some of her paintings. What qualities do you find in her work? Write an essay of your own in which you describe her essential style, as you see it.

4. Select a visual artist (or an artist in any other medium) whose work interests you. Find out about this person's life and career. Then write an essay in which you explain what you like in this artist's work and why you like it, connecting the life and work through some metaphor or concept that organizes your feelings and your essay the way that "hardness" organizes Didion's.

MAKING CONNECTIONS

Compare Didion's account of Georgia O'Keeffe to the several works by female writers collected in this anthology, such as Maya Angelou's "Graduation" (p. 29), Alice Walker's "Beauty: When the Other Dancer Is the Self" (p. 40), Isak Dinesen's "The Iguana" (p. 66), and Margaret Atwood's "The Female Body" (p. 343). What themes and concerns seem common to these women?

URBAN LEGENDS
"The Boyfriend's Death"
Jan Harold Brunvand

Trained in the study of folklore, Jan Harold Brunvand (b. 1933) has become a leading collector and interpreter of contemporary legends. These "urban legends" are stories told around campfires and in college dormitories, often as true experiences that happened to somebody other than the teller of the tale. Presently a professor at the University of Utah, Brunvand has been the editor of the Journal of American Folklore *and* American Folklore: An Encyclopedia *(1996), and is the author of the standard introduction to the field,* The Study of American Folklore: An Introduction, *fourth edition (1997). The following selection is taken from the first of his several collections of urban legends,* The Vanishing Hitchhiker: American Urban Legends and Their Meanings *(1981). Here he defines* urban legend, *gives one striking example, and offers some explanations about how and why such stories flourish even in the midst of a highly technologized society. The selection as reprinted is complete, except for the deletion of a few brief references to other discussions elsewhere in Brunvand's book.*

We are not aware of our own folklore any more than we are of the grammatical rules of our language. When we follow the ancient practice of informally transmitting "lore"—wisdom, knowledge, or accepted modes of behavior—by word of mouth and customary example from person to person, we do not concentrate on the form or content of our folklore; instead, we simply listen to information that others tell us and then pass it on—more or less accurately—to other listeners. In this stream of unselfconscious oral tradition the information that acquires a clear story line is called *narrative folklore*, and those stories alleged to be true are *legends*. This, in broad summary, is the typical process of legend formation and transmission as it has existed from time immemorial and continues to operate today. It works about the same way whether the legendary plot concerns a dragon in a cave or a mouse in a Coke bottle.

It might seem unlikely that legends—*urban* legends at that—would continue to be created in an age of widespread literacy, rapid mass communications, and restless travel. While our pioneer ancestors may have had to rely heavily on oral traditions to pass the news along about changing events and frontier dangers, surely we no longer need mere "folk" reports of what's happening, with all their tendencies to distort the facts. A moment's reflection, however, reminds us of the many weird, fascinating, but unverified rumors and tales that so frequently come to our ears—killers and madmen on the loose, shocking or funny personal experiences, unsafe manufactured products, and many other unexplained mysteries of daily life. Sometimes we encounter different oral versions of such stories, and on occasion we may read about similar events in newspapers or magazines; but seldom do we find, or even seek after, reliable documentation. The lack of verification in no way diminishes the appeal urban legends have for us. We enjoy them merely as stories, and we tend at least to half-believe them as possibly accurate reports. And the legends we tell, as with any folklore, reflect many of the hopes, fears, and anxieties of our time. In short, legends are definitely part of our modern folklore—legends which are as traditional, variable, and functional as those of the past.

Folklore study consists of collecting, classifying, and interpreting in their full cultural context the many products of everyday human interaction that have acquired a somewhat stable underlying form and that are passed traditionally from person to person, group to group, and generation to generation. Legend study is a most revealing area of such research because the stories that people believe to be true hold an important place in their worldview. "If it's true, it's important" is an axiom to be trusted, whether or not the lore really *is* true or not. Simply becoming aware of this modern folklore which we all possess to some degree is a revelation in itself, but going beyond this to compare the tales, isolate their consistent themes, and relate them to the rest of the culture can yield rich insights into the state of our current civilization. . . .

URBAN LEGENDS AS FOLKLORE

Folklore subsists on oral tradition, but not all oral communication is folklore. The vast amounts of human interchange, from casual daily conversations to formal discussions in business or industry, law, or teaching, rarely constitute straight oral folklore. However, all such "communicative events" (as scholars dub them) are punctuated routinely by various units of traditional material that are memorable, repeatable, and that fit recurring social situations well enough to serve in place of original remarks. "Tradition" is the key idea that links together such utterances as nicknames, proverbs, greeting and leave-taking formulas, wisecracks, anecdotes, and jokes as "folklore"; indeed, these are a few of the best known "conversational genres" of American folklore. Longer and more complex folk forms—fairy tales, epics, myths, legends, or ballads, for example—may thrive only in certain special situations of oral transmission. All true folklore ultimately depends upon continued oral dissemination, usually within fairly homogeneous "folk groups," and upon the retention through time of internal patterns and motifs that become traditional in the oral exchanges. The corollary of this rule of stability in oral tradition is that all items of folklore, while retaining a fixed central core, are constantly changing as they are transmitted, so as to create countless "variants" differing in length, detail, style, and performance technique. Folklore, in short, consists of oral tradition in variants.

Urban legends belong to the subclass of folk narratives, legends, that—unlike fairy tales—are believed, or at least believable, and that—unlike myths—are set in the recent past and involve normal human beings rather than ancient gods or demigods. Legends are folk history, or rather quasi-history. As with any folk legends, urban legends gain credibility from specific details of time and place or from references to source authorities. For instance, a popular western pioneer legend often begins something like, "My great-grandmother had this strange experience when she was a young girl on a wagon train going through Wyoming when an Indian chief wanted to adopt her . . ." Even though hundreds of different great-grandmothers are supposed to have had the same doubtful experience (being desired by the chief because of her beautiful long blond hair), the fact seldom reaches legend-tellers; if it does, they assume that the family lore has indeed spread far and wide. This particular popular tradition, known as "Goldilocks on the Oregon Trail," interests folklorists because of the racist implications of a dark Indian savage coveting a fair young civilized woman—this legend is familiar in the *white* folklore only—and it is of little concern that the story seems to be entirely apocryphal.

In the world of modern urban legends there is usually no geographical or generational gap between teller and event. The story is *true*; it really occurred, and recently, and always to someone else who is quite close to the narrator, or at least "a friend of a friend." Urban legends are told both in the course of casual conversations and in such special situations as campfires, slumber parties, and college dormitory bull sessions. The legends' physical settings are often close by, real, and sometimes even locally renowned for other such happenings. Though the characters in the stories are usually nameless, they are true-to-life examples of the kind of people the narrators and their audience know firsthand.

One of the great mysteries of folklore research is where oral traditions originate and who invents them. One might expect that at least in modern folklore we could come up with answers to such questions, but this is seldom, if ever, the case. . . .

THE PERFORMANCE OF LEGENDS

Whatever the origins of urban legends, their dissemination is no mystery. The tales have traveled far and wide, and have been told and retold from person to person in the same manner that myths, fairy tales, or ballads spread in earlier cultures, with the important difference that today's legends are also disseminated by the mass media. Groups of age-mates, especially adolescents, are one important American legend channel, but other paths of transmission are among office workers and club members, as well as among religious, recreational, and regional groups. Some individuals make a point of learning every recent rumor or tale, and they can enliven any coffee break, party, or trip with the latest supposed "news." The telling of one story inspires other people to share what they have read or heard, and in a short time a lively exchange of details occurs and perhaps new variants are created.

Tellers of these legends, of course, are seldom aware of their roles as "performers of folklore." The conscious purpose of this kind of storytelling is to convey a true event, and only incidentally to entertain an audience. Nevertheless, the speaker's demeanor is carefully orchestrated, and his or her delivery is low-key and soft-sell. With subtle gestures, eye movements, and vocal inflections the stories are made dramatic, pointed, and suspenseful. But, just as with jokes, some can tell them and some can't. Passive tellers of urban legends may just report them as odd rumors, but the more active legend tellers re-create them as dramatic stories of suspense and, perhaps, humor.

"THE BOYFRIEND'S DEATH"

With all these points in mind folklore's subject-matter style, and oral performance, consider this typical version of a well-known urban legend that folklorists have named "The Boyfriend's Death," collected in 1964 (the earliest documented instance of the story) by folklorist Daniel R. Barnes from an eighteen-year-old freshman at the University of Kansas. The usual tellers of the story are adolescents, and the normal setting for the narration is a college dormitory room with fellow students sprawled on the furniture and floors. 10

> This happened just a few years ago out on the road that turns off highway 59 by the Holiday Inn. This couple were parked under a tree out on this road. Well, it got to be time for the girl to be back at the dorm, so she told her boyfriend that they should start back. But the car wouldn't start, so he told her to lock herself in the car and he would go down to the Holiday Inn and call for help. Well, he didn't come back and he didn't come back, and pretty soon she started hearing a scratching noise on the roof of the car. "Scratch, scratch . . . scratch, scratch." She got scareder and scareder, but he didn't come back. Finally, when it was almost daylight, some people came along and stopped and helped her out of the car, and she looked up and there was her boyfriend hanging from the tree, and his feet were scraping against the roof of the car. This is why the road is called "Hangman's Road."

Here is a story that has traveled rapidly to reach nationwide oral circulation, in the process becoming structured in the typical manner of folk narratives. The traditional and fairly stable elements are the parked couple, the abandoned girl, the mysterious scratching (sometimes joined by a dripping sound and ghostly shadows on the windshield), the daybreak rescue, and the horrible climax. Variable traits are the precise location, the reason for her abandon-

318

ment, the nature of the rescuers, murder details, and the concluding place-name explanation. While "The Boyfriend's Death" seems to have captured teenagers' imaginations as a separate legend only since the early 1960s, it is clearly related to at least two older yarns, "The Hook" and "The Roommate's Death." All three legends have been widely collected by American folklorists, although only scattered examples have been published, mostly in professional journals. Examination of some of these variations helps to make clear the status of the story as folklore and its possible meanings.

At Indiana University, a leading American center of folklore research, folk-narrative specialist Linda Dégh and her students have gathered voluminous data on urban legends, especially those popular with adolescents. Dégh's preliminary published report on "The Boyfriend's Death" concerned nineteen texts collected from IU students from 1964 to 1968. Several storytellers had heard it in high school, often at parties; others had picked it up in college dormitories or elsewhere on campus. Several students expressed some belief in the legend, supposing either that it had happened in their own hometowns, or possibly in other states, once as far distant as "a remote part of Alabama." One informant reported that "she had been sworn to that the incident actually happened," but another, who had heard some variations of the tale, felt that "it seemed too horrible to be true." Some versions had incorporated motifs from other popular teenage horror legends or local ghost stories. . . .

One of the Indiana texts, told in the state of Washington, localizes the story there near Moses Lake, "in the country on a road that leads to a dead-end right under a big weeping willow tree . . . about four or five miles from town." As in most American versions of the story, these specific local touches make believable what is essentially a traveling legend. In a detail familiar from other variants of "The Boyfriend's Death," the body—now decapitated—is left hanging upside down from a branch of the willow tree with the fingernails scraping the top of the car. Another version studied by the Indiana researcher is somewhat aberrant, perhaps because the student was told the story by a friend's parents who claimed that "it happened a long time ago, probably thirty or forty years." Here a murderer is introduced, a "crazy old lady" on whose property the couple has parked. The victim this time is skinned rather than decapitated, and his head scrapes the car as the corpse swings to and fro in the breezy night.

A developing motif in "The Boyfriend's Death" is the character and role of the rescuers, who in the 1964 Kansas version are merely "some people." The standard identification later becomes "the police," authority figures whose presence lends further credence to the story. They are either called by the missing teenagers' parents, or simply appear on the scene in the morning to check the car. In a 1969 variant from Leonardtown, Maryland, the police give a warning, "Miss, please get out of the car and walk to the police car with us, but don't look back." . . . In a version from Texas collected in 1971, set "at this lake somewhere way out in nowhere," a policeman gets an even longer line: "Young lady, we want you to get out of the car and come with us. Whatever you do, don't turn, don't turn around, just keep walking, just keep going straight and don't look back at the car." The more detailed the police instructions are, the more plausible the tale seems to become. Of course the standard rule of folk-narrative plot development now applies: the taboo must be broken (or the "interdiction violated" as some scholars put it). The girl always *does* look back, like Orpheus in the underworld, and in a number of versions her hair turns white from the shock of what she sees, as in a dozen other American legends.

In a Canadian version of "The Boyfriend's Death," told by a fourteen-year-old boy from Willowdale, Ontario, in 1973, the words of the policemen are merely summarized, but the opening scene of the legend is developed more fully, with several special details, including . . . a warning heard on the car radio. The girl's behavior when left behind is also described in more detail. 15

> A guy and his girlfriend are on the way to a party when their car starts to give them some trouble. At that same time they catch a news flash on the radio warning all people in the area that a lunatic killer has escaped from a local criminal asylum. The girl becomes very upset and at that point the car stalls completely on the highway. The boyfriend gets out and tinkers around with the engine but can't get the car to start again. He decides that he is going to have to walk on up the road to a gas station and get a tow truck but wants his girlfriend to stay behind in the car. She is frightened and pleads with him to take her, but he says that she'll be safe on the floor of the car covered with a blanket so that anyone passing will think it is an abandoned car and not bother her. Besides he can sprint along the road and get back more quickly than if she comes with him in her high-heeled shoes and evening dress. She finally agrees and he tells her not to come out unless she hears his signal of three knocks on the window. . . .

She does hear knocks on the car, but they continue eerily beyond three; the sound is later explained as the shoes of the boyfriend's corpse bumping the car as the body swings from a limb above the car.

The style in which oral narratives are told deserves attention, for the live telling that is dramatic, fluid, and often quite gripping in actual folk performance before a sympathetic audience may seem stiff, repetitious, and awkward on the printed page. Lacking in all our examples of "The Boyfriend's Death" is the essential ingredient of immediate context—the setting of the legend-telling, the storyteller's vocal and facial expression and gestures, the audience's reaction, and the texts of other similar tales narrated at the same session. Several of the informants explained that the story was told to them in spooky situations, late at night, near a cemetery, out camping, or even "while on a hayride or out parked," occasionally near the site of the supposed murder. Some students refer to such macabre legends, therefore, as "scary stories," "screamers," or "horrors."

A widely-distributed folk legend of this kind as it travels in oral tradition acquires a good deal of its credibility and effect from the localized details inserted by individual tellers. The highway and motel identification in the Kansas text are good examples of this, and in a New Orleans version, "The Boyfriend's Death" is absorbed into a local teenage tradition about "The Grunch"—a half-sheep, half-human monster that haunts specific local sites. One teenager there reported, "A man and lady went out by the lake and in the morning they found 'em hanging upside down on a tree and they said grunches did it." Finally, rumors or news stories about missing persons or violent crimes (as mentioned in the Canadian version) can merge with urban legends, helping to support their air of truth, or giving them renewed circulation after a period of less frequent occurrence.

Even the bare printed texts retain some earmarks of effective oral tradition. Witness in the Kansas text the artful use of repetition (typical of folk narrative style): "Well, he didn't come back and he didn't come back . . . but he didn't come back." The repeated use of "well" and the building of lengthy sentences with "and" are other hallmarks of oral style which give the narrator complete control over his performance, tending to squeeze out interruptions or prevent lapses in attention among the listeners. The scene that is set for the incident— lonely road, night, a tree looming over the car, out of gas—and the sound effects—scratches or bumps on the car—contribute to the style, as does the dramatic part played by the policeman and the abrupt ending line: "She looked back, and she saw . . . !" Since the typical narrators and auditors of "The Boyfriend's Death" themselves like to "park" and may have been alarmed by rumors, strange sights and noises, or automobile emergencies (all intensified in their effects by the audience's knowing other parking legends), the abrupt, unresolved ending leaves open the possibilities of what "really happened."

URBAN LEGENDS AS CULTURAL SYMBOLS

Legends can survive in our culture as living narrative folklore if they contain three essential elements: a strong basic story-appeal, a foundation in actual belief, and a meaningful message or "moral." That is, popular stories like "The Boyfriend's Death" are not only engrossing tales, but also "true," or at least so people think, and they teach valuable lessons. Jokes are a living part of oral tradition, despite being fictional and often silly, because of their humor, brevity, and snappy punch lines, but legends are by nature longer, slower, and more serious. Since more effort is needed to tell and appreciate a legend than a joke, it needs more than just verbal art to carry it along. Jokes have significant "messages" too, but these tend to be disguised or implied. People tell jokes primarily for amusement, and they seldom sense their underlying themes. In legends the primary messages are quite clear and straightforward; often they take the form of explicit warnings or good examples of "poetic justice." Secondary mes-

321

sages in urban legends tend to be suggested metaphorically or symbolically; these may provide deeper criticisms of human behavior or social condition.

People still tell legends, therefore, and other folk take time to listen to them, 20 not only because of their inherent plot interest but because they seem to convey true, worthwhile, and relevant information, albeit partly in a subconscious mode. In other words, such stories are "news" presented to us in an attractive way, with hints of larger meanings. Without this multiple appeal few legends would get a hearing in the modern world, so filled with other distractions. Legends survive by being as lively and "factual" as the television evening news, and, like the daily news broadcasts, they tend to concern deaths, injuries, kidnappings, tragedies, and scandals. Apparently the basic human need for meaningful personal contact cannot be entirely replaced by the mass media and popular culture. A portion of our interest in what is occurring in the world must be filled by some face-to-face reports from other human beings.

On a literal level a story like "The Boyfriend's Death" simply warns young people to avoid situations in which they may be endangered, but at a more symbolic level the story reveals society's broader fears of people, especially women and the young, being alone and among strangers in the darkened world outside the security of their own home or car. Note that the young woman in the story (characterized by "her high-heeled shoes and evening dress") is shown as especially helpless and passive, cowering under the blanket in the car until she is rescued by men. Such themes recur in various forms in many other urban legends. . . .

In order to be retained in a culture, any form of folklore must fill some genuine need, whether this be the need for an entertaining escape from reality, or a desire to validate by anecdotal examples some of the culture's ideals and institutions. For legends in general, a major function has always been the attempt to explain unusual and supernatural happenings in the natural world. To some degree this remains a purpose for urban legends, but their more common role nowadays seems to be to show that the prosaic contemporary scene is capable of producing shocking or amazing occurrences which may actually have happened to friends or to near-acquaintances but which are nevertheless explainable in some reasonably logical terms. On the one hand we want our factual lore to inspire awe, and at the same time we wish to have the most fantastic tales include at least the hint of a rational explanation and perhaps even a conclusion. Thus an escaped lunatic, a possibly *real* character, not a fantastic invader from outer space or Frankenstein's monster, is said to be responsible for the atrocities committed in the gruesome tales that teenagers tell. As sometimes happens in real life, the car radio gives warning, and the police get the situation back under control. (The policemen's role, in fact, becomes larger and more commanding as the story grows in oral tradition.) Only when the young lovers are still alone and scared are they vulnerable, but society's adults and guardians come to their rescue presently.

In common with brief unverified reports ("rumors"), to which they are often closely related, urban legends gratify our desire to know about and to try to understand bizarre, frightening, and potentially dangerous or embarrassing events that *may* have happened. (In rumors and legends there is always some element of doubt concerning where and when these things *did* occur.) These floating stories appeal to our morbid curiosity and satisfy our sensation-seeking minds that demand gratification through frequent infusions of new information, "sanitized" somewhat by the positive messages. Informal rumors and stories fill in the gaps left by professional news reporting, and these marvelous, though generally false, "true" tales may be said to be carrying the folk-news—along with some editorial matter—from person to person even in today's technological world.

QUESTIONS

1. In your own words, define *urban legend.*

2. Had you ever heard the story of "The Boyfriend's Death" before? Did you believe it was true? Can you remember the circumstances in which you first heard this legend (or a similar one)? Describe your first encounter with the tale. How does your experience compare with those described by Brunvand?

3. Below is a list of other tales collected by Brunvand. Do you know any stories that might correspond to these titles?

> The Vanishing Hitchhiker
> The Mexican Pet
> The Baby-Sitter and the Man Upstairs
> The Microwaved Pet
> The Toothbrush Story
> Alligators in the Sewers
> The Nude in the RV
> The Kidney Heist

Briefly describe the stories you have heard. Compare the various versions produced by members of the class. What are the variables in the tale, and what seem to be the common features?

4. Do you know a story that sounds like an urban legend but is really true? Can you prove it?

5. Select an urban legend that you have recently heard. Write down the best version of it that you can, then analyze what you have written as an urban legend. That is, explain what features mark it as an urban legend, and discuss the elements in it that have made it interesting or appealing to you.

6. Can you remember someone who told you something as a "true" story that you now recognize as an urban legend? Write an essay in which you first describe that person and report on the legend he or she told you, and then go on to explain to that person that the story he or she told is not actually true but is an urban legend. If you think

that your explanation would not convince the person in question, try to explain why this is so. Describe the resistance you might encounter, and indicate how you might modify your explanation to make it more persuasive.

MAKING CONNECTIONS

1. Several of the pieces in "Reporting" deal with events that could provide the material for an urban legend. The AP report of the air crash (p. 284), Richard Selzer's "The Discus Thrower" (p. 276), and Michael Brown's "Love Canal and the Poisoning of America" (p. 261) are examples. What elements of these stories qualify them as urban legends? In what ways do they not qualify as urban legends?

2. Rewrite the AP report of the air crash (p. 284), "The Discus Thrower" (p. 276), or "Love Canal and the Poisoning of America" (p. 261) as an urban legend. Make any changes you find necessary to make it read like an urban legend. Then write a few paragraphs of explanation, discussing the changes you made and why you made them.

WHAT HIGH SCHOOL IS

Theodore R. Sizer

Born in New Haven, Connecticut, in 1932 and educated at Yale and Harvard Universities, Theodore R. Sizer has been headmaster at Phillips Academy in Andover, Massachusetts, dean of the Graduate School of Education at Harvard, and chairman of the Education Department at Brown University. He is the author of several influential books on educational reform and American secondary schools. His book Horace's Compromise: The Dilemma of the American High School (1984) *reports the results of a study of American high schools sponsored by the National Association of Independent Schools. The selection reprinted here is the first chapter of the second section of that book, "The Program."*

Mark, sixteen and a genial eleventh-grader, rides a bus to Franklin High School, arriving at 7:25. It is an Assembly Day, so the schedule is adapted to allow for a meeting of the entire school. He hangs out with his friends, first outside school and then inside, by his locker. He carries a pile of textbooks and notebooks; in all, it weighs eight and a half pounds.

From 7:30 to 8:19, with nineteen other students, he is in Room 304 for English class. The Shakespeare play being read this year by the eleventh grade is *Romeo and Juliet*. The teacher, Ms. Viola, has various students in turn take parts and read out loud. Periodically, she interrupts the (usually halting) recitations to ask whether the thread of the conversation in the play is clear. Mark is entertained by the stumbling readings of some of his classmates. He hopes he will not be asked to be Romeo, particularly if his current steady, Sally, is Juliet. There is a good deal of giggling in class, and much attention paid to who may be called on next. Ms. Viola reminds the class of a test on this part of the play to be given next week.

The bell rings at 8:19. Mark goes to the boys' room, where he sees a classmate who he thinks is a wimp but who constantly tries to be a buddy. Mark avoids the leech by rushing off. On the way, he notices two boys engaged in some sort of transaction, probably over marijuana. He pays them no attention. 8:24. Typing class. The rows of desks that embrace big office machines are almost filled before the bell. Mark is uncomfortable here: typing class is girl country. The teacher constantly threatens what to Mark is a humiliatingly female future: "Your employer won't like these erasures." The minutes during the period are spent copying a letter from a handbook onto business stationery. Mark struggles to keep from looking at his work; the teacher wants him to watch only the material from which he is copying. Mark is frustrated, uncomfortable, and scared that he will not complete his letter by the class's end, which would be embarrassing.

Nine tenths of the students present at school that day are assembled in the auditorium by the 9:18 bell. The dilatory tenth still stumble in, running down aisles. Annoyed class deans try to get the mob settled. The curtains part; the program is a concert by a student rock group. Their electronic gear flashes under the lights, and the five boys and one girl in the group work hard at being casual. Their movements on stage are studiously at three-quarter time, and they chat with one another as though the tumultuous screaming of their schoolmates were totally inaudible. The girl balances on a stool; the boys crank up the music. It is very soft rock, the sanitized lyrics surely cleared with the assistant principal. The girl sings, holding the mike close to her mouth, but can scarcely be heard. Her light voice is tentative, and the lyrics indecipherable. The guitars, amplified, are tuneful, however, and the drums are played with energy.

The students around Mark—all juniors, since they are seated by class—alternately slouch in their upholstered, hinged seats, talking to one another, or sit forward, leaning on the chair backs in front of them, watching the band. A boy near Mark shouts noisily at the microphone-fondling singer, "Bite it . . . ohhh," and the area around Mark explodes in vulgar male laughter, but quickly subsides. A teacher walks down the aisle. Songs continue, to great applause. Assembly is over at 9:46, two minutes early. 5

9:53 and biology class. Mark was at a different high school last year and did not take this course there as a tenth-grader. He is in it now, and all but one of his classmates are a year younger than he. He sits on the side, not taking part in the chatter that goes on after the bell. At 9:57, the public address system goes on, with the announcements of the day. After a few words from the principal ("Here's today's cheers and jeers . . ." with a cheer for the winning basketball team and a jeer for the spectators who made a ruckus at the gymnasium), the task is taken over by officers of ASB (Associated Student Bodies). There is an appeal for "bat bunnies." Carnations are for sale by the Girls' League. Miss Indian American is coming. Students are auctioning off their services (background catcalls are heard) to earn money for the prom. Nominees are needed for the ballot for school bachelor and school bachelorette. The announcements end with a "thought for the day. When you throw a little mud, you lose a little ground."

At 10:04 the biology class finally turns to science. The teacher, Mr. Robbins, has placed one of several labeled laboratory specimens—some are pinned in frames, others swim in formaldehyde—on each of the classroom's eight laboratory tables. The three or so students whose chairs circle each of these benches are to study the specimen and make notes about it or drawings of it. After a few minutes each group of three will move to another table. The teacher points out that these specimens are of organisms already studied in previous classes. He says that the period-long test set for the following day will involve observing some of these specimens—then to be without labels—and writing an identifying paragraph on each. Mr. Robbins points out that some of the printed labels ascribe the specimens names different from those given in the textbook. He explains that biologists often give several names to the same organism.

The class now falls to peering, writing, and quiet talking. Mr. Robbins comes over to Mark, and in whispered words asks him to carry a requisition form for science department materials to the business office. Mark, because of his "older" status, is usually chosen by Robbins for this kind of errand. Robbins gives Mark the form and a green hall pass to show to any teacher who might challenge him, on his way to the office, for being out of a classroom. The errand takes Mark four minutes. Meanwhile Mark's group is hard at work but gets to only three of the specimens before the bell rings at 10:42. As the students surge out, Robbins shouts a reminder about a "double" laboratory period on Thursday.

Between classes one of the seniors asks Mark whether he plans to be a candidate for schoolwide office next year. Mark says no. He starts to explain. The 10:47 bell rings, meaning that he is late for French class.

There are fifteen students in Monsieur Bates's language class. He hands out 10 tests taken the day before: "*C'est bien fait, Etienne . . . c'est mieux, Marie . . . Tch, tch, Robert . . .*" Mark notes his C+ and peeks at the A– in front of Susanna, next to him. The class has been assigned seats by M. Bates; Mark resents sitting next to prissy, brainy Susanna. Bates starts by asking a student to read a question and give the correct answer. "*James, question un.*" James haltingly reads the question and gives the answer that Bates, now speaking English, says is incomplete. In due course: "*Mark, question cinq.*" Mark does his bit, and the sequence goes on, the eight quiz questions and answers filling about twenty minutes of time.

"Turn to page forty-nine. *Maintenant, lisez après moi . . .*" and Bates reads a sentence and has the class echo it. Mark is embarrassed by this and mumbles with a barely audible sound. Others, like Susanna, keep the decibel count up, so Mark can hide. This I-say-you-repeat drill is interrupted once by the public address system, with an announcement about a meeting for the cheerleaders. Bates finishes the class, almost precisely at the bell, with a homework assignment. The students are to review these sentences for a brief quiz the following day. Mark takes note of the assignment, because he knows that tomorrow will be a day of busy-work in French class. Much though he dislikes oral drills, they are better than the workbook stuff that Bates hands out. Write, write, write, for Bates to throw away, Mark thinks.

11:36. Down to the cafeteria, talking noisily, hanging, munching. Getting to room 104 by 12:17: U.S. history. The teacher is sitting cross-legged on his desk when Mark comes in, heatedly arguing with three students over the fracas that had followed the previous night's basketball game. The teacher, Mr. Suslovic, while agreeing that the spectators from their school certainly were provoked, argues that they should neither have been so obviously obscene in yelling at the opposing cheerleaders nor have allowed Coke cans to be rolled out on the floor. The three students keep saying that "it isn't fair." Apparently they and some others had been assigned "Saturday mornings" (detentions) by the principal for the ruckus.

At 12:34, the argument appears to subside. The uninvolved students, including Mark, are in their seats, chatting amiably. Mr. Suslovic climbs off his desk and starts talking: "We've almost finished this unit, chapters nine and ten . . ." The students stop chattering among themselves and turn toward Suslovic. Several slouch down in their chairs. Some open notebooks. Most have the five-pound textbook on their desks.

Suslovic lectures on the cattle drives, from north Texas to railroads west of St. Louis. He breaks up this narrative with questions ("Why were the railroad lines laid largely east to west?"), directed at nobody in particular and eventually answered by Suslovic himself. Some students take notes. Mark doesn't. A student walks in the open door, hands Mr. Suslovic a list, and starts whispering with him. Suslovic turns from the class and hears out this messenger. He then asks, "Does anyone know where Maggie Sharp is?" Someone answers, "Sick at home"; someone else says, "I thought I saw her at lunch." Genial consternation. Finally Suslovic tells the messenger, "Sorry, we can't help you," and returns to the class: "Now, where were we?" He goes on for some minutes. The bell rings. Suslovic forgets to give the homework assignment.

1:11 and Algebra II. There is a commotion in the hallway: someone's locker is rumored to have been opened by the assistant principal and a narcotics agent. In the five-minute passing time, Mark hears the story three times and three ways. A locker had been broken into by another student. It was Mr. Gregory and a narc. It was the cops, and they did it without Gregory's knowing. Mrs. Ames, the mathematics teacher, has not heard anything about it. Several of the nineteen students try to tell her and start arguing among themselves. "O.K., that's enough." She hands out the day's problem, one sheet to each student. Mark sees with dismay that it is a single, complicated "word" problem about some train that, while traveling at 84 mph, due west, passes a car that was going due east at 55 mph. Mark struggles: Is it $d = rt$ or $t = rd$? The class becomes quiet, writing, while Mrs. Ames writes some additional, short problems on the blackboard. "Time's up." A sigh; most students still writing. A muffled "Shit." Mrs. Ames frowns. "Come on, now." She collects papers, but it takes four minutes for her to corral them all.

"Copy down the problems from the board." A minute passes. "William, try number one." William suggests an approach. Mrs. Ames corrects and cajoles, and William finally gets it right. Mark watches two kids to his right passing notes; he tries to read them, but the handwriting is illegible from his distance. He hopes he is not called on, and he isn't. Only three students are asked to puzzle out an answer. The bell rings at 2:00. Mrs. Ames shouts a homework assignment over the resulting hubbub.

Mark leaves his books in his locker. He remembers that he has homework, but figures that he can do it during English class the next day. He knows that there will be an in-class presentation of one of the *Romeo and Juliet* scenes and that he will not be in it. The teacher will not notice his homework writing, or won't do anything about it if she does.

Mark passes various friends heading toward the gym, members of the basketball teams. Like most students, Mark isn't an active school athlete. However, he is associated with the yearbook staff. Although he is not taking "Yearbook" for credit as an English course, he is contributing photographs. Mark takes twenty minutes checking into the yearbook staff's headquarters (the classroom of its faculty adviser) and getting some assignments of pictures from his boss, the senior who is the photography editor. Mark knows that if he pleases his boss and the faculty adviser, he'll take that editor's post for the next year. He'll get English credit for his work then.

After gossiping a bit with the yearbook staff, Mark will leave school by 2:35 and go home. His grocery market bagger's job is from 4:45 to 8:00, the rush hour for the store. He'll have a snack at 4:30, and his mother will save him some supper to eat at 8:30. She will ask whether he has any homework, and he'll tell her no. Tomorrow, and virtually every other tomorrow, will be the same for Mark, save for the lack of the assembly: each period then will be five minutes longer.

Most Americans have an uncomplicated vision of what secondary education 20 should be. Their conception of high school is remarkably uniform across the country, a striking fact, given the size and diversity of the United States and the politically decentralized character of the schools. This uniformity is of several generations' standing. It has, however, two appearances, each quite different from the other, one of words and the other of practice, a world of political rhetoric and Mark's world.

A California high school's general goals, set out in 1979, could serve equally well most of America's high schools, public and private. This school had as its ends:

- Fundamental scholastic achievement . . . to acquire knowledge and share in the traditionally academic fundamentals . . . to develop the ability to make decisions, to solve problems, to reason independently, and to accept responsibility for self-evaluation and continuing self-improvement.

- Career and economic competence . . .

- Citizenship and civil responsibility . . .

- Competence in human and social relations . . .

329

- Moral and ethical values . . .
- Self-realization and mental and physical health . . .
- Aesthetic awareness . . .
- Cultural diversity . . .[1]

In addition to its optimistic rhetoric, what distinguishes this list is its comprehensiveness. The high school is to touch most aspects of an adolescent's existence—mind, body, morals, values, career. No one of these areas is given especial prominence. School people arrogate to themselves an obligation to all.

An example of the wide acceptability of these goals is found in the courts. Forced to present a detailed definition of "thorough and efficient education," elementary as well as secondary, a West Virginia judge sampled the best of conventional wisdom and concluded that

> there are eight general elements of a thorough and efficient system of education: (a) Literacy, (b) The ability to add, subtract, multiply, and divide numbers, (c) Knowledge of government to the extent the child will be equipped as a citizen to make informed choices among persons and issues that affect his own governance, (d) Self-knowledge and knowledge of his or her total environment to allow the child to intelligently choose life work—to know his or her options, (e) Work-training and advanced academic training as the child may intelligently choose, (f) Recreational pursuits, (g) Interests in all creative arts such as music, theater, literature, and the visual arts, and (h) Social ethics, both behavioral and abstract, to facilitate compatibility with others in this society.[2]

That these eight—now powerfully part of the debate over the purpose and practice of education in West Virginia—are reminiscent of the influential list, "The Seven Cardinal Principles of Secondary Education," promulgated in 1918 by the National Education Association, is no surprise.[3] The rhetoric of high school purpose has been uniform and consistent for decades. Americans agree on the goals for their high schools.

---

[1]Shasta High School, Redding, California. An eloquent and analogous statement, "The Essentials of Education," one stressing explicitly the "interdependence of skills and content" that is implicit in the Shasta High School statement, was issued in 1980 by a coalition of educational associations. Organizations for the Essentials of Education (Urbana, Illinois).

[2]Judge Arthur M. Recht, in his order resulting from *Pauley v. Kelly*, 1979, as reprinted in *Education Week*, May 26, 1982, p. 10. See also, in *Education Week*, January 16, 1983, pp. 21, 24, Jonathan P. Sher, "The Struggle to Fulfill a Judicial Mandate: How Not to 'Reconstruct' Education in W. Va."

[3]Bureau of Education, Department of the Interior, "Cardinal Principles of Secondary Education: A Report of the Commission on the Reorganization of Secondary Education, appointed by the National Education Association," *Bulletin*, no. 35 (Washington: U.S. Government Printing Office, 1918).

That agreement is convenient, but it masks the fact that virtually all the words in these goal statements beg definition. Some schools have labored long to identify specific criteria beyond them; the result has been lists of daunting pseudospecificity and numbing earnestness. However, most leave the words undefined and let the momentum of traditional practice speak for itself. That is why analyzing how Mark spends his time is important: from watching him one uncovers the important purposes of education, the ones that shape practice. Mark's day is similar to that of other high school students across the country, as similar as the rhetoric of one goal statement to others'. Of course, there are variations, but the extent of consistency in the shape of school routine for a large and diverse adolescent population is extraordinary, indicating more graphically than any rhetoric the measure of agreement in America about what one does in high school, and, by implication, what it is for.

The basic organizing structures in schools are familiar. Above all, students are grouped by age (that is, freshman, sophomore, junior, senior), and all are expected to take precisely the same time—around 720 school days over four years, to be precise—to meet the requirements for a diploma. When one is out of his grade level, he can feel odd, as Mark did in his biology class. The goals are the same for all, and the means to achieve them are also similar.

Young males and females are treated remarkably alike; the schools' goals are the same for each gender. In execution, there are differences, as those pressing sex discrimination suits have made educators intensely aware. The students in metalworking classes are mostly male; those in home economics, mostly female. But it is revealing how much less sex discrimination there is in high schools than in other American institutions. For many young women, the most liberated hours of their week are in school.

School is to be like a job: you start in the morning and end in the afternoon, five days a week. You don't get much of a lunch hour, so you go home early, unless you are an athlete or are involved in some special school or extracurricular activity. School is conceived of as the children's workplace, and it takes young people off parents' hands and out of the labor market during prime-time work hours. Not surprisingly, many students see going to school as little more than a dogged necessity. They perceive the day-to-day routine, a Minnesota study reports, as one of "boredom and lethargy." One of the students summarizes: School is "boring, restless, tiresome, puts ya to sleep, tedious, monotonous, pain in the neck."[4]

The school schedule is a series of units of time: the clock is king. The base time block is about fifty minutes in length. Some schools, on what they call modular scheduling, split that fifty-minute block into two or even three pieces.

---

[4]Diane Hedin, Paula Simon, and Michael Robin, *Minnesota Youth Poll: Youth's Views on School and School Discipline*, Minnesota Report 184 (1983), Agricultural Experiment Station, University of Minnesota, p. 13.

Most schools have double periods for laboratory work, especially in the sciences, or four-hour units for the small numbers of students involved in intensive vocational or other work-study programs. The flow of all school activity arises from or is blocked by these time units. "How much time do I have with my kids" is the teacher's key question.

Because there are many claims for those fifty-minute blocks, there is little time set aside for rest between them, usually no more than three to ten minutes, depending on how big the school is and, consequently, how far students and teachers have to walk from class to class. As a result, there is a frenetic quality to the school day, a sense of sustained restlessness. For the adolescents, there are frequent changes of room and fellow students, each change giving tempting opportunities for distraction, which are stoutly resisted by teachers. Some schools play soft music during these "passing times," to quiet the multitude, one principal told me.

Many teachers have a chance for a coffee break. Few students do. In some city schools where security is a problem, students must be in class for seven consecutive periods, interrupted by a heavily monitored twenty-minute lunch period for small groups, starting as early as 10:30 A.M. and running to after 1:00 P.M. A high premium is placed on punctuality and on "being where you're supposed to be." Obviously, a low premium is placed on reflection and repose. The students rush from class to class to collect knowledge. Savoring it, it is implied, is not to be done much in school, nor is such meditation really much admired. The picture that these familiar patterns yield is that of an academic supermarket. The purpose of going to school is to pick things up, in an organized and predictable way, the faster the better.

What is supposed to be picked up is remarkably consistent among all sorts of high schools. Most schools specifically mandate three out of every five courses a student selects. Nearly all of these mandates fall into five areas—English, social studies, mathematics, science, and physical education. On the average, English is required to be taken each year, social studies and physical education three out of the four high school years, and mathematics and science one or two years. Trends indicate that in the mid-eighties there is likely to be an increase in the time allocated to these last two subjects. Most students take classes in these four major academic areas beyond the minimum requirements, sometimes in such special areas as journalism and "yearbook," offshoots of English departments.[5]

Press most adults about what high school is for, and you hear these subjects listed. *High school? That's where you learn English and math and that sort of*

[5]I am indebted to Harold F. Sizer and Lyde E. Sizer for a survey of the diploma requirements of fifty representative secondary schools, completed for A *Study of High Schools.*

thing. Ask students, and you get the same answer. High school is to "teach" these "subjects."

What is often absent is any definition of these subjects or any rationale for them. They are just there, labels. Under those labels lie a multitude of things. A great deal of material is supposed to be "covered"; most of these courses are surveys, great sweeps of the stuff of their parent disciplines.

While there is often a sequence *within* subjects—algebra before trigonometry, "first-year" French before "second-year" French—there is rarely a coherent relationship or sequence *across* subjects. Even the most logically related matters—reading ability as a precondition for the reading of history books, and certain mathematical concepts or skills before the study of some of physics—are only loosely coordinated, if at all. There is little demand for a synthesis of it all; English, mathematics, and the rest are discrete items, to be picked up individually. The incentive for picking them up is largely through tests and, with success at these, in credits earned.

Coverage within subjects is the key priority. If some imaginative teacher makes a proposal to force the marriage of, say, mathematics and physics or to require some culminating challenges to students to use several objects in the solution of a complex problem, and if this proposal will take "time" away from other things, opposition is usually phrased in terms of what may be thus forgone. If we do that, we'll have to give up colonial history. We won't be able to get to programming. We'll not be able to read *Death of a Salesman.* There isn't time. The protesters usually win out.

The subjects come at a student like Mark in random order, a kaleidoscope ³⁵ of worlds: algebraic formulae to poetry to French verbs to Ping-Pong to the War of the Spanish Succession, all before lunch. Pupils are to pick up these things. Tests measure whether the picking up has been successful.

The lack of connection between stated goals, such as those of the California high school cited earlier, and the goals inherent in school practice is obvious and, curiously, tolerated. Most striking is the gap between statements about "self-realization and mental and physical growth" or "moral and ethical values"—common rhetoric in school documents—and practice. Most physical education programs have neither the time nor the focus really to ensure fitness. Mental health is rarely defined. Neither are ethical values, save at the negative extremes, such as opposition to assault or dishonesty. Nothing in the regimen of a day like Mark's signals direct or implicit teaching in this area. The "school boy code" (not ratting on a fellow student) protects the marijuana pusher, and a leechlike associate is shrugged off without concern. The issue of the locker search was pushed aside, as not appropriate for class time.

Most students, like Mark, go to class in groups of twenty to twenty-seven students. The expected attendance in some schools, particularly those in low-income areas, is usually higher, often thirty-five students per class, but high absentee rates push the actual numbers down. About twenty-five per class is an average figure for expected attendance, and the actual numbers are somewhat lower. There are remarkably few students who go to class in groups much larger or smaller than twenty-five.[6]

A student such as Mark sees five or six teachers per day; their differing styles and expectations are part of his kaleidoscope. High school staffs are highly specialized: guidance counselors rarely teach mathematics, mathematics teachers rarely teach English, principals rarely do any classroom instruction. Mark, then, is known a little bit by a number of people, each of whom sees him in one specialized situation. No one may know him as a "whole person" — unless he becomes a special problem or has special needs.

Save in extracurricular or coaching situations, such as in athletics, drama, or shop classes, there is little opportunity for sustained conversation between student and teacher. The mode is a one-sentence or two-sentence exchange: *Mark, when was Grover Cleveland president?* Let's see, was 1890 . . . or something . . . wasn't he the one . . . he was elected twice, wasn't he . . . *Yes* . . . *Gloria, can you get the dates right?* Dialogue is strikingly absent, and as a result the opportunity of teachers to challenge students' ideas in a systematic and logical way is limited. Given the rushed, full quality of the school day, it can seldom happen. One must infer that careful probing of students' thinking is not a high priority. How one gains (to quote the California school's statement of goals again) "the ability to make decisions, to solve problems, to reason independently, and to accept responsibility for self-evaluation and continuing self-improvement" without being challenged is difficult to imagine. One certainly doesn't learn these things merely from lectures and textbooks.

Most schools are nice places. Mark and his friends enjoy being in theirs. The adults who work in schools generally like adolescents. The academic pressures are limited, and the accommodations to students are substantial. For example, if many members of an English class have jobs after school, the English teacher's expectations for them are adjusted, downward. In a word, school is sensitively accommodating, as long as students are punctual, where they are supposed to be, and minimally dutiful about picking things up from the clutch of courses in which they enroll.

This characterization is not pretty, but it is accurate, and it serves to describe the vast majority of American secondary schools. "Taking subjects" in a systematized, conveyer-belt way is what one does in high school. That this process is, in substantial respects, not related to the rhetorical purposes of education is tolerated by most people, perhaps because they do not really either believe in those ill-defined goals or, in their heart of hearts, believe that schools can or should even try to achieve them. The students are happy taking subjects. The parents are happy, because that's what they did in high school. The rituals, the most important of which is graduation, remain intact. The adoles-

40

---

[6]Education Research Service, Inc., *Class Size: A Summary of Research* (Arlington, Virginia, 1978); and *Class Size Research: A Critique of Recent Meta-Analyses* (Arlington, Virginia, 1980).

cents are supervised safely and constructively most of the time, during the morning and afternoon hours, and they are off the labor market. That is what high school is all about.

QUESTIONS

1. The first half of this essay (the first nineteen paragraphs, to be exact) is a report. What do you think of this report? Given your own experience, how accurate is it? What attitude does the report convey, or is it objective?

2. Paragraph 19 is the conclusion of the report. It ends the story of Mark's day. Does it draw or imply any conclusions from the events reported?

3. How is the explanatory section of the essay (paragraphs 20 through 41) organized? The first subtopic discussed is the goals of high school. What are the other subtopics?

4. What is the major conclusion of this explanation? To what extent do you agree with the last sentence of the essay and what it implies?

5. How does the report (paragraphs 1 through 19) function in the explanation that follows? What would be lost if the report were omitted? In considering how the two sections of the essay relate, note especially places where the explanation specifically refers to the report.

6. You may have a different view of high school, or perhaps you went to a different kind of school. Write an essay that is organized like Sizer's but that presents your own report and explanation of what school is.

7. Using the basic outline of Sizer's essay, write your own explanation of the workings of some institution: store, family, church or temple, club, team, or whatever else you know well. Think of your project in terms of Sizer's title: "What X Is."

MAKING CONNECTIONS

1. How do you suppose Sizer got this information about Mark and "what high school is"? Compare his approach to that of Farley Mowat (p. 237), Jane van Lawick-Goodall (p. 241), and Monica M. Moore (p. 469). Which one of these writers comes closest, do you think, to Sizer's method for researching his essay? Explain the resemblances and differences.

2. Sizer presents a teenage boy's high school day. Taking Carol Gilligan's "Interviewing Adolescent Girls" (p. 409) into account, write a shorter version of the high school day of a teenage girl.

ABOUT FACE
Joseph Epstein

Joseph Epstein was born in Chicago in 1937 and graduated from the University of Chicago. For many years, he wrote under the name Aristides for the journal The American Scholar; *he was its editor from 1975 to 1996. He considers the essay his specialty but has also published a collection of short stories,* The Goldin Boys *(1991), set in Chicago. This essay originally appeared in* The American Scholar *in 1981. Unlike many of his essays, which are about literary matters, here Epstein faces the mirror.*

"At fifty," wrote Orwell, "everyone has the face he deserves." I believe this and repeat it with confidence, being myself forty-six and hopeful that for me there is still time. I hope, that is, that within the next four years I shall be able to develop a noble brow, a strong chin, a deep and penetrating gaze, a nose that doesn't disappoint. This may take some doing, for I have been told by different people at different times that I resemble the following odd cast of characters: the actors Sal Mineo, Russ Tamblyn, and Ken Berry, the scholar Walter Kaufmann, the assassin Lee Harvey Oswald, and a now-deceased Yorkshire terrier named Max. Despite this, and even though no one has ever noted a resemblance in me to Alexander the Great or Lord Byron, I tend to think of myself, as I expect most men do, as a nice-enough looking chap. Beyond that I am not prepared to go, for I have long appreciated the fact that the limits of self-knowledge begin at one's own kisser. To have stared at the damned thing so long and yet still not to know what it reveals is a true tribute to the difficulties of self-analysis. So while I tend to believe, with Orwell, that everyone has the face he deserves, I gaze into the mirror and cannot tell whether justice has been done.

The notion that the face is a text to be read for clues to human character is one with a long history. It goes back at least as far as Aristotle, among whose works is that entitled *History of Animals and A Treatise on Physiognomy*. Almost all work in physiognomy, the putative science dealing with the connection between facial features and psychological characteristics, has been disqualified, and the *Encyclopaedia Britannica*, in a brief article on the subject, notes: "Since many efforts to specify such relationships [between facial features and personal character] have been discredited, the term physiognomy commonly connotes pseudoscience or charlatanry (see Fortunetelling; Palmistry)." Which makes very good sense, except that I cannot bring myself altogether to believe it. On the subject of physiognomy, I find myself in the condition of a man I once heard about who, at the end of a career of thirty-odd years working for the Anti-Defamation League, remarked that, after fighting all that time against every racial and religious stereotype, he had come to believe that perhaps there was more to these stereotypes than he had thought when he had started on the job. Rather like that man, I fear that, while I believe physiognomy to have been largely discredited, there may be more to it than an intelligent person is supposed to allow.

But let me take a paragraph to hedge, qualify, and tone down what I have just written. I do not, for example, believe that a large head implies great intelligence, or even that a high forehead implies ample intellectual capacity, though apparently Shakespeare, himself well-endowed in this respect, did. Nor do I believe that a strong jaw inevitably translates into a character of great determination. I do believe, with the poet, that the eyes are the windows of the soul; yet I do not go so far as to say that Elizabeth Taylor, who has the most beautiful public eyes of our day, therefore has the most beautiful soul. I do not believe bad teeth or bad skin symbolic of a grave flaw in character.

The mystery of personality is written in the human face—this I do believe. But, as with all truly intricate mysteries, this one must be read subtly, patiently, penetratingly.

I have always had an intense interest in faces and from as early as I can remember have watched them the way bird-watchers do birds. One of the pleasures that living in a large city provides is the delight of viewing a large human aviary. Can there be any doubt that the human face, even though it is of a very long run, is still the best game in town? Consider: we are all playing with essentially the same cards—eyes, a nose, a chin, a mouth, cheeks, eyebrows, hair, ears, a forehead—dealt out on the cloth of skin over the front of our skulls. But how inexhaustibly interestingly these cards have been dealt. Noses retroussé or Gogolian,[1] lips sensuous or forbidding, eyebrows wispy or bushy, cheeks puffy or gaunt, chins prognathous or nonexistent, eyes though available in a limited number of colors nonetheless of limitless expressive possibilities—what variety, what modalities within the variety, what variegation within the modalities!

The given in the human face is, of course, heredity. Yet I wonder if heredity—providing skin and eye and hair color, bone structure, et cetera—really furnishes anything more than the broad canvas on which the more delicate and interesting strokes are painted by time and personal fate. What usually makes a face interesting—a priggish nose, quizzical eyebrows, sarcastic lips, lines and wrinkles oddly placed—is there as a result not of heredity but of experience. What time does to a face is most fascinating of all, and I sometimes think that no face, unless it be one of rare beauty or especial hideousness, is of great interest—rather like wine that hasn't had time to age properly—much before thirty.

---

[1]*retroussé*: turned up; *Gogolian*: after Nikolai Gogol (1809–1852), Russian writer whose characters were often disfigured. "The Nose" is one of his best-known stories. [Eds.]

Perhaps it is impossible to predict the way a face will age. Most people of a physiognomic bent tend to work backward, which is to say from hindsight. Thus, to cite an example, Richard Perceval Graves, the recent biographer of A. E. Housman,[2] writes of Housman's father: "Photographs of Edward [Housman] reinforce the impression of a man who has inherited some of his father's intelligence, but more of his determination than of his judgment. The mouth and jaw are firm, even obstinate, but the eyes are weak and uncertain." But this reading is entirely ex post facto; Mr. Graves already knows that A. E. Housman's father, though in some ways determined, even obstinate, was a man of poor judgment, uncertainty, and weakness. What he first found in the man's life he afterward discovered in his face. It is the way most of us work.

Yet read faces we must, for however unreliable a method it may be, none other exists for taking at least a rough measure of others. The face, the seat of four of the five human senses, is also the meter of the emotions. The art of the actor is based on this fact. Feelings veiled in fleshy shadows, secret enmities that must not be misread, insincerities that the voice and even the mouth may be able to disguise but not the eyes—all these are to be found in the face. Goodwill and admiration, possibly even love, are writ in the disposition of facial features, and these, too, must be correctly gauged. The significance of a tic could be decisive to one's fate.

Another question is why some faces are photogenic and others are not. It may be that good bones render one more photogenic, but good bones do not necessarily make for a good face. Photographs, like statistics, often lie. Except in the hands of a photographer who is himself an artist, the camera generally misses what is most interesting in the human face. The reason is that faces are almost always most striking in animation. Some people, on the other hand, seem almost too pliantly camera-ready. Truman Capote,[3] for instance, has for me the look of someone who has been photographed much too often, the equivalent of a woman who has slept with too many men.

Does that last sentence strike you as goofy? Does it ring sexist, mystical, a mite mad? In his novel *Mr. Sammler's Planet*, Saul Bellow has a woman character whom he describes as showing, through her eyes, evidence of having slept with too many different men. Do such things show in the eyes? John Brophy, in his fine book, *The Human Face Reconsidered*, writes of the eyes, "Although the eyes can thus make vivid communications, their power of expression is restricted: they can plead but not argue; they can state but not analyze; they can declare effects but are helpless to explain causes." Still, to plead, state, or declare effects is to do a very great deal. The eyes are generally conceded to be the most expressive part of the face, though some say that the mouth can be

10

---

[2]*A. E. Housman* (1859–1936): English poet and scholar. [Eds.]
[3]*Truman Capote* (1924–1984): American author of *Breakfast at Tiffany's* (1958) and *In Cold Blood* (1966). [Eds.]

equally expressive. But in this matter I go with the Polish proverb that runs, "Watch closely the eyes of him who bows the lowest."

I know I need to look at, if not deeply into, the eyes of someone with whom I am talking. I find myself slightly resentful—perhaps irritated comes closer to it—at having to talk to someone wearing sunglasses. Worst of all are those mirrored-lens sunglasses that, when you look into them, throw back two slightly distorted pictures of yourself, rather like old-time funhouse mirrors. I like eyes not only to be up front, where God put them, but out front, where I can see them.

What goes for eyes goes for other facial features. The ears are said to be the least expressive parts of the face—some talented people can twitch theirs while the ears of others redden when they lie or are under stress—but, in men at any rate, I prefer not to shoot conversationally till I see the lobes of their ears, a thing not always possible under the dispensation of recent masculine hairdos. Charles de Gaulle had big ears; John O'Hara[4] had ears that stuck out from his head; and so do my own, though I do not own up to this fact easily. None of us, I suspect, easily owns up to his own irregularities. I was recently to be met at an airport by someone I had never met before. When I asked him what he looked like, so that I might recognize him upon arrival, he said he was blond, had a mustache, and would be wearing a blue suit. All of which turned out to be quite true, except that he neglected to mention that he also weighed around three hundred pounds.

In my neighborhood there walks a man who—through a war injury? a fire? an industrial accident?—has had the left side of his face blown away. Where features once were, a drape of flesh has been drawn. He is small, tidy, wears a cap, and through his walk and general demeanor gives an impression of thoughtfulness. The effect upon first seeing him is jolting. Life must be hard for him, and one wonders if he has ever grown inured to watching strangers re-coil upon initial sight of him. But why is one jolted, why does one recoil? As much as from anything, I think it has to do with one's inability to read his face. One cannot sense his mood or know what he is (even roughly) thinking—and the result is disconcerting in the extreme.

Reading Faces by Leopold Bellak, MD, and Samm Sinclair Baker not only maintains that the project of reading faces is a sensible one but offers a method for doing so. This method is called the Zone System, and the way it works is to divide the human face vertically down the center and horizontally under the eyes. It operates on the correct assumption that the face is asymmetrical. It speculates on the possibility that the division of the brain into left and right functions may have effects on the left and right sides of the face. One cannot

---

[4]*Charles de Gaulle* (1890–1970): French general and president; *John O'Hara* (1905–1970): American novelist. [Eds.]

say of this book, as Gibbon said of some *Lives* by Jerome, that "the only defect in these pleasing compositions is the want of truth and common sense."[5] But as a self-help book it is, I think, helpful only in a very limited way. For example, by dividing a face horizontally one can sometimes determine that, though its mouth is smiling, its eyes are cold and scrutinizing. It is also interesting to note that, divided vertically, one side of a person's face can seem cheery, while the other seems wary. One might go from there to say that a face so divided may bespeak a person riven in some fundamental way.

But whenever *Reading Faces* goes much beyond this it becomes slightly suspect. Sensibly enough, its authors write, "What one reads in the face are *potentialities*, from which further inferences can be drawn—from conversation, observation, and experience with the person over a period of time." The problem is, though, that most of the faces submitted for study are those of well-known people from politics, sports, and show business, and the analyses offered of their faces by the authors are more than a touch commonplace. In some cases, they show a political bias in favor of old-style New Deal Democrats. Of Eleanor Roosevelt they write, "It is a most unusual face about which one can only say good things." Having been brought up in a home in which Franklin and Eleanor Roosevelt were well regarded, I tend to go along with this reading. But where our authors find such traits in Mrs. Roosevelt's face as intelligence, compassion, and optimism, an old-line Taft Republican could as easily find naiveté, smugness, and self-righteousness.

One serious question about faces is whether one can find beautiful or even agreeable-looking someone whom one despises. Moral judgments, as Santayana noted,[6] take precedence over aesthetic ones, or at least do so for most of us. So when confronted with a person one detests, perhaps the best one can say is that he or she is very good-looking—yet one is likely to add, "at least to the superficial observer." What makes this observer superficial, of course, is that he is not privy to the real lowdown about the despicable character in question. Yet how much easier it is to read backward, through hindsight, from behavior to evidence of behavior in the face. As John Brophy reminds us, during Hitler's rise and early years in power, no one detected the insanity we now see so clearly in his face. The aged, puffy, baby face of Winston Churchill,[7] a cigar clamped in its mouth, might appear, to someone who has no knowledge of what Churchill accomplished, as a perfect subject for an antismoking poster.

The genius of the unknown sculptor is to have created what sometimes seems a rather limited number of human facial types yet, within this limited number of types, an infinite variety. With only rare exceptions, almost every

15

---

[5]*Edward Gibbon* (1737–1794): English historian, author of *The Decline and Fall of the Roman Empire*, referring to the writing of St. Jerome (c. 347–420). [Eds.]

[6]*George Santayana* (1863–1952): American philosopher. [Eds.]

[7]*Winston Churchill* (1874–1965): British prime minister during World War II. [Eds.]

face one sees one has seen before, if not in life, then in the work of the great painters. Walking the streets one sees here a pair of kindly Holbeinesque lips; there the porcelain cheeks of a Botticelli; elsewhere the rubicund coloring of one of Brueghel's peasants; and sometimes a face taken over from Rembrandt entire.[8] If flesh and bone be the material of the face, time supplies its varnish. And what extraordinary things time does, leaving this face unmarked, that one looking as if it were a salmon mousse left out in the rain. To read the effects of time on a face requires, as the New Critics[9] used to call it, close reading. "For in order to understand how beautiful an elderly lady can once have been," Proust wrote, "one must not only study but interpret every line of her face."[10]

Nothing so improves the appearance as a high opinion of oneself. Let this stand as the first in a paragraph riddled with risky generalizations. Love of one's work tends to make one's face interesting. Artists have animated faces, and performing musicians the most animated of all. Suffering, too, confers interest on a face, but only suffering that, if not necessarily understood, has been thought about at length. Uninterested people have uninteresting faces. In ways blatant or subtle, personality sets its seal on every face. Some people have historical seals set on their faces as well; thus some men and women walk the streets today with Romanesque, Elizabethan, or Victorian faces. Intelligence is more readily gauged in a face than is stupidity. As a final generalization, let me say that the more precisely one thinks of the relation of face to character, and the more carefully one attempts to formulate the connection between the two, the madder the entire business begins to seem.

Yet what choice have we but to continue reading faces as best we can, bringing to the job all that we have in the way of intuition, experience, intelligence? We read most subtly of course those people we know most closely: our friends, our known enemies, our families. In the faces of such people we can recognize shifting moods, hurt and pride, all the delicate shades of feeling. But of that person we supposedly know most intimately, ourself, the project remains hopeless. Study photographs of ourselves though we may, stare at ourselves in mirrors though we do, our self-scrutiny generally comes to naught. If you don't believe me, stop a moment and attempt to describe yourself to someone who has never seen you. The best I can do is the following: "I look a bit like Lee Harvey Oswald and I also rather resemble my dog, though I seem more dilapidated. You can't miss me."

---

[8]*Hans Holbein* (c. 1465–1524): German painter; *Sandro Botticelli* (c. 1445–1510): Italian painter; *Pieter Brueghel* (c. 1525–1569): Flemish painter; *Rembrandt van Rijn* (1606–1669): Dutch painter. [Eds.]

[9]*New Critics*: criticism concerned with close analysis of the language, imagery, and tensions within a work of literature. [Eds.]

[10]*Marcel Proust* (1871–1922): French author of *Remembrance of Things Past*. [Eds.]

QUESTIONS

1. How would you characterize this essay? Does Epstein explain how to read a face? If not, what does he explain?

2. In paragraph 4, Epstein says he believes that "the mystery of personality is written in the human face." From that point on, he tries to explain the difficulties of interpreting this "mystery." What purpose do his first three paragraphs serve?

3. Note that Epstein's emphasis is on reading faces in order to discern the character of a person. What are the problems he raises with such character assessment?

4. Epstein asserts that the eyes are the most expressive features of the face (paragraph 10). Which feature of someone's face do you concentrate on? Why?

5. Paragraph 18, Epstein says, is "riddled with risky generalizations." List them. Can you find other generalizations or opinions in this essay that you might question? If you were writing on this topic, how might you approach it? Are there any facts you might add?

6. Rewrite the first paragraph of this essay with yourself as the subject.

7. Epstein says, "I tend to think of myself, as I expect most men do, as a nice-enough looking chap" (paragraph 1). Write an essay in which you discuss this statement. You might want to take a poll of men you know to see whether Epstein's opinion about most men has any validity.

8. Write an essay that starts with your own version of George Orwell's statement (paragraph 1). Fill in the blanks: At _____, everyone has the _____ she/he deserves. Substitute an appropriate age and another part of the body, or substitute a thing.

MAKING CONNECTIONS

1. Compare Epstein's essay with Margaret Atwood's "The Female Body" (p. 343). If we can say that Atwood's essay has a distinctly "feminine" point of view, can we say that Epstein's point of view is "masculine"?

2. How do Lucy Grealy's conclusions in "Mirrors" (p. 48) about the image of her face compare with Epstein's views of the mirror?

THE FEMALE BODY
Margaret Atwood

Margaret Atwood, born in Ottawa, Canada, in 1939, has won numerous awards and received honorary degrees for her writing. She is best known as a poet and novelist. Her novel The Handmaid's Tale *(1986) was made into a film. In her most recent novel,* Alias Grace *(1996), she draws on nineteenth-century history and a sensational murder trial. Much of her writing deals with feminist issues, and the essay presented here is no exception, as she applies her considerable talent to fulfill a writing assignment for the* Michigan Quarterly Review, *reprinted in a collection of her short works,* Good Bones and Simple Murders *(1994).*

. . . entirely devoted to the subject of "The Female Body." Knowing how well you
have written on this topic . . . this capacious topic. . . .

—letter from *Michigan Quarterly Review*

1

I agree, it's a hot topic. But only one? Look around, there's a wide range. Take my own, for instance.

I get up in the morning. My topic feels like hell. I sprinkle it with water, brush parts of it, rub it with towels, powder it, add lubricant. I dump in the fuel and away goes my topic, my topical topic, my controversial topic, my capacious topic, my limping topic, my nearsighted topic, my topic with back problems, my badly behaved topic, my vulgar topic, my outrageous topic, my aging topic, my topic that is out of the question and anyway still can't spell, in its oversized coat and worn winter boots, scuttling along the sidewalk as if it were flesh and blood, hunting for what's out there, an avocado, an alderman, an adjective, hungry as ever.

2

The basic Female Body comes with the following accessories: garter belt, panti-girdle, crinoline, camisole, bustle, brassiere, stomacher, chemise, virgin zone, spike heels, nose ring, veil, kid gloves, fishnet stockings, fichu, bandeau, Merry Widow, weepers, chokers, barrettes, bangles, beads, lorgnette, feather boa, basic black, compact, Lycra stretch one-piece with modesty panel, designer peignoir, flannel nightie, lace teddy, bed, head.

343

3

The Female Body is made of transparent plastic and lights up when you plug it in. You press a button to illuminate the different systems. The circulatory system is red, for the heart and arteries, purple for the veins; the respiratory system is blue; the lymphatic system is yellow; the digestive system is green, with liver and kidneys in aqua. The nerves are done in orange and the brain is pink. The skeleton, as you might expect, is white.

The reproductive system is optional, and can be removed. It comes with or   5
without a miniature embryo. Parental judgment can thereby be exercised. We do not wish to frighten or offend.

4

He said, I won't have one of those things in the house. It gives a young girl a false notion of beauty, not to mention anatomy. If a real woman was built like that she'd fall on her face.

She said, If we don't let her have one like all the other girls she'll feel singled out. It'll become an issue. She'll long for one and she'll long to turn into one. Repression breeds sublimation. You know that.

He said, It's not just the pointy plastic tits, it's the wardrobes. The wardrobes and that stupid male doll, what's his name, the one with the underwear glued on.

She said, Better to get it over with when she's young. He said, All right, but don't let me see it.

She came whizzing down the stairs, thrown like a dart. She was stark naked.   10
Her hair had been chopped off, her head was turned back to front, she was missing some toes and she'd been tattooed all over her body with purple ink in a scrollwork design. She hit the potted azalea, trembled there for a moment like a botched angel, and fell.

He said, I guess we're safe.

5

The Female Body has many uses. It's been used as a door knocker, a bottle opener, as a clock with a ticking belly, as something to hold up lampshades, as a nutcracker, just squeeze the brass legs together and out comes your nut. It bears torches, lifts victorious wreaths, grows copper wings and raises aloft a ring of neon stars; whole buildings rest on its marble heads.

It sells cars, beer, shaving lotion, cigarettes, hard liquor; it sells diet plans and diamonds, and desire in tiny crystal bottles. Is this the face that launched a thousand products? You bet it is, but don't get any funny big ideas, honey, that smile is a dime a dozen.

It does not merely sell, it is sold. Money flows into this country or that country, flies in, practically crawls in, suitful after suitful, lured by all those hairless pre-teen legs. Listen, you want to reduce the national debt, don't you? Aren't you patriotic? That's the spirit. That's my girl.

She's a natural resource, a renewable one luckily, because those things wear   15
out so quickly. They don't make 'em like they used to. Shoddy goods.

6

One and one equals another one. Pleasure in the female is not a requirement. Pair-bonding is stronger in geese. We're not talking about love, we're talking about biology. That's how we all got here, daughter.

Snails do it differently. They're hermaphrodites, and work in threes.

7

Each Female Body contains a female brain. Handy. Makes things work. Stick pins in it and you get amazing results. Old popular songs. Short circuits. Bad dreams.

Anyway: each of these brains has two halves. They're joined together by a thick cord; neural pathways flow from one to the other, sparkles of electric information washing to and fro. Like light on waves. Like a conversation. How does a woman know? She listens. She listens in.

The male brain, now, that's a different matter. Only a thin connection.   20
Space over here, time over there, music and arithmetic in their own sealed compartments. The right brain doesn't know what the left brain is doing. Good for aiming through, for hitting the target when you pull the trigger. What's the target? Who's the target? Who cares? What matters is hitting it. That's the male brain for you. Objective.

This is why men are so sad, why they feel so cut off, why they think of themselves as orphans cast adrift, footloose and stringless in the deep void. What void? she asks. What are you talking about? The void of the universe, he says, and she says Oh and looks out the window and tries to get a handle on it, but it's no use, there's too much going on, too many rustlings in the leaves, too many voices, so she says, Would you like a cheese sandwich, a piece of cake, a cup of tea? And he grinds his teeth because she doesn't understand, and wanders off, not just alone but Alone, lost in the dark, lost in the skull, searching for the other half, the twin who could complete him.

Then it comes to him: he's lost the Female Body! Look, it shines in the gloom, far ahead, a vision of wholeness, ripeness, like a giant melon, like an apple, like a metaphor for "breast" in a bad sex novel; it shines like a balloon, like a foggy noon, a watery moon, shimmering in its egg of light.

Catch it. Put it in a pumpkin, in a high tower, in a compound, in a chamber, in a house, in a room. Quick, stick a leash on it, a lock, a chain, some pain, settle it down, so it can never get away from you again.

QUESTIONS

1. Why would Atwood question her assigned topic, quoted as the opening to her essay? How does she challenge the topic? How are we, finally, to read the title of her essay?

2. Consider the form of the essay. What does this arrangement allow Atwood to do? What effect does it have on the reader?

3. In what ways does Atwood present and discuss the female body in this essay?

4. What differences does Atwood draw between the male brain and the female brain? Describe the male concept of the female body presented in section 7. Consider the connotations of the metaphors in paragraph 22.

5. Write an essay on the male body, using Atwood's approach as a model. You might start by considering the metaphors you could use in your discussion. Are there as many metaphors for the male body in American culture as there are for the female body?

6. Consider the epigraph from the *Michigan Quarterly Review* that opens Atwood's essay as a prompt for writing. Then choose a quotation from Atwood's essay to generate a commentary, response, rebuttal, or analysis.

MAKING CONNECTIONS

Compare Atwood's commentary on male and female brains with Stephen Jay Gould's discussion in "Women's Brains" (p. 717). Try reading Atwood's remarks as a response to "scientific proofs" of women's inferiority.

OF SPEED READERS
AND LIP-MOVERS

William Gass

*Born in Fargo, North Dakota, in 1924, William Gass con-
tinues to live and work in the Midwest, where he has been a
professor of philosophy at Washington University. A highly
imaginative writer of philosophical bent, Gass is equally
well known for his fiction and for his essays. In his most recent novel,* The Tunnel *(1994), a midwestern history professor digs into his own history while literally digging a
tunnel from his basement. In this essay, which originally
appeared in the* New York Times Book Review *(1984),
Gass unearths his past triumphs as a speed reader.*

I was never much of an athlete, but I was once the member of a team. Indeed, I was its star, and we were champions. During high school I belonged to
a squad of speed readers in Ohio, although I was never awarded a letter for it.
Still, we took on the top 10 in our territory and read as rapidly as possible every
time we were challenged to a match, hoping to finish in front of that tow-
headed punk from Canton, the tomato-cheeked girl from Marietta, or that
silent pair of sisters, all spectacles and squints, who looked tough as German
script and who hailed from Shaker Heights or some other rough neighborhood
full of swift, mean raveners of texts.

We called ourselves the Speeders. Of course. Everybody did. There were
the Sharon Speeders, the Steubenville Speeders, and the Niles Nouns. They
never won. How could they? I lost a match myself once to a kid with green
teeth. And that's the way, I'm afraid, we appeared to others—as creeps with
squints, bad posture, unclean complexions, unscrubbed teeth, tousled hair. We
never had dates, we only memorized them; and when any real sports team
went on the road to represent the high school, we carried the socks, the Toot-
sie Rolls, the towels for them. My nemesis with the green teeth had a head of
thin red hair like rust on a saw; he revolved a suggestive little finger in his large
fungiform ears. My God, I thought . . . and the shame of that defeat still rushes
to my face whenever I remember it. Nevertheless, even today I possess a substantial, gold-colored medallion on which one sunbeaming eye seems hung
above a book like a spider. Both book and eye are open—wide. I take that
open, streaming eye to be an omen.

Our reading life has its salad days, its autumnal times. At first, of course, we
do it badly, scarcely keeping our balance, toddling along behind our finger, so
intent on remembering what each word is supposed to mean that the sentence

347

is no longer a path, and we arrive at its end without having gone anywhere. Thus it is with all the things we learn, for at first they passively oppose us; they lie outside us like mist or the laws of nature; we have to issue orders to our eyes, our limbs, our understanding: Lift this, shift that, thumb the space bar, let up on the clutch—easy! There go the gears!—and don't forget to modify the verb, or remember what an escudo's worth.[1] After a while, we find we like standing up, riding a bike, singing *Don Giovanni*,[2] making puff pastry, puppy love, or model planes. Then we are indeed like the adolescent in our eager green enthusiasms: They are plentiful as leaves. Every page is a pasture, and we are let out to graze like hungry herds.

Do you remember what magic the word *thigh* could work on you, showing up in the middle of a passage suddenly, like a whiff of cologne in a theater? I admit it: The widening of the upper thigh remains a miracle, and, honestly, many of us once read the word *thigh* as if we were exploring Africa, seeking the source of the Nile. No volume was too hefty then, no style too verbal. The weight of a big book was more comforting than Christmas candy, though you had to be lucky, strike the right text at the right time, because the special excitement Thomas Wolfe provides, for instance, can be felt only in the teens.[3] And when, again, will any of us possess the energy, the patience, the inner sympathy for volcanic bombast to read—enjoy—Carlyle?[4]

Repeating was automatic. Who needed Gertrude Stein?[5] I must have rushed through a pleasant little baseball book called *The Crimson Pennant* at least a dozen times, consuming a cake I had already cut into crumbs, yet that big base hit was never better than on that final occasion when its hero and I ran round those bases, and he shyly doffed his hat to the crowd.

No one threatened to whack our rumps if we didn't read another Nancy Drew by Tuesday; no sour-faced virgin browbeat us with *The Blithedale Romance* or held out *The Cloister and the Hearth* like a cold plate of good-for-you food.[6] We were on our own. I read Swinburne[7] and the *Adventures of the Shadow*. I read Havelock Ellis and Tom Swift and *The Idylls of the King*.[8] I read whatever came to hand, and what came to hand were a lot of naughty

---

[1] *escudo*: a Portuguese coin worth 100 centavos. [Eds.]

[2] *Don Giovanni*: a 1787 opera by Austrian composer Wolfgang Amadeus Mozart (1756–1791). [Eds.]

[3] *Thomas Wolfe* (1900–1938): American writer of lengthy semiautobiographical novels. [Eds.]

[4] *Thomas Carlyle* (1795–1881): Scottish essayist and historian. [Eds.]

[5] *Gertrude Stein* (1874–1946): American writer who made repetition a method. [Eds.]

[6] *Nancy Drew*: a fictional sleuth in a series of mysteries for girls; *The Blithedale Romance*: an 1852 novel by American writer Nathaniel Hawthorne (1804–1864); *The Cloister and the Hearth*: an 1861 historical romance by English novelist Charles Reade (1814–1884). [Eds.]

[7] *Algernon Charles Swinburne* (1837–1909): English poet. [Eds.]

[8] *Havelock Ellis* (1859–1939): English writer and scientist best known for his *Studies in the Psychology of Sex*; *Tom Swift*: the hero of a series of popular books for boys; *The Idylls of the King*: narrative poems of King Arthur and the Round Table by Alfred, Lord Tennyson (1809–1892). [Eds.]

French novels, detective stories, medical adventures, books about bees, biographies of Napoleon, and *Thus Spake Zarathustra* like a bolt of lightning.[9]

I read them all, whatever they were, with an ease that defies the goat's digestion, and with an ease that is now so easily forgotten, just as we forget the wild wobble in our bikes' wheels, or the humiliating falls we took when we began our life on spokes. That wind I felt, when I finally stayed upright around the block, continuously reaffirmed the basic joy of cycling. It told me not merely that I was moving, but that I was moving *under my own power;* just as later, when I'd passed my driver's test, I would feel another sort of exhilaration—an intense, addictive, dangerous one—that of command, of my ability to control the energy produced by another thing or person, to direct the life contained in another creature.

Yes, in those early word-drunk years, I would down a book or two a day as though they were gins. I read for adventure, excitement, to sample the exotic and the strange, for climax and resolution, to participate in otherwise forbidden passions. I forgot what it was to be under my own power, under my own steam. I was, like so many adolescents, as eager to leap from my ordinary life as the salmon is to get upstream. I sought a replacement for the world. With a surreptitious lamp lit, I stayed awake to dream. I grew reckless. I read for speed.

When you read for speed you do not read recursively, looping along the line like a sewing machine, stitching something together—say the panel of a bodice to a sleeve—linking a pair of terms, the contents of a clause, closing a seam by following the internal directions of the sentence so that the word *you* is first fastened to the word *read,* and then the phrase *for speed* is attached to both in order that the entire expression can be finally fronted by a grandly capitalized *When* ... while all of that, in turn, is gathered up to await the completion of the later segment that begins *you do not read recursively.* You can hear how long it seems to take—this patient process—and how confusing it can become. Nor do you linger over language, repeating some especially pleasant little passage, in the enjoyment, perhaps, of a modest rhyme (for example, the small clause, *when you read for speed*), or a particularly apt turn of phrase (an image, for instance, such as the one that dealt with Green Teeth's thin red hair—like rust on a saw). None of that, when you read for speed.

Nor, naturally, do you move your lips as you read the word *read* or the   10
words *moving your lips,* so that the poor fellow next to you in the reading room has to watch intently to see what your lips are saying: Are you asking him out? For the loan of his Plutarch's *Lives?*[10] And of course the poor fellow is flummoxed to find that you are moving your lips to say *moving your lips.* What can

---

[9]*Thus Spake Zarathustra:* a prophetically styled work by German philosopher Friedrich Nietzsche (1844–1900), which featured the idea of the Superman. [Eds.]

[10]*Plutarch's Lives:* biographies of Greeks and Romans by Greek essayist and biographer Plutarch (c. 46–120). [Eds.]

that mean? The lip-mover—O, such a person is low on our skill-scale. We are taught to have scorn for him, for her.

On the other hand, the speeding reader drops diagonally down across the page, on a slant like a skier, cuts across the text the way a butcher prefers to slice sausage, so that a small round can be made to yield a misleading larger oval piece. The speeding reader is after the kernel, the heart, the gist. Paragraphs become a country the eye flies over looking for landmarks, reference points, airports, restrooms, passages of sex. The speeding reader guts a book the way the skillful clean fish. The gills are gone, the tail, the scales, the fins; then the filet slides away swiftly as though fed to a seal. And only the slow reader, whose finger falters in front of long words, who moves the lips, who dances the text, will notice the odd crowd of images—flier, skier, butcher, seal—that have gathered to comment on the aims and activities of the speeding reader, perhaps like gossips at a wedding.

To the speeding reader, this jostle of images, this crazy collision of ideas—of landing strip, kernel, heart, guts, sex—will not be felt, because it is only the inner core of meaning he's after; it is the gist she wants. And the gist is: Readers who read rapidly read only for the most generalized, stereotyped sense. For them, meaning floats over the page like fluffy clouds. Cliché is forever in fashion. They read, as we say, synonymously, seeking sameness; and, indeed, it is all the same to them if they are said in one moment to be greedy as seals, and in another moment likened to descalers of fish. They—you, I, we—"get" the idea.

A speed-reading match had two halves. (I say "had" because I believe these matches long ago lit their last light.) The first consisted of the rapid reading itself, through which, of course, I whizzzzed, all the while making the sound of closing covers in order to disconcert Green Teeth or the silent Shaker Heights sisters, who were to think I had completed my reading already. I didn't wear glasses then, but I carried a glasses case to every match, and always dropped it at a pertinent moment.

Next we were required to answer questions about what we claimed we'd covered, and here quickness was again essential. The questions, however, soon disclosed their biases. They had a structure, their own gist; and it became possible, after some experience, to guess what would be asked about a text almost before it had been begun. Is it "Goldilocks" we're skimming? Then what is the favorite breakfast food of the three bears? How does Goldilocks escape from the house? Why weren't the three bears at home when Goldilocks came calling? The multiple answers we could choose from also had their own tired tilt and, like the questions, gave themselves away. The favorite breakfast foods, for instance, were: (a) Quaker Oats (which this year is paying for the prizes, and in this sly fashion gets its name in); (b) Just Rite (written like a brand name): (c) porridge (usually misspelled); (d) sugar-coated curds and whey. No one ever wondered whether Goldilocks was suffering from sibling rivalry; why she had become a teenie-trasher; or why mother bear's bowl of porridge was cold when baby bear's smaller bowl was still warm and Just Rite.

There were many other mysteries, but not for these quiz masters who didn't 15 even want to know the sexual significance of Cinderella's slipper, or why it had to be made of glass. I won my championship medal by ignoring the text entirely (it was a section from Volume Two of Oswald Spengler's *Decline of the West*,[11] the part that begins, "Regard the flowers at eventide as, one after the other, they close in the setting sun. . . ." But then, of course, you remember that celebrated passage). I skipped the questions as well, and simply encircled the gloomiest alternatives offered. Won in record time. No one's got through Spengler with such dispatch since.

What did these matches with their quizzes for comprehension, their love of literal learning, tell me? They told me that time was money (a speed reader's clearest idea); they told me what the world wanted me to read when I read, eat when I ate, see when I saw. Like the glutton, I was to get everything in and out in a hurry: Turnover was topmost. What the world wanted me to get was the gist, but the gist was nothing but an idea of trade—an idea so drearily uniform and emaciated it might have modeled dresses.

There is another way of reading I'd like to recommend. It's slow, old-fashioned, not easy either, rarely practiced. It must be learned. It is a way of life. What!—I hear your hearts exclaim—is the old wart going to go on some more about reading? Reading? When we can see the rings around his eyes for every year he's worn them out . . . reading? When we are commencing from college, leaving books, book bags, bicycles behind like pretty scenes along the highway? Yes, Just so. That's true. Most of you *are* through. Farewell, chemistry. Farewell, *Canterbury Tales*. Imagine reading *that* again. Or *The Faerie Queene* even the first time. Farewell, Sir Philip Sydney, and your golden lines.[12]

> Farewell O Sunn, Arcadias clearest light;
> Farewell O pearl, the poore mans plenteous treasure:
> Farewell O golden staffe, the weake mans might:
> Farewell O joy, the joyfulls onely pleasure.
> Wisdom farewell, the skillesse mans direction:
> Farewell with thee, farewell all our affection.

Now "Paradise" is "Lost."[13] Who cares if molecular genetics has revolutionized biology? Farewell, philosophy. Farewell, free love. From now on there

---

[11]*Oswald Spengler* (1880–1936): German historian and philosopher. [Eds.]

[12]*Canterbury Tales:* written between 1387 and 1392 by English poet Geoffrey Chaucer (c. 1342–1400); *The Faerie Queene* (1590–1609): by English poet Edmund Spenser (1552–1599); *Sir Philip Sidney* (1554–1586): English poet, statesman, and soldier. These lines are from his *Arcadia* (1590), a prose romance. [Eds.]

[13]*"Paradise" is "Lost":* a reference to *Paradise Lost* (1667), an epic poem by Englishman John Milton (1608–1674). [Eds.]

will be an interest, a carrying, a handling charge. Farewell, A *Farewell to Arms*. *Goodbye, Columbus*.[14]

You may have noticed that I am now speaking in sentence fragments. The speed reader hates subordination, qualification, refinement, deployment, ritual, decoration, order, mother, inference, country, logic, family, flag, God. Here is a little test: In that last list, what word will the speed reader pick out to stand for the rest of it—to be its gist? *God*, you guess? No. Wrong. Nor *flag*, though that's appealing. *Mother* will be the word we want.

All right. I heard your hearts heave like a slow sea. I'm adaptable. Let's talk about drinking. I belonged to a drinking club once. Defeated the Fraternal Order of Eagles on their own turf. The Chug-a-lugs, we were called. Inevitably. You don't plan, I'm sure, to give up drinking. Or reading—not altogether—I imagine. Not the letters to *Penthouse*. The inky pages of the *Washington Post*. *TV Guide*. Legal briefs. Medical romances. Business lore.

Well, there is another way of drinking I'd like to recommend. We've already dealt with the first way. Gulp. Get the gist. And the gist is the level of alcohol in your blood, the pixilated breath you blow into the test balloon. It makes appropriate the expression: Have a belt. We can toss down a text, a time of life, a love affair, that walk in the park that gets us from here to there. We can chug-a-lug them. You have, perhaps, had to travel sometime with a person whose passion was that simple: It was *getting there*. You have no doubt encountered people who impatiently wait for the payoff; they urge you to come to the point; at dinner, the early courses merely delay dessert; they look only at the bottom line (that obscene phrase); they are persons consumed by consequences; they want to climax without crescendo.

But we can read and walk and write and look in quite a different way. It is possible. I was saved from sameness by Immanuel Kant. You can't speed-read *The Critique of Pure Reason*.[15] You can't speed-read Wallace Stevens.[16] There is no gist, no simple translation, no key concept that will unlock these works; actually, there is no lock, no door, no wall, no room, no house, no world.

Reading is a complicated, profound, silent, still, very personal, very private, very solitary yet civilizing activity. Nothing is more social than speech—we are bound together by our common sounds more securely than even by our laws. Nevertheless, no one is more aware of the isolated self than the reader, for a reader communes with the word heard immaterially in that hollow of the head made only for hearing, a room nowhere in the body in any ordinary sense. On the bus, everyone of us may be deep in something different. Sitting next to a

20

---

[14]A *Farewell to Arms*: a 1929 novel by American writer Ernest Hemingway (1899–1961); *Goodbye, Columbus*: a 1959 novel by American writer Philip Roth (b. 1933). [Eds.]

[15]*Immanuel Kant* (1724–1804): German philosopher. His *Critique of Pure Reason* (1781) examines the nature and limits of reason. [Eds.]

[16]*Wallace Stevens* (1879–1955): American poet whose work, noted for its intellect, wit, and exotic diction, celebrates the imagination. [Eds.]

priest, I can still enjoy my pornography, though I may keep a thumb discreetly on top of the title.

I've grown larger, if not wiser. My vices now are visionary. That baseball book, *The Crimson Pennant*, has become *The Crimson Cancan*. What do I care if Father McIvie is reading about investments? Yet while all of us, in our verbal recreations, are full of respect for the privacy of our neighbors, the placards advertising perfume or footwear invade the public space like a visual smell; Muzak fills every unstoppered ear the way the static of the street does. The movies, the radio, television, theater, music: All run on at their own rate, and the listener or the viewer must attend, keep us, or lose out—but not the reader. The reader is free. The reader is in charge and pedals the cycle. It is easy for a reader to announce that his present run of Proust has been postponed until the holidays.[17]

Reading, that is, is not a public imposition. Of course, when we read, many 25 of us squirm and fidget. One of the closest friends of my youth would sensuously wind and unwind on his forefinger the long blond strands of his hair. How he read—that is how I remember him. Yes, our postures are often provocative, perverse. Yet these outward movements of the body really testify to the importance of the inner movements of the mind; and even those rapid flickers of the eye, as we shift from word to word, phrase to phrase, and clause to clause, hoping to keep our head afloat on a food of Faulkner or Proust or Joyce or James,[18] are registers of reason. For reading is reasoning, figuring things out through thoughts, making arrangements out of arrangements until we've understood a text so fully it is nothing but feeling and pure response, until its conceptual turns are like the reversals of mood in a marriage—petty, sad, ecstatic, commonplace, foreseeable, amazing.

In order to have this experience, however, one must learn to perform the text, say, sing, shout the words to oneself, give them, with *our* minds, *their* body. Otherwise the eye skates over every syllable like the speeder. There can be no doubt that often what we read should be skimmed, as what we are frequently asked to drink should be spilled. But the speeding reader is alone in another, less satisfactory way, one quite different from that of the reader who says the words to herself, because as we read we divide into a theater: There is the performer who shapes those silent sounds, moving the muscles of the larynx almost invisibly, and there is the listener who hears them said and who responds to their passion or their wisdom.

Such a reader sees every text as unique, greets every work as a familiar stranger. Such a reader is willing to allow another's words to become hers, his.

---

[17]*Marcel Proust* (1871–1922): French novelist. *Remembrance of Things Past* is his major work. [Eds.]

[18]*William Faulkner* (1897–1962): American novelist; *James Joyce* (1882–1941): Irish novelist; *Henry James* (1843–1916): British novelist. [Eds.]

In the next moment, let us read a wine, since I promised I would talk about drinking. We have prepared for the occasion, of course. The bottle has been allowed to breathe. Books need to breathe, too. They should be opened properly, hefted, thumbed. The paper, print, layout, should be appreciated. But now we decant the text into our wide-open and welcoming eyes. We warm the wine in the bowl of the glass with our hand. We let its bouquet collect above it just as the red of red roses seems to stain the air. We wade—shoeless, to be sure—through the color it has liquefied. We roll a bit of it about in our mouths. We sip. We savor. We say some sentences of Sir Thomas Browne: "We tearme sleepe a death, and yet it is waking that kils us, and destroyed those spirits which are the house of life. Tis indeed a part of life that best expresseth death, for every man truely lives so long as hee acts his nature, or someway makes good the faculties of himself. . . ."[19]

Are these words not from a fine field, in a splendid year? There is, of course, a sameness in all these words: *life/death, man/nature.* We get the drift. But the differences! The differences make all the difference, the way nose and eyes and cheek bones form a face, the way a muscle makes emotion pass across it. It is the differences we read. Differences are not only identifiable, distinct; they are epidemic: The wine is light, perhaps, spicy, slow to release its grip upon itself, the upper thigh is widening wonderfully, the night air has hands, words fly out of our mouths like birds. "But who knows the fate of his bones," Browne says, "or how often he is to be buried."

Yet as I say his soul out loud, he lives again; he has risen up in me, and I can be, for him, that temporary savior that every real reader is, putting his words in my mouth; not nervously, notice, as though they were pieces of gum, but in that way that is necessary if the heart is to hear them. And though they are his words and his soul, then, that return through me, I am in charge. He has asked nothing of me; his words move because I move them. It is like cycling, reading is. Can you feel the air, the pure passage of the spirit past the exposed skin?

So this reading will be like living, then—the living each of you will be off in a moment to be busy with, not always speedily, I hope, or in the continuous anxiety of consequence, the sullenness of inattention, the annoying static of distraction. But it will be only a semblance of living—this living—nevertheless, the way unspoken reading is a semblance, unless, from time to time, you perform the outer world within. Because only in that manner can it deliver itself to us. As Rainer Maria Rilke once commanded: "Dance the taste of the fruit you have been tasting. Dance the orange."[20] I should like to multiply that charge, even past all possibility. Speak the street to yourself sometimes, hear

[19]*Sir Thomas Browne* (1605–1682): English physician and writer. The lines are from his *Religio Medici*, written when he was in his twenties. [Eds.]
[20]*Rainer Maria Rilke* (1875–1926): German poet. [Eds.]

the horns in the forest, read the breeze aloud and make that inner wind yours, because, whether Nature, Man, or God has given us the text, we independently possess the ability to read, to read really well, and to move our own mind freely in tune to the moving world.

QUESTIONS

1. How does Gass present himself to his audience? How would you characterize him?

2. Extrapolate from this essay a list of rules for reading fast and one for reading slow. Do you agree with Gass's presentation of the reading experience? What rules might you add from your own experience?

3. Consider how Gass compares and contrasts speed readers and lip-movers. What metaphors or images does he use for these two types? How would you describe the figurative language connected to each?

4. Paragraph 17 marks the approximate midpoint of the essay, the point at which Gass is going to recommend his "slow" way of reading. How does he set his audience up for his explanation? How does he use "drinking" to structure his text?

5. In the course of this essay, Gass refers to quite a few writers and texts. Describe your reading experience with one of these texts or writers or with some other one that you found especially difficult, dull, or pleasurable. Try to explain why you reacted as you did.

6. Write an autobiography of yourself as a reader.

7. You have seen how Gass uses figurative language such as metaphors and similes throughout his essay, how he describes reading in terms unlike it. "Reading is drinking" is the major metaphor he uses to structure a large segment of the essay. Write a short essay of your own in which you use a metaphor to describe an activity you know well: eating, sleeping, or thinking, for example.

MAKING CONNECTIONS

Compare Gass's expression of the power and pleasure of reading with that of Frederick Douglass in "Learning to Read and Write" (p. 60). Consider how their particular motives for writing determined their approaches to the topic of reading.

THE DEVELOPMENT
OF ANNE FRANK

John Berryman

John Berryman (1914–1972) was a poet and a professor of English who was known for his semiautobiographical and sometimes eccentric writing in such poems as his Dream Songs. *He was also an astute literary critic, and in this essay from* The Freedom of the Poet *(1976), he evaluates Anne Frank's "remarkable account" of her development from young girl to woman as set forth in her* Diary.

When the first installment of the translated text of *The Diary of Anne Frank* appeared in the spring of 1952, in *Commentary*, I read it with amazement. The next day, when I went into town to see my analyst, I stopped in the magazine's offices—I often did, to argue with Clem Greenberg, who was a sort of senior adviser to what was at that time the best general magazine in the country in spite of, maybe because of, its special Jewish concerns—to see if proofs of the *Diary*'s continuation were available, and they were. Like millions of people later, I was bowled over with pity and horror and admiration for the astounding doomed little girl. But what I *thought* was: a sane person. A sane person, in the twentieth century. It was as long ago as 1889 when Tolstoy wound up his terrible story "The Devil" with this sentence:

> And, indeed, if Evgeni Irtenev was mentally deranged, then all people are mentally deranged, but undoubtedly those are most surely mentally deranged who see in others symptoms of insanity which they fail to see in themselves.

Some years later (1955), setting up a course called "Humanities in the Modern World" at the University of Minnesota, I assigned the *Diary* and reread it with feelings even more powerful than before but now highly structured. I decided that it was the most remarkable account of *normal* human adolescent maturation I had ever read, and that it was universally valued for reasons comparatively insignificant. I waited for someone to agree with me. An article by Bettelheim was announced in *Politics*, appeared, and was irrelevant. The astute Alfred Kazin and his wife, the novelist Ann Birstein, edited Anne Frank's short fiction—ah! I thought—and missed the boat.

Here we have a book only fifteen years old, the sole considerable surviving production of a young girl who died after writing it. While decisively rejecting the proposal—which acts as a blight in some areas of modern criticism—that a critic should address himself only to masterworks, still I would agree that some preliminary justification seems desirable.

It is true that the book is world-famous. I am not much impressed by this fact, which I take to be due in large part to circumstances that have nothing to do with art. The author has been made into a spokesman against one of the grand crimes of our age, and for her race, and for all its victims, and for the victims (especially children) of all the tyrannies of this horrifying century—and we could extend this list of circumstances irrelevant to the *critical* question. Some proportion of the book's fame, moreover, is even more irrelevant, as arising from the widespread success of a play adapted from it, and a film. That the book *is* by a young girl—an attractive one, as photographs show—must count heavily in its sentimental popularity. And, finally, the work has decided literary merit; it is vivid, witty, candid, astute, dramatic, pathetic, terrible—one falls in love with the girl, one finds her formidable, and she breaks one's heart. All right. It is a work infinitely superior to a similar production that has been compared to it, *The Diary of "Helena Morley,"* beautifully translated by Elizabeth Bishop in 1957. Here is a favorable specimen of the Brazilian narrative:

> When I get married I wonder if I'll love my husband as much as mama loves my father? God willing. Mama lives only for him and thinks of nothing else. When he's at home the two spend the whole day in endless conversation. When papa's in Boa Vista during the week, mama gets up singing wistful love songs and we can see she misses him, and she passes the time going over his clothes, collecting the eggs, and fattening the chickens for dinner on Saturday and Sunday. We eat best on those days.

Clearly the temperature here is nothing very unusual, and no serious reader of Anne Frank, with her extraordinary range and tension, will entertain any comparison between the two writers. But I am obliged to wonder whether Anne Frank has *had* any serious readers, for I find no indication in anything written about her that anyone has taken her with real seriousness. A moment ago we passed, after all, the critical question. *One finds her formidable:* why, and how, ought to engage us. And first it is necessary to discover what she is writing about. Perhaps, to be sure, she is not truly writing about anything—you know, "thoughts of a young girl," "Jews in hiding from the Nazis," "a poignant love affair"; but such is not my opinion.

Suppose one became interested in the phenomenon called religious conversion. There are books one can read. There is one by Sante de Sanctis entitled *Religious Conversion*, there are narratives admirably collected in William James's lectures, *The Varieties of Religious Experience*, there is an acute account of the most momentous Christian conversion, Paul's, by Maurice Goguel in the second volume (*The Birth of Christianity*) of his great history of Christian origins. If one wants, however, to experience the phenomenon, so far as one can do so at second hand—a phenomenon as gradual and intensely reluctant as it is also drastic—there is so far as I know one book and one only to be read, written by an African fifteen hundred years ago. Now in Augustine's *Confessions* we are reckoning with just one of a vast number of works by an architect of Western history, and it may appear grotesque to compare to even that one, tumultuous and gigantic, the isolated recent production of a girl who can give us nothing else. A comparison of the *authors* would be grotesque. But I am thinking of the originality and ambition and indispensability of the two books *in the heart of their substances*—leaving out of account therefore Book X of the *Confessions*, which happens to award man his deepest account of his own memory. I would call the subject of Anne Frank's *Diary* even more mysterious and fundamental than St. Augustine's, and describe it as: the conversion of a child into a person.

At once it may be exclaimed that we have thousands of books on this sub-   5
ject. I agree: autobiographies, diaries, biographies, novels. They seem to me—those that in various literatures I have come on—to bear the same sort of relation to the *Diary* that the works *on* religious conversion bear to the first seven books of the *Confessions*. Anne Frank has made the process itself available.

Why—I asked myself with astonishment when I first encountered the *Diary*, or the extracts that *Commentary* published—has this process not been described before? universal as it is, and universally interesting? And answers came. It is *not* universal, for most people do not grow up, in any degree that will correspond to Anne Frank's growing up; and it is *not* universally interesting, for nobody cares to recall his own, or can. It took, I believe, a special pressure forcing the child-adult conversion, and exceptional self-awareness and exceptional candor and exceptional powers of expression, to bring that strange or normal change into view. This, if I am right, is what she has done, and what we are to study.

The process of her development, then, is our subject. But it is not possible to examine this without some prior sense of two unusual sets of conditions in which it took place: its physical and psychological context, first, and second, the qualities that she took into it. Both, I hope to show, were *necessary* conditions.

For the context: it was both strange, sinister, even an "extreme situation" in Bettelheim's sense,[1] and pseudo-ordinary; and it is hard to say which aspect of the environment was more crippling and crushing. We take a quicksilver-active girl thirteen years old, pretty, popular, voluble, brilliant, and hide her, as it

---

[1] Bruno Bettelheim's well-known article, "Behavior in Extreme Situations," in *Politics*. I am unable to make anything of his recent article in *Harper's*, weirdly titled "The Lesson of Anne Frank," which charges that the Franks should not have gone into hiding as a family but should have dispersed for greater safety; I really do not know what to say to this, except that a man at his desk in Chicago, many years later, ought not to make such decisions perhaps; he also complains that they were not armed. Some social scientist will next inform the Buddha of *his* mistake—in leaving court at all, in austerity, in Illumination, and in teaching.

were, in prison; in a concealed annex upstairs at the rear of the business premises her father had commanded; in darkness, behind blackout curtains; in slowness—any movement might be heard—such that after a time when she peeks out to see cyclists going by they seem to be flying; in closeness—not only were she and her parents and sister hopelessly on top of each other, but so were another family with them, and another stranger—savagely bickering, in whispers, of course; in fear—of Nazis, of air raids, of betrayal by any of the Dutch who knew (this, it seems, is what finally happened, but the marvelous goodness of the responsible Dutch is one of the themes of the *Diary*), of thieves (who came)—the building, even, was once sold out from under them, and the new owner simply missed the entrance to their hiding place. All this calls for heroism, and it's clear that the personalities of the others except Mr. Frank withered and deteriorated under conditions barely tolerable. It took Anne Frank herself more than a year to make the sort of "adjustment" (detestable word) that would let her free for the development that is to be our subject.

But I said, "as it were, in prison." To prison one can become accustomed; it is *different*, and one has no responsibilities. Here there was a simulacrum of ordinary life: she studied, her family were about her, she was near—very near—the real world. The distortion and anxiety are best recorded in the dreadful letter of 1 April 1943. Her father was still (sort of) running the company and had briefed his Dutch assistant for an important conference; the assistant fell ill and there wasn't time to explain "fully" to his replacement; the responsible executive, in hiding, "was trembling with anxiety as to how the talks would go." Someone suggested that if he lay with his face on the floor he might hear. So he did, at 10:30 A.M., with the other daughter, Margot, until 2:30, when half-paralyzed he gave up. The daughters took over, understanding scarcely a word. I have seldom, even in modern literature, read a more painful scene. It takes Anne Frank, a concise writer, thirteen sentences to describe.

Let's distinguish, without resorting to the psychologists, temperament from character. The former would be the disposition with which one arrives in the world, the latter what has happened to that disposition in terms of environment, challenge, failure and success, by the time of maturity—a period individually fixed between, somewhere between, fifteen and seventy-five, say. Dictionaries will not help us; try Webster's Dictionary of Synonyms if you doubt it. Americans like dictionaries, and they are also hopeless environmentalists (although they do not let it trouble their science, as Communists do). I ought therefore perhaps to make it plain that children do differ. The small son of one of my friend would cheerfully have flung himself off the observation tower of the Empire State Building. The small son of another friend was taking a walk, hand in hand, with his father, when they came to an uneven piece of sidewalk and his father heard him say to himself, "Now, Peter, take it easy, Peter, that's all right, Peter," and they went down the other end of the slightly tilted block. My own son, a friend of both, is in between, Dionysiac with the first, Apollonian[2] with Peter. I think we ought to form some opinion of the *temperament* of Anne Frank before entering on her ordeal and thereafter trying to construct a picture of her character.

The materials are abundant, the *Diary* lies open. She was vivacious but intensely serious, devoted but playful. It may later on be a question for us as to whether this conjunction "but" is the right conjunction, in her thought. She was imaginative but practical, passionate but ironic and cold-eyed. Most of the qualities that I am naming need no illustration for a reader of the *Diary*: perhaps "cold-eyed" may have an exemplar: "Pim, who was sitting on a chair in a beam of sunlight that shone through the window, kept being pushed from one side to the other. In addition, I think his rheumatism was bothering him, because he sat rather hunched up with a miserable look on his face. . . . He looked exactly like some shriveled-up old man from an old people's home." So much for an image of the man—her adored father—whom she loves best in the world. She was self-absorbed but un-self-pitying, charitable but sarcastic, industrious but dreamy, brave but sensitive. Garrulous but secretive; skeptical but eloquent. This last "but" may engage us, too. My little word "industrious," like a refugee from a recommendation for a graduate student, finds its best instance in the letter, daunting to an American student, of 27 April 1944, where in various languages she is studying in one day matters that—if they ever came up for an American student—would take him months.

The reason this matters is that the process we are to follow displays itself in a more complicated fashion than one might have expected: in the will, in emotion, in the intellect, in libido. It is surprising what it takes to make an adult human being.

For one reason in particular, which I postpone for the present, I am willing to be extremely schematic about the development we are to follow. I see it as occupying six stages, surprisingly distinct from each other, and cumulative.

1. *Letter of 10 August 1943:* "New idea. I talk more to myself than to the others at mealtimes, which is to be recommended for two reasons. Firstly, because everyone is happy if I don't chatter the whole time, and secondly, I needn't get annoyed about other people's opinions. I don't think my opinions are stupid and the others do; so it is better to keep them to myself. I do just the same if I have to eat something that I simply can't stand. I put my plate in front of me, pretend that it is something delicious, look at it as little as possible, and before I know where I am, it is gone. When I get up in the morning, also a very unpleasant process, I jump out of bed thinking to myself: 'You'll be back in a second,' go to the window, take down the blackout, sniff at the crack of the window until I feel a bit of fresh air, and I'm awake. The bed is turned down as

---

[2]*Dionysiac:* wild or frenzied; *Apollonian:* restrained or balanced. [Eds.]

quickly as possible and then the temptation is removed. Do you know what Mummy calls this sort of thing? 'The Art of Living'—that's an odd expression."

I make no apology for quoting this remarkable passage, as it seems to me, and the crucial later ones, at length, because here there are so many points to be noticed, and because later the excessive length itself of an outburst may prove one of its most significant features. Of course the passages are interesting in themselves, but it is their bearing, in analysis, on our investigation that counts; though I take the reader probably to be acquainted with the *Diary*, a detailed knowledge of it can hardly be expected.

We notice first, then, that this "idea," as she calls it, really is "new"—there has been nothing like it in the diary hitherto—one has an impression, considering it, that she has up till now (over a year) merely been holding her own under the ordeal, assembling or reassembling her forces; and also that it addresses itself strongly to the future. Moreover, it is by no means simply an idea: it is a *program*, and a complicated one, and as different as possible from people's New Year's resolutions ("I will," "I will not," etc.). She describes, and explains, what she *is doing*. Her tone is sober and realistic, the reverse of impulsive.

Now for the burden of the program. It takes place in the Practical Will, and aims at accounting for the two *worst* problems with which her incarceration (let's call it that) confronts her. It has nothing incidental about it. These problems are meals and rising. Meals, because the exacerbated interplay of these huddled persons then is more abusive and dazing even than at other times, and because the fare is so monotonous and tasteless. Rising, because she is rising to what? the same fear, darkness, slowness, privation, exasperation as on all other days; the tendency of profoundly discouraged men to take to their beds and stay there is familiar, and got dramatic illustration—even to many deaths—in the dreadful record of our fighting men as captives in Korea. The steps taken by her against these problems are exactly opposite but verge on each other. She uses first a refraining (that is, a negative) and then her imagination (that is, a positive). I must comment on both procedures. This girl's imaginativeness— the ability to alter reality, to create a new reality—was one of her greatest mental strengths: it is here put twice, solidly, at the service of her psychological survival and tranquillity. The food, and getting up, change under her hand, in a process which *inverts* what we call daydreaming. As for the refraining, one subsidiary point seems to me so important that I want to reserve it for separate consideration, but I hope that the reader will not undervalue the main point: her decision to keep silent. Examples of garrulous persons undertaking silence are certainly not unknown, but they are spectacularly rare, as programmatic and experimental. The one comparable case that I recall is described not in the journal of a young girl but in the journal of a Nobel Prize winner, one of the greatest modern men of letters. W. B. Yeats recorded, late in life, that he once decided, attending his club, to be silent for once; and observed—to his improvement in humility—that every argument he was tempted to use was sooner

361

or later mentioned and developed by someone else. Yeats's *motive* was different from and lighter than Anne Frank's, but that we have to go so far upstairs—or is it upstairs?—for an analogy may help to retard our tendency to underestimate this girl's character as it here begins to form and unfold.

Third, the program is *submitted to her mother*. Whether my word "submitted" is quite right will be questionable. I use it tentatively, looking to an evaluation of the decidedly strange tone of her comment on her mother's comment. Her mother, clearly impressed by her daughter's account of the new administration—as who would not be?—applies an adult label; one, by the way, far from stupid. Anne Frank responds with the automatic doubt of a child about adult labels, say: children are concrete, non-categorical, and no child was ever more so perhaps than this girl. But I cannot feel that we have accounted for the sentences—in terms either of what has been taking place in the diary or in terms of what is to come. I hear *scorn* in her characterization of the mother's formula—"that's an odd expression" (I do *not* hear respect, and the expression is not neutral); and I confess to surprise that she told her mother about the program at all, much less submitted it to her—she has not been in the habit of doing anything of the sort. I take it that the referral, the telling, contained an element of competitiveness, even aggression—as if to murmur, "You are not mastering your own ordeal in this way"; and that this element emerges even more plainly in the final, almost contemptuous comment. Independence comes hard-won and is not friendly. I hardly think, however, that we can form an opinion about these suggestions except in relation to the second and third stages of the development.

The subsidiary point is this: the refraining is described as embarked on *first* in the interest of *others*—and this will interest us later.

2. Three and a half months later, 27 November: "Yesterday evening, before   20
I fell asleep, who should suddenly appear before my eyes but Lies!

"I saw her in front of me, clothed in rags, her face thin and worn. Her eyes were very big and she looked so sadly and reproachfully at me that I could read in her eyes: 'Oh, Anne, why have you deserted me? Help, oh, help me, rescue me from this hell!'

"And I cannot help her, I can only look on, how others suffer and die, and can only pray to God to send her back to us.

"*I just saw Lies, no one else* [my italics], and now I understand. I misjudged her and was too young to understand her difficulties. She was attached to a new girl friend, and to her it seemed as though I wanted to take her away. What the poor girl must have felt like, I know; I know the feeling so well myself!

"Sometimes, in a flash, I saw something of her life, but a moment later I was selfishly absorbed again in my own pleasures and problems. It was horrid of me to treat her as I did, and now she looked at me, oh so helplessly, with her pale face and imploring eyes. If only I could help her!"

There is as much again as this, in the same strain, but this will have to do.   25

362

If we had *only* this letter on this topic, I don't think we should be able to interpret it, but even so, certain observations might be made. We are dealing here with a *vision*, and a vision heavily charged with affect; nothing earlier in the *Diary* resembles it, and this very cool-headed girl seems overwhelmed. It seems, in short, to demand interpretation, as a dream would. Second, the *reason* given for the remorse (in the fourth paragraph) strikes one, I think, as inadequate; one suspects that an operation of the unconscious has thrown up a screen, if Lies is the real subject. But I have to be doubtful, third, that Lies is the real subject, in the light of the phrases that I have taken the liberty of italicizing. Why should the girl so stress the identity of an individual seen in a vision? I once as a young man experienced an hallucination of a senior writer whom I wildly admired, the poet Yeats whom I mentioned earlier, and it would never have occurred to me, in describing it, to say "I just saw Yeats, no one else." We seem bound to suppose that the emotion—passionate remorse—is real, but that both its cause (to which it is excessive, and violently so) and its object are not real—are, as we say, *transferred.*

These doubts are confirmed by a very similar letter of a month later, 29 December: "I was very unhappy again last evening. Granny and Lies came into my mind. Granny, oh, darling Granny, how little we understood of what she suffered, or how sweet she was," and so on and so on, and then back to an agony over Lies.

Now the actual circumstances—the girl friend's fate being doubtful, and the grandmother having died of cancer—were tragic. The question is whether they account for the strangeness and extremity of these outbursts, *at this point*, of love-and-remorse; and I feel certain that they cannot. Clearly, I would say the real subject is the mother—for whom the friend and the grandmother, also loved and felt as wronged, make eminently suitable screens. But how has Anne Frank wronged her mother? This emerges, *at once*, in the next letter. What I think has happened, in this second stage of the development, is that the girl is *paying beforehand*, with a torrent of affection and remorse, for the rebellion against her mother that then comes into the open.

3. 2 January 1944: "This morning when I had nothing to do I turned over some of the pages of my diary and several times I came across letters dealing with the subject 'Mummy' in such a hotheaded way that I was quite shocked, and asked myself: 'Anne, is it really you who mentioned hate? Oh, Anne, how could you!' . . .

"I used to be furious with Mummy, and still am sometimes. It's true that she doesn't understand me, but *I don't understand her either.*" "I can't really love Mummy in a dependent childlike way—I just don't have that feeling." Again I have italicized the crucial horizontal mature expression. 30

Three days later comes the remarkable letter that winds up, to my sense, this first phase of her development, concerned with her mother. The important passages are three. "One thing, which perhaps may seem rather fatuous, I have never forgiven her. It was on a day that I had to go to the dentist. Mummy and

Margot were going to come with me, and agreed that I should take my bicycle. When we had finished at the dentist, and were outside again, Margot and Mummy told me that they were going into the town *to look at something or buy something—I don't remember exactly what*. I wanted to go, too, but was not allowed to, as I had my bicycle with me. Tears of rage sprang into my eyes, and Mummy and Margot began laughing at me. Then I became so furious that I stuck my tongue out at them in the street just as an old woman happened to pass by, who looked very shocked! I rode home on my bicycle, and I know I cried for a long time." It is clear that the *meaning* of this experience is not known to the girl, and cannot become known to us, since we do not have her associations; but its *being reported*, and here, is extremely interesting. I notice that censorship has interfered with memory, in the passage I have italicized, just as it interferes with the recollections of dreams, and of course if we were in a position to interpret the account, this is where we would start. But there is no need to interpret. The traumatic incident has served its purpose, for her and for our understanding of her development, *in being recollected*: this is the sort of experience that in persons who become mentally ill is blocked, whereas the fullness here both of the recollection (with very slight blockage) and of the affect testifies to her freedom.

The next passage concerns her periods, of which she has had three, and its unexpressed tenor certainly is that of rivalry, maturity, independence of the mother, while the letter concludes with the one solid passage of physical narcissism in the whole *Diary*.

It is time to say, before we pass into the second phase of her development, that more than a year earlier (7 November 1942) Anne Frank had defined for herself with extraordinary clarity this part of her task. "I only look at her as a mother, and she just doesn't succeed in being that to me; I have to be my own mother. . . . I am always making resolutions not to notice Mummy's bad example. I want to see only the good side of her and to seek in myself what I cannot find in her. But it doesn't work. . . . Sometimes I believe that God wants to try me, both now and later on; I must become good through my own efforts, without examples and without good advice. Then later on I shall be all the stronger. Who besides me will ever read these letters? From whom but myself shall I get comfort?" Self-command and strength, virtue and independence: we have seen the struggle for them working itself out through the practical will, the imagination, an agonized vision, a trauma recovered, the physical self. The mother will remain a focus for comparison, and almost that only; not a model.

4. The second phase begins on the night of the day of the traumatic and narcissistic letter, and we hear of it in the letter of the day following—as if to say: Now that that problem's dealt with, let's get on with the next. She has sought out Peter Van Daan, exceptionally for her (he has hardly figured in the *Diary* at all to this point), in the evening in his room, and helped him with crossword puzzles. 6 January: "It gave me a queer feeling each time I looked into his deep blue eyes. . . . Whatever you do, don't think I'm in love with

Peter—not a bit of it! . . . I woke at about five to seven this morning and knew at once, quite positively, what I had dreamed. I sat on a chair and opposite me sat Peter . . . [these dots are in the original, or at any rate in the English translation] Wessel. We were looking together at a book of drawings by Mary Bos. The dream was so vivid that I can still partly remember the drawings. But that was not all—the dream went. Suddenly Peter's eyes met mine and I looked into those fine, velvet brown [*sic*] eyes for a long time. Then Peter said very softly, 'If I had only known, I would have come to you long before!' I turned around brusquely because the emotion was too much for me. And after that I felt a soft, and oh, such a cool kind cheek against mine and it felt so good, so good. . . ."

The rest of this letter, and the next, give the history of her secret calf-love for   35 Peter Wessel—of whom we have heard nothing for a year and a half, since the second entry in the *Diary*. The girl does not realize that the dream is not about him, of course. Now, again, we cannot interpret the dream with any assurance, lacking associations; but as Freud observed, some dreams are so lightly armored that they can be read at sight by a person of experience and some familiarity with the situation of the dreamer, and I think this is such a dream. I would not say that the real subject is Peter Van Daan, as perhaps a hasty impression would suggest. Two passages in the letter of the very next day confirm one's feeling that, as in the case of Lies and her grandmother, we are dealing with *two* screen figures and that the real subject is, naturally, her father: "I am completely upset by the dream. When Daddy kissed me this morning, I could have cried out: 'Oh, if only you were Peter!'" But he *was*; notice that it is otherwise hard or even impossible to account for her being "completely upset" by this very agreeable dream, and for the absence of transition from the first sentence to the second—her unconscious needed no transition, because the subject had not changed. Needless to say, in view of the well-known slang use of the word "peter," the dream has a phallic as well as a paternal level; as one would expect from the narcissism of the preceding day. The other passage is this: "Once, when we spoke about sex, Daddy told me that I couldn't possibly understand the longing yet; I always knew that I did understand it and now I understand it fully." One of the most interesting and unusual features of this girl's mind—using the term "mind" very broadly—is its astonishing vertical mobility, unconscious and conscious and half-conscious. Three letters later (22 January) she recognizes herself the formative importance of her dream: "It seems as if I've grown up a lot since my dream the other night. I'm much more of an 'independent being.'" The unsuitability of her father as object, like the unsuitability of her mother as model, later, in fact, becomes explicit.

5. This stage, comprising her intense and miserable attempt to create a post-paternal love object out of the unworthy (but solely available) Peter Van Daan, scarcely needs illustration. It fails because she cannot respect him (16 February: "I told him that he certainly had a very strong inferiority complex. He talked about the Jews. He would have found it much easier if he'd been a

365

Christian and if he could be one after the war. I asked if he wanted to be baptized, but that wasn't the case either. Who was to know whether he was a Jew when the war was over? he said. This gave me rather a pang; it seems such a pity that there's always just a tinge of dishonesty about him"); and the girl's independence and moral nature are now such that she cannot love where she does not respect. By the end of this month, February, he is already becoming unreal and shadowy: "Peter Wessel and Peter Van Daan have grown into one Peter, who is beloved and good, and for whom I long desperately." This is hardly a conception to be heard without amazement from anyone in love with another actual human being. But he has *served his purpose*, and it is just two months after the dream, 7 March, that she is able to summarize, with uncanny self-knowledge, the process with which—from our own very different point of view—we have been concerned.

6. "The first half of 1943: my fits of crying, the loneliness, how I slowly began to see all my faults and shortcomings, which are so great and which seemed much greater then. During the day I deliberately talked about anything and everything that was farthest from my thoughts, *tried to draw Pim to me* [my italics]; but couldn't. Alone I had to face the difficult task of changing myself. . . . I wanted to change in accordance with my own desires. But *one* thing that struck me even more was when I realized that even Daddy would never become my confidant over everything. I didn't want to trust anyone but myself any more.

"At the beginning of the New Year: the second great change, my dream. . . . [her dots] And with it I discovered my longing, not for a girl friend, but for a boy friend. I also discovered my inward happiness and my defensive armor of superficiality and gaiety. In due time I quieted down and discovered my boundless desire for all that is beautiful and good."

There is much more of interest in this long letter, but with a final self-comparison, later this month, to her mother, I think the process that we have been considering may be said to be completed—though what I mean by "completed" will have to have attention later. 17 March: "Although I'm only fourteen, I know quite well what I want, I know who is right and who is wrong, I have my opinions, my own ideas and principles, and although it may sound pretty mad from an adolescent, I feel more of a person than a child, I feel quite independent of anyone.

"I know that I can discuss things and argue better than Mummy, I know I'm not so prejudiced, I don't exaggerate so much, I am more precise and adroit and because of this—you may laugh—I feel superior to her over a great many things. If I love anyone, above all I must have admiration for them, admiration and respect." 40

In these passages, and particularly with the crushing phrase "more precise and adroit," we are not dealing any longer, surely, with a girl at all but with a woman, and one almost perfectly remarkable. In the sense that *Daniel*

Deronda is more "mature" than *Adam Bede*,[3] the process of maturation never ceases in interesting persons so long as they remain interesting. But in the sense—with which, you remember, we began—of the passage from childhood to adulthood, Anne Frank must appear to us here more mature than perhaps most persons ever become.

Our story, of course, can have no happy ending, and so it would be especially agreeable at this point to draw attention to the brilliant *uses* she made of this maturity during the four months of writing life left to her—the comic genius of the dramatization of "the views of the five grownups on the present situation" (14 March 1944), where a description that seemed merely amusing and acute is brought to the level of Molièrean[4] comedy by a piercing conclusion: "I, I, I . . . !"; the powerful account of her despair and ambition dated 4 April; the magnificent page that closes the very long letter of a week later, where in assessing God's responsibility for the doom of the Jews she reaches the most exalted point of the *Diary* and sounds like both spokesman and prophet. I want, indeed, presently to make some use of this last letter. But it is no part of my purpose in the present essay to praise or enjoy Anne Frank. We have been tracing a psychological and moral development to which, if I am right, no close parallel can be found. It took place under very special circumstances, which—let us now conclude, as she concluded—though superficially unfavorable, in fact highly favorable to it; she was *forced* to mature, in order to survive; the hardest challenge, let's say, that a person can face without defeat is the best for him. And anyway in the end we are all defeated; Hemingway once put it that the only point is to make the enemy pay as heavily as possible for *your* position; this she certainly did. And even on the way, life consists largely, if you aim high enough, of defeat; Churchill spent most of his years out of power. Then we said something of the qualities that went into the development: her temperament. I think that we ought to form an opinion, before leaving her, of the moral character with which she emerged—where, that is, she aimed.

It would be easy to draw up a list of the qualities she valued, but it may be more helpful to begin with an odd little remark she once, between the passages quoted above under Stage 6, made about her sister. I notice with interest, by the way, that Margot figures hardly at all in the development, and I wonder whether, on this important evidence, the psychologists have not overestimated the role played by sibling rivalry after very early childhood. "Margot is very sweet and would like me to trust her," Anne Frank writes, "but still I can't tell

---

[3]*Daniel Deronda* (1876): one of George Eliot's later novels, notable for its treatment of anti-Semitism; *Adam Bede* (1859): Eliot's first novel. [Eds.]
[4]*Molière* (1622–1673): French playwright known for satire. [Eds.]

her everything. She's a darling, she's good and pretty, but she lacks the nonchalance for conducting deep discussions...." The criticism is given as decisive, and I think it may puzzle the reader until we recall that Socrates'[5] interlocutors were frequently baffled to decide whether he was in earnest or not. She objects, let's say, to an *absence of play of mind*. But I think still further light is thrown on the expression by the formidable self-account that ends the long letter (11 April) I spoke of earlier: "I am becoming still more independent of my parents, young as I am, I face life with more courage than Mummy; my feeling for justice is immovable, and truer than hers. I know what I want, I have a goal, an opinion, I have a religion and love. Let me be myself and then I am satisfied. I know that I'm a woman, a woman with inward strength and plenty of courage.

"If God lets me live, I shall attain more than Mummy ever has done, I shall not remain insignificant, I shall work in the world and for mankind!

"And now I know that first and foremost I shall require courage and cheerfulness!"   45

Much of what we need to know of her character is to be found here, and deserves comment, but perhaps it may occasion surprise that among these high ideals should be mentioned as climactic "cheerfulness." I am not sure that its placement should occasion surprise, taken with the remark about her sister. We might seek an analogy, one singular enough, too, in the thought of Whitehead. The philosopher once cast about (the passage can be seen conveniently in Morton White's little anthology *The Age of Anxiety*) in an attempt to decide what few concepts were *indispensable* to the notion of life—not merely our life—any life; and he chose four, and he put "self-enjoyment" first. Now he was writing as a metaphysician, while she writes of course as a moralist. But the congruity seems to me remarkable, and for that matter his other three concepts—self-creation, aim (a negative notion, the rejection of all except what is decided on), creative advance—rank very high also, clearly, in her thought. It will be understood that I am not, with these exalted comparisons, claiming philosophical rank for Anne Frank; I am trying to explain what an extremely thoughtful and serious person she made herself into, and how little conventional.

For the rest, the strongly altruistic character of her immense individual ambition, as well as the scorn for anyone of lesser aim, should perhaps be signalized. And I would say finally that the author of the searching expression "my feeling for justice is immovable" has taken full account of all that which makes human justice so intolerably unattainable that Pascal[6] finally rejected it altogether (Fragment 298) in favor of might.

---

[5]*Socrates* (ca 470–399 B.C.): Greek philosopher, tried for heresy and corrupting the youth of Athens by his intellectual and moral teachings. [Eds.]

[6]*Blaise Pascal* (1623–1662): French mathematician and philosopher who believed reason to be inadequate to resolve the difficulties facing humanity. [Eds.]

We began, then, with a certain kind of freedom, which is destroyed; we passed through a long enslavement, to the creation of a new kind of freedom. Then this is destroyed, too, or rather—not so much destroyed—as turned against itself. "Let me be myself and then I am satisfied." But this, of course, was precisely what the world would not do, and in the final letter of the *Diary*, and at the end of its final sentence, we see the self-struggle failing: ". . . finally I twist my heart round again, so that the bad is on the outside and the good is on the inside and keep on trying to find a way of *becoming* what I would so like to be, and what I could be, if . . . there weren't any other people living in the world." The italics of the lacerating verb are mine, but the desperate recognition that one must advance ("self-creation," in Whitehead's term) and that there are circumstances in which one cannot, and the accusing dots, are hers. She remained able to weep with pity, in Auschwitz, for naked gypsy girls driven past to the crematory, and she died in Belsen.

QUESTIONS

1. In his opening paragraphs, Berryman considers it "desirable" to offer a "preliminary justification" for treating Anne Frank's *Diary* seriously. Why does he find it necessary, and what is the justification he offers? Do you think it is necessary?

2. In the first paragraph, Berryman recalls his first impression of reading excerpts from Anne Frank's *Diary*: "Like millions of people later, I was bowled over with pity and horror and admiration for the astounding doomed little girl. But what I *thought* was: a sane person. A sane person, in the twentieth century." Why do you think he stresses this quality? What other qualities of Anne Frank's does Berryman especially respond to?

3. Outline briefly the six stages that Berryman finds in Anne Frank's development. What are his reasons for this division into stages? Do you agree that these are discernible stages?

4. How would you evaluate Berryman as a literary critic? Does his explanation enrich the original text? If you have not read all of Anne Frank's *Diary*, what impression of it do you now have?

5. If you have kept a diary or journal, reread it. Then write an essay in which you describe the stage or stages you were going through and consider what sort of development occurred. If you've never kept a diary but have access to someone else's, give it the same evaluation.

MAKING CONNECTIONS

1. Review Berryman's essay, the excerpts from Anne Frank's *Diary* (p. 171), and the Introduction to this book (p. 1). The Introduction contains an essay by Patricia Hampl describing her process of writing a review of *The Diary of Anne Frank*, as well as the re-

view she wrote. Consider how Berryman's essay contributed to Hampl's essay and review.

2. In a footnote, Berryman refers to Bruno Bettelheim's essay "The Ignored Lesson of Anne Frank" (p. 621) in a rather dismissive way. If you have not already done so, read Bettelheim's essay and consider how Berryman's comment affects your reading of it. Write a brief essay reflecting on how reading all of the material dealing with *The Diary of Anne Frank*, as well as the excerpts from the *Diary*, demonstrates how texts and writers speak to one another—how, in other words, writing moves from text to text.

Social Sciences and Public Affairs

WHAT MADE THIS MAN?
Mengele

Robert Jay Lifton

Born in New York City in 1926, Robert Jay Lifton received his M.D. in 1948 and is presently a distinguished professor of psychiatry and psychology at John Jay College of Criminal Justice in the City University of New York. The author of books on survivors of Hiroshima and Vietnam veterans, his study of Nazi doctors, The Nazi Doctors: Killing and the Psychology of Genocide, *was published in 1986. The following essay was adapted from that book for the* New York Times *magazine in July 1985. It appeared just after Mengele's body—or what most people believe to be his body—was found in a South American grave.*

His bones do not satisfy. Josef Mengele had come to symbolize the entire Nazi killing project. The need was to capture him and put him on trial, hear his confession, put *him* at *our* mercy. For many, that anticipated event took on the significance of confronting the Holocaust and restoring a moral universe.

For Mengele has long been the focus of what could be called a cult of demonic personality. He has been seen as the embodiment of absolute evil, a doctor pledged to heal who kills instead. But this demonization made him something of a deity, a nonhuman or even superhuman force, and served as a barrier to any explanation of his behavior. One reason Auschwitz[1] survivors have hungered for his capture and trial is to divest him of this status. One of

---

[1]*Auschwitz*: Nazi concentration camp during World War II. [Eds.]

them, for instance, spoke to me of his yearning to see "this metamorphosis of turning him back into a person instead of God Almighty."

Mengele was a man, not a demon, and that is our problem.

Indeed, during recent weeks he had already begun to fall from grace as a symbol of pure evil. The most notorious Nazi fugitive, unsuccessfully pursued for decades, had suddenly appeared—as bones in a Brazilian grave. The world watched in fascination as scientific examination seemed to confirm that these were the right bones.

It was reported that Mengele had lived out much of his last 25 years in lonely, despairing isolation, that he had fallen in love with a housemaid. An exemplar of pure evil is not supposed to experience loneliness or to care for another person.

What has been lost in the preoccupation with the corpse has been the nature of the man: What made Mengele Mengele? How can we explain his murderous behavior in Auschwitz?

Over the last eight years, while conducting research for a book on Nazi doctors, I have sought answers to these questions. I have conducted psychological interviews with 28 former Nazi doctors; a number of Nazi lawyers, economists and other nonmedical professionals; and also with more than 80 former Auschwitz inmates who were engaged in medical work in the camp. The study has required me to probe moral as well as psychological issues and to raise questions about the nature of evil.

Hannah Arendt[2] gave currency to a concept of the banality of evil in her portrayal of Adolf Eichmann as a rather unremarkable bureaucrat who killed by meeting schedules and quotas. She is surely correct in her claim that an ordinary person is capable of extreme evil. But over the course of committing evil acts, an ordinary person becomes something different. In a process I call "doubling," a new self takes shape that adapts to the evil environment, and the evil acts become part of that self. At this point, the person and his behavior are anything but banal.

Mengele possessed unusually intense destructive potential, but there were no apparent signs of aberrant behavior prior to the Nazis and Auschwitz. Without Auschwitz, he would probably have kept his destructive potential under control. As a wise former inmate physician told me, "In ordinary times, Mengele could have been a slightly sadistic German professor."

It was the coming together of the man and the place, the "fit" between the two, that created the Auschwitz Mengele.

What we know about the man who arrived in Auschwitz in May 1943 is not especially remarkable. The son of a well-to-do Bavarian industrialist, Mengele is remembered by an acquaintance as a popular young man, an enthusiastic

---

[2]Hannah Arendt (1906–1975): historian and social philosopher, she published *Eichmann in Jerusalem: A Report on the Banality of Evil* in 1963. [Eds.]

friend. He was also intelligent, a serious student who showed "a very distinct ambitiousness."

In 1931, at the age of 20, Mengele joined a right-wing, nationalistic organization. He was an early Nazi enthusiast, enlisting with the SA (the storm troopers) in 1933, applying for party membership in 1937 and for SS membership the following year. There are rumors that, while studying in Munich, he met such high-ranking Nazis as Alfred Rosenberg, a leading ideologue, and even Hitler himself.

Mengele became a true ideologue: a man who understood his life to be in the service of a larger vision.

According to an Auschwitz friend and fellow-SS physician, Mengele espoused the visionary SS ideology that the Nordic race was the only truly creative race, that it had been weakened by Christian morality of Jewish origin, and that Germany needed to revert to ancient German myths in creating an SS "order" to purify the Nordic race. According to his friend, Mengele was an extreme anti-Semite, "fully convinced that the annihilation of the Jews is a provision for the recovery of the world and Germany." And Mengele considered these views to be scientifically derived. (I have preserved the anonymity of the people I interviewed. Those who are identified had previously made themselves known in books or other public documents.)

Mengele's ideology considerably influenced his intellectual choices. Matric- 15
ulating not only at Munich but also at Bonn, Vienna and Frankfurt, he came to concentrate on physical anthropology and genetics, eventually working under Professor Freiherr Otmar von Verschuer at the Institute of Hereditary Biology and Racial Hygiene at Frankfurt. He earned a degree in anthropology as well as medicine.

Mengele produced three publications before he came to Auschwitz. They dealt with physical characteristics and abnormalities and, in each case, emphasized the role of heredity—an emphasis in keeping with trends in German and international scholarship at the time. Though jammed with charts, diagrams and photographs that claim more than they prove, the papers are relatively respectable scientific works of that era. But their conclusions uniformly reflect Mengele's commitment to bringing science into the service of the Nazi vision.

Mengele seemed well on his way toward an academic career. He had the strong backing of Verschuer who, in a letter of recommendation, praised his reliability and his capacity for clear verbal presentation of difficult intellectual problems. Mengele's marriage to a professor's daughter was in keeping with his academic aspirations.

His military experience loomed large in his idea of himself. In 1938–39, Mengele served six months with a specially trained mountain light-infantry regiment, followed by a year in the reserve medical corps. He spent three years with a Waffen SS unit, mostly in the East, including action in Russia, where, according to SS records, he was wounded and declared medically unfit for combat. A commendation declared that he had "acquitted himself brilliantly in the face of the enemy," and he received five decorations, including the Iron Cross First Class and Second Class.

Mengele, his friend said, was the only doctor in Auschwitz who possessed that array of medals, and he was enormously proud of them; he frequently referred to his combat experience to bolster his arguments on a variety of matters. According to his friend, Mengele arrived at the camp with a special aura because he was coming more or less directly from the front.

His friend suggests something else special about Mengele. He had asked to [20] be sent to the Auschwitz death camp because of the opportunities it could provide for his research. He continued to have the support and collaboration of his teacher, Verschuer, who convinced the German Research Society to provide financial support for Mengele's work.

Auschwitz was both an annihilation camp and a work camp for German industry. Like other SS doctors there, Mengele had the task of "selecting" prisoners for the gas chamber—the vast majority—and for the slave labor force. SS doctors also controlled and supervised the inmate doctors who alone did whatever actual medical treatment was done. Mengele was the chief doctor of Birkenau, an Auschwitz subcamp, but seemed to many inmates to have authority beyond his position. Dr. Olga Lengyel, an inmate doctor, described Mengele as "far and away the chief provider for the gas chamber and the crematory ovens." Another inmate doctor spoke of Mengele's role as "very important, more than that of the others."

One reason he appeared to be especially important was that he was extraordinarily energetic. While many SS doctors did no more than what was required of them, Mengele was always on the move, busy with his work, initiating new projects. More than any other SS doctor, he seemed to find his calling in Auschwitz.

Many inmates thought that Mengele alone conducted the large "selections." When they arrived at Auschwitz, packed by the hundreds into freight and cattle cars, they were unloaded and herded down a ramp. The Nazi doctors were assigned, on a rotating basis, to stand on the ramp and select those prisoners who would live, as workers at the camp, and those who would be killed.

The evidence is that Mengele took his turn at the ramp, like everyone else, but he also appeared there frequently to make sure that any twins in a "transport," as the trains were called, would be collected and saved for his research. But the prisoners saw it differently. At a trial of former Auschwitz personnel, in Frankfurt in 1964, an inmate who had been assigned to unload the transports recalled only the name of Mengele. When the judge commented, "Mengele cannot have been there all the time," the witness answered: "In my opinion, always. Night and day." Mengele brought such flamboyance and posturing to the selections task that it was his image inmates remembered.

He was an elegant figure on the ramp—handsome, well groomed, extremely [25] upright in posture. Prisoners sometimes described him as "very Aryan looking" or "tall and blond," when he was actually of medium height, with dark hair and a dark complexion. Inmates said Mengele "conveyed the impression of a gentle and cultured man" and spoke of the "cheerful expression on his face . . . almost like he had fun . . . he was very playful."

There was an easy rhythm in his approach to selections. He walked back and forth, an inmate recalled, "a nice-looking man" with a riding crop in his hand who "looked at the bodies and the faces just a couple of seconds" and said, "*Links* [left], *Rechts* [right], *Links, Rechts . . . Rechts . . . Links, Rechts.*"

Prisoners were struck by the stark contrast between his calm, playful manner and the horror of what he was doing. Occasionally, though, his detachment could give way to outbreaks of rage and violence, especially when he encountered resistance to his sense of "the rules." In one instance, a mother refused to be separated from her teen-age daughter and scratched the face of the SS trooper who tried to enforce Mengele's decision. Mengele drew his gun and shot both the woman and her child. Still raging, he ordered that all the people from that transport whom he had previously selected as workers be sent to the gas chamber.

In the hospital blocks where medical treatment was given to prisoners in order to maintain the workforce, there was another kind of "selection" process. Nazi doctors would weed out for the gas chamber the weakest patients, those thought unlikely to recover in two or three weeks. Mengele, Dr. Lengyel recalled, "could show up suddenly at any hour, day or night . . . when we least expected him." The prisoners would "march before him with their arms in the air while he continued to whistle his Wagner—or it might be Verdi or Johann Strauss."

Though usually cool in his conduct of selections, Mengele was passionate in pursuing his "scientific research." His main interest was the study of twins, but he carried out a variety of projects with different groups of human subjects.

- He collected and studied dwarfs in an effort to determine the genetic reasons for their condition.

- He investigated a gangrenous condition of the face and mouth called noma. Though ordinarily a rare condition, it was common among gypsy inmates of Auschwitz. It was known to be caused by the kind of debilitation that inmates were subject to, but Mengele focused on what he deemed to be genetic and racial factors.

- He sought out inmates with a condition known as heterochromia of the iris—in which the two eyes are of different colors—and, after their death, sent their eyes to his old professor, Verschuer, at the Berlin-Dahlem Institute of Racial Biology. With some of these inmates, Mengele took the bizarre step of attempting to change eye color in an Aryan direction by injecting methylene blue into the brown eyes of blond inmate children.

30

375

But the research that most occupied Mengele, to which he devoted the greatest time and energy, was his study of twins. In fact, he probably came to Auschwitz for that specific purpose—as a continuation of work he had done under Verschuer at the University of Frankfurt a few years earlier.

As early as 1935, Verschuer had written of the absolute necessity of research on twins to achieve "complete and reliable determination of what is hereditary in man."

Because identical twins (derived from the same ovum) possess the same genetic constitution, they have traditionally been used in research on hereditary influences. Their shared physical and sometimes psychological characteristics, normal and abnormal, can be assumed to be genetically determined. Such characteristics can be assumed to be genetically determined in other people as well.   35

Mengele recognized that Auschwitz would permit him to pursue his mentor's dream. From the hundreds of thousands of prisoners, he could collect twins in quantities never before available to a scientist. What is more, he could exercise total control over them.

He could compare measurements and bodily features. He could try medications meant to prevent, treat or induce a particular illness on an individual twin, or both of a pair of twins. He could then make comparisons of various kinds, in which he sought to demonstrate the importance of heredity rather than environment. He had no need or inclination to concern himself with ethical considerations, sharing as he did the general SS doctor's view that one was doing no harm since Auschwitz inmates, especially Jews, were in any case doomed.

Mengele had a fanatic's commitment to twin research. A number of survivors reported seeing him on the transport ramp, shouting "Zwillinge heraus! [Twins out!], Zwillinge heraustreten! [Twins step forward!]." An inmate anthropologist whom Mengele had eagerly recruited to assist him described the arrival of a group of Hungarian Jews "like a river ... women, men, women with children, and suddenly I saw Mengele going quickly ... the same speed [as] the crowd [crying out] only 'Zwillinge heraus!' ... with such a face that I would think he's mad."

Mengele had the same frenzied attitude in carrying out his research. To inmates, he seemed to have an inner compulsion to get a great deal accomplished quickly in a personal race against time. He undoubtedly came to recognize increasingly that the days of the Auschwitz research bonanza were numbered.

Mainly to pursue his studies of twins, Mengele set up an Auschwitz caricature of an academic research institute. Inmate doctors, mostly Jewish, with specialized training in various laboratory and clinical areas, were called upon to contribute to his work by diagnosing, sometimes treating, X-raying and performing post-mortem examinations of his research subjects. For his pathologist, Dr. Miklos Nyiszli, he provided a special dissection room complete with porce-   40 lain sinks and a dissecting table of polished marble. The overall arrangement, as Dr. Nyiszli later wrote, was "the exact replica of any large city's institute of pathology." In addition to the area used by SS physicians, Mengele had three offices of his own, mainly for work with twins.

The precise number of twins Mengele studied is not known, but during the spring and summer of 1944, the time of the influx and mass murder of enormous numbers of Hungarian Jews, he accumulated what inmates of the men's and women's camps estimated to be a total of 175 sets of twins; it was an extraordinarily large number to have available simultaneously in a single place. Most were children, but the twins ranged up to the age of 70. The relative number of identical twins, as opposed to nonidentical twins, is also uncertain. (Nonidentical twins come from different ova and are genetically similar only to the extent of ordinary siblings.) Mengele's capacity or inclination to maintain, in his work, the crucial distinction between these two kinds of twins is unclear. Since it is known that a few ordinary siblings masqueraded as twins, upon discovering the advantages of doing so, there is reason to doubt the reliability of Mengele's research.

Being a twin gave one a much better chance to survive. That was especially true for children, who were otherwise routinely selected for the gas chamber on arrival.

Twins had unique status. They felt themselves, as one put it, "completely elevated, segregated from the hurly-burly of the camp." They lived in special blocks, usually within medical units. They were frequently permitted to keep their own clothing. Their heads were not shaved. Their diet was rich by Auschwitz standards, often including white bread and milk. They were never beaten, as one surviving twin explained—even if they were caught in such a normally "ultimate sin" as stealing food—because the word was out "not to ruin us physically."

Mothers of young female twins were sometimes allowed to stay with their children, though usually only temporarily, in order to help the twins remain in good physical and mental condition—and on occasion to contribute to information about heredity and family history. We may say that the lives of twins had unique existential value in Auschwitz.

Mengele's research method, according to the inmate anthropologist, was standard for the time—and much the same as that used by her own well-regarded professor at the Polish university where she had obtained her advanced degree. That professor, she said, stressed "the biological foundation of [the] social environment" and the delineation of "racial types." Mengele's approach was different only in being "terribly detailed."

Measurements were taken of the twins' skulls and bodies and various characteristics of the nose, lips, ears, hair and eyes. The inmate anthropologist used quality Swiss instruments and wore a white coat "like a physician."

Identical twins, Mengele's most treasured research objects, were often examined together. As one of them described: "It was like a laboratory. . . . There

45

377

isn't a piece of body that wasn't measured and compared. . . . We were always sitting together—always nude. . . . We would sit for hours together."

When Mengele himself performed the examination, they said, he was very proper and methodical: "He concentrated on one part of the body at one time . . . like [one day] he measured our eyes for about two hours." They spoke of being examined as frequently as twice a week for a period of five months in late 1944, and also remembered vividly a special visit to the Auschwitz main camp for photographs.

There were less benign research programs on twins. One twin survivor, for example, told how he and his 12-year-old twin sister would be examined and subjected to such procedures as the injection of material into their spines or the clamping of some part of the body "to see how long you could stand the pressure."

The twin survivor also spoke of Mengele's supervising "a lot of research with   50 chemicals" and of how Mengele's assistants "might stick a needle in various places from behind," including the performing of spinal taps. These procedures, when done on young children, resulted sometimes in loss of consciousness, deafness and—among the smaller children—death.

The final step in Mengele's research on a number of the twins was dissection. Auschwitz enabled him not only to observe and measure twins to compare them in life, but to arrange for them to die together. He could thereby obtain comparisons of healthy or diseased organs to show the effects of heredity.

Sometimes Mengele himself presided over the murder of his twins. A deposition given by Dr. Nyiszli in 1945 described one such event:

"In the work room next to the dissecting room, 14 gypsy twins were waiting . . . and crying bitterly. Dr. Mengele didn't say a single word to us, and prepared a 10cc. and 5cc. syringe. From a box he took evipan, and from another box he took chloroform, which was in 20 cubic-centimeter glass containers, and put these on the operating table. After that, the first twin was brought in . . . a 14-year-old girl. Dr. Mengele ordered me to undress the girl and put her on the dissecting table. Then he injected the evipan into her right arm intravenously. After the child had fallen asleep, he felt for the left ventricle of the heart and injected 10cc. of chloroform. After one little twitch the child was dead, whereupon Dr. Mengele had it taken into the corpse chamber. In this manner, all 14 twins were killed during the night."

Mengele could be totally arbitrary in his killings. An inmate radiologist told of a pair of gypsy twins, "two splendid boys of 7 or 8, whom we were studying from all aspects—from the 16 or 18 different specialties we represented." The boys both had symptoms in their joints that, according to a belief at that time, could be linked to tuberculosis. Mengele was convinced that the boys were tubercular, but the various inmate doctors, including the radiologist, found no trace of that disease.

Mengele was outraged, and he left the room, ordering the radiologist to remain. When he returned about an hour later, Mengele said calmly: "You are right. There was nothing." After some silence, Mengele added, "Yes, I dissected them." Later, the radiologist said, he heard from Dr. Nyiszli that Mengele had shot the two boys in the neck and that "while they were still warm, began to examine them: lungs first, then each organ."

The two boys, the radiologist added, had been favorites with all the doctors — including Mengele. They had been treated very well, he added, "spoiled in all respects . . . these two especially . . . they fascinated him considerably." But their post-mortem study had still greater fascination for him.

Mengele's fanatically brutal approach to his research can be understood mainly in terms of his combination of ideological zealotry and scientific ambition. Verschuer, his mentor, was taking science in a Nazi direction when he declared that research with twins would demonstrate "the extent of the damage caused by adverse hereditary influences" as well as "relations between disease, racial types, and miscegenation." In Auschwitz, Mengele saw an opportunity to deepen and extend the Nazi racial vision by means of systematic research "evidence."

He was also intent upon gaining personal recognition as a scientist. Indeed, his Auschwitz friend told me that Mengele planned to use his research with twins as the basis for his Habilitation, the presentation necessary for a formal university appointment. Mengele's ideological worship, then, included the worship of Nazified "science," and from that standpoint he told his friend that "it would be a sin, a crime . . . and irresponsible not to utilize the possibilities that Auschwitz had for twin research," and that "there would never be another chance like it."

Mengele saw himself as a biological revolutionary, part of a vanguard devoted to the bold scientific task of remaking his people and ultimately the people of the world. The German race would have to be cured and its genes improved. Many believed, as one inmate doctor said, that Mengele wanted to make use of his research on twins "to find the cause of multiple pregnancies" in order to increase such events among Aryan women. In any case, he did wish to apply his results toward German-centered racial goals.

Mengele's friend revealed something of this motivation when he told me that Mengele saw his work as having bearing on selecting national leaders "not on a political basis but on a biological basis." He might well have been unclear himself about his exact motivations, but we have reason to see in them a combination of distorted scientific claims and related ideological fantasies.

Mengele's treatment of twins provides important additional clues to his psychology. There we see displayed the full range of his adaptation to the Auschwitz environment. Survivors repeatedly commented on his confusing duality of affection and violence, an extreme manifestation of the process I call "doubling."

The twins lived in an atmosphere that combined sanctuary with terror. As one recalled, they never forgot they were in Auschwitz where, starting in the summer of 1944, they could clearly see "flames really coming up every day, every night" from the open pits in which bodies were burned, and they could "hear every evening a cacophony of screams" and breathe in "the unbearable smell."

Yet most of the twins were safe, under the protection of Mengele, and much of the time he treated them lovingly. According to an inmate doctor, Mengele in his contacts with the children was "as gentle as a father," talking to them and patting them on the head "in a loving way." He could be playful, jumping about to please them. The twin children frequently called him "Uncle Pepi." Sometimes, though, as the inmate doctor reported, Mengele would bring some gypsy twins sweets and invite them for a ride in his car which turned out to be "a little drive with Uncle Pepi, to the gas chamber."

For many of the twins, the strength of their warm feelings toward Mengele was such that they found it impossible in later years to believe the evil things they heard about him. "For us," one said, he was "like a papa, like a mama."

One inmate doctor, in his own excruciating struggles to come to terms with Mengele, thought of him as "the double man" who had "all the human feelings, pity and so on," but also had in his psyche an "impenetrable, indestructible cell, which is obedience to the received order."

He was describing Mengele's Auschwitz self, the new self that can take 65 shape in virtually anyone in adapting to an extreme environment. With the Auschwitz self, Mengele's potential for evil became actual, even as he maintained elements of his prior self that included affection toward children. In this process, each part-self behaved as a functioning whole: the Auschwitz self enabling him to function in that murderous environment and to exploit its human resources with considerable efficiency; the prior self enabling him to maintain a sense of decency. His powerful commitment to Nazi ideology served as a bridge, a necessary connection between the two.

Mengele's Auschwitz behavior reflects important pre-existing psychological tendencies that contributed greatly to that doubling process. His inclinations toward omnipotence and total control over others could be given extreme expression in Auschwitz.

The man and the place were dramatically summed up by a survivor who did art work for him and spoke of herself as Mengele's "pet," someone who was pleasant to have around. The death camp, she said, was like a city dog pound, with Mengele as the inspector checking up on the keepers—the inmate doctors—and on the dogs—the inmates.

The inspector, she recalled, would often admonish the keepers to "wash up the excrement" in the pound, "to keep it clean, to keep the dogs healthy." Then he would examine "these chambers where they are killed" and he would inquire about the dog population: "How many are you? Well, it's too crowded—you better put in two more [gas chambers] today."

This image, with its blending of omnipotence and sadism, was relevant to much of Mengele's relationship to twins. "It was an axiom," one of them told me, "that Mengele is God. He used to come always with an entourage, very well decked out, very elegant. He always carried around him an aura of some terrifying threat, which is, I suspect, unexplainable to normal human beings who didn't see this." It was "literally impossible," the survivor said, "to transmit the edge of this terror."

Only in Auschwitz could Mengele assume that aura and become what the 70 inmate artist described as "a very charismatic man" with "star quality." But when she added, "Marilyn Monroe flashed through my mind," she was perhaps suggesting the strong element of mannered self-display, what is loosely called "narcissism"—and perhaps a certain amount of kitsch and absurdity—contained in Mengele's assumption of omnipotence.

Another prior trait, Mengele's schizoid tendencies, were reflected in survivors' accounts of his "dead eyes"—eyes that showed no emotion, that avoided looking into the eyes of others. The inmate artist described him as so distant from others that "he seemed to be from a different planet." That kind of schizoid person, however friendly or affectionate at times, remains fundamentally removed from others, with inner divisions that can contribute to the doubling process.

Mengele's exaggerated immaculateness was consistent with such tendencies toward withdrawal. He was "very sensitive about bad smells," an inmate doctor reported, so that before he arrived, "the doors and windows had to be opened." He was "Clean, clean, clean!" one survivor said. This passion for cleanliness actually became part of Mengele's selection esthetic. He often sent prisoners with skin blemishes—even those with small abscesses or old appendectomy scars—to the gas chamber.

All people are capable of psychic numbing, a diminished tendency or inclination to feel. But Mengele's version of the Auschwitz self—his ease in harming and killing—carried psychic numbing to a remarkable extreme. "The main thing about him," an observant inmate-doctor stated, "was that he totally lacked feeling." He was enabled to feel nothing in killing a young twin, even one he had been fond of, to make a medical point.

Mengele's sadism was of a piece with these other traits. The pleasure he could take in causing pain was an aspect of his omnipotence, a means of maintaining his schizoid withdrawal and his renunciation of anything in the realm of fellow-feeling toward his victims. That kind of sadism was manifest in his smiling enthusiasm at selections. It was present in his remark to a Jewish woman doctor who was pleading vainly for the life of her father: "Your father is 70 years old. Don't you think he has lived long enough?" And survivors tell of Mengele's proclaiming on Tisha B'Av, the commemoration of the destruction of the first and second temples, "We will have a concert." There was a concert, then a roll-call, then an enormous selection for the gas chamber.

In his play "The Deputy," Rolf Hochhuth creates a fiendish Nazi character 75 known only as "the Doctor," modeled after Mengele, who is described as having "the stature of Absolute Evil," as "only playing the part of a human being."

381

Some inmate-doctors also viewed Mengele as a demon and wished to divest him of his professional status. One described him as "a monster, period," and another as "no more doctor than anything else."

But being a doctor was part of Mengele's demonology: he took on the dark side of the omnipotent Svengali-like physician-shaman.

The myth of Mengele's demonic stature was given added support by the often misleading rumors about his life after Auschwitz. He was said to be living in comfort in South America, advising dictators such as Gen. Alfredo Stroessner of Paraguay on how to annihilate the Indian population, growing wealthy in an extensive drug trade run by former Nazis. Nobody could touch Mengele.

We have seen that his death has partly dispelled this demonology. His continuing "metamorphosis" into an ordinary mortal can be enhanced by probing his motivations and behavior.

The psychological traits Mengele brought to Auschwitz exist in many of us, 80 but in him they took exaggerated form. His impulse toward omnipotence and total control of the world around him were a means of fending off anxiety and doubt, fears of falling apart—ultimately, fear of death. That fear also activated his sadism and extreme psychic numbing. He could quiet his fears of death in that death-dominated environment by performing the ultimate act of power over another person: murder.

Yet, as far as we know, he had neither killed nor maimed prior to Auschwitz, and had in fact functioned in a more or less integrated way.

The perfect match between Mengele and Auschwitz changed all that. Through doubling, he could call forth his evil potential. That evil, generally speaking, is neither inherent in any self nor foreign to it. Under certain kinds of psychological and moral conditions it can emerge. Crucial to that emergence is an ideology or world view, a theory or vision that justifies or demands evil actions.

Viewed in this light, Josef Mengele emerges as he really was: a visionary ideologue, an efficiently murderous functionary, a diligent careerist—and disturbingly human.

QUESTIONS

1. As paragraph 6 makes clear, this essay seeks to explain Mengele. Summarize in your own words the explanation that it offers.

2. Why were twins so important to Mengele, according to Lifton? Are the reasons psychological, scientific, or both? What has his interest in twins got to do with the process Lifton calls "doubling" in paragraph 8?

3. Much of this essay is devoted to reporting. Where do these reports come from? What sources does Lifton identify in the article?

4. In paragraph 70 Lifton speaks of "narcissism." In what ways does Mengele seem to conform to, or depart from, this psychological type?

5. "Viewed in this light," Lifton concludes, "Josef Mengele emerges as he really was: a visionary ideologue, an efficiently murderous functionary, a diligent careerist—and disturbingly human." Do you agree? Would you like to offer a different interpretation?

6. Do some research on another person supposed to have been a human monster, such as the Roman emperors Nero or Caligula or some more modern tyrant, terrorist, or torturer. (You may find legend at odds with history as you look into things.) Incorporate your research in an essay considering the kind of figure that humans find horrifying. What is it that makes these creatures both terrible and fascinating?

MAKING CONNECTIONS

1. Read Bruno Bettelheim's "The Ignored Lesson of Anne Frank" (p. 621), paying special attention to his description of Mengele. How are the terms for Bettelheim's argument about Mengele different from Lifton's?

2. Lifton speaks in paragraph 73 of "psychic numbing." Can you think of other instances of this phenomenon that you have encountered in your reading or in your experience? Is a play like Shakespeare's *Macbeth*, for instance, about psychic numbing? Write an essay in which you discuss this phenomenon, defining and illustrating the concept.

SOME CONDITIONS OF OBEDIENCE AND DISOBEDIENCE TO AUTHORITY

Stanley Milgram

Stanley Milgram (1933–1984) was born in New York, went to Queens College and Harvard University, and was a professor of social psychology at the Graduate Center of the City University of New York. The following explanation of Milgram's experiment first appeared in the professional journal Human Relations *in 1965 and made him famous, causing a storm of controversy over his method of experimentation and the results of his experiment. Milgram once said of his work, "As a social psychologist, I look at the world not to master it in any practical sense, but to understand it and to communicate that understanding to others."*

The situation in which one agent commands another to hurt a third turns up time and again as a significant theme in human relations.[1] It is powerfully expressed in the story of Abraham, who is commanded by God to kill his son. It is no accident that Kierkegaard,[2] seeking to orient his thought to the central themes of human experience, chose Abraham's conflict as the springboard to his philosophy.

War too moves forward on the triad of an authority which commands a person to destroy the enemy, and perhaps all organized hostility may be viewed as a theme and variation on the three elements of authority, executant, and victim.[3] We describe an experimental program, recently concluded at Yale Uni-

---

[1]This research was supported by two grants from the National Science Foundation: NSF G-7916 and NSF G-24152. Exploratory studies carried out in 1960 were financed by a grant from the Higgins Funds of Yale University. I am grateful to John T. Williams, James J. McDonough, and Emil Elges for the important part they played in the project. Thanks are due also to Alan Elms, James Miller, Taketo Murata, and Stephen Stier for their aid as graduate assistants. My wife, Sasha, performed many valuable services. Finally, I owe a profound debt to the many persons in New Haven and Bridgeport who served as subjects.

[2]*Søren Kierkegaard* (1813–1855): Danish philosopher and theologian. [Eds.]

[3]Consider, for example, J. P. Scott's analysis of war in his monograph on aggression:

. . . while the actions of key individuals in a war may be explained in terms of direct stimulation to aggression, vast numbers of other people are involved simply by being part of an organized society.

. . . For example, at the beginning of World War I an Austrian archduke was assassinated in Sarajevo. A few days later soldiers from all over Europe were marching toward each other, not because they were stimulated by the archduke's misfortune, but because they had been trained to obey orders.

(Slightly rearranged from Scott (1958), *Aggression*, p. 103.)

versity, in which a particular expression of this conflict is studied by experimental means.

In its most general form the problem may be defined thus: if X tells Y to hurt Z, under what conditions will Y carry out the command of X and under what conditions will he refuse? In the more limited form possible in laboratory research, the question becomes: If an experimenter tells a subject to hurt another person, under what conditions will the subject go along with this instruction, and under what conditions will he refuse to obey? The laboratory problem is not so much a dilution of the general statement as one concrete expression of the many particular forms this question may assume.

One aim of the research was to study behavior in a strong situation of deep consequence to the participants, for the psychological forces operative in powerful and lifelike forms of the conflict may not be brought into play under diluted conditions.

This approach meant, first, that we had a special obligation to protect the welfare and dignity of the persons who took part in the study; subjects were, of necessity, placed in a difficult predicament, and steps had to be taken to ensure their wellbeing before they were discharged from the laboratory. Toward this end, a careful, post-experimental treatment was devised and has been carried through for subjects in all conditions.[4]

TERMINOLOGY

If Y follows the command of X we shall say that he has obeyed X; if he fails to carry out the command of X, we shall say that he has disobeyed X. The terms to *obey* and to *disobey*, as used here, refer to the subject's overt action only, and carry no implication for the motive or experiential states accompanying the action.[5]

---

[4]It consisted of an extended discussion with the experimenter and, of equal importance, a friendly reconciliation with the victim. It is made clear that the victim did *not* receive painful electric shocks. After the completion of the experimental series, subjects were sent a detailed report of the results and full purposes of the experimental program. A formal assessment of this procedure points to its overall effectiveness. Of the subjects, 83.7 percent indicated that they were glad to have taken part in the study; 15.1 percent reported neutral feelings; and 1.3 percent stated that they were sorry to have participated. A large number of subjects spontaneously requested that they be used in further experimentation. Four-fifths of the subjects felt that more experiments of this sort should be carried out, and 74 percent indicated that they had learned something of personal importance as a result of being in the study. Furthermore, a university psychiatrist, experienced in outpatient treatment, interviewed a sample of experimental subjects with the aim of uncovering possible injurious effects resulting from participation. No such effects were in evidence. Indeed, subjects typically felt that their participation was instructive and enriching. A more detailed discussion of this question can be found in Milgram (1964)

[5]To *obey* and to *disobey* are not the only terms one could use in describing the critical action of Y. One could say that Y is cooperating with X, or displays conformity with regard to X's commands. However, *cooperation* suggests that X agrees with Y's ends, and understands the relationship between his own behavior and the attainment of those ends. (But the experimental procedure, and,

To be sure, the everyday use of the word *obedience* is not entirely free from complexities. It refers to action within varying situations, and connotes diverse motives within those situations: a child's obedience differs from a soldier's obedience, or the love, honor, and *obey* of the marriage vow. However, a consistent behavioral relationship is indicated in most uses of the term: in the act of obeying, a person does what another person tells him to do. Y obeys X if he carries out the prescription for action which X has addressed to him; the term suggests, moreover, that some form of dominance-subordination, or hierarchical element, is part of the situation in which the transaction between X and Y occurs.

A subject who complies with the entire series of experimental commands will be termed an *obedient* subject; one who at any point in the command series defies the experimenter will be called a *disobedient* or *defiant* subject. As used in this report the terms refer only to the subject's performance in the experiment, and do not necessarily imply a general personality disposition to submit to or reject authority.

SUBJECT POPULATION

The subjects used in all experimental conditions were male adults, residing in the greater New Haven and Bridgeport areas, aged 20 to 50 years, and engaged in a wide variety of occupations. Each experimental condition described in this report employed 40 fresh subjects and was carefully balanced for age and occupational types. The occupational composition for each experiment was: workers, skilled and unskilled: 40 percent; white collar, sales, business: 40 percent; professionals: 20 percent. The occupations were intersected with three

---

in particular, the experimenter's command that the subject shock the victim even in the absence of a response from the victim, preclude such understanding.) Moreover, cooperation implies status parity for the co-acting agents, and neglects the asymmetrical, dominance-subordination element prominent in the laboratory relationship between experimenter and subject. *Conformity* has been used in other important contexts in social psychology, and most frequently refers to imitating the judgments or actions of others when no explicit requirement for imitation has been made. Furthermore, in the present study there are two sources of social pressure; pressure from the experimenter issuing the commands, and pressure from the victim to stop the punishment. It is the pitting of a common man (the victim) against an authority (the experimenter) that is the distinctive feature of the conflict. At a point in the experiment the victim demands that he be let free. The experimenter insists that the subject continue to administer shocks. Which act of the subject can be interpreted as conformity? The subject may conform to the wishes of his peer or to the wishes of the experimenter, and conformity in one direction means the absence of conformity in the other. Thus the word has no useful reference in this setting, for the dual and conflicting social pressures cancel out its meaning.

In the final analysis, the linguistic symbol representing the subject's action must take its meaning from the concrete context in which that action occurs; and there is probably no word in everyday language that covers the experimental situation exactly, without omissions or irrelevant connotations. It is partly for convenience, therefore, that the terms *obey* and *disobey* are used to describe the subject's actions. At the same time, our use of the words is highly congruent with dictionary meaning.

age categories (subjects in 20's, 30's, and 40's, assigned to each condition in the proportions of 20, 40, and 40 percent, respectively).

THE GENERAL LABORATORY PROCEDURE[6]

The focus of the study concerns the amount of electric shock a subject is willing to administer to another person when ordered by an experimenter to give the "victim" increasingly more severe punishment. The act of administering shock is set in the context of a learning experiment, ostensibly designed to study the effect of punishment on memory. Aside from the experimenter, one naïve subject and one accomplice perform in each session. On arrival each subject is paid $4.50. After a general talk by the experimenter, telling how little scientists know about the effect of punishment on memory, subjects are informed that one member of the pair will serve as teacher and one as learner. A rigged drawing is held so that the naïve subject is always the teacher, and the accomplice becomes the learner. The learner is taken to an adjacent room and strapped into an "electric chair."

The naïve subject is told that it is his task to teach the learner a list of paired associates, to test him on the list, and to administer punishment whenever the learner errs in the test. Punishment takes the form of electric shock, delivered to the learner by means of a shock generator controlled by the naïve subject. The teacher is instructed to increase the intensity of electric shock one step on the generator on each error. The learner, according to plan, provides many wrong answers, so that before long the naïve subject must give him the strongest shock on the generator. Increases in shock level are met by increasingly insistent demands from the learner that the experiment be stopped because of the growing discomfort to him. However, in clear terms the experimenter orders the teacher to continue with the procedure in disregard of the learner's protests. *Thus, the naïve subject must resolve a conflict between two mutually incompatible demands from the social field. He may continue to follow the orders of the experimenter and shock the learner with increasing severity, or he may refuse to follow the orders of the experimenter and heed the learner's pleas. The experimenter's authority operates not in a free field, but against ever-mounting countervailing pressure from the person being punished.*

A few technical points need to be considered before the findings of the study are described. For the purpose of delivering shock, a simulated shock generator is used, with 30 clearly marked voltage levels that range from 15 to 450 volts. (Each level is activated by one of 30 individual lever switches set in a

---

[6]A more detailed account of the laboratory procedure can be found in Milgram (1963). A similar and independently evolved experimental procedure, employing a shock generator, victim, and learning task, was reported by Buss (1961). Buss used the technique for studying aggression, not obedience, and did not make use of the fundamental measure employed in the present study: breakoff points.

horizontal line.) The naïve subject is given a sample shock of 45 volts to convince him of the authenticity of the instrument. The generator bears verbal designations that range from "Slight Shock" to "Danger: Severe Shock."

The responses of the victim are standardized on tape, and each protest is coordinated to a particular voltage level on the shock generator. Starting with 75 volts the learner begins to grunt and moan. At 150 volts he demands to be let out of the experiment. At 180 volts he cries out that he can no longer stand the pain. At 300 volts he refuses to provide any more answers to the memory test, insisting that he is no longer a participant in the experiment and must be freed. In response to this last tactic, the experimenter instructs the naïve subject to treat the absence of an answer as equivalent to a wrong answer, and to follow the usual shock procedure. The experimenter reinforces his demand with the statement: "You have no other choice, you must go on!" (This imperative is used whenever the naïve subject tries to break off the experiment.) If the subject refuses to give the next higher level of shock, the experiment is considered at an end. A quantitative value is assigned to the subject's performance based on the maximum-intensity shock he administered before breaking off. Thus any subject's score may range from zero (for a subject unwilling to administer the first shock level) to 30 (for a subject who proceeds to the highest voltage level on the board). For any particular subject and for any particular experimental condition, the degree to which participants have followed the experimenter's orders may be specified with a numerical value, corresponding to the metric on the shock generator.

This laboratory situation gives us a framework in which to study the subject's reactions to the principal conflict of the experiment. Again, this conflict is between the experimenter's demands that he continue to administer the electric shock, and the learner's demands, which become increasingly more insistent, that the experiment be stopped. The crux of the study is to vary systematically the factors believed to alter the degree of obedience to the experimental commands, to learn under what conditions submission to authority is most probable and under what conditions defiance is brought to the fore.

PILOT STUDIES

Pilot studies for the present research were completed in the winter of 1960; 15 they differed from the regular experiments in a few details: for one, the victim was placed behind a silvered glass, with the light balance on the glass such that the victim could be dimly perceived by the subject (Milgram, 1961).

Though essentially qualitative in treatment, these studies pointed to several significant features of the experimental situation. At first no vocal feedback was used from the victim. It was thought that the verbal and voltage designations on the control panel would create sufficient pressure to curtail the subject's obedience. However, this was not the case. In the absence of protests from the learner, virtually all subjects, once commanded, went blithely to the end of the board, seemingly indifferent to the verbal designations ("Extreme Shock" and "Danger: Severe Shock"). This deprived us of an adequate basis for scaling obedient tendencies. A force had to be introduced that would strengthen the subject's resistance to the experimenter's commands, and reveal individual differences in terms of a distribution of break-off points.

This force took the form of protests from the victim. Initially, mild protests were used, but proved inadequate. Subsequently, more vehement protests were inserted into the experimental procedure. To our consternation, even the strongest protests from the victim did not prevent all subjects from administering the harshest punishment ordered by the experimenter; but the protests did lower the mean maximum shock somewhat and created some spread in the subject's performance; therefore, the victim's cries were standardized on tape and incorporated into the regular experimental procedure.

The situation did more than highlight the technical difficulties of finding a workable experimental procedure: It indicated that subjects would obey authority to a greater extent than we had supposed. It also pointed to the importance of feedback from the victim in controlling the subject's behavior.

One further aspect of the pilot study was that subjects frequently averted their eyes from the person they were shocking, often turning their heads in an awkward and conspicuous manner. One subject explained: "I didn't want to see the consequences of what I had done." Observers wrote:

> ... subjects showed a reluctance to look at the victim, whom they could see through the glass in front of them. When this fact was brought to their attention they indicated that it caused them discomfort to see the victim in agony. We note, however, that although the subject refuses to look at the victim, he continues to administer shocks.

This suggested that the salience of the victim may have, in some degree, regulated the subject's performance. If, in obeying the experimenter, the subject found it necessary to avoid scrutiny of the victim, would the converse be true? If the victim were rendered increasingly more salient to the subject, would obedience diminish? The first set of regular experiments was designed to answer this question.

IMMEDIACY OF THE VICTIM

This series consisted of four experimental conditions. In each condition the victim was brought "psychologically" closer to the subject giving him shocks.

In the first condition (Remote Feedback) the victim was placed in another room and could not be heard or seen by the subject, except that, at 300 volts, he pounded on the wall in protest. After 315 volts he no longer answered or was heard from.

The second condition (Voice Feedback) was identical to the first except that voice protests were introduced. As in the first condition the victim was placed in an adjacent room, but his complaints could be heard clearly through a door left slightly ajar and through the walls of the laboratory.[7]

The third experimental condition (Proximity) was similar to the second, except that the victim was now placed in the same room as the subject, and 1⅜ feet from him. Thus he was visible as well as audible, and voice cues were provided.

The fourth, and final, condition of this series (Touch-Proximity) was identical to the third, with this exception: The victim received a shock only when his hand rested on a shockplate. At the 150-volt level the victim again demanded to be let free and, in this condition, refused to place his hand on the shockplate. The experimenter ordered the naïve subject to force the victim's hand onto the plate. Thus obedience in this condition required that the subject have physical contact with the victim in order to give him punishment beyond the 150-volt level.

Forty adult subjects were studied in each condition. The data revealed that obedience was significantly reduced as the victim was rendered more immediate to the subject. The mean maximum shock for the conditions is shown in Figure 1.

Expressed in terms of the proportion of obedient to defiant subjects, the findings are that 34 percent of the subjects defied the experimenter in the Re-

---

[7]It is difficult to convey on the printed page the full tenor of the victim's responses, for we have no adequate notation for vocal intensity, timing, and general qualities of delivery. Yet these features are crucial to producing the effect of an increasingly severe reaction to mounting voltage levels. (They can be communicated fully only by sending interested parties the recorded tapes.) In general terms, however, the victim indicates no discomfort until the 75-volt shock is administered, at which time there is a light grunt in response to the punishment. Similar reactions follow the 90- and 105-volt shocks, and at 120 volts the victim shouts to the experimenter that the shocks are becoming painful. Painful groans are heard on administration of the 135-volt shock, and at 150 volts the victim cries out, "Experimenter, get me out of here! I won't be in the experiment any more! I refuse to go on!" Cries of this type continue with generally rising intensity, so that at 180 volts the victim cries out, "I can't stand the pain," and by 270 volts his response to the shock is definitely an agonized scream. Throughout, he insists that he be let out of the experiment. At 300 volts the victim shouts in desperation that he will no longer provide answers to the memory test; and at 315 volts, after a violent scream, he reaffirms with vehemence that he is no longer a participant. From this point on, he provides no answers, but shrieks in agony whenever a shock is administered; this continues through 450 volts. Of course, many subjects will have broken off before this point.

A revised and stronger set of protests was used in all experiments outside the Proximity series. Naturally, new baseline measures were established for all comparisons using the new set of protests.

There is overwhelming evidence that the great majority of subjects, both obedient and defiant, accepted the victims' reactions as genuine. The evidence takes the form of: (a) tension created in the subjects (see discussion of tension); (b) scores on "estimated-pain" scales filled out by subjects immediately after the experiment; (c) subjects' accounts of their feelings in post-experimental interviews; and (d) quantifiable responses to questionnaires distributed to subjects several months after their participation in the experiments. This matter will be treated fully in a forthcoming monograph.

(The procedure in all experimental conditions was to have the naïve subject announce the voltage level before administering each shock, so that—independently of the victim's responses—he was continually reminded of delivering punishment of ever-increasing severity.)

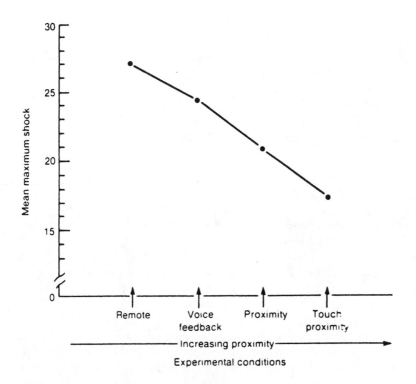

FIGURE 1. Mean maxima in proximity series.

mote condition, 37.5 percent in Voice Feedback, 60 percent in Proximity, and 70 percent in Touch-Proximity.

How are we to account for this effect? A first conjecture might be that as the victim was brought closer the subject became more aware of the intensity of his suffering and regulated his behavior accordingly. This makes sense, but our evidence does not support the interpretation. There are no consistent differences in the attributed level of pain across the four conditions (i.e. the amount of pain experienced by the victim as estimated by the subject and expressed on a 14-point scale). But it is easy to speculate about alternative mechanisms:

Empathic cues. In the Remote and to a lesser extent the Voice Feedback conditions, the victim's suffering possesses an abstract, remote quality for the subject. He is aware, but only in a conceptual sense, that his actions cause pain to another person; the fact is apprehended, but not felt. The phenomenon is common enough. The bombardier can reasonably suppose that his weapons will inflict suffering and death, yet this knowledge is divested of af-

391

fect and does not move him to a felt, emotional response to the suffering resulting from his actions. Similar observations have been made in wartime. It is possible that the visual cues associated with the victim's suffering trigger empathic responses in the subject and provide him with a more complete grasp of the victim's experience. Or it is possible that the empathic responses are themselves unpleasant, possessing drive properties which cause the subject to terminate the arousal situation. Diminishing obedience, then, would be explained by the enrichment of empathic cues in the successive experimental conditions.

Denial and narrowing of the cognitive field. The Remote condition allows a 30 narrowing of the cognitive field so that the victim is put out of mind. The subject no longer considers the act of depressing a lever relevant to moral judgment, for it is no longer associated with the victim's suffering. When the victim is close it is more difficult to exclude him phenomenologically. He necessarily intrudes on the subject's awareness since he is continuously visible. In the Remote condition his existence and reactions are made known only after the shock has been administered. The auditory feedback is sporadic and discontinuous. In the Proximity conditions his inclusion in the immediate visual field renders him a continuously salient element for the subject. The mechanism of denial can no longer be brought into play. One subject in the Remote condition said: "It's funny how you really begin to forget that there's a guy out there, even though you can hear him. For a long time I just concentrated on pressing the switches and reading the words."

Reciprocal fields. If in the Proximity condition the subject is in an improved position to observe the victim, the reverse is also true. The actions of the subject now come under proximal scrutiny by the victim. Possibly, it is easier to harm a person when he is unable to observe our actions than when he can see what we are doing. His surveillance of the action directed against him may give rise to shame, or guilt, which may then serve to curtail the action. Many expressions of language refer to the discomfort or inhibitions that arise in face-to-face confrontation. It is often said that it is easier to criticize a man "behind his back" than to "attack him to his face." If we are in the process of lying to a person it is reputedly difficult to "stare him in the eye." We "turn away from others in shame" or in "embarrassment" and this action serves to reduce our discomfort. The manifest function of allowing the victim of a firing squad to be blindfolded is to make the occasion less stressful for him, but it may also serve a latent function of reducing the stress of the executioner. In short, in the Proximity conditions, the subject may sense that he has become more salient in the victim's field of awareness. Possibly he becomes more self-conscious, embarrassed, and inhibited in his punishment of the victim.

Phenomenal unity of act. In the Remote condition it is more difficult for the subject to gain a sense of *relatedness* between his own actions and the consequences of these actions for the victim. There is a physical and spatial separation of the act and its consequences. The subject depresses a lever in one room, and protests and cries are heard from another. The two events are in correlation, yet they lack a compelling phenomenological unity. The structure of a meaningful act—*I am hurting a man*—breaks down because of the spatial arrangements, in a manner somewhat analogous to the disappearance of phi phenomena[8] when the blinking lights are spaced too far apart. The unity is more fully achieved in the Proximity condition as the victim is brought closer to the action that causes him pain. It is rendered complete in Touch-Proximity.

Incipient group formation. Placing the victim in another room not only takes him further from the subject, but the subject and the experimenter are drawn relatively closer. There is incipient group formation between the experimenter and the subject, from which the victim is excluded. The wall between the victim and the others deprives him of an intimacy which the experimenter and subject feel. In the Remote condition, the victim is truly an outsider, who stands alone, physically and psychologically.

When the victim is placed close to the subject, it becomes easier to form an alliance with him against the experimenter. Subjects no longer have to face the experimenter alone. They have an ally who is close at hand and eager to collaborate in a revolt against the experimenter. Thus, the changing set of spatial relations leads to a potentially shifting set of alliances over the several experimental conditions.

Acquired behavior dispositions. It is commonly observed that laboratory mice will rarely fight with their litter mates. Scott (1958) explains this in terms of passive inhibition. He writes: "By doing nothing under . . . circumstances [the animal] learns to do nothing, and this may be spoken of as passive inhibition . . . this principle has great importance in teaching an individual to be peaceful, for it means that he can learn not to fight simply by not fighting." Similarly, we may learn not to harm others simply by not harming them in everyday life. Yet this learning occurs in a context of proximal relations with others, and may not be generalized to that situation in which the person is physically removed from us. Or possibly, in the past, aggressive actions against others who were physically close resulted in retaliatory punishment which extinguished the original form of response. In contrast, aggression against others at a distance may have only sporadically led to retaliation.

35

---

[8]*phi phenomena:* the optical impression of motion generated when similar stationary objects are presented one after another at a certain interval. [Eds.]

Thus the organism learns that it is safer to be aggressive toward others at a distance, and precarious to be so when the parties are within arm's reach. Through a pattern of rewards and punishments, he acquires a disposition to avoid aggression at close quarters, a disposition which does not extend to harming others at a distance. And this may account for experimental findings in the remote and proximal experiments.

Proximity as a variable in psychological research has received far less attention than it deserves. If men were sessile[9] it would be easy to understand this neglect. But we move about; our spatial relations shift from one situation to the next, and the fact that we are near or remote may have a powerful effect on the psychological processes that mediate our behavior toward others. In the present situation, as the victim is brought closer to the subject ordered to give him shocks, increasing numbers of subjects break off the experiment, refusing to obey. The concrete, visible, and proximal presence of the victim acts in an important way to counteract the experimenter's power to generate disobedience.[10]

CLOSENESS OF AUTHORITY

If the spatial relationship of the subject and victim is relevant to the degree of obedience, would not the relationship of subject to experimenter also play a part?

There are reasons to feel that, on arrival, the subject is oriented primarily to the experimenter rather than to the victim. He has come to the laboratory to fit into the structure that the experimenter—not the victim—would provide. He has come less to understand his behavior than to *reveal* that behavior to a competent scientist, and he is willing to display himself as the scientist's purposes require. Most subjects seem quite concerned about the appearance they are making before the experimenter, and one could argue that this preoccupation in a relatively new and strange setting makes the subject somewhat insensitive to the triadic nature of the social situation. In other words, the subject is so concerned about the show he is putting on for the experimenter that influences from other parts of the social field do not receive as much weight as they ordinarily would. This overdetermined orientation to the experimenter would account for the relative insensitivity of the subject to the victim, and would also

---

[9]*sessile*: permanently attached. [Eds.]

[10]Admittedly, the terms *proximity, immediacy, closeness,* and *salience-of-the-victim* are used in a loose sense, and the experiments themselves represent a very coarse treatment of the variable. Further experiments are needed to refine the notion and tease out such diverse factors as spatial distance, visibility, audibility, barrier interposition, etc.

The Proximity and Touch-Proximity experiments were the only conditions where we were unable to use taped feedback from the victim. Instead, the victim was trained to respond in these conditions as he had in Experiment 2 (which employed taped feedback). Some improvement is possible here, for it should be technically feasible to do a proximity series using taped feedback.

lead us to believe that alterations in the relationship between subject and experimenter would have important consequences for obedience.

In a series of experiments we varied the physical closeness and degree of surveillance of the experimenter. In one condition the experimenter sat just a few feet away from the subject. In a second condition, after giving initial instructions, the experimenter left the laboratory and gave his orders by telephone. In still a third condition the experimenter was never seen, providing instructions by means of a tape recording activated when the subjects entered the laboratory.

Obedience dropped sharply as the experimenter was physically removed   40
from the laboratory. The number of obedient subjects in the first condition (Experimenter Present) was almost three times as great as in the second, where the experimenter gave his orders by telephone. Twenty-six subjects were fully obedient in the first condition, and only nine in the second (Chi square obedient vs. defiant in the two conditions, df = 14.7; $p < 0.001$). Subjects seemed able to take a far stronger stand against the experimenter when they did not have to encounter him face to face, and the experimenter's power over the subject was severely curtailed.[11]

Moreover, when the experimenter was absent, subjects displayed an interesting form of behavior that had not occurred under his surveillance. Though continuing with the experiment, several subjects administered lower shocks than were required and never informed the experimenter of their deviation from the correct procedure. (Unknown to the subjects, shock levels were automatically recorded by an Esterline-Angus event recorder wired directly into the shock generator; the instrument provided us with an objective record of the subjects' performance.) Indeed, in telephone conversations some subjects specifically assured the experimenter that they were raising the shock level according to instruction, whereas in fact they were repeatedly using the lowest shock on the board. This form of behavior is particularly interesting: although these subjects acted in a way that clearly undermined the avowed purposes of the experiment, they found it easier to handle the conflict in this manner than to precipitate an open break with authority.

Other conditions were completed in which the experimenter was absent during the first segment of the experiment, but reappeared at the point that the subject definitely refused to give higher shocks when commanded by telephone. Although he had exhausted his power via telephone, the experimenter could frequently force further obedience when he reappeared in the laboratory.

Experiments in this series show that the *physical presence* of an authority is an important force contributing to the subject's obedience or defiance. Taken

---

[11]The third condition also led to significantly lower obedience than this first situation in which the experimenter was present, but it contains technical difficulties that require extensive discussion.

together with the first experimental series on the proximity of the victim, it would appear that something akin to fields of force, diminishing in effectiveness with increasing psychological distance from their source, have a controlling effect on the subject's performance. As the victim is brought closer, the subject finds it harder to administer shocks to him. When the victim's position is held constant relative to the subject, and the authority is made more remote, the subject finds it easier to break off the experiment. This effect is substantial in both cases, but manipulation of the experimenter's position yielded the more powerful results. Obedience to destructive commands is highly dependent on the proximal relations between authority and subject.

TENSIONS

The description of final scores does not fully convey the character of the subjects' performance, and it would be useful to interrupt our reporting of quantitative relationships to remark on the subjects' general reaction to the situation.

One might suppose that a subject would simply break off or continue as his 45 conscience and temperament dictated. Yet this is very far from what happened. There were powerful reactions of tension and emotional strain in a substantial proportion of the participants. Persons were observed to sweat, tremble, stutter, bite their lips, and groan as they found themselves increasingly implicated in the experimental conflict. Some sense of the subjects' mood can be found in a transcript of their remarks at break-off point. Here are the remarks of two defiant subjects:

> Is he banging? ... Is he hurt out there? Well, I don't want to be responsible for anything that happens to him. No, I can't go on with it. I don't know whether he's all right or not. I mean he may have a heart condition or something; I wouldn't feel right doing it. He's banging for help. He's evidently in trouble or he wouldn't bang ... I don't see any sense to this—to knocking him out or something. I just can't see it.
> [*Subject refuses to administer shocks*]　　　　　　　　[*Subject 0108*]

> The man is banging. He wants to get out ... I'm sorry. If the man wants to get out I'd just as soon stop ... I don't want to administer any more [extremely excited] ... I will gladly refund the check, but I will not harm this man ... I'm sorry, I will not give him any more if he obviously wants to get out. There is no money in the world that will make me hurt another individual.
> 　　　　　　　　　　　　　　　　　　　[*Subject 010X*]

And here is a transcript from an obedient subject. He began the experiment calmly, but became increasingly tense as the experiment proceeded. After administering the 150-volt shock, he began to address the experimenter in agitated tones:

150 volts delivered. You want me to keep going?

165 volts delivered. That guy is hollering in there. There's a lot of them here. He's liable to have a heart condition. You want me to go?

180 volts delivered. He can't stand it! I'm not going to kill that man in there! You hear him hollering? He's hollering. He can't stand it. What if something happens to him? . . . I'm not going to get that man sick in there. He's hollering in there. You know what I mean? I mean I refuse to take responsibility. He's getting hurt in there. He's in there hollering. Too many left here. Geez, if he gets them wrong. There's too many of them left. I mean who is going to take responsibility if anything happens to that gentleman?

[The experimenter accepts responsibility.] All right.

195 volts delivered. You see he's hollering. Hear that. Gee, I don't know.

[The experimenter says: "The experiment requires that you go on."] —I know it does, sir, but I mean—hugh—he don't know what he's in for. He's up to 195 volts.

210 volts delivered.

225 volts delivered.

240 volts delivered. Aw, no. You mean I've got to keep going up with the scale? No sir. I'm not going to kill that man! I'm not going to give him 450 volts!

[The experimenter says: "The experiment requires that you go on."] —I know it does, but that man is hollering there, sir . . .

Despite his numerous, agitated objections, which were constant accompaniments to his actions, the subject unfailingly obeyed the experimenter, proceeding to the highest shock level on the generator. He displayed a curious dissociation between word and action. Although at the verbal level he had resolved not to go on, his actions were fully in accord with the experimenter's commands. This subject did not want to shock the victim, and he found it an extremely disagreeable task, but he was unable to invent a response that would free him from E's authority. Many subjects cannot find the specific verbal formula that would enable them to reject the role assigned to them by the experimenter. Perhaps our culture does not provide adequate models for disobedience.

One puzzling sign of tension was the regular occurrence of nervous laughing fits. In the first four conditions 71 of the 160 subjects showed definite signs of nervous laughter and smiling. The laughter seemed entirely out of place, even bizarre. Full-blown, uncontrollable seizures were observed for 15 of these subjects. On one occasion we observed a seizure so violently convulsive that it was necessary to call a halt to the experiment. In the post-experimental interviews subjects took pains to point out that they were not sadistic types and that the laughter did not mean they enjoyed shocking the victim.

In the interview following the experiment subjects were asked to indicate on a 14-point scale just how nervous or tense they felt at the point of maximum tension

(Figure 2). The scale ranged from "not at all tense and nervous" to "extremely tense and nervous." Self-reports of this sort are of limited precision and at best provide only a rough indication of the subject's emotional response. Still, taking the reports for what they are worth, it can be seen that the distribution of responses spans the entire range of the scale, with the majority of subjects concentrated at the center and upper extreme. A further breakdown showed that obedient subjects reported themselves as having been slightly more tense and nervous than the defiant subjects at the point of maximum tension.

How is the occurrence of tension to be interpreted? First, it points to the presence of conflict. If a tendency to comply with authority were the only psychological force operating in the situation, all subjects would have continued to the end and there would have been no tension. Tension, it is assumed, results from the simultaneous presence of two or more incompatible response tendencies (Miller, 1944). If sympathetic concern for the victim were the exclusive force, all subjects would have calmly defied the experimenter. Instead, there were both obedient and defiant outcomes, frequently accompanied by extreme tension. A conflict develops between the deeply ingrained disposition

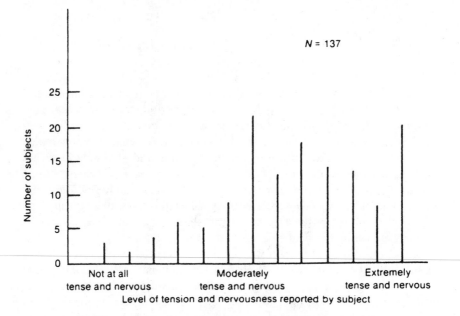

FIGURE 2. Level of tension and nervousness: the self-reports on "tension and nervousness" for 137 subjects on the Proximity experiments. Subjects were given a scale with 14 values ranging from "not at all tense and nervous" to "extremely tense and nervous." They were instructed: "Thinking back to that point in the experiment when you felt the most tense and nervous, indicate just how you felt by placing an X at the appropriate point on the scale." The results are shown in terms of midpoint values.

not to harm others and the equally compelling tendency to obey others who are in authority. The subject is quickly drawn into a dilemma of a deeply dynamic character, and the presence of high tension points to the considerable strength of each of the antagonistic vectors.

Moreover, tension defines the strength of the aversive state from which the subject is unable to escape through disobedience. When a person is uncomfortable, tense, or stressed, he tries to take some action that will allow him to terminate this unpleasant state. Thus tension may serve as a drive that leads to escape behavior. But in the present situation, even where tension is extreme, many subjects are unable to perform the response that will bring about relief. Therefore there must be a competing drive, tendency, or inhibition that precludes activation of the disobedient response. The strength of this inhibiting factor must be of greater magnitude than the stress experienced, or else the terminating act would occur. Every evidence of extreme tension is at the same time an indication of the strength of the forces that keep the subject in the situation.

Finally, tension may be taken as evidence of the reality of the situations for the subjects. Normal subjects do not tremble and sweat unless they are implicated in a deep and genuinely felt predicament.

BACKGROUND AUTHORITY

In psychophysics, animal learning, and other branches of psychology, the fact that measures are obtained at one institution rather than another is irrelevant to the interpretation of the findings, so long as the technical facilities for measurement are adequate and the operations are carried out with competence.

But it cannot be assumed that this holds true for the present study. The effectiveness of the experimenter's commands may depend in an important way on the larger institutional context in which they are issued. The experiments described thus far were conducted at Yale University, an organization which most subjects regarded with respect and sometimes awe. In post-experimental interviews several participants remarked that the locale and sponsorship of the study gave them confidence in the integrity, competence, and benign purposes of the personnel; many indicated that they would not have shocked the learner if the experiments had been done elsewhere.

This issue of background authority seemed to us important for an interpretation of the results that had been obtained thus far; moreover it is highly relevant to any comprehensive theory of human obedience. Consider, for example, how closely our compliance with the imperatives of others is tied to particular institutions and locales in our day-to-day activities. On request, we expose our throats to a man with a razor blade in the barber shop, but would not do so in a shoe store; in the latter setting we willingly follow the clerk's request to stand in our stockinged feet, but resist the command in a bank. In the laboratory of a great university, subjects may comply with a set of commands that would be resisted if given elsewhere. *One must always question the relationship of obedience to a person's sense of the context in which he is operating.*

To explore the problem we moved our apparatus to an office building in industrial Bridgeport and replicated experimental conditions, without any visible tie to the university.   55

Bridgeport subjects were invited to the experiment through a mail circular similar to the one used in the Yale study, with appropriate changes in letterhead, etc. As in the earlier study, subjects were paid $4.50 for coming to the laboratory. The same age and occupational distributions used at Yale and the identical personnel were employed.

The purpose in relocating in Bridgeport was to assure a complete dissociation from Yale, and in this regard we were fully successful. On the surface, the study appeared to be conducted by Research Associates of Bridgeport, an organization of unknown character (the title had been concocted exclusively for use in this study).

The experiments were conducted in a three-room office suite in a somewhat run-down commercial building located in the downtown shopping area. The laboratory was sparsely furnished, though clean, and marginally respectable in appearance. When subjects inquired about professional affiliations, they were informed only that we were a private firm conducting research for industry.

Some subjects displayed skepticism concerning the motives of the Bridgeport experimenter. One gentleman gave us a written account of the thoughts he experienced at the control board:

> ... Should I quit this damn test? Maybe he passed out? What dopes we were not to check up on this deal. How do we know that these guys are legit? No furniture, bare walls, no telephone. We could of called the Police up or the Better Business Bureau. I learned a lesson tonight. How do I know that Mr. Williams [the experimenter] is telling the truth ... I wish I knew how many volts a person could take before lapsing into unconsciousness ...   [Subject 2414]

Another subject stated:

> I questioned on my arrival my own judgment [about coming]. I had doubts as to the legitimacy of the operation and the consequences of participation. I felt it was a heartless way to conduct memory or learning processes on human beings and certainly dangerous without the presence of a medical doctor.   [Subject 2440V]

There was no noticeable reduction in tension for the Bridgeport subjects.   60
And the subjects' estimation of the amount of pain felt by the victim was slightly, though not significantly, higher than in the Yale study.

A failure to obtain complete obedience in Bridgeport would indicate that the extreme compliance found in New Haven subjects was tied closely to the background authority of Yale University; if a large proportion of the subjects remained fully obedient, very different conclusions would be called for.

As it turned out, the level of obedience in Bridgeport, although somewhat reduced, was not significantly lower than that obtained at Yale. A large proportion of the Bridgeport subjects were fully obedient to the experimenter's commands (48 percent of the Bridgeport subjects delivered the maximum shock versus 65 percent in the corresponding condition at Yale).

How are these findings to be interpreted? It is possible that if commands of a potentially harmful or destructive sort are to be perceived as legitimate they must occur within some sort of institutional structure. But it is clear from the study that it need not be a particularly reputable or distinguished institution. The Bridgeport experiments were conducted by an unimpressive firm lacking any credentials; the laboratory was set up in a respectable office building with a title listed in the building directory. Beyond that, there was no evidence of benevolence or competence. It is possible that the *category* of institution, judged according to its professed function, rather than its qualitative position within that category, wins our compliance. Persons deposit money in elegant, but also in seedy-looking banks, without giving much thought to the differences in security they offer. Similarly, our subjects may consider one laboratory to be as competent as another, so long as it is a scientific laboratory.

It would be valuable to study the subjects' performance in other contexts which go even further than the Bridgeport study in denying institutional support to the experimenter. It is possible that, beyond a certain point, obedience disappears completely. But that point had not been reached in the Bridgeport office: almost half the subjects obeyed the experimenter fully.

FURTHER EXPERIMENTS

We may mention briefly some additional experiments undertaken in the Yale series. A considerable amount of obedience and defiance in everyday life occurs in connection with groups. And we had reason to feel in light of the many group studies already done in psychology that group forces would have a profound effect on reactions to authority. A series of experiments was run to examine these effects. In all cases only one naïve subject was studied per hour, but he performed in the midst of actors who, unknown to him, were employed by the experimenter. In one experiment (Groups for Disobedience) two actors broke off in the middle of the experiment. When this happened 90 percent of the subjects followed suit and defied the experimenter. In another condition the actors followed the orders obediently; this strengthened the experimenter's power only slightly. In still a third experiment the job of pushing the switch to shock the learner was given to one of the actors, while the naïve subject performed a subsidiary act. We wanted to see how the teacher would respond if he were involved in the situation but did not actually

401

give the shocks. In this situation only three subjects out of forty broke off. In a final group experiment the subjects themselves determined the shock level they were going to use. Two actors suggested higher and higher shock levels; some subjects insisted, despite group pressure, that the shock level be kept low; others followed along with the group.

Further experiments were completed using women as subjects, as well as a set dealing with the effects of dual, unsanctioned, and conflicting authority. A final experiment concerned the personal relationship between victim and subject. These will have to be described elsewhere, lest the present report be extended to monographic length.

It goes without saying that future research can proceed in many different directions. What kinds of response from the victim are most effective in causing disobedience in the subject? Perhaps passive resistance is more effective than vehement protest. What conditions of entry into an authority system lead to greater or lesser obedience? What is the effect of anonymity and masking on the subject's behavior? What conditions lead to the subject's perception of responsibility for his own actions? Each of these could be a major research topic in itself, and can readily be incorporated into the general experimental procedure described here.

LEVELS OF OBEDIENCE AND DEFIANCE

One general finding that merits attention is the high level of obedience manifested in the experimental situation. Subjects often expressed deep disapproval of shocking a man in the face of his objections, and others denounced it as senseless and stupid. Yet many subjects complied even while they protested. The proportion of obedient subjects greatly exceeded the expectations of the experimenter and his colleagues. At the outset, we had conjectured that subjects would not, in general, go above the level of "Strong Shock." In practice, many subjects were willing to administer the most extreme shocks available when commanded by the experimenter. For some subjects the experiment provided an occasion for aggressive release. And for others it demonstrated the extent to which obedient dispositions are deeply ingrained and engaged, irrespective of their consequences for others. Yet this is not the whole story. Somehow, the subject becomes implicated in a situation from which he cannot disengage himself.

The departure of the experimental results from intelligent expectation, to some extent, has been formalized. The procedure was to describe the experimental situation in concrete detail to a group of competent persons, and to ask them to predict the performance of 100 hypothetical subjects. For purposes of indicating the distribution of break-off points, judges were provided with a diagram of the shock generator and recorded their predictions before being informed of the actual results. Judges typically underestimated the amount of obedience demonstrated by subjects.

In Figure 3, we compare the predictions of forty psychiatrists at a leading 70 medical school with the actual performance of subjects in the experiment. The psychiatrists predicted that most subjects would not go beyond the tenth shock level (150 volts; at this point the victim makes his first explicit demand to be freed). They further predicted that by the twentieth shock level (300 volts; the victim refuses to answer) 3.73 percent of the subjects would still be obedient; and that only a little over one-tenth of one percent of the subjects would administer the highest shock on the board. But, as the graph indicates, the obtained behavior was very different. Sixty-two percent of the subjects obeyed the experimenter's commands fully. Between expectation and occurrence there is a whopping discrepancy.

Why did the psychiatrists underestimate the level of obedience? Possibly, because their predictions were based on an inadequate conception of the determinants of human action, a conception that focuses on motives *in vacuo.* This orientation may be entirely adequate for the repair of bruised impulses as

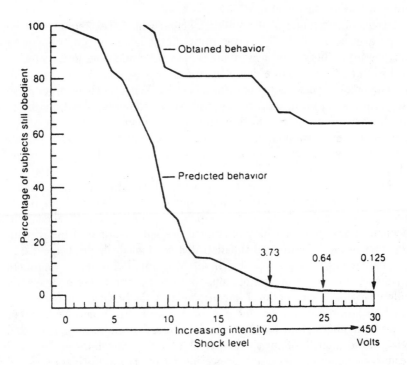

FIGURE 3. Predicted and obtained behavior in voice feedback.

revealed on the psychiatrist's couch, but as soon as our interest turns to action in larger settings, attention must be paid to the situations in which motives are expressed. A situation exerts an important press on the individual. It exercises constraints and may provide push. In certain circumstances it is not so much the kind of person a man is, as the kind of situation in which he is placed, that determines his actions.

Many people, not knowing much about the experiment, claim that subjects who go to the end of the board are sadistic. Nothing could be more foolish than an overall characterization of these persons. It is like saying that a person thrown into a swift-flowing stream is necessarily a fast swimmer, or that he has great stamina because he moves so rapidly relative to the bank. The context of action must always be considered. The individual, upon entering the laboratory, becomes integrated into a situation that carries its own momentum. The subject's problem then is how to become disengaged from a situation which is moving in an altogether ugly direction.

The fact that disengagement is so difficult testifies to the potency of the forces that keep the subject at the control board. Are these forces to be conceptualized as individual motives and expressed in the language of personality dynamics, or are they to be seen as the effects of social structure and pressures arising from the situational field?

A full understanding of the subject's action will, I feel, require that both perspectives be adopted. The person brings to the laboratory enduring dispositions toward authority and aggression, and at the same time he becomes enmeshed in a social structure that is no less an objective fact of the case. From the standpoint of personality theory one may ask: What mechanisms of personality enable a person to transfer responsibility to authority? What are the motives underlying obedient and disobedient performance? Does orientation to authority lead to a short-circuiting of the shame-guilt system? What cognitive and emotional defenses are brought into play in the case of obedient and defiant subjects?

The present experiments are not, however, directed toward an exploration 75 of the motives engaged when the subject obeys the experimenter's commands. Instead, they examine the situational variables responsible for the elicitation of obedience. Elsewhere, we have attempted to spell out some of the structural properties of the experimental situation that account for high obedience, and this analysis need not be repeated here (Milgram, 1963). The experimental variations themselves represent our attempt to probe that structure, by systematically changing it and noting the consequences for behavior. It is clear that some situations produce greater compliance with the experimenter's commands than others. However, this does not necessarily imply an increase or decrease in the strength of any single definable motive. Situations producing the greatest obedience could do so by triggering the most powerful, yet perhaps the most idiosyncratic, of motives in each subject confronted by the setting. Or they may simply recruit a greater number and variety of motives in their service. But whatever the motives involved—and it is far from certain that they can ever be known—action may be studied as a direct function of the situation in which it occurs. This has been the approach of the present study, where we sought to plot behavioral regularities against manipulated properties of the social field. Ultimately, social psychology would like to have a compelling *theory of situations* which will, first, present a language in terms of which situations can be defined; proceed to a typology of situations; and then point to the manner in which definable properties of situations are transformed into psychological forces in the individual.[12]

POSTSCRIPT

Almost a thousand adults were individually studied in the obedience research, and there were many specific conclusions regarding the variables that control obedience and disobedience to authority. Some of these have been discussed briefly in the preceding sections, and more detailed reports will be released subsequently.

There are now some other generalizations I should like to make, which do not derive in any strictly logical fashion from the experiments as carried out, but which, I feel, ought to be made. They are formulations of an intuitive sort that have been forced on me by observation of many subjects responding to the pressures of authority. The assertions represent a painful alteration in my own thinking; and since they were acquired only under the repeated impact of direct observation, I have no illusion that they will be generally accepted by persons who have not had the same experience.

With numbing regularity good people were seen to knuckle under the demands of authority and perform actions that were callous and severe. Men who are in everyday life responsible and decent were seduced by the trappings of authority, by the control of their perceptions, and by the uncritical acceptance of the experimenter's definition of the situation, into performing harsh acts.

What is the limit of such obedience? At many points we attempted to establish a boundary. Cries from the victim were inserted; not good enough. The victim claimed heart trouble; subjects still shocked him on command. The victim pleaded that he be let free, and his answers no longer registered on the signal box; subjects continued to shock him. At the outset we had not conceived that such drastic procedures would be needed to generate disobedience, and each step was added only as the ineffectiveness of the earlier techniques became clear. The final effort to establish a limit was the Touch-Proximity condition. But the very first subject in this condition subdued the victim on command, and proceeded to the highest shock level. A quarter of the subjects in this condition performed similarly.

---

[12]My thanks to Professor Howard Leventhal of Yale for strengthening the writing in this paragraph.

The results, as seen and felt in the laboratory, are to this author disturbing. ⁸⁰ They raise the possibility that human nature or, more specifically, the kind of character produced in American democratic society cannot be counted on to insulate its citizens from brutality and inhumane treatment at the direction of malevolent authority. A substantial proportion of people do what they are told to do, irrespective of the content of the act and without limitations of conscience, so long as they perceive that the command comes from a legitimate authority. If in this study an anonymous experimenter could successfully command adults to subdue a fifty-year-old man and force on him painful electric shocks against his protests, one can only wonder what government, with its vastly greater authority and prestige, can command of its subjects. There is, of course, the extremely important question of whether malevolent political institutions could or would arise in American society. The present research contributes nothing to this issue.

In an article titled "The Danger of Obedience," Harold J. Laski wrote:

> . . . civilization means, above all, an unwillingness to inflict unnecessary pain. Within the ambit of that definition, those of us who heedlessly accept the commands of authority cannot yet claim to be civilized men.
>
> . . . Our business, if we desire to live a life, not utterly devoid of meaning and significance, is to accept nothing which contradicts our basic experience merely because it comes to us from tradition or convention or authority. It may well be that we shall be wrong; but our self-expression is thwarted at the root unless the certainties we are asked to accept coincide with the certainties we experience. That is why the condition of freedom in any state is always a widespread and consistent skepticism of the canons upon which power insists.

REFERENCES

Buss, Arnold H. 1961. *The Psychology of Aggression.* New York and London: John Wiley.

Kierkegaard, S. 1843. *Fear and Trembling.* English edition, Princeton: Princeton University Press, 1941.

Laski, Harold J. 1929. "The dangers of obedience." *Harper's Monthly Magazine,* 15 June, 1–10.

Milgram, S. 1961. "Dynamics of obedience: experiments in social psychology." Mimeographed report, *National Science Foundation,* January 25.

—— 1963. "Behavioral study of obedience." *J. Abnorm. Soc. Psychol.* 67, 371–378.

—— 1964. "Issues in the study of obedience: a reply to Baumrind." *Amer. Psychol.* 1, 848–852.

Miller, N. E. 1944. "Experimental studies of conflict." In J. McV. Hunt (ed.), *Personality and the Behavior Disorders.* New York: Ronald Press.

Scott, J. P. 1958. *Aggression.* Chicago: University of Chicago Press.

QUESTIONS

1. What did Milgram want to determine by his experiment? What were his anticipated outcomes?

2. What conclusions did Milgram reach about the extent to which ordinary individuals would obey the orders of an authority figure? Under what conditions is this submission most probable? Under what conditions is defiance most likely?

3. Describe the general procedures of this experiment. Some people have questioned Milgram's methods. Do you think it is ethical to expose subjects without warning to experiments that might have a lasting effect on them? What such effects might this experiment have had?

4. One characteristic of this article is Milgram's willingness to consider several possible explanations of the same phenomenon. Study the interpretations in paragraphs 28 through 35. What do you make of the range of interpretation there and elsewhere in the article? How does Milgram achieve such a range?

5. A report such as Milgram's is not structured in the same way as a conventional essay. His research is really a collection of separate but related experiments, each one of which requires its own interpretation. Describe the groups into which these experiments fall. Which results seemed most surprising to you? Which were easiest to anticipate?

6. In Milgram's experiment, people who are responsible and decent in everyday life were seduced, he says, by trappings of authority. Most of us, however, like to believe that we would neither engage in brutality on our own nor obey directions of this kind. Has Milgram succeeded in getting you to question your own behavior? Would you go so far as to say that he forces you to question your own human nature?

7. In paragraph 46 Milgram comments, "Perhaps our culture does not provide adequate models for disobedience." What do you think of this hypothesis? Are there such models? Ought there to be? Have such models appeared since the experiment was conducted? Explain your stand on Milgram's statement.

8. If research in social psychology takes place in your school today, there is probably a panel of some sort that enforces guidelines on research with human subjects. Locate that board, if it exists, and find out whether this experiment could take place today. Report to your class on the rules that guide researchers today. Do you think those rules are wise?

9. What, in your opinion, should be the guidelines for psychological research with human subjects? List the guidelines you think are appropriate, and compare your list with the lists of your classmates. Would your guidelines have allowed Milgram's experiment?

10. Think of a situation in which you were faced with the moral and ethical dilemma of whether or not to obey a figure of authority. How did you behave? Did your behavior surprise you? Describe and explain that experience.

MAKING CONNECTIONS

1. One of the conditions of valid scientific research is the replicability of its experiments. When we are persuaded that results are replicable, we are inclined to believe

them valid. What provisions for replicability does Milgram make in his experiments? Compare his stance to that of Bruno Bettelheim (p. 621) or Oliver Sacks (p. 511), whose observations are not replicable but who are also concerned with writing authoritative science.

2. Think of other essays in this collection in which ethical matters are at issue, particularly the ethics of composing some kind of story. Consider Richard Selzer's "A Mask on the Face of Death" (p. 121) and Michael Brown's "Love Canal and the Poisoning of America" (p. 261). In each of those studies, human subjects seem manipulated a little for the sake of the writer's interests. Perhaps you would prefer to offer another example. Whatever study you choose, compare it to Milgram's, and discuss the two writers' sensitivity to their human subjects. Note also the last sentence of Milgram's first footnote. What choices do the writers have in the cases that interest you most?

INTERVIEWING ADOLESCENT GIRLS
Carol Gilligan

*Carol Gilligan (b. 1936) is a professor in the human devel-
opment and psychology program at the Harvard Graduate
School of Education. Her research on women's identity formation and moral development in adolescence and adulthood was the subject of* In a Different Voice: Psychological
Theory and Women's Development *(1982), a book that
brought her wide attention in the academic community and
beyond. The following selection is from an essay called
"Teaching Shakespeare's Sister: Notes from the Underground of Adolescence," a synthesis of the preface and pro-
logue to* Making Connections: The Relational Worlds of
Adolescent Girls at Emma Willard School *(1990), which
Gilligan coauthored with Nona Lyons and Trudy Hanmer.*

Interviewing girls in adolescence, in the time between the twelve-year-old's
knowing and the adult woman's remembering, I felt at times that I had entered
an underground world, that I was led in by girls to caverns of knowledge that
were then suddenly covered over, as if nothing were known and nothing were
happening. What I heard was at once familiar and surprising: girls' knowledge
of the human social world, a knowledge gleaned by seeing and listening, by
piecing together thoughts and feelings, sounds and glances, responses and reactions, until they compose a pattern, compelling in its explanatory power and
often intricate in its psychological logic. Such knowledge on the part of girls is
not represented in descriptions of psychological development nor in clinical
case studies, and, more disturbingly, it is disclaimed by adolescent girls themselves, who often seem divided from their own knowledge and preface their observations by saying "I don't know."

At a school for girls in a large midwestern city, twelve-year-olds, when asked
to describe a powerful learning experience, were as likely to describe an experience that took place inside as outside of school. By fifteen more than twice as
many girls located powerful learning experiences outside of school rather than
inside. With respect to the nature of such experiences, girls at fifteen were
more likely than girls at twelve to talk about experiences outside of school in
which family or friends or other people they knew were the central catalysts of
learning.[1] Between the ages of twelve and fifteen—the time when dropping out

---

[1] Alan Braun, "Themes of Connection: Powerful Learning among Adolescent Girls" (Working
Paper, Laurel/Harvard Study, Project on the Psychology of Women and the Development of Girls,
Harvard Graduate School of Education), 3.

of school becomes common in the inner city—the education of girls seems to be moving out of the public sphere and into the private realm. Is this the time, I wondered, when girls' knowledge becomes buried? Was girls' learning going underground?

The question surfaced in reflecting on my experiences in interviewing adolescent girls at Emma Willard School in Troy, New York. The isolated setting of the residential school and its walled enclosure made it something of a strange island in the stream of contemporary living, an odd mixture of old world and new. In this resonant setting I heard girls speak about storms in relationships and pleasure in relationships, revealing a knowledge of relationships that often was grounded in detailed descriptions of inner psychic worlds—relational worlds through which girls sometimes moved freely and which at other times seemed blocked or walled. Listening for this knowledge, I felt myself entering, to some extent, the underground city of female adolescence, the place where powerful learning experiences were happening. The gateway to this underworld was marked by the statement "I don't know"—the sign of repression—and the code word of membership or the password was the phrase "you know." I wondered about the relationship between this knowledge and girls' other life of notebooks, lessons, and homework.

One afternoon, in the second year of the study, toward the end of an interview with Gail, a girl with whom I had not made much contact, I asked if she were curious about the "it" that she was describing—"the problem" that stood between her and her being "able to achieve anywhere near [her] potential," the thing that kept her from "getting [her] act together." Gail said that she did not know whether she would "ever understand what the problem was," but, she said, "I hope that someday it will be gone and I will be happy." I asked how it will go away. She said she did not know, but that it would be "sad if it doesn't." I asked if she were curious; she said she did not know. We went on with the interview questions. As she thought about herself in the future, I asked, how did she imagine her life, what expectations did she feel others had for her, what were her hopes for herself? She was waiting, she said, to see if "it happens." She felt she had come up against "this big wall." We went on. At the end Gail said, "Maybe someday I will draw it." It seemed that she knew what it looked like. I asked what color she would make it: "Kind of deep ivory," she said. What shape? "A giant block of ice. This tall . . . very thick. A cube standing in front of me." She said that she could melt it, but that she would "have to use very high temperatures."

The following year Gail, now a senior, began by talking to me in the language of social science. "I would like to mention," she said, "that, having thought about my last two interviews, it occurs to me that it is hard to get the real opinions of teenage girls as young as we are because a lot of girls really don't know what they think." If I had interviewed her on another day, or if I were a different person, I would "get very different things," especially because "a lot of the questions you asked are not questions that I have ever put to myself . . . and afterwards I wondered, you know, did I really mean that. . . . I don't feel you are getting what is important to me; you are getting that and other things in equal weight." I asked, "So there is no way of knowing [what's true and what's important]?" She agreed.

I began with the interview questions. "Looking back over the past year. . . ." I suggested that as we went along she might tell me which questions were ones that she had put to herself and which—Gail suddenly switched modes of discourse. She said, "I actually feel a great deal older this year." One way of speaking about herself ("Teenage girls . . . really don't know what they think") yielded to another ("I actually feel . . ."). The relationship between these two ways of speaking about herself seemed critical. In the terms of her own imagery, one way of speaking shored up the wall between herself and her knowledge, and one provided a sense of an opening, a place of entry, which led through knowing how she was feeling. "I really feel able," Gail explained, taking the opening,

> to put myself in perspective about a lot of things that were confusing me about myself, and I have a tendency to keep things to myself, things that bother me. I keep them in and then I start feeling like this, just harassed and I can't really—everything just warps my perception of everything. . . . But I have discovered the reason for my whole block. I mean, I was getting bad grades, and I told you about a mysterious block last year that was like a wall.
>
> *I remember that.*
>
> Now, I figured out what was going on. I figured this out last week. It is that, all through my childhood, I interpreted what my parents were saying to me in my mind. I never voiced this interpretation.

The unvoiced or unspoken, being out of relationship, had gotten out of perspective—"just warp[ing] my perception of everything." What Gail interpreted her parents as saying to her was that she should "be independent and self-sufficient from a very early age." Thus, Gail said, "anything that interrupted my sense of what I should be I would soak up into myself, as though I were a big sponge and had tremendous shock capacity to just bounce back." What Gail was taking in was clearly something that she found shocking, but she felt that she should act as though she were a sponge and just soak up the shock by herself. So, she said, "I would feel bad about things, [but] I wouldn't do anything about them. I wouldn't say anything. That goes with grades and personal problems and relationships"—much of her adolescent life. And then, she said, "last week, last Wednesday, this whole thing came over me, and I can really feel that now I can understand what was going on with me. I can put my life in perspective." Thus, Gail explained that she no longer had to not know: "What's happening, what's happening with me? What is going on? Why am I not being able to see? Why is this so hard for me? And then of course when I finally let it out, maybe every six months, it is like a chair casting shadows and

411

making tremendous spokes. Everything becomes monumental. I feel terrible, and it is really very disturbing." With this powerful image of "it" as "a chair casting shadows and making tremendous spokes," Gail conveys how the ordinary can become monumental and very disturbing. What is explicit in this passage is that Gail became disconnected from her own thoughts and feelings and found herself asking questions about herself that she then could not answer. In threatening this disconnection, the process of knowing had become overwhelming. I asked Gail if she had a sense of what had led her to the understanding she described, and she spoke about a conversation with a friend:

> It started when my friend was telling me how angry she was at her math teacher, who when she asked for extra help must have been in a bad mood and was angry with her. I was thinking about the way my stepfather would do the same thing. And then I was thinking about my stepfather, and then I decided that I really have been abused as a child, not physically, but even last summer, whenever he has insecurity, he is very jealous of me, he is insecure with my mother, and then he just lashes out at me and criticizes me to no end, very angrily. And for a person who has grown up with that and who really doesn't understand herself—instead of saying, "Wait a minute. What are you doing? I am a person."—I would just cuddle up and make like a rock. Tense all my muscles and just sit there and listen to it and be relieved when it was over. And then I was thinking about myself and my reactions to things, and I was thinking all year about all the problems I had last year.... It is all my holding back. And I really feel I have made a tremendous breakthrough.

Joining her friend in voicing anger in response to anger rather than just soaking it up like a sponge or tensing her muscles and becoming like a rock, Gail felt she had broken through the wall that was holding back her "reactions to things," her feelings and thoughts.

"It was amazing," I said, "to see it that way," responding to Gail's precise description of psychological processes—the step-by-step tracing of her own feelings and thoughts in response to her friend's story about anger and the math teacher as well as her analysis of how insecurity and jealousy breed attack. "My mother," Gail said, turning to the missing person in the drama (and signaling by the phrase "you know" that this was in part an underground story):

> came down the day before yesterday, and I told her about it. She has been worried about me day and night since I was little because of my holding back. She would say, "You are holding your light under a bushel," and then, you know, get very upset once or twice a year, because everything would get [to be] too much, you know. Of course, my mother would have tremendous guilt.... "What have I done to this poor child? I don't really know what I have done, but there is something. What is it?"

"You have read *Oedipus Rex?*"[2] Gail asks me. I had. "Well, Oedipus went through his entire life weighing himself by himself, and I have done that, and that is what allows me to get out of proportion. I don't talk about anything with anybody, anything that is bothering me."

I thought of the queen in the Oedipus story. Gail's description of her   10
mother had caught the franticness of Jocasta as she tries to keep Oedipus from knowing the truth about family relations. No more truth, she pleads. Was Gail hearing a similar plea from her mother? The problem was that "it"—the un-named or unspoken truth—"just rolls up like a snowball, and it gets bigger and bigger, and my perception just warps out of shape" so that, like Oedipus, Gail cannot see what in another sense she knows. Her question to herself—"Why am I not able to see?"—resonates with the question she attributes to her mother: "What have I done to this poor child?" But Gail also lays out the logic that suppressed her questions about suffering and about women. Gail reasoned that, if her stepfather's attacks had truly been hurtful to her, then her mother would have taken action to stop them. Because her mother did nothing, at least as far as Gail was aware of, Gail concluded that her stepfather's verbal lashings could not really have hurt her. To feel her feelings then posed difficult questions: what does it mean to be a good mother, what does it mean for a mother to love her daughter, and what does it mean for a daughter to love both her mother and herself?

The either/or logic that Gail was learning as an adolescent, the straight-line categories of Western thinking (self/other, mind/body, thought/feelings, past/present) and the if/then construction of linear reasoning threatened to under-mine Gail's knowledge of human relationships by washing out the logic of feel-ings. To understand psychological processes means to follow the both/and logic of feelings and to trace the currents of associations, memories, sounds, and images that flow back and forth, connecting self and other, mind and body, past and present, consciousness and culture. To separate thinking from relationship, and thus to make a division between formal education and power-ful learning experiences, is to become like Oedipus, who got things out of pro-portion by "weighing himself by himself." Gail ties the return of perspective to the return of relationship and describes the insight and knowledge that sud-denly came out of the back-and-forth play of her conversation with her friend: "I talked to my friend, and she talked about her math teacher, and I was think-ing about my stepfather, and then, with all my thinking about it beforehand, wondering what makes a difference, I finally put it together and bang! . . . Be-fore, when I was getting all tied up, everything was a huge wall that isn't a wall anymore." The "it" is no longer a wall but a relationship that joins Gail with herself and with her friend.

---

[2]*Oedipus Rex:* Sophocles play in which Oedipus unknowingly murders his father and marries his mother. [Eds.]

413

The image of a wall recurred in interviews with adolescent girls—a physical rendering of the blocks preventing connection, the impasses in relationships, which girls acutely described and which were associated with intense feelings of anger and sadness. Girls' wishes to make connection with others reflected the pleasure that they found in relationships.

Pleasure in relationships is linked to knowledge gained through relationships, and girls voice their desire to know more about others and also to be known better themselves. "I wish to become better in the relationship with my mother," Ellen says—"to be able more easily to disagree with her." Disagreement here is a sign of relationship, a manifestation of two people coming together. And it is in close relationships that girls are most willing to argue or disagree, wanting most to be known and seen by those to whom they feel closest and also believing more that those who are close will be there, will listen, and will try to understand. "If you love someone," Anna explains, "you are usually comfortable with them. And, feeling comfortable, you can easily argue with one another and say, look, I want you to see my side. It's a lot easier to fight with someone you love, because you know they will always forgive you, at least usually they will . . . and you know that they are still going to be there for you after the disagreement."

Perhaps it is because of this feeling of being comfortable that girls most often speak about conflict in their relationships with their mothers—the person who, one girl said, "will always welcome me." Girls' willingness to fight for genuine connection with their mothers is well illustrated by Kate, a fifteen-year-old who says, paradoxically:

> I called my mother up and said, "Why can't I speak to you anymore? What is going on?" And I ended up crying and hanging up on her because she wouldn't listen to me. She had her own opinion about what was truth and what was reality, and she gave me no opening. . . . What she had on her mind was the truth. And you know, I kept saying, "Well, you hurt me," and she said, "No, I did not." And I said, "Well, why am I hurt?" you know, and she is just denying my feelings as if they did not exist and as if I had no right to feel them, you know, even though they were.

The counterpart to the image of a wall is the search for an opening, a way 15 of reaching another person, of finding a place of entry. Yet to open oneself to another person creates a great vulnerability, and thus the strength of girls' desire for relationship also engenders the need for protection from fraudulent relationships and psychic wounding. "To me," Jane says, "love means an attachment to a person," by which she means a willingness or wish

> to share a lot of things with that person and not feel as though you are opening up your soul and it is going to be misrepresented or misunderstood. Rather, so that person . . . will know kind of inside how far to go and, if they go too far, they will understand when you say, that's

not what I want . . . where people accept your idiosyncrasies . . . that you can have fun and you can disagree but that the argument isn't something that wounds you for months. . . . Some people are too quick to say "I love you." It takes time to learn someone. I don't think you can love on first sight. . . . You can feel a connection with someone, but you can't just love them.

These carefully drawn distinctions, the contrast between feeling connected with someone and loving them and between having fun and disagreeing and having an argument that wounds you for months, bespeak close observation of relationships and psychological processes and also experiences of being misrepresented, misunderstood, and not listened to, which have left both knowledge and scars. Jane says she is looking for someone who will understand when she says, "that's not what I want." Mira, in contrast, has chosen silence as a way of avoiding being hurt:

I personally have had a hard time asking questions . . . because I was shy and did not really like to talk to people about what I was really thinking.
Why not?
I thought it was much safer just to keep it to myself, and this way nobody would have so much of a vulnerable spot that they could get to me with. And so I thought, just the thought of having somebody having something on me that could possibly hurt me, that scared me and kept me from speaking up a lot of the time.

Like the character in Woolf's story, "An Unwritten Novel," Mira keeps her life to herself; her speaking self also is "entombed . . . driven in, in, in to the central catacomb. . . . Flit[ting] with its lanterns restlessly up and down the dark corridor."[3] Mary Belenky and her colleagues have described how women retreat into silence when words become weapons and are used to wound.[4] Adolescent girls invoke images of violence and talk in the language of warfare or about winning and losing when they describe the inner workings of explosive relationships, fearing also that such relationships can "throw us apart forever."

What is the worst thing that can happen in a relationship?
I guess if people build up resentments and don't talk about them, things can just keep building up until they reach the boiling point, and then there is like a cold war going on. People are just fencing on either side of a wall, but not admitting it to the other person until there is an explosion or something.

---

[3]Virginia Woolf, "An Unwritten Novel," *Haunted House and Other Short Stories* (1921; reprint, New York: Harcourt Brace Jovanovich, 1972), 19.

[4]Mary Belenky, Blythe Clinchy, Nancy Goldberger and Jill Tarule, *Women's Ways of Knowing* (New York: Basic Books, 1986).

Other girls, like Emma, describe "building a wall" that serves to undermine relationships:

> *What is the worst thing that can happen in a relationship?*
> Not talking it out. Building a wall . . . I think that can lead to a lot more because you don't give a chance to the other person to say anything. . . . You are too close-minded to listen to what they have to say. . . . If you don't listen to your friends, they are not your friends, there is no relationship there, because you don't listen.

Taken together, these observations of the ways in which people move and affect, touch and are touched by one another, appear and disappear in relationships with themselves and with others, reveal an understanding of psychic processes that is closer to a physics than a metaphysics of relationship—based on tracking voices and images, thoughts and feelings, across the cloud chamber of daily life. Certain observations are breathtakingly simple in their logic although profound in their implications, especially given the pace of contemporary living. Emma says that, "if you don't listen to your friends, they are not your friends. There is no relationship there." Others are more complex, like Joan's exegesis of the indirect discourse of betrayal: "If you don't trust someone to know a secret . . . you sort of grow apart . . . or you will feel like you are with them and down underneath you are angry . . . but you don't say anything, so it comes out . . . in other ways." Or Maria's explication of the confusing mixing of anger and hurt:

> I am not sure of the difference when I feel angry and hurt. . . . I don't even know if they are separate emotions. . . . I was angry, I think at myself in that relationship, that I had let myself be used . . . that I had let down my guard so much. I was completely vulnerable. And I chose to do that. . . . I kept saying, "I hate him," but I realized that he didn't even notice me there because he was in his own world. So that I think . . . all my anger comes out of being hurt, and it's a confusion there.

Repeatedly, girls emphasize the need for open conflict and voicing disagreement. Catherine describes the fruitful quality of disagreement in her relationship with her friend:

> We have learned more about ourselves . . . I think . . . she had never really had a close friend but lots of acquaintances. She didn't get into fights and things like that. . . . I think she realizes that you have to have disagreements and things like that for a relationship to last.
> *How come?*
> Because if you don't really voice your disagreements, then you don't really have anything going, do you know what I mean? It's just another way, it is another side of you that you are letting someone else see.

And Liza describes the raw pain of finding, at the end of a long journey, that you are not able to talk with someone on whom you had depended:

> *What is the worst thing that can happen in a relationship?*
> That you grow up, or sideways, and not be able to talk to each other, especially if you depend on being able to talk to someone and not being able to. That hurts a lot, because you have been dependent on that. It is like walking fifty miles for a glass of water in a hot desert, and you have been depending on it for days, and getting there and finding it is not there anymore; you made the wrong turn ten miles back.

The knowledge about relationships and the life of relationships that flourish on this remote island of female adolescence are, to shift the metaphor, like notes from the underground. Much of what psychologists know about relationships is also known by adolescent girls. But, as girls themselves say clearly, they will speak only when they feel that someone will listen and will not leave in the face of conflict or disagreement. Thus, the fate of girls' knowledge and girls' education becomes tied to the fate of their relationships.

When women's studies is joined with the study of girls' development, it becomes clearer why adolescence is a critical time in girls' lives—a time when girls are in danger of losing their voices and thus losing connection with others, and also a time when girls, gaining voice and knowledge, are in danger of knowing the unseen and speaking the unspoken and thus losing connection with what is commonly taken to be "reality." This crisis of connection in girls' lives at adolescence links the psychology of women with the most basic questions about the nature of relationships and the definition of reality. Girls' questions about relationships and about reality, however, also tug at women's silences.

At the edge of adolescence, eleven- and twelve-year-old girls observe where and when women speak and when they are silent.[5] As resisters, they may be especially prone to notice and question the compliance of women to male authority. One of Woolf's questions in *A Room of One's Own* is why mothers do not provide more rooms for their daughters, why they do not leave more of a legacy for their daughters, and why, more specifically, mothers do not endow their daughters' education with greater comfort.[6] A teacher of twelve-year-olds, after a faculty meeting where women's reluctance to disagree in public became a subject of discussion, told the following story: her eleven-year-old daughter had commented on her reluctance to disagree with her husband (the girl's father). She was angry at her mother, she said, for always giving in. In response,

---

[5]Lyn Mikel Brown, "A Problem of Vision: The Development of Voice and Relational Knowledge in Girls Ages Seven to Sixteen," *Women's Studies Quarterly* 1991:1 & 2.

[6]Virginia Woolf, *A Room of One's Own* (1928; reprint, New York: Harcourt, Brace, and World, 1957), 20–24.

the mother began to explain that, although the girl's father sometimes raised his voice, he was loving and well-intentioned—at which point her daughter interrupted her, saying that it was she, her mother, who she was angry at for always giving in. "I was so humiliated," the teacher said, "so ashamed." Later that year, when her colleague announced a new rule about lunch in homeroom one day, she suppressed her disagreement with him and did not voice her objections—because, she said, she did not want to undermine his authority. Perhaps it was as a result of her previous humiliation that she thought twice on a day when the rule seemed particularly senseless and excused some girls, in spite of the rule, before others who had arrived late at lunch had finished eating. "Good for you," the girls said, "we're proud of you." It was clear that they had noticed everything.

In his appreciation of the poetry of Sylvia Plath, Seamus Heaney reads a famous passage by William Wordsworth as a parable of the three stages in a poet's journey.[7] At first one goes out into the woods and whistles to hear if the owls will respond. Then, once one discovers that one can speak in a way that calls forth a response from the world of nature, one has to learn to perfect one's craft, to enter the world of sounds—of birdcalls, traditions, and poetic conventions—until, Heaney says, if one is blessed or fortunate, one becomes the instrument through which the sounds of the world pass. Heaney traces this transformation in Plath's poetry, drawing the reader into his own exhilaration as her language takes off. But Plath's relationship to the tradition of male voices, which she was entering and changing by entering, was not the same as Heaney's, and her entrance was more deeply disruptive. And the same can be said for women students.

A student first must learn how to call forth a response from the world: to ask a question to which people will listen, which they will find interesting and respond to. Then she must learn the craft of inquiry so that she can tune her questions and develop her ear for language and thus speak more clearly and more freely, can say more and also hear more fully. But if the world of nature, as Heaney implies, is equally responsive to the calls of women and men, the world of civilization is not, or at least has not been up to the present. The wind of tradition blowing through women is a chill wind because it brings a message of exclusion: stay out. It brings a message of subordination: stay under. It brings a message of objectification: become the object of another's worship or desire; see yourself as you have been seen for centuries, through a male gaze. And because all of the suffering, the endless litany of storm and shipwreck, is presented as necessary or even good for civilization, the message to women is: keep quiet, notice the absence of women, and say nothing.

---

[7]Seamus Heaney, *The Government of the Tongue: Selected Prose, 1978–1987* (New York: Farrar, Straus and Giroux, 1989).

At the present moment the education of women presents genuine dilemmas and real opportunities. Women's questions—especially questions about relationships and questions about violence—often feel disruptive to women because at present they are disruptive both in private and public life. And relationships between women are often strained. It is not at all clear what it means to be a good mother or teacher to an adolescent girl coming of age in Western culture. The choices that women make in order to survive or to appear good in the eyes of others and thus sustain their protection are often at the expense of women's relationships with one another, and girls begin to observe and comment on these choices around the age of eleven or twelve. If women can stay in the gaze of girls so that girls do not have to look and not see, if women can be seen by girls, including the twelve-year-old in themselves, if women can sustain girls' gazes and respond to girls' voices, then, perhaps as Woolf envisioned, "the opportunity will come and the dead poet who is Shakespeare's sister will put on the body which she has so often laid down and find it possible to live and write her poetry"[8]—as Plath did for a moment before taking her life. Yet as Woolf reminds us, before Shakespeare's sister can come, we must have the habit of freedom and the courage to write and say exactly what we think.

QUESTIONS

1. Where did your most powerful learning experience occur? Poll your class. How do the answers break down according to sex (and age, if relevant)?

2. In your discussion of learning experiences, did men and women participate equally, or is there a pattern of domination in your classroom?

3. Gilligan is interested in the metaphors her subjects use to express their emotional states. Gail talks about her "block . . . like a wall" (paragraph 6). What other metaphors does she use? Are they unusual or common? How would you interpret them? What other metaphors are used by Gilligan's subjects?

4. Gilligan says in her conclusion, "It is not at all clear what it means to be a good mother or teacher to an adolescent girl coming of age in Western culture." Discuss some of the reasons why this is so, or disagree with this statement.

5. Take the statement quoted in Question 4 and substitute *father* for *mother* and *boy* for *girl*. Then discuss why you agree or disagree with the statement.

6. On the subject of learning experiences, extend your interviews and observations to a wider group of students, or to a different age group. You may, for example, want to talk to a group of public high school or junior high school students, to see if their experiences are similar to those of the private school students Gilligan interviewed. Write up your findings.

---

[8]Woolf, *A Room of One's Own*, 117.

MAKING CONNECTIONS

Gilligan ends by saying that adolescents—indeed, all women—"must have . . . the courage to write and say exactly what we think." Compare Lucy Grealy's description of her adolescence in "Mirrors" (p. 48) with those described by Gilligan's interviewees. How does Grealy's essay comment on Gilligan's statement?

ON THE FEAR OF DEATH

Elisabeth Kübler-Ross

Elisabeth Kübler-Ross (b. 1926), a Swiss-American psychia-
trist, is one of the leaders of the movement that may help
change the way Americans think about death. Born in
Zurich, she received her M.D. from the University of Zurich
in 1957 and came to the United States as an intern the
following year. Kübler-Ross began her work with terminally
ill patients while teaching psychiatry at the University of
Chicago Medical School. She founded the hospice care
movement in the United States and runs Shanti Nilaya
(Sanskrit for "home of peace"), an organization "dedicated
to the promotion of physical, emotional, and spiritual
health." This selection is taken from her first and most fa-
mous book, On Death and Dying *(1969).*

> Let me not pray to be sheltered from
> dangers but to be fearless in facing them.
> Let me not beg for the stilling of my
> pain but for the heart to conquer it.
> Let me not look for allies in life's battle-
> field but to my own strength.
> Let me not crave in anxious fear to be
> saved but hope for the patience to win my
> freedom.
> Grant me that I may not be a coward,
> feeling your mercy in my success alone;
> but let me find the grasp of your hand in
> my failure.

Rabindranath Tagore, *Fruit-Gathering*

Epidemics have taken a great toll of lives in past generations. Death in infancy and early childhood was frequent and there were few families who didn't
lose a member of the family at an early age. Medicine has changed greatly in
the last decades. Widespread vaccinations have practically eradicated many
illnesses, at least in western Europe and the United States. The use of chemotherapy, especially the antibiotics, has contributed to an ever-decreasing number of fatalities in infectious diseases. Better child care and education have effected a low morbidity and mortality among children. The many diseases that
have taken an impressive toll among the young and middle-aged have been

421

conquered. The number of old people is on the rise, and with this fact come the number of people with malignancies and chronic diseases associated more with old age.

Pediatricians have less work with acute and life-threatening situations as they have an ever-increasing number of patients with psychosomatic disturbances and adjustment and behavior problems. Physicians have more people in their waiting rooms with emotional problems than they have ever had before, but they also have more elderly patients who not only try to live with their decreased physical abilities and limitations but who also face loneliness and isolation with all its pains and anguish. The majority of these people are not seen by a psychiatrist. Their needs have to be elicited and gratified by other professional people, for instance, chaplains and social workers. It is for them that I am trying to outline the changes that have taken place in the last few decades, changes that are ultimately responsible for the increased fear of death, the rising number of emotional problems, and the greater need for understanding of and coping with the problems of death and dying.

When we look back in time and study old cultures and people, we are impressed that death has always been distasteful to man and will probably always be. From a psychiatrist's point of view this is very understandable and can perhaps best be explained by our basic knowledge that, in our unconscious, death is never possible in regard to ourselves. It is inconceivable for our unconscious to imagine an actual ending of our own life here on earth, and if this life of ours has to end, the ending is always attributed to a malicious intervention from the outside by someone else. In simple terms, in our unconscious mind we can only be killed; it is inconceivable to die of a natural cause or of old age. Therefore death in itself is associated with a bad act, a frightening happening, something that in itself calls for retribution and punishment.

One is wise to remember these fundamental facts as they are essential in understanding some of the most important, otherwise unintelligible communications of our patients.

The second fact that we have to comprehend is that in our unconscious 5 mind we cannot distinguish between a wish and a deed. We are all aware of some of our illogical dreams in which two completely opposite statements can exist side by side—very acceptable in our dreams but unthinkable and illogical in our wakening state. Just as our unconscious mind cannot differentiate between the wish to kill somebody in anger and the act of having done so, the young child is unable to make this distinction. The child who angrily wishes his mother to drop dead for not having gratified his needs will be traumatized greatly by the actual death of his mother—even if this event is not linked closely in time with his destructive wishes. He will always take part or the whole blame for the loss of his mother. He will always say to himself—rarely to others—"I did it, I am responsible, I was bad, therefore Mommy left me." It is well to remember that the child will react in the same manner if he loses a parent by divorce, separation, or desertion. Death is often seen by a child as an impermanent thing and has therefore little distinction from a divorce in which he may have an opportunity to see a parent again.

Many a parent will remember remarks of their children such as, "I will bury my doggy now and next spring when the flowers come up again, he will get up." Maybe it was the same wish that motivated the ancient Egyptians to supply their dead with food and goods to keep them happy and the old American Indians to bury their relatives with their belongings.

When we grow older and begin to realize that our omnipotence is really not so omnipotent, that our strongest wishes are not powerful enough to make the impossible possible, the fear that we have contributed to the death of a loved one diminishes—and with it the guilt. The fear remains diminished, however, only so long as it is not challenged too strongly. Its vestiges can be seen daily in hospital corridors and in people associated with the bereaved.

A husband and wife may have been fighting for years, but when the partner dies, the survivor will pull his hair, whine and cry louder and beat his chest in regret, fear and anguish, and will hence fear his own death more than before, still believing in the law of talion—an eye for an eye, a tooth for a tooth—"I am responsible for her death, I will have to die a pitiful death in retribution."

Maybe this knowledge will help us understand many of the old customs and rituals which have lasted over the centuries and whose purpose is to diminish the anger of the gods or the people as the case may be, thus decreasing the anticipated punishment. I am thinking of the ashes, the torn clothes, the veil, the *Klage Weiber* of the old days[1]—they are all means to ask you to take pity on them, the mourners, and are expressions of sorrow, grief, and shame. If someone grieves, beats his chest, tears his hair, or refuses to eat, it is an attempt at self-punishment to avoid or reduce the anticipated punishment for the blame that he takes on the death of a loved one.

This grief, shame, and guilt are not very far removed from feelings of anger 10 and rage. The process of grief always includes some qualities of anger. Since none of us likes to admit anger at a deceased person, these emotions are often disguised or repressed and prolong the period of grief or show up in other ways. It is well to remember that it is not up to us to judge such feelings as bad or shameful but to understand their true meaning and origin as something very human. In order to illustrate this I will again use the example of the child— and the child in us. The five-year-old who loses his mother is both blaming himself for her disappearance and being angry at her for having deserted him and for no longer gratifying his needs. The dead person then turns into something the child loves and wants very much but also hates with equal intensity for this severe deprivation.

The ancient Hebrews regarded the body of a dead person as something unclean and not to be touched. The early American Indians talked about the evil

---

[1] *Klage Weiber*: wailing wives. [Eds.]

spirits and shot arrows in the air to drive the spirits away. Many other cultures have rituals to take care of the "bad" dead person, and they all originate in this feeling of anger which still exists in all of us, though we dislike admitting it. The tradition of the tombstone may originate in the wish to keep the bad spirits deep down in the ground, and the pebbles that many mourners put on the grave are leftover symbols of the same wish. Though we call the firing of guns at military funerals a last salute, it is the same symbolic ritual as the Indian used when he shot his spears and arrows into the skies.

I give these examples to emphasize that man has not basically changed. Death is still a fearful, frightening happening, and the fear of death is a universal fear even if we think we have mastered it on many levels.

What has changed is our way of coping and dealing with death and dying and our dying patients.

Having been raised in a country in Europe where science is not so advanced, where modern techniques have just started to find their way into medicine, and where people still live as they did in this country half a century ago, I may have had an opportunity to study a part of the evolution of mankind in a shorter period.

I remember as a child the death of a farmer. He fell from a tree and was not 15 expected to live. He asked simply to die at home, a wish that was granted without question. He called his daughters into the bedroom and spoke with each one of them alone for a few moments. He arranged his affairs quietly, though he was in great pain, and distributed his belongings and his land, none of which was to be split until his wife should follow him in death. He also asked each of his children to share in the work, duties, and tasks that he had carried on until the time of the accident. He asked his friends to visit him once more, to bid goodbye to them. Although I was a small child at the time, he did not exclude me or my siblings. We were allowed to share in the preparations of the family just as we were permitted to grieve with them until he died. When he did die, he was left at home, in his own beloved home which he had built, and among his friends and neighbors who went to take a last look at him where he lay in the midst of flowers in the place he had lived in and loved so much. In that country today there is still no make-believe slumber room, no embalming, no false makeup to pretend sleep. Only the signs of very disfiguring illnesses are covered up with bandages and only infectious cases are removed from the home prior to the burial.

Why do I describe such "old-fashioned" customs? I think they are an indication of our acceptance of a fatal outcome, and they help the dying patient as well as his family to accept the loss of a loved one. If a patient is allowed to terminate his life in the familiar and beloved environment, it requires less adjustment for him. His own family knows him well enough to replace a sedative with a glass of his favorite wine; or the smell of a home-cooked soup may give him the appetite to sip a few spoons of fluid which, I think, is still more enjoyable than an infusion. I will not minimize the need for sedatives and infusions and realize full well from my own experience as a country doctor that they are sometimes life-saving and often unavoidable. But I also know that patience and familiar people and foods could replace many a bottle of intravenous fluids given for the simple reason that it fulfills the physiological need without involving too many people and/or individual nursing care.

The fact that children are allowed to stay at home where a fatality has struck and are included in the talk, discussions, and fears gives them the feeling that they are not alone in their grief and gives them the comfort of shared responsibility and shared mourning. It prepares them gradually and helps them view death as part of life, an experience which may help them grow and mature.

This is in great contrast to a society in which death is viewed as taboo, discussion of it is regarded as morbid, and children are excluded with the presumption and pretext that it would be "too much" for them. They are then sent off to relatives, often accompanied by some unconvincing lies of "Mother has gone on a long trip" or other unbelievable stories. The child senses that something is wrong, and his distrust in adults will only multiply if other relatives add new variations of the story, avoid his questions or suspicions, shower him with gifts as a meager substitute for a loss he is not permitted to deal with. Sooner or later the child will become aware of the changed family situation and, depending on the age and personality of the child, will have an unresolved grief and regard this incident as a frightening, mysterious, in any case very traumatic experience with untrustworthy grownups, which he has no way to cope with.

It is equally unwise to tell a little child who lost her brother that God loved little boys so much that he took little Johnny to heaven. When this little girl grew up to be a woman she never solved her anger at God, which resulted in a psychotic depression when she lost her own little son three decades later.

We would think that our great emancipation, our knowledge of science and of man, has given us better ways and means to prepare ourselves and our families for this inevitable happening. Instead the days are gone when a man was allowed to die in peace and dignity in his own home.

The more we are making advancements in science, the more we seem to fear and deny the reality of death. How is this possible?

We use euphemisms, we make the dead look as if they were asleep, we ship the children off to protect them from the anxiety and turmoil around the house if the patient is fortunate enough to die at home, we don't allow children to visit their dying parents in the hospitals, we have long and controversial discussions about whether patients should be told the truth—a question that rarely arises when the dying person is tended by the family physician who has known him from delivery to death and who knows the weaknesses and strengths of each member of the family.

I think there are many reasons for this flight away from facing death calmly. One of the most important facts is that dying nowadays is more gruesome in

20

425

many ways, namely, more lonely, mechanical, and dehumanized; at times it is even difficult to determine technically when the time of death has occurred.

Dying becomes lonely and impersonal because the patient is often taken out of his familiar environment and rushed to an emergency room. Whoever has been very sick and has required rest and comfort especially may recall his experience of being put on a stretcher and enduring the noise of the ambulance siren and hectic rush until the hospital gates open. Only those who have lived through this may appreciate the discomfort and cold necessity of such transportation which is only the beginning of a long ordeal—hard to endure when you are well, difficult to express in words when noise, light, pumps, and voices are all too much to put up with. It may well be that we might consider more the patient under the sheets and blankets and perhaps stop our well-meant efficiency and rush in order to hold the patient's hand, to smile, or to listen to a question. I include the trip to the hospital as the first episode in dying, as it is for many. I am putting it exaggeratedly in contrast to the sick man who is left at home—not to say that lives should not be saved if they can be saved by a hospitalization but to keep the focus on the patient's experience, his needs and his reactions.

When a patient is severely ill, he is often treated like a person with no right   25
to an opinion. It is often someone else who makes the decision if and when and where a patient should be hospitalized. It would take so little to remember that the sick person too has feelings, has wishes and opinions, and has—most important of all—the right to be heard.

Well, our presumed patient has now reached the emergency room. He will be surrounded by busy nurses, orderlies, interns, residents, a lab technician perhaps who will take some blood, an electrocardiogram technician who takes the cardiogram. He may be moved to X-ray and he will overhear opinions of his condition and discussions and questions to members of the family. He slowly but surely is beginning to be treated like a thing. He is no longer a person. Decisions are made often without his opinion. If he tries to rebel he will be sedated, and after hours of waiting and wondering whether he has the strength, he will be wheeled into the operating room or intensive treatment unit and become an object of great concern and great financial investment.

He may cry for rest, peace, and dignity, but he will get infusions, transfusions, a heart machine, or tracheotomy if necessary. He may want one single person to stop for one single minute so that he can ask one single question— but he will get a dozen people around the clock, all busily preoccupied with his heart rate, pulse, electrocardiogram or pulmonary functions, his secretions or excretions but not with him as a human being. He may wish to fight it all but it is going to be a useless fight since all this is done in the fight for his life, and if they can save his life they can consider the person afterwards. Those who consider the person first may lose precious time to save his life! At least this seems to be the rationale or justification behind all this—or is it? Is the reason for this increasingly mechanical, depersonalized approach our own defensiveness? Is this approach our own way to cope with and repress the anxieties that a terminally or critically ill patient evokes in us? Is our concentration on equipment, on blood pressure, our desperate attempt to deny the impending death which is so frightening and discomforting to us that we displace all our knowledge onto machines, since they are less close to us than the suffering face of another human being which would remind us once more of our lack of omnipotence, our own limits and failures, and last but not least perhaps our own mortality?

Maybe the question has to be raised: Are we becoming less human or more human? . . . It is clear that whatever the answer may be, the patient is suffering more—not physically, perhaps, but emotionally. And his needs have not changed over the centuries, only our ability to gratify them.

QUESTIONS

1. Why does Kübler-Ross describe the death of a farmer? What point is she making in explaining "such 'old-fashioned' customs" (paragraph 16)?

2. To what extent is this essay explanatory? Summarize a particular explanation of hers that you find intriguing. Is it persuasive?

3. At what point in this essay does Kübler-Ross turn from explanation to argument? Do you think she has taken a stand on her subject? How sympathetic are you to her position?

4. In paragraphs 2 and 10, Kübler-Ross indicates a specialized audience for her writing. Who is that audience, and how do you relate to it?

5. Think of the audience you described in question 4 as a primary audience and of yourself as a member of a secondary audience. To what extent do the two audiences overlap? How thoroughly can you divide one from the other?

6. What experience of death have you had so far? Write of a death that you know something about, even if your relation to it is distant, perhaps only through the media. Can you locate elements of fear and anger in your own behavior or in the behavior of other people involved? Does Kübler-Ross's interpretation of those reactions help you come to terms with the experience?

7. What kind of balance do you think best between prolonging life and allowing a person to die with dignity? What does the phrase "dying with dignity" mean?

8. If you were told you had a limited time to live, how would that news change the way you are living? Or would it? Offer an explanation for your position.

MAKING CONNECTIONS

Kübler-Ross suggests that we have significant lessons to learn from the dying and warns that we avoid thinking about death only at our own peril. In "Dialogues with the Dead" (p. 68), Christopher Clausen suggests that the dead will eat us up if we pay too much or too little attention to them. Imagine a conversation between these two essayists and write an essay in which you create a dialog between them.

THE SCIENCE OF SHOPPING
Malcolm Gladwell

Malcolm Gladwell (b. 1963), an astute observer of the con-
temporary scene, is a frequent contributor to such periodi-
cals as the New Yorker, Vogue, *and* New York *and he has*
worked as a reporter for the Washington Post. *In this essay,*
which originally appeared in the New Yorker *(1996), Glad-*
well investigates a researcher into a new science—the sci-
ence of shopping—and puts his theories to the test.

Human beings walk the way they drive, which is to say that Americans tend to keep to the right when they stroll down shopping-mall concourses or city sidewalks. This is why in a well-designed airport travelers drifting toward their gate will always find the fast-food restaurants on their left and the gift shops on their right: people will readily cross a lane of pedestrian traffic to satisfy their hunger but rarely to make an impulse buy of a T-shirt or a magazine. This is also why Paco Underhill tells his retail clients to make sure that their window displays are canted, preferably to both sides but especially to the left, so that a potential shopper approaching the store on the inside of the sidewalk—the shopper, that is, with the least impeded view of the store window—can see the display from at least twenty-five feet away.

Of course, a lot depends on how fast the potential shopper is walking. Paco, in his previous life, as an urban geographer in Manhattan, spent a great deal of time thinking about walking speeds as he listened in on the great debates of the nineteen-seventies over whether the traffic lights in midtown should be timed to facilitate the movement of cars or to facilitate the movement of pedestrians and so break up the big platoons that move down Manhattan sidewalks. He knows that the faster you walk the more your peripheral vision narrows, so you become unable to pick up visual cues as quickly as someone who is just ambling along. He knows, too, that people who walk fast take a surprising amount of time to slow down—just as it takes a good stretch of road to change gears with a stick-shift automobile. On the basis of his research, Paco estimates the human downshift period to be anywhere from twelve to twenty-five feet, so if you own a store, he says, you never want to be next door to a bank: potential shoppers speed up when they walk past a bank (since there's nothing to look at), and by the time they slow down they've walked right past your business. The downshift factor also means that when potential shoppers enter a store it's going to take them from five to fifteen paces to adjust to the light and refocus and gear down from walking speed to shopping speed—particularly if they've just had to navigate a treacherous parking lot or hurry to make the light at Fifty-seventh and Fifth.

Paco calls that area inside the door the Decompression Zone, and something he tells clients over and over again is never, *ever* put anything of value in that zone—not shopping baskets or tie racks or big promotional displays—because no one is going to see it. Paco believes that, as a rule of thumb, customer interaction with any product or promotional display in the Decompression Zone will increase at least thirty percent once it's moved to the back edge of the zone, and even more if it's placed to the right, because another of the fundamental rules of how human beings shop is that upon entering a store—whether it's Nordstrom or K mart, Tiffany or the Gap—the shopper invariably and reflexively turns to the right. Paco believes in the existence of the Invariant Right because he has actually verified it. He has put cameras in stores trained directly on the doorway, and if you go to his office, just above Union Square, where videocassettes and boxes of Super-eight film from all his work over the years are stacked in plastic Tupperware containers practically up to the ceiling, he can show you reel upon reel of grainy entryway video—customers striding in the door, down-shifting, refocusing, and then, again and again, making that little half turn.

Paco Underhill is a tall man in his mid-forties, partly bald, with a neatly trimmed beard and an engaging, almost goofy manner. He wears baggy khakis and shirts open at the collar, and generally looks like the academic he might have been if he hadn't been captivated, twenty years ago, by the ideas of the urban anthropologist William Whyte. It was Whyte who pioneered the use of time-lapse photography as a tool of urban planning, putting cameras in parks and the plazas in front of office buildings in midtown Manhattan, in order to determine what distinguished a public space that worked from one that didn't. As a Columbia undergraduate, in 1974, Paco heard a lecture on Whyte's work and, he recalls, left the room "walking on air." He immediately read everything Whyte had written. He emptied his bank account to buy cameras and film and make his own home movie, about a pedestrian mall in Poughkeepsie. He took his "little exercise" to Whyte's advocacy group, the Project for Public Spaces, and was offered a job. Soon, however, it dawned on Paco that Whyte's ideas could be taken a step further—that the same techniques he used to establish why a plaza worked or didn't work could also be used to determine why a store worked or didn't work. Thus was born the field of retail anthropology, and, not long afterward, Paco founded Envirosell, which in just over fifteen years has counseled some of the most familiar names in American retailing, from Levi Strauss to Kinney, Starbucks, McDonald's, Blockbuster, Apple Computer, A.T.&T., and a number of upscale retailers that Paco would rather not name.

When Paco gets an assignment, he and his staff set up a series of videocameras throughout the test store and then back the cameras up with Envirosell staffers—trackers, as they're known—armed with clipboards. Where the cameras go and how many trackers Paco deploys depends on exactly what the store 5 wants to know about its shoppers. Typically, though, he might use six cameras and two or three trackers, and let the study run for two or three days, so that at the end he would have pages and pages of carefully annotated tracking sheets and anywhere from a hundred to five hundred hours of film. These days, given the expansion of his business, he might tape fifteen thousand hours in a year, and, given that he has been in operation since the late seventies, he now has well over a hundred thousand hours of tape in his library.

Even in the best of times, this would be a valuable archive. But today, with the retail business in crisis, it is a gold mine. The time per visit that the average American spends in a shopping mall was sixty-six minutes last year—down from seventy-two minutes in 1992—and is the lowest number ever recorded. The amount of selling space per American shopper is now more than double what it was in the mid-seventies, meaning that profit margins have never been narrower, and the costs of starting a retail business—and of failing—have never been higher. In the past few years, countless dazzling new retailing temples have been built along Fifth and Madison Avenues—Barneys, Calvin Klein, Armani, Valentino, Banana Republic, Prada, Chanel, Nike Town, and on and on—but it is an explosion of growth based on no more than a hunch, a hopeful multimillion-dollar gamble that the way to break through is to provide the shopper with spectacle and more spectacle. "The arrogance is gone," Millard Drexler, the president and C.E.O. of the Gap, told me. "Arrogance makes failure. Once you think you know the answer, it's almost always over." In such a competitive environment, retailers don't just want to know how shoppers behave in their stores. They *have* to know. And who better to ask than Paco Underhill, who in the past decade and a half has analyzed tens of thousands of hours of shopping videotape and, as a result, probably knows more about the strange habits and quirks of the species *Emptor americanus*[1] than anyone else alive?

Paco is considered the originator, for example, of what is known in the trade as the butt-brush theory—or, as Paco calls it, more delicately, *le facteur bousculade*[2]—which holds that the likelihood of a woman's being converted from a browser to a buyer is inversely proportional to the likelihood of her being brushed on her behind while she's examining merchandise. Touch—or brush or bump or jostle—a woman on the behind when she has stopped to look at an item, and she will bolt. Actually, calling this a theory is something of a misnomer, because Paco doesn't offer any explanation for why women react that way, aside from venturing that they are "more sensitive back there." It's really an observation, based on repeated and close analysis of his videotape library, that Paco has transformed into a retailing commandment: a women's product that requires extensive examination should never be placed in a narrow aisle.

---

[1] *Emptor americanus*: American buyer. [Eds.]
[2] *le facteur bousculade*: the jostling or pushing factor. [Eds.]

Paco approaches the problem of the Invariant Right the same way. Some retail thinkers see this as a subject crying out for interpretation and speculation.
The design guru Joseph Weishar, for example, argues, in his magisterial "Design for Effective Selling Space," that the Invariant Right is a function of the
fact that we "absorb and digest information in the left part of the brain" and
"assimilate and logically use this information in the right half," the result being
that we scan the store from left to right and then fix on an object to the right
"essentially at a 45 degree angle from the point that we enter." When I asked
Paco about this interpretation, he shrugged, and said he thought the reason
was simply that most people are right-handed. Uncovering the fundamentals of
"why" is clearly not a pursuit that engages him much. He is not a theoretician
but an empiricist, and for him the important thing is that in amassing his huge
library of in-store time-lapse photography he has gained enough hard evidence
to know how often and under what circumstances the Invariant Right is expressed and how to take advantage of it.

What Paco likes are facts. They come tumbling out when he talks, and, because he speaks with a slight hesitation—lingering over the first syllable in, for
example, "re-tail" or "de-sign"—he draws you in, and you find yourself truly
hanging on his words. "We have reached a historic point in American history,"
he told me in our very first conversation. "Men, for the first time, have begun
to buy their own underwear." He then paused to let the comment sink in, so
that I could absorb its implications, before he elaborated: "Which means that
we have to *totally* rethink the way we sell that product." In the parlance of Hollywood scriptwriters, the best endings must be surprising and yet inevitable;
and the best of Paco's pronouncements take the same shape. It would never
have occurred to me to wonder about the increasingly critical role played by
touching—or, as Paco calls it, petting—clothes in the course of making the decision to buy them. But then I went to the Gap and to Banana Republic and
saw people touching and fondling and, one after another, buying shirts and
sweaters laid out on big wooden tables, and what Paco told me—which was no
doubt based on what he had seen on his videotapes—made perfect sense: that
the reason the Gap and Banana Republic have tables is not merely that
sweaters and shirts look better there, or that tables fit into the warm and relaxing residential feeling that the Gap and Banana Republic are trying to create
in their stores, but that tables invite—indeed, symbolize—touching. "Where
do we eat?" Paco asks. "We eat, we pick up food, on tables."

Paco produces for his clients a series of carefully detailed studies, totaling   10
forty to a hundred and fifty pages, filled with product-by-product breakdowns
and bright-colored charts and graphs. In one recent case, he was asked by a
major clothing retailer to analyze the first of a new chain of stores that the firm
planned to open. One of the things the client wanted to know was how successful the store was in drawing people into its depths, since the chances that
shoppers will buy something are directly related to how long they spend shopping, and how long they spend shopping is directly related to how deep they

get pulled into the store. For this reason, a supermarket will often put dairy products on one side, meat at the back, and fresh produce on the other side, so that the typical shopper can't just do a drive-by but has to make an entire circuit of the store, and be tempted by everything the supermarket has to offer. In the case of the new clothing store, Paco found that ninety-one percent of all shoppers penetrated as deep as what he called Zone 4, meaning more than three-quarters of the way in, well past the accessories and shirt racks and belts in the front, and little short of the far wall, with the changing rooms and the pants stacked on shelves. Paco regarded this an an extraordinary figure, particularly for a long, narrow store like this one, where it is not unusual for the rate of penetration past, say, Zone 3 to be under fifty percent. But that didn't mean the store was perfect—far from it. For Paco, all kinds of questions remained.

Purchasers, for example, spent an average of eleven minutes and twenty-seven seconds in the store, nonpurchasers two minutes and thirty-six seconds. It wasn't that the nonpurchasers just cruised in and out: in those two minutes and thirty-six seconds, they went deep into the store and examined an average of 3.42 items. So why didn't they buy? What, exactly, happened to cause some browsers to buy and other browsers to walk out the door?

Then, there was the issue of the number of products examined. The purchasers were looking at an average of 4.81 items but buying only 1.33 items. Paco found this statistic deeply disturbing. As the retail market grows more cut-throat, store owners have come to realize that it's all but impossible to increase the number of customers coming in, and have concentrated instead on getting the customers they do have to buy more. Paco thinks that if you can sell someone a pair of pants you must also be able to sell that person a belt, or a pair of socks, or a pair of underpants, or even do what the Gap does so well: sell a person a complete outfit. To Paco, the figure 1.33 suggested that the store was doing something very wrong, and one day when I visited him in his office he sat me down in front of one of his many VCRs to see how he looked for the 1.33 culprit.

It should be said that sitting next to Paco is a rather strange experience. "My mother says that I'm the best-paid spy in America," he told me. He laughed, but he wasn't entirely joking. As a child, Paco had a nearly debilitating stammer, and, he says, "since I was never that comfortable talking I always relied on my eyes to understand things." That much is obvious from the first moment you meet him: Paco is one of those people who look right at you, soaking up every nuance and detail. It isn't a hostile gaze, because Paco isn't hostile at all. He has a big smile, and he'll call you "chief" and use your first name a lot and generally act as if he knew you well. But that's the awkward thing: he has looked at you so closely that you're sure he does know you well, and you, meanwhile, hardly know him at all.

This kind of asymmetry is even more pronounced when you watch his shopping videos with him, because every movement or gesture means something to Paco—he has spent his adult life deconstructing the shopping experience—but nothing to the outsider, or, at least, not at first. Paco had to keep stopping the video to get me to see things through his eyes before I began to understand. In one sequence, for example, a camera mounted high on the wall outside the changing rooms documented a man and a woman shopping for a pair of pants for what appeared to be their daughter, a girl in her midteens. The tapes are soundless, but the basic steps of the shopping dance are so familiar to Paco that, once I'd grasped the general idea, he was able to provide a running commentary on what was being said and thought. There is the girl emerging from the changing room wearing her first pair. There she is glancing at her reflection in the mirror, then turning to see herself from the back. There is the mother looking on. There is the father—or, as fathers are known in the trade, the "wallet carrier"—stepping forward and pulling up the jeans. There's the girl trying on another pair. There's the primp again. The twirl. The mother. The wallet carrier. And then again, with another pair. The full sequence lasted twenty minutes, and at the end came the take-home lesson, for which Paco called in one of his colleagues, Tom Moseman, who had supervised the project.

"This is a very critical moment," Tom, a young, intense man wearing little round glasses, said, and he pulled up a chair next to mine. "She's saying, 'I don't know whether I should wear a belt.' Now here's the salesclerk. The girl says to him, 'I need a belt,' and he says, 'Take mine.' Now there he is taking her back to the full-length mirror." 15

A moment later, the girl returns, clearly happy with the purchase. She wants the jeans. The wallet carrier turns to her, and then gestures to the salesclerk. The wallet carrier is telling his daughter to give back the belt. The girl gives back the belt. Tom stops the tape. He's leaning forward now, a finger jabbing at the screen. Beside me, Paco is shaking his head. I don't get it—at least, not at first—and so Tom replays that last segment. The wallet carrier tells the girl to give back the belt. She gives back the belt. And then, finally, it dawns on me why this store has an average purchase number of only 1.33. "Don't you see?" Tom said. "*She wanted the belt.* A great opportunity to make an add-on sale . . . *lost!*"

Should we be afraid of Paco Underhill? One of the fundamental anxieties of the American consumer, after all, has always been that beneath the pleasure and the frivolity of the shopping experience runs an undercurrent of manipulation, and that anxiety has rarely seemed more justified than today. The practice of prying into the minds and habits of American consumers is now a multibillion-dollar business. Every time a product is pulled across a supermarket checkout scanner, information is recorded, assembled, and sold to a market-research firm for analysis. There are companies that put tiny cameras inside frozen-food cases in supermarket aisles; market-research firms that feed census data and behavioral statistics into algorithms and come out with complicated maps of the American consumer; anthropologists who sift through the garbage of carefully targeted households to analyze their true consumption patterns; and endless rounds of highly organized focus groups and questionnaire takers and phone surveyors. That some people are now tracking our every shopping move with video cameras seems in many respects the last straw: Paco's movies are, after all, creepy. They look like the surveillance videos taken during convenience-store holdups—hazy and soundless and slightly warped by the angle of the lens. When you watch them, you find yourself waiting for something bad to happen, for someone to shoplift or pull a gun on a cashier.

The more time you spend with Paco's videos, though, the less scary they seem. After an hour or so, it's no longer clear whether simply by watching people shop—and analyzing their every move—you can learn how to control them. The shopper that emerges from the videos is not pliable or manipulable. The screen shows people filtering in and out of stores, petting and moving on, abandoning their merchandise because checkout lines are too long, or leaving a store empty-handed because they couldn't fit their stroller into the aisle between two shirt racks. Paco's shoppers are fickle and headstrong, and are quite unwilling to buy anything unless conditions are perfect—unless the belt is presented at *exactly* the right moment. His theories of the butt-brush and petting and the Decompression Zone and the Invariant Right seek not to make shoppers conform to the desires of sellers but to make sellers conform to the desires of shoppers. What Paco is teaching his clients is a kind of slavish devotion to the shopper's every whim. He is teaching them humility.

Paco has worked with supermarket chains, and when you first see one of his videos of grocery aisles it looks as if he really had—at least in this instance—got one up on the shopper. The clip he showed me was of a father shopping with a small child, and it was an example of what is known in the trade as "advocacy," which basically means what happens when your four-year-old goes over and grabs a bag of cookies that the store has conveniently put on the bottom shelf, and demands that it be purchased. In the clip, the father takes what the child offers him. "Generally, dads are not as good as moms at saying no," Paco said as we watched the little boy approach his dad. "Men tend to be more impulse-driven than women in grocery stores. We know that they tend to shop less often with a list. We know that they tend to shop much less frequently with coupons, and we know, simply by watching them shop, that they can be marching down the aisle and something will catch their eye and they will stop and buy." This kind of weakness on the part of fathers might seem to give the supermarket an advantage in the cookie-selling wars, particularly since more and more men go grocery shopping with their children. But then Paco let drop a hint about a study he'd just done in which he discovered, to his and everyone else's amazement, that shoppers had already figured this out, that they were already one step ahead—that *families were avoiding the cookie aisle.*

This may seem like a small point. But it begins to explain why, even though 20
retailers seem to know more than ever about how shoppers behave, even

though their efforts at intelligence-gathering have rarely seemed more intrusive and more formidable, the retail business remains in crisis. The reason is that shoppers are a moving target. They are becoming more and more complicated, and retailers need to know more and more about them simply to keep pace.

This fall, for example, Estée Lauder is testing in a Toronto shopping mall a new concept in cosmetics retailing. Gone is the enclosed rectangular counter, with the sales staff on one side, customers on the other, and the product under glass in the middle. In its place the company has provided an assortment of product-display, consultation, and testing kiosks arranged in a broken circle, with a service desk and a cashier in the middle. One of the kiosks is a "makeup play area," which allows customers to experiment on their own with a hundred and thirty different shades of lipstick. There are four self-service displays—for perfumes, skin-care products, and makeup—which are easily accessible to customers who have already made up their minds. And, for those who haven't, there is a semiprivate booth for personal consultations with beauty advisers and makeup artists. The redesign was prompted by the realization that the modern working woman no longer had the time or the inclination to ask a salesclerk to assist her in every purchase, that choosing among shades of lipstick did not require the same level of service as, say, getting up to speed on new developments in skin care, that a shopper's needs were now too diverse to be adequately served by just one kind of counter.

"I was going from store to store, and the traffic just wasn't there," Robin Burns, the president and C.E.O. of Estée Lauder U.S.A. and Canada, told me. "We had to get rid of the glass barricade." The most interesting thing about the new venture, though, is what it says about the shifting balance of power between buyer and seller. Around the old rectangular counter, the relationship of clerk to customer was formal and subtly paternalistic. If you wanted to look at a lipstick, you had to ask for it. "Twenty years ago, the sales staff would consult with you and *tell* you what you needed, as opposed to asking and recommending," Burns said. "And in those days people believed what the salesperson told them." Today, the old hierarchy has been inverted. "Women want to draw their own conclusions," Burns said. Even the architecture of the consultation kiosk speaks to the transformation: the beauty adviser now sits beside the customer, not across from her.

This doesn't mean that marketers and retailers have stopped trying to figure out what goes on in the minds of shoppers. One of the hottest areas in market research, for example, is something called typing, which is a sophisticated attempt to predict the kinds of products that people will buy or the kind of promotional pitch they will be susceptible to on the basis of where they live or how they score on short standardized questionnaires. One market-research firm in Virginia, Claritas, has divided the entire country, neighborhood by neighborhood, into sixty-two different categories—Pools & Patios, Shotguns & Pickups, Bohemia Mix, and so on—using census data and results from behavioral surveys. On the basis of my address in Greenwich Village, Claritas classifies me as Urban Gold Coast, which means that I like Kellogg's Special K, spend more than two hundred and fifty dollars on sports coats, watch "Seinfeld," and buy metal polish. Such typing systems—and there are a number of them—can be scarily accurate. I actually do buy Kellogg's Special K, have spent more than two hundred and fifty dollars on a sports coat, and watch "Seinfeld." (I don't buy metal polish.) In fact, when I was typed by a company called Total Research, in Princeton, the results were so dead-on that I got the same kind of creepy feeling that I got when I first watched Paco's videos. On the basis of a seemingly innocuous multiple-choice test, I was scored as an eighty-nine-percent Intellect and a seven-percent Relief Seeker (which I thought was impressive until John Morton, who developed the system, told me that virtually everyone who reads *The New Yorker* is an Intellect). When I asked Morton to guess, on the basis of my score, what kind of razor I used, he riffed, brilliantly, and without a moment's hesitation. "If you used an electric razor, it would be a Braun," he began. "But, if not, you're probably shaving with Gillette, if only because there really isn't an Intellect safety-razor positioning out there. Schick and Bic are simply not logical choices for you although I'm thinking, You're fairly young, and you've got that Relief Seeker side. It's possible you would use Bic because you don't like that all-American, overly confident masculine statement of Gillette. It's a very, very conventional positioning that Gillette uses. But then they've got the technological angle with the Gillette Sensor. . . . I'm thinking Gillette. It's Gillette."

He was right. I shave with Gillette—though I didn't even know that I do. I had to go home and check. But information about my own predilections may be of limited usefulness in predicting how I shop. In the past few years, market researchers have paid growing attention to the role in the shopping experience of a type of consumer known as a Market Maven. "This is a person you would go to for advice on a car or a new fashion," said Linda Price, a marketing professor at the University of South Florida, who first came up with the Market Maven concept, in the late eighties. "This is a person who has information on a lot of different products or prices or places to shop. This is a person who likes to initiate discussions with consumers and respond to requests. Market Mavens like to be helpers in the marketplace. They take you shopping. They go shopping for you, and it turns out they are a lot more prevalent than you would expect." Mavens watch more television than almost anyone else does, and they read more magazines and open their junk mail and look closely at advertisements and have an awful lot of influence on everyone else. According to Price, sixty percent of Americans claim to know a Maven.

The key question, then, is not what I think but what my Mavens think. The 25 challenge for retailers and marketers, in turn, is not so much to figure out and influence my preferences as to figure out and influence the preferences of my Mavens, and that is a much harder task. "What's really interesting is that the

436

distribution of Mavens doesn't vary by ethnic category, by income, or by professional status," Price said. "A working woman is just as likely to be a Market Maven as a nonworking woman. You might say that Mavens are likely to be older, unemployed people, but that's wrong, too. There is simply not a clear demographic guide to how to find these people." More important, Mavens are better consumers than most of the rest of us. In another of the typing systems, developed by the California-based SRI International, Mavens are considered to be a subcategory of the consumer type known as Fulfilled, and Fulfilleds, one SRI official told me, are "the consumers from Hell—they are very feature oriented." He explained, "They are not pushed by promotions. You can reach them, but it's an intellectual argument." As the complexity of the marketplace grows, in other words, we have responded by appointing the most skeptical and the most savvy in our midst to mediate between us and sellers. The harder stores and manufacturers work to sharpen and refine their marketing strategies, and the harder they try to read the minds of shoppers, the more we hide behind Mavens.

Imagine that you want to open a clothing store, men's and women's, in the upper-middle range—say, khakis at fifty dollars, dress shirts at forty dollars, sports coats and women's suits at two hundred dollars and up. The work of Paco Underhill would suggest that in order to succeed you need to pay complete and concentrated attention to the whims of your customers. What does that mean, in practical terms? Well, let's start with what's called the shopping gender gap. In the retail-store study that Paco showed me, for example, male buyers stayed an average of nine minutes and thirty-nine seconds in the store and female buyers stayed twelve minutes and fifty-seven seconds. This is not atypical. Women always shop longer than men, which is one of the major reasons that in the standard regional mall women account for seventy percent of the dollar value of all purchases. "Women have more patience than men," Paco says. "Men are more distractible. Their tolerance level for confusion or time spent in a store is much shorter than women's." If you wanted, then, you could build a store designed for men, to try to raise that thirty-percent sales figure to forty or forty-five percent. You could make the look more masculine— more metal, darker woods. You could turn up the music. You could simplify the store, put less product on the floor. "I'd go narrow and deep," says James Adams, the design director for NBBJ Retail Concepts, a division of one of the country's largest retail-design firms. "You wouldn't have fifty different cuts of pants. You'd have your four basics with lots of color. You know the Garanimals they used to do to help kids pick out clothes, where you match the giraffe top with the giraffe bottom? I'm sure every guy is like 'I wish I could get those, too.' You'd want to stick with the basics. Making sure most of the color story goes together. That is a big deal with guys, because they are always screwing the colors up." When I asked Carrie Gennuso, the Gap's regional vice-president for

New York, what she would do in an all-male store, she laughed and said, "I might do fewer displays and more signage. Big signs. Men! Smalls! Here!"

As a rule, though, you wouldn't want to cater to male customers at the expense of female ones. It's no accident that many clothing stores have a single look in both men's and women's sections, and that the quintessential nineties look—light woods, white walls—is more feminine than masculine. Women are still the shoppers in America, and the real money is to be made by making retailing styles *more* female-friendly, not less. Recently, for example, NBBJ did a project to try to increase sales of the Armstrong flooring chain. Its researchers found that the sales staff was selling the flooring based on its functional virtues—the fact that it didn't scuff, that it was long-lasting, that it didn't stain, that it was easy to clean. It was being sold by men to men, as if it were a car or a stereo. And that was the problem. "It's a wonder product technologically," Adams says. "But the woman is the decision-maker on flooring, and that's not what's she's looking for. This product is about fashion, about color and design. You don't want to get too caught up in the man's way of thinking."

To appeal to men, then, retailers do subtler things. At the Banana Republic store on Fifth Avenue in midtown, the men's socks are displayed near the shoes and between men's pants and the cash register (or cash/wrap, as it is known in the trade), so that the man can grab them easily as he rushes to pay. Women's accessories are by the fitting rooms, because women are much more likely to try on pants first, and then choose an item like a belt or a bag. At the men's shirt table, the display shirts have matching ties on them—the tie table is next to it—in a grownup version of the Garanimals system. But Banana Republic would never match scarves with women's blouses or jackets. "You don't have to be that direct with women," Jeanne Jackson, the president of Banana Republic, told me. "In fact, the Banana woman is proud of her sense of style. She puts her own looks together." Jackson said she liked the Fifth Avenue store because it's on two floors, so she can separate men's and women's sections and give men what she calls "clarity of offer," which is the peace of mind that they won't inadvertently end up in, say, women's undergarments. In a one-floor store, most retailers would rather put the menswear up front and the women's wear at the back (that is, if they weren't going to split the sexes left and right), because women don't get spooked navigating through apparel of the opposite sex, whereas men most assuredly do. (Of course, in a store like the Gap at Thirty-ninth and Fifth, where, Carrie Gennuso says, "I don't know if I've ever seen a man," the issue is moot. There, it's safe to put the women's wear out front.)

The next thing retailers want to do is to encourage the shopper to walk deep into the store. The trick there is to put "destination items"—basics, staples, things that people know you have and buy a lot of—at the rear of the store. Gap stores, invariably, will have denim, which is a classic destination item for them, on the back wall. Many clothing stores also situate the cash/wrap and the fitting rooms in the rear of the store, to compel shoppers to walk back into Zone 3 or 4. In the store's prime real estate—which, given Paco's theory of the Decompression Zone and the Invariant Right, is to the right of the front entrance and five to fifteen paces in—you always put your hottest and newest merchandise, because that's where the maximum number of people will see it. Right now, in virtually every Gap in the country, the front of the store is devoted to the Gap fall look—casual combinations in black and gray, plaid shirts and jackets, sweaters, black wool and brushed-twill pants. At the Gap at Fifth Avenue and Seventeeth Street, for example, there is a fall ensemble of plaid jacket, plaid shirt, and black pants in the first prime spot, followed, three paces later, by an ensemble of gray sweater, plaid shirt, T-shirt, and black pants, followed, three paces after that, by an ensemble of plaid jacket, gray sweater, white T-shirt, and black pants. In all, three variations on the same theme, each placed so that the eye bounces naturally from the first to the second to the third, and then, inexorably, to a table deep inside Zone 1 where merchandise is arrayed and folded for petting. Every week or ten days, the combinations will change, the "look" highlighted at the front will be different, and the entryway will be transformed.

Through all of this, the store environment—the lighting, the colors, the fixtures—and the clothes have to work together. The point is not so much beauty as coherence. The clothes have to match the environment. "In the nineteen-seventies, you didn't have to have a complete wardrobe all the time," Gabriella Forte, the president and chief operating officer of Calvin Klein, says. "I think now the store has to have a complete point of view. It has to have all the options offered, so people have choices. It's the famous one-stop shopping. People want to come in, be serviced, and go out. They want to understand the clear statement the designer is making."

At the new Versace store on Fifth Avenue, in the restored neoclassical Vanderbilt mansion, Gianni Versace says that the "statement" he is making with the elaborate mosaic and parquet floors, the marble façade and the Corinthian columns is "quality—my message is always a scream for quality." At her two new stores in London, Donna Karan told me, she never wants "customers to think that they are walking into a clothing store." She said, "I want them to think that they are walking into an environment, that I am transforming them out of their lives and into an experience, that it's not about clothes, it's about who they are as people." The first thing the shopper sees in her stark, all-white DKNY store is a video monitor and café: "It's about energy," Karan said, "and nourishment." In her more sophisticated, "collection" store, where the walls are black and ivory and gold, the first thing that the customer notices is the scent of a candle: "I wanted a nurturing environment where you feel that you will be taken care of." And why, at a Giorgio Armani store, is there often only a single suit in each style on display? Not because the store has only the one suit in stock but because the way the merchandise is displayed has to be consistent

30

with the message of the designers: that Armani suits are exclusive, that the Armani customer isn't going to run into another man wearing his suit every time he goes to an art opening at Gagosian.[3]

The best stores all have an image—or what retailers like to call a "point of view." The flagship store for Ralph Lauren's Polo collection, for example, is in the restored Rhinelander mansion, on Madison Avenue and Seventy-second Street. The Polo Mansion, as it is known, is alive with color and artifacts that suggest a notional prewar English gentility. There are fireplaces and comfortable leather chairs and deep-red Oriental carpets and soft, thick drapes and vintage photographs and paintings of country squires and a color palette of warm crimsons and browns and greens—to the point that after you've picked out a double-breasted blazer or a cashmere sweater set or an antique silver snuffbox you feel as though you ought to venture over to Central Park for a vigorous morning of foxhunting.

The Calvin Klein flagship store, twelve blocks down Madison Avenue, on the other hand, is a vast, achingly beautiful minimalist temple, with white walls, muted lighting, soaring ceilings, gray stone flooring, and, so it seems, less merchandise in the entire store than Lauren puts in a single room. The store's architect, John Pawson, says, "People who enter are given a sense of release. They are getting away from the hustle and bustle of the street and New York. They are in a calm space. It's a modern idea of luxury, to give people space."

The first thing you see when you enter the Polo Mansion is a display of two hundred and eight sweaters, in twenty-eight colors, stacked in a haberdasher's wooden fixture, behind an antique glass counter; the first thing you see at the Klein store is a white wall, and then, if you turn to the right, four clear-glass shelves, each adorned with three solitary-looking black handbags. The Polo Mansion is an English club. The Klein store, Pawson says, is the equivalent of an art gallery, a place where "neutral space and light make a work of art look the most potent." When I visited the Polo Mansion, the stereo was playing Bobby Short. At Klein, the stereo was playing what sounded like Brian Eno. At the Polo Mansion, I was taken around by Charles Fagan, a vice-president at Polo Ralph Lauren. He wore pale-yellow socks, black loafers, tight jeans, a pale-purple polo shirt, blue old-school tie, and a brown plaid jacket—which sounds less attractive on paper than it was in reality. He looked, in a very Ralph Lauren way, *fabulous*. He was funny and engaging and bounded through the store, keeping up a constant patter ("This room is sort of sportswear, Telluride-y, vintage"), all the while laughing and hugging people and having his freshly cut red hair tousled by the sales assistants in each section. At the Calvin Klein store, the idea that the staff—tall, austere, somber-suited—might laugh and hug and tousle each other's hair is unthinkable. Lean over and whisper, per-

---

[3]*Gagosian:* prominent art gallery in New York City. [Eds.]

haps. At the most, murmur discreetly into tiny black cellular phones. Visiting the Polo Mansion and the Calvin Klein flagship in quick succession is rather like seeing a "Howards End"–"The Seventh Seal" double feature.

Despite their differences, though, these stores are both about the same thing—communicating the point of view that shoppers are now thought to demand. At Polo, the "life style" message is so coherent and all-encompassing that the store never has the 1.33 items-per-purchase problem that Paco saw in the retailer he studied. "We have multiple purchases in excess—it's the cap, it's the tie, it's the sweater, it's the jacket, it's the pants," Fagan told me, plucking each item from its shelf and tossing it onto a tartan-covered bench seat. "People say, 'I *have* to have the belt.' It's a life-style decision." 35

As for the Klein store, it's really concerned with setting the tone for the Calvin Klein clothes and products sold *outside* the store—including the designer's phenomenally successful underwear line, the sales of which have grown nearly fivefold in the past two and a half years, making it one of the country's dominant brands. Calvin Klein underwear is partly a design triumph: lowering the waistband just a tad in order to elongate, and flatter, the torso. But it is also a triumph of image—transforming, as Gabriella Forte says, a "commodity good into something desirable," turning a forgotten necessity into *fashion*. In the case of women's underwear, Bob Mazzoli, president of Calvin Klein Underwear, told me that the company "obsessed about the box being a perfect square, about the symmetry of it all, how it would feel in a woman's hand." He added, "When you look at the boxes they are little works of art." And the underwear itself is without any of the usual busyness—without, in Mazzoli's words, "the excessive detail" of most women's undergarments. It's a clean look, selling primarily in white, heather gray, and black. It's a look, in other words, not unlike that of the Calvin Klein flagship store, and it exemplifies the brilliance of the merchandising of the Calvin Klein image: preposterous as it may seem, once you've seen the store and worn the underwear, it's difficult not to make a connection between the two.

All this imagemaking seeks to put the shopping experience in a different context, to give it a story line. "I wish that the customers who come to my stores feel the same comfort they would entering a friend's house—that is to say, that they feel at ease, without the impression of having to deal with the 'sanctum sanctorum' of a designer," Giorgio Armani told me. Armani has a house. Donna Karan has a kitchen and a womb. Ralph Lauren has a men's club. Calvin Klein has an art gallery. These are all very different points of view. What they have in common is that they have nothing to do with the actual act of shopping. (No one buys anything at a friend's house or a men's club.) Presumably, by engaging in this kind of misdirection designers aim to put us at ease, to create a kind of oasis. But perhaps they change the subject because they must, because they cannot offer an ultimate account of the shopping experience itself. After all, what do we really know, in the end, about why people

441

buy? We know about the Invariant Right and the Decompression Zone. We know to put destination items at the back and fashion at the front, to treat male shoppers like small children, to respect the female derrière, and to put the socks between the cash/wrap and the men's pants. But this is grammar; it's not prose. It is enough. But it is not much.

One of the best ways to understand the new humility in shopping theory is to go back to the work of William Whyte. Whyte put his cameras in parks and in the plazas in front of office buildings because he believed in the then radical notion that the design of public spaces had been turned inside out—that planners were thinking of their designs first and of people second, when they should have been thinking of people first and of design second.

In his 1980 classic, "The Social Life of Small Urban Spaces," for example, Whyte trained his cameras on a dozen or so of the public spaces and small parks around Manhattan, like the plaza in front of the General Motors Building, on Fifth Avenue, and the small park at 77 Water Street, downtown, and Paley Park, on Fifty-third Street, in order to determine why some, like the tiny Water Street park, averaged well over a hundred and fifty people during a typical sunny lunch hour and others, like the much bigger plaza at 280 Park Avenue, were almost empty. He concluded that all the things used by designers to attempt to lure people into their spaces made little or no difference. It wasn't the size of the space, or its beauty, or the presence of waterfalls, or the amount of sun, or whether a park was a narrow strip along the sidewalk or a pleasing open space. What mattered, overwhelmingly, was that there were plenty of places to sit, that the space was in some way connected to the street, and—the mystical circularity—that it was already well frequented. "What attracts people most, it would appear, is other people," Whyte noted:

> If I labor the point, it is because many urban spaces still are being designed as though the opposite were true—as though what people liked best were the places they stay away from. People often do talk along such lines, and therefore their responses to questionnaires can be entirely misleading. How many people would say they like to sit in the middle of a crowd? Instead, they speak of "getting away from it all," and use words like "escape," "oasis," "retreat." What people *do*, however, reveals a different priority.

Whyte's conclusions demystified the question of how to make public space 40
work. Places to sit, streets to enjoy, and people to watch turned out to be the simple and powerful rules for park designers to follow, and these rules demolished the orthodoxies and theoretical principles of conventional urban design. But in a more important sense—and it is here that Whyte's connection with Paco Underhill and retail anthropology and the stores that line Fifth and Madison is most striking—what Whyte did was to remystify the art of urban plan-

ning. He said, emphatically, that people could not be manipulated, that they would enter a public space only on their own terms, that the goal of observers like him was to find out what people wanted, not why they wanted it. Whyte, like Paco, was armed with all kinds of facts and observations about what it took to build a successful public space. He had strict views on how wide ledges had to be to lure passersby (at least thirty inches, or two backsides deep), and what the carrying capacity of prime outdoor sitting space is (total number of square feet divided by three). But, fundamentally, he was awed by the infinite complexity and the ultimate mystery of human behavior. He took people too seriously to think that he could control them. Here is Whyte, in "The Social Life of Small Urban Spaces," analyzing hours of videotape and describing what he has observed about the way men stand in public. He's talking about feet. He could just as easily be talking about shopping:

> Foot movements ... seem to be a silent language. Often, in a schmoozing group, no one will be saying anything. Men stand bound in amiable silence, surveying the passing scene. Then, slowly, rhythmically, one of the men rocks up and down; first on the ball of the foot, then back on the heel. He stops. Another man starts the same movement. Sometimes there are reciprocal gestures. One man makes a half turn to the right. Then, after a rhythmic interval, another responds with a half turn to the left. Some kind of communication seems to be taking place here, but I've never broken the code.

QUESTIONS

1. How would you describe the "science" that is the subject of this piece? Locate examples of the terminology of this science and of its methods of research.

2. How much research did Gladwell have to do to write this essay? How many people did he interview? How many stores did he visit? What sort of knowledge did he need to acquire and from what sources? Is there any indication that he enjoys shopping?

3. In paragraph 17, Gladwell raises the question of our anxiety regarding manipulation as consumers. How does he answer this question? Do you agree with his conclusions?

4. Apply some of Paco Underhill's methods of observation and data gathering to your favorite store, and write a report describing its layout and the effectiveness of its sales staff. Be sure to include a description of the store's point of view or lifestyle message.

5. Bring some of the observations of Paco Underhill and William Whyte to bear on a public space on your campus or in your city or town. Do you think the space was designed to appeal to people? Explain why or why not, and describe what might be done to improve it.

MAKING CONNECTIONS

In what ways would the information gathered by Monica M. Moore for her article "Nonverbal Courtship Patterns in Women" (p. 469) be useful to Paco Underhill were he asked to advise on the layout and design of a singles bar?

BABEL IN AMERICA
Or, The Politics of Language Diversity in the United States

Marc Shell

Marc Shell (b. 1947) is a professor of comparative literature and of English and American literature at Harvard University. The author of a number of books on literature, economics, politics, and nationhood, Shell has been the recipient of the prestigious MacArthur Fellowship Award. Among his recent publications are Children of the Earth: Literature, Politics, and Nationhood *(1993) and* Art and Money *(1995). In this essay, which originally appeared in the journal* Critical Inquiry *(1993), Shell approaches the controversial topic of an official national language through a provocative question.*

What really is the language of the United States?

The common American response to this question is to dismiss it as outlandishly naive and as lacking cultural or political significance. After all, isn't the United States, that land of immigrants, fundamentally English-speaking, or essentially anglophone?[1] Didn't founder John Jay, for example, insist in the *Federalist Papers* "that Providence has been pleased to give this one connected country, to one united people . . . speaking the same language"?[2] And isn't America's linguistic union one of the great historical feats of social language-engineering?[3]

The familiar rhetoric of inevitable linguistic union ranges from the humorous to the imperialistically oppressive. ("Melting pot, yes. Tower of Babel, no!" is the saying.)[4] And it still informs manifestly most studies of the politics of lan-

---

[1]*anglophone:* an English-speaking population [Ed.].

[2]John Jay writes "that Providence has been pleased to give this one connected country, to one united people; a people descended from the same ancestors, speaking the same language, professing the same religion" (Alexander Hamilton, James Madison, and John Jay, *The Federalist Papers: A Collection of Essays Written in Support of the Constitution of the United States,* ed. Roy P. Fairfield [Garden City, N.Y., 1966], p. 6).

[3]In this essay, I use the terms *America* and *United States* as near synonyms while at the same time examining the international and intranational political significance of how the rhetoric of the term *American*—indicating here the English language as spoken in the United States—takes the part for the whole (the United States for the Americas North and South, for example) or the one for the many (anglophone unilingualism for plurilingualism).

[4]Saul Bellow is perhaps wrongly reported to have said this about the goals of U.S. English, a group bent on making English the one and only official language of the U.S. Bellow has said that he is not a member of U.S. English (quoted in S. I. Hayakawa, *One Nation—Indivisible? The English Language Amendment,* excerpted as "The Case for Official English," in *Language Loyalties: A Source Book on the Official Language Controversy,* ed. James Crawford [Chicago, 1992], p. 100).

guage in America and histories of the anglicization of America.[5] That rhetoric serves, as we shall see, to obscure or explain away the facts that the revolutionary colonies were markedly polyglot,[6] that neither the Constitution of the United States nor other such official documents name an official language,[7] and that there is a crucial dialogue, nowadays generally submerged but nevertheless ready to surface, about whether the United States should have an official language—or several official languages—and, if so, which one.

What, besides the predilection to confuse America with the world before Babel, impels Americans to take the fiction of original American monoglottism for the reality of American polyglottism? What is the link between the impressive bilingualism of America's former population and its current population's high rate of illiteracy in even one language?

1. MANY LANGUAGES

The actual linguistic makeup of people inside and outside the often changing borders of the American colonies between 1750 and 1850 is relevant here. For if ever there were a polyglot place on the globe—other than Babel's spire—this was it. Here three continents—North America, Africa, and Europe[8]—met one another. This is the polyglot situation in America that, in 1789, Frenchmen reported.[9]

Inside the colonies at the time, there were not so many native English speakers as generally assumed. First, non-English European settlers made up

---

Compare Arthur M. Schlesinger's complaint: "The national ideal had once been *e pluribus unum.* Are we now to belittle *unum* and glorify *pluribus*? Will the center hold? or will the melting pot yield to the Tower of Babel?" (quoted in Werner Sollors, "*E Pluribus Unum;* or, Matthew Arnold Meets George Orwell in the Multiculturalism Debate," Working Paper, no. 53, for the John F. Kennedy-Institut für Nordamerikastudien at Freie Universität Berlin [1992]: 22).

[5]The telling silence about official language in America characterizes analyses from the left and right sides of the political spectrum. Both sides assume the hegemony of English as a fact of life and define the politics of language in the United States mainly in terms of the characteristics of a specifically American English. Among such analysts are Michael P. Kramer, *Imagining Language in America: From the Revolution to the Civil War* (Princeton, N.J., 1992), and David Simpson, *The Politics of American English 1776–1850* (New York, 1986); they fail to consider fully the significance of America's polyglot past and its unofficially official monoglottal present.

[6]See Shirley Brice Heath, "English in our Language Heritage," in *Language in the USA,* ed. Charles A. Ferguson and Heath (Cambridge, 1981), pp. 6–20. *polyglot:* speaking or writing several languages. [Eds.]

[7]However, it is worth recalling the following extenuating factors: (1) Various treaties with the Indians and the Spanish seem to have meant to guarantee some sort of official language parity with English; (2) the Constitution was translated into other languages; (3) as discussed below (section 7), in our own century there have been movements to make English the one official language. For translation of the Constitution into French, see Benjamin Franklin, letter to Robert R. Livingston, 22 July 1783, *Franklin: Writings,* ed. J. A. Leo Lemay (New York, 1987), p. 1071.

[8]And later Asia.

[9]See Richard W. Bailey, *Images of English: A Cultural History of the Language* (Ann Arbor, Mich., 1991), p. 102.

one quarter of the total white population.[10] (Two-fifths of Pennsylvania's population alone spoke German.)[11] Second, the languages of the Amerindian populations—called "Aborigines" by George Washington[12]—were numerous and widespread.[13] Third were the blacks, mostly slaves, with their many African languages, who numbered more than one-fifth of the total population.[14] (Had a slave the courage to speak his native language, punishment was sometimes severe; there are reports of blacks having their tongues removed.)

Outside the colonies too there were mostly non-English speakers, principally the various Amerindians and next the French and Spanish. Hence Thomas Jefferson suggested that Americans should travel to Canada in order to acquire a knowledge of French, and he emphasized that Spanish was an important influence in the New World. Of course, Jefferson's internationalist pose was partly a short-term strategy for a border-changing, expansionist period.[15] After the Louisiana Purchase (1803)—under President Jefferson—francophones were Americanized. A later example is the Treaty of Guadalupe Hidalgo (1848). By this treaty Mexico ceded almost half its territory to the United States, and language rights were supposed to devolve to the newly Americanized Spanish-speaking population.[16] (It is worth comparing here the language rights guaranteed to francophone Catholics by the British North America Act of 1867, which was for a century or more Canada's constitutive document.)

---

[10]See *The Federalist Papers*, pp. 287–88 n. 4. The linguistic "stock" of some of the white people of 1790 has been studied with some care; see American Council of Learned Societies, *Report of Committee on Linguistic and National Stocks in the Population of the United States*, in *The Annual Report of the American Historical Association*, 3 vols. (Washington, D.C., 1932), 1:103–441. Compare Jack Citrin, "Language Politics and American Identity," *The Public Interest* 99 (Spring 1990): 96–109.

[11]See American Council of Learned Societies, *Committee on Linguistic and National Stocks in the Population of the United States*, pp. 291–94. See also Frank Ried Diffenderffer, *The German Immigration into Pennsylvania through the Port of Philadelphia, 1770–1775* (Lancaster, Pa., 1990), pp. 102–6.

[12]George Washington, letter to the Marquis de Lafayette, 10 Jan. 1788, *The Writings of George Washington from the Original Manuscript Sources, 1745–1799*, ed. John C. Fitzpatrick, 39 vols. (Washington, D.C., 1931–44), 29:374.

[13]Their numbers, though probably great, are not known because the official census reports for Amerindians were ludicrously and inaccurately low.

[14]For black population figures, see Lisa A. Bull, "The Negro," in *The Ethnic Contribution to the American Revolution*, ed. Frederick Harling and Martin Kaufman (Westfield, Mass., 1976), pp. 67–74. The study of the process whereby slaves lost their various tribal languages (hence also a comparative history of those languages) has yet to be fully undertaken; but see Daniel C. Littlefield, *Rice and Slaves: Ethnicity and the Slave Trade in Colonial South Carolina* (Baton Rouge, La., 1981), and Guion Griffis Johnson, *A Social History of the Sea Islands, with Special Reference to St. Helena Island, South Carolina* (Chapel Hill, N.C., 1930), pp. 77–78.

[15]See R. Merritt Cox, "Thomas Jefferson and Spanish: 'To Every Inhabitant Who Means to Look beyond the Limits of His Farm,'" *Romance Notes* 14 (Autumn 1972): 116–21. Merritt focuses more on Spain than the local areas.

[16]By 1878 in New Mexico and Arizona—after the large influx of English speakers during the gold rush—Spanish language rights, if ever they existed, were rescinded. See Rodolofo Acuña, *Occupied America: The Chicano's Struggle toward Liberation* (San Francisco, 1972), p. 104.

447

2. ONE LANGUAGE

The polyglot situation in the newly constituted United States had its problems. How could people of one language get along with others? Thus Thomas Paine wrote, "if there is a country in the world where concord, according to common calculation, would be least expected, it is America. Made up, as it is, of people . . . speaking different languages."[17]

Concern for commercial and political concord, as well as an "enlightenment" search for affinity among languages or for a universal language—abetted by American missionaries' and presidents' research into Amerindian languages[18]—led to discussion, still itself little researched, about the need or desire to have only one language in America. A principal purpose of this research into the diversity of languages was thus generally to foster linguistic homogeneity rather than to encourage linguistic heterogeneity.[19]

The chief question was, of course, what *one* language should predominate   10
in America. The factors that militated for English are well known. The commercially dominant plurality of people were English speakers schooled in the rhetoric of the British Empire, and many believed in the manifest destiny of their own tongue. Not a few figured that English would soon become something like what Latin had been among Catholics or European intellectuals: a universal language.[20] In a letter to Noah Webster, Benjamin Franklin thus noted that one day English would outflank French as the universal secular language.[21]

---

[17] Quoted in Hayakawa, "The Case for Official English," p. 95.

[18] See note 19 below.

[19] The European settlers, including Thomas Jefferson, researched myriad languages of the Amerindians. See Alexander F. Chamberlain, "Thomas Jefferson's Ethnological Opinions and Activities," *American Anthropologist* 9 (July–Sept. 1907): 499–509. George Washington, in a letter to Lafayette with which he included a *Vocabulary of the Shawanese and Delaware Languages* compiled by Richard Butler, wrote that "to know the affinity of tongues seems to be one step towards promoting the affinity of nations" (Washington, letter to Lafayette, 10 Jan. 1788, p. 374). The compilers of Indian vocabularies were generally either military men or missionaries; Washington also sent Lafayette a book about Delaware Indian (and English) "spellings" by the Reverend David Zeisberger, a Moravian missionary (see ibid., p. 377). See also below, section 6, on the Amerindian languages.

[20] Thomas Paine reminds us of the religious aspect to the problem of unilingualism. He recalls the situation of Jesus: "But how was Jesus Christ to make anything known to all nations? He could speak but one language, which was Hebrew, and there are in the world several hundred languages. Scarcely any two nations speak the same language, or understand each other; and as to translations, every man who knows anything of languages knows that it is impossible to translate from one language into another, not only without losing a great part of the original, but frequently mistaking the sense" (Thomas Paine, *The Age of Reason*, in *The Life and Works of Thomas Paine*, ed. William M. Van der Weyde, 10 vols. [New Rochelle, N.Y., 1925], 8:42). Saint Paul, that great traveler, might say that in the New Dispensation there will be no longer Hebrew or Greek; but language differences are not transcended—except in silence or, in the "old" elevation, as uniquely sacred Hebrew (among the Jews) and, in the "new" elevation, as Roman imperial Latin or Christian Church Latin.

[21] Franklin, noting that the universal language of the eighteenth century was French, wrote that "our English bids fair to obtain the second Place" and expressed the conviction that one day it would be English that would be first (Franklin, letter to Noah Webster, 26 Dec. 1789, *Franklin*, p. 1175).

But there were also factors that militated against English. Thus some American republicans argued that independence from England—and from British imperialism—required independence from English. This notion, with its shades of English anti-Normanism, led to discussion of several strategies.[22] Some of these may seem bizarre, as we shall see, but the outlandishly successful social language-engineering projects in our own century—the miraculous Israeli renaissance of Hebrew, say, and the imperialist Russification of the Soviet colonies[23]—suggest that very few strategic proposals were preposterous and that all speak eloquently of their designers' hopes and fears.

First was the idea of starting a new language—something like Esperanto or Boontling (a unique language experiment in a California town).[24] *The Quarterly Review* commented, "Nor have [Americans] been wanting projects among them for getting rid of the English language . . . by substituting a new language of their own."[25] Second was the idea of the renaissance of an ancient language. Here Hebrew and Greek played roles. Concerning Hebrew—the language of that other "'chosen people'" (G, p. 12), founders of the famously tolerant and much discussed ancient "Hebrew commonwealth"[26]—one Frenchman, the Marquis de Chastellux, reported in the 1780s that "the Americans have carried [their anti-British aversion] so far, as seriously to propose introducing a new language; and some persons were desirous, for the convenience of the public,

---

[22]The English colonists' rebellious discussions of ridding the United States of the English language and concomitant English political institutions were themselves variations of English nationalist demands, common since Anglo-Norman times, that the English language be purged of its "foreign" elements, chiefly Norman, and that pure English become, as Edmund Spenser puts it, "the kingdom of our own language" (quoted in Richard Helgerson, Forms of Nationhood: The Elizabethan Writing of England [Chicago, 1992], p. 25). Hugh MacDougall points out that John Hare had argued for freedom from French, saying that English usages—and constitutive laws—of Norman origin should be "'devested of their French rages . . . be restored into the ["original"] English or Latine tongue.' All French words should be purged from the language and replaced with words and terms 'from the old Saxon and the learned tongues'" (Hugh A. MacDougall, Racial Myth in English History: Trojans, Teutons, and Anglo-Saxons [Montréal, 1992], p. 61).

[23]Concerning Stalin's Soviet empire: The political underdog generally conflates oppression by a conquering *people* with oppression by that people's *language*. Likewise the conqueror often argues that no language is inherently—that is, lexically or syntactically—oppressive. Stalin led a murderous experiment in social language-engineering and argued implicitly, in *Marxism and Linguistics*, that a new Russian unilingualism would help destroy economic inequalities. See Joseph Stalin, *Marxism and Linguistics*, trans. Margaret Schlauch (New York, 1951).

[24]Boontling was spoken from 1880 to 1920 in the area near Boonville (in northern California); it was not intelligible to outsiders. See Charles C. Adams, *Boontling: An American Lingo* (Austin, Tex., 1971). (*Esperanto*: an artificial language invented in 1887 and intended for international use. [Eds.])

[25]Quoted in Dennis E. Baron, *Grammar and Good Taste: Reforming the American Language* (New Haven, Conn., 1982), p. 12; hereafter abbreviated G.

[26]On ideas about the commonwealth in England and Amsterdam in the seventeenth century, see Marc Shell, "Marranos (Pigs), or from Coexistence to Toleration," *Critical Inquiry* 17 (Winter 1991): 306–35.

that the *Hebrew* should be substituted for the English. The proposal was, that it should be taught in the schools, and made use of in all public acts" (quoted in G, p. 12). Concerning ancient Greek, Charles Astor Bristed wrote in 1855 that "it is still on record that a legislator seriously proposed that the young republic should complete its independence by adopting a different language from that of the mother-country, 'the Greek for instance,' which proposition was summarily extinguished by a suggestion of a fellow representative [Roger Sherman of Connecticut, delegate to the Continental Congress and a member of the committee that drafted the Declaration of Independence] that 'it would be more convenient for us to keep the language as it was, and *make the English speak Greek*'" (quoted in G, pp. 12–13). Third were the modern languages. Among these was French, of which the etymologist Herbert Croft wrote in 1797 (in his *A Letter from Germany to the Princess Royal of England*, published in Hamburg) that "during the American revolution, the idea was started of revenging themselves on England, by rejecting its language and adopting that of France" (quoted in G, p. 12). And there was German, whose experience in the United States belies the widespread belief in America that there were no serious attempts to make the country or its states officially bilingual.[27]

3. OFFICIAL GERMAN

A brief history of the controversies surrounding German as official American language might begin with the biography of that quintessential American, Benjamin Franklin, ace newspaper publisher, book seller, and editor of the *The New England Courant*. He opened his own printing shop in 1724, at age eighteen, and operated the *Pennsylvania Gazette* as proprietor at twenty-three. In the early 1730s Franklin taught himself French, German, Italian, Spanish, and Latin. And he would seem to have believed enough in multilingualism to publish in 1732 the first German-language newspaper in North America, the *Philadelphische Zeitung*.[28]

However, Franklin's German newspaper failed, and "a better qualified German printer" cornered the German book market. The failure may have been critical for the subsequent linguistic history of Pennsylvania—if not the entire continent. Forever thereafter Franklin's writings about American "foreign"-language speakers took a sharply xenophobic turn. In 1750, for example, he complained that Pennsylvania "will in a few Years become a German colony: Instead of their

---

[27]For an example of the myth: "Despite persistent folklore promulgated by subsequent writers, there were no serious attempts to adopt some language other than English for the new nation" (Bailey, *Images of English*, p. 104).

[28]See Franklin. "The German Language in Pennsylvania," in *Language Loyalties*, p. 18 n.9. See also Oswald Seidensticker, *The First Century of German Printing in America, 1728–1830; Preceded by a Notice of the Literary Work of F. D. Pastorius* (Philadelphia, 1893).

Learning our Language, we must learn their's, or live as in a foreign country."[29] In "Observations Concerning the Increase of Mankind" (1751), he grumbled likewise about *"Palatine Boors"* who "swarm into our Settlements and . . . establish their Language"; he asked, "Why should *Pennsylvania*, founded by the *English*, become a Colony of Aliens, who will shortly be so numerous as to Germanize us instead of our Anglifying them, and will never adopt our Language or Customs any more than they can acquire our Complexion?" ("O," p. 401).[30] Even in 1784, in the face of the considerable distrust of Englishmen that one would expect in the revolutionary period, Franklin complained about "Foreigners of all Nations and Languages, who by their Numbers may drown and stifle the English," and he argued that only with such immigration of Englishmen would English "become in the course of two Centuries the most extensive Language in the World, the Spanish only excepted."[31]

It is unclear how much influence Franklin had, or how many shared his   15
views. But, whether thanks to English speakers' fear of another language's parity with English or to non-English speakers' desire for it, stories, with at least a germ of truth, began to circulate about how one or another language, usually German, "almost" became official. A Congressional committee recommended that "'it will be necessary that the laws be translated, and printed in the German language'" ("O," p. 399).[32] And an American German book reported about attempts at German language parity in Pennsylvania that "in the vote on this question: whether the dominant speech in the Assembly, in the courts, and in the records of Pennsylvania should be the German language—the votes were tied" (quoted in "O," p. 395).[33]

---

[29]Quoted in Robert A. Feer, "Official Use of the German Language in Pennsylvania," *Pennsylvania Magazine of History and Biography* 76 (Oct. 1952): 401; hereafter abbreviated "O." This passage is from Franklin, letter to James Parker, 20 Mar. 1750, *The Papers of Benjamin Franklin*, ed. Leonard W. Labaree et al., 29 vols. (New Haven, Conn., 1959–), 4:120.

[30]See Franklin's diatribe against the Germans in a letter to Peter Collinson, 9 May 1753, *The Papers of Benjamin Franklin*, 4:479–86. In the same tradition as Franklin, William Smith wrote in 1755 that "I know nothing that will hinder them, either from soon being able to give us Law and Language, or else, by joining with the *French*, to eject all the *English* Inhabitants" (quoted in "O," p. 402).

[31]Franklin, letter to William Strahan, 19 Aug. 1784, *Franklin*, p. 1102. Franklin offers the Irish of Pennsylvania as an example of how a minority group can dominate the government.

[32]The committee recommendation followed an incident in the Third Congress of the United States: "'a petition of a number of Germans, residing in the State of Virginia' was presented to the House of Representatives . . . 'praying that a certain proportion of the laws of the United States may be printed in the German language'" ("O," p. 398).

[33]In this same book the author, Franz Löhrer, says that "half of them [in the Assembly] were for the introduction of the German language, and this was certainly of great importance when one considers that here it was a question of making a German state where English had previously been the official language. Then the speaker of the Assembly, a Muhlenberg, through his vote, gave the decision in favor of the English language" ("O," p. 395). What was "involved was a request, made by a group of Virginia Germans, to have certain laws issued in German *as well as* in English. The proposal was rejected by [only] one vote" (David Crystal, *Cambridge Encyclopedia of Language* [Cambridge, 1987], p. 365). See also Heath and Frederick Mandabach, "Language Status Decision and the Law in the United States," in *Progress in Language Planning*, ed. Juan Cobarrius and Joshua A. Fishman (Berlin, 1983), pp. 87–105.

The German language remained a strong, unofficial presence in the United States throughout the nineteenth century. Many argued that anglophone Americans should learn German[34] and endorsed the view of Benjamin Rush, who argued that there should be a German-language college;[35] and bilingual schools were not unusual. But thanks partly to the hostilities of World War I and fears of a third column, anti-German and isolationist sentiment was strengthened. In 1916 it was made illegal even to teach many foreign languages in American schools![36] President Theodore Roosevelt, in his still influential 1917 appeal called "The Children of the Crucible," said that "we must . . . have but one language. That must be the language of the Declaration of Independence."[37]

The problem was partly one of "language loyalty."[38] Roosevelt, characterizing all Americans as willing immigrants, did not consider that blacks and Amerindians were, one way or another, conquered peoples. Nor did he mention the French, whose territory was bought from under them, nor the Dutch and Germans, who had been settlers before the signing of the Declaration of Independence.[39] More tellingly, Roosevelt did not consider the Spanish, for whom the Treaty of Guadalupe Hidalgo might have involved official language rights, or the bilingual constitution of New Mexico (1912), which actually partly provided those rights. (During debates in 1878 about whether the Spanish territories should become states, Spanish-Americans had been called simply

---

[34]Joseph Ehrenfried argued in 1834 that "the prevalence of the German language in many parts of the United States should form a powerful inducement of men in every situation of life to become, at least partially acquainted with it" (quoted by Heath, "English in Our Language Heritage," p. 11).

[35]Rush was a member of the Continental Congress and signer of the Declaration of Independence. See Benjamin Rush, *The Letters of Benjamin Rush*, ed. L. H. Butterfield, 2 vols. (Princeton, N.J., 1951), 1:356–66. See also Rush, *Information to Europeans Who Are Disposed to Migrate to the United States* (Philadelphia, 1790).

[36]See Edward Sagarin and Robert J. Kelly, "Polylingualism in the United States of America: A Multitude of Tongues amid a Monolingual Majority," in *Language Policy and National Unity*, ed. William R. Beer and James E. Jacob (Totowa, N.J., 1985), pp. 20–44. One might also consider here the conflict between the Germanic (Hegelian) philosophers of Missouri (as well as Ohio and Chicago) and the New England transcendentalists. See Carl Wittke, *German-Americans and the World War with Special Emphasis on Ohio's German-Language Press* (Columbus, Ohio, 1936). On the bilingual German schools, see Carolyn Toth, *German-English Bilingual Schools in America: The Cincinnati Tradition in Historical Context* (New York, 1990).

[37]Roosevelt continued, "The greatness of this nation depends on the swift assimilation of the aliens she welcomes to her shores" (Theodore Roosevelt, "The Children of the Crucible," excerpted as "One Flag, One Language," in *Language Loyalties*, p. 85).

[38]See Joshua A. Fishman, *Language Loyalty in the United States: The Maintenance and Perpetuation of Non-English Mother Tongues by American Ethnic and Religious Groups* (The Hague, 1966).

[39]On the long-term use of "Dutch" elsewhere than in Pennsylvania, see Philip E. Webber, *Pella Dutch: The Portrait of a Language and Its Use in One of Iowa's Ethnic Communities* (Ames, Iowa, 1988) and various linguistic histories of New York, once called "New Amsterdam."

"foreigners,"[40] but when the state constitution of New Mexico was finally ratified in 1912, Spanish-Americans were promised official language rights on a two-decade "trial basis.")[41] About these matters Roosevelt remained as silent as are most Americans—both anglophone and Spanish speaking—today.

President Roosevelt's wartime ideology—that the United States has to have only one language just as it has one flag and that this language must be English—has remained the effective unofficial view of America's political officers ever since. But, of course, more than the wartime xenophobia of World War I explains how the unofficial culture of English as the one official American language gained its considerable influence.

4. NON-ENGLISH AND DIALECT

Since 1750, we have seen, there had been a dialogue about whether there should be only one official language and which language that should be: English or one of the "foreign," that is, non-English languages, whether ancient or modern. The dialogue, barely recognizable, was sometimes expressed in the form of literary debates about whether the American language itself was not essentially a "foreign"—that is, non-English—language. This expression helps to explain the still-widespread phenomenon in America of treating the politics of language mainly in terms of changes, called politically symptomatic, to the English language. This phenomenon, like so much else, served to divert attention from the question of an official or national language.

To begin with, the view that the American language ought to become something essentially other than the English language seemed to involve notions about fundamental lexis, syntax, and even truth.[42] Early on, William Thornton wrote in *Cadmus* that American English should become a language of new political truth: "You have corrected the dangerous doctrines of European powers, correct now

---

[40]Thus we read in the record:

> Mr. Tinnin: We have here in the Capitol now tons and tons of documents published in Spanish for the benefit of foreigners.
> Mr. Rolfe: Do you call the native population of this State foreigners?
> [Quoted in *Language Loyalties*, p. 53]

[41]See U.S. Commission on Civil Rights, *The Excluded Student: Educational Practices Affecting Mexican Americans in the Southwest*, excerpted as "Language Rights and New Mexico Statehood," in *Language Loyalties*, p. 62. On the bilingualism of the older New Mexico constitutions, see New Mexico's constitutions in vol. 3 of *Constitutions of the United States, National and State*, 2d ed., eds. Mark Chen and F. Grad (New York, 1990), and Dorothy Cline, *New Mexico's 1910 Constitution: A Nineteenth-Century Product* (Santa Fe, N. Mex., 1985). The bilingual provision was renewed in 1931 and 1943 but was apparently omitted in 1949.

[42]Larzer Ziff writes that Americans at the time of the revolution had "inherited a medium shaped by centuries of monarchal government . . . encoded in its diction, syntax, and especially its literary conventions the values of hierarchal society" (quoted in David Bromwich, "When Books Are to Blame," review of *Writing in the New Nation: Prose, Print, and Politics in the Early United States* by Larzer Ziff, *Times Literary Supplement*, 22 May 1992, p. 13).

the language you have imported . . . The AMERICAN LANGUAGE will thus be as distinct as the government, free from all the follies of unphilosophical fashion, and resting upon truth as its only regulator."[43] But James Herron saw, in the polyglot heritage of the new republic, the possibility of creating a new language. Thus he wrote in *American Grammar* that "we express our own free thoughts in *language* our own, adopted from the tongues of the many nations, of our forefathers. . . . Consequently, LANGUAGE in the UNITED STATES is *Polyglot*—national with our people—not borrowed from any one distinct tongue" (quoted in G, p. 14). In this polyglot tradition, Noah Webster claimed that the United States "will produce, in a course of time, a language in North America, as different from the future language of England, as the modern Dutch, Danish and Swedish are from German, or from one another."[44]

Webster was wrong about this. And just why America did not develop as Webster envisioned is an interesting question in "sociolinguistics." Yet the thought of an apparently non-English American language emerging from polyglot populations in America was no more exotic than that of the United States or one of its states—say, Pennsylvania (German) or New Mexico (Spanish)—becoming officially bilingual. Moreover, the Americanist "assimilationist" vision of the "natural" metamorphosis of one language into another language—that is, the hypothesis of an American English language that would be both "foreign" and "familiar" to English—made it easier to forget the question, Why should English predominate? Now it could be said that it was not English that ruled, or would soon rule, but some new language.

In the ensuing years, Webster and his followers came to realize that the English language would predominate, or they now argued outright that it should. (The revisionist Webster now said that "our language is the *English* and it is desirable that the language of the United States and Great Britain should continue to be the same.")[45] And so, whereas once it had been said that the declared political separation from the English people meant also a linguistic separation from the English language, now everything became merely a matter of practical (supposedly "fonetic") spellings and the like.[46] Debate about

---

[43]Quoted in Geoffrey Nunberg. "The Official English Movement: Reimagining America," in *Language Loyalties*, p. 485.

[44]Quoted in Bailey, *Images of English*, p. 104. Webster also said that in the Federal Procession there was "a scroll, containing the principles of a [new] *Federal* language" (Webster, *The New York Packet*, 5, 1788).

[45]Noah Webster, *Dissertations on the English Language: With Notes, Historical and Critical*, excerpted as "Declaration of Linguistic Independence," in *Language Loyalties*, p. 35 n. 33. The two languages—English and American—should be the same, Webster wrote, "except so far as local circumstances, laws and institutions shall require a few particularities in each country" (ibid.).

[46]Webster's ideas for his "*Federal* English"—to which Adams, Franklin, Jefferson, and Madison contributed their notions—were not so "revolutionary" as the "fonetic" pronunciation-spellings used by some writers in France in the eighteenth century. William Thornton's proposed phonetic alphabet was sometimes discussed; see also Charles Jared Ingersoll, *Remarks on the Review of Inchinquin's Letters* (Boston, 1815), pp. 138–39; cited in G, p. 12.

official language was thus displaced into questions of dialect and race. Dialect as such became a popular subject and medium for anglophone fiction writers in America—Irving, Poe, Melville, Twain, and myriad others.

Comparing the language issue in an officially biracial United States and in an officially bilingual Québec may be helpful here for understanding the distinctive American linkage between dialect and race. Whereas in Québec the subject of dialect *supplemented* without supplanting that of language, in the unofficially monoglottal and officially biracial United States, an often-exclusive focus on dialect serves to mask the disappearance of actual languages.[47] Whereas some Québécois call themselves the *nègres* of Canada, refuse to "speak white"[48] (that is, English, *FrAnglais*, or *joual*—a quasi-dialect sometimes loosely translated as "French jive talk" or "French gumbo"), and try in various ways to return to "pure French," the once legally defined "group" of American blacks lost its various "original mother tongues" and adopted its "master's" language along with his religion. (The brutal Philomelan history has yet to be told thanks partly to a continuing failure on both sides[49]—"white" and "black"—to acknowledge fully as their inheritance the effective conditions of American race slavery. The failure is abetted and masked by diversions into such interesting and otherwise important topical areas as Africanisms in American English,[50] Gullah as an essentially African language rather than as an essentially English one,[51] syntactic similarities between Creole and African-American,[52] and African-American bidialectalism.)[53]

In Twain's properly unsettling and bidialectal *Pudd'nhead Wilson*, for example, the nursemother-slave Roxana looks white and is legally black (that is, she

---

[47]"As soon as I began to write," Gérald Godin had written in *Parti pris* in 1965, "I realized that I was a barbarian, i.e. a foreigner, according to the etymological meaning of the term. My mother tongue was not French but *franglais*. I had to learn French almost as a foreign language" (quoted in Lise Gauvin, "From Octave Crémazie to Victor-Lévy Beaulieu: Language, Literature, and Ideology," trans. Emma Henderson, *Yale French Studies*, no. 65 [1983]: 38–39). Gaston Miron discussed in 1973 the linguistic schizophrenia and alienation that informed the diseased cultural life of Québec; and briefly considering the "debilitating effects" of bilingual signs on the "purity" of the "French language," he had called for a new "linguistic decolonization" ("Décoloniser la langue: Interview/témoignage with Gaston Miron," *Maintenant* 125 [Apr. 1973]:12). Jacques Godbout had claimed similarly in 1975 that the "ideology" of *joual* was an "infantile disease of nationalism" (quoted in Gauvin, "From Crémazie to Victor-Lévy Beaulieu," p. 43).

[48]See Pierre Vallières, *Nègres blancs d'amérique: Autobiographie précoce d'un 'terroriste' québécois* (Paris, 1969); Kathy Mezei, "Speaking White: Literary Translation as a Vehicle of Assimilation in Québec," *Canadian Literature*, no. 117 (Summer 1988): 11–23; and Michèle Lalonde, "Speak White," *Change* 30–31 (Mar. 1977): 100–104. Malcolm X compares some American blacks' intention not to assimilate (with the white racial majority of the United States) to some French Canadians' intention not to assimilate (with the linguistic majority of Canada). See Malcolm X and Alex Haley, *The Autobiography of Malcolm X* (New York, 1965), p. 277.

[49]*Philomela*: in Greek mythology, the Athenian princess raped by her brother-in-law Tereus, who then cut out her tongue. [Eds.]

[50]On distinct Africanisms in African-American language, see *Africanisms in Afro-American Language Varieties*, ed. Salikoko S. Mufwene and Nancy Condon (Athens, Ga., 1993), which concerns the influence of African languages on English. Compare Joseph E. Holloway and Winifred K. Vass, *The African Heritage of American English* (Bloomington, Ind., 1993).

[51]On Gullah as a "language" or "dialect," see Charles W. Joyner, *Down by the Riverside: A South Carolina Slave Community* (Urbana, Ill., 1984), and on some of its social implications, see

has one-sixteenth black blood), but she is treated as *black* because she speaks black. Similarly, Roxana's changeling "Tom Driscoll" (né *Valet de Chambres*, in the "malapropriated" French of Mississippi planters) looks white and is legally black (that is, he has one-thirty-second black blood), but he is treated as *white* because he talks white. Finally, Roxana's master's changeling "*Valet de Chambres*" (né Tom Driscoll) looks white and is legally white (he has fully white blood), but, even after everyone learns he is "really" white, he is treated as black and thinks of himself as black because he talks black.[54] (America's often-prosperous elocution schools and best-selling elocution manuals offered to rid clients of just such foreign, regional, and black accents.)[55] Spanish *limpieza de sangre* [blood purity], adapted to the needs of the distinctively American institution of race slavery, thus infected America's peculiarly unspoken rhetoric of "language purity."[56]

5. LANGUAGE AND RACE

Mon pays, ce n'est pas un pays, c'est l'hiver.[57]
—GILLES VIGNEAULT

The rhetoric for speaking about language is, of course, often like that for 25
race. The linguistic and natural historians' term for genus and species are thus

---

my *Money, Language, and Thought: Literary and Philosophical Economies from the Medieval to the Modern Era* (Berkeley, 1982), chap. 1.

[52]See the views that "black English" is a type of Creole (*Verb Phrase Patterns in Black English and Creole*, ed. Walter F. Edwards and Donald Winford [Detroit, 1991]) and relevant views about its syntax (Edgar W. Schneider, *Morphologische und syntaktische Variablen im amerikanischen Early Black English* [Tuscaloosa, Fla., 1989]).

[53]Hanni U. Taylor, *Standard English, Black English, and Bidialectalism: A Controversy* (New York, 1991).

[54]Compare David R. Sewell, *Mark Twain's Languages: Discourse, Dialogue, and Linguistic Variety* (Berkeley, 1987) and Shelley Fisher Fishkin, *Was Huck Black? Mark Twain and African-American Voices* (New York, 1993). In his Uncle Remus stories, Joel Chandler Harris blended everyone—both "black" and "white"—into a society of dialectally like-speaking humanoid "brethren." (The word *brer* in such names as Brer Rabbit and Brer B'ar means "brother.")

[55]A few examples of early general manuals may be helpful here. Noah Webster's *Grammatical Institute of the English Language (Pt. 3)*, 3d ed. (Philadelphia, 1787) already included in its subtitle "rules in elocution, and directions for expressing the principal passions of the mind." John Walker's *Elements of Elocution* includes "copper-plates explaining the nature of accent" (Boston, 1810). John Frost's *The American Speaker* (Philadelphia, 1839) likewise announces its stress "on pronunciation, pauses, inflections, accent, and emphasis" and its goal "to improve the pupil in . . . recitation." See also William Russell, *The American Elocutionist; Comprising 'Lessons in Enunciation', 'Exercises in Elocution', and 'Rudiments of Gesture'* (Boston, 1844). Closer to Twain's period, see Alexander Melville Bell, *Elocutionary Manual: The Principles of Elocution*, 4th ed. (Salem, Mass., 1878), with its focus on, as its subtitle has it, "the principles of elocution, with exercises and notations for pronunciation, intonation, emphasis, gesture and emotional expression," and Loomis J. Campbell, *The New Franklin Fourth Reader* (New York, 1884).

[56]See Shell, "Marranos (Pigs)."

[57]My country is not a country, it's winter.

often the same,[58] and, as Charles Darwin puts it, "the proofs that [different languages and distinct species] have been developed through a gradual process, are curiously the same."[59] Despite various intelligent protests about this rhetoric,[60] nineteenth-century ideologies of linguistic historiography (Grimm), in their dialectics of universal-particular and terminus-origin, differ little from those of species historiography (Darwin) or racial historiography (Gobineau).[61] The common sentiment remains that "language is by itself the nearest approach to a perfect test of national extraction."[62]

How language mediates the politics of race or nationhood in North America depends on whether the state is essentially unilingual or multilingual. On the one hand, there are purportedly unilingual places where citizens generally have political rights (including that of "free speech") as individuals rather than as members of one or another particular linguistic or racial group. Thus every

---

[58]Even the term *Aryan*, once applied only to language families—as in Thomas Young's article in *The Quarterly Review* (1813)—came to be applied also to biological groupings. Language thus became a test for race.

[59]Charles Darwin, *The Descent of Man, and Selection in Relation to Sex* (1871; Princeton, N.J., 1981), p. 59.

[60]Thus Max Müller, recanting some of his earlier views, wrote in 1888 that "to me an ethnologist who speaks of an Aryan race, Aryan blood, Aryan eyes and hair, is as great a sinner as a linguist who speaks of a *dolichocephalic* dictionary or a *barchycephalic* grammar. It is worse than a Babylonian confusion of tongues—it is downright theft. We [linguists] have made our own terminology for the classification of languages; let ethnologists make their own for the classification of skulls, and hair, and blood" (Max Müller, *Biographies of Words and the Home of the Aryas* [London, 1888], pp. 120–21).

[61]Thus many natural historians have hypothesized a human "monogenesis"—one genetic origin of all presently living human beings, sketching a family tree that illustrates a supposed divergence of humankind from a single DNA stock. The hypothesis of "'Eve, mother of all humankind'" in the logic of this natural history (Robert Wright, "Quest for the Mother Tongue," *Atlantic Monthly* 267 [Apr. 1991]: 64; see also Philip E. Ross, "Hard Words," *Scientific American* 264 [Apr. 1991]: 138–47, and compare Gen. 4:20—"The man called his wife's name Eve, because she was mother of all living things"), like the apostle's claim that "God made of one blood all the peoples of this earth" in the logic of Christian kinship (Acts 17:26; compare John 3:16) and in some versions of American abolitionist rhetoric, is both comfortingly unitarian ("All men are my consanguineous kin") and critically divisive ("Only my consanguineous kin are brothers, all others are animals"). Many historical linguists likewise hypothesize a single original source or locale for all human languages, some claiming to "have reconstructed the ancestor of all living languages" (Vitaly Shevoroshkin, "The Mother Tongue: How Linguists Have Reconstructed the Ancestor of All Living Languages," *The Sciences* 30 [May/June 1990]: 20–28); this was, of course, the pre-Babel, Ur language that seventeenth-century theorists called Adamic, the "language" that modern linguists sometimes call Nostratic. See David S. Katz, *Philo-Semitism and the Readmission of the Jews to England, 1603–1655* (Oxford, 1982), esp. chap. 2. Belief in the historical existence of this unitarian language is "a kind of religion" that "emphasize[s] the unity of humankind and the need of brotherhood" (Juha Janhunen, quoted in Wright, "Quest for the Mother Tongue," p. 48). On the racialist rhetoric of German romantic linguistics in the eighteenth and nineteenth centuries, see also Martin Bernal, *The Fabrication of Ancient Greece, 1785–1985*, vol. 1 of *Black Athena: The Afroasiatic Roots of Classical Civilization* (New Brunswick, N.J., 1987), pp. 224–72. On Gobineau, see Shell, *Children of the Earth: Literature, Politics, and Nationhood* (Oxford, 1992), pp. 178–79, 276 n. 15.

[62]William Stubbs, *The Constitutional History of England in Its Origin and Development*, 3 vols. (1870; Oxford, 1891), 1:7.

American universally has the same de facto right to go to school or to argue in court, but there is no constitutionally or officially *guaranteed* right in the United States to attend school or to plead in court in the language of one's choice, if one's choice is *not* English—perhaps, officially, even if one's choice is English. American courts do sometimes grant permission to plead in a non-English language, especially where there are many people who speak Spanish, but when differences between the meaning of the law as written in English and its meaning in the non-English translation appear, the courts make their disposition according to the "original" English.

On the other hand, there are such North American places as Québec.[63] Québec heeds the group rights of Canada's two constitutive nations (variously called English-speakers and French-speakers, or Protestants and Catholics, or British stock and French stock), generally subordinating the rights of these two official groups *both* to the individual rights of any particular citizen *and* to the group rights, if any, of linguistic, religious, and racial groups other than the official two. In this respect, Québec differs from the United States, which generally heeds the equal rights of individuals as members of one ideally unilingual nation, generally subordinating the status of citizens as members of particular linguistic groups, unless their group is the anglophone one. (Exceptionally or not, the United States does grant to some people, as members of groups, an anomalous treatment under the law. The fact that Hispanics are covered by various affirmative action rulings tends to lessen the difference in American ideology between race and language; the term *Hispanic* seems to indicate now a racial group, now a linguistic one.)

Official bilingualism in Québec has included the constitutive right of members of the two "originary" national groups, Protestants and Catholics, to attend schools in their respective religions. (There are no purely "secular" schools of the American sort.)[64] On the basis of this right, guaranteed by the British North America Act (1867), Protestant and Catholic leaders argued successfully that they had the derivative right to attend school in their respective language, Protestants being generally English-speaking and Catholics French-speaking.[65] Further, they asserted the religious and linguistic rights of the groups of persons who are British "blood stock," or *brittanique de souche*, and who are French Canadian "blood stock," or *québécois de souche*.

---

[63]For relevant details about the language issue in Québec, see Shell, *Children of the Earth*, esp. chap. 3, "The Road Not Taken in Québec," and "La Publicité bilingue au Québec: Une Langue fourchue," *Journal canadien de recherche sémiotique* 5, no. 2 (1977): 55–76.

[64]The Québec government's Parent Act of 1964 introduced a few supposedly nonconfessional (or secular) schools. Various governments since then have tried to secularize the entire school system.

[65]In this same vein Martin Luther wrote in 1518 that "I thank God that I am able to hear and find my God in the German language, Whom neither I nor you could ever find in Latin or Greek or Hebrew" (quoted in Arno Borst, *Der Turmbau von Babel: Geschichte der Meinungen über Ursprung und vielfalt der Sprachen und Völker*, 4 vols. in 6 [Stuttgart, 1957–63], 3:1:1006).

One way to understand the nationalist workings of such states as Québec is to ask, What happens to those "immigrants" to Québec who are, by racial or linguistic generation, neither French-speaking nor English-speaking, or neither "English" nor "French"?[66] The answer tempers unrealistic enthusiasms for the Canadian cultural "mosaic" or "salad." In the United States, diverse immigrants all become American citizens by virtue of the civic ritual of naturalization (they are reborn or regenerated fictively as American: *e pluribus unum*); in Québec all immigrants become members of one official group *or* the other. Official *nationhood* in Québec thus has a bi- or multilateral meaning.

In Québec in the 1980s, for example, immigrants from non-English-speaking countries (called allophones) and those from most English-speaking countries (anglophones) were classified, for educational and taxation purposes, as "French" (francophone). This meant that a person with Greek-speaking, Greek Orthodox parents was "francophone," and by the same legal *fiction*, a monolingual English-speaking person from Singapore who was not *britannique de souche* was classified as "francophone." By a similar fiction, Jews in Québec were generally classified as "English Protestants" (and so attended Protestant schools) even when they were, like the Morocco-born Sephardim, "native" French- or Arabic-speakers.[67] The fact that the Jews of Montréal, whether European Ashkenazim or African Sephardim, both constituted something like one nation as a *group* (with one sacred written language) and spoke various native languages besides French or English as *individuals*, tended discomfortingly to challenge the thesis, dear to European linguistic nationalists, that a common spoken language is the main distinguishing characteristic of nationhood.

6. THE VEIL OF CULTURAL DIVERSITY

Out of an anxiety about cultural dependence on the English "mother tongue" and a romantic competition with English writers, anglophone American writers and literary critics have fabricated the idea of American as a primary—even independent—language and literature.[68] (This American fabrication contrasts with the Canadian experience. The latter involves the dependence both of the English language and of the French language on their respective "mother countries," Britain and France—a dependence fostered and

---

[66]On routing of Montréal's "ethnic minorities" into French language schools, see Conseil de la langue française, *Vivre la diversité en français: Le Défi de l'école française à clientèle pluriethnique de l'île de Montréal* (Québec, 1987). For an analysis of "immigrant anglicisation" and the *commission des écoles catholiques de Montréal* in the 1980s (as seen from the viewpoint of the Italian community), see Donat J. Taddeo and Raymond C. Taras, *Le Débat linguistique au Québec* (Montréal, 1987). On Montréal's efforts at the trilingual education of "Néo-Canadiens," see Michael D. Behiels, "The Commission des écoles catholiques de Montréal and the Neo-Canadian Question: 1947–63," *Canadian Ethnic Studies* 13, no. 2 (1986): 38–64.

[67]In previous decades some members of the Jewish community, including the "Bundists," had favored the assimilationist tendencies of this arrangement.

[68]See Walt Whitman, *An American Primer*, ed. Horace Traubel (Boston, 1904).

abetted by the competition within Québec itself between English and French. That is why there is no Canadian national literature in the American sense of the term.)

Anglophone Americans' various fictive idealizations of an independent American language buttressed the spectacular development in the United States of a distinctly monoglottal and linguistically amnesic national literature and culture. For neither in literature nor in American politics generally did the question of official language assert itself successfully. Among American French and American German writers the story is different, but despite the plethora of their books in America's parish churches and great public and private libraries, their work is little studied by scholars in the institutionalized academic discipline called American language and civilization. In many American universities, professors of literature still say that nonanglophone American literature — American German, say, or American Chinese — belongs properly neither to departments of foreign languages nor to departments of English and American language and literature.

The American academy's passing over most nonanglophone American languages and literatures is, of course, partly explicable by the fact that it is easier to talk about other peoples' cultures in English than to learn other people's talk. But the main explanation is that America, faltering always between its horror of race slavery and its ideal of race blindness, has always liked to emphasize racial difference instead of language difference. The contrast between emphasizing cultural diversity and deemphasizing language difference arises from the traditional American pretense that culture is not largely linguistic or, rather, that culture ought to be English.[69] The monoglottal Tereus fears the nightingale's song.[70]

Even as the American university claims to foster a tolerant heterogeneity of cultures, then, it perseveres in the traditional American homogenization of the world as English. At Hampshire College in Amherst, for example, one third of the curriculum is devoted to courses in "cultural diversity," but there is not a single foreign language course. Such obliviousness to how Hispanic literature written in translation is still Anglo — the name Hispanics sometimes give to monoglottal "white" anglophones — serves to obscure the fact of an ineradicable tension, crucial to understanding American ideology, between the argument that other languages should be assimilated to English and the argument that they really cannot be assimilated because, as Herder suggested, culture *is* (essentially) language. This is the tension informing thoughtful American writ-

---

[69]See Johann Gottfried Herder's suggestion that the essential "constituent" in national *culture* is language: "Jede Nation spricht also, nach dem sie denkt, und denkt, nach dem sie spricht" (Johann Gottfried Herder, *Über die neüre Deutsche Litteratur: Fragmente erste Sammlung* [1768], *Sämmtliche Werke*, ed. Bernhard Suphan, 33 vols. [Berlin, 1877–1913], 2:18). See also Herder, pt. 1 of *Ideen zur Philosophie der Geschichte der Menschheit* (1784), *Sämmtliche Werke*, 13:354–66.

[70]*Tereus*: in Greek mythology, the Thracian prince who raped Philomela and cut out her tongue. She was transformed into a nightingale. [Eds.]

ers in a tradition extending from Roger William's *Key into the Language of America* (1643) to Benjamin Whorf's *Language, Thought, and Reality* (1956), in which "standard average European" is compared with the language of the Hopi.[71] (Much relevant anthropological, linguistic, and missionary investigation similarly concerns "culturally" non-European aspects of the languages of Amerindian tribes and thus often seems, like Whorf's book itself, ventriloquistically to transform American silence about Amerindian genocide into something like the whisper of America.)[72]

It is useful here to compare the academic fields of literary criticism in the United States and Québec. On the one hand, few American literary critics work on the vast multilingual literature of the United States. Most simply raise up English-language works written by Philomelan members of America's various "ethnic" and "racial" groups—often in the name of multicultural diversity—even as they erase, or put down, American literary works written in languages other than English. Thus they encourage reading English-language literature by Americans of Chinese "ethnicity" but don't bother with Chinese-language American literature.[73]

When scholars in the field of American studies, so called, do read nonanglophone American writings in the "original" language, they still generally exhibit distinctly monolingual methodological tendencies; they treat American German literature as a discretely non-American entity,[74] for example, or they provide a five hundred-year history of an unrealistically remote Spanish litera-

35

---

[71]Whorf's teacher Edward Sapir had served as head of anthropology at the Canadian Museum (1910–25) before becoming professor of anthropology and linguistics at the University of Chicago (1925–31) and Yale (1931–39), where he met Whorf. Sapir, author of the influential *Language* (New York, 1921), was German-born (in Pomerania, now Poland), as was Franz Boas, the influential scholar of British Columbia's Amerindians. (Boas ultimately made his career as professor at Columbia from 1899.) Boas worked to refute eugenic theories of the time and to preserve details of cultures becoming extinct; his books include *Handbook of American Indian Languages* (Washington, D.C., 1911) and *Race, Language, and Culture* (New York, 1940).

[72]See especially Jonathan Edwards, *Observations on the Language of the Muhhekaneew Indians; in which the Extent of that Language in North-America is Shewn; its Genius is Grammatically Traced; some of its Peculiarities, and Some Instances of Analogy between that and the Hebrew are Pointed Out* (New Haven, Conn., 1788). For the many works written in the Amerindian languages themselves, see Robert Kruse, *The Henry Rowe Schoolcraft Collection: A Catalogue of Books in Native American Languages in the Library of the Boston Athenaeum* (Boston, 1991). Being encouraged by economic or political circumstances—and sometimes being compelled by law—to speak a language other than one's own, at least in the public sphere, is part of the experience of most nonanglophone immigrants. Some critics of this ambiguously involuntary anglicization call it cultural or linguistic genocide. However, a better analogy than genocide would be forced conversion.

[73]Sollors, *Beyond Ethnicity: Consent and Descent in American Culture* (Oxford, 1986) has barely a word to say about linguistic difference and official language, but see *Ethnicity and Language*, ed. Winston A. Van Horne (Milwaukee, 1987).

[74]See Robert Elmer Ward, *A Bio-Bibliography of German-American Writers, 1670–1970* (White Plains, N.Y., 1985); Brent Orlyn Peterson, *Popular Narratives and Ethnic Identity: Literature and Community in Die Abendschule* (Ithaca, N.Y., 1991); and Stephen Clausing, *English Influence on American German and American Icelandic* (New York, 1986).

ture of New Mexico,[75] or they depict American Yiddish as a language basically disconnected from American English.[76] (Not surprisingly, non-American students of American literature have often been better at this sort of work: European, Canadian, and Chinese scholars have made important contributions.)[77]

Tellingly, the American brand of comparative literature, so called, has been domesticated in such a way that, despite its multilingualism and its historical origin (at the beginning of the nineteenth century) in problems of linguistic and national difference, it generally avoids studying the linguistically multifaceted American literary experience and sometimes even serves to conceal that experience. The problem here is not so much that Americanized comparative literature has become a political rest home for professorial refugees and discards from linguistically unilingual literature departments (although, of course, in some cases it has). The problem is rather that professors project uncritically the linguistically homogenized domestic agenda of the United States onto the screens of faraway literary theories and national differentiations.

Among scholars in Québec, on the other hand, the emphasis is tellingly bifocal almost to the point of myopia. Here there is not only the traditional literary history of Québec's various languages and literatures. There is also a fascination with diglossia (as in such works as Anne Hébert's *Kamouraska*),[78] a

---

[75]See several essays in *Pasó por aquí: Critical Essays on the New Mexican Literary Tradition, 1542–1988*, ed. Erlinda Gonzales-Berry (Albuquerque, N. Mex., 1989). As Heinz Kloss argues, "the entire life of New Mexico is colored by the coexistence of these two language groups," that is, Spanish and English (Heinz Kloss, *American Bilingual Tradition* [Rowley, Mass., 1977], p. 126); however, it would be worth considering also the role of the unofficial languages, that is, the so-called native American languages, in a quasi-bilingual New Mexico as in an officially bilingual Québec.

[76]Yiddish might provide a good case study, thanks in part to Henry James's *American Scene* in which he writes concerning the possible effects of Yiddish on English that "the accent of the very ultimate future, in the States, may be destined to become the most beautiful on the globe . . . ; but whatever we shall know it for, certainly, we shall not know it for English—in any sense for which there is existing literary measure" (Henry James, *The American Scene* [1907; New York, 1946], p. 139). See also Cynthia Ozick, "Envy; or, Yiddish in America," *The Pagan Rabbi and Other Stories* (New York, 1971), pp. 39–100.

[77]For American German, see Sigrid Bauschinger, *Die Posaune der Reform: Deutsche Literatur im Neuengland des 19. Jahrhunderts* (Bern, 1989). For American "Dutch": Kurt Rein, *Religiöse Minderheiten als Sprachgemeinschaftsmodelle: Deutsch Sprachinseln täufer ischen Ursprungs in den Vereinigten Staaten von Amerika* (Wiesbaden, 1977). For American Spanish: Antonio Blanco S., *La lengua española en la historia de California: Contribución a su estudio* (Madrid, 1971); Yves-Charles Grandjeat et al., *Écritures hispaniques aux États-Unis: Mémoires et mutations* (Aix-en-Provence, 1990); *European Perspectives on Hispanic Literature of the United States*, ed. Geneviève Fabre (Paris, 1986); and parts of *Spanish in the United States: Sociolinguistic Aspects*, ed. Jon Amastae and Lucía Elías-Olivares (New York, 1982). For American Chinese: Mimi Chan and Helen Kwok, *A Study of Lexical Borrowing from Chinese into English with Special Reference to Hong Kong* (Hong Kong, 1985). For North America as a whole: Gilles Bibeau, *L'Éducation bilingue en Amérique du Nord* (Montréal, 1982), and Fernand Baldensperger, *Note sur les moyens d'action intellectuelle de la France à l'étranger* (Paris, 1917).

[78]On this aspect of Anne Hébert's *Kamouraska* (Paris, 1970), see, among others, Ben-Z. Shek, "Diglossia and Ideology: Socio-Cultural Aspects of 'Translation' in Québec," *Études sur le texte et ses transformations: Traductions et Cultures* 1, no. 1 (1988): 85–91. *diglossia:* formal and informal versions of a language coexisting in a society. [Eds.]

scholarly respect for *joual* together with the old distrust of it, a rejuvenating interest in the theory of translating French texts that contain English words into English and translating English texts that contain French words into French (as in such works as Jacques Poulin's *Volkswagen Blues*),[79] much concern with the role of so-called *transfuge* writers,[80] a still-growing movement to increase the number of French anthologies of English writers,[81] and a renewing focus on publishing bilingual journals.[82]

It would be tempting here to look outside the American academy to such popular American counterparts to these critical Québecois tendencies as the contemporary bilingual novel of the American Southwest[83] and the multilingual—Spanish, English, and Haitian French—rap or hip-hop of Miami.[84] But American popular culture has always been *just* beginning to comprehend its own multilingual elements. And American cultural criticism, in its inability or unwillingness to recognize America's centuries-long negotiations with such issues (or in its buoyant service to the national anglophone identity of the American literary tradition), still turns a blind eye to America's past—and its future.

7. A CONCLUSION

What the United States evidences nowadays is both a continual rise in the 40 number of non-English speakers and a unilingual policy without overt official sanction.[85] Any social or intellectual movement towards official bilingualism—

---

[79]The Volkswagen in this Québecois author's French novel has the Heideggerian inscription "Die Sprache ist das Haus des Seins" (Jacques Poulin, *Volkswagen Blues* [Montréal, 1984], p. 85; trans. Sheila Fischman, under the title *Volkswagen Blues* [Toronto, 1988]). Compare Mezei, "Speaking White."

[80]Pierre Monette, "Mon français mais Montréal," in *L'Avenir du français au Québec*, ed. Jacques Folch-Ribas (Montréal, 1987), p. 115. Monette, author also of *Traduit du jour le jour* (Montréal, 1978), points out that "la plupart des écrivains majeurs sont des transfuges" (ibid.). (*transfuge*: fugitive, deserter. [Eds.])

[81]See Paul Morisset, "La Face cachée de la culture québécoise," in *Le Québec en textes: Anthologie 1940–1986*, ed. Gérard Boismenu, Laurent Mailhot, and Jacques Rouillard (Montréal, 1986), pp. 531–38.

[82]See the bilingual journals *Vice Versa, Montréal Now,* and *Ellipse.*

[83]See Cormac McCarthy's novel *All the Pretty Horses* (New York, 1992), one part of *The Border Trilogy.* Set in Texas and Mexico, this book includes a good deal of Spanish.

[84]On Miami's current multilingualism generally, see *Miami Now! Immigration, Ethnicity, and Social Change*, ed. Guillermo Grenier and Alex Stepick (Gainesville, Fla., 1992).

[85]In the 1980s, the total number of United States residents five years old and over who spoke a language other than English at home rose by 14 percent to 31,845,000 in 1990. The number of people who speak Spanish and French—the two most frequently spoken non-English languages—rose by 50.1 percent to 17,339,000 and by 8.3 percent to 1,703,000 respectively. (The figure for French speakers includes French Canadians in New Hampshire and Maine, but it does not include Haitian Creole-speakers, whose number rose by 65.4 percent to 188,000 or Louisiana Cajun-speakers.) It is not only the rate of immigration (50.1 percent) that explains the high number of Spanish speakers. (Some immigrant groups have higher rates of immigration: Chinese up 97.7 percent to 1,249,000, Tagalog up 88.6 percent to 843,000, Korean up 127.2 percent to 626,000, and Vietnamese up 149.5 percent to 507,000.) It is also the feeling that Spanish has a certain staying

legally mandated bilingualism in court, say, with equally weighted versions of the law—would have little positive means of expression in current culture. (It does have a negative means, however, as when the self-styled "Japanese-American" former senator S. I. Hayakawa, in a legal tradition dating back to 1923, introduced a bill to make English the one and only official language of the country.)[86] Moreover, legislative bills with doublespeak misnomers like Bilingual Education Act—bills that turn out to mean something like "help for the linguistically disabled"[87]—divert public attention from official language as much as does talk about quirkily "regional" literary traditions. And, for many Americans, caught up in problems of civil warring and an almost official biracialism, the example of an always apparently dividing, officially bilingual Canada looms as a warning against any experiments in bilingualism. (Thus Edward A. Steiner wrote in 1916 that "a cleavage in the language [of the United States] now would mean to us a cleavage of the nation in its most vulnerable if not in its most essential part.")[88] So it is that a country once polyglot, with thousands of bilingual schools, has become unilingual, barely, in the twentieth century.[89]

More startling than American lack of intellectual concern with official bilingualism is the lack of political interest in the problems and opportunities of actual multilingualism. After all, America's longstanding attempts to decentralize

---

power deriving, on the one hand, from the feeling in some parts of the country—principally such border states as New Mexico and California, with 33.5 percent and 31.5 percent non-English speakers—that enough people already speak Spanish to make the language self-sustaining" and, on the other hand, from the belief that Spanish speakers have a historical "right" to the land. A similar belief may help account for the rise in the number of French speakers and of Navaho speakers (up 20.6 percent to 149,000).

[86]Hayakawa, a former senator from California, proposed the constitutional amendment that would have made English the official language of the United States. See Jon Stewart, "Saving America from Foreign Tongues," *Seattle Post-Intelligencer*, 31 May 1981, p. B2. For a discussion of this amendment, see Hayakawa, *One Nation—Indivisible?* The twentieth-century legal movement to make "American" the official language of the United States dates from about 1923, when Congressman Washington J. McCormick introduced a bill to Congress that, though it died in committee, was later adopted by Illinois. See Washington J. McCormick, "'American' as the Official Language of the United States," in *Language Loyalties*, pp. 40–41. The 1986 debate about California's English Language Amendment is exemplary. During the debate, Richard D. Lamm argued that "we should be color-blind but linguistically cohesive" (Richard D. Lamm, "English Comes First," *New York Times*, 1 July 1986, p. 23); compare Lamm and Gary Imhoff, *The Immigration Time Bomb: The Fragmenting of America* (New York, 1985); on the other side, the American Civil Liberties Union stated that it does not "believe that the ability to be protected by the State Constitution should be dependent upon proficiency in English" (quoted in Marcia Chambers, "California Braces for Change with English as Official Language," *New York Times*, 26 Nov. 1986, p. 20).

[87]On "bilingual education" see, among others, Alfred Bruce Gaarder, *Bilingual Schooling and the Survival of Spanish in the United States* (Rowley, Mass., 1977); Joshua A. Fishman et al., *Bilingualism in the Barrio: The Measurement and Description of Language Dominance in Bilinguals* (1968; New York, 1971); *The New Bilingualism: An American Dilemma*, ed. Martin Ridge (New Brunswick, N.J., 1981); and perhaps Nathan Glazer, *Towards a Bilingual Democracy?* (Chicago, 1982). See too Fishman, "Bilingualism and Separatism," *The Annals of the American Academy of Political and Social Science* 487 (Sept. 1986): 169–80.

[88]Quoted in Heath, "English in Our Language Heritage," p. 8.

[89]This is the regular condition, we say, of "developing" nations. See *Language Problems of Developing Nations*, ed. Fishman, Charles A. Ferguson, and Jyotirindra Das Gupta (New York, 1968).

political power by "balancing" one power against another would seem almost to make official bilingualism palatable. (Such bilingualism would mean that the Spanish version of the Constitution would have equal "weight" with the English version; translation would thus partly replace interpretation of the English words of the document's authors.) There are controversies about language in the workplace that would seem to goad America to consider the legal issue, as when commercial corporations seek to outlaw the use of Asian languages or Spanish in the lunch room.[90] Also there are disagreements about the appropriate language for private or public signs, as when anglophones want to outlaw unilingual non-English signs in California.[91] In this latter case, the court certified the right to have unilingual non-English signs, but it is significant that the court made its ruling not on the basis of any argument about official (or unofficial) language but only on one about First Amendment rights—free speech. Thus America's generally laudable concern with free speech served, as usual, to distract Americans from the issue of official language and even to veil it. (It is the apparent contrast in North America between the rights of individuals [American free speech] and the rights of groups [American race rights, Canadian language rights] that sheds light on why the free speech arena is not the politically realistic place to stage effectively an American debate about official languages and multilingualism.)

It might seem easier nowadays to raise the issue of constitutional bilingualism thanks to contemporary discussions of American statehood for Puerto Rico or to current debates about North American union for Canada, the United States, and Mexico. Concerning Puerto Rico, for example, its altercations about whether to "elevate" English to the status of official language has again made many terms of the language debate quasi-official. In January of this year "Governor Pedro Rosselló [of Puerto Rico] signed into law a bill that [gave] English equal status with Spanish as the official language of this American territory. 'Now we have two hymns, two flags, two languages,' Mr. Rosselló, a statehood advocate, declared to hundreds of cheering supporters at a signing ceremony. . . . He dismissed as 'a rhetorical storm' the arguments of critics who had

---

[90]*Gutiérrez v. Municipal Court* (838 F.2d 1031 [9th Cir. 1988]) outlawed English-only rules in the workplace. Concerning various other English-only rulings, see Edward M. Chen, "Language Rights in the Private Sector," in *Language Loyalties*, pp. 269–77. For various cases relating to the Spanish language, see Bill Piatt, *Language on the Job: Balancing Business Needs and Employee Rights* (Albuquerque, N. Mex., 1993) and *Only English? Law and Language Policy in the United States* (Albuquerque, N. Mex., 1990).

[91]In 1988 the city of Pomona enacted an ordinance providing that if local businesses "displayed signs featuring 'foreign alphabetical characters,' they must 'devote at least one-half of the sign area to advertising copy in English alphabetical characters'" (Crawford, introduction to *Asian American Business Group v. City of Ponoma*, in *Language Loyalties*, pp. 284–85). See also *Bilingualism in the Southwest*, ed. Paul R. Turner (Tucson, Ariz., 1973) and "Indian Language Renewal," in *Human Organization* 47 (Winter 1988): 283–329. Law cases include discrimination in the workplace against not only those who speak a non-English language but also those who speak English dialects and those who speak English with a foreign accent.

sought to safeguard Spanish's 21-month-old status as the island's sole official language."[92] To an unofficially unilingual American populace, still undecided even whether the term *Hispanic* refers to a linguistic or a racial grouping, official Spanish/English bilingualism in Washington, D.C., still means only "a rhetorical storm"—and babble in education, law, and the workplace. (It is useful to rephrase the question of Spanish/English bilingualism with the crucible-metaphor that has informed discussion of ethnicity since even before Israel Zangwill's *Melting-Pot* [1908] and Theodore Roosevelt's "Children of the Crucible" [1917]. In these perhaps too-familiar terms, the main question is not how long the Spanish language can resist melting in the anglophone pot of America. Nor is the question whether Spanish will "break the [linguistic] melting pot" in the sense that Webster meant when he surveyed the linguistic diversity of the United States in the late eighteenth century and predicted that all the American languages—English, German, French, and so on—would eventually melt together to become a distinctly nonanglophone language.[93] Rather, the main question involving bilingualism would concern whether the Spanish language will become, in the United States, *another* linguistic melting pot, just as the English language has already become a second official linguistic pot in Puerto Rico. As such the Spanish language in the United States would become not just the language of a "nation within a nation"—which is what Martin Delany called American blacks[94] and Clermont-Tonnerre called French Jews[95]—but a twin language alongside English, whether as an officially unofficial language, which is what English is in the present, or, more fractious toward the ideology of one melting pot, as an official language, which is what the English language itself would also be likely to become in such circumstances.)

Similarly, it might appear simpler these days to raise issues of official multilingualism thanks to contemporary American hopes for—or fears of—a North American economic union (NAFTA) joining together the United States, Mexico, and Canada. This union, should it ever amount to more than "free trade," would seem to project and fulfill Americans' dream of manifest destiny north and south, Mexicans' vision of again crossing legally the Rio Grande, and francophone Canadians' traditional conviction that they would have been better off with anglophone Americans than with anglophone Canadians. In the first years, moreover, such a union might well weaken federal governments and simultaneously strengthen local cultures (hence languages), much as the con-

---

[92]"Puerto Rico Elevates English," *New York Times* 29 Jan. 1993, p. A6.

[93]Compare Thomas Weyr, *Hispanic U.S.A.: Breaking the Melting Pot* (New York, 1988).

[94]Martin Robison Delany, *The Condition, Elevation, Emigration, and Destiny of the Colored People of the United States* (1852; New York, 1968), p. 12.

[95]See Comte Stanislas de Clermont-Tonnerre, *Opinion relativement aux persecutions qui menacent les juifs d'Alsace* (Versailles, 1789).

temporary political unification of multilingual Europe seems to be doing. But the problems and opportunities for this North American future are properly accessible to debate only in a discourse to which Americans still show the specific "nationalizing" resistance that was, for centuries, part of America's unifying motive.

Thus the story of America's social language-engineering is there to be understood and perhaps wisely redirected. It is a remarkable, and some would say heroic, story of immigration: forced, illegal, and voluntary; of treaties, purchases, and constitutions by which Spanish-, French-, German-, and Amerindian-speakers' languages, among many others, were subsumed; of a once new and powerfully nationalist literary movement that still informs devotedly monoglottal American university departments. Most Americans, however, cannot yet tell the story, or they do not want to tell the real story, not so much because the languages are forgotten (which they are), but mainly because forgetting language difference—and hence, more critically, partly suppressing the category of "language" itself—is still the urgent component of unofficially anglophone America's understanding of itself. America's otherwise laudable concerns with free speech, dialect, bilingual education, ethnicity, and cultural diversity serve effectively to mask substantive language issues. Comprehending the full magnitude of multilingualism in the United States—and defining the problem of the language rights of "peoples" both within it and without it—thus probably requires a radical revision of the political history of languages in North America. "Babel in America" is, I hope, an introductory essay in that direction.

If ever we work our way beyond discussing free speech to seriously debating official national language—and there is no sign yet that we will and no clear imperative that we should—the change will involve linguistic history and law. On an ideal plane, perhaps, the Treaty of Guadalupe Hidalgo and the original constitution of New Mexico will play roles. But practically speaking, the change would probably concern Puerto Rico. For Puerto Ricans, the question of statehood entails establishing officially bilingual government at the federal as well as the state levels. And so, for good or ill, Spanish-speaking Puerto Ricans may yet have the official status for which German-speaking Pennsylvanians once struggled and that both French-speaking Québecois and English-speaking Quebeckers have, for now.

Monoglottal anglophone Americans often say they believe in the equality of all language groups, when they mean only the equality of language groups other than the definitively, if not officially, anglophone one. Yet American Spanish-speakers, among others we have considered, may have a winning legal or demographic case for language equality with anglophones—hence for the same inequality with speakers of other languages that English speakers have. Time has told already what implications this long-primed scenario will have for defining anew the American language and America.

QUESTIONS

1. How does this article contribute to the debate about whether English should be the official language of the United States?

2. Recent statistics suggest that around 95 percent of Americans today speak English. Does this high percentage suggest that immigrants willingly assimilated English, demonstrating what Theodore Roosevelt called "language loyalty"? How might Shell respond to this?

3. In a recent article on the official language issue, Robert D. King described Canada as a country "whose unity is gravely imperiled by language and ethnic conflicts." How does Shell's exposition of language issues in Québec comment on King's statement?

4. Shell compares "the language issue in an officially biracial United States and in an officially bilingual Québec" in order to discuss the "linkage between dialect and race" (paragraph 23). What does he mean by the United States being "officially biracial"?

5. In his conclusion, Shell suggests that "a radical revision of the political history of languages in North America" is required to understand multilingualism in the United States and to define "the problem of language rights" (paragraph 44). His essay is intended as an introduction to that history. What historical facts in this article seem to contribute most toward the definition of the problem?

6. The subject of this article, the question of an official national language, is controversial and has been heavily debated and highly politicized. Write an essay setting forth your position on this subject. In addition to your own experience, refer to Shell and his sources and to any recent developments you know of.

MAKING CONNECTIONS

How would Shell respond to James Baldwin's argument in "If Black English Isn't a Language, Then Tell Me, What Is?" (p. 577)? You might want to bring the recent debate over teaching "Ebonics" to bear on this issue.

NONVERBAL COURTSHIP PATTERNS IN WOMEN
Context and Consequences

Monica M. Moore

Monica M. Moore (b. 1953) is a professor of psychology at Webster University in St. Louis, Missouri. Moore has conducted research on nonverbal courtship behavior in women since 1978, publishing articles in such journals as Semiotica *and the* Journal of Sex Research. *In this article, which originally appeared in the journal* Ethology and Sociobiology, *Moore applied the research methods of psychology to study the mating habits of the human female.*

[Abstract.] *There is a class of nonverbal facial expressions and gestures, exhibited by human females, that are commonly labeled "flirting behaviors." I observed more than 200 randomly selected adult female subjects in order to construct a catalog of these nonverbal solicitation behaviors. Pertinent behaviors were operationally defined through the use of consequential data; these behaviors elicited male attention. Fifty-two behaviors were described using this method. Validation of the catalog was provided through the use of contextual data. Observations were conducted on 40 randomly selected female subjects in one of four contexts: a singles' bar, a university snack bar, a university library, and at university Women's Center meetings. The results indicated that women in "mate relevant" contexts exhibited higher average frequencies of nonverbal displays directed at males. Additionally, women who signaled often were also those who were most often approached by a man; and this relationship was not context specific.*

I suggest that the observation of women in field situations may provide clues to criteria used by females in the initial selection of male partners. As much of the work surrounding human attraction has involved laboratory studies or data collected from couples in established relationships, the observation of nonverbal behavior in field settings may provide a fruitful avenue for the exploration of human female choice in the preliminary stages of male–female interaction.

INTRODUCTION

Biologically, one of the most important choices made by an organism is the selection of a mate. The evolution of traits that would assist in the identification of "superior mates" prior to the onset of mating is clearly advantageous.

One legacy of anisogamy is that errors in mate selection are generally more expensive to females than to males (Trivers 1972).[1] Hence, the females of a wide variety of species may be expected to exhibit traits that would facilitate the assessment of the quality of potential suitors in respect to their inherited attributes and acquired resources. There are many examples of female selectivity in a variety of species, including elephant seals (LeBoeuf and Peterson 1969; Bertram 1975), mice (McClearn and Defries 1973), fish (Weber and Weber 1975), rats (Doty 1974), gorillas (Nadler 1975), monkeys (Beach 1976), birds (Selander 1972; Wiley 1973; Williams 1975), and a few ungulates[2] (Beuchner and Schloeth 1965; Leuthold 1966).

Very few studies in the area of human mate selection and attraction have focused on the issue of female choice. Fowler (1978) interviewed women to identify the parameters of male sexual attractiveness. The results showed that the male's value as a sexual partner correlated with the magnitude of emotional and material security he provided. Baber (1939) found that women emphasize qualities such as economic status, disposition, family religion, morals, health, and education in a prospective marriage partner, whereas men most frequently chose good looks, morals, and health as important qualities. More recent studies (Coombs and Kenkel 1966; Tavris 1977) also found women rating attributes such as physical attractiveness as less important than did men. Reiss (1960) believes that many more women than men choose "someone to look up to" and Hatkoff and Luswell (1977) presented data that indicated that women want the men with whom they fall in love to be persons whom they can respect and depend on. Daly and Wilson (1978) conclude from cross-cultural data that a male's financial status is an important determinant of his mating success.

Although these reports are valuable, it is clear that the mechanisms and expression of male assessment and female choice in humans have received little attention. In addition, much of the information available regarding human female choice is derived from interviews or questionnaires. Few studies have focused on initial choice situations in field observations. There are several difficulties with a field approach. A major problem surrounds the determination that a choice situation is being observed when verbal information is unavailable. I suggest that this problem may be solved through observations of nonverbal behavior. Indeed, there appears to be a repertoire of gestures and facial expressions that are used by humans as courtship signals (Birdwhistell 1970), much as there is signaling between members of the opposite sex in other species. Even in humans courtship and the choice of a mate have been characterized as largely nonverbal, with the cues being so persuasive that they can,

[1] *anisogamy:* the union of unlike gametes—or mates, in this case. [Eds.]
[2] *ungulate:* a group of hoofed, herbivorous mammals, including camels, horses, and swine. [Eds.]

as one observer put it, "turn a comment about the weather into a seductive invitation" (Davis 1971, p. 97).

The focus of much study in the area of nonverbal communication has been description (Scheflen 1965; Birdwhistell 1970; Mehrabian 1972). The primary aim of this research has been the categorization and analysis of nonverbal behaviors. By employing frame-by-frame analysis of films, Birdwhistell and his associates have been able to provide detailed descriptions of the facial expressions and movements or gestures of subjects in a variety of contexts. Observations conducted in this fashion as well as field studies have resulted in the labeling of many nonverbal behaviors as courtship signals. For example, Givens (1978) has described five phases of courtship between unacquainted adults. Scheflen (1965) investigated flirting gestures in the context of psychotherapy, noting that both courtship behaviors and qualifiers of the courtship message were exhibited by therapists and clients. Eibl-Eibesfeldt (1971) used two approaches to describe flirting behavior in people from diverse cultural backgrounds. Employing a camera fitted with right angle lenses to film people without their knowledge, he found that an eyebrow flash combined with a smile was a common courtship behavior. Through comments made to women, Eibl-Eibesfeldt has been able to elicit the "coy glance," an expression combining a half-smile and lowered eyes. Kendon (1975) filmed a couple seated on a park bench in order to document the role of facial expression during a kissing round. He discovered that it was the female's behavior, particularly her facial expressions that functioned as a regulator in modulating the behavior of the male. Cary (1976) has shown that the female's behavior is important in initiating conversation between strangers. Both in laboratory settings and singles' bars conversation was initiated only after the female glanced at the male. These results are valuable in documenting the importance of nonverbal behavior in human courtship. But what is lacking is an ethogram of female solicitation behavior.[3]

The purpose of this study was to describe an ensemble of visual and tactile displays emitted by women during initial meetings with men. I shall argue here that these nonverbal displays are courtship signals; they serve as attractants and elicit the approach of males or ensure the continued attention of males. In order to establish the immediate function of the described behaviors as courtship displays, I employed two classes of evidence described by Hinde (1975) for use in the establishment of the immediate function of a behavior; contextual evidence and consequential evidence. The rationale behind the use of consequential data was that behavior has certain consequences and that if the consequence appears to be a "good thing" it should have relevance for the immediate function of the behavior in question. It should be noted, however, that Eibl-Eibesfeldt (1970) has pointed out the danger in this approach because of interpretations of value on the part of the observer. Therefore, contex-

---

[3]*ethogram*: a pictorial catalog of behavior patterns shown by members of a species. [Eds.]

tual information was provided as further documentation that the nonverbal behaviors in question were courtship signals. Hinde has noted that if certain behaviors are seen in some contexts but are absent in others their function must relate to those contexts in which they were observed. Together these two classes of information provide an indication of the immediate function of the behavior, in this case nonverbal behavior in women interacting with men. Thus, this study consisted of two parts: catalog compilation based on consequential information and validation of the catalog obtained through contextual data.

DEVELOPMENT OF THE CATALOG

Method

Subjects

For the initial study, more than 200 subjects were observed in order to obtain data to be used in the development of the catalog of nonverbal solicitation signals. Subjects were judged to be between the ages of 18 and 35 years. No systematic examination was made of background variables due to restrictions imposed by anonymity. All subjects were white and most were probably college students.

Procedure

Subjects were covertly observed in one social context where opportunities for male–female interaction were available, a singles' bar. Subjects were observed for 30 minutes by two trained observers. Focal subjects were randomly selected from the pool of possible subjects at the start of the observation period. We observed a woman only if she was surrounded by at least 25 other people (generally there were more than 50 others present) and if she was not accompanied by a male. In order to record all instances of the relevant behaviors, observers kept a continuous narrative account of all behaviors exhibited by a single subject and the observable consequences of those actions (Altmann 1974). The following criteria were used for identifying behaviors: a nonverbal solicitation behavior was defined as a movement of body part(s) or whole body that resulted in male attention, operationally defined, within 15 seconds following the behavior. Male attention consisted of the male performing one of the following behaviors: approaching the subject, talking to her, leaning toward her or moving closer to her, asking the subject to dance, touching her, or kissing her. Field notes were transcribed from concealed audio tape recorders. Estimates of interobserver reliability were calculated for 35 hours of observation using the formula:

$$\frac{\text{No. of agreements (A + B)}}{\text{No. of agreements (A + B) + No. seen by B only + No. seen by A only}}$$

(McGrew 1972). The range of interobserver reliability scores was 0.72–0.98, with the average score equaling .88. Low reliability scores were obtained only for behaviors difficult for an observer to catch in a darkened room, such as glancing behaviors.

Subsequently, five randomly selected subjects were observed for a period of at least 1 hour. Again observers kept a continuous narrative account of all nonverbal behavior exhibited by the woman.

The behaviors observed in courting women can be conceptualized in various ways: distance categories (Crook 1972), directional versus nondirectional, or on the basis of body part and movement employed in the exhibition of the nonverbal pattern (McGrew 1972). The third framework was chosen because the displays were most discretely partitioned along these dimensions.

Results

Fifty-two different behaviors were exhibited by the subjects in the present study. Nonverbal solicitation behaviors and their frequencies are summarized in Table 1 according to category. These behaviors were highly visible and most appeared very similar in form in each subject. In other words, each behavior was discrete, or distinct from all other solicitation behaviors.

Descriptions of Nonverbal Solicitation Behaviors

FACIAL AND HEAD PATTERNS. A number of different facial and head patterns were seen in the women we observed. All women performed glancing behaviors, although the particular pattern varied among the individual subjects in the duration or length of time involved in eye to eye contact.

Type I glance (the room encompassing glance) was not restricted to an identifiable recipient. It was usually exhibited early in the evening and often was not seen later in the evening, particularly if the woman made contact with a man. The woman moved her head rapidly, orienting her face around the room. This movement was followed by another head movement that reoriented the woman's face to its original position. The total duration of the glance was brief, 5–10 seconds, with the woman not making eye contact with any specific individual. In some women this pattern of behavior was exaggerated: the woman stood up as her glance swept about the room.

The glancing behavior called the *type II glance (the short darting glance)* was a solicitation behavior that appeared directed at a particular man. The woman directed her gaze at the man, then quickly away (within 3 seconds). The target axis of the horizontal rotation of the head was approximately 25–45 degrees. This behavior was usually repeated in bouts, with three glances the average number per bout.

473

Table 1. Catalog of Nonverbal Solicitation Behaviors

Facial and Head Patterns	Frequency	Gestures	Frequency	Posture Patterns	Frequency
Type I glance (room-encompassing glance)	253	Arm flexion	10	Lean	121
		Tap	8	Brush	28
		Palm	18	Breast touch	6
Type II glance (short darting glance)	222				
Type III glance (gaze fixate)	117				
Eyebrow flash	4	Gesticulation	62	Knee touch	25
Head toss	102	Hand hold	20	Thigh touch	23
Neck presentation	58	Primp	46	Foot to foot	14
Hair flip	139	Hike skirt	4	Placement	19
Head nod	66	Object caress	56	Shoulder hug	25
Lip lick	48	Caress (face/hair)	5	Hug	11
Lipstick application	1	Caress (leg)	32	Lateral body contact	1
Pout	27	Caress (arm)	23	Frontal body contact	7
Smile	511	Caress (torso)	8	Hang	2
Coy smile	20	Caress (back)	17	Parade	41
Laugh	249	Buttock pat	8	Approach	18
Giggle	61			Request dance	12
Kiss	6			Dance (acceptance)	59
Whisper	60			Solitary dance	253
Face to face	9			Point/permission grant	62
				Aid solicitation	34
				Play	31

In contrast, *type III glance (gaze fixate)* consisted of prolonged (more than 3 seconds) eye contact. The subject looked directly at the man; sometimes her glance was returned. Again, this behavior was seen several times in a period of minutes in some subjects.

Another movement involving the eye area was an *eyebrow flash*, which consisted of an exaggerated raising of the eyebrows of both eyes, followed by a rapid lowering to the normal position. The duration of the raised eyebrow portion of the movement was approximately 2 seconds. This behavior was often combined with a smile and eye contact.

Several behaviors involved the head and neck region. In *head tossing*, the head was flipped backwards so that the face was tilted upwards briefly (less than 5 seconds). The head was then lowered to its original position. The head toss was often combined with or seen before the *hair flip*. The hair flip consisted of the woman raising one hand and pushing her fingers through her hair or running her palm along the surface of her hair. Some women made only one hand movement, while in others there were bouts of hair stroking; the woman put her hand to her hair several times within a 30-second interval. The *head nod* was seen when the woman was only a short distance from the man. Usually exhibited during conversation, the head was moved forward and backward on the neck, which resulted in the face of the subject moving up and down. Another head pattern was called *face to face*. In this behavior pattern the head and face of the woman were brought directly opposite another person's face so that the noses almost touched, a distance of approximately 5 cm. A final behavior involving the head and neck was the *neck presentation*. The woman tilted her head sideways to an angle of approximately 45 degrees. This resulted in the ear almost touching the ipsilateral shoulder,[4] thereby exposing the opposite side of the neck. Occasionally the woman stroked the exposed neck area with her fingers.

There were a number of signals that involved the lips and mouth of the observed subjects. *Lipstick application* was a rare behavior. The woman directed her gaze so that she made eye contact with a particular man. She then slowly applied lipstick to her lips. She engaged in this behavior for some time (15 seconds), repeatedly circling her lips. In contrast, the *lip lick* was seen quite often, particularly in certain subjects. The woman opened her mouth slightly and drew her tongue over her lips. Some women used a single lip lick, wetting only the upper or the lower lip, while others ran the tongue around the entire lip area. The *lip pout* was another behavior involving the mouth. The lips were placed together and protruded. Generally, the lower lip was extended somewhat farther than the upper lip, so that it was fuller in appearance.

Smiling was among the most prevalent behaviors observed in the sampled women. The smile consisted of the corners of the mouth being turned upward.

20

---

[4]*ipsilateral*: situated on the same side of the body. [Eds.]

This resulted in partial or sometimes full exposure of the teeth. In some women the smile appeared fixed and was maintained for long periods of time. The *coy smile* differed from the smile in that the woman displaying a coy smile combined a half-smile (the teeth were often not displayed or only partially shown) with a downward gaze or eye contact which was very brief (less than 3 seconds). In the latter case the woman's glance slid quickly away from an on-looker who had become aware that he was being looked at.

Laughing and giggling were generally responses to another person's comments or behavior and were very common. In some women the *laugh* was preceded by a head toss. *Giggling* was less intense laughter. The mouth of the woman was often closed and generally the sounds were softer.

Kissing was rather unusual in the bar context. The slightly protruded lips were brought into contact with another person's body by a forward head movement. Variations consisted of the area touched by the woman's lips. The most common targets were the lips, face, and neck of the man. The woman, however, sometimes puckered her lips and waited, as if "offering" them to the male.

Finally, the *whisper* was used by most of the subjects in the sample. The woman moved her mouth near another person's ear and soft vocalizations presumedly were produced. Sometimes body contact was made.

GESTURES. There were several nonverbal patterns that involved movement of the hands and arms. Most were directed at a particular person. Some involved touching another individual. Others functioned at a distance.

Arm flexion occurred when the arm was flexed at wrist and elbow and was moved toward the body. It was often repeated two or three times in a bout. This behavior was often followed by the approach of another individual toward whom the subject gazed. If the male was in close physical proximity, the female sometimes used *tapping* instead to get his attention. The elbow or wrist was flexed repeatedly so that the woman's finger was moved vertically on an object (usually another person's arm).

Women occasionally *palmed*. Palming occurred when the hand was extended or turned so that the palm faced another person for a brief period of time, less than 5 seconds. In this study, palming was also recorded when the woman coughed or touched herself with the palm up.

In several women rapid movements of the hands and arms were seen accompanying speech. This behavior was labeled *gesticulation*. Arms and hands, while held in front of the woman's torso, were waved or extended upwards in an exaggerated, conspicuous manner. This behavior was often followed by a lean forward on the part of the man.

A hand gesture sometimes initiated by a woman was the *hand hold*. The woman grasped the man's hand so that her palm was next to the man's palm. This occurred on the dance floor as well as when the man was seated at the table with the woman. Generally, this behavior had a long duration, more than 1 minute.

There were several behaviors that appeared related to each other because they involved inanimate objects. The first of these was the *primp*. In this gesture the clothing was patted or smoothed, although to the observer it appeared in no need of adjustment. A shirt was tucked in or a skirt was pulled down. On the other hand, the *skirt hike* was performed by raising the hem of the skirt with a movement of the hand or arm so that more leg was exposed. This behavior was only performed by two women and was directed at a particular man. When another man looked the skirt was pushed rapidly into place. Instead of patting or smoothing clothing, subjects sometimes "played with" an object, called *object caress*. For example, keys or rings were often fondled. Glasses were caressed with the woman sliding her palm up and down the surface of the glass. A cigarette pack was another item frequently toyed with in an object caress.

Finally, many women touched other people in a caressing fashion. Each incidence of caressing was considered separately in terms of the part of the body that was touched, because the message, in each case, may have been quite different. In *caress (face/hair)* the woman moved her hand slowly up and down the man's face and neck area or tangled her hands in his hair. While the couple was seated, women have been observed stroking the man's thigh and inner leg, *caress (leg)*. The *buttock pat*, however, occurred while the couple was standing, often while dancing. In this gesture the woman moved her hand, palm side down, up and down the man's buttocks. Other items in this group included *caress (arm)*, *caress (torso)*, and *caress (back)*.

POSTURE PATTERNS. Compared to the two categories just presented, there were some behaviors which involved more of the body in movement. These I called posture patterns. Many of these behaviors could only be accomplished while the woman was standing or moving about the room.

Lean was a common solicitation pattern. Generally while seated, the woman moved her torso and upper body forward, which resulted in closer proximity to the man. This movement was sometimes followed by a *brush* or a *breast touch*. The brush occurred when brief body contact (less than 5 seconds) was initiated by the woman against another individual. This occurred when a woman was walking across the room; she bumped into a man. The result was often conversation between the man and the woman. The breast touch also appeared accidental; and it was difficult to tell, except by length of time of contact, whether or not the movement was purposeful. The upper torso was moved so the breast made contact with the man's body (usually his arm). Most often the contact was brief (less than 5 seconds), but sometimes women maintained this position for several minutes.

There were four other actions that were similar to the brush and breast touch in that the woman made bodily contact with the man. In the *knee touch* the legs were brought into contact with the man's legs so that the knees touched. Interactants were always facing one another while seated. If the man

477

and woman were sitting side by side, the woman may have initiated a *thigh touch*. The leg was brought into contact with the man's upper leg. *Foot to foot* resulted in the woman moving her foot so that it rested on top of the man's foot. Finally, rather than make contact with some part of her own body, an observed woman sometimes took the man's hand and placed it on her body. I called this behavior *placement*. For example, on two occasions, a woman put a man's hand in her lap. Other targets were the thigh or arm.

There was another constellation of behaviors that appeared related to each other. All of these behaviors were variations of some contact made between the woman's upper body and her partner's upper body. These were generally behaviors of long duration, more than 1 minute. The most common of these behaviors was the *shoulder hug*. In this signal, the partially flexed arm was draped on and around another person's shoulder. In contrast, the *hug* occurred when both arms were moved forward from a widespread position and around the man, thereby encircling him. The duration of this behavior, however, was brief (less than 10 seconds). *Lateral body contact* was similar to shoulder hug except that the woman moved under the man's arm so that his arm was draped around her shoulders rather than vice versa. Similarly, *frontal body contact* occurred when the chest and thighs of the woman rested against the chest and thighs of the man. This behavior was like the hug except that there was no squeeze pressure and the arms did not necessarily encircle the other person. This posture pattern was often seen on the dance floor or when a couple was standing at the bar. *Hanging* was similar to frontal body contact except that the man was supporting the woman's weight. This behavior was initiated by the woman who placed her arms around the man's neck. She was then lifted off her feet while her torso and hips rested against the man's chest and hip. This was a behavior low in frequency and brief in duration, less than 5 seconds.

There were two behaviors that involved whole body movement. These were called *parade* and *approach*. Parade consisted of the woman walking across the room, perhaps on her way to the bar or the restroom. Yet rather than maintaining a relaxed attitude, the woman exaggerated the swaying motion of her hips. Her stomach was held in and her back was arched so that her breasts were pushed out; her head was held high. In general she was able to make herself "look good." The other behavior that involved walking was approach. The woman went up to the man and stood very close to him, within 2 feet. Usually verbal interaction ensued.

Some women followed an approach with a *request dance*. This was demonstrated nonverbally by the woman pointing and/or nodding in the direction of the dance floor. Two other categories involving dancing behavior were included in the catalog. *Dance (female acceptance)* was included because by accepting a dance with the man the woman maintained his attention. Another dancing behavior was one of the most frequently seen signals. It was called the *solitary dance* because, while seated or standing, the woman moved her body in time to the music. A typical male response was to request a dance.

35

Just as a woman, in agreeing to dance with a man, was telling him, nonverbally, that he was acceptable for the moment she also told him so when she allowed him to sit at her table with her. Thus, *point/permission grant* was given a place in the catalog. The woman pulled out the chair for the man or pointed or nodded in the direction of the chair. There was generally a verbal component to the signal which could not be overheard.

Aid solicitation consisted of several behaviors that involved the request of help by the subject. For example, the woman handed her jacket to the man and allowed him to help her put it on. Other patterns in this category included indicating that a drink be refilled, waiting to be seated, or holding a cigarette for lighting.

The final category of solicitation behavior was also a variety of posture patterns. Called *play*, these behaviors consisted of the woman pinching the man, tickling him, sticking out her tongue at him, or approaching him from behind covering his eyes. Some women sat on the man's lap, and several women in the sample came up behind men and stole their hats. All of these behaviors were simply recorded as play behavior.

VALIDATION OF THE CATALOG

Method

Subjects

Forty women were covertly observed for the second portion of the study, validation of the catalog. Subjects were judged between the ages of 18 and 35. All subjects were white. Again no systematic examination of background variables was possible.

Procedure

To justify the claim that the nonverbal behaviors described above were courtship signals, that is, carried a message of interest to the observing man, women were covertly observed in different social contexts. The four contexts selected for study were a singles' bar, a university snack bar, a university library, and university Women's Center meetings. These contexts were chosen in order to sample a variety of situations in which nonverbal solicitation might be expected to occur as well as situations in which it was unlikely to be exhibited. The selection of contexts was based on information collected through interviews and pilot observations. If nonverbal solicitation was found in situations where male–female interaction was likely but either was not found or occurred in lower frequencies where male–female interactions were impossible, then the immediate function of nonverbal solicitation can be said to be the enhancement of male–female relationships.

The methodology employed in this section was similar to that used in the development of the catalog. Focal individual sampling was the method of choice for the 40 subjects, 10 in each of the 4 contexts. Each subject was randomly selected from those individuals present at the beginning of the observation period. Sessions were scheduled to begin at 9:00 P.M. and end at 11:00 P.M. in the bar context. This time was optimal because crowd density was at its peak. Sessions in the Women's Center context always began at noon or at 7:00 P.M. because that was the time at which programs were scheduled. Observations were randomly made in both the library and the snack bar contexts; for each context, four sessions were conducted at 11:00 A.M., three at 2:00 P.M., and three at 7:00 P.M. Subjects were observed for a period of 1 hour. (Any subject who did not remain for 1 hour of observation was excluded from the analyses.) Observations were conducted using either a concealed audio recorder or, when appropriate, paper and pen. No subject evidenced awareness of being observed. Again, we observed a woman only if she was surrounded by at least 25 other people and if she was not accompanied by a male.

Data for each woman consisted of a frequency measure, the number of nonverbal solicitation behaviors, described above, that she exhibited during the hour of observation. Observers counted not only the total number of nonverbal solicitation behaviors, but also kept a tally of the specific behaviors that were used by each woman.

Results

Frequency and Categorization of Nonverbal Solicitation Behaviors

Data collected on 40 subjects and the respective frequencies of their solicitation displays are given in Table 2. The results show that the emission of the cataloged behaviors was context specific in respect to both the frequency of displays and the number of different categories of the repertoire. The subjects observed in the singles' bar emitted an average of 70.6 displays in the sampled interval, encompassing a mean number of 12.8 different categories of the catalog. In contrast, the corresponding data from the snack bar, library, and women's meetings were 18.6 and 7.5, 9.6 and 4.0, and 4.7 and 2.1, respectively. The asymmetry in display frequency was highly significant ($\chi^2 = 25.079$, df = 3, $p < 0.001$). In addition, the asymmetry in the number of categories utilized was also significant ($\chi^2 = 23.099$, df = 3, $p < 0.001$).

Rate of Display

The quartile display frequencies for the four contexts are given in Figure 1. As can be seen, the display frequency accelerated over time in the singles' bar context but was relatively invariant in the other three contexts. [45]

Table 2. Social Context: Display Frequency and Number of Approaches[a]

	Singles' Bar	Snack Bar	Library	Women's Meetings
Number of subjects	10	10	10	10
Total number of displays	706	186	96	47
Mean number of displays	70.6	18.6	9.6	4.7
Mean number of catagories utilized	12.8	7.5	4.0	2.1
Number of approaches to the subject by a male	38	4	4	0
Number of approaches to a male by the subject	11	4	1	0

[a]The tabulated data are for a 60-minute observation interval. Assymetry in display frequency: $\chi^2 = 25.079$, df = 3, $p < 0.001$; assymetry in number of categories utilized: $\chi^2 = 23.099$, df = 3, $p < 0.001$.

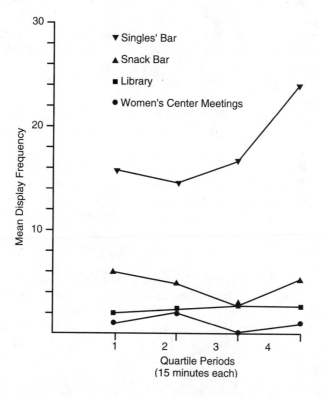

FIGURE 1. Frequency of occurrence for all solicitation behaviors for each quartile of the observation interval for each of the four social contexts.

Frequency of Approach

If subjects are pooled across contexts in which males are present and partitioned into high- and low-display categories, where the high display category is defined as more than 35 displays per hour, the data show that the high-display subjects elicited greater than 4 approaches per hour, whereas low display subjects elicited less than 0.48 approaches per hour. The number of approaches to subjects by a male in each context is presented in Table 2. Approaches were most frequent in the singles' bar where displays were also most frequent.

For the three contexts in which males were present (the singles' bar, the snack bar, and the library), the number of approaches to the subject was compared to the number of categories employed in solicitation displays. Subjects were pooled across these contexts and divided into two groups—those who utilized less than ten categories and those who employed ten or more categories. The results were highly significant ($\chi^2 = 12.881$, df = 1, $p < 0.025$): regardless of when the woman utilized a high number of categories she was more likely to be approached by a male.

Also given in Table 2 are the figures for female-to-male approaches. In both cases (female to male, and male to female), approaches were much higher in the bar context. To show that the number of male approaches correlated with frequency of female solicitation, Spearman rank correlations[5] were determined for these measures. The correlation between number of male approaches and total number of solicitations, across all three contexts, equaled 0.89 ($p < 0.05$). Clearly, those women who signaled often were also those who were most often approached by a man; and this relationship was not context specific.

DISCUSSION

The results of this study are in no way discoveries of "new" behaviors. The behaviors cataloged here have been described as courtship behaviors by others. But there has been little firm evidence to support this claim of their function, aside from references to context. This study was the first attempt to bring all the behaviors together in catalog form and provide documentation of their function.

When we compare those behaviors contained in the catalog compiled in   50
this study to other descriptions of courtship in humans, we find many areas of congruence. Scheflen (1965) has outlined four categories of heterosexual courtship behavior: courtship readiness, preening behavior, positional cues, and actions of appeal or invitation. Many of the behaviors observed in courting

---

[5]*Spearman rank correlations:* when in a statistical study it is not possible to give actual values to variables, the rank order to instances of each variable is assigned. [Eds.]

women are similar to those seen by Scheflen during psychotherapy sessions. For example, Scheflen's category of courtship readiness bears resemblance to parade behavior. Preening behaviors, as described by Scheflen, are similar to the hair flip, primp, skirt hike, and object caress cataloged here. Positional cues are found in the catalog under leaning, brushing, and caressing or touching signals. Finally, Scheflen's actions of appeal or invitation are included as aid solicitation, point/permission grant, request dance, palm and solitary dance. What appears to be absent in courting women are the qualifiers of the courtship message observed by Scheflen during psychotherapy.

There is significant continuity between the expressions and gestures described in this study and those Givens (1978) believed to be important during the first four phrases of courtship. According to Givens, the essence of the first stage, the attention phase, is ambivalence. Behaviors seen by Givens during this stage and observed in this study include primping, object caressing, and glancing at and then away from the male. During the recognition phase Givens has observed head cocking, pouting, primping, eyebrow flashing and smiling, all of which were seen by me. During the interaction stage, conversation is initiated and the participants appear highly animated. Indeed, women in this study, while talking to men, appeared excited, laughing, smiling, and gesticulating frequently. Givens has indicated that in the fourth stage, the sexual arousal phase, touching gestures are exchanged. Similarly, it was not unusual to see couples hold hands, caress, hug, or kiss after some period of interaction.

Given's work has indicated that it is often the female who controls interaction in these early phases. The observations of Cary (1976) seem to bear this out and glancing behavior appears to be a significant part of the female role. In this study glancing often took place over a period of time prior to a male approach. As Crook (1972) has stated, males are generally hesitant to approach without some indication of interest from the partner, and repeated eye contact seems to demonstrate that interest. Rejection behaviors were not cataloged here, but it is entirely possible that one way women reject suitors is by failing to recognize their presence through eye contact.

Eibl-Eibesfeldt has also stressed importance of the eye area in two flirting gestures he has observed in several cultures. The first, a rapid raising and lowering of the eyebrows, accompanied by a smile and a nod, was seen rarely in this study. Raised eyebrows were sometimes seen in the bar context and when directed at a man with a quick glance to the dance floor were often followed by a request to dance. Raised eyebrows also sometimes followed comments by a man when he had joined a woman at her table. Eibl-Eibesfeldt (1970) has also presented pictures of women exhibiting what he calls the coy glance. Although the coy glance was sometimes seen in this study (here called the coy smile), it was more usual for a young American woman to use direct eye contact and a full smile. Yet the fact that these behaviors were observed is signifi-

cant, and later cross-cultural studies may demonstrate that there are more behaviors that share the courtship message.

It appears then that although glancing behaviors were important in signaling interest, initially, other behaviors seemed to reaffirm the woman's interest
later in the observation period. Behaviors such as nodding, leaning close to the
man, smiling and laughing were seen in higher frequencies after the man had
made contact with the woman and was dancing with her or was seated at her
table. This accounts for the rise in frequency of solicitation near the end of the
observation period in the bar context. Yet it is difficult to make any firm statements about a sequential pattern in the exhibition of solicitation behavior. Although these behaviors are distinct in form, variability among subjects with regard to timing was great. Neither was it possible to determine the potency of
particular behaviors. Indeed, it often appeared as though behaviors had a cumulative effect; that is, the man waited to respond to the woman until after he
had observed several solicitations.

However, it is clear that there is a constellation of nonverbal behaviors asso- 55
ciated with female solicitation that has been recognized by many investigators
in several contexts and with similar results (Morris 1971; Kerdon and Feber
1973; Nieremberg and Calero 1973; Clore et al. 1975; Key 1975; Knapp 1978;
Lockard and Adams 1980). This is strong circumstantial evidence supporting
the current results that these are "real" contextually valid movements, not random behaviors. Furthermore, these expressions and gestures appear to function
as attractants and advertisers of female interest.

Traditionally, women have had more control in choosing men for relationships, being able to pace the course of sexual advances and having the preroga-
tive to accept or decline proposals (Hatkoff and Luswell 1977). Nonverbal solicitation is only one of the first steps in the sequence of behaviors beginning
with mate attraction and culminating with mate selection. However, these
courtship gestures and expressions appear to aid the woman in her role as discriminating chooser. Females are able to determine when and where they wish
to survey mate potential by exhibiting or withholding displays. They can elicit
a high number of male approaches, allowing them to choose from a number of
available men. Or they may direct solicitations at a particular male.

What happens after the approach of a man then becomes increasingly important. Much of the basis of actual choice must rest on what the man says to
the woman in addition to his behavior toward her and others. It seems reasonable that females would enhance their fitness by making the most informed
judgment possible. Yet before interaction is initiated some initial choice is
made. These initial impressions and the selection of those men deemed interesting enough to warrant further attention by a woman have been virtually ignored. If, indeed, the woman is exercising her right to choose, what sort of filter system is she using? Which men are chosen for further interaction and
which are rejected? Literature cited earlier indicates that behaviors that indicate status, wealth, and dependability are attributes that women may assess in

initial encounters. At present data are not available to address these issues. But I believe that hypotheses regarding the particulars of human female choice can be tested through covert observation of female invitational behavior. Information obtained through observations in field settings can be added to verbal reports. The results of such a venture may present us with a more complete picture of the levels of selection involved in human female choice.

REFERENCES

Altmann, J. Observational study of behavior: sampling methods. *Behavior* 49: 227–267 (1974).

Baber, R. E. *Marriage and Family.* New York: McGraw-Hill, 1939.

Beach, R. A. Sexual attractivity, proceptivity and receptivity in female mammals. *Hormones and Behavior* 7: 105–138 (1976).

Bertram, B. C. Social factors influencing reproduction in wild lions. *Journal of Zoology* 177: 463–482 (1975).

Beuchner, H. K., Schloeth, R. Ceremonial mating system in Uganda kob (*Adenota kob thomase* Neuman). *Zeitschrift fur Tierpsychologie* 22: 209–225 (1965).

Birdwhistell, R. L. *Kinesics and Context.* Philadelphia: University of Pennsylvania Press, 1970.

Cary, M. S. Talk? Do you want to talk? Negotiation for the initiation of conversation between the unacquainted. Ph.D. dissertation, University of Pennsylvania, 1976.

Clore, G. L., Wiggins, N. H., Itkin, I. Judging attraction from nonverbal behavior: the gain phenomenon. *Journal of Consulting and Clinical Pyschology* 43: 491–497 (1975).

Coombs, R. H., Kenkel, W. F. Sex differences in dating aspirations and satisfaction with computer selected partners. *Journal of Marriage and the Family* 28: 62–66 (1966).

Crook, J. H. Sexual selection, dimorphism, and social organization in primates. In *Sexual Selection and the Descent of Man 1871–1971*, B. Campbell (Ed.). Chicago: Aldine, 1972.

—— The socio-ecology of primates. In *Social Behavior in Birds and Mammals: Essays on the Social Ethology of Animals and Man*, J. H. Crook (Ed.). London: Academic, 1972.

Daly, M., Wilson, M. *Sex, Evolution, and Behavior.* North Scituate, MA: Duxbury, 1978.

Davis, F. *Inside Intuition.* New York: McGraw-Hill, 1971.

Doty, R. L. A cry for the liberation of the female rodent: Courtship and copulation in Rodentia. *Psychological Bulletin* 81: 159–172 (1974).

Eibl-Eibesfeldt, I. *Ethology: The Biology of Behavior.* New York: Holt, Rinehart, and Winston, 1970.

—— *Love and Hate.* New York: Holt, Rinehart and Winston, 1971.

Fowler, H. F. Female choice: An investigation into human breeding system strategy. Paper presented to Animal Behavior Society, Seattle, June 1978.

Givens, D. The nonverbal basis of attraction: Flirtation, courtship, and seduction. *Psychiatry* 41:346–359 (1978).

Hatkoff, T. S., Luswell, T. E. Male–female similarities and differences in conceptualizing love. In *Love and Attraction*, M. Cook, G. Wilson (Eds.). Oxford: Pergamon, 1977.

Hinde, R. A. The concept of function. In *Function and Evolution in Behavior*, S. Bariends, C. Beer, and A. Manning (Eds.). Oxford: Clarendon, 1975.

Kendon, A. Some functions of the face in a kissing round. *Semiotica* 15: 299–334 (1975).

——, Ferber, A. A description of some human greetings. In *Comparative Ecology and Behavior of Primates*, R. P. Michael and J. H. Crook (Eds.). London: Academic, 1973.

Key, M. R. *Male/Female Language*. Metuchen NJ: Scarecrow, 1975.

Knapp, M. L. *Nonverbal Communication in Human Interaction*. New York: Holt, Rinehart, and Winston, 1978.

LeBoeuf, B. J., Peterson, R. S. Social status and mating activity in elephant seals. *Science* 163: 91–93 (1969).

Leuthold, W. Variations in territorial behavior of Uganda kob *Adenota kob thomasi* (Neumann 1896). *Behaviour* 27: 215–258 (1966).

Lockard, J. S., Adams, R. M. Courtship behaviors in public: Different age/sex roles. *Ethology and Sociobiology* 1(3): 245–253 (1980).

McClearn, G. E., Defries, J. C. *Introduction to Behavioral Genetics*. San Francisco: Freeman, 1973.

McGrew, W. C. *An Ethological Study of Children's Behavior*. New York: Academic, 1972.

Mehrabian, A. *Nonverbal Communication*. Chicago: Aldine, 1972.

Morris, D. *Intimate Behavior*. New York: Random House, 1971.

Nadler, R. D. Sexual cyclicity in captive lowland gorillas. *Science* 189: 813–814 (1975).

Nieremberg, G. I., Calero, H. H. *How to Read a Person Like a Book*. New York: Hawthorne, 1973.

Reiss, I. L. Toward a sociology of the heterosexual love relationship. *Marriage and Family Living* 22: 139–145 (1960).

Scheflen, A. E. Quasi-courtship behavior in psychotherapy. *Psychiatry* 28: 245–257 (1965).

Selander, R. K. Sexual selection and dimorphism in birds. In *Sexual Selection and the Descent of Man 1871–1971*, B. Campbell (Ed.). Chicago: Aldine, 1972.

Tavris, C. Men and women report their views on masculinity. *Psychology Today* 10: 34–42 (1977).

Trivers, R. L. Parental investment and sexual selection. In *Sexual Selection and the Descent of Man 1871–1971*, B. Campbell (Ed.). Chicago: Aldine, 1972.

Weber, P. G., Weber, S. P. The effect of female color, size, dominance and early experience upon mate selection in male convict cichlids, *cichlosoma nigrofasciatum Gunther* (pisces, cichlidae). *Behaviour* 56: 116–135 (1975).

Wiley, R. H. Territoriality and nonrandom mating in sage grouse. *Centrocerus urophasiamis*. *Animal Behavior Monographs* 6: 85–169 (1973).

Williams, G. C. *Sex and Evolution*. Princeton NJ: Princeton University Press, 1975.

QUESTIONS

1. Which of Moore's observations or conclusions do you find the most interesting or unusual? Explain.

2. The interest of this piece lies in its subject—flirting—which is more frequently treated in popular how-to books and on talk shows. Based on your familiarity with these popular treatments and on your knowledge of the subject through your own observations, how accurate a report do you find Moore's article to be?

3. Moore suggests that different courtship behavior may pertain in other cultures. If you have knowledge of another culture's courtship rituals, explain how they compare with Moore's findings.

4. Moore concludes by suggesting that further study should be made on women's "filter system," meaning how they choose a man for further interaction. She suggests that this can be done through additional "covert observation" (paragraph 57). Do you agree? What would one look for?

5. What does Moore mean when she writes, "It seems reasonable that females would enhance their fitness by making the most informed judgment possible" (paragraph 57)? What sort of "fitness" do you think Moore means?

6. Would it be possible to replicate this experiment by studying courtship behavior in males? Write an essay in which you suggest some of the categories of male courtship behavior that such a study might reveal.

MAKING CONNECTIONS

What similarities in method or substantive findings can you find between Moore's study and Jane van Lawick-Goodall's "First Observations" (p. 241) or Farley Mowat's "Observing Wolves" (p. 237)? Note that Moore presented portions of this article before publication at a meeting of the Animal Behavior Society.

Sciences and Technologies

WHY THE SKY IS BLUE

James Jeans

Sir James Jeans (1877–1946) was a British physicist and as-
tronomer. Educated at Trinity College, Cambridge, he lec-
tured there and was a professor of applied mathematics at
Princeton University from 1905 to 1909. He later did re-
search at Mount Wilson Observatory in California. Jeans
won many honors for his work and wrote a number of schol-
arly and popular scientific books. The following selection is
from The Stars in Their Courses *(1931), a written version*
of what began as a series of radio talks for an audience as-
sumed to have no special knowledge of science.

Imagine that we stand on any ordinary seaside pier, and watch the waves
rolling in and striking against the iron columns of the pier. Large waves pay
very little attention to the columns—they divide right and left and re-unite
after passing each column, much as a regiment of soldiers would if a tree stood
in their road; it is almost as though the columns had not been there. But the
short waves and ripples find the columns of the pier a much more formidable
obstacle. When the short waves impinge on the columns, they are reflected
back and spread as new ripples in all directions. To use the technical term,
they are "scattered." The obstacle provided by the iron columns hardly affects
the long waves at all, but scatters the short ripples.

We have been watching a sort of working model of the way in which sunlight struggles through the earth's atmosphere. Between us on earth and outer
space the atmosphere interposes innumerable obstacles in the form of molecules of air, tiny droplets of water, and small particles of dust. These are represented by the columns of the pier.

The waves of the sea represent the sunlight. We know that sunlight is a
blend of lights of many colors—as we can prove for ourselves by passing it
through a prism, or even through a jug of water, or as Nature demonstrates to
us when she passes it through the raindrops of a summer shower and produces

489

a rainbow. We also know that light consists of waves, and that the different colors of light are produced by waves of different lengths, red light by long waves and blue light by short waves. The mixture of waves which constitutes sunlight has to struggle through the obstacles it meets in the atmosphere, just as the mixture of waves at the seaside has to struggle past the columns of the pier. And these obstacles treat the light-waves much as the columns of the pier treat the sea-waves. The long waves which constitute red light are hardly affected, but the short waves which constitute blue light are scattered in all directions.

Thus, the different constituents of sunlight are treated in different ways as they struggle through the earth's atmosphere. A wave of blue light may be scattered by a dust particle, and turned out of its course. After a time a second dust particle again turns it out of its course, and so on, until finally it enters our eyes by a path as zigzag as that of a flash of lightning. Consequently the blue waves of the sunlight enter our eyes from all directions. And that is why the sky looks blue.

QUESTIONS

1. Analogy, the comparison of something familiar with something less familiar, occurs frequently in scientific explanation. Jeans introduces an analogy in his first paragraph. How does he develop that analogy as he develops his explanation?

2. The analogy Jeans provides enables him to explain the process by which the blue light-waves scatter throughout the sky. Hence he gives us a brief process analysis of that phenomenon. Summarize that process in your own words.

3. Try rewriting this essay without the analogy. Remove paragraph 1 and all the references to ocean waves and pier columns in paragraphs 2 and 3. How clear an explanation is left?

4. Besides the sea-waves, what other familiar examples does Jeans use in his explanation?

5. This piece opens with "Imagine that we stand. . . ." Suppose that every *we* was replaced with a *you*. How would the tone of the essay change?

6. While analogy can be effective in helping to explain difficult scientific concepts, it can be equally useful in explaining and interpreting familiar things by juxtaposing them in new ways. Suppose, for example, that you wish to explain to a friend why you dislike a course you are taking. Select one of the following ideas for an analogy (or find a better one): a forced-labor camp, a three-ring circus, squirrels on a treadmill, a tea party, a group-therapy session. Think through the analogy to your course, and write a few paragraphs of explanation. Let Jeans's essay guide you in organizing your own.

MAKING CONNECTIONS

1. Jeans's essay is a clear explanation of a complex phenomenon, yet it is quite short. Where else in this volume have you found explanations as clear? A number of short passages in the essays by Francis Crick (p. 492), Stephen W. Hawking (p. 500),

Bruno Bettelheim (p. 621), and Farley Mowat (p. 237) could provide examples. Choose a descriptive passage that you find clear in the work of one of these writers, and compare it to Jeans's. Is an analogy central to the passage you selected? If not, what are the differences in the authors' explanations?

2. Describe the audience Jeans seems to have in mind for his explanation. How does that sense of audience differ for Francis Crick (p. 492), Margaret Atwood (p. 343), William Gass (p. 347), or Malcolm Gladwell (p. 428)? Compare one or two of those essays with Jeans's account of "Why the Sky Is Blue," and discuss how the task of explaining shifts according to the writer's assumptions about an audience.

TIMES AND DISTANCES, LARGE AND SMALL

Francis Crick

Francis Crick (b. 1916), a British molecular biologist, shared the 1962 Nobel Prize for medicine with James D. Watson for their report on the structure of DNA. Their work probably constitutes the single most important scientific discovery of the century, having generated revolutions in biology, chemistry, physics, and medicine. Crick, known for an incessant inquisitiveness that has taken him into many fields, was once described in the pages of Nature as "fractious," a quality that shows in his research in the neuroscience of brain modeling. Both Watson and Crick have made special efforts to explain their studies to the general public. The essay reprinted here is the first chapter of Crick's book, Life Itself: Its Origin and Nature *(1981). Other books intended for a larger audience include* What Mad Pursuit *(1988) and* The Astonishing Hypothesis: The Scientific Search for the Soul *(1994).*

There is one fact about the origin of life which is reasonably certain. Whenever and wherever it happened, it started a very long time ago, so long ago that it is extremely difficult to form any realistic idea of such vast stretches of time. Our own personal experience extends back over tens of years, yet even for that limited period we are apt to forget precisely what the world was like when we were young. A hundred years ago the earth was also full of people, bustling about their business, eating and sleeping, walking and talking, making love and earning a living, each one steadily pursuing his own affairs, and yet (with very rare exceptions) not one of them is left alive today. Instead, a totally different set of persons inhabits the earth around us. The shortness of human life necessarily limits the span of direct personal recollection.

Human culture has given us the illusion that our memories go further back than that. Before writing was invented, the experience of earlier generations, embodied in stories, myths and moral precepts to guide behavior, was passed down verbally or, to a lesser extent, in pictures, carvings and statues. Writing has made more precise and more extensive the transmission of such information and in recent times photography has sharpened our images of the immediate past. Cinematography will give future generations a more direct and vivid impression of their forebears than we can now easily get from the written word.

What a pity we don't have a talking picture of Cleopatra;[1] it would not only reveal the true length of her nose but would make more explicit the essence of her charm.

We can, with an effort, project ourselves back to the time of Plato and Aristotle,[2] and even beyond to Homer's Bronze Age heroes.[3] We can learn something of the highly organized civilizations of Egypt, the Middle East, Central America and China and a little about other primitive and scattered habitations. Even so, we have difficulty in contemplating steadily the march of history, from the beginnings of civilization to the present day, in such a way that we can truly experience the slow passage of time. Our minds are not built to deal comfortably with periods as long as hundreds or thousands of years.

Yet when we come to consider the origin of life, the time scales we must deal with make the whole span of human history seem but the blink of an eyelid. There is no simple way to adjust one's thinking to such vast stretches of time. The immensity of time passed is beyond our ready comprehension. One can only construct an impression of it from indirect and incomplete descriptions, much as a blind man laboriously builds up, by touch and sound, a picture of his immediate surroundings.

The customary way to provide a convenient framework for one's thoughts is   5 to compare the age of the universe with the length of a single earthly day. Perhaps a better comparison, along the same lines, would be to equate the age of our earth with a single week. On such a scale the age of the universe, since the Big Bang,[4] would be about two or three weeks. The oldest macroscopic fossils (those from the start of the Cambrian)[5] would have been alive just one day ago. Modern man would have appeared in the last ten seconds and agriculture in the last one or two. Odysseus would have lived only half a second before the present time.[6]

Even this comparison hardly makes the longer time scale comprehensible to us. Another alternative is to draw a linear map of time, with the different events marked on it. The problem here is to make the line long enough to show our own experience on a reasonable scale, and yet short enough for convenient reproduction and examination. For easy reference such a map has been printed at the beginning of [the next page]. But perhaps the most vivid method is to compare time to the lines of print themselves. Let us make [a

---

[1]*Cleopatra* (69–30 B.C.): Egyptian queen who charmed Julius Caesar and Marc Antony. [Eds.]

[2]*Plato* (c. 428–348 B.C.) and *Aristotle* (384–322 B.C.): Greek philosophers. [Eds.]

[3]*Homer's Bronze Age heroes*: the heroes of *The Iliad* and *The Odyssey*, epic poems written by Greek poet Homer about 750 B.C. Homer's heroes fought in the Trojan war (c. 1200 B.C.) at the end of the Bronze Age (3500–1000 B.C.). [Eds.]

[4]*Big Bang*: a cosmological model in which all matter in the universe originated in a giant explosion about eighteen billion years ago. [Eds.]

[5]*Cambrian*: the earliest period of the Paleozoic era, beginning about six-hundred million years ago. [Eds.]

[6]*Odysseus*: the most famous Greek hero of antiquity; he is the hero of Homer's *Odyssey* and a prominent character in *The Iliad*. [Eds.]

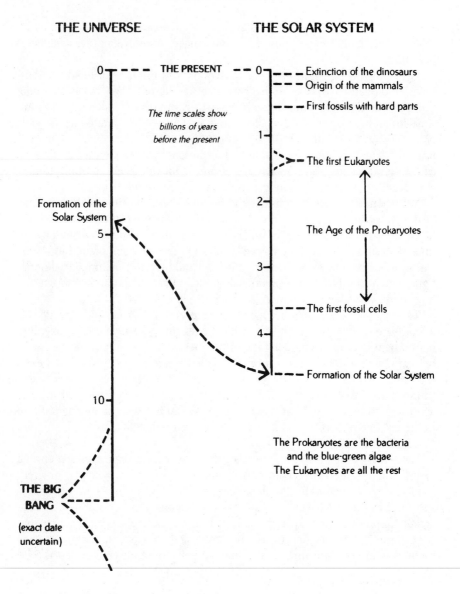

THE UNIVERSE   THE SOLAR SYSTEM

0 — THE PRESENT — 0 — Extinction of the dinosaurs
Origin of the mammals

First fossils with hard parts

The time scales show billions of years before the present

1 —

The first Eukaryotes

Formation of the Solar System

5 —

The Age of the Prokaryotes

2 —

3 —

The first fossil cells

4 —

Formation of the Solar System

10 —

The Prokaryotes are the bacteria and the blue-green algae
The Eukaryotes are all the rest

THE BIG BANG

(exact date uncertain)

200-page] book equal in length to the time from the start of the Cambrian to the present; that is, about 600 million years. Then each full page will represent roughly 3 million years, each line about ninety thousand years and each letter or small space about fifteen hundred years. The origin of the earth would be about seven books ago and the origin of the universe (which has been dated only approximately) ten or so books before that. Almost the whole of recorded human history would be covered by the last two or three letters of the book.

If you now turn back the pages of the book, slowly reading *one letter at a time*—remember, each letter is fifteen hundred years—then this may convey to you something of the immense stretches of time we shall have to consider. On this scale the span of your own life would be less than the width of a comma.

If life really started here we need hardly be concerned with the rest of the universe, but if it started elsewhere the magnitude of large distances must be squarely faced. Though it is difficult to convey a vivid and precise impression of the age of the universe, to grasp its size is almost beyond human comprehension, however we try to express it. The main stumbling block is the extreme emptiness of space; not merely the few atoms in between the stars but the immense distance from one star to another. The visible world close to us is cluttered with objects and our intuitive estimates of their distance depend mainly on various clues provided by their apparent size and their visual interrelationships. It is much more difficult to judge the distance of an unfamiliar object floating in the emptiness of the clear, blue sky. I once heard a Canadian radio interviewer say, when challenged, that he thought the moon "was about the size of a balloon," though admittedly this was before the days of space travel.

This is how two astronomers, Jastrow and Thompson, try to describe, by analogy, the size and the distance of objects in space:

> Let the sun be the size of an orange; on that scale the earth is a grain of sand circling in orbit around the sun at a distance of thirty feet; Jupiter, eleven times larger than the earth, is a cherry pit revolving at a distance of 200 feet or one city block from the sun. The galaxy on this scale is 100 billion oranges, each orange separated from its neighbors by an average distance of 1,000 miles.[7]

The difficulty with an analogy of this type is that it is almost impossible for us to estimate distances in empty space. A comparison with a city block is misleading, because we too easily visualize the buildings in it, and in doing so lose the idea of emptiness. If you try to imagine an orange floating even a mile up in the sky you will find that its distance seems to become indefinite. An "orange" a thousand miles away would be too small to see unless it were incandescent.

Another possible method is to convert distances to time. Pretend you are on a spaceship which is traveling faster than any present-day spaceship. For various reasons, which will become clear later, let us take its speed to be one-hundredth the velocity of light; that is, about 1,800 miles per second. At this

10

---

[7]Robert Jastrow and Malcolm M. Thompson, *Astronomy: Fundamentals and Frontiers*, 2nd ed. (New York: Wiley, 1972).

speed one could go from New York to Europe in about three seconds (Concorde takes roughly three hours), so we are certainly traveling fairly fast by everyday standards. It would take us two minutes to reach the moon and fifteen hours to reach the sun. To go right across the solar system from one side to the other—let us take this distance rather arbitrarily as the diameter of the orbit of Neptune—would take us almost three and one-half weeks. The main point to grasp is that this journey is not unlike a very long train journey, rather longer than the distance from Moscow to Vladivostok and back. Such a trip would probably be monotonous enough, even though the landscape were constantly flowing past the train window. While going across the solar system, there would be nothing at all just outside the window of the spaceship. Very slowly, day after day, the sun would change in size and position. As we traveled farther away from it, its apparent diameter would decrease, till near the orbit of Neptune it would look "little bigger than a pin's head," as I have previously described it, assuming that its apparent size, as viewed from the earth, corresponds roughly to that of a silver dollar. In spite of traveling so fast—remember that at this speed we could travel from any spot to any other on the earth's surface in less than seven seconds—this journey would be tedious in the extreme. Our main impression would be of the almost total emptiness of space. At this distance a planet would appear to be little more than an occasional speck in this vast wilderness.

This feeling of an immense three-dimensional emptiness is bad enough while we are focusing on the solar system. (Almost all of the scale models of the solar system one sees in museums are grossly misleading. The sun and the planets are almost always shown as far too big by comparison with the distances between them.) It is when we try to go farther afield that the enormity of space really hits us. To reach the nearest star—actually a group of three stars fairly close together—would take our spaceship 430 years and the chances are we would pass nothing significant on the way there. A whole lifetime of one hundred years, traveling at this very high speed, would take us less than a quarter of the way there. We would be constantly traveling from emptiness to emptiness with nothing but a few gas molecules and an occasional tiny speck of dust to show that we were not always in the same place. Very, very slowly a few of the nearest stars would change their positions slightly, while the sun itself would fade imperceptibly until it was just another star in the brilliant panorama of stars visible on all sides of the spaceship. Long though it would seem, this journey to the nearest star is, by astronomical standards, a very short one. To cross our own galaxy from side to side would take no less than ten million years. Such distances are beyond anything we can conceive except in the most abstract way. And yet, on a cosmic scale, the distance across the galaxy is hardly any distance at all. Admittedly it is only about twenty times as far to Andromeda, the nearest large galaxy, but to reach the limits of space visible to us in our giant telescopes we would have to travel more than a thousand times farther than that. To me it is remarkable that this astonishing discovery, the vastness and the emptiness of space, has not attracted the imaginative attention of poets and religious thinkers. People are happy to contemplate the limitless powers of God—a doubtful proposition at best—but quite unwilling to meditate creatively on the size of this extraordinary universe in which, through no virtue of their own, they find themselves. Naïvely one might have thought that both poets and priests would be so utterly astonished by these scientific revelations that they would be working with a white-hot fury to try to embody them in the foundation of our culture. The psalmist who said, "When I consider Thy heavens, the work of Thy fingers, the moon and the stars, which Thou hast ordained; what is man, that Thou art mindful of him? . . ." was at least trying, within the limitations of his beliefs, to express his wonder at the universe visible to the naked eye and the pettiness of man by comparison. And yet *his* universe was a small, almost cozy affair compared to the one modern science has revealed to us. It is almost as if the utter insignificance of the earth and the thin film of its biosphere has totally paralyzed the imagination, as if it were too dreadful to contemplate and therefore best ignored.

I shall not discuss here how these very large distances are estimated. The distance of the main objects in the solar system can now be obtained very accurately by a combination of the theory of solar mechanics and radar ranging, the distances of the nearest stars by the way their relative positions change slightly when viewed from the different positions of the earth in its yearly orbit around the sun. After that the arguments are more technical and less precise. But that the distances are the sort of size astronomers estimate there is not the slightest doubt.

So far we have been considering very large magnitudes. Fortunately, when we turn to very small distances and times things are not quite so bad. We need to know the size of atoms—the size and contents of the tiny nucleus within each atom will concern us less—compared to everyday things. This we can manage in two relatively small hops. Let us start with a millimeter. This distance (about a twenty-fifth of an inch) is easy for us to see with the naked eye. One-thousandth part of this is called a micron. A bacteria cell is about two microns long. The wavelength of visible light (which limits what we can see in a high-powered light microscope) is about half a micron long.

We now go down by another factor of a thousand to reach a length known as a nanometer. The typical distance between adjacent atoms bonded strongly together in an organic compound lies between a tenth and a fifth of this. Under the best conditions we can see distances of a nanometer, or a little less, using an electron microscope, provided the specimen can be suitably prepared. Moreover, it is possible to exhibit pictures of a whole series of natural objects at every scale between a small group of atoms and a flea, so that with a little practice we can feel one scale merging into another. By contrast with the emptiness of space, the living world is crammed with detail at every level. The ease with which we can go from one scale to another should not blind us to the fact that the numbers of objects within a *volume* can be uncomfortably large. For example, a drop of water contains rather more than a thousand billion billion water molecules.

The short time we shall be concerned with will rarely be less than a picosecond, that is, one-millionth of a millionth of a second, though very much shorter times occur in nuclear reactions and in studies of subatomic particles. This minute interval is the sort of time scale on which molecules are vibrating, but looked at another way, it does not seem so outlandish. Consider the velocity of sound. In air this is relatively slow—little faster than most jet planes—being about a thousand feet per second. If a flash of lightning is only a mile away, it will take a full five seconds for its sound to reach us. This velocity is, incidentally, approximately the same as the average speed of the molecules of gas in the air, in between their collisions with each other. The speed of sound in most solids is usually a little faster.

Now we ask, how long will it take a sound wave to pass over a small molecule? A simple calculation shows this time to be in the picosecond range. This is just what one would expect, since this is about the time scale on which the atoms of the molecule are vibrating against one another. What is important is that this is, roughly speaking, the pulse rate *underlying* chemical reactions. An enzyme—an organic catalyst—can react a thousand or more times a second. This may appear fast to us but this rate is really rather slow on the time scale of atomic vibration.

Unfortunately, it is not so easy to convey the time scales in between a second and a picosecond, though a physical chemist can learn to feel at home over this fairly large range. Fortunately, we shall not be concerned directly with these very short times, though we shall see their effects indirectly. Most chemical reactions are really very rare events. The molecules usually move around intermittently and barge against one another many times before a rare lucky encounter allows them to hit each other strongly enough and in the correct direction to surmount their protective barriers and produce a chemical reaction. It is only because there are usually so many molecules in one small volume, all doing this at the same time, that the rate of chemical reaction appears to proceed quite smoothly. The chance variations are smoothed out by the large numbers involved.

When we stand back and review once again these very different scales—the minute size of an atom and the almost unimaginable size of the universe; the pulse rate of chemical reaction compared to the deserts of vast eternity since the Big Bang—we see that in all these instances our intuitions, based on our experience of everyday life, are likely to be highly misleading. By themselves, large numbers mean very little to us. There is only one way to overcome this handicap, so natural to our human condition. We must calculate and recalculate, even though only approximately, to check and recheck our initial impressions until slowly, with time and constant application, the real world, the world of the immensely small and the immensely great, becomes as familiar to us as the simple cradle of our common earthly experience.

QUESTIONS

1. Study the diagram that accompanies the essay. How does one line relate to the other? What is the diagram trying to convey?

2. Why are the first three paragraphs devoted to the history and historical memory of humankind?

3. Compare the analogies Crick uses to explain the long passage of universal time in paragraphs 5, 6, and 7. What does the analogy of the book add to that of the week?

4. In paragraph 8, what is the implication of *elsewhere* in the first sentence? This essay is the first chapter of a book called *Life Itself*. What do you imagine to be at least one idea treated in the rest of the book?

5. Paragraph 11 is an extremely long paragraph, and paragraph 12 is even longer. Their lengths seem to correspond to the subjects they take up. Can you think of other ways to imagine the kind of emptiness these paragraphs describe?

6. Paragraph 11 implies an unusual definition of *wilderness*, its last word. Explain why you consider Crick's idea of wilderness the essential one or an eccentric notion.

7. Why do you think that poets and priests have not, as Crick observes, been "working with a white-hot fury to try to embody [these scientific revelations] in the foundation of our culture" (paragraph 12)? What does that last phrase, "foundation of our culture," mean in this context?

8. Why do you think Crick treats the very large before the very small? Which are the more astonishing measurements?

9. Think of a way of estimating, closely but reasonably, something quite numerous—for example, the number of blades of grass in a yard, the number of leaves or pine needles on a tree, the number of hairs on the tail of a cat, or the number of cars on all the roads, during a single day, in your state or city. Describe your system of estimation, and explain the answer it yields.

MAKING CONNECTIONS

1. Compare the diagrams in the articles by Crick and Stephen W. Hawking (p. 500). What differences do you find in the purposes for these diagrams? Identify the one that you find particularly successful, and explain its success.

2. Consider several of the following essays: Isak Dinesen's "The Iguana" (p. 66), Alice Walker's "Beauty: When the Other Dancer Is the Self" (p. 40), George Orwell's "Shooting an Elephant" (p. 104), N. Scott Momaday's "The Way to Rainy Mountain" (p. 98), and Joan Didion's "Georgia O'Keeffe" (p. 311). How do you think one or more of these writers would respond to Crick's assertion in paragraph 12 that our poets and priests are not trying to deal with the wonders of the universe?

OUR PICTURE OF THE UNIVERSE

Stephen W. Hawking

Stephen W. Hawking (b. 1942), the Lucasian Professor of Mathematics at Cambridge University, is one of the world's leading theoretical physicists. Carl Sagan described the moment in 1974 when he observed "an ancient rite, the investiture of new fellows into the Royal Society, one of the most ancient scholarly organizations on the planet. In the front row a young man in a wheelchair was, very slowly, signing his name in a book that bore on its earliest pages the signature of Isaac Newton. When at last he finished, there was a stirring ovation. Stephen Hawking was a legend even then." Hawking's extraordinary achievements have drawn broad popular admiration in part because he suffers from the serious physical disabilities associated with Lou Gehrig's disease. Hawking is known especially for his work on "black holes" and their implications for a unified theory of physical phenomena. His best-selling book A Brief History of Time *(1988) made his thinking available to the general reader, with over a million copies in print. (In 1992, filmmaker Erroll Morris released a fascinating documentary portrait of Hawking under the same title.) The essay reprinted below is the first chapter of that book, unchanged except for the removal of references to the book as a whole.*

A well-known scientist (some say it was Bertrand Russell) once gave a public lecture on astronomy. He described how the earth orbits around the sun and how the sun, in turn, orbits around the center of a vast collection of stars called our galaxy. At the end of the lecture, a little old lady at the back of the room got up and said: "What you have told us is rubbish. The world is really a flat plate supported on the back of a giant tortoise." The scientist gave a superior smile before replying, "What is the tortoise standing on?" "You're very clever, young man, very clever," said the old lady. "But it's turtles all the way down!"

Most people would find the picture of our universe as an infinite tower of tortoises rather ridiculous, but why do we think we know better? What do we know about the universe, and how do we know it? Where did the universe come from, and where is it going? Did the universe have a beginning, and if so, what happened *before* then? What is the nature of time? Will it ever come to an end? Recent breakthroughs in physics, made possible in part by fantastic new technologies, suggest answers to some of these longstanding questions.

500

Someday these answers may seem as obvious to us as the earth orbiting the sun—or perhaps as ridiculous as a tower of tortoises. Only time (whatever that may be) will tell.

As long ago as 340 B.C. the Greek philosopher Aristotle, in his book *On the Heavens*, was able to put forward two good arguments for believing that the earth was a round sphere rather than a flat plate. First, he realized that eclipses of the moon were caused by the earth coming between the sun and the moon. The earth's shadow on the moon was always round, which would be true only if the earth was spherical. If the earth had been a flat disk, the shadow would have been elongated and elliptical, unless the eclipse always occurred at a time when the sun was directly under the center of the disk. Second, the Greeks knew from their travels that the North Star appeared lower in the sky when viewed in the south than it did in more northerly regions. (Since the North Star lies over the North Pole, it appears to be directly above an observer at the North Pole, but to someone looking from the equator, it appears to lie just at the horizon.) From the difference in the apparent position of the North Star in Egypt and Greece, Aristotle even quoted an estimate that the distance around the earth was 400,000 stadia. It is not known exactly what length a stadium was, but it may have been about 200 yards, which would make Aristotle's estimate about twice the currently accepted figure. The Greeks even had a third argument that the earth must be round, for why else does one first see the sails of a ship coming over the horizon, and only later see the hull?

Aristotle thought that the earth was stationary and that the sun, the moon, the planets, and the stars moved in circular orbits about the earth. He believed this because he felt, for mystical reasons, that the earth was the center of the universe, and that circular motion was the most perfect. This idea was elaborated by Ptolemy in the second century A.D. into a complete cosmological model. The earth stood at the center, surrounded by eight spheres that carried the moon, the sun, the stars, and the five planets known at the time, Mercury, Venus, Mars, Jupiter, and Saturn (Fig. 1). The planets themselves moved on smaller circles attached to their respective spheres in order to account for their rather complicated observed paths in the sky. The outermost sphere carried the so-called fixed stars, which always stay in the same positions relative to each other but which rotate together across the sky. What lay beyond the last sphere was never made very clear, but it certainly was not part of mankind's observable universe.

Ptolemy's model provided a reasonably accurate system for predicting the positions of heavenly bodies in the sky. But in order to predict these positions correctly, Ptolemy had to make an assumption that the moon followed a path that sometimes brought it twice as close to the earth as at other times. And that meant that the moon ought sometimes to appear twice as big as at other times! Ptolemy recognized this flaw, but nevertheless his model was generally, although not universally, accepted. It was adopted by the Christian church as the picture of the universe that was in accordance with Scripture, for it had the great advantage that it left lots of room outside the sphere of fixed stars for heaven and hell.

A simpler model, however, was proposed in 1514 by a Polish priest, Nicholas Copernicus. (At first, perhaps for fear of being branded a heretic by his church, Copernicus circulated his model anonymously.) His idea was that the sun was stationary at the center and that the earth and the planets moved in circular orbits around the sun. Nearly a century passed before this idea was taken seriously. Then two astronomers—the German, Johannes Kepler, and the Italian, Galileo Galilei—started publicly to support the Copernican theory, despite the fact that the orbits it predicted did not quite match the ones observed. The death blow to the Aristotelian/Ptolemaic theory came in 1609. In that year, Galileo started observing the night sky with a telescope, which had just been invented. When he looked at the planet Jupiter, Galileo found that it was accompanied by several small satellites or moons that orbited around it. This implied that everything did *not* have to orbit directly around the earth, as Aristotle and Ptolemy had thought. (It was, of course, still possible to believe that the earth was stationary at the center of the universe and that the moons of Jupiter moved on extremely complicated paths around the earth, giving the *appearance* that they orbited Jupiter. However, Copernicus's theory was much simpler.) At the same time, Johannes Kepler had modified Copernicus's the-

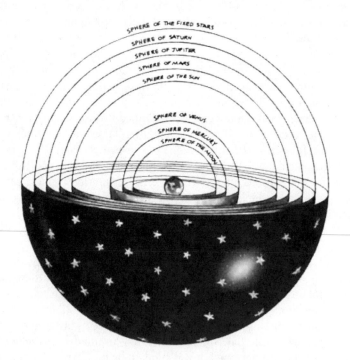

FIGURE 1

ory, suggesting that the planets moved not in circles but in ellipses (an ellipse is an elongated circle). The predictions now finally matched the observations.

As far as Kepler was concerned, elliptical orbits were merely an ad hoc hypothesis, and a rather repugnant one at that, because ellipses were clearly less perfect than circles. Having discovered almost by accident that elliptical orbits fit the observations well, he could not reconcile them with his idea that the planets were made to orbit the sun by magnetic forces. An explanation was provided only much later, in 1687, when Sir Isaac Newton published his *Philosophiae Naturalis Principia Mathematica*, probably the most important single work ever published in the physical sciences. In it Newton not only put forward a theory of how bodies move in space and time, but he also developed the complicated mathematics needed to analyse those motions. In addition, Newton postulated a law of universal gravitation according to which each body in the universe was attracted toward every other body by a force that was stronger the more massive the bodies and the closer they were to each other. It was this same force that caused objects to fall to the ground. (The story that Newton was inspired by an apple hitting his head is almost certainly apocryphal. All Newton himself ever said was that the idea of gravity came to him as he sat "in a contemplative mood" and "was occasioned by the fall of an apple.") Newton went on to show that, according to his law, gravity causes the moon to move in an elliptical orbit around the earth and causes the earth and the planets to follow elliptical paths around the sun.

The Copernican model got rid of Ptolemy's celestial spheres, and with them, the idea that the universe had a natural boundary. Since "fixed stars" did not appear to change their positions apart from a rotation across the sky caused by the earth spinning on its axis, it became natural to suppose that the fixed stars were objects like our sun but very much farther away.

Newton realized that, according to his theory of gravity, the stars should attract each other, so it seemed they could not remain essentially motionless. Would they not fall together at some point? In a letter in 1691 to Richard Bentley, another leading thinker of his day, Newton argued that this would indeed happen if there were only a finite number of stars distributed over a finite region of space. But he reasoned that if, on the other hand, there were an infinite number of stars, distributed more or less uniformly over infinite space, this would not happen, because there would not be any central point for them to fall to.

This argument is an instance of the pitfalls that you can encounter in talking about infinity. In an infinite universe, every point can be regarded as the center, because every point has an infinite number of stars on each side of it. The correct approach, it was realized only much later, is to consider the finite situation, in which the stars all fall in on each other, and then to ask how things change if one adds more stars roughly uniformly distributed outside this region. According to Newton's law, the extra stars would make no difference at all to the original ones on average, so the stars would fall in just as fast. We can add as many stars as we like, but they will still always collapse in on themselves. We now know it is impossible to have an infinite static model of the universe in which gravity is always attractive.

It is an interesting reflection on the general climate of thought before the twentieth century that no one had suggested that the universe was expanding or contracting. It was generally accepted that either the universe had existed forever in an unchanging state, or that it had been created at a finite time in the past more or less as we observe it today. In part this may have been due to people's tendency to believe in eternal truths, as well as the comfort they found in the thought that even though they may grow old and die, the universe is eternal and unchanging.

Even those who realized that Newton's theory of gravity showed that the universe could not be static did not think to suggest that it might be expanding. Instead, they attempted to modify the theory by making the gravitational force repulsive at very large distances. This did not significantly affect their predictions of the motions of the planets, but it allowed an infinite distribution of stars to remain in equilibrium—with the attractive forces between nearby stars balanced by the repulsive forces from those that were farther away. However, we now believe such an equilibrium would be unstable: if the stars in some region got only slightly nearer each other, the attractive forces between them would become stronger and dominate over the repulsive forces so that the stars would continue to fall toward each other. On the other hand, if the stars got a bit farther away from each other, the repulsive forces would dominate and drive them farther apart.

Another objection to an infinite static universe is normally ascribed to the German philosopher Heinrich Olbers, who wrote about this theory in 1823. In fact, various contemporaries of Newton had raised the problem, and the Olbers article was not even the first to contain plausible arguments against it. It was, however, the first to be widely noted. The difficulty is that in an infinite static universe nearly every line of sight would end on the surface of a star. Thus one would expect that the whole sky would be as bright as the sun, even at night. Olbers's counterargument was that the light from distant stars would be dimmed by absorption by intervening matter. However, if that happened the intervening matter would eventually heat up until it glowed as brightly as the stars. The only way of avoiding the conclusion that the whole of the night sky should be as bright as the surface of the sun would be to assume that the stars had not been shining forever but had turned on at some finite time in the past. In that case the absorbing matter might not have heated up yet or the light from distant stars might not yet have reached us. And that brings us to the question of what could have caused the stars to have turned on in the first place.

The beginning of the universe had, of course, been discussed long before this. According to a number of early cosmologies and the Jewish/Christian/Muslim tradition, the universe started at a finite, and not very distant, time in the past. One argument for such a beginning was the feeling that it was necessary to have "First Cause" to explain the existence of the universe. (Within the universe, you always explained one event as being caused by some earlier event, but the existence of the universe itself could be explained in this way only if it had some beginning.) Another argument was put forward by St. Augustine in his book *The City of God*. He pointed out that civilization is progressing and we remember who performed this deed or developed that technique. Thus man, and so also perhaps the universe, could not have been around all that long. St. Augustine accepted a date of about 5000 B.C. for the Creation of the universe according to the book of Genesis. (It is interesting that this is not so far from the end of the last Ice Age, about 10,000 B.C. which is when archaeologists tell us that civilization really began.)

Aristotle, and most of the other Greek philosophers, on the other hand, did 15 not like the idea of a creation because it smacked too much of divine intervention. They believed, therefore, that the human race and the world around it had existed, and would exist, forever. The ancients had already considered the argument about progress described above, and answered it by saying that there had been periodic floods or other disasters that repeatedly set the human race right back to the beginning of civilization.

The questions of whether the universe had a beginning in time and whether it is limited in space were later extensively examined by the philosopher Immanuel Kant in his monumental (and very obscure) work, *Critique of Pure Reason*, published in 1781. He called these questions antinomies (that is, contradictions) of pure reason because he felt that there were equally compelling arguments for believing the thesis, that the universe had a beginning, and the antithesis, that it had existed forever. His argument for the thesis was that if the universe did not have a beginning, there would be an infinite period of time before any event, which he considered absurd. The argument for the antithesis was that if the universe had a beginning, there would be an infinite period of time before it, so why should the universe begin at any one particular time? In fact, his cases for both the thesis and the antithesis are really the same argument. They are both based on his unspoken assumption that time continues back forever, whether or not the universe had existed forever. As we shall see, the concept of time has no meaning before the beginning of the universe. This was first pointed out by St. Augustine. When asked: What did God do before he created the universe? Augustine didn't reply: He was preparing Hell for people who asked such questions. Instead, he said that time was a property of the universe that God created, and that time did not exist before the beginning of the universe.

When most people believed in an essentially static and unchanging universe, the question of whether or not it had a beginning was really one of metaphysics or theology. One could account for what was observed equally well on the theory that the universe had existed forever or on the theory that it was set in motion at some finite time in such a manner as to look as though it had existed forever. But in 1929, Edwin Hubble made the landmark observation that wherever you look, distant galaxies are moving rapidly away from us. In other words, the universe is expanding. This means that at earlier times objects would have been closer together. In fact, it seemed that there was a time, about ten or twenty thousand million years ago, when they were all at exactly the same place and when, therefore, the density of the universe was infinite. This discovery finally brought the question of the beginning of the universe into the realm of science.

Hubble's observations suggested that there was a time, called the big bang, when the universe was infinitesimally small and infinitely dense. Under such conditions all the laws of science, and therefore all ability to predict the future, would break down. If there were events earlier than this time, then they could not affect what happens at the present time. Their existence can be ignored because it would have no observational consequences. One may say that time had a beginning at the big bang, in the sense that earlier times simply would not be defined. It should be emphasized that this beginning in time is very different from those that had been considered previously. In an unchanging universe a beginning in time is something that has to be imposed by some being outside the universe; there is no physical necessity for a beginning. One can imagine that God created the universe at literally any time in the past. On the other hand, if the universe is expanding, there may be physical reasons why there had to be a beginning. One could still imagine that God created the universe at the instant of the big bang, or even afterwards in just such a way as to make it look as though there had been a big bang, but it would be meaningless to suppose that it was created *before* the big bang. An expanding universe does not preclude a creator, but it does place limits on when he might have carried out his job!

In order to talk about the nature of the universe and to discuss questions such as whether it has a beginning or an end, you have to be clear about what a scientific theory is. I shall take the simpleminded view that a theory is just a model of the universe, or a restricted part of it, and a set of rules that relate quantities in the model to observations that we make. It exists only in our minds and does not have any other reality (whatever that might mean). A theory is a good theory if it satisfies two requirements: It must accurately describe a large class of observations on the basis of a model that contains only a few arbitrary elements, and it must make definite predictions about the results of future observations. For example, Aristotle's theory that everything was made out of four elements, earth, air, fire, and water, was simple enough to qualify, but it did not make any definite predictions. On the other hand, Newton's theory of gravity was based on an even simpler model, in which bodies attracted each other with a force that was proportional to a quantity called their mass and inversely proportional to the square of the distance between them. Yet it predicts the motions of the sun, the moon, and the planets to a high degree of accuracy.

Any physical theory is always provisional, in the sense that it is only a hypothesis: you can never prove it. No matter how many times the results of experiments agree with some theory, you can never be sure that the next time the result will not contradict the theory. On the other hand, you can disprove a theory by finding even a single observation that disagrees with the predictions of the theory. As philosopher of science Karl Popper has emphasized, a good theory is characterized by the fact that it makes a number of predictions that could in principle be disproved or falsified by observation. Each time new experiments are observed to agree with the predictions the theory survives, and our confidence in it is increased; but if ever a new observation is found to disagree, we have to abandon or modify the theory. At least that is what is supposed to happen, but you can always question the competence of the person who carried out the observation.

In practice, what often happens is that a new theory is devised that is really an extension of the previous theory. For example, very accurate observations of the planet Mercury revealed a small difference between its motion and the predictions of Newton's theory of gravity. Einstein's general theory of relativity predicted a slightly different motion from Newton's theory. The fact that Einstein's predictions matched what was seen, while Newton's did not, was one of the crucial confirmations of the new theory. However, we still use Newton's theory for all practical purposes because the difference between its predictions and those of general relativity is very small in the situations that we normally deal with. (Newton's theory also has the great advantage that it is much simpler to work with than Einstein's!)

The eventual goal of science is to provide a single theory that describes the whole universe. However, the approach most scientists actually follow is to separate the problem into two parts. First, there are the laws that tell us how the universe changes with time. (If we know what the universe is like at any one time, these physical laws tell us how it will look at any later time.) Second, there is the question of the initial state of the universe. Some people feel that science should be concerned with only the first part; they regard the question of the initial situation as a matter for metaphysics or religion. They would say that God, being omnipotent, could have started the universe off any way he wanted. That may be so, but in that case he also could have made it develop in a completely arbitrary way. Yet it appears that he chose to make it evolve in a very regular way according to certain laws. It therefore seems equally reasonable to suppose that there are also laws governing the initial state.

It turns out to be very difficult to devise a theory to describe the universe all in one go. Instead, we break the problem up into bits and invent a number of partial theories. Each of these partial theories describes and predicts a certain limited class of observations, neglecting the effects of other quantities, or representing them by simple sets of numbers. It may be that this approach is completely wrong. If everything in the universe depends on everything else in a fundamental way, it might be impossible to get close to a full solution by investigating parts of the problem in isolation. Nevertheless, it is certainly the way that we have made progress in the past. The classic example again is the Newtonian theory of gravity, which tells us that the gravitational force between two bodies depends only on one number associated with each body, its mass, but is otherwise independent of what the bodies are made of. Thus one does not need to have a theory of the structure and constitution of the sun and the planets in order to calculate their orbits.

Today scientists describe the universe in terms of two basic partial theories—the general theory of relativity and quantum mechanics. They are the great intellectual achievements of the first half of this century. The general theory of relativity describes the force of gravity and the large-scale structure of the universe, that is, the structure on scales from only a few miles to as large as a million million million million (1 with twenty-four zeros after it) miles, the size of the observable universe. Quantum mechanics, on the other hand, deals with phenomena on extremely small scales, such as a millionth of a millionth of an inch. Unfortunately, however, these two theories are known to be inconsistent with each other—they cannot both be correct. One of the major endeavors in physics today . . . is the search for a new theory that will incorporate them both—a quantum theory of gravity. We do not yet have such a theory, and we may still be a long way from having one, but we do already know many of the properties that it must have. And . . . we already know a fair amount about the predictions a quantum theory of gravity must make.

Now, if you believe that the universe is not arbitrary, but is governed by definite laws, you ultimately have to combine the partial theories into a complete unified theory that will describe everything in the universe. But there is a fundamental paradox in the search for such a complete unified theory. The ideas about scientific theories outlined above assume we are rational beings who are free to observe the universe as we want and to draw logical deductions from what we see. In such a scheme it is reasonable to suppose that we might progress even closer toward the laws that govern our universe. Yet if there really is a complete unified theory, it would also presumably determine our actions. And so the theory itself would determine the outcome of our search for it! And why should it determine that we come to the right conclusions from the evidence? Might it not equally well determine that we draw the wrong conclusion? Or no conclusion at all?

The only answer that I can give to this problem is based on Darwin's principle of natural selection. The idea is that in any population of self-reproducing organisms, there will be variations in the genetic material and upbringing that different individuals have. These differences will mean that some individuals are better able than others to draw the right conclusions about the world around them and to act accordingly. These individuals will be more likely to survive and reproduce and so their pattern of behavior and thought will come to dominate. It has certainly been true in the past that what we call intelligence and scientific discovery has conveyed a survival advantage. It is not so

508

clear that this is still the case: our scientific discoveries may well destroy us all, and even if they don't, a complete unified theory may not make much difference to our chances of survival. However, provided the universe has evolved in a regular way, we might expect that the reasoning abilities that natural selection has given us would be valid also in our search for a complete unified theory, and so would not lead us to the wrong conclusions.

Because the partial theories that we already have are sufficient to make accurate predictions in all but the most extreme situations, the search for the ultimate theory of the universe seems difficult to justify on practical grounds. (It is worth noting, though, that similar arguments could have been used against both relativity and quantum mechanics, and these theories have given us both nuclear energy and the microelectronics revolution!) The discovery of a complete unified theory, therefore, may not aid the survival of our species. It may not even affect our life-style. But ever since the dawn of civilization, people have not been content to see events as unconnected and inexplicable. They have craved an understanding of the underlying order in the world. Today we still yearn to know why we are here and where we came from. Humanity's deepest desire for knowledge is justification enough for our continuing quest. And our goal is nothing less than a complete description of the universe we live in.

QUESTIONS

1. There is a break in the essay after paragraph 18, indicated by extra space between paragraphs. If you had to provide a subtitle for each of the two sections demarcated by that break, what would these subtitles be?

2. What is the function of the anecdote in paragraph 1? Why do you suppose Hawking begins with that story?

3. What is the function of paragraph 2? What kind of sentence structure predominates in this paragraph? Why?

4. The first date mentioned in the essay comes in paragraph 3. Make a list of all the other exact dates that are given, noting the paragraphs in which they appear. Discuss any patterns (or violations of pattern) that you note. What does this list tell you about the organization of the essay?

5. Hawking uses the word *God* with some frequency. How would you describe the notion of God generated by his text? Is it different from your own views? How important is God to Hawking's view of the universe?

6. What is the notion of science that can be derived from Hawking's use of that word? That is, with what definition or concept of science is he working? Is it the same as your own? Discuss.

7. In the latter part of his essay, Hawking takes up the philosophical question of how we can know that we know what we know. Describe and discuss the view that he presents, bringing in any other theories of knowledge that you have encountered in your studies or reading on the subject.

MAKING CONNECTIONS

Read Carl Sagan's essay, "Can We Know the Universe? Reflections on a Grain of Salt" (p. 132). Are Sagan and Hawking talking about the same universe? Note Sagan's strongest beliefs as expressed in his final paragraphs. Are Sagan and Hawking thinking along the same lines? To what extent does Hawking seem to be answering the challenge that Sagan makes?

THE MAN WHO MISTOOK
HIS WIFE FOR A HAT

Oliver Sacks

Oliver Sacks was born in London, England, in 1933, and educated in London and Oxford before coming to the United States to complete his education in California and New York. At present he is clinical professor of neurology at Albert Einstein College of Medicine. He is best known, however, for his extraordinary writing on matters related to his medical studies, in such books as Awakenings *(1974),* Seeing Voices: A Journey into the World of the Deaf *(1989),* An Anthropologist on Mars *(1995),* The Island of the Colorblind *(1997), and his national best-seller,* The Man Who Mistook His Wife for a Hat *(1986), in which the following selection appeared. Interested in the art of storytelling as well as in clinical neurology, Sacks subtitled the book in which this essay appeared, "and Other Clinical Tales." He insists that his essays are not just case studies, though they are that, but also tales or fables of "heroes, victims, martyrs, warriors." In his writing, he says, "the scientific and romantic . . . come together at the intersection of fact and fable." Sacks's prose style is lyrical as well as accurate; his explanation of prosopagnosia (perception without recognition) seeks to engage our interest and emotions while it defines and illustrates a syndrome unfamiliar to many readers.*

Dr. P. was a musician of distinction, well-known for many years as a singer, and then, at the local School of Music, as a teacher. It was here, in relation to his students, that certain strange problems were first observed. Sometimes a student would present himself, and Dr. P. would not recognize him; or, specifically, would not recognize his face. The moment the student spoke, he would be recognized by his voice. Such incidents multiplied, causing embarrassment, perplexity, fear—and, sometimes, comedy. For not only did Dr. P. increasingly fail to see faces, but he saw faces when there were no faces to see: genially, Magoo-like, when in the street he might pat the heads of water hydrants and parking meters, taking these to be the heads of children; he would amiably address carved knobs on the furniture and be astounded when they did not reply. At first these odd mistakes were laughed off as jokes, not least by Dr. P. himself. Had he not always had a quirky sense of humor and been given to Zen-like paradoxes and jests? His musical powers were as dazzling as ever; he did not feel ill—he had never felt better; and the mistakes were so ludicrous—and so ingenious—that they could hardly be serious or betoken anything serious. The notion of there being "something the matter" did not emerge until some three years later, when diabetes developed. Well aware that diabetes could affect his eyes, Dr. P. consulted an ophthalmologist, who took a careful history and examined his eyes closely. "There's nothing the matter with your eyes," the doctor concluded. "But there is trouble with the visual parts of your brain. You don't need my help, you must see a neurologist." And so, as a result of this referral, Dr. P. came to me.

It was obvious within a few seconds of meeting him that there was no trace of dementia in the ordinary sense. He was a man of great cultivation and charm who talked well and fluently, with imagination and humor. I couldn't think why he had been referred to our clinic.

And yet there *was* something a bit odd. He faced me as he spoke, was oriented towards me, and yet there was something the matter—it was difficult to formulate. He faced me with his *ears*, I came to think, but not with his eyes. These, instead of looking, gazing, at me, "taking me in," in the normal way, made sudden strange fixations—on my nose, on my right ear, down to my chin, up to my right eye—as if noting (even studying) these individual features, but not seeing my whole face, its changing expressions, "me," as a whole. I am not sure that I fully realized this at the time—there was just a teasing strangeness, some failure in the normal interplay of gaze and expression. He saw me, he *scanned* me, and yet . . .

"What seems to be the matter?" I asked him at length.

"Nothing that I know of," he replied with a smile, "but people seem to   5 think there's something wrong with my eyes."

"But *you* don't recognize any visual problems?"

"No, not directly, but I occasionally make mistakes."

I left the room briefly to talk to his wife. When I came back, Dr. P. was sitting placidly by the window, attentive, listening rather than looking out. "Traffic," he said, "street sounds, distant trains—they make a sort of symphony, do they not? You know Honegger's[1] *Pacific 234?*"

What a lovely man, I thought to myself. How can there be anything seriously the matter? Would he permit me to examine him?

"Yes, of course, Dr. Sacks."   10

I stilled my disquiet, his perhaps, too, in the soothing routine of a neurological exam—muscle strength, coordination, reflexes, tone. . . . It was while examining his reflexes—a trifle abnormal on the left side—that the first bizarre experience occurred. I had taken off his left shoe and scratched the sole of his foot with a key—a frivolous-seeming but essential test of a reflex—and then, ex-

---

[1]*Arthur Honegger* (1892–1955): French composer. [Eds.]

cusing myself to screw my ophthalmoscope together, left him to put on the shoe himself. To my surprise, a minute later, he had not done this.

"Can I help?" I asked.

"Help what? Help whom?"

"Help you put on your shoe."

"Ach," he said, "I had forgotten the shoe," adding, *sotto voce*, "The shoe? The shoe?" He seemed baffled.   15

"Your shoe," I repeated. "Perhaps you'd put it on."

He continued to look downwards, though not at the shoe, with an intense but misplaced concentration. Finally his gaze settled on his foot: "That is my shoe, yes?"

Did I mis-hear? Did he mis-see?

"My eyes," he explained, and put a hand to his foot. "*This* is my shoe, no?"

"No, it is not. That is your foot. *There* is your shoe."   20

"Ah! I thought that was my foot."

Was he joking? Was he mad? Was he blind? If this was one of his "strange mistakes," it was the strangest mistake I had ever come across.

I helped him on with his shoe (his foot), to avoid further complication. Dr. P. himself seemed untroubled, indifferent, maybe amused. I resumed my examination. His visual acuity was good: he had no difficulty seeing a pin on the floor, though sometimes he missed it if it was placed to his left.

He saw all right, but what did he see? I opened out a copy of the *National Geographic Magazine* and asked him to describe some pictures in it.

His responses here were very curious. His eyes would dart from one thing to   25
another, picking up tiny features, individual features, as they had done with my face. A striking brightness, a color, a shape would arrest his attention and elicit comment—but in no case did he get the scene-as-a-whole. He failed to see the whole, seeing only details, which he spotted like blips on a radar screen. He never entered into relation with the picture as a whole—never faced, so to speak, *its* physiognomy. He had no sense whatever of a landscape or scene.

I showed him the cover, an unbroken expanse of Sahara dunes.

"What do you see here?" I asked.

"I see a river," he said. "And a little guest-house with its terrace on the water. People are dining out on the terrace. I see colored parasols here and there." He was looking, if it was "looking," right off the cover into mid-air and confabulating nonexistent features, as if the absence of features in the actual picture had driven him to imagine the river and the terrace and the colored parasols.

I must have looked aghast, but he seemed to think he had done rather well. There was a hint of a smile on his face. He also appeared to have decided that the examination was over and started to look around for his hat. He reached out his hand and took hold of his wife's head, tried to lift it off, to put it on. He had apparently mistaken his wife for a hat! His wife looked as if she was used to such things.

I could make no sense of what had occurred in terms of conventional neu-   30
rology (or neuropsychology). In some ways he seemed perfectly preserved, and
in others absolutely, incomprehensibly devastated. How could he, on the one
hand, mistake his wife for a hat and, on the other, function, as apparently he
still did, as a teacher at the Music School?

I had to think, to see him again—and to see him in his own familiar habitat,
at home.

A few days later I called on Dr. P. and his wife at home, with the score of
the *Dichterliebe* in my briefcase (I knew he liked Schumann),[2] and a variety of
odd objects for the testing of perception. Mrs. P. showed me into a lofty apartment, which recalled fin-de-siècle Berlin. A magnificent old Bösendorfer stood
in state in the center of the room, and all around it were music stands, instruments, scores. . . . There were books, there were paintings, but the music was
central. Dr. P. came in, a little bowed, and, distracted, advanced with outstretched hands to the grandfather clock, but, hearing my voice, corrected himself, and shook hands with me. We exchanged greetings and chatted a little of
current concerts and performances. Diffidently, I asked him if he would sing.

"The *Dichterliebe!*" he exclaimed. "But I can no longer read music. You
will play them, yes?"

I said I would try. On that wonderful old piano even my playing sounded
right, and Dr. P. was an aged but infinitely mellow Fischer-Dieskau,[3] combining a perfect ear and voice with the most incisive musical intelligence. It was
clear that the Music School was not keeping him on out of charity.

Dr. P.'s temporal lobes were obviously intact: he had a wonderful musical   35
cortex. What, I wondered, was going on in his parietal and occipital lobes, especially in those areas where visual processing occurred? I carry the Platonic
solids in my neurological kit and decided to start with these.

"What is this?" I asked, drawing out the first one.

"A cube, of course."

"Now this?" I asked, brandishing another.

He asked if he might examine it, which he did swiftly and systematically: "A
dodecahedron, of course. And don't bother with the others—I'll get the icosa-
hedron, too."

Abstract shapes clearly presented no problems. What about faces? I took out   40
a pack of cards. All of these he identified instantly, including the jacks, queens,
kings, and the joker. But these, after all, are stylized designs, and it was impossible to tell whether he saw faces or merely patterns. I decided I would show
him a volume of cartoons which I had in my briefcase. Here, again, for the
most part, he did well. Churchill's cigar, Schnozzle's nose: as soon as he had
picked out a key feature he could identify the face. But cartoons, again, are for-

---

[2]*Robert Schumann* (1810–1856): German romantic composer. [Eds.]
[3]*Dietrich Fischer-Dieskau* (b. 1925): German baritone, noted for his interpretations of Schumann.

mal and schematic. It remained to be seen how he would do with real faces, realistically represented.

I turned on the television, keeping the sound off, and found an early Bette Davis film. A love scene was in progress. Dr. P. failed to identify the actress—but this could have been because she had never entered his world. What was more striking was that he failed to identify the expressions on her face or her partner's, though in the course of a single torrid scene these passed from sultry yearning through passion, surprise, disgust, and fury to a melting reconciliation. Dr. P. could make nothing of any of this. He was very unclear as to what was going on, or who was who or even what sex they were. His comments on the scene were positively Martian.

It was just possible that some of his difficulties were associated with the unreality of a celluloid, Hollywood world; and it occurred to me that he might be more successful in identifying faces from his own life. On the walls of the apartment there were photographs of his family, his colleagues, his pupils, himself. I gathered a pile of these together and, with some misgivings, presented them to him. What had been funny, or farcical, in relation to the movie, was tragic in relation to real life. By and large, he recognized nobody: neither his family, nor his colleagues, nor his pupils, nor himself. He recognized a portrait of Einstein because he picked up the characteristic hair and mustache; and the same thing happened with one or two other people. "Ach, Paul!" he said, when shown a portrait of his brother. "That square jaw, those big teeth—I would know Paul anywhere!" But was it Paul he recognized, or one or two of his features, on the basis of which he could make a reasonable guess as to the subject's identity? In the absence of obvious "markers," he was utterly lost. But it was not merely the cognition, the *gnosis*, at fault; there was something radically wrong with the whole way he proceeded. For he approached these faces—even of those near and dear—as if they were abstract puzzles or tests. He did not relate to them, he did not behold. No face was familiar to him, seen as a "thou," being just identified as a set of features, an "it." Thus, there was formal, but no trace of personal, gnosis. And with this went his indifference, or blindness, to expression. A face, to us, is a person looking out—we see, as it were, the person through his *persona*, his face. But for Dr. P. there was no *persona* in this sense—no outward *persona*, and no person within.

I had stopped at a florist on my way to his apartment and bought myself an extravagant red rose for my buttonhole. Now I removed this and handed it to him. He took it like a botanist or morphologist given a specimen, not like a person given a flower.

"About six inches in length," he commented. "A convoluted red form with a linear green attachment."

"Yes," I said encouragingly, "and what do you think it *is*, Dr. P.?"

"Not easy to say." He seemed perplexed. "It lacks the simple symmetry of the Platonic solids, although it may have a higher symmetry of its own. . . . I think this could be an inflorescence or flower."

45

"Could be?" I queried.

"Could be," he confirmed.

"Smell it," I suggested, and he again looked somewhat puzzled, as if I had asked him to smell a higher symmetry. But he complied courteously, and took it to his nose. Now, suddenly, he came to life.

"Beautiful!" he exclaimed. "An early rose. What a heavenly smell!" He started to hum *"Die Rose, die Lillie . . ."* Reality, it seemed, might be conveyed by smell, not by sight.

I tried one final test. It was still a cold day, in early spring, and I had thrown my coat and gloves on the sofa.

"What is this?" I asked, holding up a glove.

"May I examine it?" he asked, and, taking it from me, he proceeded to examine it as he had examined the geometrical shapes.

"A continuous surface," he announced at last, "infolded on itself. It appears to have"—he hesitated—"five outpouchings, if this is the word."

"Yes," I said cautiously. "You have given me a description. Now tell me what it is."

"A container of some sort?"

"Yes," I said, "and what would it contain?"

"It would contain its contents!" said Dr. P., with a laugh. "There are many possibilities. It could be a change purse, for example, for coins of five sizes. It could . . ."

I interrupted the barmy flow. "Does it not look familiar? Do you think it might contain, might fit, a part of your body?"

No light of recognition dawned on his face.[4]

No child would have the power to see and speak of "a continuous surface . . . infolded on itself," but any child, any infant, would immediately know a glove as a glove, see it as familiar, as going with a hand. Dr. P. didn't. He saw nothing as familiar. Visually, he was lost in a world of lifeless abstractions. Indeed, he did not have a real visual world, as he did not have a real visual self. He could speak about things, but did not see them face-to-face. Hughlings Jackson, discussing patients with aphasia and left-hemisphere lesions, says they have lost "abstract" and "propositional" thought—and compares them with dogs (or, rather, he compares dogs to patients with aphasia). Dr. P., on the other hand, functioned precisely as a machine functions. It wasn't merely that he displayed the same indifference to the visual world as a computer but—even more strikingly—he construed the world as a computer construes it, by means of key features and schematic relationships. The scheme might be identified—in an "identi-kit" way—without the reality being grasped at all.

---

[4]Later, by accident, he got it on, and exclaimed, "My God, it's a glove!" This was reminiscent of Kurt Goldstein's patient "Lanuti," who could only recognize objects by trying to use them in action.

The testing I had done so far told me nothing about Dr. P.'s inner world. Was it possible that his visual memory and imagination were still intact? I asked him to imagine entering one of our local squares from the north side, to walk through it, in imagination or in memory, and tell me the buildings he might pass as he walked. He listed the buildings on his right side, but none of those on his left. I then asked him to imagine entering the square from the south. Again he mentioned only those buildings that were on the right side, although these were the very buildings he had omitted before. Those he had "seen" internally before were not mentioned now; presumably, they were no longer "seen." It was evident that his difficulties with leftness, his visual field deficits, were as much internal as external, bisecting his visual memory and imagination.

What, at a higher level, of his internal visualization? Thinking of the almost hallucinatory intensity with which Tolstoy visualizes and animates his characters, I questioned Dr. P. about *Anna Karenina*. He could remember incidents without difficulty, had an undiminished grasp of the plot, but completely omitted visual characteristics, visual narrative, and scenes. He remembered the words of the characters but not their faces; and though, when asked, he could quote, with his remarkable and almost verbatim memory, the original visual descriptions, these were, it became apparent, quite empty for him and lacked sensorial, imaginal, or emotional reality. Thus, there was an internal agnosia as well.[5]

But this was only the case, it became clear, with certain sorts of visualization. The visualization of faces and scenes, of visual narrative and drama—this was profoundly impaired, almost absent. But the visualization of *schemata* was preserved, perhaps enhanced. Thus, when I engaged him in a game of mental chess, he had no difficulty visualizing the chessboard or the moves—indeed, no difficulty in beating me soundly.

Luria[6] said of Zazetsky that he had entirely lost his capacity to play games but that his "vivid imagination" was unimpaired. Zazetsky and Dr. P. lived in worlds which were mirror images of each other. But the saddest difference between them was that Zazetsky, as Luria said, "fought to regain his lost faculties with the indomitable tenacity of the damned," whereas Dr. P. was not fighting, did not know what was lost, did not indeed know that anything was lost. But

65

---

[5] I have often wondered about Helen Keller's visual descriptions, whether these, for all their eloquence, are somehow empty as well? Or whether, by the transference of images from the tactile to the visual, or, yet more extraordinarily, from the verbal and the metaphorical to the sensorial and the visual, she *did* achieve a power of visual imagery, even though her visual cortex had never been stimulated, directly, by the eyes? But in Dr. P.'s case it is precisely the cortex that was damaged, the organic prerequisite of all pictorial imagery. Interestingly and typically he no longer dreamed pictorially—the "message" of the dream being conveyed in nonvisual terms.

[6] *Alexander Luria* (1902–1977): Russian neuropsychologist who worked with victims of traumatic head injuries. [Eds.]

who was more tragic, or who was more damned—the man who knew it, or the man who did not?

When the examination was over, Mrs. P. called us to the table, where there was coffee and a delicious spread of little cakes. Hungrily, hummingly, Dr. P. started on the cakes. Swiftly, fluently, unthinkingly, melodiously, he pulled the plates towards him and took this and that in a great gurgling stream, an edible song of food, until, suddenly, there came an interruption: a loud, peremptory rat-tat-tat at the door. Startled, taken aback, arrested by the interruption, Dr. P. stopped eating and sat frozen, motionless, at the table, with an indifferent, blind bewilderment on his face. He saw, but no longer saw, the table; no longer perceived it as a table laden with cakes. His wife poured him some coffee: the smell titillated his nose and brought him back to reality. The melody of eating resumed.

How does he do anything? I wondered to myself. What happens when he's dressing, goes to the lavatory, has a bath? I followed his wife into the kitchen and asked her how, for instance, he managed to dress himself. "It's just like the eating," she explained. "I put his usual clothes out, in all the usual places, and he dresses without difficulty, singing to himself. He does everything singing to himself. But if he is interrupted and loses the thread, he comes to a complete stop, doesn't know his clothes—or his own body. He sings all the time—eating songs, dressing songs, bathing songs, everything. He can't do anything unless he makes it a song."

While we were talking my attention was caught by the pictures on the walls.

"Yes," Mrs. P. said, "he was a gifted painter as well as a singer. The School exhibited his pictures every year."

I strolled past them curiously—they were in chronological order. All his ear-   70
lier work was naturalistic and realistic, with vivid mood and atmosphere, but finely detailed and concrete. Then, years later, they became less vivid, less concrete, less realistic and naturalistic, but far more abstract, even geometrical and cubist. Finally, in the last paintings, the canvases became nonsense, or nonsense to me—mere chaotic lines and blotches of paint. I commented on this to Mrs. P.

"Ach, you doctors, you're such Philistines!"[7] she exclaimed. "Can you not see *artistic development*—how he renounced the realism of his earlier years, and advanced into abstract, nonrepresentational art?"

"No, that's not it," I said to myself (but forbore to say it to poor Mrs. P.). He had indeed moved from realism to nonrepresentation to the abstract, yet this was not the artist, but the pathology, advancing—advancing towards a profound visual agnosia, in which all powers of representation and imagery, all sense of the concrete, all sense of reality, were being destroyed. This wall of paintings was a tragic pathological exhibit, which belonged to neurology, not art.

---

[7]*Philistines:* insult for ignorant or smug people who disdain intellectual or artistic values. [Eds.]

And yet, I wondered, was she not partly right? For there is often a struggle, and sometimes, even more interestingly, a collusion between the powers of pathology and creation. Perhaps, in his cubist period, there might have been both artistic and pathological development, colluding to engender an original form; for as he lost the concrete, so he might have gained in the abstract, developing a greater sensitivity to all the structural elements of line, boundary, contour—an almost Picasso-like power to see, and equally depict, those abstract organizations embedded in, and normally lost in, the concrete.... Though in the final pictures, I feared, there was only chaos and agnosia.

We returned to the great music room, with the Bösendorfer in the center, and Dr. P. humming the last torte.

"Well, Dr. Sacks," he said to me. "You find me an interesting case, I perceive. Can you tell me what you find wrong, make recommendations?"

"I can't tell you what I find wrong," I replied, "but I'll say what I find right. You are a wonderful musician, and music is your life. What I would prescribe, in a case such as yours, is a life which consists entirely of music. Music has been the center, now make it the whole, of your life."

This was four years ago—I never saw him again, but I often wondered about how he apprehended the world, given his strange loss of image, visuality, and the perfect preservation of a great musicality. I think that music, for him, had taken the place of image. He had no body-image, he had body-music: this is why he could move and act as fluently as he did, but came to a total confused stop if the "inner music" stopped. And equally with the outside, the world . . . [8]

In *The World as Representation and Will*, Schopenhauer[9] speaks of music as "pure will." How fascinated he would have been by Dr. P., a man who had wholly lost the world as representation, but wholly preserved it as music or will.

And this, mercifully, held to the end—for despite the gradual advance of his disease (a massive tumor or degenerative process in the visual parts of his brain) Dr. P. lived and taught music to the last days of his life.

POSTSCRIPT

How should one interpret Dr. P.'s peculiar inability to interpret, to judge, a glove as a glove? Manifestly, here, he could not make a cognitive judgment, though he was prolific in the production of cognitive hypotheses. A judgment is intuitive, personal, comprehensive, and concrete—we "see" how things stand, in relation to one another and oneself. It was precisely this setting, this relating, that Dr. P. lacked (though his judging, in all other spheres, was

---

[8]Thus, as I learned later from his wife, though he could not recognize his students if they sat still, if they were merely "images," he might suddenly recognize them if they *moved*. "That's Karl," he would cry. "I know his movements, his body-music."

[9]*Arthur Schopenhauer* (1788–1860): German philosopher whose work included a theory to explain the life and work of the artist. [Eds.]

prompt and normal). Was this due to lack of visual information, or faulty processing of visual information? (This would be the explanation given by a classical, schematic neurology.) Or was there something amiss in Dr. P.'s attitude, so that he could not relate what he saw to himself?

These explanations, or modes of explanation, are not mutually exclusive—being in different modes they could coexist and both be true. And this is acknowledged, implicitly or explicitly, in classical neurology: implicitly, by Macrae, when he finds the explanation of defective schemata, or defective visual processing and integration, inadequate; explicitly, by Goldstein, when he speaks of "abstract attitude." But abstract attitude, which allows "categorization," also misses the mark with Dr. P.—and, perhaps, with the concept of "judgment" in general. For Dr. P. *had* abstract attitude—indeed, nothing else. And it was precisely this, his absurd abstractness of attitude—absurd because unleavened with anything else—which rendered him incapable of perceiving identity, or particulars, rendered him incapable of judgment.

Neurology and psychology, curiously, though they talk of everything else, almost never talk of "judgment"—and yet it is precisely the downfall of judgment . . . which constitutes the essence of so many neuropsychological disorders. Judgment and identity may be casualties—but neuropsychology never speaks of them.

And yet, whether in a philosophic sense (Kant's sense),[10] or an empirical and evolutionary sense, judgment is the most important faculty we have. An animal, or a man, may get on very well without "abstract attitude" but will speedily perish if deprived of judgment. Judgment must be the *first* faculty of higher life or mind—yet it is ignored, or misinterpreted, by classical (computational) neurology. And if we wonder how such an absurdity can arise, we find it in the assumptions, or the evolution, of neurology itself. For classical neurology (like classical physics) has always been mechanical—from Hughlings Jackson's mechanical analogies to the computer analogies of today.

Of course, the brain *is* a machine and a computer—everything in classical neurology is correct. But our mental processes, which constitute our being and life, are not just abstract and mechanical, but personal, as well—and, as such, involve not just classifying and categorizing, but continual judging and feeling also. If this is missing, we become computer-like, as Dr. P. was. And, by the same token, if we delete feeling and judging, the personal, from the cognitive sciences, we reduce *them* to something as defective as Dr. P.—and we reduce *our* apprehension of the concrete and real.

By a sort of comic and awful analogy, our current cognitive neurology and psychology resemble nothing so much as poor Dr. P.! We need the concrete and real, as he did; and we fail to see this, as he failed to see it. Our cognitive sciences are themselves suffering from an agnosia essentially similar to Dr. P.'s.

85

---

[10]*Immanuel Kant* (1724–1804): German philosopher; some of his work concerned ethics and moral judgment. [Eds.]

Dr. P. may therefore serve as a warning and parable—of what happens to a science which eschews the judgmental, the particular, the personal, and becomes entirely abstract and computational.

It was always a matter of great regret to me that, owing to circumstances beyond my control, I was not able to follow his case further, either in the sort of observations and investigations described, or in ascertaining the actual disease pathology.

One always fears that a case is "unique," especially if it has such extraordinary features as those of Dr. P. It was, therefore, with a sense of great interest and delight, not unmixed with relief, that I found, quite by chance—looking through the periodical *Brain* for 1956—a detailed description of an almost comically similar case, similar (indeed identical) neuropsychologically and phenomenologically, though the underlying pathology (an acute head injury) and all personal circumstances were wholly different. The authors speak of their case as "unique in the documented history of this disorder"—and evidently experienced, as I did, amazement at their own findings.[11] The interested reader is referred to the original paper, Macrae and Trolle (1956), of which I here subjoin a brief paraphrase, with quotations from the original.

Their patient was a young man of 32, who, following a severe automobile accident, with unconsciousness for three weeks, ". . . complained, exclusively, of an inability to recognize faces, even those of his wife and children." Not a single face was "familiar" to him, but there were three he could identify; these were workmates: one with an eye-blinking tic, one with a large mole on his cheek, and a third "because he was so tall and thin that no one else was like him." Each of these, Macrae and Trolle bring out, was "recognized solely by the single prominent feature mentioned." In general (like Dr. P.) he recognized familiars only by their voices.

He had difficulty even recognizing himself in a mirror, as Macrae and Trolle describe in detail: "In the early convalescent phase he frequently, especially when shaving, questioned whether the face gazing at him was really his own, and even though he knew it could physically be none other, on several occasions grimaced or stuck out his tongue 'just to make sure.' By carefully studying his face in the mirror he slowly began to recognize it, but 'not in a flash' as in the past—he relied on the hair and facial outline, and on two small moles on his left cheek."

---

[11]Only since the completion of this book have I found that there is, in fact, a rather extensive literature on visual agnosia in general, and prosopagnosia in particular. In particular I had the great pleasure recently of meeting Dr. Andrew Kertesz, who has himself published some extremely detailed studies of patients with such agnosias (see, for example, his paper on visual agnosia, Kertesz 1979). Dr. Kertesz mentioned to me a case known to him of a farmer who had developed prosopagnosia and in consequence could no longer distinguish (the faces of) his *cows*, and of another such patient, an attendant in a Natural History Museum, who mistook his own reflection for the diorama of an *ape*. As with Dr. P., and as with Macrae and Trolle's patient, it is especially the animate which is so absurdly misperceived. The most important studies of such agnosias, and of visual processing in general, are now being undertaken by A. R. and H. Damasio.

In general he could not recognize objects "at a glance," but would have to   90
seek out, and guess from, one or two features—occasionally his guesses were
absurdly wrong. In particular, the authors note, there was difficulty with the
animate.

On the other hand, simple schematic objects—scissors, watch, key, etc.—
presented no difficulties. Macrae and Trolle also note that: "His *topographical
memory* was strange: the seeming paradox existed that he could find his way
from home to hospital and around the hospital, but yet could not name streets
en route [unlike Dr. P., he also had some aphasia] or appear to visualize the
topography."

It was also evident that visual memories of people, even from long before
the accident, were severely impaired—there was memory of conduct, or perhaps a mannerism, but not of visual appearance or face. Similarly, it appeared,
when he was questioned closely, that he no longer had visual images in his
dreams. Thus, as with Dr. P., it was not just visual perception, but visual imagination and memory, the fundamental powers of visual representation, which
were essentially damaged in this patient—at least those powers insofar as they
pertained to the personal, the familiar, the concrete.

A final, humorous point. Where Dr. P. might mistake his wife for a hat,
Macrae's patient, also unable to recognize his wife, needed her to identify herself by a visual *marker*, by ". . . a conspicuous article of clothing, such as a large
hat."

QUESTIONS

1. Summarize as clearly as you can the nature of Dr. P.'s problem. What are the
symptoms? What seems to have caused them?

2. What conclusions can be drawn from the case of Dr. P. about the way our visual
systems work? Using what Sacks himself says and whatever additional conclusions you
yourself can draw, what does the case of Dr. P. tell us about the way we see things and
what it means to recognize what we see?

3. Sacks has a way of drawing readers into his case studies, of making them concerned about the individuals whose cases he presents. How does he do this? That is,
considering him as a writer rather than as a doctor, what aspects of his writing arouse interest and concern? Look at the opening paragraphs of the essay in particular.

4. Is this essay to any degree a story with a plot? Most people find Sacks a very compelling writer. What is it about his way of writing that causes this response? How does
he keep readers reading?

5. This essay is not only a single case history and an explanation of some very curious behavior. It also contains or sketches out an argument about the nature of the cognitive sciences—how they should and should not proceed. What is that argument? Do
you agree or disagree with the view of cognitive science that Sacks is advocating? Write
an essay in which you present his position and develop one of your own on this matter.

6. Write an essay in which you discuss Sacks as a writer and a scientist. Consider such matters as his style of writing, his interest in the arts, his clinical procedures, and the values he expresses or implies in his work. If your instructor wishes, you may look further into his work in order to write this essay.

MAKING CONNECTIONS

1. Compare Sacks's essay with Robert Jay Lifton's "What Made This Man? Mengele" (p. 371). How do they differ as case studies? What kinds of evidence do they call on? How do they evaluate it? What kinds of stories do they tell? Do you find evidence in this comparison for Sacks's claim that his essays are "not just case studies . . . but also tales or fables of 'heroes, victims, martyrs, warriors'"?

2. Compare Sacks's essay to the reports of John Hersey, "Hatsuyo Nakamura" (p. 181), and Roy C. Selby Jr. "A Delicate Operation" (p. 280). What elements of a case study do these reports contain? Are they also tales or fables similar to Sacks's essay?

THE ACTION OF NATURAL SELECTION

Charles Darwin

Charles Darwin (1809–1882), British botanist, geologist, and naturalist, is best known for his discovery that natural selection is responsible for changes in organisms during evolution. After an undistinguished academic career and a five-year voyage to South America with a British survey ship, he began keeping his Transmutation Notebooks (1837–1839), *developing the idea of "selection owing to struggle." In 1842 and 1844 he published short accounts of his views and in 1859 published* On the Origin of Species, *which made him famous—even notorious—as the father of the theory of evolution. He preferred to avoid controversy and left the debates over his theories to others whenever possible. But he was a keen observer and continued to study and write on natural history all his life. The essay that follows here is a brief excerpt from* On the Origin of Species, *in which Darwin explains his principle of "natural selection."*

In order to make it clear how, as I believe, natural selection acts, I must beg permission to give one or two imaginary illustrations. Let us take the case of a wolf, which preys on various animals, securing some by craft, some by strength, and some by fleetness; and let us suppose that the fleetest prey, a deer for instance, had from any change in the country increased in numbers, or that other prey had decreased in numbers, during that season of the year when the wolf is hardest pressed for food. I can under such circumstances see no reason to doubt that the swiftest and slimmest wolves would have the best chance for surviving, and so be preserved or selected—provided always that they retained strength to master their prey at this or at some other period of the year, when they might be compelled to prey on other animals. I can see no more reason to doubt this, than that man can improve the fleetness of his greyhounds by careful and methodical selection, or by that unconscious selection which results from each man trying to keep the best dogs without any thought of modifying the breed.

Even without any change in the proportional numbers of the animals on which our wolf preyed, a cub might be born with an innate tendency to pursue certain kinds of prey. Nor can this be thought very improbable; for we often observe great differences in the natural tendencies of our domestic animals; one cat, for instance, taking to catch rats, another mice; one cat, according to

Mr. St. John, bringing home winged game, another hares or rabbits, and another hunting on marshy ground and almost nightly catching woodcocks or snipes. The tendency to catch rats rather than mice is known to be inherited. Now, if any slight innate change of habit or of structure benefited an individual wolf, it would have the best chance of surviving and of leaving offspring. Some of its young would probably inherit the same habits or structure, and by the repetition of this process, a new variety might be formed which would either supplant or coexist with the parent-form of wolf. Or, again, the wolves inhabiting a mountainous district, and those frequenting the lowlands, would naturally be forced to hunt different prey; and from the continued preservation of the individuals best fitted for the two sites, two varieties might slowly be formed. These varieties would cross and blend where they met; but to this subject of intercrossing we shall soon have to return. I may add, that, according to Mr. Pierce, there are two varieties of the wolf inhabiting the Catskill Mountains in the United States, one with a light greyhound-like form, which pursues deer, and the other more bulky, with shorter legs, which more frequently attacks the shepherd's flocks.

Let us now take a more complex case. Certain plants excrete a sweet juice, apparently for the sake of eliminating something injurious from their sap: this is effected by glands at the base of the stipules in some Leguminosae, and at the back of the leaf of the common laurel. This juice, though small in quantity, is greedily sought by insects. Let us now suppose a little sweet juice or nectar to be excreted by the inner bases of the petals of a flower. In this case insects in seeking the nectar would get dusted with pollen, and would certainly often transport the pollen from one flower to the stigma of another flower. The flowers of two distinct individuals of the same species would thus get crossed; and the act of crossing, we have good reason to believe (as will hereafter be more fully alluded to), would produce very vigorous seedlings, which consequently would have the best chance of flourishing and surviving. Some of these seedlings would probably inherit the nectar-excreting power. Those individual flowers which had the largest glands or nectaries, and which excreted most nectar, would be oftenest visited by insects, and would be oftenest crossed; and so in the long-run would gain the upper hand. Those flowers, also, which had their stamens and pistils placed, in relation to the size and habits of the particular insects which visited them, so as to favor in any degree the transportal of their pollen from flower to flower, would likewise be favored or selected. We might have taken the case of insects visiting flowers for the sake of collecting pollen instead of nectar; and as pollen is formed for the sole object of fertilization, its destruction appears a simple loss to the plant; yet if a little pollen were carried, at first occasionally and then habitually, by the pollen-devouring insects from flower to flower, and a cross thus effected, although nine-tenths of the pollen were destroyed, it might still be a great gain to the plant; and those individuals which produced more and more pollen, and had larger and larger anthers, would be selected.

When our plant, by this process of the continued preservation or natural selection of more and more attractive flowers, had been rendered highly attractive to insects, they would, unintentionally on their part, regularly carry pollen from flower to flower; and that they can most effectually do this, I could easily show by many striking instances. I will give only one—not as a very striking case, but as likewise illustrating one step in the separation of the sexes of plants, presently to be alluded to. Some holly-trees bear only male flowers, which have four stamens producing rather a small quantity of pollen, and a rudimentary pistil; other holly-trees bear only female flowers; these have a full-sized pistil and four stamens with shrivelled anthers, in which not a grain of pollen can be detected. Having found a female tree exactly sixty yards from a male tree, I put the stigmas of twenty flowers, taken from different branches, under the microscope, and on all, without exception, there were pollen-grains, and on some a profusion of pollen. As the wind had set for several days from the female to the male tree, the pollen could not thus have been carried. The weather had been cold and boisterous, and therefore not favorable to bees, nevertheless every female flower which I examined had been effectually fertilized by the bees, accidentally dusted with pollen, having flown from tree to tree in search of nectar. But to return to our imaginary case: as soon as the plant had been rendered so highly attractive to insects that pollen was regularly carried from flower to flower, another process might commence. No naturalist doubts the advantage of what has been called the "physiological division of labor"; hence we may believe that it would be advantageous to a plant to produce stamens alone in one flower or on one whole plant, and pistils alone in another flower or on one whole plant. In plants under culture and placed under new conditions of life, sometimes the male organs and sometimes the female organs become more or less impotent; now if we suppose this to occur in ever so slight a degree under nature, then as pollen is already carried regularly from flower to flower, and as a more complete separation of the sexes of our plant would be advantageous on the principle of the division of labor, individuals with this tendency more and more increased would be continually favored or selected, until at last a complete separation of the sexes would be effected.

Let us now turn to the nectar-feeding insects in our imaginary case: we may suppose the plant of which we have been slowly increasing the nectar by continued selection, to be a common plant; and that certain insects depended in main part on its nectar for food. I could give many facts, showing how anxious bees are to save time; for instance, their habit of cutting holes and sucking the nectar at the bases of certain flowers, which they can, with a very little more trouble, enter by the mouth. Bearing such facts in mind, I can see no reason to doubt that an accidental deviation in the size and form of the body, or in the curvature and length of the proboscis, &c., far too slight to be appreciated by us, might profit a bee or other insect, so that an individual so characterized would be able to obtain its food more quickly, and so have a better chance of living and leaving descendants. Its descendants would probably inherit a tendency to a similar slight deviation of structure. The tubes of the corollas of the common red and incarnate clovers (Trifolium pratense and incarnatum) do not on a hasty glance appear to differ in length; yet the hive-bee can easily suck the nectar out of the incarnate clover, but not out of the common red clover, which is visited by humble-bees alone; so that whole fields of the red clover offer in vain an abundant supply of precious nectar to the hive-bee. Thus it might be a great advantage to the hive-bee to have a slightly longer or differently constructed proboscis. On the other hand, I have found by experiment that the fertility of clover greatly depends on bees visiting and moving parts of the corolla, so as to push the pollen on to the stigmatic surface. Hence, again, if humble-bees were to become rare in any country, it might be a great advantage to the red clover to have a shorter or more deeply divided tube to its corolla, so that the hive-bee could visit its flowers. Thus I can understand how a flower and a bee might slowly become, either simultaneously or one after the other, modified and adapted in the most perfect manner to each other, by the continued preservation of individuals presenting mutual and slightly favorable deviations of structure.

I am well aware that this doctrine of natural selection, exemplified in the above imaginary instances, is open to the same objections which were at first urged against Sir Charles Lyell's[1] noble views on "the modern changes of the earth, as illustrative of geology;" but we now very seldom hear the action, for instance, of the coast-waves, called a trifling and insignificant cause, when applied to the excavation of gigantic valleys or to the formation of the longest lines of inland cliffs. Natural selection can act only by the preservation and accumulation of infinitesimally small inherited modifications, each profitable to the preserved being; and as modern geology has almost banished such views as the excavation of a great valley by a single diluvial wave, so will natural selection, if it be a true principle, banish the belief of the continued creation of new organic beings, or of any great and sudden modification in their structure.

QUESTIONS

1. What does Darwin mean by "natural selection"?

2. The short title of Darwin's major book is often mistakenly given as *The Origin of the Species*. What is the difference between that and the book's correct title, *On the Origin of Species*? Why do you suppose so many people get it wrong?

3. Why does Darwin "beg permission" in the first sentence? In the same sentence, what does he mean by "imaginary illustrations"? Are they untrue?

4. We use the name *bumblebee* for what Darwin (and other English writers before him) called a "humble-bee." Find out something about the word *humble* and about the different kinds of bees. (What is the difference between a hive-bee and a humble-bee,

---

[1]*Sir Charles Lyell* (1797–1875): British geologist. [Eds.]

anyway?) For the word *humble*, go to a good dictionary, but don't depend on a dictionary for information about different kinds of bees. Play with the words *humble* and *bumble* to see which of their meanings can be appropriately applied to bees.

5. Darwin's illustrative explanations are excellent examples of process analysis, a type of writing that presents a complicated chain of events as clearly as possible. Select some subject that you know well and that involves an intricate linkage of events. Explain an "imaginary" process taken from that subject. That is, imagine how some little change in an intricate pattern of events would lead to other changes that would cause other changes, until a whole new pattern was established. For example, how would some change in your behavior, appearance, or abilities change the patterns of school and family life around you? Explain the process you imagine as accurately and "scientifically" as you can. Complete your explanation by drawing some conclusion about the principles exemplified by the process you have described.

MAKING CONNECTIONS

1. To what extent could you read Francis Crick's "Times and Distances, Large and Small" (p. 492) as a commentary on this explanation of Darwin's? Or could you just as well read Darwin as a commentary on Crick?

2. Compare Darwin's illustrations of the wolf, the bee, and the flower to James Jeans's explanation in "Why the Sky Is Blue" (p. 489). How are their explanations similar? Are there any striking differences?

FACE PERCEPTION
WITHOUT RECOGNITION

Antonio R. Damasio

Antonio R. Damasio was born in Portugal in 1944, where he studied medicine, receiving both an M.D. and a Ph.D. from the University of Lisbon. He is professor and head of the Department of Neurology at the University of Iowa College of Medicine and adjunct professor at the Salk Institute in La Jolla, California. Most of Damasio's publications are on anatomical aspects of higher brain functions, parkinsonism, and dementia. His research focuses on understanding the cerebral basis of vision, language, and memory. Oliver Sacks has written that "the most important studies of . . . agnosias, and of visual processing in general, are now being undertaken by A. R. and H. Damasio." In 1989, Damasio was one of four American scientists and scholars named to review progress in Western studies of consciousness for the Dalai Lama. He recently published Descartes' Error: Emotion, Reason, and the Human Brain *(1994) and co-edited* Neurobiology of Decision-Making *(1996). The article reprinted here, a review of research on prosopagnosia, the phenomenon of perception without recognition, first appeared in* Trends in NeuroScience *(March 1985).*

REVIEW OF RESEARCH ON PROSOPAGNOSIA

[Abstract.] *The impaired recognition of previously known familiar faces (prosopagnosia), when it appears in isolation, is one of the most extreme forms of behavioral dissociation encountered in human pathology. Its research provides an outstanding opportunity to understand better the organization of the visual system and of memory mechanisms in humans. Recent evidence indicates that the disorder is associated with bilateral lesions of the central visual system, located in the mesial occipito-temporal region. These lesions either destroy a specific sector of the visual association cortex or disconnect it from limbic structures located anteriorly in the temporal lobe. This evidence is in keeping with the demonstration, in normals, that both hemispheres are capable of facial recognition, but should not be seen to indicate that each hemisphere uses the same mechanisms to process faces or is equally efficient in the process. Cognitive analysis of prosopagnosia reveals that the defect is not specific to human faces*

529

but also appears in relation to other visual stimuli whose recognition depends on the evocation of specific contextual attributes and associations, and which are visually "ambiguous" (different stimuli belonging to the same group but having similar physical structure). Physiopathologically, prosopagnosia is the result of a failure to activate, on the basis of visual stimuli, memories pertinent to those stimuli.

The description of prosopagnosia dates from the turn of the century although the designation was only coined in 1947 by Bodamer.[1] In isolation, the condition is so extreme and infrequent that many investigators doubted its reality. Otherwise normal individuals suddenly lose their ability to recognize the faces of relatives, friends, and even their own faces in the mirror, while being able to recognize other objects visually. They also lose the ability to learn to identify the faces of new persons they come into contact with. In short, the visual inspection of these familiar faces no longer generates an experience of even vague familiarity and thus facial recognition is forever precluded. The patients can still recognize, by the sound of their voices, the people whose faces have become meaningless. All the remote memories that pertain to those people remain intact. Cognitive skills also remain intact and so do complex visual abilities, i.e. most prosopagnosic patients describe their visual environment accurately, localize stimuli in space flawlessly, inspect visual arrays in normal fashion, and some can even read. Needless to say, their visual acuity is normal. The only symptoms that commonly accompany prosopagnosia are achromatopsia, an acquired defect in color perception which may affect part or all of the visual field, an acquired defect in the appreciation of textures visually, and some partial field cut for the vision of forms. (Prosopagnosia may also be found as a component of global amnesic syndrome. In such instances no field defects for color or form accompany the manifestation, and visual perception is manifestly intact.) .

Even after it became clear that the condition was indeed real, considerable controversy surfaced regarding its physiopathological nature and anatomical basis. This review focuses on some of these issues as well as on new developments in the understanding of prosopagnosia.

ANATOMICAL BASIS

The early descriptions of prosopagnosia indicated that the condition was associated with the bilateral damage to the occipital lobes.[26,3] But when after decades of neglect, there was a resurgence of interest in prosopagnosia, several investigators conceptualized it as a sign of unilateral damage of the right hemisphere. At the time, the 1960s, fresh neuropsychological investigations had revealed the major role of the right hemisphere in visual processing and it appeared reasonable to assume that the right hemisphere might possess the sole key to a refined visual process such as facial recognition. Hecaen and Angelergues[2] added strength to this hypothesis by noting that most prosopagnosic patients had exclusive left visual field defects, and suggesting that this was due to exclusive right hemisphere damage. Later, in a comprehensive review of the data available in 1974, Meadows concluded "that patients with prosopagnosia have right anterior inferior occipital lesions in the region of the occipital temporal junction. Many if not all cases have an additional lesion in the left hemisphere."[4] Although these interpretations were consonant with the anatomical localization methods at the time, the evidence uncovered in the years that followed revealed that they were not supportable. The current view is that bilateral lesions are indeed necessary, a notion that is based on: (1) a critical review of the meaning of visual field data: (2) a reassessment of post-mortem studies of prosopagnosic patients; (3) Computed Tomography (CT), Nuclear Magnetic Resonance (NMR) and Emission Tomography (ET) studies of patients with and without prosopagnosia; (4) a study of patients with cerebral hemispherectomy, callosal surgery and amnesic syndromes. The fundamental evidence is as follows:

(1) The one patient of Hecaen and Angelergues to come to post-mortem, turned out to have a bilateral lesion.[2] The lesion in the left hemisphere was "silent" as far as visual field findings were concerned. Similar "silent" lesions were uncovered at autopsy in patients described by Benson[5] and by Lhermitte.[6] It is now apparent that when lesions of the central visual system fail to involve optic radiations or primary visual cortex they do not produce an overt defect of form vision even when they can cause major disturbances of complex visual processing such as a defect in recognition or color processing.[7] While the presence of a field defect correctly indicates the presence of a lesion, its absence does not exclude focal damage. Thus while the detailed study of field defects is mandatory for the appropriate study of visual agnosia, its details cannot be used for the prediction of lesion localization.

(2) Analysis of the post-mortem records of all patients that have come to autopsy[8,9] indicate that they all have bilateral lesions. Furthermore, it is clear that those lesions preferably involve the inferior visual association cortices, i.e. the occipito-temporal region. Finally, patients with bilateral lesions involving the superior visual association cortices, i.e. the occipito-parietal region, never develop prosopagnosia, presenting instead either a full Balint syndrome or some of its components, i.e. visual disorientation, optic ataxia or ocular apraxia.[7] Patients with Balint syndrome can recognize faces provided their attention is properly directed to the stimuli.

(3) Computed Tomography (CT) has permitted the study of many cases of prosopagnosia and of numerous controls with unilateral lesions of the left or right occipito-temporal region, or with bilateral lesions of the occipito-parietal region. With one exception all the instances of permanent prosopagnosia studied in appropriate patients with technically advanced scanning techniques have shown bilateral lesions.[8-11] Furthermore, numerous instances of unilateral

lesion in the right and left hemispheres have been described and there has been no report of prosopagnosia appearing in those circumstances. (The possible exception was reported in a hypertensive patient on the basis of a single cut of an acute CT scan;[12] it is important to consider the possibility of an undetected lesion in the opposite hemisphere.)

Patients with bilateral occipito-parietal lesions consistently show Balint syndrome or its components but not prosopagnosia.[7] In the only two cases studied with Nuclear Magnetic Resonance (NMR) the lesions were bilateral. In the only two cases studies with Single Photon Emission Tomography there were bilateral regions of diminished cerebral blood flow.[7]

(4) Evidence from hemispherectomy and from cases of surgical callosal section has also been helpful. Patients with right hemispherectomy maintain their ability to recognize faces with their single left hemisphere.[13] The split-brain subjects continue to recognize faces with each isolated hemisphere although, as expected, the mechanisms of recognition appear to be different on the left and on the right.[27]

Final evidence for the bilaterality of damage in prosopagnosia comes from the analysis of patients with amnesic syndromes. Patients with global amnesic syndromes associated with temporal lobe damage have prosopagnosia as a component. All have bilateral lesions.[15,16] The finding simply underscores the fact that memory processing of the type involved in facial recognition is of crucial importance for the individual and is clearly operated by both hemispheres. This is not to say that the left and right hemispheres perform the task in the same way or equally well. On the contrary, we believe each hemisphere learns, recognizes and recalls faces with different strategies and that the right hemisphere's approach is probably more efficient than the left.

THE NATURE OF THE DEFECT

The bizarre nature of prosopagnosia, when it appears in isolation, has prompted all sorts of explanations for the phenomenon. Those who have never seen a prosopagnosic patient may be tempted to dismiss the phenomenon as the result of psychiatric illness or dementia. None of these interpretations obtain, considering that these patients show no evidence of language impairment, have intact cognitive skills and do not have psychiatric symptomatology before or after the onset of prosopagnosia. In his review of the neuropsychological investigation of prosopagnosia, Benton noted how some authors have seen prosopagnosia as a primary perceptual defect that would preclude the analysis and synthesis of complex visual stimuli; how others have postulated an incapacity to perceive individuality within a single class of objects; and yet others have proposed a material specific defect in memory, that is, a defect of integrating current facial percepts with past experience of them.[17]

Some of these issues are more clear today. There is substantial evidence against the notion that prosopagnosia is due to a primary perceptual disturbance. Firstly, prosopagnosic patients can discriminate unfamiliar faces well. Some of these patients perform normally in Benton and Van Allen's test of facial discrimination—a difficult task in which they are called to match unfamiliar and differently lit photographs of faces but obviously not asked to recognize any of them;[8,17] they can perform complex visual tasks such as the anomalous contours test and they have normal stereopsis;[8] they can draw accurately complex figures shown in photographs, drawings or in real models;[8,17] more importantly, they can recognize, at a generic level, any visual stimulus provided that no contextual memory cues are required.[6,8] Secondly, severe disorders of visual perception such as seen in patients with Balint syndrome or comparable disorders, do not have prosopagnosia.[7,18,19] Patients with prosopagnosia can perceive and recognize accurately many stimuli that are visually more complex than human faces, i.e., that have a greater number of individual components arranged in just as complicated a manner but crowded in smaller areas or volumes.[8] On the other hand, there is evidence that the particular class of visual stimuli, as well as the ability to integrate facial percepts with pertinent past experience, are important factors in the physiopathology of prosopagnosia. The evidence is as follows.

Prosopagnosia does not occur in relation to human faces alone. All of the patients with prosopagnosia have defects of recognition for other stimuli.[4,6,8] The types of stimuli for which they have agnosia, however, are rather special. They include: (a) automobiles (prosopagnosics cannot recognize their own car and do not recognize different makes of cars; however, these patients can recognize different types of car, such as a passenger car, a fire engine, an ambulance, or a funeral car); (b) clothes of the same type and general shape, i.e. dresses, suits, shirts, etc.; (c) food ingredients with similar forms and volumes; (d) specific animals within a group (a farmer suddenly became unable to recognize, within a herd, specific animals that he could easily recognize before; birdwatchers have become unable to recognize different birds, etc.). In all of these instances, the process of recognition operates normally up to the point in which specific recognition of a given member within the group is required. In other words, all of these patients can recognize an automobile as an automobile, a cow as a cow, or a dress as a dress. They can also recognize all of the subcomponents of these stimuli correctly, i.e. eyes, noses, windshields, wheels, sleeves, etc. But when, as is the case with human faces, the patient is requested to identify precisely the specific possessor of that visual appearance, the process breaks down and the within-class-membership of the stimulus cannot be ascertained.

An analysis of the shared characteristics of the stimuli which can cause prosopagnosia reveals that: (a) these are stimuli for which a specific recognition is mandatory and for which a generic recognition is either socially unacceptable (human faces), or incompatible with normal activity (cars, clothing, foodstuffs); (b) the specific recognition of all of the stimuli depends on contextual (episodic) memory, i.e. it depends on the evocation of multiple traces of memory previously associated with the currently perceived stimulus; those traces depend on a personal, temporally and spatially bound, memory process; (c) that all of the stimuli belong to groups in which numerous members are physically *similar* (in visual terms), and yet individually *different*; we have designated these stimuli as visually "ambiguous" (an operational definition of visual ambiguity is the presence in a group of numerous *different* members with *similar* visual characteristics). Prosopagnosia patients have no difficulty with the correct, individual recognition of "non-ambiguous" stimuli, i.e. visual stimuli that belong to groups with numerous members but in which *different* individual members have a *different* (distinctive) visual structure.[8]

According to the analysis above, the basic perceptual mechanisms in prosopagnosic patients are normal. There is no evidence that the varied partial defects of color, texture or form perception, alone or in combination, can cause prosopagnosia. When patients are called on to recognize stimuli that belong to visually ambiguous classes, they fail to evoke the pertinent, associated traces of contextual memory on the basis of which familiarity and recognition of the stimulus would be based. Seen in this light, the defect must be described, physiopathologically, as a disorder of visually-triggered contextual memory. It is important to distinguish this from a disorder of memory in general (memory traces can be normally activated through other sensory channels) and even from a disorder of visual memory (auditory stimulation can bring forward numerous traces of visual memory testifying to the intactness of many visual memory stores). The malfunction is in the triggering system for the associated evocations. We believe this defect can be explained by one of three possible mechanisms: (1) a defect in the highest level of visual analysis, that which permits the distinction of finest structural details necessary for the separation of visually "ambiguous" stimuli but unnecessary for visually unambiguous ones; (2) a defect of the plotting of the ongoing percept into the pre-existing, templated information, acquired for each specific stimulus (this mechanism would assume the normalcy of the perceptual step referred to above); (3) a defect in the activation of pertinent associated memories occurring after both steps above operate normally. Current research in our laboratory and others is aimed at investigating the validity of these possible mechanisms.

NEW DEVELOPMENTS

Autonomic Evidence for Nonconscious Recognition

One of the intriguing problems posed by visual agnosia and, more generally, by amnesia has to do with the level at which the failure of recognition occurs. Some investigators have hypothesized that the failure to evoke both non-verbal and verbal memories capable of generating recognition does not preclude some process of recognition at a lower, nonconscious level of processing. In other words, it is possible that some part of the brain does recognize stimulus even if the subject is not aware of that process taking place. Patients with prosopagnosia are ideal subjects to test this hypothesis and that is what has recently been accomplished using paradigms aimed at detecting autonomic responses to stimuli that patients are clearly not aware of recognizing. In available studies (Ref. 20 and Tranel, D., and Damasio, A.), there is persuading evidence that at a nonconscious level, faces of relatives, friends, and self, generated strong psychophysiological responses clearly different from the weak or nonexistent responses to faces unfamiliar to the subject. The implications of this discovery are far-reaching. The findings support the notion that perception and recognition processes evolve by steps and that failure at the top of the cascade does not necessarily imply failure at more elementary levels. On the issue of facial recognition itself, they argue for the existence of a template system for each individual familiar face, and suggest that, at least in some of the patients, such a template system is intact. It is important to note that in our model the template system is not conceived in the Humian[1] sense, as a static facsimile of a given face, but rather as a dynamic, evolving record of computations built on multiple exposure to the stimulus and probably stored at multiple levels of CNS, but especially anchored in visual association cortices.

Ocular Motor Activity in Visual Recognition

It has been suggested that patients with prosopagnosia might have an impairment of the proper scanning of the face, a disturbance of the ability to search appropriately for elements crucial to facial perception, i.e. eyes, nose, mouth, hairline, facial contour. A recent study carried out in prosopagnosic patients shows that this is not the case (Rizzo, M., Hurtig, R. and Damasio, A., unpublished observations). Using electro-oculographic techniques the investigators showed that prosopagnosic patients scan fundamental elements of the face as do controls, using a natural progression in their scanning and spending comparable times in the analysis of separate features. The prosopagnosic patients also scan a complex picture (e.g. the Cookie Theft plate from the Boston Diagnostic Battery) in exactly the same manner as controls. Once again, the results lend credence to the notion that basic perception proceeds normally and that prosopagnosic subjects search and accumulate information as do normal individuals but fail, at a later stage, either to bring that information together in an integrated pattern, or to lead the integrated pattern to activate the pertinent associated memories.

Perception of Contrast Sensitivity in Visual Agnosia

It has been suggested that object recognition may be especially dependent on the processing of low visuospatial frequencies.[21] It might follow that prosopagnosia would be caused by selective impairment of low spatial fre-

---

[1]*Humian:* from the Scottish philosopher and historian David Hume (1711–1776). [Eds.]

quency vision. A recent study investigated this possibility in a prosopagnosic patient and has revealed exactly the contrary: the patient's processing of low spatial frequencies was intact, entirely comparable to matched controls, while the processing of high spatial frequencies showed a defect (Rizzo, M., Hurtig, R. and Damasio, A., unpublished observations). Further studies are necessary to clarify the role of different spatial frequencies in the recognition of objects and faces, in both normals and agnosics. Nonetheless, there is evidence to suggest that normal facial recognition calls for both low and high visuospatial frequencies.[22]

Cognitive Strategies in Facial Processing

While it is clear that both hemispheres can learn, recognize and recall faces, recent investigations demonstrate that, as one might have expected, the left and the right hemispheres utilize different strategies to accomplish the task. The findings obtained in patients with callosal surgery,[14] or in normals,[23-25] suggest that the right hemisphere of most individuals is likely to be the most efficient processor of faces and of comparable visual stimuli.

Studies in Animals

The electrophysiological study of neurons responsive to visual stimuli in nonhuman primates is likely to shed some light on the mechanisms of facial recognition and prosopagnosia. E. T. Rolls and E. Perrett have reported the presence of neurons in the temporal lobe of the monkey that respond powerfully to faces.[28]

20

SELECTED REFERENCES[2]

1. Bodamer, J. (1947) *Arch. Psychiatr. Nervenkr.* 179, 6–54
2. Hecaen, H. and Angelergues, R. (1962) *Soc. for Inf. Disp. Arch. Neurol.* 7, 92–100
3. Wilbrand, H. (1892) *Deutche Z Nervenheilkd.* 2, 361–387
4. Meadows, J. C. (1974) *J. Neurol. Neurosurg. Psychiatry* 37, 498–501
5. Benson, D., Segarra, J. and Albert, M. L. (1974) *Arch. Neurol. (Chicago)* 30, 307–310
6. Lhermitte, J., Chain, F., Escourolle, R., Ducarne, B. and Pillon, B. (1972) *Rev. Neurol.* 126, 329–346

[2]These references work somewhat in the manner of footnotes. That is, they are listed roughly in order of their citation in the text. Number 1 is the first cited, and so on, but there are many exceptions to this and sometimes more than one reference is cited as bearing on a particular statement made in the text. The second citation in the text, for instance, is 26, 3, indicating that both references 26 and 3 bear on the issue under discussion. The third citation is numbered 2, the fourth 4, and the fifth is 2 again. This method avoids the needless proliferation of numbers. Why 3 comes before 2, however, is one of the mysteries of science. [Eds.]

7. Damasio, A. R. (1985) in *Principles of Behavioral Neurology* (Mesulam, M. M., ed.), Davis, Philadelphia

8. Damasio, A. R., Damasio, H. and Van Hoesen, G. W. (1982) *Neurology* 32, 331–341

9. Nardelli, E., Buonanno, F., Coccia, G., Fiaschi, A., Terzian, H. and Rizzuto, N. (1982) *Eur. Neurol.* 21, 289–297

10. Brazis, P. W., Biller, J. and Fine, M. (1981) *Neurology* 31, 920

11. Bruyer, R., Laterre, C., Seron, X., Feyereisen, P., Strypstein, E., Pierrand, E. and Rectem, D. (1983) *Brain Cognition* 2, 257–284

12. Whitely, A. M. and Warrington, E. K. (1977) *J. Neurol. Neurosurg. Psychiatry* 40, 395–403

13. Damasio, A. R., Lima, P. A. and Damasio, H. (1975) *Neurology* 25, 89–93

14. Gazzaniga, M. S., Smylie, C. S. (1983) *Ann Neurol.* 13, 537–540

15. Corkin, S. (1984) *Semin. Neurol.* 4, 249–259

16. Damasio, A. R., Eslinger, P. J., Damasio, H., Van Hoesen, G. W. and Cornell, S. (1985) *Arch. Neurol.* 42, 252–259

17. Benton, A. (1980) *Am. Psychol.* 35, 176–186

18. Meier, M. J. and French, L. A. (1965) *Neuropsychologia* 3, 261–272

19. Orgass, B., Poeck, K., Kerchensteiner, M. and Hartje, W. (1972) *Z. Neurol.* 202, 177–195

20. Bauer, R. M. (1984) *Neuropsychologia* 22, 457–469; Tranel, D. and Damasio, A. (1985) *Science* 228, 1453–1454

21. Ginsburg, A. P. (1980) *Proc. of the Soc. for Inf. Dis.* 21, 219–227

22. Fiorentini, A., Maffei, L. and Sandini, G. (1983) *Perception* 12, 195–201

23. Ellis, H. D. (1983) in *Functions of the Right Cerebral Hemisphere* (Young, A. W., ed.), Academic Press, London

24. Sergent, J. and Bindra, D. (1981) *Psycol. Bull.* 89, 541–554

25. Warrington, E. K. and James, M. (1967) *Cortex* 3, 317–326

26. Heidenhain, A. (1927) *Monatschr. Psychiatr. Neurol.* 66, 61–116

27. Levy, J., Trevarthen, C. and Sperry, R. W. (1972) *Brain* 95, 61–78

28. Perrett, D. I., Rolls, E. T. and Caan, W. (1982) *Exp. Brain. Res.* 47, 329–342

QUESTIONS

1. This article is a review of research on prosopagnosia. Analyze how it is organized. Divide the text into sections, and explain the function of each. How do you account for the order or arrangement of the sections?

2. Like many pieces written for scientific journals, this one begins with an abstract. What does the full text provide that is not in the abstract?

3. Consider the relationship between the style of this article (format, vocabulary, sentence structure, and so on) and the audience for whom it was written. Does audience always have an effect on style? Explain why or why not.

4. What portions of this article give you the most vivid sense of prosopagnosia? What accounts for your clearer understanding of those sections?

5. Using this article as a model, write a review of research in a field that you know something about. What is the purpose of such a review? What does your own review of research put you in a position to do?

ANTONIO R. DAMASIO

MAKING CONNECTIONS

1. Consider this essay along with Oliver Sacks's "The Man Who Mistook His Wife for a Hat" (p. 511). Obviously, Sacks generates a good deal of interest in a case similar to the problem Damasio describes. Damasio, on the other hand, gives us a good deal of additional information on the problem. Describe the differences in form and content between the two essays.

2. Although Oliver Sacks (p. 511) mentions agnosia and frequently refers to Dr. P.'s case as an example of prosopagnosia (see footnote 4), some of the details he gives do not square with the description of prosopagnosia that Damasio offers. Make a list of those differences, and describe the ways in which Dr. P. does not behave as a prosopagnosiac would.

"WHAT, PRECISELY, IS THINKING?"
. . . EINSTEIN'S ANSWER

Gerald Holton

*Gerald James Holton was born in Berlin in 1922 and be-
came an American citizen in 1945. He has been professor of
physics and the history of science at Harvard University
since 1959. The recipient of numerous awards and honorary
degrees, Holton is the author of physics textbooks and scholarly and popular books on physics and the history of science. His latest book,* Einstein, History, and Other Passions
*(1995), focuses on the life and work of Albert Einstein, con-
siders issues in science, and reflects on Holton's own teaching. This essay is a chapter taken from that book, with references to the book as a whole removed.*

How did Albert Einstein do his thinking? At first glance an answer seems
impossible. His work was carried out at the very frontiers of physics and of
human ability. And his mind was not open to easy study from the outside, even
by those who worked with him—as was discovered by the physicist Banesh
Hoffmann who, with Leopold Infeld, was Einstein's assistant in 1937. Hoffmann has given an account of what it was like when he and Infeld, having
come to an impassable obstacle in their work, would seek out Einstein's help.
At such a point, Hoffmann related,

> We would all pause and Einstein would stand up quietly and say, in
> his quaint English, "I will a little think." So saying, he would pace up
> and down and walk around in circles, all the time twirling a lock of his
> long grey hair around his forefinger. At these moments of high drama,
> Infeld and I would remain completely still, not daring to move or
> make a sound, lest we interrupt his train of thought.

Many minutes would pass this way, and then, all of a sudden,

> Einstein would visibly relax and a smile would light up his face . . .
> then he would tell us the solution to the problem, and almost always
> the solution worked. . . . The solution sometimes was so simple we
> could have kicked ourselves for not having been able to think of it by
> ourselves. But the magic was performed invisibly in the recesses of
> Einstein's mind, by a process that we could not fathom. From this
> point of view the whole thing was completely frustrating.[1]

---

[1] Quoted from a report by Banesh Hoffmann in *Einstein, the Man and His Achievement*, by
G. J. Whitrow (New York: Dover, 1967), p. 75.

But if not accessible from the outside, Einstein's mind was accessible from the inside, because like many of the best scientists, he was interested in the way the scientific imagination works, and wrote about it frankly. As far as possible, we shall follow the description, quite accessible and in his own words, of how he wrestled with theories of fundamental importance. Needless to say, we shall not be under any illusion that by doing so we can imitate or even fully "explain" his detailed thought processes, nor will we forget that other scientists have other styles. But Einstein's humane and thoughtful description of scientific reasoning will serve as a reminder of how false the popular, hostile caricatures are that depict contemporary scientific thought. . . .

There are numerous sources to draw on, for Einstein wrote about his view of the nature of scientific discovery, in a generally consistent way, on many occasions, notably in the essays collected in the book *Ideas and Opinions* and in his letters. He was also intrigued enough by this problem to discuss it with researchers into the psychology of scientific ideas and with philosophers of science. Indeed, from his earliest student days, Einstein was deeply interested in the theory of knowledge (epistemology). He wrote, "The reciprocal relationship of epistemology and science is of noteworthy kind. They are dependent upon each other. Epistemology without contact with science becomes an empty scheme. Science without epistemology is—insofar as it is thinkable at all—primitive and muddled."[2]

There are two especially suitable routes to Einstein's thoughts. One is a set of pages near the beginning of the "Autobiographical Notes," which he wrote in 1946.[3] It is the only serious autobiographical essay he ever wrote, and he called it jokingly his own "obituary." It gives a fascinating picture of Einstein's contributions as he viewed them, looking back at the age of sixty-seven. The essay is chiefly an account of his intellectual development rather than an autobiography in the usual sense. We shall now use this remarkable document to learn from his own words, while avoiding the use of technical, philosophical terminology, as he himself avoided it. All quotations not otherwise identified are from the pages of this text.

The other path to an understanding of Einstein's way of thinking is found in some letters he wrote to an old friend after publication of the "Autobiographical Notes." These allow Einstein to rebut, so to speak, a few of the objections a reader of the autobiographical essay might have, and I discuss them therefore at the end of this chapter, where Einstein should have the final word.

THE COURAGE TO THINK

It certainly is curious to start one's autobiography, not with where and when one was born, the names of one's parents, and similar personal details, but to

---

[2]Paul Arthur Schilpp, ed., *Albert Einstein: Philosopher-Scientist* (Evanston, Ill.: Library of Living Philosophers, Inc., 1949)), pp. 683–84.

[3]Albert Einstein, "Autobiographical Notes" (in German and English), in Schilpp, pp. 1–95.

focus instead on a question which Einstein phrases simply: "What, precisely, is thinking?" Einstein explains why he has to start his "obituary" in this way: "For the essential in the being of a man of my type lies precisely in *what* he thinks and *how* he thinks, not in what he does or suffers."[4]

From this viewpoint, thinking is not a joy or a chore added to the daily existence. It is the essence of a person's very being, and the tool by which the transient sorrows, the primitive forms of feeling, and what he calls the other "merely personal" parts of existence can be mastered. For it is through such thought that one can lift oneself up to a level where one can think about "great, eternal riddles." It is a "liberation" which can yield inner freedom and security. When the mind grasps the "extra-personal" part of the world—that part which is not tied to shifting desires and moods—it gains knowledge which all men and women can share regardless of individual conditions, customs, and other differences.

This, of course, is precisely why the laws of nature, toward which these thoughts can be directed, are so powerful: their applicability in principle can be demonstrated by anyone, anywhere, at any time. The laws of nature are utterly shareable. Insofar as the conclusions are right, the laws discovered by a scientist are equally valid for different thinkers, or *invariant* with respect to the individual personal situations. Einstein's interest in this matter seems to be not unrelated to his work in the physics of relativity: The essence of relativity theory is precisely that it provides a tool for expressing the laws of nature in such a manner that they are invariant with respect to differently moving observers.

As his "Autobiographical Notes" show, Einstein was also aware that life cannot be all thought, that even the enjoyment of thought can be carried to a point where it may be "at the cost of other sides" of one's personality. But the danger which more ordinary persons face is not that they will abandon their very necessary personal ties, but that the society surrounding them will not say often enough what Einstein here suggests to his wide audience: that the purpose of thinking is more than merely solving problems and puzzles. It is instead, and most importantly, the necessary tool for permitting one's intellectual talent to come through, so that "gradually the major interest disengages itself . . . from the momentary and merely personal." Here Einstein is saying: Have the courage to take your own thoughts seriously, for they will shape you. And significantly, Einstein meant his whole analysis to apply to thinking on any topic, not only on scientific matters.

THINKING WITH IMAGES

Having touched on the *why* of thinking, the autobiography takes up the *how* 10 of thinking and strangely seems to be concerned with "pictures" (*Bilder*):

---

[4] Ibid., p. 33.

What, precisely, is "thinking"? When, at the reception of sense-impressions, memory-pictures emerge, this is not yet "thinking." And when such pictures form series, each member of which calls forth another, this too is not yet "thinking." When, however, a certain picture turns up in many such series, then—precisely through such return—it becomes an ordering element for such series, in that it connects series which in themselves are unconnected. Such an element becomes an instrument, a concept.

Adhering to one of several contesting traditions in psychology and philosophy and perhaps particularly influenced by Helmholtz and Boltzmann,[5] Einstein holds that the repeated encounter with images (such as "memory pictures") in a different context leads to the formation of "concepts." Thus, a small child might form the concept "glass" when he or she experiences that a variety of differently shaped solids are hard, transparent, and break on being dropped.

A concept must of course eventually be put into a form where it can be communicated to others; but for private thought it is not necessary to wait for this stage. For some people, including such physicists as Faraday and Rutherford,[6] the most important part of thinking may occur without the use of words. Einstein writes: "I have no doubts but that our thinking goes on for the most part without use of signs (words) and beyond that to a considerable degree unconsciously." Such persons tend to think in terms of images to which words may or may not be assignable; Einstein tells of his pleasure in discovering, as a boy, his skill in contemplating relationships among geometrical "objects"—triangles and other nonverbal elements of the imagination.... Einstein explained in a letter to the mathematician Jacques Hadamar that in his thinking he used not words but "certain signs and more or less clear images which can be voluntarily produced and combined." Einstein's letter continued as follows:

> The psychical entities which seem to serve as elements in thought are certain signs and more or less clear images which can be "voluntarily" reproduced and combined.... But taken from a psychological viewpoint, this combinatory play seems to be the essential feature in productive thought—before there is any connection in words or other kinds of signs which can be communicated to others. The above-mentioned elements are, in my case, of visual and some muscular type. Conventional words or other signs have to be sought for laboriously only in a secondary stage, when the mentioned associative play is sufficiently established and can be reproduced at will.[7]

---

[5]*Hermann Helmholtz* (1821–1894): German physicist; *Ludwig Boltzmann* (1844–1906): Austrian physicist. [Eds.]

[6]*Michael Faraday* (1791–1867): English physicist; *Ernest Rutherford* (1871–1937): English physicist. [Eds.]

[7]Albert Einstein, *Ideas and Opinions*, new translations and revisions by Sonja Bergmann (New York: Crown, 1954), pp. 25–26.

Einstein's ability to visualize is evident in the brilliant use he made of "thought experiments" (*Gedankenexperimente*). His first came to him at the age of about sixteen, when he tried to imagine that he was pursuing a beam of light and wondered what the observable values of the electric and magnetic field vectors would be in the electromagnetic wave making up the light beam. For example, looking back along the beam over the space of one whole wavelength, one should see that the local magnitudes of the electric and magnetic field vectors increase point by point from, say, zero to full strength, and then decrease again to zero, one wavelength away. This seemed to him a paradoxical conclusion. Already at that age, he seems to have assumed that Maxwell's equations must remain unchanged in form for the observer moving along the beam;[8] but from those equations one did not expect to find such a stationary oscillatory pattern of electric and magnetic field vectors in free space. He realized later that in this problem "the germ of the special relativity theory was contained." (Among other examples of visualized *Gedankenexperimente*, Einstein related one which he said had led him to the general theory of relativity. . . .)

THE FREE PLAY WITH CONCEPTS

Having stressed the role of images and memory pictures, including *Gedankenexperimente*, in thinking, and having defined "concepts" as the crystallized products, the unvarying elements found to be common to many series of such memory pictures, Einstein now makes a startling assertion: "All our thinking is of the nature of a free play with concepts." This sentence has to be unraveled for it deals with two opposite but equally indispensable elements in all human thought, the empirical and the rational.

Even if one grants that "free play" is still play within some set of rules—similar to tentatively trying out a word to see if it fits into a crossword puzzle—by no means all philosophers would agree with Einstein's position. Some would argue that the external world imposes itself strongly on us and gives us little leeway for play, let alone for choosing the rules of the game. In Einstein's youth, most of his contemporaries believed in Immanuel Kant's description of the boundaries of such "play," namely, that they were to be fixed by two intuitions which are present in one's mind already at birth (i.e., *a priori*): Newtonian absolute space and absolute time. Only a few disagreed, including Ernst Mach,[9] who called absolute space "a conceptual monstrosity, purely a thought-thing which cannot be pointed to in experience."

Thus Einstein was struggling anew with the old question: What precisely is the relation between our knowledge and the sensory raw material, "the only

15

---

[8]*James Clerk Maxwell* (1831–1879): Scottish physicist. [Eds.]
[9]*Ernst Mach* (1838–1916): Austrian physicist, psychologist, and philosopher. [Eds.]

source of our knowledge"?[10] If we could be sure that there is one unchanging, external, "objective" world that is connected to our brains and our sensations in a reliable, causal way, then pure thought can lead to truths about physical science. But since we cannot be certain of this, how can we avoid falling constantly into error or fantasy? David Hume had shown that "habit may lead us to belief and expectation but not to the knowledge, and still less to the understanding, of lawful relations."[11] Einstein concluded that, "In error are those theorists who believe that theory comes inductively from experience."[12]

In fact, he was skeptical about both of the major opposing philosophies. He wrote that there is an "aristocratic illusion [of subjectivism or idealism] concerning the unlimited penetrating power of thought," just as there is a "plebian illusion of naive realism, according to which things are as they are perceived by us through our senses."[13] Einstein held that there is no "real world" which one can access directly—the whole concept of the "real world"[14] being justified only insofar as it refers to the mental connections that weave the multitude of sense impressions into some connected net. Sense impressions are "conditioned by an 'objective' and by a 'subjective' factor."[15] Similarly, reality itself is a relation between what is outside us and inside us. "The real world is not given to us, but put to us (by way of a riddle)."[16]

Since the world as dealt with by a scientist is more complex than was allowed for in the current philosophies, Einstein thought that the way to escape illusion was by avoiding being a captive of any one school of philosophy. He would take from any system the portions he found useful. Such a scientist, he realized "therefore must appear to the systematic epistemologist as a type of unscrupulous opportunist: he appears as a *realist* insofar as he seeks to describe the world independent of the acts of perception; as *idealist* insofar as he looks upon the concepts and theories as the free inventions of the human spirit (not logically derivable from what is empirically given); as *positivist* insofar as he considers his concepts and theories justified *only* to the extent to which they furnish a logical representation of relations among sensory experiences. He may even appear as *Platonist* or *Pythagorean* insofar as he considers the viewpoint of logical simplicity as an indispensable and effective tool of his research."[17]

---

[10]Ibid., p. 22.
[11]Ibid. (David Hume [1711–1776]: Scottish philosopher and historian. [Eds.])
[12]Ibid., p. 301.
[13]Ibid., p. 20.
[14]Ibid., p. 291
[15]Schilpp, p. 673.
[16]Ibid., p. 680.
[17]Ibid., p. 684. (The Greek philosopher Plato [c. 428–348 B.C.] regarded mathematics and its method far more highly than sense knowledge. Followers of Pythagoras [c. 580–500 B.C.], Greek philosopher and mathematician, supposed that the substances of all things were numbers and that all phenomena were sensuous apprehensions of mathematical ratios. [Eds.])

But what justifies this "free play with concepts"? There is only one justification: that it can result, perhaps after much labor, in a thought structure which gives us the testable realization of having achieved meaningful order over a large range of sense experiences that would otherwise seem separate and unconnected. In the important essay "Physics and Reality,"[18] which covers much of the same ground as the early pages of the "Autobiographical Notes," Einstein makes the same point with this fine image: "By means of such concepts and mental relations between them we are able to orient ourselves in the labyrinth of sense impressions."[19]

This important process is described by Einstein in a condensed paragraph of the "Autobiographical Notes." "Imagine," he says, "on one side the totality of sense experiences," such as the observation that the needle on a meter is seen to deflect. On the other side, he puts the "totality of concepts and propositions which are laid down in books," which comprises the distilled products of past progress such as the concepts of force or momentum, propositions or axioms that make use of such concepts (for example, the law of conservation of momentum), and more generally, any concepts of ordinary thinking (for example, "black" and "raven"). Investigating the relations that exist among the concepts and propositions is "the business of logical thinking," which is carried out along the "firmly laid-down rules" of logic. The rules of logic, like the concepts themselves, are of course not God-given but are the "creation of humans." However, once they are agreed upon and are part of a widely held convention—the rules of syllogism, for example—they tell us with (only seemingly) inescapable finality that *if* all ravens are black and a particular bird is a raven, then the bird is black. They allow us to deduce from the law of conservation of momentum that in a closed system containing only a neutron and proton, the momentum gained by one is accompanied by the loss experienced by the other. Without the use of logic to draw conclusions, no disciplined thinking, and hence no science, could exist.

But all such conclusions, Einstein warns, are empty of useful "meaning" or "content" until there is some definition by which the particular concept (e.g., "raven" or "neutron") is correlated with actual instances of the concept which have consequences in the world of experience rather than in the world of words and logical rules. Necessary though the correlation or connection between concepts and sense experience is, Einstein warns that it is "not itself of a logical nature." It is an act in which, Einstein holds, "intuition" is one guide, even if not an infallible one. Without it, one could not be led to the assertion that a particular bird, despite some differences in its exact size or degree of blackness from all other birds, does belong to the species raven; or that the start of a particular track, visible in the cloud chamber, is the place where a neutron has struck a proton.

---

[18]Einstein, *Ideas and Opinions*, p. 290ff.
[19]Ibid., p. 291.

One might wish that Einstein had used a notion more firm than the dangerous-sounding one of "intuition." But he saw no other way. He rejected the use of the word *abstraction* to characterize the transition from observation to concept, e.g., from individual black birds to the idea of "raven." He rejected it precisely because, he said, "I do not consider it justifiable to veil the logical independence of the concept from the sense experiences" (whereas the use of the term *abstraction* or *induction* might make it seem as if there *were* a logical dependence).

The danger is evidently that delusion or fantasy can and does make similar use of the elements of thinking: and since there are no hard, utterly reliable connections between the concepts, propositions, and experience, one cannot know with absolute certainty whether one has escaped the trap of false conclusion. That is why it was thought for so long that observations proved the earth was fixed and the sun went around the earth; that time had a universal meaning, the same for all moving observers; and that Euclidean geometry is the only one that has a place in the physical world. But this is just where Einstein's view is most helpful: Only those who think they *can* play freely with concepts can pull themselves out of such error. His message is even more liberal: The concepts themselves, in our thoughts and verbal expressions, are, "when viewed logically, the free creation of thought which cannot inductively be gained from sense experience." We must be continually aware that it is not necessity but habit which leads us to identify certain concepts (for example, "bread") with corresponding sense experience (feel, smell, taste, satisfaction); for, since this works well enough most of the time, "we do not become conscious of the gulf—logically unbridgeable—which separates the world of sense experience from the world of concepts and propositions." Einstein is perhaps so insistent on the point because he had to discover it the hard way: as a young man, he had to overcome the accepted meanings of such concepts as space, time, simultaneity, energy, etc., and to propose redefinitions that reshaped all our physics, and hence our very concept of reality itself. One might well add here that Einstein demanded the same freedom to challenge orthodoxy outside science. Thus, as a boy he rejected the malignant militarism he saw entrenched in the life of his native country.

Once a conceptual structure has tentatively been erected, how can one check whether it is scientifically "true"? It depends on how nearly the aim of making the system deal with a large amount of diverse sense experience has been achieved, and how economical or parsimonious the introduction of separate basic concepts or axioms into the system has been. Einstein doubted a physical theory, and would say that it failed to "go to the heart of the matter," if it had to be jerry-built with the aid of ad hoc hypotheses, each specially introduced to produce greater agreement between theory and experience (experiment). He also was rarely convinced by theories that dealt with only a small part of the range of physical phenomena, applicable only here or there under special circumstances. In this view, a really good theory, one that has high scientific "truth" value, is considered to be correct not merely when it does not harbor any logical contradictions, but when it allows a close check on the correspondence between the predictions of the theory and a large range of possible experimental experiences. He summarized all this in the following way: "One comes nearer to the most superior scientific goal, to embrace a maximum of experimental content through logical deduction from a minimum of hypotheses. . . . One must allow the theoretician his imagination, for there is no other possible way for reaching the goal. In any case, it is not an aimless imagination but a search for the logically simplest possibilities and their consequences."

This search may take "years of groping in the dark"; hence, the ability to hold onto a problem for a long time, and not to be destroyed by repeated failure, is necessary for any serious researcher. As Einstein once said, "Now I know why there are so many people who love chopping wood. In that activity one immediately sees the results." But for him, the goal of "embracing a maximum of experimental content . . . with a minimum of hypotheses" meant nothing less than endless devotion to the simplification and unification of our world picture, for example, by producing fusions in hitherto separate fundamental concepts such as space and time, mass and energy, gravitation and inertial mass, electric and magnetic fields, and inertial and accelerating systems.

KEEPING ALIVE THE SENSE OF WONDER

Embedded in Einstein's views on how to think scientifically about the deep problems, there is an engaging passage in the "Autobiographical Notes" in which Einstein speaks of the importance of the sense of marvel, of deep curiosity, of "wonder," such as his two experiences, when, at the age of four or five, he was shown a magnetic compass by his father, and when, at the age of twelve, a book on Euclidean geometry came into his hands. A person's thought-world develops in part by the mastering of certain new experiences which were so inexplicable, in terms of the previous stage of development, that a sense of wonder or enchantment was aroused. As we learn more, both through science and other approaches, we progressively find that the world around us, as it becomes more rational, also becomes more "disenchanted." But Einstein repeatedly insisted in other writings that there is a limit to this progressive disenchantment, and even the best scientist must not be so insensitive or falsely proud as to forget it. For, as Einstein said in a famous paragraph: "It is a fact that the totality of sense experiences is so constituted as to permit putting them in order by means of thinking—a fact which can only leave us astonished, but which we shall never comprehend. One can say: The eternally incomprehensible thing about the world is its comprehensibility."

He went on: "In speaking here of 'comprehensibility,' the expression is used in its most modest sense. It implies: the production of some sort of order among sense impressions, this order being produced by the creation of general concepts, by relations among these concepts, and by relations of some kind between the concepts and sense experience. It is in this sense that the world of our sense experiences is comprehensible. The fact that it is comprehensible is a wonder."[20]

That wonder [*Wunder*], that sense of awe, can only grow stronger, Einstein implied, the more successfully our scientific thoughts find order to exist among the separate phenomena of nature. This success aroused in him a "deep conviction of the rationality of the universe." To this conviction he gave the name "cosmic religious feeling," and he saw it as the "strongest and noblest motive for scientific research."[21] Indeed, "The most beautiful experience we can have is the mysterious. It is the fundamental emotion which stands at the cradle of true art and true science. Whoever does not know it and can no longer wonder, no longer marvel, is as good as dead. . . ."[22]

After the publication of such sentiments, Einstein received a worried letter from one of his oldest and best friends, Maurice Solovine. They had met in Bern in 1902 when Einstein was twenty-three years old, and they became close friends. Solovine was then a young philosophy student at the University of Bern, to which he had come from Romania, and, together with Conrad Habicht, who was also a student at the university, they banded together to meet regularly to read and discuss works in science and philosophy. With high irony they called themselves the "Olympia Academy." Their "dinners" were no banquets: They all lived on the edge of poverty, and Solovine tells us that their idea of a special dinner was two hard-boiled eggs each. But the talk was that much better, as they discussed works by Ernst Mach, J. S. Mill, David Hume, Plato, Henri Poincaré, Karl Pearson, Spinoza, Hermann Helmholtz, Ampère — and also those of Sophocles, Racine, and Dickens.[23] Many of Einstein's epistemological ideas might be traced back to these discussions.

Now, half a century later, Maurice Solovine was concerned. He asked Einstein how there could be a puzzle about the comprehensibility of our world. For us it is simply an undeniable necessity, which lies in our very nature. No doubt Solovine was bothered that Einstein's remarks seemed to allow into science, that most rational activity of mankind, a function for the human mind which is not rational in the sense of being coldly logical. But Einstein rejected as a "malady"[24] the kind of accusation that implied that he had become "metaphysical." Instead, he saw the opportunity of using *all* one's faculties and skills to do science as a sign of strength rather than of weakness.

30

---

[20]Ibid., p. 292 (but in corrected translation).
[21]Ibid., p. 39.
[22]Ibid., p. 11.
[23]*John Stuart Mill* (1806–1873): English philosopher and economist; *Henri Poincaré* (1854–1912): French mathematician; *Karl Pearson* (1857–1936): English statistician; *Baruch Spinoza* (1632–1677): Dutch philosopher; *André Ampère* (1775–1836): French physicist; *Sophocles* (c. 496–406 B.C.): Greek dramatist; *Jean Baptiste Racine* (1639–1699): French dramatist; *Charles Dickens* (1812–1870): English novelist. [Eds.]
[24]Ibid., p. 24.

Certainly, he did not propose to abandon rationality, nor to guess where one must puzzle things out in a careful, logical way. But he saw that there is, and has to be, a role for those other elements of thinking which properly used, can help scientific thought. Specifically, this could become necessary at two points in Einstein's scheme. One is the courageous use of an intuitive feeling for nature *when there is simply no other guide at all*—as when one has tentatively to propose an axiom that by definition is unproved (as Einstein did at the start of the first paper on relativity, where he simply proposed the principle of relativity and the principle of constancy of light velocity); or when one decides which sense experiences to select in order to make an operational definition of a concept. The other point is the sense of wonder at being able to discern something of the grand design of the world, a feeling that motivates and sustains many a scientist.

Einstein's reply (in his letter of 30 March 1952) to Solovine addresses this second point.

> You find it remarkable that the comprehensibility of the world (insofar as we are justified to speak of such a comprehensibility) seems to me a wonder or eternal secret. Now, *a priori*, one should, after all, expect a chaotic world that is in no way graspable through thinking. One could (even *should*) expect that the world turns out to be lawful only insofar as we make an ordering intervention. It would be a kind of ordering like putting into alphabetic order the words of a language. On the other hand, the kind of order which, for example, was created through [the discovery of] Newton's theory of gravitation is of quite a different character. Even if the axioms of the theory are put forward by human agents, the success of such an enterprise does suppose a high degree of order in the objective world, which one had no justification whatever to expect *a priori*. Here lies the sense of "wonder" which increases even more with the development of our knowledge.
>
> And here lies the weak point for the positivists and the professional atheists, who are feeling happy through the consciousness of having successfully made the world not only God-free, but even "wonder-free." The nice thing is that we must be content with the acknowledgment of the "wonder," without there being a legitimate way beyond it. I feel I must add this explicitly, so you wouldn't think that I—weakened by age—have become a victim of the clergy.

In one of Einstein's other letters to Maurice Solovine, Einstein goes over some of these questions—but this time with the aid of a diagram, as befits a person who prefers to think visually.[25] In this and all these writings, Einstein asks his reader to take the business of making progress in science into one's

---

[25]The analysis is the subject of "Einstein's Model for Constructing a Scientific Theory," chapter 2 in G. Holton, *The Advancement of Science, and Its Burdens: The Jefferson Lecture and Other Essays* (New York: Cambridge University Press, 1986).

own hands; to insist on thinking one's own thoughts even if they are not blessed by consent from the crowd; to rebel against the presumed inevitability or orthodoxy of ideas that do not meet the test of an original mind; and to live and think in all segments of our rich world—at the level of everyday experience, the level of scientific reasoning, and the level of deeply felt wonder.

QUESTIONS

1. Albert Einstein himself posed the question, "What, precisely, is thinking?" (paragraph 6). Why was this an important question for him? What particular values does he connect with thinking?

2. What place do emotions have in Einstein's thinking process?

3. How are these key terms defined in this essay: *thought experiments, free play, concept, intuition, wonder?*

4. What does Einstein mean by this statement: "The eternally incomprehensible thing about the world is its comprehensibility" (paragraph 26)?

5. Intuition appears to be an important part of thinking, of making connections. But the danger is that delusion or fantasy operates the same way, leading one to false conclusions. Holton, paraphrasing Einstein, states, "Only those who think they *can* play freely with concepts can pull themselves out of such error" (paragraph 23). How do you interpret this statement? Does Einstein suggest that one can learn free play?

6. Why was Maurice Solovine concerned that Einstein was becoming "metaphysical"? How might Solovine define scientific thinking?

7. When was the last time you felt a sense of wonder? Write an essay in which you describe the experience and explain how you came to learn the meaning of the event. On the other hand, if you find wonder too "unscientific" or too metaphysical, you can write about that.

MAKING CONNECTIONS

Consider some of the other scientists in this section, such as James Jeans (p. 489), Francis Crick (p. 492), or Stephen W. Hawking (p. 500). Do you discern in their writing evidence of the sense of wonder that Einstein considers so important? How would you describe their attitudes toward the topics they're writing about?

ARGUING

Here in "Arguing" you will find authors taking positions on a wide range of controversial subjects—from the issue of cigarette smoking to the status of black English, from the nature of scientific discovery to the use of animals in psychological research. No matter what their academic fields or professions, these authors energetically defend their stands on the issues and questions they address. But this should come as no surprise. None of us, after all, holds lightly to our beliefs and ideas about what is true or beautiful or good. Indeed, most of us get especially fired up when our views are pitted against the ideas and beliefs of others. So, you will find these authors vigorously engaged in the give-and-take of argument. As a consequence, you will repeatedly find yourself having to weigh the merits of competing positions in a debate or disagreement about some controversial issue.

The distinctive quality of arguing can be seen in the following passage from Frederick A. King's "Animals in Research: The Case for Experimentation":

> A recent pamphlet published by the MFA [Mobilization for Animals Coalition] stated, "Of all these experiments, those conducted in psychology are the most painful, pointless, and repulsive." . . .
>
> Such irresponsible accusations of research cruelty have consistently characterized the publications of the MFA. However, a recent study by psychologists D. Caroline Coile and Neal E. Miller of Rockefeller University counters these charges. Coile and Miller looked at every article (a total of 608) appearing in the past five years in journals of the American Psychological Association that report animal research. They concluded that none of the extreme allegations made by the MFA could be supported. . . .
>
> Furthermore, there are standards and mechanisms to ensure that research animals are treated in a humane and scientifically sensible way. These mechanisms include the Federal Animal Welfare Act of 1966 (amended in Congress in 1970, 1976, and 1979); periodic inspection of all animal-research facilities by the Department of Agriculture . . .

This excerpt comes from the opening section of a piece in which King attempts to defend the use of animals in psychological research. In taking this view, King realizes that he is at odds with "more than 400 animal-protectionist organizations" that are united by "an adamant opposition to animal research." Given the significant disagreements that exist between his view and those of the animal protectionists, he is not free just to make a straightforward case for his own position on the matter. He must instead contend with his opponents, refuting their positions while providing evidence in support of his own. He is, in short, engaged in arguing. The argumentative situation is immediately reflected in the subtitle of his piece, which implicitly acknowledges that there is a case *against* experimentation, and in the debatelike structure of the paragraphs that follow. King begins by identifying the views of his opponents, namely that the use of animals in psychological research is "painful, pointless, and repulsive." He then moves into a discussion intended to refute those claims. So it is that argument puts ideas to the test by forcing them to stand up against opposing beliefs or theories.

As the King passage also reveals, argument naturally arises over significant issues or questions that are open to sharply differing points of view. Questions about the use of animals in research, for example, are of crucial interest to people in a wide range of fields—not only to experimental psychologists such as King, but also to medical researchers, zoologists, environmentalists, and naturalists in general, as well as to philosophers, theologians, social planners, lawyers, and politicians. And people in each of these fields might well be inclined to approach the question from markedly different points of view that involve different assumptions as well as different bodies of knowledge and experience. Many experimental psychologists and medical researchers, for example, perceive animals as being absolutely necessary in their investigations, whereas a number of philosophers, lawyers, and specialists in biomedical ethics are intensely committed to establishing and protecting the rights of animals, and thus with defining the point at which those rights have been violated by researchers. Each point of view necessarily leads to substantially different claims about the use of animals in research, and none of the claims can be conclusively proven to be true. Indeed, if conclusive evidence had existed for one view or another, the argument would never have arisen, or it would have been resolved as quickly as the evidence had been discovered. So, like all controversial issues, the question remains open to debate, and anyone involved in such an argument can at best hope to make a persuasive case for a particular viewpoint—a case that will move thoughtful readers to consider that position seriously and possibly even convince them to accept it.

As readers of argumentative writing, we in turn should try to be as impartial as the members of a jury. We should try to set aside any biases or prejudices that we might have about one view or another. Then, we should weigh all the evidence, logic, claims, and appeals for each viewpoint before arriving at a decision about which one we find most convincing. By the same token, as writers of argument we should assume that readers are not likely to be persuaded by a one-sided view of a complex situation. Thus, we should be ready to present a case that not only will support our position, but will respond to the crucial challenges of views that differ from our own. Both as readers and writers, then, we should strive to understand the balanced methods of persuasion that can be found throughout the broad range of argumentative writing.

THE RANGE OF ARGUMENTATIVE WRITING

Argumentative writing so pervades our lives that we may not even recognize it as such in the many brochures and leaflets that come our way, urging us to vote for one candidate rather than another or to support one cause rather than another. Argumentative writing also figures heavily in newspaper editorials, syndicated columns, and letters to the editor, which are typically given over to debating the pros and cons of one public issue or another, from local taxes to national defense policies. Argument, of course, is fundamental in the judicial process, crucial in the legislative process, and serves the basic aims of the academic world, enabling different ideas and theories to be tested by pitting them against each other. Whatever the field or profession, argument is an important activity in the advancement of knowledge and society.

The broad range of argumentative writing can be understood by considering the kinds of issues and questions that typically give rise to disagreement and debate. The most basic sources of controversy are questions of fact—the who, what, when, and where of things, as well as how much. Intense arguments over questions of fact can develop in any academic or professional field, especially when the facts in question have a significant bearing on the explanation or judgment of a particular subject, body of material, or type of investigation. In his piece on animals in research, for example, King, as we have seen, cites a study conducted by Coile and Miller who "looked at every article (a total of 608) appearing in the past five years in journals of the American Psychological Association that report animal research," in which "they concluded that none of the extreme allegations made by the MFA could be supported." So, in a very real sense, the argument in this piece arises over questions of fact as well as questions of how to interpret the facts.

Even when there is no question about the facts themselves, there are likely to be arguments about how to explain the facts. Disagreements of this kind abound across the full range of academic and professional fields. And the arguments inevitably arise out of sharply differing points of view on the facts, as can be seen in Bruno Bettelheim's "The Ignored Lesson of Anne Frank." Bettelheim is attacking not the facts of the Frank family's story, but the play and movie versions, which "eulogiz[e] how they lived in their hiding place while neglecting to examine first whether it was a reasonable or an effective choice." In attacking "the universal admiration of their way of coping, or rather of not coping," Bettelheim is taking a stand quite opposite to that of people who interpret the Frank family's attempt at hiding from the Nazis as touching or noble.

Differing viewpoints, of course, ultimately reflect differing beliefs and values. The way we view any particular subject is, after all, a matter of personal choice, an outgrowth of what our experience and knowledge have led us to hold as being self-evident. In this sense, beliefs and values are always to some extent at issue in any argumentative situation, even when they remain more or less in the background. But in some cases the conflicting values themselves are so clearly at the heart of the argument that they become a central focus in the debate, as you can see in this well-known passage from the Declaration of Independence:

> We hold these truths to be self-evident, that all men are created equal, that they are endowed by their Creator with certain unalienable Rights, that among these are Life, Liberty and the pursuit of Happiness. That to secure these rights, Governments are instituted among Men, deriving their just powers from the consent of the governed. That whenever any Form of Government becomes destructive of these ends, it is the Right of the People to alter or to abolish it, and to institute new Government, laying its foundation on such principles and organizing its powers in such form, as to them shall seem most likely to affect their Safety and Happiness.

In this crucial passage, which comes at the opening of the second paragraph of the Declaration, Thomas Jefferson and his congressional colleagues directly challenged several fundamental assumptions about the rights of people and the sources of governmental power that were then held not only by the British king but also by many British people and others throughout the world. Only in this way was it possible for them to make the compelling case for their ultimate claim that the colonies should be "FREE AND INDEPENDENT STATES . . . absolved from all Allegiance to the British Crown."

Though Jefferson and his colleagues did not outline a new system of government in the Declaration itself, the document does enable us to see that conflicts over beliefs and values can, and often do, have a decisive bearing on questions of policy and planning. For a clear-cut example of how conflicts over beliefs lead to debates over policy, you need only look at Vicki Hearne's "What's Wrong with Animal Rights." Hearne starts her essay by carefully establishing her definition of happiness as it pertains to animals. She then asserts that animal rights advocates are wrong to place suffering "at the iconographic center of a skewed value system," one with an emphasis on the "avoidance of suffering rather than . . . the pursuit of happiness."

After attacking that value system, she must then argue for her own. She does so by employing definition, asserting that the question one should ask is not whether animals have rights or what those rights might be, but rather, "What is a right?" Since the issue primarily involves pets, she must consider rights of ownership: the case of possession of one being by another, a condition she defines as reciprocal. She uses her experience with her own dog, backed by the knowledge she has acquired as a trainer, to return to the issue of happiness as it occurs within reciprocal possession. In the process, she attacks popular notions about happiness and praise that she considers misconceived.

Just as her argument against popular notions of animal rights requires Hearne to establish her working definitions of basic values such as rights and happiness, so every other kind of question imposes on writers a particular set of argumentative obligations. King's argument in favor of using animals in research, for example, obliges him to cite extensive data concerning the humaneness and purposefulness of psychological research on animals, and Bettelheim's argument against the sanctification of the Anne Frank story requires him to present historical evidence against maintaining peacetime "family values" in time of war. A writer who aims to be persuasive cannot simply assert that something is or is not the case, for readers in general are not willing to be bullied, hoodwinked, or otherwise manipulated into accepting a particular claim. But they are capable of being reached by civilized and rational methods of persuasion that are appropriate to controversial issues—by evidence, logic, and eloquence.

METHODS OF ARGUING

In any piece of argumentative writing, your primary purpose is to bring readers around to your point of view. Some readers, of course, will agree with you in advance, but others will disagree, and still others will be undecided. So, in planning a piece of argumentative writing, you should begin by examining your material with an eye to discovering the issues that have to be addressed and the points that have to be made to present your case most persuasively to readers, especially those who oppose you or are undecided. This means that you will have to deal not only with issues that you consider relevant, but also with matters that have been raised by your opponents. In other words, you will have to show readers that you have considered both sides of the controversy. In arguing about the use of animals in research, for example, King repeatedly takes into account the views of his opponents. Likewise, Hearne not only presents her view of animal rights, but also argues against existing practices and beliefs.

After you have identified the crucial points to be addressed, you should then select the methods you'll need to make a convincing case with respect to each of the points. Some methods, of course, are imperative no matter what point you are trying to prove. Every piece of argumentation requires that you offer readers evidence to support your position. To do so, you will need to gather and present specific details that bear on each of the points you are trying to make. This basic concern for providing readers with appropriate evidence will lead you inevitably into the activity of reporting. Jefferson, for example, provides a lengthy and detailed list of "injuries" that the king of Great Britain inflicted on the colonies in his attempt to demonstrate the right of the colonies "to throw off such Government." Reporting appropriate evidence constitutes the most basic means of making a persuasive case for any point under consideration. So, any point for which evidence cannot be provided, or for which only weak or limited evidence can be offered, is likely to be much less convincing to readers than one that can be amply and vividly substantiated.

But evidence alone will not be persuasive to readers unless it is brought to bear on a point in a reasonable or logical way. In one of its most familiar forms, induction, logic involves the process of moving from bits of evidence to a generalization or a conclusion that is based on that evidence. King, for example, tells in detail about several different kinds of psychological experiments involving animals to refute the charge of his opponents that animal research is "pointless." Although this evidence is appropriate for showing that some research on animals has been purposeful and beneficial, it does not demonstrate the necessity of using animals in research. To do that, King attempts to show that certain kinds of research problems "do not lend themselves" to alternative methods of investigation. Based on this evidence, he claims that in some instances "animals are necessary if the research is to be done at all." This particular claim appears reasonable not just because King has gathered and presented evidence that pertains to the issue at hand, but also because he has carefully worded his claim so as not to overstate the case. But like all generalizations, it is a hypothesis and not a certainty. To prove his claim beyond any doubt, King would have had to examine every instance of animal research that had ever been conducted and consider alternative methods that might have been available at the time. So, he has no choice but to make what is known as an inductive leap from a reasonable, but necessarily limited, body of evidence to a generalization. So, too, his generalization is at best a statement of probability.

Deduction, another form of logic, involves the movement from general assumptions or hypotheses to particular conclusions that can be derived from them. For example, having made the general claim that "a long train of abuses" entitles people "to throw off such Government" and having cited, in turn, a long list of abuses that Great Britain had inflicted on the colonies, Jefferson is able to reach the conclusion that the colonies "are Absolved from all Allegiance to the British Crown." Given his initial assumptions about government and the rights of the people, together with his evidence about British abuse of the colonists, Jefferson's deduction seems to be a logical conclusion, as indeed it is. But as in any case of deductive logic, the conclusion is only as convincing as the premises on which it is based. Great Britain, obviously, did not accept Jefferson's premises, so it did not accept his conclusions, logical though they were. Other countries of the time, just as obviously, took a different view of the matter. So, in developing an argument deductively, you need to keep in mind not only the logic of your case, but also the appeal its premises are likely to have for those whom you are most interested in convincing.

As you can see just from the cases of Jefferson, King, and Hearne, presenting evidence and using it in a logical way can take a variety of common forms, and all of these forms are likely to be present in subtle and complicated ways in virtually every piece of argumentative writing. Arguing calls on writers to be especially resourceful in developing and presenting their positions. Actually, logic is a necessary—and powerful—tool in every field and profession because it serves to fill in gaps where evidence does not exist or, as in a court case, to move beyond the accumulated evidence to conclusions that follow from it. But like any powerful tool it must be used with care. One weak link in a logical chain of reasoning can lead, after all, to a string of falsehood.

Explanatory techniques, as discussed in the introduction to "Explaining" (p. 303), also can play a role in argument, as you may already have inferred from the passages we have just been discussing. Hearne's argument about animal rights, for example, is based on her interpretation of key terms, such as rights, and Bettelheim's attack on the sanctification of the Franks' unrealistic approach to a terrible situation relies on causal analysis to make its case. Any piece of argument, in other words, is likely to draw on a wide range of techniques, for argument is always attempting to achieve the complex purpose not only of getting at the truth about something and making that truth intelligible to readers, but also of persuading them to accept it as such.

No matter what particular combination of techniques a writer favors, when carrying out an argument, most save a very telling point or bit of evidence or well-turned phrase for last. Like effective storytellers or successful courtroom lawyers, writers know that a memorable detail makes for a powerful climax. In the pieces that follow in this section, you will see how different writers use the various resources of language to produce some very striking and compelling pieces of argument.

Arts and Humanities

HIROSHIMA
John Berger

After beginning his career as a painter and drawing instructor, John Berger (b. 1926) came to be one of Britain's most influential art critics. He has achieved recognition as a screenwriter, novelist, and documentary writer. As a Marxist, he is concerned with the ideological and technological conditioning of our ways of seeing both art and the world. In Ways of Seeing *(1972), he explores the interrelation between words and images, between verbal and visual meaning. "Hiroshima" first appeared in 1981 in the journal* New Society, *and later in a collection of essays,* The Sense of Sight *(1985). Berger examines how the facts of nuclear holocaust have been hidden through "a systematic, slow and thorough process of suppression and elimination . . . within the reality of politics." Images, rather than words, Berger asserts, can help us see through the "mask of innocence" that evil wears.*

The whole incredible problem begins with the need to reinsert those events of 6 August 1945 back into living consciousness.

I was shown a book last year at the Frankfurt Book Fair. The editor asked me some question about what I thought of its format. I glanced at it quickly and gave some reply. Three months ago I was sent a finished copy of the book. It lay on my desk unopened. Occasionally its title and cover picture caught my eye, but I did not respond. I didn't consider the book urgent, for I believed that I already knew about what I would find within it.

Did I not clearly remember the day—I was in the army in Belfast—when we first heard the news of the bomb dropped on Hiroshima? At how many meetings during the first nuclear disarmament movement had I and others not recalled the meaning of that bomb?

And then, one morning last week, I received a letter from America, accompanying an article written by a friend. This friend is a doctor of philosophy and a Marxist. Furthermore, she is a very generous and warm-hearted woman. The article was about the possibilities of a third world war. Vis-à-vis the Soviet Union she took, I was surprised to read, a position very close to Reagan's. She concluded by evoking the likely scale of destruction which would be caused by nuclear weapons, and then welcomed the positive possibilities that this would offer the socialist revolution in the United States.

It was on that morning that I opened and read the book on my desk. It is 5 called *Unforgettable Fire.*[1]

The book consists of drawings and paintings made by people who were in Hiroshima on the day that the bomb was dropped, thirty-six years ago today. Often the pictures are accompanied by a verbal record of what the image represents. None of them is by a professional artist. In 1974, an old man went to the television center in Hiroshima to show to whomever was interested a picture he had painted, entitled "At about 4 pm, 6th August 1945, near Yurozuyo bridge."

This prompted an idea of launching a television appeal to other survivors of that day to paint or draw their memories of it. Nearly a thousand pictures were sent in, and these were made into an exhibition. The appeal was worded: "Let us leave for posterity pictures about the atomic bomb, drawn by citizens."

Clearly, my interest in these pictures cannot be an art-critical one. One does not musically analyze screams. But after repeatedly looking at them, what began as an impression became a certainty. These were images of hell.

I am not using the word as hyperbole. Between these paintings by women and men who have never painted anything else since leaving school, and who have surely, for the most part, never traveled outside Japan, between these traced memories which had to be exorcised, and the numerous representations of hell in European medieval art, there is a very close affinity.

This affinity is both stylistic and fundamental. And fundamentally it is to do 10 with the situations depicted. The affinity lies in the degree of the multiplication of pain, in the lack of appeal or aid, in the pitilessness, in the equality of wretchedness, and in the disappearance of time.

> I am 78 years old. I was living at Midorimachi on the day of the A-bomb blast. Around 9 am that morning, when I looked out of my window, I saw several women coming along the street one after another towards the Hiroshima prefectural hospital. I realized for the first time, as it is sometimes said, that when people are very much frightened hair really does stand on end. The women's hair was, in fact, standing straight up and the skin of their arms was peeled off. I suppose they were around 30 years old.

Time and again, the sober eyewitness accounts recall the surprise and horror of Dante's verses about the Inferno. The temperature at the center of the

HOW SURVIVORS SAW IT. A painting by Kazuhiro Ishizu, aged 68

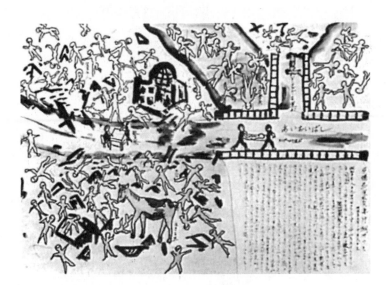

AT THE AIOI BRIDGE, by Sawami Katagiri, aged 76

Hiroshima fireball was 300,000 degrees centigrade. The survivors are called in Japanese *hibakuska*—"those who have seen hell."

> Suddenly, one man who was stark naked came up to me and said in a quavering voice, "Please help me!" He was burned and swollen all over from the effects of the A-bomb. Since I did not recognize him as my neighbor, I asked who he was. He answered that he was Mr. Sasaki, the son of Mr. Ennosuke Sasaki, who had a lumber shop in Funairi town. That morning he had been doing volunteer labor service, evacuating the houses near the prefectural office in Kato town. He had been burned black all over and had started back to his home in Funairi. He looked miserable—burned and sore, and naked with only pieces of his gaiters trailing behind as he walked. Only the part of his hair covered by his soldier's hat was left, as if he was wearing a bowl. When I touched him, his burned skin slipped off. I did not know what to do, so I asked a passing driver to take him to Eba hospital.

Does not this evocation of hell make it easier to forget that these scenes belonged to life? Is there not something conveniently unreal about hell? The whole history of the twentieth century proves otherwise.

Very systematically in Europe the conditions of hells have been constructed. It is not even necessary to list the sites. It is not even necessary to repeat the calculations of the organizers. We know this, and we choose to forget it.

We find it ridiculous or shocking that most of the pages concerning, for example, Trotsky were torn out of official Soviet history. What has been torn out of our history are the pages concerning the experience of the two atom bombs dropped on Japan.

Of course, the facts are there in the textbooks. It may even be that school children learn the dates. But what these facts mean—and originally their meaning was so clear, so monstrously vivid, that every commentator in the world was shocked, and every politician was obliged to say (whilst planning differently), "Never again"—what these facts mean has now been torn out. It has been a systematic, slow and thorough process of suppression and elimination. This process has been hidden within the reality of politics.

Do not misunderstand me. I am not here using the word "reality" ironically, 15 I am not politically naïve. I have the greatest respect for political reality, and I believe that the innocence of political idealists is often very dangerous. What we are considering is how in this case in the West—not in Japan for obvious reasons and not in the Soviet Union for different reasons—political and military realities have eliminated another reality.

The eliminated reality is both physical—

> Yokogawa bridge above Tenma river, 6th August 1945, 8:30 am.
> People crying and moaning were running towards the city. I did not know why. Steam engines were burning at Yokogawa station.

Skin of cow tied to wire.
Skin of girl's hip was hanging down.
"My baby is dead, isn't she?"

and moral.

The political and military arguments have concerned such issues as deterrence, defense systems, relative strike parity, tactical nuclear weapons and—pathetically—so-called civil defense. Any movement for nuclear disarmament today has to contend with those considerations and dispute their false interpretation. To lose sight of them is to become as apocalyptic as the Bomb and all utopias. (The construction of hells on earth was accompanied in Europe by plans for heavens on earth.)

What has to be redeemed, reinserted, disclosed and never be allowed to be forgotten, is the other reality. Most of the mass means of communication are close to what has been suppressed.

These paintings were shown on Japanese television. Is it conceivable that the BBC would show these pictures on Channel One at a peak hour? Without any reference to "political" and "military" realities, under the straight title, *This is How It Was, 6th August 1945*? I challenge them to do so.

What happened on that day was, of course, neither the beginning nor the end of the act. It began months, years before, with the planning of the action, and the eventual final decision to drop two bombs on Japan. However much the world was shocked and surprised by the bomb dropped on Hiroshima, it has to be emphasized that it was not a miscalculation, an error, or the result (as can happen in war) of a situation deteriorating so rapidly that it gets out of hand. What happened was consciously and precisely planned. Small scenes like this were part of the plan:

> I was walking along the Hihiyama bridge about 3 pm on 7th August. A woman, who looked like an expectant mother, was dead. At her side, a girl of about three years of age brought some water in an empty can she had found. She was trying to let her mother drink from it.
>
> As soon as I saw this miserable scene with the pitiful child, I embraced the girl close to me and cried with her, telling her that her mother was dead.

There was a preparation. And there was an aftermath. The latter included long, lingering deaths, radiation sickness, many fatal illnesses which developed later as a result of exposure to the bomb, and tragic genetical effects on generations yet to be born.

I refrain from giving the statistics: how many hundreds of thousands of dead, how many injured, how many deformed children. Just as I refrain from pointing out how comparatively "small" were the atomic bombs dropped on Japan. Such statistics tend to distract. We consider numbers instead of pain. We calculate instead of judging. We relativize instead of refusing.

It is possible today to arouse popular indignation or anger by speaking of the threat and immorality of terrorism. Indeed, this appears to be the central plank of the rhetoric of the new American foreign policy ("Moscow is the world-base of all terrorism") and of British policy towards Ireland. What is able to shock people about terrorist acts is that often their targets are unselected and inno-cent—a crowd in a railway station, people waiting for a bus to go home after work. The victims are chosen indiscriminately in the hope of producing a shock effect on political decision-making by their government.

The two bombs dropped on Japan were terrorist actions. The calculation was terrorist. The indiscriminacy was terrorist. The small groups of terrorists operating today are, by comparison, humane killers.

Another comparison needs to be made. Today terrorist groups mostly repre- 25 sent small nations or groupings, who are disputing large powers in a position of strength. Whereas Hiroshima was perpetrated by the most powerful alliance in the world against an enemy who was already prepared to negotiate, and was ad-mitting defeat.

To apply the epithet "terrorist" to the acts of bombing Hiroshima and Na-gasaki is logically justifiable, and I do so because it may help to reinsert that act into living consciousness today. Yet the word changes nothing in itself.

The first-hand evidence of the victims, the reading of the pages which have been torn out, provokes a sense of outrage. This outrage has two natural faces. One is a sense of horror and pity at what happened; the other face is self-defensive and declares: *this should not happen again (here).* For some the *here* is in brackets, for others it is not.

The face of horror, the reaction which has now been mostly suppressed, forces us to comprehend the reality of what happened. The second reaction, unfortunately, distances us from that reality. Although it begins as a straight declaration, it quickly leads into the labyrinth of defense policies, military ar-guments and global strategies. Finally it leads to the sordid commercial absur-dity of private fall-out shelters.

This split of the sense of outrage into, on one hand, horror, and, on the other hand, expediency occurs because the concept of evil has been aban-doned. Every culture, except our own in recent times, has had such a concept.

That its religious or philosophical bases vary is unimportant. The concept of 30 evil implies a force or forces which have to be continually struggled against so that they do not triumph over life and destroy it. One of the very first written texts from Mesopotamia, 1,500 years before Homer, speaks of this struggle, which was the first condition of human life. In public thinking nowadays, the concept of evil has been reduced to a little adjective to support an opinion or hypothesis (abortions, terrorism, ayatollahs).

Nobody can confront the reality of 6th August 1945 without being forced to acknowledge that what happened was evil. It is not a question of opinion or in-terpretation, but of events.

The memory of these events should be continually before our eyes. This is why the thousand citizens of Hiroshima started to draw on their little scraps of paper. We need to show their drawings everywhere. These terrible images can now release an energy for opposing evil and for the life-long struggle of that opposition.

And from this a very old lesson may be drawn. My friend in the United States is, in a sense, innocent. She looks beyond a nuclear holocaust without considering its reality. This reality includes not only its victims but also its planners and those who support them. Evil from time immemorial has often worn a mask of innocence. One of evil's principal modes of being is *looking beyond* (with indifference) that which is before the eyes.

> August 9th: On the west embankment of a military training field was a young boy four or five years old. He was burned black, lying on his back, with his arms pointing towards heaven.

Only by looking beyond or away can one come to believe that such evil is relative, and therefore under certain conditions justifiable. In reality—the reality to which the survivors and the dead bear witness—it can never be justified.

NOTE

1. Edited by Japan Broadcasting Corporation, London, Wildwood House, 1981; New York, Pantheon, 1981.

QUESTIONS

1. Berger begins his essay with this powerful sentence: "The whole incredible problem begins with the need to reinsert those events of 6 August 1945 back into living consciousness." What is "the whole incredible problem" as Berger describes and defines it?

2. Berger argues that what happened on August 6, 1945, was "consciously and precisely planned" (paragraph 20). What evidence does he present to support this claim? How does this argument advance his larger purpose?

3. Berger tells his readers that he refrains from giving statistics because "statistics tend to distract" (paragraph 22). What do statistics distance us from understanding about Hiroshima?

4. The content in Berger's essay ranges from thoughts about Hiroshima, to images of hell, to political realities, to terrorist actions, to concepts of evil. How does he connect these various subjects? What is the chain of reasoning?

5. Berger offers various images from the book *Unforgettable Fire*, such as "August 9th: On the west embankment of a military training field was a young boy four or five years old. He was burned black, lying on his back, with his arms pointing towards heaven" (paragraph 33). Look at the various places in the essay where Berger presents

such images from *Unforgettable Fire*. What effect does this evidence have on you? How does this evidence strengthen Berger's argument?

6. Spend some time looking at and thinking about the paintings by the survivors, Kazuhiro Ishizu and Sawami Katagiri, reprinted on page 561. What do you *see* in these paintings? What do these images represent to you?

MAKING CONNECTIONS

1. Berger insists on closing the distance between ourselves and the essential horror of Hiroshima. Look at some other essays that struggle with issues of distance. Jonathan Swift's "A Modest Proposal" (p. 632) and Alice Walker's "Am I Blue?" (p. 567) would both be examples, but you might propose another. To what an extent is distance an issue in arguing? Compare how two or three arguers handle problems of distance in their essays.

2. One of Berger's strategies in this essay is to challenge and invert popular definitions, as of *terrorism* and *terrorists*, for example (paragraphs 23–26). Similar inversions take place or are hinted at in Jane van Lawick-Goodall's "First Observations" (p. 241) and Alice Walker's "Am I Blue?" (p. 567). In these examples, the inversion involves humans and animals. Write an argument in which you invert the definition of a key term, of *safe* and *unsafe*, for example, or *capitalist* and *communist*, or *fair* and *foul*, or *villain* and *victim*. Experiment with the leverage for arguing that you find in such a radical redefinition.

AM I BLUE?

Alice Walker

Alice Walker (b. 1944) is an essayist, poet, novelist, and short-story writer. The following essay comes from her collection Living by the Word: Selected Writings, 1973–1987 *(1988). About this collection, Walker writes, "In my travels I found many people sitting and thinking thoughts similar to my own. In this study I was taught by these other people, by the art and history of past cultures, by the elements, and by the trees, the flowers, and, most especially, the animals." In the essay reprinted here, Walker questions the distinctions commonly made between human and animal.*

For about three years my companion and I rented a small house in the country that stood on the edge of a large meadow that appeared to run from the end of our deck straight into the mountains. The mountains, however, were quite far away, and between us and them there was, in fact, a town. It was one of the many pleasant aspects of the house that you never really were aware of this.

It was a house of many windows, low, wide, nearly floor to ceiling in the living room, which faced the meadow, and it was from one of these that I first saw our closest neighbor, a large white horse, cropping grass, flipping its mane, and ambling about—not over the entire meadow, which stretched well out of sight of the house, but over the five or so fenced-in acres that were next to the twenty-odd that we had rented. I soon learned that the horse, whose name was Blue, belonged to a man who lived in another town, but was boarded by our neighbors next door. Occasionally, one of the children, usually a stocky teenager, but sometimes a much younger girl or boy, could be seen riding Blue. They would appear in the meadow, climb up on his back, ride furiously for ten or fifteen minutes, then get off, slap Blue on the flanks, and not be seen again for a month or more.

There were many apple trees in our yard, and one by the fence that Blue could almost reach. We were soon in the habit of feeding him apples, which he relished, especially because by the middle of summer the meadow grasses — so green and succulent since January—had dried out from lack of rain, and Blue stumbled about munching the dried stalks half-heartedly. Sometimes he would stand very still just by the apple tree, and when one of us came out he would whinny, snort loudly, or stamp the ground. This meant, of course: I want an apple.

It was quite wonderful to pick a few apples, or collect those that had fallen to the ground overnight, and patiently hold them, one by one, up to his large, toothy mouth. I remained as thrilled as a child by his flexible dark lips, huge, cubelike teeth that crunched the apples, core and all, with such finality, and his high, broad-breasted *enormity*; beside which, I felt small indeed. When I was a child, I used to ride horses, and was especially friendly with one named Nan until the day I was riding and my brother deliberately spooked her and I was thrown, head first, against the trunk of a tree. When I came to, I was in bed and my mother was bending worriedly over me; we silently agreed that perhaps horseback riding was not the safest sport for me. Since then I have walked, and prefer walking to horseback riding—but I had forgotten the depth of feeling one could see in horses' eyes.

I was therefore unprepared for the expression in Blue's. Blue was lonely. Blue was horribly lonely and bored. I was not shocked that this should be the case; five acres to tramp by yourself, endlessly, even in the most beautiful of meadows—and his was—cannot provide many interesting events, and once the rainy season turned to dry that was about it. No, I was shocked that I had forgotten that human animals and nonhuman animals can communicate quite well; if we are brought up around animals as children we take this for granted. By the time we are adults we no longer remember. However, the animals have not changed. They are in fact *completed* creations (at least they seem to be, so much more than we) who are not likely *to* change; it is their nature to express themselves. What else are they going to express? And they do. And, generally speaking, they are ignored.

After giving Blue the apples, I would wander back to the house, aware that he was observing me. Were more apples not forthcoming then? Was that to be his sole entertainment for the day? My partner's small son had decided he wanted to learn how to piece a quilt; we worked in silence on our respective squares as I thought . . .

Well, about slavery: about white children, who were raised by black people, who knew their first all-accepting love from black women, and then, when they were twelve or so, were told they must "forget" the deep levels of communication between themselves and "mammy" that they knew. Later they would be able to relate quite calmly, "My old mammy was sold to another good family." "My old mammy was _____." Fill in the blank. Many more years later a white woman would say: "I can't understand these Negroes, these blacks. What do they want? They're so different from us."

And about the Indians, considered to be "like animals" by the "settlers" (a very benign euphemism for what they actually were), who did not understand their description as a compliment.

And about the thousands of American men who marry Japanese, Korean, Filipina, and other non-English-speaking women and of how happy they report they are, "*blissfully*," until their brides learn to speak English, at which point the marriages tend to fall apart. What then did the men see, when they looked into the eyes of the women they married, before they could speak English? Apparently only their own reflections.

I thought of society's impatience with the young. "Why are they playing the music so loud?" Perhaps the children have listened to much of the music of oppressed people their parents danced to before they were born, with its passionate but soft cries for acceptance and love, and they have wondered why their parents failed to hear.

I do not know how long Blue had inhabited his five beautiful, boring acres before we moved into our house; a year after we had arrived—and had also traveled to other valleys, other cities, other worlds—he was still there.

But then, in our second year at the house, something happened in Blue's life. One morning, looking out the window at the fog that lay like a ribbon over the meadow, I saw another horse, a brown one, at the other end of Blue's field. Blue appeared to be afraid of it, and for several days made no attempt to go near. We went away for a week. When we returned, Blue had decided to make friends and the two horses ambled or galloped along together, and Blue did not come nearly as often to the fence underneath the apple tree.

When he did, bringing his new friend with him, there was a different look in his eyes. A look of independence, of self-possession, of inalienable *horse*ness. His friend eventually became pregnant. For months and months there was, it seemed to me, a mutual feeling between me and the horses of justice, of peace. I fed apples to them both. The look in Blue's eyes was one of unabashed "this is *it*ness."

It did not, however, last forever. One day, after a visit to the city, I went out to give Blue some apples. He stood waiting, or so I thought, though not beneath the tree. When I shook the tree and jumped back from the shower of apples, he made no move. I carried some over to him. He managed to half-crunch one. The rest he let fall to the ground. I dreaded looking into his eyes—because I had of course noticed that Brown, his partner, had gone—but I did look. If I had been born into slavery, and my partner had been sold or killed, my eyes would have looked like that. The children next door explained that Blue's partner had been "put with him" (the same expression that old people used, I had noticed, when speaking of an ancestor during slavery who had been impregnated by her owner) so that they could mate and she conceive. Since that was accomplished, she had been taken back by her owner, who lived somewhere else.

Will she be back? I asked.

They didn't know.

Blue was like a crazed person. Blue *was*, to me, a crazed person. He galloped furiously, as if he were being ridden, around and around his five beautiful acres. He whinnied until he couldn't. He tore at the ground with his hooves. He butted himself against his single shade tree. He looked always and always toward the road down which his partner had gone. And then, occasionally, when he came up for apples, or I took apples to him, he looked at me. It was a look so piercing, so full of grief, a look so *human*, I almost laughed (I felt too sad to cry) to think there are people who do not know that animals suffer. People like me who have forgotten, and daily forget, all that animals try to tell us. "Everything you do to us will happen to you; we are your teachers, as you are ours. We are one lesson" is essentially it, I think. There are those who never once have even considered animals' rights: those who have been taught that animals actually want to be used and abused by us, as small children "love" to be frightened, or women "love" to be mutilated and raped. . . . They are the great-grandchildren of those who honestly thought, because someone taught them this: "Woman can't think" and "niggers can't faint." But most disturbing of all, in Blue's large brown eyes was a new look, more painful than the look of despair: the look of disgust with human beings, with life; the look of hatred. And it was odd what the look of hatred did. It gave him, for the first time, the look of a beast. And what that meant was that he had put up a barrier within to protect himself from further violence; all the apples in the world wouldn't change that fact.

And so Blue remained, a beautiful part of our landscape, very peaceful to look at from the window, white against the grass. Once a friend came to visit and said, looking out on the soothing view: "And it *would* have to be a *white* horse; the very image of freedom." And I thought, yes, the animals are forced to become for us merely "images" of what they once so beautifully expressed. And we are used to drinking milk from containers showing "contented" cows, whose real lives we want to hear nothing about, eating eggs and drumsticks from "happy" hens, and munching hamburgers advertised by bulls of integrity who seem to command their fate.

As we talked of freedom and justice one day for all, we sat down to steaks. I am eating misery, I thought, as I took the first bite. And spit it out.

QUESTIONS

1. Why does Walker begin her argument by setting the scene ("[We] rented a small house in the country . . .") and by leisurely describing the meadow where she first saw Blue?

2. Walker takes great pleasure in describing Blue for her readers. In paragraph 4, she tells us, "I remained as thrilled as a child by his flexible dark lips, huge, cubelike teeth that crunched the apples, core and all, with such finality, and his high, broadbreasted *enormity*; beside which, I felt small indeed." What does Blue represent to Walker? What does she learn from observing him?

3. In paragraph 7, Walker switches from thinking about Blue to thinking about slavery. This kind of transition is the work of the essayist—to link together through language horses, slavery, Indians, and non-English-speaking women. How does Walker make these various connections? What is her argument?

4. Walker writes in paragraph 18, "And I thought, yes, the animals are forced to become for us merely 'images' of what they once so beautifully expressed. And we are

used to drinking milk from containers showing 'contented' cows, whose real lives we want to hear nothing about, eating eggs and drumsticks from 'happy' hens, and munching hamburgers advertised by bulls of integrity who seem to command their fate." How would you respond to this comment? Write a response to Walker's essay in which you argue your position.

5. Some animal rights activists argue that animal rights will emerge as the civil rights movement of the twenty-first century. A central issue in this movement is the question, What distinguishes humans from other animals? Write an essay in which you argue your position on this issue.

MAKING CONNECTIONS

1. Walker's strategies for arguing differ from those of a more formal argument, such as Thomas Jefferson's Declaration of Independence (p. 640) or Diana Baumrind's "Review of Stanley Milgram's Experiments on Obedience" (p. 645). Describe the strategies Walker uses and how they differ from Jefferson's or Baumrind's or those of another writer of your choice from this section.

2. Walker's other essay in this volume, "Beauty: When the Other Dancer Is the Self" (p. 40), is categorized as reflective rather than argumentative. Presumably, her approaches to these two essays differ. Compare her two essays. In what passages in "Am I Blue?" do you find Walker most intensely absorbed in arguing? How do those passages stand out? How are they prepared for? Is there an argument embedded in the earlier essay as well? If so, how can you describe it?

JOHN KEATS VERSUS BOB DYLAN
Why Value Judgments Matter

Simon Frith

Simon Frith (b. 1946) is a professor and research director of the John Logie Baird Center and professor of English studies at Strathclyde University in Scotland. He has written music criticism for the Sunday Times *of London and the* Village Voice *of New York City, and he has chaired the International Association for the Study of Popular Music. His latest book is* Performing Rites: On the Value of Popular Music *(1996). This essay first appeared in the* Chronicle of Higher Education *on their "Point of View" page (1997).*

A couple of years ago, the British playwright David Hare had his moment of mass-media fame after remarking tetchily on television that, in the end, Keats was just better than Bob Dylan. The remark caused a stir because Hare is a left-leaning writer and was talking on the British Broadcasting Corporation's "Late Show," an arts slot that self-consciously played down the distinctions between high and low culture. As with any other media storm, the reported details of Hare's argument were vague; the context for his comment and his exact words were not major features of the furor that they provoked.

If he simply had meant that John Keats was a better poet than Bob Dylan, the remark was incontrovertible. But what he was taken to mean—hence the attention—was that Keats, a poet, was more *valuable* than Dylan, a rock star. His comment was read as a statement less about specific works than about cultural hierarchies. And it was a statement welcomed by the press (which uses far more space to orchestrate pop culture than to celebrate high culture) for its educational implications: Here was someone explaining pithily why the traditional school curriculum matters; why the "relativizing" effects of media and cultural studies—with their tendency to have students study soap operas alongside Shakespeare—should be deplored.

As a sociologist, I found the resulting pronouncements from tabloid pulpits illuminating, if not in their own terms. After all, for a sociologist (or anthropologist), all cultural items and activities are important—as evidence of beliefs and values, as ways of organizing social relations. For me, the question was less whether Keats is more valuable then Dylan, than what "valuable" meant in this public discussion, and why the issue seemed to matter so much to people who were rather more likely to listen to Dylan's songs than to read Keats's poems.

This was the media version of a debate that was already well entrenched in the academy concerning the rise of cultural studies and the crisis of confidence in literature departments over what should be studied and why. I remembered an earlier assertion in the media: the American columnist George Will's dismissing the idea that there could be a feminist reading of the Brontës or a post-colonialist interpretation of *The Tempest*. As usual, he had slightly missed the point. What irritated him was that such (perfectly feasible) sociological approaches as considering gender relations in novels about love or race relations in a play about power might be viewed as challenging traditional close readings of the works themselves. Again, what was at stake was less our understanding of the Brontës and Shakespeare than the importance of literary evaluation (and authority) in the first place.

In 1987, I left the sociology department at Warwick University (where I had   5 been involved in media and cultural studies from a social-science perspective) and joined the English department at Strathclyde University (with a brief to develop media and cultural studies in the context of the humanities). My sociological training meant that I was well aware that this academic shift would bring a fundamental change in how I was expected to analyze literary and other cultural phenomena. In sociology, all social phenomena are equal, equally the products of social forces and institutions, while English departments depend on value judgments' being made, on Keats's being better than Dylan. I knew (having read my Pierre Bourdieu[1]) that to draw my new colleagues' attention to the social bases of "transcendent" aesthetic categories would be tactless.

What has continued to surprise me, though, is how tentative my colleagues in English are when it comes to the evaluative process itself. Creative writing, I was informed when I made the switch, is a tricky subject to add to the undergraduate curriculum because it is so difficult to assess: Who is to say whether a student's poem or story is any good or not? The curriculum for the contemporary-literature course turns out to be a constant source of controversy: How can we know that Martin Amis or Margaret Atwood is going to last? Because the underlying value of literature is taken for granted, students are not actually encouraged to use their own responses to a text as a legitimate ground for evaluating it.

The resulting confusion over what is meant by "good," in and out of the classroom (among students and professors, as well as newspaper readers and columnists), is most evident in film studies, with which I also have become involved. The first pedagogical task of an academic film course is to wean students from their accustomed conversations about the films they see—"I liked the bit when ..." and "Wasn't X good?" Film students must put aside their everyday assessments of films to treat them analytically; they have to learn a

---

[1]*Pierre Bourdieu* (b. 1930): French sociologist eminent in the field of cultural analysis. [Eds.]

new, more technical language of film judgment, drawn from film theory and professorial authority.

As a sociologist, I knew this teaching approach was inevitable. To make films the object of academic study is to turn them into academic objects, assessed according to their pedagogical value. But while students are well used to this kind of analysis in literature classes—in high school they learn to distinguish between books read for pleasure and books read for the teacher—film students generally have to make the move from subjective response to objective assessment instantly. I now began to realize what was lost: any discussion of the processes of popular evaluation itself, the ways in which non-academic filmgoers come to decide—and assert—what is a "good" or a "bad" film.

This is also apparent in music studies. The problem is not just that musicologists resist sociological accounts of how "good" music came to be that way, but, equally, that sociologists in music studies (like myself) think that once we have explained how particular popular songs or stars came to be produced and consumed, not much more need be said. Whether the songs or stars are any good is not seen as a sociological question. Does it really matter whether Bryan Adams is better than Michael Bolton, Boyzone better than East 17?

Yes, it does—to the people who make such judgments, whether they be record companies deciding which performers to sign, radio programmers deciding what to play, or consumers deciding which CD's to buy. And as someone who is making a living as a rock critic as well as a professor, it matters to me, too. What seems obvious is that popular cultural activities—like all cultural activities—depend on judgments. They are organized around patterns of discrimination and difference, through arguments about the good and the bad. And if evaluation is a key cultural activity, then the sociological task is to chart how such evaluation works—in what terms, under what circumstances.

In the course of my exploration of the value of popular music, three issues, in particular, have intrigued me. First, the difference between the ways in which musicians make judgments and the ways in which listeners do: A pop concert is as much a source of tension between performers and audience as a celebration of their community. Second, the ways in which aesthetic and ethical judgments are mixed up in pop practice: We like singers or genres less for technical, musical reasons than as sources of identity and idealism. Which means, third, that musical evaluation is tied up with our sense of sociability: Even the most atomized, Walkman-wrapped listener takes pleasure from placing herself in a social world.

But how should these questions of popular evaluation be addressed, if at all, in the classroom? This takes me back to the problems of relativism and authority: If what's at stake is everyday evaluation, then why should a professor's pop judgments be any more authoritative than a student's?

I see two problems here. The evaluation that occurs in the classroom (unlike the evaluation that occurs in the rehearsal or the living room) has to follow classroom conventions: textual analysis, agreed-upon descriptive terms, an as-

10

sumed objectivity, a suspension of personal prejudice. One effect is that complex texts are much more satisfying for classroom purposes than simple ones. Students would rather study a George Eliot than a Jeffrey Archer novel or, for that matter, a Keats than a Dylan poem, because there is more, in classroom terms, to say about them.

In this respect, then, a teacher's authority derives from greater experience of, and adeptness with, academic discourse. But there is also the authority of the instructor's personal investment in the music and enjoyment of it. Great teachers are great for subjective, not objective, reasons. I will always remember the excitement of watching the film scholar David Bordwell lecture to his undergraduates at the University of Wisconsin. At a certain moment his account of the movie M shifted from the objective—how the film worked analytically—to the subjective, why the film mattered so much to him. This wasn't a conscious movement: Bordwell couldn't help his own engagement with the film from emerging and inspiring everyone present, not necessarily to rate M as he did, but to understand why value matters in cinema.

It is in this context that I find some bad faith in what we know as cultural   15
studies. Some scholars treat popular texts only for their ideological significance, without addressing the question of value. They leave it to sales figures to determine what matters. The point is not that students should share their teachers' tastes—whether in literature, film, or music—but that they should have to think about evaluation and why it matters.

For the last five years, I've been chairman of the judges of the Mercury Music Prize, which is awarded annually to the best British record of any sort of music. From the beginning, we agreed that our decisions would be determined not by vote but by persuasion. The winning records are those with the most articulate supporters, and my biggest pleasure in the judging room is to have my mind changed or to change those of other people. This is a pedagogic pleasure, and its something we should not forgo in the classroom.

Cultural studies, if nothing else, is about challenging students to think about their cultural values, to change their minds about television programs and films and rock acts, or, if not, to help them argue their own views more convincingly in those daily conversations in which passing judgment is already the cement of our social lives.

QUESTIONS

1. What issues are set forth in Frith's opening anecdote and his commentary on it (paragraphs 1–4)?

2. When we say a book or film is "good," what do we mean? Consider your own experience with evaluation in and out of the classroom. What is your process of evaluation for a recent film? For an assigned novel, such as *The Scarlet Letter?*

3. What arguments are being made for the validity of subjective responses? Does Frith consider subjectivity more important or as important as objectivity in evaluation?

4. In what ways is Frith's essay an argument for the importance of cultural studies in the academic curriculum?

5. Frith's essay, originally published in a weekly newspaper on higher education, is addressed primarily to teachers. What is he urging them to do to (or for) you, the student?

6. Do some research on a film, a TV series, or a popular music group you particularly like. Gather reviews and articles from several different sources, such as popular magazines, fanzines, and academic journals specializing in popular culture, film, or music. Compare and contrast the kinds of analysis and the implicit or explicit standards and modes of evaluation in these reviews or articles. How do they compare with your own evaluation?

7. Take a position in the culture wars: Does popular material—romance novels, films, TV shows, rock or rap music, for example—have a place in the academic curriculum? If not, why not? If you think it does, describe its place. You may want to use some specific examples to make your case.

MAKING CONNECTIONS

Compare Frith's statements on objectivity and subjectivity in evaluation with Barbara Tuchman's discussion of it in "When Does History Happen?" (p. 604).

IF BLACK ENGLISH ISN'T
A LANGUAGE, THEN TELL ME,
WHAT IS?

James Baldwin

James Baldwin was born in Harlem in 1924 and followed his father's vocation, becoming a preacher at the age of fourteen. At seventeen, he left the ministry and devoted himself to writing until his death in 1987. Baldwin's most frequent subject was the relationship between blacks and whites, about which he wrote, "The color of my skin made me automatically an expert." Baldwin himself might also have added that his life's work lay in defining and legitimizing the black voice; like Orwell, Baldwin argued that language is "a political instrument, means, and proof of power." He wrote five novels, a book of stories, one play, and several collections of essays. The following essay on language and legitimacy first appeared in 1979 in the New York Times *and later was included in* The Price of the Ticket: Collected Nonfiction, 1948–1985 *(1985).*

The argument concerning the use, or the status, or the reality, of black English is rooted in American history and has absolutely nothing to do with the question the argument supposes itself to be posing. The argument has nothing to do with language itself but with the role of language. Language, incontestably, reveals the speaker. Language, also, far more dubiously, is meant to define the other—and, in this case, the other is refusing to be defined by a language that has never been able to recognize him.

People evolve a language in order to describe and thus control their circumstances or in order not to be submerged by a situation that they cannot articulate. (And if they cannot articulate it, they are submerged.) A Frenchman living in Paris speaks a subtly and crucially different language from that of the man living in Marseilles; neither sounds very much like a man living in Quebec; and they would all have great difficulty in apprehending what the man from Guadeloupe, or Martinique, is saying, to say nothing of the man from Senegal—although the "common" language of all these areas is French. But each has paid, and is paying, a different price for this "common" language, in which, as it turns out, they are not saying, and cannot be saying, the same things: They each have very different realities to articulate, or control.

What joins all languages, and all men, is the necessity to confront life, in order, not inconceivably, to outwit death: The price for this is the acceptance, and achievement, of one's temporal identity. So that, for example, though it is not taught in the schools (and this has the potential of becoming a political issue) the south of France still clings to its ancient and musical Provençal, which resists being described as a "dialect." And much of the tension in the Basque countries, and in Wales, is due to the Basque and Welsh determination not to allow their languages to be destroyed. This determination also feeds the flames in Ireland for among the many indignities the Irish have been forced to undergo at English hands is the English contempt for their language.

It goes without saying, then, that language is also a political instrument, means, and proof of power. It is the most vivid and crucial key to identity: It reveals the private identity, and connects one with, or divorces one from, the larger, public, or communal identity. There have been, and are, times and places, when to speak a certain language could be dangerous, even fatal. Or, one may speak the same language, but in such a way that one's antecedents are revealed, or (one hopes) hidden. This is true in France, and is absolutely true in England: The range (and reign) of accents on that damp little island make England coherent for the English and totally incomprehensible for everyone else. To open your mouth in England is (if I may use black English) to "put your business in the street." You have confessed your parents, your youth, your school, your salary, your self-esteem, and, alas, your future.

Now, I do not know what white Americans would sound like if there had never been any black people in the United States, but they would not sound the way they sound. *Jazz*, for example, is a very specific sexual term, as in *jazz me, baby*, but white people purified it into the Jazz Age. *Sock it to me*, which means, roughly, the same thing, has been adopted by Nathaniel Hawthorne's descendants with no qualms or hesitations at all, along with *let it all hang out* and *right on! Beat to his socks*, which was once the black's most total and despairing image of poverty, was transformed into a thing called the Beat Generation, which phenomenon was, largely, composed of *uptight*, middle-class white people, imitating poverty, trying to *get down*, to *get with it*, doing their *thing*, doing their despairing best to be *funky*, which we, the blacks, never dreamed of doing—we were funky, baby, like *funk* was going out of style.

Now, no one can eat his cake, and have it, too, and it is late in the day to attempt to penalize black people for having created a language that permits the nation its only glimpse of reality, a language without which the nation would be even more *whipped* than it is.

I say that the present skirmish is rooted in American history, and it is. Black English is the creation of the black diaspora. Blacks came to the United States chained to each other, but from different tribes. Neither could speak the other's language. If two black people, at that bitter hour of the world's history, had been able to speak to each other, the institution of chattel slavery could never have lasted as long as it did. Subsequently, the slave was given, under the eye, and the gun, of his master, Congo Square, and the Bible—or, in other words, and under those conditions, the slave began the formation of the black church, and it is within this unprecedented tabernacle that black English began to be formed. This was not, merely, as in the European example, the adoption of a foreign tongue, but an alchemy that transformed ancient elements into a new language: *A language comes into existence by means of brutal necessity, and the rules of the language are dictated by what the language must convey.*

There was a moment, in time, and in this place, when my brother, or my mother, or my father, or my sister, had to convey to me, for example, the danger in which I was standing from the white man standing just behind me, and to convey this with a speed and in a language, that the white man could not possibly understand, and that, indeed, he cannot understand, until today. He cannot afford to understand it. This understanding would reveal to him too much about himself and smash that mirror before which he has been frozen for so long.

Now, if this passion, this skill, this (to quote Toni Morrison) "sheer intelligence," this incredible music, the mighty achievement of having brought a people utterly unknown to, or despised by "history"—to have brought this people to their present, troubled, troubling, and unassailable and unanswerable place—if this absolutely unprecedented journey does not indicate that black English is a language, I am curious to know what definition of languages is to be trusted.

A people at the center of the western world, and in the midst of so hostile a   10 population, has not endured and transcended by means of what is patronizingly called a "dialect." We, the blacks, are in trouble, certainly, but we are not inarticulate because we are not compelled to defend a morality that we know to be a lie.

The brutal truth is that the bulk of the white people in America never had any interest in educating black people, except as this could serve white purposes. It is not the black child's language that is despised. It is his experience. A child cannot be taught by anyone who despises him, and a child cannot afford to be fooled. A child cannot be taught by anyone whose demand, essentially, is that the child repudiate his experience, and all that gives him sustenance, and enter a limbo in which he will no longer be black, and in which he knows that he can never become white. Black people have lost too many black children that way.

And, after all, finally, in a country with standards so untrustworthy, a country that makes heroes of so many criminal mediocrities, a country unable to face why so many of the nonwhite are in prison, or on the needle, or standing, futureless, in the streets—it may very well be that both the child, and his elder, have concluded that they have nothing whatever to learn from the people of a country that has managed to learn so little.

QUESTIONS

1. Baldwin begins his essay by challenging the standard argument concerning black English: "The argument has nothing to do with language itself but with the role of language." What distinctions does Baldwin note between "language itself" and "the role of language"? Why is this distinction central to his argument?

2. Baldwin's position on black English is at odds with those who would like to deny black English status as a language. Summarize Baldwin's position. Summarize the position of Baldwin's opponents.

3. In paragraph 4, Baldwin writes, "It goes without saying, then, that language is also a political instrument, means, and proof of power." How, according to Baldwin, does language connect or divide one from "public or communal identity"? What evidence does he provide to support this claim that language is a political instrument?

4. Baldwin asks his readers, "What is language?" and thus leads them to define for themselves "what definition of languages is to be trusted" (paragraph 9). Do you find Baldwin's definition and position persuasive?

5. Reread Baldwin's memorable conclusion. How does he prepare you for this conclusion? What are you left to contemplate?

6. How has Baldwin's essay made you think about your own use of language and the role language plays in your identity? Baldwin makes an important distinction between *dialect* and *language*. Write an essay in which you take a position on the role of language in shaping your identity.

7. Select a dialect with which you are familiar. Analyze the features of this dialect. Write an essay in which you develop a position showing how this dialect reflects the richness of its culture.

MAKING CONNECTIONS

1. Read Alice Walker's essay, "Am I Blue?" (p. 567), paying particular attention to paragraph 17 on Blue's language and to Walker's sense of Blue's power of communication. To what extent does her argument support Baldwin's position on black English?

2. Consider Baldwin's argument about language as a political instrument that forges and reveals identity in relation to the writings of several female writers in "Explaining"—Joan Didion (p. 311), Margaret Atwood (p. 343), and Carol Gilligan (p. 409), in particular. Can you find and describe in those writings evidence of a women's English parallel in some ways to black English? Or is there a men's English you would prefer to describe, drawing on another set of writers?

POLITICS AND THE ENGLISH LANGUAGE

George Orwell

The rise of totalitarianism in Europe led George Orwell (1903–1950) to write about its causes in his most famous novels, 1984 *(1949) and* Animal Farm *(1945), and in essays like "Politics and the English Language." In this essay, written in 1946, Orwell tells his readers that "in our time, political speech and writing are largely the defense of the indefensible." He attacks language that consists "largely of euphemism, question begging, and sheer cloudy vagueness." Orwell, like John Berger earlier in this section, is concerned with the ways in which language is often used to conceal unpleasant and horrifying realities.*

Most people who bother with the matter at all would admit that the English language is in a bad way, but it is generally assumed that we cannot by conscious action do anything about it. Our civilization is decadent and our language—so the argument runs—must inevitably share in the general collapse. It follows that any struggle against the abuse of language is a sentimental archaism, like preferring candles to electric light or hansom cabs to aeroplanes. Underneath this lies the half-conscious belief that language is a natural growth and not an instrument which we shape for our own purposes.

Now, it is clear that the decline of a language must ultimately have political and economic causes: it is not due simply to the bad influence of this or that individual writer. But an effect can become a cause, reinforcing the original cause and producing the same effect in an intensified form, and so on indefinitely. A man may take to drink because he feels himself to be a failure, and then fail all the more completely because he drinks. It is rather the same thing that is happening to the English language. It becomes ugly and inaccurate because our thoughts are foolish, but the slovenliness of our language makes it easier for us to have foolish thoughts. The point is that the process is reversible. Modern English, especially written English, is full of bad habits which spread by imitation and which can be avoided if one is willing to take the necessary trouble. If one gets rid of these habits one can think more clearly, and to think clearly is a necessary first step towards political regeneration: so that the fight against bad English is not frivolous and is not the exclusive concern of professional writers. I will come back to this presently, and I hope that by that time the meaning of what I have said here will have become clearer. Meanwhile, here are five specimens of the English language as it is now habitually written.

These five passages have not been picked out because they are especially bad—I could have quoted far worse if I had chosen—but because they illustrate various of the mental vices from which we now suffer. They are a little below the average, but are fairly representative samples. I number them so that I can refer back to them when necessary:

"(1) I am not, indeed, sure whether it is not true to say that the Milton who once seemed not unlike a seventeenth-century Shelley had not become, out of an experience ever more bitter in each year, more alien [*sic*] to the founder of that Jesuit sect which nothing could induce him to tolerate."

Professor Harold Laski (Essay in *Freedom of Expression*)

"(2) Above all, we cannot play ducks and drakes with a native battery of idioms which prescribes such egregious collocations of vocables as the Basic *put up with* for *tolerate* or *put at a loss* for *bewilder*."

Professor Lancelot Hogben (*Interglossa*)

"(3) On the one side we have the free personality: by definition it is not neurotic, for it has neither conflict nor dream. Its desires, such as they are, are transparent, for they are just what institutional approval keeps in the forefront of consciousness; another institutional pattern would alter their number and intensity; there is little in them that is natural, irreducible, or culturally dangerous. But *on the other* side, the social bond itself is nothing but the mutual reflection of these self-secure integrities. Recall the definition of love. Is not this the very picture of a small academic? Where is there a place in this hall of mirrors for either personality or fraternity?"

Essay on psychology in *Politics* (New York)

"(4) All the 'best people' from the gentlemen's clubs, and all the frantic fascist captains, united in common hatred of Socialism and bestial horror of the rising tide of the mass revolutionary movement, have turned to acts of provocation, to foul incendiarism, to medieval legends of poisoned wells, to legalize their own destruction of proletarian organizations, and rouse the agitated petty-bourgeoisie to chauvinistic fervour on behalf of the fight against the revolutionary way out of the crisis."

Communist pamphlet

"(5) If a new spirit *is* to be infused into this old country, there is one thorny and contentious reform which must be tackled, and that is the humanization and galvanization of the B.B.C. Timidity here will bespeak cancer and atrophy of the soul. The heart of Britain may be sound and of strong beat, for instance, but the British lion's roar at present is like that of Bottom in Shakespeare's *Midsummer Night's*

Dream—as gentle as any sucking dove. A virile new Britain cannot continue indefinitely to be traduced in the eyes or rather ears, of the world by the effete languors of Langham Place, brazenly masquerading as 'standard English.' When the Voice of Britain is heard at nine o'clock, better far and infinitely less ludicrous to hear aitches honestly dropped than the present priggish, inflated, inhibited, school-ma'amish arch braying of blameless bashful mewing maidens!"

Letter in Tribune

Each of these passages has faults of its own, but, quite apart from avoidable ugliness, two qualities are common to all of them. The first is staleness of imagery: the other is lack of precision. The writer either has a meaning and cannot express it, or he inadvertently says something else, or he is almost indifferent as to whether his words mean anything or not. This mixture of vagueness and sheer incompetence is the most marked characteristic of modern English prose, and especially of any kind of political writing. As soon as certain topics are raised, the concrete melts into the abstract and no one seems able to think of turns of speech that are not hackneyed: prose consists less and less of *words* chosen for the sake of their meaning, and more and more of *phrases* tacked together like the sections of a prefabricated hen-house. I list below, with notes and examples, various of the tricks by means of which the work of prose-construction is habitually dodged:

DYING METAPHORS

A newly invented metaphor assists thought by evoking a visual image, while on the other hand a metaphor which is technically "dead" (e.g. *iron resolution*) has in effect reverted to being an ordinary word and can generally be used without loss of vividness. But in between these two classes there is a huge dump of worn-out metaphors which have lost all evocative power and are merely used because they save people the trouble of inventing phrases for themselves. Examples are: *Ring the changes on, take up the cudgels for, toe the line, ride roughshod over, stand shoulder to shoulder with, play into the hands of, no axe to grind, grist to the mill, fishing in troubled waters, on the order of the day, Achilles' heel, swan song, hotbed.* Many of these are used without knowledge of their meaning (what is a "rift," for instance?), and incompatible metaphors are frequently mixed, a sure sign that the writer is not interested in what he is saying. Some metaphors now current have been twisted out of their original meaning without those who use them even being aware of the fact. For example, *toe the line* is sometimes written *tow the line*. Another example is *the hammer and the anvil*, now always used with the implication that the anvil gets the worst of it. In real life it is always the anvil that breaks the hammer, never the other way about: a writer who stopped to think what he was saying would be aware of this, and would avoid perverting the original phrase.

OPERATORS OR VERBAL FALSE LIMBS

These save the trouble of picking out appropriate verbs and nouns, and at the same time pad each sentence with extra syllables which give it an appearance of symmetry. Characteristic phrases are: *render inoperative, militate against, make contact with, be subjected to, give rise to, give grounds for, have the effect of, play a leading part (role) in, make itself felt, take effect, exhibit a tendency to, serve the purpose of, etc., etc.* The keynote is the elimination of simple verbs. Instead of being a single word, such as *break, stop, spoil, mend, kill,* a verb becomes a *phrase,* made up of a noun or adjective tacked on to some general-purposes verb such as *prove, serve, form, play, render.* In addition, the passive voice is wherever possible used in preference to the active, and noun constructions are used instead of gerunds (*by examination of* instead of *by examining*). The range of verbs is further cut down by means of the *-ize* and *de-* formation, and the banal statements are given an appearance of profundity by means of the *not un-* formation. Simple conjunctions and prepositions are replaced by such phrases as *with respect to, having regard to, the fact that, by dint of, in view of, in the interests of, on the hypothesis that;* and the ends of sentences are saved from anticlimax by such resounding commonplaces as *greatly to be desired, cannot be left out of account, a development to be expected in the near future, deserving of serious consideration, brought to a satisfactory conclusion,* and so on and so forth.

PRETENTIOUS DICTION

Words like *phenomenon, element, individual* (as noun), *objective, categorical, effective, virtual, basic, primary, promote, constitute, exhibit, exploit, utilize, eliminate, liquidate,* are used to dress up simple statements and give an air of scientific impartiality to biased judgments. Adjectives like *epoch-making, epic, historic, unforgettable, triumphant, age-old, inevitable, inexorable, veritable,* are used to dignify the sordid processes of international politics, while writing that aims at glorifying war usually takes on an archaic color, its characteristic words being: *realm, throne, chariot, mailed fist, trident, sword, shield, buckler, banner, jackboot, clarion.* Foreign words and expressions such as *cul de sac, ancien régime, deus ex machina, mutatis mutandis, status quo, gleichschaltung, weltanschauung,* are used to give an air of culture and elegance. Except for the useful abbreviations *i.e., e.g.,* and *etc.,* there is no real need for any of the hundreds of foreign phrases now current in English. Bad writers, and especially scientific, political and sociological writers, are nearly always haunted by the notion that Latin or Greek words are grander than Saxon ones, and unnecessary words like *expedite, ameliorate, predict, extraneous, deracinated, clandestine, subaqueous* and hundreds of others constantly gain ground from their Anglo-Saxon opposite numbers.[1] The jargon peculiar to Marxist writing (*hyena, hangman, cannibal, petty bourgeois, these gentry, lackey, flunky, mad dog, White Guard,* etc.) consists largely of words and phrases translated from Russian, German or French; but the normal way of coining a new word is to use a Latin or Greek root with the appropriate affix and, where necessary, the *-ize* formation. It is often easier to make up words of this kind (*deregionalize, impermissible, extramarital, nonfragmentatory* and so forth) than to think up the English words that will cover one's meaning. The result, in general, is an increase in slovenliness and vagueness.

MEANINGLESS WORDS

In certain kinds of writing, particularly in art criticism and literary criticism, it is normal to come across long passages which are almost completely lacking in meaning.[2] Words like *romantic, plastic, values, human, dead, sentimental, natural, vitality,* as used in art criticism, are strictly meaningless in the sense that they not only do not point to any discoverable object, but are hardly ever expected to do so by the reader. When one critic writes, "The outstanding feature of Mr. X's work is its living quality," while another writes, "The immediately striking thing about Mr. X's work is its peculiar deadness," the reader accepts this as a simple difference of opinion. If words like *black* and *white* were involved, instead of the jargon words *dead* and *living,* he would see at once that language was being used in an improper way. Many political words are similarly abused. The word *Fascism* has now no meaning except in so far as it signifies "something not desirable." The words *democracy, socialism, freedom, patriotic, realistic, justice,* have each of them several different meanings which cannot be reconciled with one another. In the case of a word like *democracy,* not only is there no agreed definition, but the attempt to make one is resisted from all sides. It is almost universally felt that when we call a country democratic we are praising it: consequently the defenders of every kind of régime claim that it is a democracy, and fear that they might have to stop using the word if it were tied down to any one meaning. Words of this kind are often used in a consciously dishonest way. That is, the person who uses them has his

---

[1]An interesting illustration of this is the way in which the English flower names which were in use till very recently are being ousted by Greek ones, *snapdragon* becoming *antirrhinum, forget-me-not* becoming *myosotis,* etc. It is hard to see any practical reason for this change of fashion: it is probably due to an instinctive turning-away from the more homely word and a vague feeling that the Greek word is scientific.

[2]Example: "Comfort's catholicity of perception and image, strangely Whitmanesque in range, almost the exact opposite in aesthetic compulsion, continues to evoke that trembling atmospheric accumulative hinting at a cruel, an inexorably serene timelessness ... Wrey Gardiner scores by aiming at simple bull's-eyes with precision. Only they are not so simple, and through this contented sadness runs more than the surface bittersweet of resignation" (*Poetry Quarterly*).

own private definition, but allows his hearer to think he means something quite different. Statements like *Marshal Pétain was a true patriot, The Soviet Press is the freest in the world, The Catholic Church is opposed to persecution,* are almost always made with intent to deceive. Other words used in variable meanings, in most cases more or less dishonestly, are: *class, totalitarian, science, progressive, reactionary, bourgeois, equality.*

Now that I have made this catalog of swindles and perversions, let me give another example of the kind of writing that they lead to. This time it must of its nature be an imaginary one. I am going to translate a passage of good English into modern English of the worst sort. Here is a well-known verse from *Ecclesiastes:*

> "I returned and saw under the sun, that the race is not to the swift, nor the battle to the strong, neither yet bread to the wise, nor yet riches to men of understanding, nor yet favor to men of skill; but time and chance happeneth to them all."

Here it is in modern English: 10

> "Objective consideration of contemporary phenomena compels the conclusion that success or failure in competitive activities exhibits no tendency to be commensurate with innate capacity, but that a considerable element of the unpredictable must invariably be taken into account."

This is a parody, but not a very gross one. Exhibit (3), above, for instance, contains several patches of the same kind of English. It will be seen that I have not made a full translation. The beginning and ending of the sentence follow the original meaning fairly closely, but in the middle the concrete illustrations—race, battle, bread—dissolve into the vague phrase "success or failure in competitive activities." This had to be so, because no modern writer of the kind I am discussing—no one capable of using phrases like "objective consideration of contemporary phenomena"—would ever tabulate his thoughts in that precise and detailed way. The whole tendency of modern prose is away from concreteness. Now analyse these two sentences a little more closely. The first contains forty-nine words but only sixty syllables, and all its words are those of everyday life. The second contains thirty-eight words of ninety syllables: eighteen of its words are from Latin roots, and one from Greek. The first sentence contains six vivid images, and only one phrase ("time and chance") that could be called vague. The second contains not a single fresh, arresting phrase, and in spite of its ninety syllables it gives only a shortened version of the meaning contained in the first. Yet without a doubt it is the second kind of sentence that is gaining ground in modern English. I do not want to exaggerate. This kind of writing is not yet universal, and outcrops of simplicity will occur here and there in the worst-written page. Still, if you or I were told to write a few lines on the uncertainty of human fortunes, we should probably come much nearer to my imaginary sentence than to the one from *Ecclesiastes*.

As I have tried to show, modern writing at its worst does not consist in picking out words for the sake of their meaning and inventing images in order to make the meaning clearer. It consists in gumming together long strips of words which have already been set in order by someone else, and making the results presentable by sheer humbug. The attraction of this way of writing is that it is easy. It is easier—even quicker, once you have the habit—to say *In my opinion it is a not unjustifiable assumption that* than to say *I think*. If you use ready-made phrases, you not only don't have to hunt about for words; you also don't have to bother with the rhythms of your sentences, since these phrases are generally so arranged as to be more or less euphonious. When you are composing in a hurry—when you are dictating to a stenographer, for instance, or making a public speech—it is natural to fall into a pretentious, Latinized style. Tags like *a consideration which we should do well to bear in mind* or *a conclusion to which all of us would readily assent* will save many a sentence from coming down with a bump. By using stale metaphors, similes and idioms, you save much mental effort, at the cost of leaving your meaning vague, not only for your reader but for yourself. This is the significance of mixed metaphors. The sole aim of a metaphor is to call up a visual image. When these images clash— as in *The Fascist octopus has sung its swan song, the jackboot is thrown into the melting pot*—it can be taken as certain that the writer is not seeing a mental image of the objects he is naming; in other words he is not really thinking. Look again at the examples I gave at the beginning of this essay. Professor Laski (1) uses five negatives in fifty-three words. One of these is superfluous, making nonsense of the whole passage, and in addition there is the slip *alien* for akin, making further nonsense, and several avoidable pieces of clumsiness which increase the general vagueness. Professor Hogben (2) plays ducks and drakes with a battery which is able to write prescriptions, and, while disapproving of the everyday phrase *put up with*, is unwilling to look *egregious* up in the dictionary and see what it means. (3), if one takes an uncharitable attitude towards it, is simply meaningless: probably one could work out its intended meaning by reading the whole of the article in which it occurs. In (4), the writer knows more or less what he wants to say, but an accumulation of stale phrases chokes him like tea leaves blocking a sink. In (5), words and meaning have almost parted company. People who write in this manner usually have a general emotional meaning—they dislike one thing and want to express solidarity with another—but they are not interested in the detail of what they are saying. A scrupulous writer, in every sentence that he writes, will ask himself at least four questions, thus: What am I trying to say? What words will express it? What image or idiom will make it clearer? Is this image fresh enough to have an effect? And he will probably ask himself two more: Could I put it more shortly? Have I said anything that is avoidably ugly? But you are not obliged to go to all this trouble. You can shirk it by simply throwing your mind open and letting the ready-made phrases come crowding in. They will construct your sentences for you—even think your thoughts for you, to a certain extent—and at need they will perform the important service of partially concealing your meaning even from yourself. It is at this point that the special connection between politics and the debasement of language becomes clear.

In our time it is broadly true that political writing is bad writing. Where it is not true, it will generally be found that the writer is some kind of rebel, expressing his private opinions and not a "party line." Orthodoxy, of whatever color, seems to demand a lifeless, imitative style. The political dialects to be found in pamphlets, leading articles, manifestos, White Papers and the speeches of under-secretaries do, of course, vary from party to party, but they are all alike in that one almost never finds in them a fresh, vivid, home-made turn of speech. When one watches some tired hack on the platform mechanically repeating the familiar phrases—*bestial atrocities, iron heel, bloodstained tyranny, free peoples of the world, stand shoulder to shoulder*—one often has a curious feeling that one is not watching a live human being but some kind of dummy: a feeling which suddenly becomes stronger at moments when the light catches the speaker's spectacles and turns them into blank discs which seem to have no eyes behind them. And this is not altogether fanciful. A speaker who uses that kind of phraseology has gone some distance towards turning himself into a machine. The appropriate noises are coming out of his larynx, but his brain is not involved as it would be if he were choosing his words for himself. If the speech he is making is one that he is accustomed to make over and over again, he may be almost unconscious of what he is saying, as one is when one utters the responses in church. And this reduced state of consciousness, if not indispensable, is at any rate favorable to political conformity.

In our time, political speech and writing are largely the defense of the indefensible. Things like the continuance of British rule in India, the Russian purges and deportations, the dropping of the atom bombs on Japan, can indeed be defended, but only by arguments which are too brutal for most people to face, and which do not square with the professed aims of political parties. Thus political language has to consist largely of euphemism, question-begging and sheer cloudy vagueness. Defenseless villages are bombarded from the air, the inhabitants driven out into the countryside, the cattle machine-gunned, the huts set on fire with incendiary bullets: this is called *pacification*. Millions of peasants are robbed of their farms and sent trudging along the roads with no more than they can carry: this is called *transfer of population* or *rectification of frontiers*. People are imprisoned for years without trial, or shot in the back of the neck or sent to die of scurvy in Arctic lumber camps: this is called *elimination of unreliable elements*. Such phraseology is needed if one wants to name things without calling up mental pictures of them. Consider for instance some comfortable English professor defending Russian totalitarianism. He cannot say outright, "I believe in killing off your opponents when you can get good results by doing so." Probably, therefore, he will say something like this:

"While freely conceding that the Soviet régime exhibits certain features which the humanitarian may be inclined to deplore, we must, I think, agree that a certain curtailment of the right to political opposition is an unavoidable concomitant of transitional periods, and that the rigors which the Russian people have been called upon to undergo have been amply justified in the sphere of concrete achievement."

The inflated style is itself a kind of euphemism. A mass of Latin words falls upon the facts like soft snow, blurring the outlines and covering up all the details. The great enemy of clear language is insincerity. When there is a gap between one's real and one's declared aims, one turns as it were instinctively to long words and exhausted idioms, like a cuttlefish squirting out ink. In our age there is no such thing as "keeping out of politics." All issues are political issues, and politics itself is a mass of lies, evasions, folly, hatred and schizophrenia. When the general atmosphere is bad, language must suffer. I should expect to find—this is a guess which I have not sufficient knowledge to verify—that the German, Russian and Italian languages have all deteriorated in the last ten or fifteen years, as a result of dictatorship.

But if thought corrupts language, language can also corrupt thought. A bad usage can spread by tradition and imitation, even among people who should and do know better. The debased language that I have been discussing is in some ways very convenient. Phrases like *a not unjustifiable assumption, leaves much to be desired, would serve no good purpose, a consideration which we should do well to bear in mind,* are a continuous temptation, a packet of aspirins always at one's elbow. Look back through this essay, and for certain you will find that I have again and again committed the very faults I am protesting against. By this morning's post I have received a pamphlet dealing with conditions in Germany. The author tells me that he "felt impelled" to write it. I open it at random, and here is almost the first sentence that I see: "(The Allies) have an opportunity not only of achieving a radical transformation of Germany's social and political structure in such a way as to avoid a nationalistic reaction in Germany itself, but at the same time of laying the foundations of a cooperative and unified Europe." You see, he "feels impelled" to write—feels, presumably, that he has something new to say—and yet his words, like cavalry horses answering the bugle, group themselves automatically into the familiar dreary pattern. This invasion of one's mind by ready-made phrases (*lay the foundations, achieve a radical transformation*) can only be prevented if one is constantly on guard against them, and every such phrase anaesthetizes a portion of one's brain.

I said earlier that the decadence of our language is probably curable. Those who deny this would argue, if they produced an argument at all, that language merely reflects existing social conditions, and that we cannot influence its development by any direct tinkering with words and constructions. So far as the general tone or spirit of a language goes, this may be true, but it is not true in detail. Silly words and expressions have often disappeared, not through any evolutionary process but owing to the conscious action of a minority. Two recent examples were *explore every avenue* and *leave no stone unturned*, which were killed by the jeers of a few journalists. There is a long list of flyblown metaphors which could similarly be got rid of if enough people would interest themselves in the job; and it should also be possible to laugh the *not un-* formation out of existence,[3] to reduce the amount of Latin and Greek in the average sentence, to drive out foreign phrases and strayed scientific words, and, in general, to make pretentiousness unfashionable. But all these are minor points. The defense of the English language implies more than this, and perhaps it is best to start by saying what it does *not* imply.

To begin with it has nothing to do with archaism, with the salvaging of obsolete words and turns of speech, or with the setting up of a "standard English" which must never be departed from. On the contrary, it is especially concerned with the scrapping of every word or idiom which has outworn its usefulness. It has nothing to do with correct grammar and syntax, which are of no importance so long as one makes one's meaning clear, or with the avoidance of Americanisms, or with having what is called a "good prose style." On the other hand it is not concerned with fake simplicity and the attempt to make written English colloquial. Nor does it even imply in every case preferring the Saxon word to the Latin one, though it does imply using the fewest and shortest words that will cover one's meaning. What is above all needed is to let the meaning choose the word, and not the other way about. In prose, the worst thing one can do with words is to surrender to them. When you think of a concrete object, you think wordlessly, and then, if you want to describe the thing you have been visualizing you probably hunt about till you find the exact words that seem to fit. When you think of something abstract you are more inclined to use words from the start, and unless you make a conscious effort to prevent it, the existing dialect will come rushing in and do the job for you, at the expense of blurring or even changing your meaning. Probably it is better to put off using words as long as possible and get one's meaning as clear as one can through pictures or sensations. Afterwards one can choose—not simply *accept*—the phrases that will best cover the meaning, and then switch round and decide what impression one's words are likely to make on another person. This last effort of the mind cuts out all stale or mixed images, all prefabricated phrases, needless repetitions, and humbug and vagueness generally. But one can often be in doubt about the effect of a word or a phrase, and one needs rules that one can rely on when instinct fails. I think the following rules will cover most cases:

---

[3]One can cure oneself of the *not un-* formation by memorizing this sentence: A *not unblack dog was chasing a not unsmall rabbit across a not ungreen field.*

(i) Never use a metaphor, simile or other figure of speech which you are used to seeing in print.

(ii) Never use a long word where a short one will do.

(iii) If it is possible to cut a word out, always cut it out.

(iv) Never use the passive where you can use the active.

(v) Never use a foreign phrase, a scientific word or a jargon word if you can think of an everyday English equivalent.

(vi) Break any of these rules sooner than say anything outright barbarous.

These rules sound elementary, and so they are, but they demand a deep change of attitude in anyone who has grown used to writing in the style now fashionable. One could keep all of them and still write bad English, but one could not write the kind of stuff that I quoted in those five specimens at the beginning of this article.

I have not here been considering the literary use of language, but merely language as an instrument for expressing and not for concealing or preventing thought. Stuart Chase and others have come near to claiming that all abstract words are meaningless, and have used this as a pretext for advocating a kind of political quietism. Since you don't know what Fascism is, how can you struggle against Fascism? One need not swallow such absurdities as this, but one ought to recognize that the present political chaos is connected with the decay of language, and that one can probably bring about some improvement by starting at the verbal end. If you simplify your English, you are freed from the worst follies of orthodoxy. You cannot speak any of the necessary dialects, and when you make a stupid remark its stupidity will be obvious, even to yourself. Political language—and with variations this is true of all political parties, from Conservatives to Anarchists—is designed to make lies sound truthful and murder respectable, and to give an appearance of solidity to pure wind. One cannot change this all in a moment, but one can at least change one's own habits, and from time to time one can even, if one jeers loudly enough, send some worn-out and useless phrase—some *jackboot*, *Achilles' heel*, *hotbed*, *melting pot*, *acid test*, *veritable inferno* or other lump of verbal refuse—into the dustbin where it belongs.

20

QUESTIONS

1. What is Orwell's position on the ways in which modern writers are destroying the English language?

2. Orwell argues that "thought corrupts language," but he also argues that "language can also corrupt thought" (paragraph 17). What argument is he making? How does language corrupt thought?

3. Orwell writes in paragraph 17, "Look back through this essay, and for certain you will find that I have again and again committed the very faults I am protesting against." Does Orwell, in fact, break his own rules? If so, what might his purpose be in doing so?

4. What sense of himself does Orwell present to his readers? How would you describe his persona, his character?

5. Why do people write badly, according to Orwell? What causes does he identify in his essay? Do you agree with him?

6. Orwell presents guidelines for good writing in paragraph 19. Take one of your recent essays and analyze how your writing measures up to Orwell's standards.

7. Spend one week developing a list of examples of bad writing from newspapers or popular magazines. Use this material as the basis for an essay in which you develop a thesis to argue your position on politics and language.

8. Written more than fifty years ago, this is probably the best known of all of Orwell's essays. How insightful and current do you find it today? Take five examples from your reading, as Orwell takes from his, and use them as evidence in an argument of your own about the state of contemporary written English. Take your examples from anything you like, including this book—even this question—if you wish. Be careful to choose recent pieces of writing.

MAKING CONNECTIONS

1. Read Orwell's essay, "Shooting an Elephant" (p. 104), in "Reflecting." What do you learn about Orwell, the essayist, from reading these two essays?

2. John Berger (p. 559) and James Baldwin (p. 577), as represented by their essays in this section, are two writers likely to have been influenced by this essay of Orwell's. Choose the essay you responded to more strongly of those two, and write an essay of your own explaining the connections that you find between Orwell and either Berger or Baldwin.

THE HISTORIAN AND HIS FACTS
Edward Hallet Carr

E. H. Carr (1892–1982) was a distinguished British historian whose major work was The History of Soviet Russia *in fourteen volumes. A fellow of Trinity College, Cambridge, Carr delivered a series of lectures there in 1961 under the general title of "What Is History?" The lectures were later published in a book, which opened with the selection reprinted here. It is addressed to the general question— What is history?—in terms of a more specific question: What is a historical fact? Like Barbara Tuchman's "When Does History Happen?" Carr's essay addresses the practice of history. He warns against a "fetishism of facts" and urges that more attention be given to the way that the historian processes the facts.*

What is history? Lest anyone think the question meaningless or superfluous, I will take as my text two passages relating respectively to the first and second incarnations of *The Cambridge Modern History*. Here is Acton in his report of October 1896 to the Syndics of the Cambridge University Press on the work which he had undertaken to edit.[1]

> It is a unique opportunity of recording, in the way most useful to the greatest number, the fullness of the knowledge which the nineteenth century is about to bequeath.... By the judicious division of labour we should be able to do it, and to bring home to every man the last document, and the ripest conclusions of international research.
>
> Ultimate history we cannot have in this generation; but we can dispose of conventional history, and show the point we have reached on the road from one to the other, now that all information is within reach, and every problem has become capable of solution.[2]

And almost exactly sixty years later Professor Sir George Clark, in his general introduction to the second *Cambridge Modern History*, commented on this belief of Acton and his collaborators that it would one day be possible to produce "ultimate history," and went on:

---

[1]*John Dalberg Acton* (1834–1902): British historian and editor of the first *Cambridge Modern History*. [Eds.]

[2]*The Cambridge Modern History: Its Origin, Authorship and Production* (Cambridge University Press; 1907), pp. 10–12.

Historians of a later generation do not look forward to any such prospect. They expect their work to be superseded again and again. They consider that knowledge of the past has come down through one or more human minds, has been "processed" by them, and therefore cannot consist of elemental and impersonal atoms which nothing can alter.... The exploration seems to be endless, and some impatient scholars take refuge in scepticism, or at least in the doctrine that, since all historical judgments involve persons and points of view, one is as good as another and there is no "objective" historical truth.[3]

Where the pundits contradict each other so flagrantly the field is open to enquiry. I hope that I am sufficiently up-to-date to recognize that anything written in the 1890's must be nonsense. But I am not yet advanced enough to be committed to the view that anything written in the 1950's necessarily makes sense. Indeed, it may already have occurred to you that this enquiry is liable to stray into something even broader than the nature of history. The clash between Acton and Sir George Clark is a reflection of the change in our total outlook on society over the interval between these two pronouncements. Acton speaks out of the positive belief, the clear-eyed self-confidence of the later Victorian age; Sir George Clark echoes the bewilderment and distracted scepticism of the beat generation. When we attempt to answer the question, What is history?, our answer, consciously or unconsciously, reflects our own position in time, and forms part of our answer to the broader question, what view we take of the society in which we live. I have no fear that my subject may, on closer inspection, seem trivial. I am afraid only that I may seem presumptuous to have broached a question so vast and so important.

The nineteenth century was a great age for facts. "What I want," said Mr. Gradgrind in *Hard Times*,[4] "is Facts.... Facts alone are wanted in life." Nineteenth-century historians on the whole agreed with him. When Ranke in the 1830's,[5] in legitimate protest against moralizing history, remarked that the task of the historian was "simply to show how it really was (*wie es eigentlich gewesen*)" this not very profound aphorism had an astonishing success. Three generations of German, British, and even French historians marched into battle intoning the magic words, "*Wie es eigentlich gewesen*" like an incantation— designed, like most incantations, to save them from the tiresome obligation to think for themselves. The Positivists, anxious to stake out their claim for history as a science, contributed the weight of their influence to this cult of facts. First ascertain the facts, said the positivists, then draw your conclusions from them. In Great Britain, this view of history fitted in perfectly with the empiricist tradition which was the dominant strain in British philosophy from Locke to

---

[3]*The New Cambridge Modern History*, I (Cambridge University Press; 1957), pp. xxiv–xxv.
[4]*Hard Times*: a novel by Charles Dickens. [Eds.]
[5]*Leopold von Ranke* (1795–1886): German historian. [Eds.]

Bertrand Russell.[6] The empirical theory of knowledge presupposes a complete separation between subject and object. Facts, like sense-impressions, impinge on the observer from outside, and are independent of his consciousness. The process of reception is passive: having received the data, he then acts on them. *The Shorter Oxford English Dictionary*, a useful but tendentious work of the empirical school, clearly marks the separateness of the two processes by defining a fact as "a datum of experience as distinct from conclusions." This is what may be called the common-sense view of history. History consists of a corpus of ascertained facts. The facts are available to the historian in documents, inscriptions, and so on, like fish on the fishmonger's slab. The historian collects them, takes them home, and cooks and serves them in whatever style appeals to him. Acton, whose culinary tastes were austere, wanted them served plain. In his letter of instructions to contributors to the first *Cambridge Modern History* he announced the requirement "that our Waterloo must be one that satisfies French and English, German and Dutch alike; that nobody can tell, without examining the list of authors where the Bishop of Oxford laid down the pen, and whether Fairbairn or Gasquet, Liebermann or Harrison took it up."[7] Even Sir George Clark, critical as he was of Acton's attitude, himself contrasted the "hard core of facts" in history with the "surrounding pulp of disputable interpretation"[8]—forgetting perhaps that the pulpy part of the fruit is more rewarding than the hard core. First get your facts straight, then plunge at your peril into the shifting sands of interpretation—that is the ultimate wisdom of the empirical, common-sense school of history. It recalls the favorite dictum of the great liberal journalist C. P. Scott: "Facts are sacred, opinion is free."

Now this clearly will not do. I shall not embark on a philosophical discussion of the nature of our knowledge of the past. Let us assume for present purposes that the fact that Caesar crossed the Rubicon and the fact that there is a table in the middle of the room are facts of the same or of a comparable order, that both these facts enter our consciousness in the same or in a comparable manner, and that both have the same objective character in relation to the person who knows them. But, even on this bold and not very plausible assumption, our argument at once runs into the difficulty that not all facts about the past are historical facts, or are treated as such by the historian. What is the criterion which distinguishes the facts of history from other facts about the past?

What is a historical fact? This is a crucial question into which we must look a little more closely. According to the common-sense view, there are certain basic facts which are the same for all historians and which form, so to speak, the backbone of history—the fact, for example, that the Battle of Hastings was fought in 1066. But this view calls for two observations. In the first place, it is

---

[6]*John Locke* (1632–1704): English philosopher; *Bertrand Russell* (1872–1970): English philosopher and mathematician. [Eds.]

[7]Acton: *Lectures on Modern History* (London: Macmillan & Co.; 1906), p. 318.

[8]Quoted in *The Listener* (June 19, 1952), p. 992.

not with facts like these that the historian is primarily concerned. It is no doubt important to know that the great battle was fought in 1066 and not in 1065 or 1067, and that it was fought at Hastings and not at Eastbourne or Brighton. The historian must not get these things wrong. But when points of this kind are raised, I am reminded of Housman's remark that "accuracy is a duty, not a virtue."[9] To praise a historian for his accuracy is like praising an architect for using well-seasoned timber or properly mixed concrete in his building. It is a necessary condition of his work, but not his essential function. It is precisely for matters of this kind that the historian is entitled to rely on what have been called the "auxiliary sciences" of history—archaeology, epigraphy, numismatics, chronology, and so forth. The historian is not required to have the special skills which enable the expert to determine the origin and period of a fragment of pottery or marble, to decipher an obscure inscription, or to make the elaborate astronomical calculations necessary to establish a precise date. These so-called basic facts which are the same for all historians commonly belong to the category of the raw materials of the historian rather than of history itself. The second observation is that the necessity to establish these basic facts rests not on any quality in the facts themselves, but on an *a priori* decision of the historian. In spite of C. P. Scott's motto, every journalist knows today that the most effective way to influence opinion is by the selection and arrangement of the appropriate facts. It used to be said that facts speak for themselves. This is, of course, untrue. The facts speak only when the historian calls on them: it is he who decides to which facts to give the floor, and in what order or context. It was, I think, one of Pirandello's characters who said that a fact is like a sack[10]— it won't stand up till you've put something in it. The only reason why we are interested to know that the battle was fought at Hastings in 1066 is that historians regard it as a major historical event. It is the historian who has decided for his own reasons that Caesar's crossing of that petty stream, the Rubicon, is a fact of history, whereas the crossing of the Rubicon by millions of other people before or since interests nobody at all. The fact that you arrived in this building half an hour ago on foot, or on a bicycle, or in a car, is just as much a fact about the past as the fact that Caesar crossed the Rubicon. But it will probably be ignored by historians. Professor Talcott Parsons once called science "a selective system of cognitive orientations to reality."[11] It might perhaps have been put more simply. But history is, among other things, that. The historian is necessarily selective. The belief in a hard core of historical facts existing objectively and independently of the interpretation of the historian is a preposterous fallacy, but one which it is very hard to eradicate.

---

[9]M. Manilius: *Astronomicon: Liber Primus*, 2nd ed. (Cambridge University Press; 1937), p. 87. (A. E. Housman [1859–1936]: poet and classical scholar who edited Manilius. [Eds.])

[10]*Luigi Pirandello* (1867–1936): Italian playwright. [Eds.]

[11]Talcott Parsons and Edward A. Shils: *Toward a General Theory of Action*, 3rd ed. (Cambridge, Mass.: Harvard University Press; 1954), p. 167.

Let us take a look at the process by which a mere fact about the past is trans- 5 formed into a fact of history. At Stalybridge Wakes in 1850, a vendor of ginger-bread, as the result of some petty dispute, was deliberately kicked to death by an angry mob. Is this a fact of history? A year ago I should unhesitatingly have said "no." It was recorded by an eyewitness in some little-known memoirs;[12] but I had never seen it judged worthy of mention by any historian. A year ago Dr. Kitson Clark cited it in his Ford lectures in Oxford.[13] Does this make it into a historical fact? Not, I think, yet. Its present status, I suggest, is that it has been proposed for membership of the select club of historical facts. It now awaits a seconder and sponsors. It may be that in the course of the next few years we shall see this fact appearing first in footnotes, then in the text, of articles and books about nineteenth-century England, and that in twenty or thirty years' time it may be a well established historical fact. Alternatively, nobody may take it up, in which case it will relapse into the limbo of unhistorical facts about the past from which Dr. Kitson Clark has gallantly attempted to rescue it. What will decide which of these two things will happen? It will depend, I think, on whether the thesis or interpretation in support of which Dr. Kitson Clark cited this incident is accepted by other historians as valid and significant. Its status as a historical fact will turn on a question of interpretation. This element of interpretation enters into every fact of history.

May I be allowed a personal reminiscence? When I studied ancient history in this university many years ago, I had as a special subject "Greece in the period of the Persian Wars." I collected fifteen or twenty volumes on my shelves and took it for granted that there, recorded in these volumes, I had all the facts relating to my subject. Let us assume—it was very nearly true—that those volumes contained all the facts about it that were then known, or could be known. It never occurred to me to enquire by what accident or process of attrition that minute selection of facts, out of all the myriad facts that must have once been known to somebody, had survived to become *the* facts of history. I suspect that even today one of the fascinations of ancient and medieval history is that it gives us the illusion of having all the facts at our disposal within a manageable compass: the nagging distinction between the facts of history and other facts about the past vanishes because the few known facts are all facts of history. As Bury, who had worked in both periods, said, "the records of ancient and medieval history are starred with lacunae."[14] History has been called an enormous jig-saw with a lot of missing parts. But the main trouble does not consist of the lacunae. Our picture of Greece in the fifth century B.C. is defective not primarily because so many of the bits have been accidentally lost, but

---

[12]Lord George Sanger: *Seventy Years a Showman* (London: J. M. Dent & Sons; 1962); pp. 188–9.
[13]These will shortly be published under the title *The Making of Victorian England.*
[14]John Bagnell Bury: *Selected Essays* (Cambridge University Press; 1930), p. 52. (*lacunae:* empty spaces or gaps. [Eds.])

because it is, by and large, the picture formed by a tiny group of people in the city of Athens. We know a lot about what fifth-century Greece looked like to an Athenian citizen; but hardly anything about what it looked like to a Spartan, a Corinthian, or a Theban—not to mention a Persian, or a slave or other noncitizen resident in Athens. Our picture has been pre-selected and predetermined for us, not so much by accident as by people who were consciously or unconsciously imbued with a particular view and thought the facts which supported that view worth preserving. In the same way, when I read in a modern history of the Middle Ages that the people of the Middle Ages were deeply concerned with religion, I wonder how we know this, and whether it is true. What we know as the facts of medieval history have almost all been selected for us by generations of chroniclers who were professionally occupied in the theory and practice of religion, and who therefore thought it supremely important, and recorded everything relating to it, and not much else. The picture of the Russian peasant as devoutly religious was destroyed by the revolution of 1917. The picture of medieval man as devoutly religious, whether true or not, is indestructible, because nearly all the known facts about him were pre-selected for us by people who believed it, and wanted others to believe it, and a mass of other facts, in which we might possibly have found evidence to the contrary, has been lost beyond recall. The dead hand of vanished generations of historians, scribes, and chroniclers has determined beyond the possibility of appeal the pattern of the past. "The history we read," writes Professor Barraclough, himself trained as a medievalist, "though based on facts, is, strictly speaking, not factual at all, but a series of accepted judgments."[15]

But let us turn to the different, but equally grave, plight of the modern historian. The ancient or medieval historian may be grateful for the vast winnowing process which, over the years, has put at his disposal a manageable corpus of historical facts. As Lytton Strachey said in his mischievous way, "ignorance is the first requisite of the historian, ignorance which simplifies and clarifies, which selects and omits."[16] When I am tempted, as I sometimes am, to envy the extreme competence of colleagues engaged in writing ancient or medieval history, I find consolation in the reflection that they are so competent mainly because they are so ignorant of their subject. The modern historian enjoys none of the advantages of this built-in ignorance. He must cultivate this necessary ignorance for himself—the more so the nearer he comes to his own times. He has the dual task of discovering the few significant facts and turning them into facts of history, and of discarding the many insignificant facts as unhistorical. But this is the very converse of the nineteenth-century heresy that history consists of the compilation of a maximum number of irrefutable and objective

---

[15]Geoffrey Barraclough: *History in a Changing World* (London: Basil Blackwell & Mott; 1955), p. 14.

[16]Lytton Strachey: Preface to *Eminent Victorians.*

facts. Anyone who succumbs to this heresy will either have to give up history as a bad job, and take to stamp-collecting or some other form of antiquarianism, or end in a madhouse. It is this heresy, which during the past hundred years has had such devastating effects on the modern historian, producing in Germany, in Great Britain, and in the United States a vast and growing mass of dry-as-dust factual histories, of minutely specialized monographs, of would-be historians knowing more and more about less and less, sunk without trace in an ocean of facts. It was, I suspect, this heresy—rather than the alleged conflict between liberal and Catholic loyalties—which frustrated Acton as a historian. In an early essay he said of his teacher Döllinger: "He would not write with imperfect materials, and to him the materials were always imperfect."[17] Acton was surely here pronouncing an anticipatory verdict on himself, on the strange phenomenon of a historian whom many would regard as the most distinguished occupant the Regius Chair of Modern History in this university has ever had—but who wrote no history. And Acton wrote his own epitaph in the introductory note to the first volume of *The Cambridge Modern History*, published just after his death, when he lamented that the requirements pressing on the historian "threaten to turn him from a man of letters into the compiler of an encyclopedia."[18] Something had gone wrong. What had gone wrong was the belief in this untiring and unending accumulation of hard facts as the foundation of history, the belief that facts speak for themselves and that we cannot have too many facts, a belief at that time so unquestioning that few historians then thought it necessary—and some still think it unnecessary today—to ask themselves the question: What is history?

The nineteenth-century fetishism of facts was completed and justified by a fetishism of documents. The documents were the Ark of the Covenant in the temple of facts. The reverent historian approached them with bowed head and spoke of them in awed tones. If you find it in the documents, it is so. But what, when we get down to it, do these documents—the decrees, the treaties, the rent-rolls, the blue books, the official correspondence, the private letters and diaries—tell us? No document can tell us more than what the author of the document thought—what he thought had happened, what he thought ought to happen or would happen, or perhaps only what he wanted others to think he thought, or even only what he himself thought he thought. None of this means anything until the historian has got to work on it and deciphered it. The facts, whether found in documents or not, have still to be processed by the historian before he can make any use of them: the use he makes of them is, if I may put it that way, the processing process.

---

[17]Quoted in George P. Gooch: *History and Historians in the Nineteenth Century* (London: Longmans, Green & Company; 1952), p. 385. Later Acton said of Döllinger that "it was given him to form his philosophy of history on the largest induction ever available to man" (*History of Freedom and Other Essays* [London: Macmillan & Co.; 1907], p. 435).

[18]*The Cambridge Modern History*, I (1902), p. 4.

Let me illustrate what I am trying to say by an example which I happen to know well. When Gustav Stresemann, the Foreign Minister of the Weimar Republic,[19] died in 1929, he left behind him an enormous mass—300 boxes full—of papers, official, semi-official, and private, nearly all relating to the six years of his tenure of office as Foreign Minister. His friends and relatives naturally thought that a monument should be raised to the memory of so great a man. His faithful secretary Bernhardt got to work; and within three years there appeared three massive volumes, of some 600 pages each, of selected documents from the 300 boxes, with the impressive title *Stresemanns Vermächtnis*.[20] In the ordinary way the documents themselves would have moldered away in some cellar or attic and disappeared for ever; or perhaps in a hundred years or so some curious scholar would have come upon them and set out to compare them with Bernhardt's text. What happened was far more dramatic. In 1945 the documents fell into the hands of the British and the American governments, who photographed the lot and put the photostats at the disposal of scholars in the Public Record Office in London and in the National Archives in Washington, so that, if we have sufficient patience and curiosity, we can discover exactly what Bernhardt did. What he did was neither very unusual nor very shocking. When Stresemann died, his Western policy seemed to have been crowned with a series of brilliant successes—Locarno, the admission of Germany to the League of Nations, the Dawes and Young plans and the American loans, the withdrawal of allied occupation armies from the Rhineland. This seemed the important and rewarding part of Stresemann's foreign policy; and it was not unnatural that it should have been over-represented in Bernhardt's selection of documents. Stresemann's Eastern policy, on the other hand, his relations with the Soviet Union, seemed to have led nowhere in particular; and, since masses of documents about negotiations which yielded only trivial results were not very interesting and added nothing to Stresemann's reputation, the process of selection could be more rigorous. Stresemann in fact devoted a far more constant and anxious attention to relations with the Soviet Union, and they played a far larger part in his foreign policy as a whole, than the reader of the Bernhardt selection would surmise. But the Bernhardt volumes compare favorably, I suspect, with many published collections of documents on which the ordinary historian implicitly relies.

This is not the end of my story. Shortly after the publication of Bernhardt's volumes, Hitler came into power. Stresemann's name was consigned to oblivion in Germany, and the volumes disappeared from circulation: many, perhaps most, of the copies must have been destroyed. Today *Stresemanns Vermächtnis* is a rather rare book. But in the West Stresemann's reputation stood high. In 1935 an English publisher brought out an abbreviated translation of Bern-

---

[19]*Weimar Republic*: the government of Germany, established in the city of Weimar after World War I (1919) and lasting until Adolf Hitler rose to power in 1933. [Eds.]
[20]*Stresemanns Vermächtnis*: this title may be translated as "Stresemann's Legacy." [Eds.]

hardt's work—a selection from Bernhardt's selection; perhaps one third of the original was omitted. Sutton, a well-known translator from the German, did his job competently and well. The English version, he explained in the preface, was "slightly condensed, but only by the omission of a certain amount of what, it was felt, was more ephemeral matter . . . of little interest to English readers or students."[21] This again is natural enough. But the result is that Stresemann's Eastern policy, already under-represented in Bernhardt, recedes still further from view, and the Soviet Union appears in Sutton's volumes merely as an occasional and rather unwelcome intruder in Stresemann's predominantly Western foreign policy. Yet it is safe to say that, for all except a few specialists, Sutton and not Bernhardt—and still less the documents themselves—represents for the Western world the authentic voice of Stresemann. Had the documents perished in 1945 in the bombing, and had the remaining Bernhardt volumes disappeared, the authenticity and authority of Sutton would never have been questioned. Many printed collections of documents gratefully accepted by historians in default of the originals rest on no securer basis than this.

But I want to carry the story one step further. Let us forget about Bernhardt and Sutton, and be thankful that we can, if we choose, consult the authentic papers of a leading participant in some important events of recent European history. What do the papers tell us? Among other things they contain records of some hundreds of Stresemann's conversations with the Soviet ambassador in Berlin and of a score or so with Chicherin.[22] These records have one feature in common. They depict Stresemann as having the lion's share of the conversations and reveal his arguments as invariably well put and cogent, while those of his partner are for the most part scanty, confused, and unconvincing. This is a familiar characteristic of all records of diplomatic conversations. The documents do not tell us what happened, but only what Stresemann thought had happened, or what he wanted others to think, or perhaps what he wanted himself to think, had happened. It was not Sutton or Bernhardt, but Stresemann himself, who started the process of selection. And, if we had, say, Chicherin's records of these same conversations, we should still learn from them only what Chicherin thought, and what really happened would still have to be reconstructed in the mind of the historian. Of course, facts and documents are essential to the historian. But do not make a fetish of them. They do not by themselves constitute history; they provide in themselves no ready-made answer to this tiresome question: What is history?

At this point I should like to say a few words on the question of why nineteenth-century historians were generally indifferent to the philosophy of history. The term was invented by Voltaire,[23] and has since been used in differ-

---

[21]*Gustav Stresemann: His Diaries, Letters, and Papers* (London: Macmillan & Co.; 1935), I, Editor's Note.

[22]*Grigory Chicherin* (1872–1936): a powerful Russian diplomat. [Eds.]

[23]*Voltaire* (1694–1778): French dramatist, philosopher, and social critic. [Eds.]

ent senses; but I shall take it to mean, if I use it at all, our answer to the question: What is history? The nineteenth century was, for the intellectuals of Western Europe, a comfortable period exuding confidence and optimism. The facts were on the whole satisfactory; and the inclination to ask and answer awkward questions about them was correspondingly weak. Ranke piously believed that divine providence would take care of the meaning of history if he took care of the facts; and Burckhardt with a more modern touch of cynicism observed that "we are not initiated into the purposes of the eternal wisdom." Professor Butterfield as late as 1931 noted with apparent satisfaction that "historians have reflected little upon the nature of things and even the nature of their own subject."[24] But my predecessor in these lectures, Dr. A. L. Rowse, more justly critical, wrote of Sir Winston Churchill's *The World Crisis*—his book about the First World War—that, while it matched Trotsky's *History of the Russian Revolution* in personality, vividness, and vitality, it was inferior in one respect: it had "no philosophy of history behind it."[25] British historians refused to be drawn, not because they believed that history had no meaning, but because they believed that its meaning was implicit and self-evident. The liberal nineteenth-century view of history had a close affinity with the economic doctrine of *laissez-faire*—also the product of a serene and self-confident outlook on the world. Let everyone get on with his particular job, and the hidden hand would take care of the universal harmony. The facts of history were themselves a demonstration of the supreme fact of a beneficent and apparently infinite progress towards higher things. This was the age of innocence, and historians walked in the Garden of Eden, without a scrap of philosophy to cover them, naked and unashamed before the god of history. Since then, we have known Sin and experienced a Fall; and those historians who today pretend to dispense with a philosophy of history are merely trying, vainly and self-consciously, like members of a nudist colony, to recreate the Garden of Eden in their garden suburb. Today the awkward question can no longer be evaded.

QUESTIONS

1. Carr's essay answers the question, What is a historical fact? Summarize his answer to that question.

2. In paragraph 7, Carr says the historian must "cultivate . . . ignorance." What does this expression mean in its context? What is the point of the discussion of Acton and Döllinger in that paragraph? How does this discussion contribute to the larger theme of the essay?

---

[24]Herbert Butterfield: *The Whig Interpretation of History* (London: George Bell & Sons; 1931), p. 67.
[25]Alfred L. Rowse: *The End of an Epoch* (London: Macmillan & Co.; 1947), pp. 282–3.

3. In presenting an argument, especially a controversial one, a writer must often seek to gain the confidence of the reader. How does Carr go about this? What sort of picture does he present of himself? What impression of him do you get from his references to himself in paragraphs 1 and 6, and how does that impression affect your evaluation of his position?

4. Carr's essay is an argumentative essay on interpretation. Locate the many uses of the words *interpret* and *interpretation* in the essay, and consider how they function in the larger discussion. What view of the relationship between facts and interpretation is presented here?

5. Carr's essay contradicts previously existing explanations of the relationship between historians and the facts they must deal with in writing history. Where does Carr summarize the opposing position? State in your own words the views of historical facts with which Carr takes issue.

6. Consider several facts generally known to you and your classmates. Limit your attention to recent facts, specifically from the last year. (You might first discuss in class what sorts of facts merit your attention.) Which of those facts has the best chance of becoming "a historical fact," in Carr's terms? On what does that process depend? Write an explanation of the historicity of a fact you choose, trying to convince your classmates that your fact will become a historical fact.

7. Select an accepted historical fact not mentioned by Carr, and write an essay in which you argue why your fact is a historical fact and what grounds we have for understanding it and accepting it as a fact.

MAKING CONNECTIONS

How does John Berger's essay, "Hiroshima" (p. 559), comment on the use of facts? How might Carr comment on Berger's interpretation of history?

WHEN DOES HISTORY HAPPEN?

Barbara Tuchman

*Like E. H. Carr, Barbara Tuchman (1912–1989) is con-
cerned with the role of facts. According to Tuchman, "The
historian's task is . . . to tell what happened within the discipline of facts." The following essay comes from her collection,* Practicing History: Selected Essays *(1981). In this selection, Tuchman offers a lucid argument for her attitudes
toward history and historical research. For further biographical information on Tuchman, see the headnote on page
219.*

Within three months of the Conservative party crisis in Britain last October
[1963] a book by Randolph Churchill on the day-to-day history of the affair
had been written and published. To rush in upon an event before its significance has had time to separate from the surrounding circumstances may be
enterprising, but is it useful? An embarrassed author may find, when the excitement has died down, that his subject had little significance at all. The recent prevalence of these hot histories on publishers' lists raises the question:
Should—or perhaps can—history be written while it is still smoking?

Before taking that further, one must first answer the question: What is history? Professional historians have been exercising themselves vehemently over
this query for some time. A distinguished exponent, E. H. Carr of Cambridge
University, made it the subject of his Trevelyan Lectures and the title of a book
in 1962.

Is history, he asked, the examination of past events or is it the past events
themselves? By good luck I did not read the book until after I had finished an
effort of my own at historical narrative, otherwise I should have never dared to
begin. In my innocence I had not been aware that the question posed by Mr.
Carr had ever come up. I had simply assumed that history was past events existing independently, whether we examined them or not.

I had thought that we who comment on the past were extraneous to it; helpful, perhaps, to its understanding but not integral to its existence. I had supposed that the Greeks' defeat of the Persians would have given the same direction to Western history whether Herodotus chronicled it or not. But that is not
Mr. Carr's position. "The belief in a hard core of historical facts existing independently of the interpretation of the historian," he says, "is a preposterous fallacy but one that is very hard to eradicate."

On first reading, this seemed to me to be preposterous nonsense. Was it 5
some sort of recondite joke? But a thinker of such eminence must be taken se-

riously, and after prolonged silent arguments with Mr. Carr of which he remained happily unaware, I began to see what he was driving at. What he means, I suppose, is that past events cannot exist independently of the historian because without the historian we would know nothing about them; in short, that the unrecorded past is none other than our old friend, the tree in the primeval forest which fell where there was no one to hear the sound of the crash. If there was no ear, was there a sound?

I refuse to be frightened by that conundrum because it asks the wrong question. The point is not whether the fall of the tree made a noise but whether it left a mark on the forest. If it left a space that let in the sun on a hitherto shade-grown species, or if it killed a dominant animal and shifted rule of the pack to one of different characteristics, or if it fell across a path of animals and caused some small change in their habitual course from which larger changes followed, then the fall made history whether anyone heard it or not.

I therefore declare myself a firm believer in the "preposterous fallacy" of historical facts existing independently of the historian. I think that if Domesday Book and all other records of the time had been burned, the transfer of land ownership from the Saxons to the Normans would be no less a fact of British history. Of course Domesday Book was a record, not an interpretation, and what Mr. Carr says is that historical facts do not exist independently of the *interpretation* of historians. I find this untenable. He might just as well say the Grecian Urn would not exist without Keats.[1]

As I see it, evidence is more important than interpretation, and facts are history whether interpreted or not. I think the influence of the receding frontier on American expansion was a phenomenon independent of Frederick Jackson Turner,[2] who noticed it, and the role of the leisure class independent of Thorstein Veblen,[3] and the influence of sea power upon history independent of Admiral Mahan. In the last case lurks a possible argument for the opposition, because Admiral Mahan's book *The Influence of Sea Power upon History* so galvanized the naval policy of Imperial Germany and Great Britain in the years before 1914 that in isolating and describing a great historical fact he himself made history. Mr. Carr might make something of that.

Meanwhile I think his main theme unnecessarily metaphysical. I am content to define history as the past events of which we have knowledge and refrain from worrying about those of which we have none—until, that is, some archeologist digs them up.

I come next to historians. Who are they: contemporaries of the event or 10 those who come after? The answer is obviously both. Among contemporaries, first and indispensable are the more-or-less unconscious sources: letters, diaries,

---

[1] *John Keats* (1795–1821): British poet, author of "Ode on a Grecian Urn." [Eds.]
[2] *Frederick Jackson Turner* (1861–1932): American historian. [Eds.]
[3] *Thorstein Veblen* (1857–1929): American economist, author of *The Theory of the Leisure Class.* [Eds.]

memoirs, autobiographies, newspapers and periodicals, business and government documents. These are historical raw material, not history. Their authors may be writing with one eye or possibly both on posterity, but that does not make them historians. To perform that function requires a view from the outside and a conscious craft.

At a slightly different level are the I-was-there recorders, usually journalists, whose accounts often contain golden nuggets of information buried in a mass of daily travelogue which the passage of time has reduced to trivia. Some of the most vivid details that went into my book *The Guns of August* came from the working press: the rag doll crushed under the wheel of a German gun carriage from Irvin Cobb, the smell of half a million unwashed bodies that hung over the invaded villages of Belgium from Will Irwin, the incident of Colonel Max Hoffmann yelling insults at the Japanese general from Frederick Palmer, who reported the Russo-Japanese War. Daily journalism, however, even when collected in book form, is, like letters and the rest, essentially source material rather than history.

Still contemporary but dispensable are the Compilers who hurriedly assemble a book from clippings and interviews in order to capitalize on public interest when it is high. A favorite form of these hasty puddings is the overnight biography, like *The Lyndon Johnson Story*, which was in the bookstores within a few weeks of the incident that gave rise to it. The Compilers, in their treatment, supply no extra understanding and as historians are negligible.

All these varieties being disposed of, there remains a pure vein of conscious historians of whom, among contemporaries, there are two kinds. First, the Onlookers, who deliberately set out to chronicle an episode of their own age—a war or depression or strike or social revolution or whatever it may be—and shape it into a historical narrative with character and validity of its own. Thucydides' *Peloponnesian War*, on a major scale, and Theodore White's *The Making of a President*, undertaken in the same spirit though on a tiny scale in comparison, are examples.

Second are the Active Participants or Axe-Grinders, who attempt a genuine history of events they have known, but whose accounts are inevitably weighted, sometimes subtly and imperceptibly, sometimes crudely, by the requirements of the role in which they wish themselves to appear. Josephus' *The Jewish War*, the Earl of Clarendon's *History of the Rebellion*, and Winston Churchill's *World Crisis* and *Second World War* are classics of this category.

For the latter-day historian, these too become source material. Are we now 15 in possession of history when we have these accounts in hand? Yes, in the sense that we are in possession of wine when the first pressing of the grapes is in hand. But it has not fermented, and it has not aged. The great advantage of the latter-day historian is the distance conferred by the passage of time. At a distance from the events he describes and with a wider area of vision, he can see more of what was going on at the time and distinguish what was significant from what was not.

The contemporary has no perspective; everything is in the foreground and appears the same size. Little matters loom big, and great matters are sometimes missed because their outlines cannot be seen. Vietnam and Panama are given four-column headlines today, but the historian fifty or a hundred years hence will put them in a chapter under a general heading we have not yet thought of.

The contemporary, especially if he is a participant, is inside his events, which is not an entirely unmixed advantage. What he gains in intimacy through personal acquaintance—which we can never achieve—he sacrifices in detachment. He cannot see or judge fairly both sides in a quarrel, for example the quarrel as to who deserves chief credit for the French victory at the Battle of the Marne in 1914. All contemporary chroniclers were extreme partisans of either Joffre or Gallieni. So violent was the partisanship that no one (except President Poincaré) noticed what is so clearly visible when viewed from a distance, that both generals had played an essential role. Gallieni saw the opportunity and gave the impetus; Joffre brought the Army and the reinforcements into place to fight, but it took fifty years before this simple and just apportionment could be made.

Distance does not always confer objectivity; one can hardly say Gibbon[4] wrote objectively of the Roman Empire or Carlyle[5] of the French Revolution. Objectivity is a question of degree. It is possible for the latter-day historian to be at least *relatively* objective, which is not the same thing as being neutral or taking no sides. There is no such thing as a neutral or purely objective historian. Without an opinion a historian would be simply a ticking clock, and unreadable besides.

Nevertheless, distance does confer a kind of removal that cools the judgment and permits a juster appraisal than is possible to a contemporary. Once long ago as a freshman journalist I covered a campaign swing by Franklin D. Roosevelt during which he was scheduled to make a major speech at Pittsburgh or Harrisburg, I forget which. As we were leaving the train, one of the newspapermen remained comfortably behind in the club car with his feet up, explaining that as a New Dealer writing for a Republican paper he had to remain "objective" and he could "be a lot more objective right here than within ten feet of that fellow." He was using distance in space if not in time to acquire objectivity.

I found out from personal experience that I could not write contemporary history if I tried. Some people can, William Shirer,[6] for one; they are not affected by involvement. But I am, as I discovered when working on my first book, *Bible and Sword*. It dealt with the historical relations between Britain

---

[4]*Edward Gibbon* (1737–1794): British historian, author of *The History of the Decline and Fall of the Roman Empire.* [Eds.]

[5]*Thomas Carlyle* (1795–1881): Scottish historian. [Eds.]

[6]*William Shirer* (1904–1993): American journalist and historian, author of *The Rise and Fall of the Third Reich.* [Eds.]

and Palestine from the time of the Phoenicians to the present. Originally I had intended to bring the story down through the years of the British Mandate to the Arab-Israeli War and the re-establishment of the state of Israel in 1948.

I spent six months of research on the bitter history of those last thirty years: the Arab assaults and uprisings, the Round Tables, the White Papers, the cutting off of Jewish immigration, the Commissions of Inquiry, the ultimate historical irony when the British, who had issued the Balfour Declaration, rammed the ship *Exodus*, the whole ignominious tale of one or more chapters of appeasement.

When I tried to write this as history, I could not do it. Anger, disgust, and a sense of injustice can make some writers eloquent and evoke brilliant polemic, but these emotions stunted and twisted my pen. I found the tone of my concluding chapter totally different from the seventeen chapters that went before. I had suddenly walked over the line into contemporary history; I had become involved, and it showed. Although the publisher wanted the narrative brought up to date, I knew my final chapter as written would destroy the credibility of all the preceding, and I could not change it. I tore it up, discarded six months' work, and brought the book to a close in 1918.

I am not saying that emotion should have no place in history. On the contrary, I think it is an essential element of history, as it is of poetry, whose origin Wordsworth[7] defined as "emotion recollected in tranquillity." History, one might say, is emotion plus action recollected or, in the case of latter-day historians, reflected on in tranquillity after a close and honest examination of the records. The primary duty of the historian is to stay within the evidence. Yet it is a curious fact that poets, limited by no such rule, have done very well with history, both of their own times and of times long gone before.

Tennyson[8] wrote the "Charge of the Light Brigade" within three months of the event at Balaclava in the Crimea. "Cannon in front of them volleyed and thundered ... Flashed all their sabres bare ... Plunged in the battery-smoke ... Stormed at with shot and shell ... When can their glory fade? O the wild charge they made!" His version, even including the Victorian couplet "Theirs not to reason why / Theirs but to do and die," as poetry may lack the modern virtue of incomprehensibility, but as history it captures that combination of the glorious and the ridiculous which was a nineteenth-century cavalry charge against cannon. As an onlooker said, *"C'est magnifique, mais ce n'est pas la guerre"* ("It is magnificent, but it is not war"), which is exactly what Tennyson conveyed better than any historian.

To me who grew up before Bruce Catton[9] began writing, the Civil War will   25
always appear in terms of

---

[7]*William Wordsworth* (1770–1850): British poet. [Eds.]

[8]*Alfred Tennyson* (1809–1892): British poet. [Eds.]

[9]*Bruce Catton* (1899–1978): American historian, author of a number of books on the Civil War. [Eds.]

> Up from the meadows rich with corn,
> Clear in the cool September morn,
> The clustered spires of Frederick stand.

Whittier,[10] too, was dealing in contemporary history. Macaulay,[11] on the other hand, wrote "Horatius at the Bridge" some 2,500 years after the event. Although he was a major historian and only secondarily a poet, would any of us remember anything about Tarquin the Tyrant or Roman history before Caesar if it were not for "Lars Porsena of Clusium / By the Nine Gods he swore," and the rest of the seventy stanzas? We know how the American Revolution began from Longfellow's[12] signal lights in the old North Church.

> "One, if by land, and two, if by sea,
> And I on the opposite shore will be,
> Ready to ride and spread the alarm
> Through every Middlesex village and farm."

The poets have familiarized more people with history than have the historians, and sometimes they have given history a push. Kipling[13] did it in 1899 with his bidding "Take up the White Man's Burden," addressed to Americans, who, being plunged into involuntary imperialism by Admiral Dewey's adventure at Manila, were sorely perplexed over what to do about the Philippines. "Send forth the best ye breed," Kipling told them firmly,

> To want in heavy harness,
> On fluttered folk and wild—
> Your new-caught, sullen peoples,
> Half-devil and half-child.
>
> Take up the White Man's burden,
> The savage wars of peace—
> Fill full the mouth of Famine
> And bid the sickness cease;
>
> Take up the White Man's burden—
> Ye dare not stoop to less.

The advice, published in a two-page spread by *McClure's Magazine*, was quoted across the country within a week and quickly reconciled most Americans to the expenditure of bullets, brutality, and trickery that soon proved necessary to implement it.

---

[10]*John Greenleaf Whittier* (1807–1892): American poet. [Eds.]
[11]*Thomas Macaulay* (1800–1859): British historian and statesman. [Eds.]
[12]*Henry Wadsworth Longfellow* (1807–1882): American poet, author of "Paul Revere's Ride." [Eds.]
[13]*Rudyard Kipling* (1865–1936): British author. [Eds.]

Kipling had a peculiar gift for recognizing history at close quarters. He wrote "Recessional" in 1897 at the time of the Queen's Diamond Jubilee when he sensed a self-glorification, a kind of hubris, in the national mood that frightened him. In *The Times* on the morning after, when people read his reminder—

> Lo, all our pomp of yesterday
> Is one with Nineveh and Tyre!
> Judge of the Nations, spare us yet,
> Lest we forget—lest we forget!

—it created a profound impression. Sir Edward Clark, the distinguished barrister who defended Oscar Wilde, was so affected by the message that he pronounced "Recessional" "the greatest poem written by any living man."

What the poets did was to convey the *feeling* of an episode or a moment of history as they sensed it. The historian's task is rather to tell what happened within the discipline of the facts.

What his imagination is to the poet, facts are to the historian. His exercise of judgment comes in their selection, his art in their arrangement. His method is narrative. His subject is the story of man's past. His function is to make it known.

QUESTIONS

1. What position is Tuchman taking in declaring herself a firm believer in "the 'preposterous fallacy' of historical facts existing independently of the historian" (paragraph 7)?

2. According to Tuchman, what advantage does the latter-day historian have over the contemporary historian? What does this advantage suggest about when history happens?

3. Tuchman tells her readers about the problems she had in working on her first book, *Bible and Sword*. Tuchman writes, "Anger, disgust, and a sense of injustice can make some writers eloquent and evoke brilliant polemic, but these emotions stunted and twisted my pen" (paragraph 22). What is the effect of these personal reflections? How do they serve to strengthen her argument?

4. Why does Tuchman choose to quote from Tennyson, Longfellow, and Kipling? How does this evidence from poetry support her argument?

5. How do you respond to Tuchman's claim that emotion "is an essential element of history" (paragraph 23)?

MAKING CONNECTIONS

1. Both E. H. Carr (p. 593) and Tuchman ask, in one way or another, What is history? Outline the major areas of agreement and disagreement between these writers. Where do you find the most significant areas of agreement? Of disagreement?

2. Consider an episode or event you know a good deal about, and think about how you might write its history. You could write of a recent year or season, a local political campaign, curricular reform at your high school or college, the birth of an organization in which you know some members, a recent criminal case, a school controversy. How would you approach that event if you were to write under the influence of E. H. Carr (p. 593) or Tuchman? What would you have to know, discover, worry, and think about if you were to take Carr as your guide? What if you were to follow Tuchman? Write an explanation of where your research, in one case or the other, would lead you.

3. Tuchman asks an important question: "Should—or perhaps can—history be written while it is still smoking" (paragraph 1)? Consider your responses to the selections by E. H. Carr (p. 593) and Tuchman. What is your position?

UNDER THE BED
Jincy Willett

Jincy Willett first published this essay in The Massachusetts Review *in 1983. She has since written a collection of
short stories,* Jenny and the Jaws of Life *(1987). In this
essay, Willett presents the story of a rape, and in the process
she presents an argument on the nature of the tragedy of the
event.*

On November 6 of last year, at around 8:15 p.m., I was beaten and raped by
a man named Raymond C. Moreau, Jr., who had entered our first floor apartment through a living room window while I was taking a shower. This is neither the most significant event in my life nor the most interesting; nevertheless
it is a fact, around which cluster many other facts, and the truth is always worth
telling. As I approach forty I am learning to value the truth for its own sake; I
discover that most people have little use for it, beyond its practical applications,
except as the glue which holds together rickety constructs of theory and opinion. As a rule the brighter and better educated select their facts with great care.

I teach philosophy at our mediocre state junior college. My husband
teaches physics at the University. He is the real philosopher, like all good scientists, although, like most good scientists, he amiably resists this description.
We self-styled philosophers window shop through metaphysics, epistemology
and ethics, until we settle on those views which suit us, and then we tailor
them to fit our idiosyncrasies. The more cynical among us deliberately choose
unpopular or bizarre philosophies the more easily to establish a reputation. My
husband is a born verificationist. He does not ask unanswerable questions; he
does not whine, or posture, or plead, or shake his fist at the stars. His agnosti-
cism, unlike mine, is consistent throughout, utterly free of petulance and despair. It is he who taught me to hold the truth in such high regard, as he has
taught me so many things. He believes in a rational universe. How I love him
for that! He is worth a hundred humanists, a thousand priests.

My husband was at an evening seminar on November 6 (or, as we now refer
to it, with some humor, "The Night of the Thing") and did not return until
9:00, when I was again alone in the apartment. Of course he blamed himself,
especially at first, for having been away, for not coming right home when the
seminar concluded. I am very glad he stayed for coffee. Had he interrupted us
he would have had to do something, as would Raymond C. Moreau, Jr., who
had a gun.

As it happened, and for reasons I shall try to explain, when he came home I
was under our double bed, asleep. He did not notice that our television set was

missing; there were damp towels on the living room floor, and the bedspread was considerably rumpled, but this did not alarm him so much (for I am not very neat) as the apparent fact of my absence. He was smiling when he opened the front door—I know this, because I am usually there to meet him, and he always smiles—but when he sat on our bed to puzzle out where I might be he was not smiling. I imagine that at that moment he looked his age (he is older than I) and that he let his shoulders sag, and that his expression was blank and vulnerable. I cannot imagine how he looked when, bending down to untie his shoes, he saw the fingertips of my right hand protruding from behind the gray chenille spread. Thank god he has a good heart. He dropped to his knees and took my hand and lifted the spread, at which point I woke up. A farce ensued. (Unfunny, as farces so often are.) I immediately realized, from the way his voice cracked when he called my name, that he was badly frightened, as who wouldn't be; since I did not want to frighten him further I determined not to let him see my face, which was bloody and ugly with bruises. "I'm fine," I said, idiotically, in an exaggerated reasonable tone. "What the hell do you mean," he said, and yanked on my arm. "Come out of there." I braced my other arm against the rail. "I will in a minute. I have to tell you something." Then, unfortunately, and rather horribly, I began to laugh, at the picture we would have made to an impartial observer, at our outlandish dialogue. This is usually called the "hysterical laugh," to distinguish it substantially from genuine laughter. Now my husband—and good for him—wasted no time, but gave the bed a hard sideways push. It flew on well-oiled casters and thumped against wall and windowsill; and for the second time in an hour I was well exposed. A pitiful and wrenching sight I must have been, clutching my old red bathrobe tight around me like a cartoon spinster, hiding my ugly face in the dusty green shag. (To this day a breath of dust makes me flush a little, with artificial shame. The body remembers.) Well, then there was reconciliation, and explanation, and generally the sort of behavior you would expect from lovers to whom such a thing has happened. These events were not extraordinary, except to us, and I shall not record them, here or anywhere else. These are private matters. We are very private people.

Raymond C. Moreau was twenty years old and looked thirty. He had long sand-colored hair, which hung in greasy ropes; small deep-set eyes, I don't know what color; thin lips and receding chin; and a rough, ravaged complexion: the right side of his face especially was seamed and pitted. I gave this information to the police artist and he drew me a picture of Charlie Goodby, a paperboy we had in Worcester when I was a little girl. He—the rapist—wore a soiled yellow windbreaker, an undershirt, beige chinos, and jockey shorts. Obviously he must have worn shoes, but I never noticed. His breath was terrible. He looked, as you would expect, like a bad man and a loser.

During the fifteen or so minutes of our association he said the following:
Get it off. Drop it.

613

In there, lady.

On the bed.

You got a husband? You all alone, you stupid bitch?   10

Spread them, bitch.

You're all alike. All alike. All alike.

Shut up. I'll kill you.

That's right.

Oh. Love. Love, love love, ahhh, love. Ahhh.   15

Stay there. Stay away from the phone. I'll come back and I'll kill you.

That he said "love, love, love" at the point of orgasm does not, in retrospect, strike me as ironic. On the back of his windbreaker the initials "C H S E" and the numerals "1972" were stencilled in brown. "C H S E 1972" is heavier with implication than "love, love, love." "C H S E 1972," now that I think of it, is eloquent as hell.

He never looked me in the eye. But he did not, I think, purposely avoid my eyes. He was not nervous, or ashamed, or fearful. It just never occurred to him to look there.

I used to be afraid of everything. That is, I was a functioning, relatively happy person with a great deal of fear. Spiders, heights, closed-in places—I had all the phobias in moderation. I never answered the phone without first composing myself for bad news—I always waited a beat before I picked up the receiver. (The ring of a telephone on a late sunny afternoon was particularly menacing to me.) Every time I got on a plane I knew I was going to die; and I was ever aware of the dangers inherent in any form of transportation. If I had to enter a dark room I hurried to the light switch, even though my night vision is excellent. At night I never let my hand or my foot dangle over the side of the bed.

Once or twice a year I would experience a few days of serious dread,   20
touched off by something Walter Cronkite said, or a remark overheard at a sherry hour. Once a colleague mentioned a Roman Catholic legend to the effect that the last Pope would be the first non-Italian. "Then what," I asked him, with a false conspiratorial smile. "The end of the world," he said, and lifted his glass as if to toast this hideous prophecy. Oh, I despised him then, and all the laughing doomsayers, who spread terror all unmindful, precisely because they do not know what terror is. Cassandra never laughed.

It is not that I have ever believed the holocaust inevitable, or even probable; rather, I was forced on some occasions to admit the possibility. And on these occasions suicide had a certain appeal for me. I would lie beside my sleeping husband and try to think about a universe purged of human beings—surely there was some comfort in this concept; but then, I would be reminded, there would be no concepts either. A universe of particles, normally neutral: black, a pitiless black whole, with no memories, not even of the finest of us. I kept imagining the moment of purging, the dying, the knowing, and terror froze me so I could not even cry. I feared most that we would see it coming, that we would be spared nothing; that I would be separated from my husband, unable to get to him in time—in the last moments of time; or that we would be together but helpless to end in our own way. Plans must be made, I would think: emergency rations of cyanide. But even then we would not both die at once; one would have to endure alone, for however long it took. . . .

When I had had enough of this I always sought to calm myself, with craven prayer, and with the warmth of my husband's body, and the cool dry cross-grain of his skin; and magically, on the third or fourth sleepless night the terror would slip away.

And other nights, when nothing weighed on me at all, and fearless as a movie hero I lay in wait for sleep, I would suddenly have to rise on one elbow, just like a robot, and strain to hear the sound of my husband breathing; and if I could not be sure of it I would brush and push against him, as though by accident, until I had drawn out a sigh or shaken him into motion.

I was not so much neurotic as superstitious, as though through occasional ritualistic suffering I could save us all. I carefully hid this, and only this, from my husband, my talisman, because I did not want to worry or disappoint him; and if he ever suspected the depth of my perverse irrationality he kindly left me to it.

I am not superstitious now. Whatever else he did to me, Raymond C. 25 Moreau measurably improved the quality of my life. My body sometimes jumps or shrinks from the unexpected casual touch, and this can be awkward. But I know no fear. I don't worry any more.

I used to have a good friend. Regina Montgomery is the only woman outside my family for whom I have ever felt physical affection. She is an Amazon, sturdy and large-breasted, with plain coarse features; she smiles like a big cat and is made beautiful. We are opposites physically, emotionally, politically; she is ten years my junior. She pleased me. She was exotic in her proportions and in her strength; earthy, passionate, intense, everything I was not.

She gave me two weeks to start talking on my own about my experience with Raymond C. Moreau. Actually I did not let her see me the first week, until the marks faded; and when she came to the door it was she, not I, whose eyes were red-rimmed and puffy. I remember she had part of a foil-wrapped fruitcake in her hand, and that she kissed my husband on the cheek and hugged him fiercely—it was so strange to see them embracing, she had always been so shy around him; and that she waited for some sign from me and didn't get it, for she kept her distance, fluttering like a great clumsy bird, saying how wonderful I looked. I was cruel to her, surprising myself; I was bland and cheerful and gracious, serving up the fruitcake, making light, maddening conversation, meticulously avoiding even oblique allusion to the single topic she had come to discuss. Her anxiety, so ingenuously displayed, was as comical as it was touching. I kept thinking that at any moment I would let down, but after awhile she left, unsatisfied and bewildered.

"I understood," she told me after, when we finally had it out. "You couldn't stand to be touched in any way." I let her think this. The truth is, I have a mean streak. Obvious people bring out the worst in me. I was not proud of having tortured her like that; I loved her for her genuine concern, her simple candor, her trust. I made a gift of my confession, describing the attack in detail, answering all her questions. It was not enough for her. "You talk as though this—this horror—happened to someone else. How do you feel? Or don't you even know?" "A total stranger invades my home, hurts me, rapes me, calls me names, turns my life into a melodrama. How do you suppose I feel?" She opened her mouth, shut it again. She had decided, I could see, that I was still not "over it." She would bide her time.

And she watched me closely, obviously, over the next few months, impatiently waiting, I suppose, for me to start drinking, or break into sobs at a faculty meeting, or something like that. Armchair psychoanalysis has always annoyed me, it is such an undisciplined activity. I deeply resented such presumption on the part of a friend.

We went out for wine one afternoon and had an awful fight. Our friendship has not recovered. 30

"All you can say is, you're not changed, not outraged, not afraid, not anything. Christ, you make it seem like a—an embarrassing *incident!*"

"Or a shaggy dog horror story?" I said, smiling, and poured us wine from our third carafe. Wine makes me happy and reckless.

"But you have changed," said Regina, who was not happy at all. "You're icy. Icy. Not like your old reserve. You've become rude, do you know that? Well, not actively, but I swear you look at people with such—I don't know—contempt—"

"You're just a bad sport," I said, teasing her. The difference in our ages was never more apparent. She was flushed, earnest and drunk, and childishly adamant. "Reggie, look. He just got me on a good day, all right? You know how sometimes a movie will make you cry, and other days you laugh yourself sick—"

"That's disgusting! You were violated! Violence was done to you!" 35

"You say that with such an air of discovery."

"And not just to you. To me. To all women."

"Oh, really?" I was angry now. We had argued the political point before, but this was personal. "Then why don't you tell me about it, Regina? It must have been a ghastly experience."

"You are bitter! You see." She was triumphant.

"Only about you. You want me to be a martyr, a role I find repellent in the extreme. I was victimized, yes, but I am not a victim. And I am not a symbol. I am not in the symbolizing business." 40

In the end I said she was no different from Raymond Moreau. Always willing to take a metaphor and run with it, she stared up at me, stupid and openmouthed, trying to understand in what way she had been "raping" me. I could see clear into her skull. I threw my money down in disgust and left her there. I had meant only, she thought we were all alike, all alike. All alike.

I padded on damp feet into the living room, wrapped in a big yellow towel, another towel on my clean hair. I was going to turn on the television, for the comforting noise. He was winding the cord around its handle; a nice breeze came in the open window. I said, "Hello." I thought to say, "I've been expecting you," for this was true; I had been expecting him all my life. I thought to scream, but then the gun was out. Another woman—Regina—might have screamed without thinking first. I never do anything without thinking first.

I let my body have the fear. Bodies are designed to handle fright. It rippled and shuddered, the heart panicked, the blood scampered in terror. I watched. Really, it was not so bad. It was nothing like the end of the world.

He lay me on my back, arranged my legs this way and that, pushed against me like a vacant idiot child; his belly was soft and slack, it rested on mine light and warm and unmuscled; when my flesh shrank away it followed, spread thick, a cloying intimate layer of skin and fat. His upper body he kept to himself, propped up on rosy eczematous elbows. I could see each row in the machine-weave of his undershirt, the irregular rows of tiny hairs and diamond-shaped skin segments in his neck and jaw, the arch of his upper teeth, filigreed with silver. If there is a god, I remember thinking, he certainly attends to detail. He hit my face, alternating open palm and knuckles, with precise unhurried rhythm; and from my mouth came a terrible sound, as from a grunting pig. But I did not make the sound. I could never make a sound like that.

At no time did I need to remind myself that this was happening, and not a dream. There was no feeling of displacement. Nor did I wonder why he did it. After all, he never wondered about me.

Where is the tragedy here? He did not touch me. Of course, it was unpleasant and wearing, but I have been more deeply hurt by rude bus drivers. It was just a collision of machines.

When he left I was faced with the problem of how to tell my husband. It does not seem now like such a great problem but then I had been under a strain and could not think clearly. Once, when I was in college, I was playing bridge with some friends in my dormitory room when a girl from down the hall—a secretive, nervous girl, a bare acquaintance—shuffled in, in nightgown and slippers, asked if she could sit and watch. She was very pale, apparently exhausted from crying. She sat still for half an hour, peculiarly ominous but circumspect, until finally, blushing with shame, she confessed, in an offhand way, that she had taken a lot of pills and didn't know what to do. There is just no proper way to inform a roomful of strangers that you have attempted suicide.

45

There is no way at all to tell your husband that you have been raped. Should I stay as I was, naked, unseemly? This seemed a gratuitously cruel method, almost amounting to accusation. Look what's been done to me! I put on my robe and wandered through the apartment, looking for a place to light. Well, I could sit down, on the couch for instance, with a single dim lamp on, and greet him that way—but with what words? For a while I thought seriously of cleaning up, combing my hair; I could stay in shadow, avert my face, never mention it at all. But now my body, which had served me so well, let me down: I was tired and could not even lift a cloth to wash myself. I needed a hiding place, where decisions could be held in abeyance; a place of noncommitment. Intending to rest for only a minute I slid underneath the bed, where the monsters used to be; and there were no monsters there, just me; and I slept without dreaming.

To say the least I have never been effusive or easygoing, but before the rape I got along well enough with my colleagues. There was mutual respect. I have no respect for most of them now; they have shown little for me. We live in an age when self-control, competence, discretion—all are thought abnormal, symptomatic of dysfunction. "But how do you *feel*," they all want to know; their eyes betray them, they are so obvious; some of them dare to ask. "I'm sorry," said our Kant and Leibniz specialist, a man I had always credited with sense. "I'm sorry!" "What for," I asked him, infuriated by his gloomy hangdog look, "are you responsible in some way? Did you once have adolescent rape fantasies? Do you believe in a common consciousness?" Shoddy, second-rate thinkers; bullies. Sentimentalists. *Why, look you now, how unworthy a thing you make of me!*

A police detective came to my office with a high school photograph of Raymond Moreau. After I identified him the detective told me he was dead, shot dead by some woman better prepared than I, a woman with her own gun. (What a stupid criminal was Raymond Moreau!) "Well, that's convenient, isn't it?" I said, and shook his hand. And even he, this stolid, unimaginative fellow, even he paused, surprised, disappointed, waiting for some further response. Tears of relief, perhaps; a primitive whoop of joy.

There are so many like Raymond Moreau.

50

My disgust is not unreasonable. I know, because I have talked to my husband, and he agrees with me. He does urge me, from time to time, not to be too harsh: they mean no harm, he says. He contends that people usually do the best they can. I suppose he is right, although I do wonder if this is not really a tautology in lush disguise. He has always been a compassionate man. He alone sees me as I am, and loves me as he loves the truth.

We are closer now than ever. We seldom go out; neither of us spends unnecessary time at school. Evenings find us here, laughing, talking into the night. We seem again to have as much to say to each other as when we first were lovers. I have fixed up the apartment quite differently—the bedroom is completely rearranged, with all new linens and a white bedspread and a thick white carpet. (I happen to like white. White does not symbolize.) Often we have picnics, as we did when we were young, only now we hold them indoors on the living room floor; and we drink good wine, '66 burgundies, '61 bordeaux, rich wines of every hue from purple black to brick red. And I have never been so content.

But lately, and too often, as we lie in the dark, I curl away from him, peaceful and fearless, he rises, stealthy, gentle, and leans over me, watching my face; I can feel his breath on my cheek; and I must give him a sign, a sigh, a dreamy moan to ease his mind. Just like a robot he must rise, prompted by my old foolish impulse, unworthy of him, as though by watching he could keep me safe; as though the universe concerned itself with us.

There's the violation. There's the damage, and the tragedy.

QUESTIONS

1. What are Willett's reasons for comparing her friend Regina and the policeman to Raymond Moreau?

2. How does Willett structure her argument?

3. Consider how this essay comments on Willett's opening statement about truth, that "the truth is always worth telling," but that "most people have little use for it."

4. After presenting the facts of the rape, Willett asks, "Where is the tragedy here? . . . It was just a collision of machines" (paragraph 46). What does she mean?

5. Why does Willett refuse to be characterized as a victim? Comment on how the term *victim* is currently used in American society.

6. According to Willett, what, finally, is the tragedy in this case?

MAKING CONNECTIONS

Referring to E. H. Carr's discussion of facts and interpretation of history (p. 593), comment on Willett's view of facts and truth, and her interpretation of the facts she presents.

Social Sciences
and Public Affairs

THE IGNORED LESSON
OF ANNE FRANK
Bruno Bettelheim

Psychoanalyst Bruno Bettelheim (1903–1990) survived imprisonment in Nazi concentration camps. Here he writes about Anne Frank, one of the better-known victims of World War II. After hiding in an attic in Amsterdam for two years, her family was betrayed to the Nazis, and Anne perished in a concentration camp. Her diary, kept during her time in hiding, was published in 1947 and later was turned into a play and a film. The following essay originally appeared in Harper's *magazine (November 1960) and was reprinted in Bettelheim's book* Surviving and Other Essays *(1979). In this essay, Bettelheim seeks to revise our moral understanding of Anne Frank's story.*

When the world first learned about the Nazi concentration and death camps, most civilized people felt the horrors committed in them to be so uncanny as to be unbelievable. It came as a severe shock that supposedly civilized nations could stoop to such inhuman acts. The implication that modern man has such inadequate control over his cruel and destructive proclivities was felt as a threat to our views of ourselves and our humanity. Three different psychological mechanisms were most frequently used for dealing with the appalling revelation of what had gone on in the camps:

(1) its applicability to man in general was denied by asserting—contrary to evidence—that the acts of torture and mass murder were committed by a small group of insane or perverted persons;

(2) the truth of the reports was denied by declaring them vastly exaggerated and ascribing them to propaganda (this originated with the German govern-

ment, which called all reports on terror in the camps "horror propaganda"—
Greuel-propaganda);

(3) the reports were believed, but the knowledge of the horror repressed as
soon as possible.

All three mechanisms could be seen at work after liberation of those prisoners remaining. At first, after the discovery of the camps and their death-dealing,
a wave of extreme outrage swept the Allied nations. It was soon followed by a
general repression of the discovery in people's minds. Possibly this reaction was
due to something more than the blow dealt to modern man's narcissism by the
realization that cruelty is still rampant among men. Also present may have
been the dim but extremely threatening realization that the modern state now
has available the means for changing personality, and for destroying millions it
deems undesirable. The ideas that in our day a people's personalities might be
changed against their will by the state, and that other populations might be
wholly or partially exterminated, are so fearful that one tries to free oneself of
them and their impact by defensive denial, or by repression.

The extraordinary world-wide success of the book, play, and movie *The
Diary of Anne Frank* suggests the power of the desire to counteract the realization of the personality-destroying and murderous nature of the camps by concentrating all attention on what is experienced as a demonstration that private
and intimate life can continue to flourish even under the direct persecution by
the most ruthless totalitarian system. And this although Anne Frank's fate
demonstrates how efforts at disregarding in private life what goes on around
one in society can hasten one's own destruction.

What concerns me here is not what actually happened to the Frank family,
how they tried—and failed—to survive their terrible ordeal. It would be very
wrong to take apart so humane and moving a story, which aroused so much
well-merited compassion for gentle Anne Frank and her tragic fate. What is at
issue is the universal and uncritical response to her diary and to the play and
movie based on it, and what this reaction tells about our attempts to cope with
the feelings her fate—used by us to serve as a symbol of a most human reaction
to Nazi terror—arouses in us. I believe that the world-wide acclaim given her
story cannot be explained unless we recognize in it our wish to forget the gas
chambers, and our effort to do so by glorifying the ability to retreat into an extremely private, gentle, sensitive world, and there to cling as much as possible
to what have been one's usual daily attitudes and activities, although surrounded by a maelstrom apt to engulf one at any moment.

The Frank family's attitude that life could be carried on as before may well   5
have been what led to their destruction. By eulogizing how they lived in their
hiding place while neglecting to examine first whether it was a reasonable or
an effective choice, we are able to ignore the crucial lesson of their story—that
such an attitude can be fatal in extreme circumstances.

While the Franks were making their preparations for going passively into hiding, thousands of other Jews in Holland (as elsewhere in Europe) were trying to escape to the free world, in order to survive and/or fight. Others who could not escape went underground—into hiding—each family member with, for example, a different gentile family. We gather from the diary, however, that the chief desire of the Frank family was to continue living as nearly as possible in the same fashion to which they had been accustomed in happier times.

Little Anne, too, wanted only to go on with life as usual, and what else could she have done but fall in with the pattern her parents created for her existence? But hers was not a necessary fate, much less a heroic one; it was a terrible but also a senseless fate. Anne had a good chance to survive, as did many Jewish children in Holland. But she would have had to leave her parents and go live with a gentile Dutch family, posing as their own child, something her parents would have had to arrange for her.

Everyone who recognized the obvious knew that the hardest way to go underground was to do it as a family; to hide out together made detection by the SS most likely; and when detected, everybody was doomed. By hiding singly, even when one got caught, the others had a chance to survive. The Franks, with their excellent connections among gentile Dutch families, might well have been able to hide out singly, each with a different family. But instead, the main principle of their planning was continuing their beloved family life—an understandable desire, but highly unrealistic in those times. Choosing any other course would have meant not merely giving up living together, but also realizing the full measure of the danger to their lives.

The Franks were unable to accept that going on living as a family as they had done before the Nazi invasion of Holland was no longer a desirable way of life, much as they loved each other; in fact, for them and others like them, it was most dangerous behavior. But even given their wish not to separate, they failed to make appropriate preparations for what was likely to happen.

There is little doubt that the Franks, who were able to provide themselves 10 with so much while arranging for going into hiding, and even while hiding, could have provided themselves with some weapons had they wished. Had they had a gun, Mr. Frank could have shot down at least one or two of the "green police" who came for them. There was no surplus of such police, and the loss of an SS with every Jew arrested would have noticeably hindered the functioning of the police state. Even a butcher knife, which they certainly could have taken with them into hiding, could have been used by them in self-defense. The fate of the Franks wouldn't have been very different, because they all died anyway except for Anne's father. But they could have sold their lives for a high price, instead of walking to their death. Still, although one must assume that Mr. Frank would have fought courageously, as we know he did when a soldier in the first World War, it is not everybody who can plan to kill those who are bent on killing him, although many who would not be ready to contemplate doing so would be willing to kill those who are bent on murdering not only them but also their wives and little daughters.

An entirely different matter would have been planning for escape in case of discovery. The Franks' hiding place had only one entrance; it did not have any other exit. Despite the fact, during their many months of hiding, they did not try to devise one. Nor did they make other plans for escape, such as that one of the family members—as likely as not Mr. Frank—would try to detain the police in the narrow entrance way—maybe even fight them, as suggested above— thus giving other members of the family a chance to escape, either by reaching the roofs of adjacent houses, or down a ladder into the alley behind the house in which they were living.

Any of this would have required recognizing and accepting the desperate straits in which they found themselves, and concentrating on how best to cope with them. This was quite possible to do, even under the terrible conditions in which the Jews found themselves after the Nazi occupation of Holland. It can be seen from many other accounts, for example from the story of Marga Minco, a girl of about Anne Frank's age who lived to tell about it. Her parents had planned that when the police should come for them, the father would try to detain them by arguing and fighting with them, to give the wife and daughter a chance to escape through a rear door. Unfortunately it did not quite work out this way, and both parents got killed. But their short-lived resistance permitted their daughter to make her escape as planned and to reach a Dutch family who saved her.[1]

This is not mentioned as a criticism that the Frank family did not plan or behave along similar lines. A family has every right to arrange their life as they wish or think best, and to take the risks they want to take. My point is not to criticize what the Franks did, but only the universal admiration of their way of coping, or rather of not coping. The story of little Marga who survived, every bit as touching, remains totally neglected by comparison.

Many Jews—unlike the Franks, who through listening to British radio news were better informed than most—had no detailed knowledge of the extermination camps. Thus it was easier for them to make themselves believe that complete compliance with even the most outrageously debilitating and degrading Nazi orders might offer a chance for survival. But neither tremendous anxiety that inhibits clear thinking and with it well-planned and determined action, nor ignorance about what happened to those who responded with passive waiting for being rounded up for their extermination, can explain the reaction of audiences to the play and movie retelling Anne's story, which are all about such waiting that results finally in destruction.

I think it is the fictitious ending that explains the enormous success of this play and movie. At the conclusion we hear Anne's voice from the beyond, say-

---

[1] Marga Minco, *Bitter Herbs* (New York: Oxford University Press), 1960.

ing, "In spite of everything, I still believe that people are really good at heart." This improbable sentiment is supposedly from a girl who had been starved to death, had watched her sister meet the same fate before she did, knew that her mother had been murdered, and had watched untold thousands of adults and children being killed. This statement is not justified by anything Anne actually told her diary.

Going on with intimate family living, no matter how dangerous it might be to survival, was fatal to all too many during the Nazi regime. And if all men are good, then indeed we can all go on with living our lives as we have been accustomed to in times of undisturbed safety and can afford to forget about Auschwitz. But Anne, her sister, her mother, may well have died because her parents could not get themselves to believe in Auschwitz.

While play and movie are ostensibly about Nazi persecution and destruction, in actuality what we watch is the way that, despite this terror, lovable people manage to continue living their satisfying intimate lives with each other. The heroine grows from a child into a young adult as normally as any other girl would, despite the most abnormal conditions of all other aspects of her existence, and that of her family. Thus the play reassures us that despite the destructiveness of Nazi racism and tyranny in general, it is possible to disregard it in one's private life much of the time, even if one is Jewish.

True, the ending happens just as the Franks and their friends had feared all along: their hiding place is discovered, and they are carried away to their doom. But the fictitious declaration of faith in the goodness of all men which concludes the play falsely reassures us since it impresses on us that in the combat between Nazi terror and continuance of intimate family living the latter wins out, since Anne has the last word. This is simply contrary to fact, because it was she who got killed. Her seeming survival through her moving statement about the goodness of men releases us effectively of the need to cope with the problems Auschwitz presents. That is why we are so relieved by her statement. It explains why millions loved play and movie, because while it confronts us with the fact that Auschwitz existed it encourages us at the same time to ignore any of its implications. If all men are good at heart, there never really was an Auschwitz; nor is there any possibility that it may recur.

The desire of Anne Frank's parents not to interrupt their intimate family living, and their inability to plan more effectively for their survival, reflect the failure of all too many others faced with the threat of Nazi terror. It is a failure that deserves close examination because of the inherent warnings it contains for us, the living.

Submission to the threatening power of the Nazi state often led both to the [20] disintegration of what had once seemed well-integrated personalities and to a return to an immature disregard for the dangers of reality. Those Jews who submitted passively to Nazi persecution came to depend on primitive and infantile thought processes: wishful thinking and disregard for the possibility of death. Many persuaded themselves that they, out of all the others, would be spared.

Many more simply disbelieved in the possibility of their own death. Not believing in it, they did not take what seemed to them desperate precautions, such as giving up everything to hide out singly; or trying to escape even if it meant risking their lives in doing so; or preparing to fight for their lives when no escape was possible and death had become an immediate possibility. It is true that defending their lives in active combat before they were rounded up to be transported into the camps might have hastened their deaths, and so, up to a point, they were protecting themselves by "rolling with the punches" of the enemy.

But the longer one rolls with the punches dealt not by the normal vagaries of life, but by one's eventual executioner, the more likely it becomes that one will no longer have the strength to resist when death becomes imminent. This is particularly true if yielding to the enemy is accompanied not by a commensurate strengthening of the personality, but by an inner disintegration. We can observe such a process among the Franks, who bickered with each other over trifles, instead of supporting each other's ability to resist the demoralizing impact of their living conditions.

Those who faced up to the announced intentions of the Nazis prepared for the worst as a real and imminent possibility. It meant risking one's life for a self-chosen purpose, but in doing so, creating at least a small chance for saving one's own life or those of others, or both. When Jews in Germany were restricted to their homes, those who did not succumb to inertia took the new restrictions as a warning that it was high time to go underground, join the resistance movement, provide themselves with forged papers, and so on; if they had not done so long ago. Many of them survived.

Some distant relatives of mine may furnish an example. Early in the war, a young man living in a small Hungarian town banded together with a number of other Jews to prepare against a German invasion. As soon as the Nazis imposed curfews on the Jews, his group left for Budapest—because the bigger capital city with its greater anonymity offered chances for escaping detection. Similar groups from other towns converged in Budapest and joined forces. From among themselves they selected typically "Aryan" looking men who equipped themselves with false papers and immediately joined the Hungarian SS. These spies were then able to warn of impending persecution and raids.

Many of these groups survived intact. Furthermore, they had also equipped themselves with small arms, so that if they were detected, they could put up enough of a fight for the majority to escape while a few would die fighting to make the escape possible. A few of the Jews who had joined the SS were discovered and immediately shot, probably a death preferable to one in the gas chambers. But most of even these Jews survived, hiding within the SS until liberation.

Compare these arrangements not just to the Franks' selection of a hiding place that was basically a trap without an outlet but with Mr. Frank's teaching typically academic high-school subjects to his children rather than how to make a getaway: a token of his inability to face the seriousness of the threat of death. Teaching high-school subjects had, of course, its constructive aspects. It relieved the ever-present anxiety about their fate to some degree by concentrating on different matters, and by implication it encouraged hope for a future in which such knowledge would be useful. In this sense such teaching was purposeful, but it was erroneous in that it took the place of much more pertinent teaching and planning: how best to try to escape when detected.

Unfortunately the Franks were by no means the only ones who, out of anxiety, became unable to contemplate their true situation and with it to plan accordingly. Anxiety, and the wish to counteract it by clinging to each other, and to reduce its sting by continuing as much as possible with their usual way of life incapacitated many, particularly when survival plans required changing radically old ways of living that they cherished, and which had become their only source of satisfaction.

My young relative, for example, was unable to persuade other members of his family to go with him when he left the small town where he had lived with them. Three times, at tremendous risk to himself, he returned to plead with his relatives, pointing out first the growing persecution of the Jews, and later the fact that transport to the gas chambers had already begun. He could not convince these Jews to leave their homes and break up their families to go singly into hiding.

As their desperation mounted, they clung more determinedly to their old living arrangements and to each other, became less able to consider giving up the possessions they had accumulated through hard work over a lifetime. The more severely their freedom to act was reduced, and what little they were still permitted to do restricted by insensible and degrading regulations imposed by the Nazis, the more did they become unable to contemplate independent action. Their life energies drained out of them, sapped by their ever-greater anxiety. The less they found strength in themselves, the more they held on to the little that was left of what had given them security in the past—their old surroundings, their customary way of life, their possessions—all these seemed to give their lives some permanency, offer some symbols of security. Only what had once been symbols of security now endangered life, since they were excuses for avoiding change. On each successive visit the young man found his relatives more incapacitated, less willing or able to take his advice, more frozen into inactivity, and with it further along the way to the crematoria where, in fact, they all died.

Levin renders a detailed account of the desperate but fruitless efforts made by small Jewish groups determined to survive to try to save the rest. She tells how messengers were "sent into the provinces to warn Jews that deportation meant death, but their warnings were ignored because most Jews refused to contemplate their own annihilation."[2] I believe the reason for such refusal has

---

[2]Nora Levin, *The Holocaust* (New York: Thomas Y. Crowell, 1968).

to be found in their inability to take action. If we are certain that we are help-less to protect ourselves against the danger of destruction, we cannot contem-plate it. We can consider the danger only as long as we believe there are ways to protect ourselves, to fight back, to escape. If we are convinced none of this is possible for us, then there is no point in thinking about the danger; on the con-trary, it is best to refuse to do so.

As a prisoner in Buchenwald, I talked to hundreds of German Jewish pris-oners who were brought there as part of the huge pogrom in the wake of the murder of vom Rath in the fall of 1938. I asked them why they had not left Germany, given the utterly degrading conditions they had been subjected to. Their answer was: How could we leave? It would have meant giving up our homes, our work, our sources of income. Having been deprived by Nazi perse-cution and degradation of much of their self-respect, they had become unable to give up what still gave them a semblance of it: their earthly belongings. But instead of using possessions, they became captivated by them, and this posses-sion by earthly goods became the fatal mask for their possession by anxiety, fear, and denial.

How the investment of personal property with one's life energy could make people die bit by bit was illustrated throughout the Nazi persecution of the Jews. At the time of the first boycott of Jewish stores, the chief external goal of the Nazis was to acquire the possessions of the Jews. They even let Jews take some things out of the country at that time if they would leave the bulk of their property behind. For a long time the intention of the Nazis, and the goal of their first discriminatory laws, was to force undesirable minorities, including Jews, into emigration.

Although the extermination policy was in line with the inner logic of Nazi racial ideology, one may wonder whether the idea that millions of Jews (and other foreign nationals) could be submitted to extermination did not partially result from seeing the degree of degradation Jews accepted without fighting back. When no violent resistance occurred, persecution of the Jews worsened, slow step by slow step.

Many Jews who on the invasion of Poland were able to survey their situation and draw the right conclusions survived the Second World War. As the Ger-mans approached, they left everything behind and fled to Russia, much as they distrusted and disliked the Soviet system. But there, while badly treated, they could at least survive. Those who stayed on in Poland believing they could go on with life-as-before sealed their fate. Thus in the deepest sense the walk to the gas chamber was only the last consequence of these Jews' inability to com-prehend what was in store; it was the final step of surrender to the death in-stinct, which might also be called the principle of inertia. The first step was taken long before arrival at the death camp.

We can find a dramatic demonstration of how far the surrender to inertia can be carried, and the wish not to know because knowing would create unbearable anxiety, in an experience of Olga Lengyel.[3] She reports that although she and her fellow prisoners lived just a few hundred yards from the crematoria and the gas chambers and knew what they were for, most prisoners denied knowledge of them for months. If they had grasped their true situation, it might have helped them save either the lives they themselves were fated to lose, or the lives of others.

When Mrs. Lengyel's fellow prisoners were selected to be sent to the gas chambers, they did not try to break away from the group, as she successfully did. Worse, the first time she tried to escape the gas chambers, some of the other selected prisoners told the supervisors that she was trying to get away. Mrs. Lengyel desperately asks the question: How was it possible that people denied the existence of the gas chambers when all day long they saw the crematoria burning and smelled the odor of burning flesh? Why did they prefer ignoring the exterminations to fighting for their very own lives? She can offer no explanation, only the observation that they resented anyone who tried to save himself from the common fate, because they lacked enough courage to risk action themselves. I believe they did it because they had given up their will to live and permitted their death tendencies to engulf them. As a result, such prisoners were in the thrall of the murdering SS not only physically but also psychologically, while this was not true for those prisoners who still had a grip on life.

Some prisoners even began to serve their executioners, to help speed the death of their own kind. Then things had progressed beyond simple inertia to the death instinct running rampant. Those who tried to serve their executioners in what were once their civilian capacities were merely continuing life as usual and thereby opening the door to their death.

For example, Mrs. Lengyel speaks of Dr. Mengele, SS physician at Auschwitz, as a typical example of the "business as usual" attitude that enabled some prisoners, and certainly the SS, to retain whatever balance they could despite what they were doing. She described how Dr. Mengele took all correct medical precautions during childbirth, rigorously observing all aseptic principles, cutting the umbilical cord with greatest care, etc. But only half an hour later he sent mother and infant to be burned in the crematorium.

Having made his choice, Dr. Mengele and others like him had to delude themselves to be able to live with themselves and their experience. Only one personal document on the subject has come to my attention, that of Dr. Nyiszli, a prisoner serving as "research physician" at Auschwitz.[4] How Dr. Nyiszli deluded himself can be seen, for example, in the way he repeatedly refers to himself as working in Auschwitz as a physician, although he worked as

_____

[3]Olga Lengyel, *Five Chimneys: The Story of Auschwitz* (Chicago: Ziff-Davis, 1947).
[4]Miklos Nyiszli, *Auschwitz: A Doctor's Eyewitness Account* (New York: Frederick Fell, 1960).

the assistant of a criminal murderer. He speaks of the Institute for Race, Biological, and Anthropological Investigation as "one of the most qualified medical centers of the Third Reich," although it was devoted to proving falsehoods. That Nyiszli was a doctor didn't alter the fact that he—like any of the prisoner foremen who served the SS better than some SS were willing to serve it—was a participant in the crimes of the SS. How could he do it and live with himself?

The answer is: by taking pride in his professional skills, irrespective of the purpose they served. Dr. Nyiszli and Dr. Mengele were only two among hundreds of other—and far more prominent—physicians who participated in the Nazis' murderous pseudo-scientific human experiments. It was the peculiar pride of these men in their professional skill and knowledge, without regard for moral implications, that made them so dangerous. Although the concentration camps and crematoria are no longer here, this kind of pride still remains with us; it is characteristic of a modern society in which fascination with technical competence has dulled concern for human feelings. Auschwitz is gone, but so long as this attitude persists, we shall not be safe from cruel indifference to life at the core.

I have met many Jews as well as gentile anti-Nazis, similar to the activist   40
group in Hungary described earlier, who survived in Nazi Germany and in the occupied countries. These people realized that when a world goes to pieces and inhumanity reigns supreme, man cannot go on living his private life as he was wont to do, and would like to do; he cannot, as the loving head of a family, keep the family living together peacefully, undisturbed by the surrounding world; nor can he continue to take pride in his profession or possessions, when either will deprive him of his humanity, if not also of his life. In such times, one must radically reevaluate all of what one has done, believed in, and stood for in order to know how to act. In short, one has to take a stand on the new reality—a firm stand, not one of retirement into an even more private world.

If today, Negroes in Africa march against the guns of a police that defends *apartheid*—even if hundreds of dissenters are shot down and tens of thousands rounded up in camps—their fight will sooner or later assure them of a chance for liberty and equality. Millions of the Jews of Europe who did not or could not escape in time or go underground as many thousands did, could at least have died fighting as some did in the Warsaw ghetto at the end, instead of passively waiting to be rounded up for their own extermination.

QUESTIONS

1. As part of his evidence, Bettelheim repeatedly refers to and sometimes summarizes parts of the story of Anne Frank. What are the main outlines of her story? What makes it so important?

2. What is Bettelheim's thesis? What is his most urgent message?

3. At times Bettelheim's thesis bears on Nazi resistance during World War II; at times it appears more universal. When does it tip one way, and when another? How do these two messages work together in the essay to strengthen Bettelheim's argument?

4. Bettelheim writes in paragraph 15, "I think it is the fictitious ending that explains the enormous success of this play and movie." Why does Bettelheim suggest that the ending must be fictitious? What evidence does he provide to support this claim?

5. Bettelheim refers to four other stories in print, those of Minco, Levin, Lengyel, and Nyiszli, as well as the case of his own distant relatives. How do these stories serve as evidence? Why do you think Bettelheim decided to arrange them in the order in which they appear?

6. Have you ever observed or learned of a situation in which someone's inaction seemed to increase, rather than decrease, some form of persecution? If so, analyze this situation in light of Bettelheim's essay.

7. Bettelheim seeks to revise his readers' moral understanding of Anne Frank's story. Write an essay in which you argue for revising your readers' understanding of some belief or some conventionally understood situation or story.

MAKING CONNECTIONS

1. Read Robert Jay Lifton's "What Made This Man? Mengele" (p. 371). Bettelheim mentions Mengele, too (paragraphs 37–39). More than that, he offers at least a few hints of what else went into making that man. What would Bettelheim add to Lifton's explanation?

2. Considering the cases Bettelheim discusses in his essay, whatever you know about the struggles of South African blacks, and your knowledge of other contemporary freedom movements, write a position paper on when, if ever, you find it proper to rebel. You may bring any other doctrine you like into this paper—whether it be political, religious, or moral—as long as you explain it clearly and relate its principles to your thesis.

A MODEST PROPOSAL

Jonathan Swift

Jonathan Swift (1667–1745) was born in Dublin, Ireland, of English parents and was educated in Irish schools. A graduate of Trinity College, Dublin, he received a master's degree from Oxford and was ordained a priest in the Church of England in 1695. He was active in politics as well as religion, becoming an editor and pamphlet writer for the Tory party in 1710. After becoming Dean of St. Patrick's Cathedral, Dublin, in 1713, he settled in Ireland and began to take an interest in the English economic exploitation of Ireland, gradually becoming a fierce Irish patriot. By 1724 the English were offering a reward for the discovery of the writer of the Drapier's Letters, *a series of pamphlets secretly written by Swift, attacking the British for their treatment of Ireland. In 1726 Swift produced the first volume of a more universal satire, known to modern readers as* Gulliver's Travels, *which has kept his name alive for 250 years. "A Modest Proposal," his best-known essay on Irish affairs, appeared in 1729.*

A Modest Proposal
*for Preventing the Children of Poor People in Ireland
from Being a Burden to Their Parents or Country,
and for Making Them Beneficial to the Public*

It is a melancholy object to those who walk through this great town,[1] or travel in the country, when they see the streets, the roads and cabin-doors crowded with beggars of the female sex, followed by three, four, or six children, all in rags, and importuning every passenger for an alms. These mothers, instead of being able to work for their honest livelihood, are forced to employ all their time in strolling, to beg sustenance for their helpless infants, who, as they grow up, either turn thieves for want of work, or leave their dear native country to fight for the Pretender in Spain,[2] or sell themselves to the Barbadoes.[3]

---

[1] *this great town:* Dublin. [Eds.]

[2] *Pretender in Spain:* a Catholic descendant of the British royal family (James I, Charles I, and Charles II) of Stuart. Exiled so that England could be governed by Protestant rulers, the Stuarts lurked in France and Spain, preparing various disastrous schemes for regaining the throne. [Eds.]

[3] *sell themselves to the Barbadoes:* sell themselves as indentured servants, a sort of temporary slavery, to the sugar merchants of the British Caribbean islands. [Eds.]

I think it is agreed by all parties that this prodigious number of children, in the arms, or on the backs, or at the heels of their mothers, and frequently of their fathers, is in the present deplorable state of the kingdom a very great additional grievance; and therefore whoever could find out a fair, cheap, and easy method of making these children sound and useful members of the commonwealth would deserve so well of the public as to have his statue set up for a preserver of the nation.

But my intention is very far from being confined to provide only for the children of professed beggars; it is of a much greater extent, and shall take in the whole number of infants at a certain age who are born of parents in effect as little able to support them as those who demand our charity in the streets.

As to my own part, having turned my thoughts for many years upon this important subject, and maturely weighed the several schemes of other projectors, I have always found them grossly mistaken in their computation. It is true a child just dropped from its dam may be supported by her milk for a solar year with little other nourishment, at most not above the value of two shillings,[4] which the mother may certainly get, or the value in scraps, by her lawful occupation of begging, and it is exactly at one year old that I propose to provide for them, in such a manner as, instead of being a charge upon their parents, or the parish, or wanting food and raiment for the rest of their lives, they shall, on the contrary, contribute to the feeding and partly to the clothing of many thousands.

There is likewise another great advantage to my scheme, that it will prevent those voluntary abortions, and that horrid practice of women murdering their bastard children, alas, too frequent among us, sacrificing the poor innocent babes, I doubt, more to avoid the expense than the shame, which would move tears and pity in the most savage and inhuman breast.

The number of souls in Ireland being usually reckoned one million and a half, of these I calculate there may be about two hundred thousand couples whose wives are breeders, from which number I subtract thirty thousand couples who are able to maintain their own children, although I apprehend there cannot be so many under the present distresses of the kingdom, but this being granted, there will remain an hundred and seventy thousand breeders. I again subtract fifty thousand for those women who miscarry, or whose children die by accident or disease within the year. There only remain an hundred and twenty thousand children of poor parents annually born: the question therefore is, how this number shall be reared, and provided for, which as I have already said, under the present situation of affairs is utterly impossible by all the methods hitherto proposed, for we can neither employ them in handicraft or agriculture; we neither build houses (I mean in the country), nor cultivate land: they can very seldom pick up a livelihood by stealing until they arrive at six years old, except where they are of towardly parts, although I confess they learn

---

[4]*shillings:* a shilling used to be worth about one day's labor. [Eds.]

the rudiments much earlier, during which time they can however be properly looked upon only as probationers, as I have been informed by a principal gentleman in the County of Cavan, who protested to me that he never knew above one or two instances under the age of six, even in a part of the kingdom so renowned for the quickest proficiency in that art.

I am assured by our merchants that a boy or girl before twelve years old, is no saleable commodity, and even when they come to this age, they will not yield above three pounds, or three pounds and half-a-crown at most on the Exchange, which cannot turn to account either to the parents or the kingdom, the charge of nutriment and rags having been at least four times that value.

I shall now therefore humbly propose my own thoughts, which I hope will not be liable to the least objection.

I have been assured by a very knowing American of my acquaintance in London, that a young healthy child well nursed is at a year old a most delicious, nourishing and wholesome food, whether stewed, roasted, baked, or boiled, and I make no doubt that it will equally serve in a fricassee, or a ragout.

I do therefore humbly offer it to public consideration, that of the hundred and twenty thousand children already computed, twenty thousand may be reserved for breed, whereof only one fourth part to be males, which is more than we allow to sheep, black-cattle, or swine, and my reason is that these children are seldom the fruits of marriage, a circumstance not much regarded by our savages, therefore one male will be sufficient to serve four females. That the remaining hundred thousand may at a year old be offered in sale to the persons of quality, and fortune, through the kingdom, always advising the mother to let them suck plentifully in the last month, so as to render them plump, and fat for a good table. A child will make two dishes at an entertainment for friends, and when the family dines alone, the fore or hind quarters will make a reasonable dish, and seasoned with a little pepper or salt will be very good boiled on the fourth day, especially in winter.

I have reckoned upon a medium, that a child just born will weigh twelve pounds, and in a solar year if tolerably nursed increaseth to twenty-eight pounds.

I grant this food will be somewhat dear, and therefore very proper for landlords, who, as they have already devoured most of the parents, seem to have the best title to the children.

Infant's flesh will be in season throughout the year, but more plentiful in March, and a little before and after, for we are told by a grave author, an eminent French physician,[5] that fish being a prolific diet, there are more children born in Roman Catholic countries about nine months after Lent than at any other season; therefore reckoning a year after Lent, the markets will be more glutted than usual, because the number of Popish infants is at least three to

---

[5]*French physician:* François Rabelais (1494?–1553), physician and satirist known for his *Gargantua and Pantagruel.* [Eds.]

one in this kingdom, and therefore it will have one other collateral advantage by lessening the number of Papists among us.

I have already computed the charge of nursing a beggar's child (in which list I reckon all cottagers, laborers, and four-fifths of the farmers) to be about two shillings *per annum*, rags included, and I believe no gentleman would repine to give ten shillings for the carcass of a good fat child, which, as I have said, will make four dishes of excellent nutritive meat, when he hath only some particular friend of his own family to dine with him. Thus the Squire will learn to be a good landlord and grow popular among his tenants, the mother will have eight shillings net profit, and be fit for work until she produces another child.

Those who are more thrifty (as I must confess the times require) may flay the carcass; the skin of which artificially dressed, will make admirable gloves for ladies, and summer boots for fine gentlemen.   15

As to our city of Dublin, shambles[6] may be appointed for this purpose, in the most convenient parts of it, and butchers we may be assured will not be wanting, although I rather recommend buying the children alive, and dressing them hot from the knife, as we do roasting pigs.

A very worthy person, a true lover of his country, and whose virtues I highly esteem was lately pleased, in discoursing on this matter to offer a refinement upon my scheme. He said that many gentlemen of this kingdom, having of late destroyed their deer, he conceived that the want of venison might be well supplied by the bodies of young lads and maidens, not exceeding fourteen years of age, nor under twelve, so great a number of both sexes in every county being now ready to starve, for want of work and service: and these to be disposed of by their parents if alive, or otherwise by their nearest relations. But with due deference to so excellent a friend, and so deserving a patriot, I cannot be altogether in his sentiments. For as to the males, my American acquaintance assured me from frequent experience that their flesh was generally tough and lean, like that of our schoolboys, by continual exercise, and their taste disagreeable, and to fatten them would not answer the charge. Then as to the females, it would, I think with humble submission, be a loss to the public, because they soon would become breeders themselves: and besides, it is not improbable that some scrupulous people might be apt to censure such a practice (although indeed very unjustly) as a little bordering upon cruelty, which I confess, hath always been with me the strongest objection against any project, howsoever well intended.

But in order to justify my friend, he confessed that this expedient was put into his head by the famous Psalmanazar, a native of the island Formosa, who came from thence to London, above twenty years ago, and in conversation told my friend that in his country when any young person happened to be put to death, the executioner sold the carcass to persons of quality, as a prime dainty,

---

[6]*shambles:* slaughterhouses. [Eds.]

and that, in his time, the body of a plump girl of fifteen, who was crucified for an attempt to poison the emperor, was sold to his Imperial Majesty's Prime Minister of State, and other great Mandarins of the Court, in joints from the gibbet, at four hundred crowns. Neither indeed can I deny that if the same use were made of several plump young girls in this town who, without one single groat to their fortunes, cannot stir abroad without a chair, and appear at the playhouse and assemblies in foreign fineries, which they never will pay for, the kingdom would not be the worse.

Some persons of a desponding spirit are in great concern about that vast number of poor people, who are aged, diseased, or maimed, and I have been desired to employ my thoughts what course may be taken to ease the nation of so grievous an encumbrance. But I am not in the least pain upon that matter, because it is very well known that they are every day dying, and rotting, by cold, and famine, and filth, and vermin, as fast as can be reasonably expected. And as to the younger laborers they are now in almost as hopeful a condition. They cannot get work, and consequently pine away from want of nourishment, to a degree that if at any time they are accidentally hired to common labor, they have not strength to perform it; and thus the country and themselves are in a fair way of being soon delivered from the evils to come.

I have too long digressed, and therefore shall return to my subject. I think the advantages by the proposal which I have made are obvious and many, as well as of the highest importance. 20

For first, as I have already observed, it would greatly lessen the number of Papists, with whom we are yearly over-run, being the principal breeders of the nation, as well as our most dangerous enemies, and who stay at home on purpose with a design to deliver the kingdom to the Pretender, hoping to take their advantage by the absence of so many good Protestants, who have chosen rather to leave their country than stay at home and pay tithes against their conscience to an idolatrous Episcopal curate.

Secondly, the poorer tenants will have something valuable of their own, which by law may be made liable to distress, and help to pay their landlord's rent, their corn and cattle being already seized, and money a thing unknown.

Thirdly, whereas the maintenance of an hundred thousand children, from two years old, and upwards, cannot be computed at less than ten shillings a piece *per annum*, the nation's stock will be thereby increased fifty thousand pounds *per annum*, besides the profit of a new dish, introduced to the tables of all gentlemen of fortune in the kingdom, who have any refinement in taste, and the money will circulate among ourselves, the goods being entirely of our own growth and manufacture.

Fourthly, the constant breeders, besides the gain of eight shillings sterling *per annum*, by the sale of their children, will be rid of the charge of maintaining them after the first year.

Fifthly, this food would likewise bring great custom to taverns, where the vintners will certainly be so prudent as to procure the best receipts for dressing 25

636

it to perfection, and consequently have their houses frequented by all the fine gentlemen, who justly value themselves upon their knowledge in good eating; and a skillful cook, who understands how to oblige his guests, will contrive to make it as expensive as they please.

Sixthly, this would be a great inducement to marriage, which all wise nations have either encouraged by rewards, or enforced by laws and penalties. It would increase the care and tenderness of mothers towards their children, when they were sure of a settlement for life, to the poor babes, provided in some sort by the public to their annual profit instead of expense. We should soon see an honest emulation among the married women, which of them could bring the fattest child to the market. Men would become as fond of their wives, during the time of their pregnancy, as they are now of their mares in foal, their cows in calf, or sows when they are ready to farrow, nor offer to beat or kick them (as it is too frequent a practice) for fear of a miscarriage.

Many other advantages might be enumerated. For instance, the addition of some thousand carcasses in our exportation of barreled beef; the propagation of swine's flesh, and improvement in the art of making good bacon, so much wanted among us by the great destruction of pigs, too frequent at our tables, are no way comparable in taste or magnificence to a well-grown, fat yearling child, which roasted whole will make a considerable figure at a Lord Mayor's feast, or any other public entertainment. But this and many others I omit, being studious of brevity.

Supposing that one thousand families in this city would be constant customers for infants' flesh, besides others who might have it at merry meetings, particularly weddings and christenings; I compute that Dublin would take off annually about twenty thousand carcasses, and the rest of the kingdom (where probably they will be sold somewhat cheaper) the remaining eighty thousand.

I can think of no one objection that will possibly be raised against this proposal, unless it should be urged that the number of people will be thereby much lessened in the kingdom. This I freely own, and it was indeed one principal design in offering it to the world. I desire the reader will observe, that I calculate my remedy *for this one individual Kingdom of* Ireland, *and for no other that ever was, is, or, I think, ever can be upon earth.* Therefore let no man talk to me of other expedients: *Of taxing our absentees at five shillings a pound: Of using neither clothes, nor household furniture, except what is of our own growth and manufacture: Of utterly rejecting the materials and instruments that promote foreign luxury: Of curing the expensiveness of pride, vanity, idleness, and gaming in our women: Of introducing a vein of parsimony, prudence, and temperance: Of learning to love our country, wherein we differ even from* Laplanders, *and the inhabitants of* Topinamboo: *Of quitting our animosities and factions, nor act any longer like the* Jews, *who were murdering one another at the very moment their city was taken: Of being a little cautious not to sell our country and consciences for nothing: Of teaching landlords to have at least one de-*

gree of mercy towards their tenants. Lastly, *of putting a spirit of honesty, industry, and skill into our shopkeepers, who, if a resolution could now be taken to buy only our native goods, would immediately unite to cheat and exact upon us in the price, the measure and the goodness, nor could ever yet be brought to make one fair proposal of just dealing, though often and earnestly invited to it.*

Therefore I repeat, let no man talk to me of these and the like expedients, till he hath at least a glimpse of hope that there will ever be some hearty and sincere attempt to put them in practice. 30

But as to myself, having been wearied out for many years with offering vain, idle, visionary thoughts, and at length utterly despairing of success, I fortunately fell upon this proposal, which as it is wholly new, so it hath something solid and real, of no expense and little trouble, full in our own power, and whereby we can incur no danger in disobliging England. For this kind of commodity will not bear exportation, the flesh being of too tender a consistence to admit a long continuance in salt, *although perhaps I could name a country which would be glad to eat up our whole nation without it.*

After all I am not so violently bent upon my own opinion as to reject any offer, proposed by wise men, which shall be found equally innocent, cheap, easy and effectual. But before some thing of that kind shall be advanced in contradiction to my scheme, and offering a better, I desire the author, or authors, will be pleased maturely to consider two points. First, as things now stand, how they will be able to find food and raiment for a hundred thousand useless mouths and backs? And secondly, there being a round million of creatures in human figure, throughout this kingdom, whose whole subsistence put into a common stock would leave them in debt two millions of pounds sterling; adding those who are beggars by profession, to the bulk of farmers, cottagers, and laborers with their wives and children, who are beggars in effect; I desire those politicians who dislike my overture, and may perhaps be so bold to attempt an answer, that they will first ask the parents of these mortals whether they would not at this day think it a great happiness to have been sold for food at a year old, in the manner I prescribe, and thereby have avoided such a perpetual scene of misfortunes as they have since gone through, by the oppression of landlords, the impossibility of paying rent without money or trade, the want of common sustenance, with neither house nor clothes to cover them from the inclemencies of weather, and the most inevitable prospect of entailing the like, or greater miseries upon their breed for ever.

I profess in the sincerity of my heart that I have not the least personal interest in endeavoring to promote this necessary work, having no other motive than the *public good of my country, by advancing our trade, providing for infants, relieving the poor, and giving some pleasure to the rich.* I have no children by which I can propose to get a single penny; the youngest being nine years old, and my wife past child-bearing.

QUESTIONS

1. A proposal always involves a proposer. What is the character of the proposer here? Do we perceive his character to be the same throughout the essay? Compare, for example, paragraphs 21, 26, and 33.

2. When does the proposer actually offer his proposal? What does he do before making his proposal? What does he do after making his proposal? How does the order in which he does things affect our impression of him and of his proposal?

3. What kinds of counterarguments to his own proposal does this proposer anticipate? How does he answer and refute proposals that might be considered alternatives to his?

4. In reading this essay, most people are quite certain that the author, Swift, does not himself endorse the proposer's idea. How do we distinguish the two of them? What details of style help us make this distinction?

5. Consider the proposer, the counterarguments he acknowledges and refutes, and Swift himself, who presumably does not endorse the proposal. To what extent is Swift's position essentially that which his proposer refutes? To what extent is it a somewhat different position still?

6. To what extent does an ironic essay like this depend on the author and reader sharing certain values without question or reservation? Can you discover any such values explicitly or implicitly present in Swift's essay?

7. Use Swift's technique to write a "modest proposal" of your own about some contemporary situation. That is, use some outlandish proposal as a way of drawing attention to a situation that needs correcting. Consider carefully the character you intend to project for your proposer and the way you intend to make your own view distinguishable from hers or his.

MAKING CONNECTIONS

Jack E. Henningfield et al.'s "A Proposal to Develop Meaningful Labeling for Cigarettes" (p. 734) follows a form commonly used in the sciences. How does the form of Swift's proposal compare with theirs? Can we consider Henningfield et al.'s proposal truly modest?

THE DECLARATION OF INDEPENDENCE

Thomas Jefferson

Thomas Jefferson (1743–1826) was born in Shadwell, Virginia, attended William and Mary College, and became a lawyer. He was elected to the Virginia House of Burgesses in 1769 and was a delegate to the Continental Congress in 1776. When the Congress voted in favor of Richard Henry Lee's resolution that the colonies "ought to be free and independent states," a committee of five members, including John Adams, Benjamin Franklin, and Jefferson, was appointed to draw up a declaration. Jefferson, because of his eloquence as a writer, was asked by this committee to draw up a first draft. Jefferson's text, with a few changes suggested by Franklin and Adams, was presented to the Congress. After a debate in which further changes were made, including striking out a passage condemning the slave trade, the Declaration was approved on July 4, 1776. Jefferson said of it, "Neither aiming at originality of principles or sentiments, nor yet copied from any particular and previous writing, it was intended to be an expression of the American mind."

In Congress, July 4, 1776
The unanimous Declaration of the
thirteen united States of America

When in the Course of human events it becomes necessary for one people to dissolve the political bands which have connected them with another, and to assume among the powers of the earth, the separate and equal station to which the Laws of Nature and of Nature's God entitle them, a decent respect to the opinions of mankind requires that they should declare the causes which impel them to the separation.

We hold these truths to be self-evident, that all men are created equal, that they are endowed by their Creator with certain unalienable Rights, that among these are Life, Liberty and the pursuit of Happiness. That to secure these rights, Governments are instituted among Men, deriving their just powers from the consent of the governed. That whenever any Form of Government becomes destructive of these ends, it is the Right of the People to alter or to abolish it, and to institute new Government, laying its foundation on such principles and organizing its powers in such form, as to them shall seem most likely to affect their Safety and Happiness. Prudence, indeed, will dictate that Governments long established should not be changed for light and transient causes; and accordingly all experience hath shewn that mankind are more disposed to suffer, while evils are sufferable, than to right themselves by abolishing the forms to which they are accustomed. But when a long train of abuses and usurpations, pursuing invariably the same Object evinces a design to reduce them under absolute Despotism, it is their right, it is their duty, to throw off such Government, and to provide new Guards for their future security. Such has been the patient sufferance of these Colonies; and such is now the necessity which constrains them to alter their former Systems of Government. The history of the present King of Great Britain is a history of repeated injuries and usurpations, all having in direct object the establishment of an absolute Tyranny over these States. To prove this, let Facts be submitted to a candid world.

He has refused his Assent to Laws, the most wholesome and necessary for the public good.

He has forbidden his Governors to pass laws of immediate and pressing importance, unless suspended in their operation till his Assent should be obtained; and when so suspended, he has utterly neglected to attend to them.

He has refused to pass other Laws for the accommodation of large districts 5 of people, unless those people would relinquish the right of Representation in the Legislature, a right inestimable to them and formidable to tyrants only.

He has called together legislative bodies at places unusual, uncomfortable, and distant from the depository of their Public Records, for the sole purpose of fatiguing them into compliance with his measures.

He has dissolved Representative Houses repeatedly, for opposing with manly firmness his invasions on the rights of the people.

He has refused for a long time, after such dissolutions, to cause others to be elected; whereby the Legislative Powers, incapable of Annihilation, have returned to the People at large for their exercise; the State remaining in the mean time exposed to all the dangers of invasion from without, and convulsions within.

He has endeavored to prevent the population of these States; for that purpose obstructing the Laws for Naturalization of Foreigners; refusing to pass others to encourage their migration hither, and raising the conditions of new Appropriations of Lands.

He has obstructed the Administration of Justice, by refusing his Assent to 10 Laws for Establishing Judiciary Powers.

He has made Judges dependent on his Will alone, for the tenure of their offices, and the amount and payment of their salaries.

He has erected a multitude of New Offices, and sent hither swarms of Officers to harass our people, and eat out their substance.

He has kept among us, in times of peace, Standing Armies without the Consent of our legislatures.

He has affected to render the Military independent of and superior to the Civil Power.

He has combined with others to subject us to a jurisdiction foreign to our constitution, and unacknowledged by our laws; giving his Assent to the Acts of pretended Legislation: For quartering large bodies of armed troops among us: For protecting them, by a mock Trial, from punishment for any Murders which they should commit on the Inhabitants of these States: For cutting off our Trade with all parts of the world: For imposing Taxes on us without our Consent: For depriving us in many cases, of the benefits of Trial by Jury: For Transporting us beyond Seas to be tried for pretended offenses: For abolishing the free System of English Laws in a neighboring Province, establishing therein an Arbitrary government, and enlarging its Boundaries so as to render it at once an example and fit instrument for introducing the same absolute rule into these Colonies: For taking away our Charters, abolishing our most valuable Laws and altering fundamentally the Forms of our Governments: For suspending our own Legislatures, and declaring themselves invested with power to legislate for us in all cases whatsoever.

He has abdicated Government here, by declaring us out of his Protection and waging War against us.

He has plundered our seas, ravaged our Coasts, burnt our towns, and destroyed the lives of our people.

He is at this time transporting large Armies of foreign Mercenaries to complete the works of death, desolation and tyranny, already begun with circumstances of Cruelty & Perfidy scarcely paralleled in the most barbarous ages, and totally unworthy the Head of a civilized nation.

He has constrained our fellow Citizens taken Captive on the high Seas to bear Arms against their Country, to become the executioners of their friends and Brethren, or to fall themselves by their Hands.

He has excited domestic insurrections amongst us, and has endeavored to bring on the inhabitants of our frontiers, the merciless Indian Savages, whose known rule of warfare is an undistinguished destruction of all ages, sexes, and conditions.

In every stage of these Oppressions We have Petitioned for Redress in the most humble terms: Our repeated petitions have been answered only by repeated injury. A Prince, whose character is thus marked by every act which may define a Tyrant, is unfit to be the ruler of a free people.

Nor have we been wanting in attention to our British brethren. We have warned them from time to time of attempts by their legislature to extend an unwarrantable jurisdiction over us. We have reminded them of the circumstances of our emigration and settlement here. We have appealed to their native justice and magnanimity, and we have conjured them by the ties of our common kindred to disavow these usurpations, which would inevitably interrupt our connections and correspondence. They too have been deaf to the voice of justice and of consanguinity. We must, therefore, acquiesce in the necessity, which denounces our Separation, and hold them, as we hold the rest of mankind, Enemies in War, in Peace Friends.

We, THEREFORE, the Representatives of the UNITED STATES OF AMERICA, in General Congress, Assembled, appealing to the Supreme Judge of the world for the rectitude of our intentions, do, in the Name, and by Authority of the good People of these Colonies, solemnly publish and declare, That these United Colonies are, and of Right ought to be FREE AND INDEPENDENT STATES; that they are Absolved from all Allegiance to the British Crown, and that all political connection between them and the State of Great Britain, is and ought to be totally dissolved; and that as Free and Independent States; they have full Power to levy War, conclude Peace, contract Alliances, establish Commerce, and to do all the Acts and Things which Independent States may of right do. And for the support of this Declaration, with a firm reliance on the protection of Divine Providence, we mutually pledge to each other our Lives, our Fortunes, and our sacred Honor.

QUESTIONS

1. The Declaration of Independence is frequently cited as a classic deductive argument. A deductive argument is based on a general statement, or premise, that is assumed to be true. What does this document assume that the American colonists are entitled to and on what basis? Look at the reasoning in paragraph 2. What are these truths that are considered self-evident? What does *self-evident* mean?

2. What accusations against the king of Great Britain are the facts presented meant to substantiate? If you were the British king presented with this document, how might you reply to it? Would you attack its premise or reply to its accusations? Or would you do both? (How did George III respond?)

3. To what extent is the audience of the Declaration intended to be the king and people of Great Britain?

4. What other audiences were intended for this document? Define at least two other audiences, and describe how each might be expected to respond.

5. Although this declaration could have been expected to lead to war and all the horrors thereof, it is a most civilized document, showing great respect throughout for certain standards of civility among people and among nations. Try to define the civilized standards that the declaration assumes. Write an essay that tries to identify and characterize the nature and variety of those expectations.

6. Write a declaration of your own, announcing your separation from some injurious situation (an incompatible roommate, a noisy sorority or fraternity house, an awful job, or whatever). Start with a premise, give reasons to substantiate it, provide facts that illustrate the injurious conditions, and conclude with a statement of what your new condition will mean to you and to other oppressed people.

MAKING CONNECTIONS

1. If Jefferson's declaration is a classic deductive argument, as the first question above suggests, Alice Walker's "Am I Blue?" (p. 567) might stand as a clear example of inductive arguing. Review the structure of her argument. Where does she express her thesis most precisely? Why doesn't she announce it more quickly? What would the Declaration look like if Jefferson had approached it inductively? Write an inductive version of the Declaration of Independence.

2. What if, rather than writing the Declaration of Independence, Jefferson had offered "a modest proposal" to the British king? What do you suppose he would have said? How would he have formulated his argument? Write your own "modest proposal" to the king, addressing him more or less in the manner of Jonathan Swift (p. 632), but drawing on the evidence that Jefferson provides in the Declaration.

REVIEW OF STANLEY MILGRAM'S EXPERIMENTS ON OBEDIENCE

Diana Baumrind

Diana Baumrind (b. 1927) is a developmental and clinical psychologist with the Institute of Human Development at the University of California at Berkeley. Her research specialties are "the effects of family socialization on the development of social responsibility and personal agency in children and adolescents" and "the ethics of research with human subjects." That last subject is her topic here as she discusses the experiment conducted by Stanley Milgram (pages 384–408). This article appeared originally in 1964 in American Psychologist, *the journal of the American Psychological Association.*

Certain problems in psychological research require the experimenter to balance his career and scientific interests against the interests of his prospective subjects. When such occasions arise the experimenter's stated objective frequently is to do the best possible job with the least possible harm to his subjects. The experimenter seldom perceives in more positive terms an indebtedness to the subject for his services, perhaps because the detachment which his functions require prevents appreciation of the subject as an individual.

Yet a debt does exist, even when the subject's reason for volunteering includes course credit or monetary gain. Often a subject participates unwillingly in order to satisfy a course requirement. These requirements are of questionable merit ethically, and do not alter the experimenter's responsibility to the subject.

Most experimental conditions do not cause the subjects pain or indignity, and are sufficiently interesting or challenging to present no problem of an ethical nature to the experimenter. But where the experimental conditions expose the subject to loss of dignity, or offer him nothing of value, then the experimenter is obliged to consider the reasons why the subject volunteered and to reward him accordingly.

The subject's public motives for volunteering include having an enjoyable or stimulating experience, acquiring knowledge, doing the experimenter a favor which may some day be reciprocated, and making a contribution to science. These motives can be taken into account rather easily by the experimenter who is willing to spend a few minutes with the subject afterwards to thank him for his participation, answer his questions, reassure him that he did well, and chat with him a bit. Most volunteers also have less manifest, but equally legitimate, motives. A subject may be seeking an opportunity to have contact with, be noticed by, and perhaps confide in a person with psychological training. The dependent attitude of most subjects toward the experimenter is an artifact of the experimental situation as well as an expression of some subjects' personal need systems at the time they volunteer.

The dependent, obedient attitude assumed by most subjects in the experimental setting is appropriate to that situation. The "game" is defined by the experimenter and he makes the rules. By volunteering, the subject agrees implicitly to assume a posture of trust and obedience. While the experimental conditions leave him exposed, the subject has the right to assume that his security and self-esteem will be protected. 5

There are other professional situations in which one member—the patient or client—expects help and protection from the other—the physician or psychologist. But the interpersonal relationship between experimenter and subject additionally has unique features which are likely to provoke initial anxiety in the subject. The laboratory is unfamiliar as a setting and the rules of behavior ambiguous compared to a clinician's office. Because of the anxiety and passivity generated by the setting, the subject is more prone to behave in an obedient, suggestible manner in the laboratory than elsewhere. Therefore, the laboratory is not the place to study degree of obedience or suggestibility, as a function of a particular experimental condition, since the base line for these phenomena as found in the laboratory is probably much higher than in most other settings. Thus experiments in which the relationship to the experimenter as an authority is used as an independent condition are imperfectly designed for the same reason that they are prone to injure the subjects involved. They disregard the special quality of trust and obedience with which the subject appropriately regards the experimenter.

Other phenomena which present ethical decisions, unlike those mentioned above, *can* be reproduced successfully in the laboratory. Failure experience, conformity to peer judgment, and isolation are among such phenomena. In these cases we can expect the experimenter to take whatever measures are necessary to prevent the subject from leaving the laboratory more humiliated, insecure, alienated, or hostile than when he arrived. To guarantee that an especially sensitive subject leaves a stressful experimental experience in the proper state sometimes requires special clinical training. But usually an attitude of compassion, respect, gratitude, and common sense will suffice, and no amount of clinical training will substitute. The subject has the right to expect that the psychologist with whom he is interacting has some concern for his welfare, and the personal attributes and professional skill to express his good will effectively.

Unfortunately, the subject is not always treated with the respect he deserves. It has become more commonplace in sociopsychological laboratory studies to manipulate, embarrass, and discomfort subjects. At times the insult to the subject's sensibilities extends to the journal reader when the results are reported.

Milgram's (1963) study is a case in point. The following is Milgram's abstract of his experiment:

> This article describes a procedure for the study of destructive obedience in the laboratory. It consists of ordering a naïve S to administer increasingly more severe punishment to a victim in the context of a learning experiment. Punishment is administered by means of a shock generator with 30 graded switches ranging from Slight Shock to Danger: Severe Shock. The victim is a confederate of E.[1] The primary dependent variable is the maximum shock the S is willing to administer before he refuses to continue further.[2] 26 Ss obeyed the experimental commands fully, and administered the highest shock on the generator. 14 Ss broke off the experiment at some point after the victim protested and refused to provide further answers. The procedure created extreme levels of nervous tension in some Ss. Profuse sweating, trembling, and stuttering were typical expressions of this emotional disturbance. One unexpected sign of tension—yet to be explained—was the regular occurrence of nervous laughter, which in some Ss developed into uncontrollable seizures. The variety of interesting behavioral dynamics observed in the experiment, the reality of the situation for the S, and the possibility of parametric variation within the framework of the procedure,[3] point to the fruitfulness of further study [p. 371].

The detached, objective manner in which Milgram reports the emotional disturbance suffered by his subjects contrasts sharply with his graphic account of that disturbance. Following are two other quotes describing the effects on his subjects of the experimental conditions:

> I observed a mature and initially poised businessman enter the laboratory smiling and confident. Within 20 minutes he was reduced to a twitching, stuttering wreck, who was rapidly approaching a point of nervous collapse. He constantly pulled on his earlobe, and twisted his hands. At one point he pushed his fist into his forehead and muttered: "Oh God, let's stop it." And yet he continued to respond to every word of the experimenter, and obeyed to the end [p. 377].

> In a large number of cases the degree of tension reached extremes that are rarely seen in sociopsychological laboratory studies. Subjects were observed to sweat, tremble, stutter, bite their lips, groan, and dig their fingernails into their flesh. These were characteristic rather than

---

[1]S: stands for subject; E: stands for experimenter. [Eds.]

[2]*dependent variable:* that which changes as a result of other changes made in the experiment. [Eds.]

[3]*parametric variation:* statistical term suggesting variables within the experiment that would influence the results and so leave some questions unanswered. [Eds.]

exceptional responses to the experiment. One sign of tension was the regular occurrence of nervous laughing fits. Fourteen of the 40 subjects showed definite signs of nervous laughter and smiling. The laughter seemed entirely out of place, even bizarre. Full-blown, uncontrollable seizures were observed for 3 subjects. On one occasion we observed a seizure so violently convulsive that it was necessary to call a halt to the experiment . . . [p. 375].

Milgram does state that,

> After the interview, procedures were undertaken to assure that the subject would leave the laboratory in a state of well being. A friendly reconciliation was arranged between the subject and the victim, and an effort was made to reduce any tensions that arose as a result of the experiment [p. 374].

It would be interesting to know what sort of procedures could dissipate the type of emotional disturbance just described. In view of the effects on subjects, traumatic to a degree which Milgram himself considers nearly unprecedented in sociopsychological experiments, his casual assurance that these tensions were dissipated before the subject left the laboratory is unconvincing.

What could be the rational basis for such a posture of indifference? Perhaps 10 Milgram supplies the answer himself when he partially explains the subject's destructive obedience as follows, "Thus they assume that the discomfort caused the victim is momentary, while the scientific gains resulting from the experiment are enduring [p. 378]." Indeed such a rationale might suffice to justify the means used to achieve his end if that end were of inestimable value to humanity or were not itself transformed by the means by which it was attained.

The behavioral psychologist is not in as good a position to objectify his faith in the significance of his work as medical colleagues at points of breakthrough. His experimental situations are not sufficiently accurate models of real-life experience; his sampling techniques are seldom of a scope which would justify the meaning with which he would like to endow his results; and these results are hard to reproduce by colleagues with opposing theoretical views. Unlike the Sabin vaccine,[4] for example, the concrete benefit to humanity of his particular piece of work, no matter how competently handled, cannot justify the risk that real harm will be done to the subject. I am not speaking of physical discomfort, inconvenience, or experimental deception per se, but of permanent harm, however slight. I do regard the emotional disturbance described by Milgram as potentially harmful because it could easily effect an alteration in the subject's self-image or ability to trust adult authorities in the future. It is potentially harmful to a subject to commit, in the course of an experiment, acts

---

[4]*Sabin vaccine:* an oral vaccine against polio, developed by Albert Bruce Sabin (1906–1993), Polish-born American physician and microbiologist. [Eds.]

which he himself considers unworthy, particularly when he has been entrapped into committing such acts by an individual he has reason to trust. The subject's personal responsibility for his actions is not erased because the experimenter reveals to him the means which he used to stimulate these actions. The subject realizes that he would have hurt the victim if the current were on. The realization that he also made a fool of himself by accepting the experimental set results in additional loss of self-esteem. Moreover, the subject finds it difficult to express his anger outwardly after the experimenter in a self-acceptant but friendly manner reveals the hoax.

A fairly intense corrective interpersonal experience is indicated wherein the subject admits and accepts his responsibility for his own actions, and at the same time gives vent to his hurt and anger at being fooled. Perhaps an experience as distressing as the one described by Milgram can be integrated by the subject,[5] provided that careful thought is given to the matter. The propriety of such experimentation is still in question even if such a reparational experience were forthcoming. Without it I would expect a naive, sensitive subject to remain deeply hurt and anxious for some time, and a sophisticated, cynical subject to become even more alienated and distrustful.

In addition the experimental procedure used by Milgram does not appear suited to the objectives of the study because it does not take into account the special quality of the set which the subject has in the experimental situation. Milgram is concerned with a very important problem, namely, the social consequences of destructive obedience. He says,

> Gas chambers were built, death camps were guarded, daily quotas of corpses were produced with the same efficiency as the manufacture of appliances. These inhumane policies may have originated in the mind of a single person, but they could only be carried out on a massive scale if a very large number of persons obeyed orders [p. 371].

But the parallel between authority-subordinate relationships in Hitler's Germany and in Milgram's laboratory is unclear. In the former situation the SS man or member of the German Officer Corps, when obeying orders to slaughter, had no reason to think of his superior officer as benignly disposed towards himself or their victims. The victims were perceived as subhuman and not worthy of consideration. The subordinate officer was an agent in a great cause. He did not need to feel guilt or conflict because within his frame of reference he was acting rightly.

It is obvious from Milgram's own descriptions that most of his subjects were concerned about their victims and did trust the experimenter, and that their distressful conflict was generated in part by the consequences of these two dis-

---

[5]*integrated:* a technical term in psychology suggesting the process by which we adjust to and incorporate traumatic experience. [Eds.]

parate but appropriate attitudes. Their distress may have resulted from shock at what the experimenter was doing to them as well as from what they thought they were doing to their victims. In any case there is not a convincing parallel between the phenomena studied by Milgram and destructive obedience as that concept would apply to the subordinate-authority relationship demonstrated in Hitler's Germany. If the experiments were conducted "outside of New Haven and without any visible ties to the university," I would still question their validity on similar although not identical grounds. In addition, I would question the representativeness of a sample of subjects who would voluntarily participate within a noninstitutional setting.

In summary, the experimental objectives of the psychologist are seldom incompatible with the subject's ongoing state of well being, provided that the experimenter is willing to take the subject's motives and interests into consideration when planning his methods and correctives. Section 4b in *Ethical Standards of Psychologists* (American Psychological Association, undated) reads in part:

> Only when a problem is significant and can be investigated in no other way, is the psychologist justified in exposing human subjects to emotional stress or other possible harm. In conducting such research, the psychologist must seriously consider the possibility of harmful aftereffects, and should be prepared to remove them as soon as permitted by the design of the experiment. Where the danger of serious aftereffects exists, research should be conducted only when the subjects or their responsible agents are fully informed of this possibility and volunteer nevertheless [p. 12].

From the subject's point of view procedures which involve loss of dignity, self-esteem, and trust in rational authority are probably most harmful in the long run and require the most thoughtfully planned reparations, if engaged in at all. The public image of psychology as a profession is highly related to our own actions, and some of these actions are changeworthy. It is important that as research psychologists we protect our ethical sensibilities rather than adapt our personal standards to include as appropriate the kind of indignities to which Milgram's subjects were exposed. I would not like to see experiments such as Milgram's proceed unless the subjects were fully informed of the dangers of serious aftereffects and his correctives were clearly shown to be effective in restoring their state of well being.

REFERENCES

American Psychological Association. Ethical Standards of Psychologists: A summary of ethical principles. Washington, D.C.: APA, undated.

Milgram, S. Behavioral study of obedience. *J. abnorm. soc. Psychol.*, 1963, 67, 371–378.

QUESTIONS

1. Baumrind challenges Milgram's experiment on two grounds. Distinguish and summarize the two.

2. Baumrind speaks generally for a couple of pages before even mentioning the Milgram experiment. Why do you think she introduces her argument this way? Are there moments during this opening when Milgram's experiment is very much in mind, even without being mentioned?

3. At the end of her article, Baumrind challenges the applicability of Milgram's experiment to events in Hitler's Germany. Does Baumrind represent Milgram's thinking fairly? Do you agree with her that the application does not work? Explain your views.

4. Study Milgram's abstract, quoted by Baumrind in paragraph 8. How do you understand its next-to-last sentence? Do you really find the "nervous laughter" unexplained?

5. See whether your school has a policy about the use of human subjects in experiments. If it has, and its standards are available to the public, get a copy. After studying the policy, write a paper either supporting it or arguing for its amendment.

6. Have you ever been coerced by a situation to mistreat another person, or have you witnessed such mistreatment? Write an analysis of that situation as you remember it. Try to explain the degree to which the situation itself seemed to elicit the questionable behavior. How do you weigh individual responsibility against institutional or group responsibility in this instance?

MAKING CONNECTIONS

1. Stanley Milgram's professed aims (p. 384) included the question of why people obeyed their leaders in Nazi Germany as they did. Read Robert Jay Lifton's essay, "What Made This Man? Mengele" (p. 371), and decide whether Milgram's experiment helps answer that question. How does Baumrind's criticism of Milgram contribute to the discussion?

2. The ethical points that Baumrind raises have certain connections with the issues of animal rights addressed in "Just like Us: A Forum on Animal Rights" by Arthur Caplan et al. (p. 652) and "Animals in Research: The Case for Experimentation" by Frederick A. King (p. 695). What connections do you find among these selections? To what extent is Baumrind addressing something quite different?

3. What do you make of Baumrind's claim that "the laboratory is not the place to study degree of obedience or suggestibility" (paragraph 6)? Do Baumrind's reasons successfully undercut Milgram (p. 384), or has he anticipated that worry?

JUST LIKE US
A Forum on Animal Rights
Arthur Caplan, Gary Francione, Roger Goldman, and Ingrid Newkirk

This discussion of animal rights was held at the Cooper Union for the Advancement of Science and Art, in New York City. The participants approach the subject from a variety of viewpoints. Arthur Caplan is the director of the Center for Biomedical Ethics at the University of Minnesota. Gary Francione is a professor at the University of Pennsylvania Law School and frequently litigates animal rights cases. Roger Goldman is a constitutional law scholar and professor at St. Louis University School of Law. Ingrid Newkirk is the national director of People for the Ethical Treatment of Animals, in Washington. The forum was moderated by Jack Hitt, a contributing editor at Harper's *magazine. The participants debate what qualities determine a right to life. They raise the question of what the proper relationship between humans and animals should be: Do animals have the same rights as humans? During the discussion they seek to expose the assumptions that underlie their opponents' arguments.*

The relationship of man to animal has long been one of sympathy, manifested in such welfare organizations as the kindly Bide-A-Wee or the avuncular ASPCA. In the last few years, the politics of that relationship have been questioned by a number of new and vociferous interest groups which hold to the credo that animals are endowed with certain inalienable rights.

Typically, when animal rights advocates are called upon by the media to defend their views, they are seated across the table from research scientists. The discussion turns on the treatment of laboratory animals or the illegal efforts of fanatics who smuggle animals out of research facilities via latter-day underground railroads to freedom.

Behind these easy headlines, however, stand serious philosophical questions: How should we treat animals? Why do humans have rights and other animals not? If animals had rights, what would they be? To address these questions, *Harper's Magazine* asked two leading animal rights activists to sit down with a philosopher and a constitutional scholar to examine the logic of their opinions.

BUNNIES AND SEWER RATS

JACK HITT: Let me ask a question that many readers might ask: Gary, why have you—a former Supreme Court law clerk and now a professor of law at the University of Pennsylvania—devoted your life to animal rights?

GARY FRANCIONE: I believe that animals have *rights*. This is not to say that animals have the same rights that we do, but the reasons that lead us to accord certain rights to human beings are equally applicable to animals. The problem is that our value system doesn't permit the breadth of vision necessary to understand that. We currently use the category of "species" as the relevant criterion for determining membership in our moral community, just as we once used race and sex to determine that membership.

If you asked white men in 1810 whether blacks had rights, most of them would have laughed at you. What was necessary then is necessary now. We must change the *way* we think: a paradigm shift in the way we think about animals. Rights for blacks and women were *the* constitutional issues of the nineteenth and twentieth centuries. Animal rights, once more people understand the issue, will emerge as *the* civil rights movement of the twenty-first century.

HITT: I want to see where the logic of your beliefs takes us. Suppose I am the head of a company that has invented a dynamite new shampoo. It gives your hair great body; everyone is going to look like Lisa Bonet. But my preliminary tests show that it may cause some irritation or mild damage to the eye. So I've purchased 2,000 rabbits to test this shampoo on their eyes first. Roger, do you find anything offensive about testing shampoo this way?

ROGER GOLDMAN: As someone new to the animal rights issue, I don't find it particularly offensive.

HITT: What if the only thing new about my shampoo is that it is just a different color?

GOLDMAN: If everything else is equal, then I would say the testing is unnecessary.

INGRID NEWKIRK: I think Roger hit the nail on the head. The public has absolutely no idea what the tests involve or whether they're necessary. I think Roger might object if he knew that there were alternatives, that a human-skin patch test can be substituted for the rabbit-blinding test. If consumers were informed, then no compassionate consumer would abide such cruelty.

FRANCIONE: The problem is that we can use animals in any way we like because they are *property*. The law currently regards animals as no different from that pad of paper in front of you, Roger. If you own that pad, you can rip it up or burn it. By and large we treat animals no different than glasses, cups, or paper.

ARTHUR CAPLAN: I know you lawyers love to talk about the property status of these little creatures, but there are other factors. We treat animals as property

653

because people don't believe that animals have any moral worth. People look at rabbits and say, "There are many rabbits. If there are a few less rabbits, who cares?"

NEWKIRK: Not true. Many people, who don't support animal rights, *would* care if you stuck a knife in their rabbit or dog. They're deeply offended by acts of *individual* cruelty.

CAPLAN: Yes, but I suspect that if in your test we substituted ugly sewer rats for button-nosed rabbits, people might applaud the suffering. There are some animals that just don't register in the human consciousness. Rats don't, rabbits might, dogs and horses definitely do.   15

NEWKIRK: Not always. If the test were done to a sewer rat in *front* of a person, the average person would say, "Don't do that" or "Kill him quickly."

HITT: Why?

NEWKIRK: It's institutionalized cruelty, born of our hideous compartmentalized thinking. If the killing is done behind closed doors, if the government says it must be done, or if some man or woman in a white coat assures us that it's for our benefit, we ignore our own ethical good sense and allow it to happen.

HITT: If the frivolity of the original test bothers us, what if we up the ante? What if the product to be tested might yield a cure for baldness?

FRANCIONE: Jack, that is a "utilitarian" argument which suggests that the rightness or wrongness of an action is determined by the *consequences* of that action. In the case of animals, it implies that animal exploitation produces benefits that justify that exploitation. I don't believe in utilitarian moral thought. It's dangerous because it easily leads to atrocious conclusions, both in how we treat humans and how we treat animals. I don't believe it is morally permissible to exploit weaker beings even if we derive benefits.   20

GOLDMAN: So not even the cancer cure?

FRANCIONE: No, absolutely not.

CAPLAN: But you miss the point about moral selfishness. By the time you get to the baldness cure, people start to say, "I don't *care* about animals. My interests are a hell of a lot more important than the animals' interests. So if keeping hair on my head means sacrificing those animals, painlessly or not, I want it." It's not utilitarian—it's selfish.

FRANCIONE: But you certainly wouldn't put that forward as a justification, would you?

CAPLAN: No, it's just a description.   25

FRANCIONE: I can't argue with your assertion that people are selfish. But aren't we morally obliged to assess the consequences of that selfishness? To begin that assessment, people must become aware of the ways in which we exploit animals.

Maybe I'm just a hopeless optimist, but I believe that once people are confronted with these facts, they will reassess. The backlash that we're seeing from the exploitation industries—the meat companies and the biomedical research laboratories — is a reaction of fear. They know that the more people learn, the more people will reject this painful exploitation.

HITT: But won't your movement always be hampered by that mix of moral utilitarianism and moral egotism? People will say, "Yes, be kind to animals up to a point of utilitarianism (so I can have my cancer cure) and up to a point of moral egotism (so I can have my sirloin)." There may be some shift in the moral center, but it will move only so far.

CAPLAN: I agree. Gary can remain optimistic, but confronting people with the facts won't get him very far. Moral egotism extends even into human relations. Let's not forget that we are in a city where you have to step over people to enter this building. People don't say, "Feed, clothe, and house them, and then tax me: I'll pay." We have a limited moral imagination. It may be peculiarly American, but you can show people pictures of starving children or homeless people or animals in leg traps, and many will say, "That's too bad. Life is hard, but I still want my pleasures, my enjoyments."

NEWKIRK: There are two answers to that. First, people accept the myth. They were brought up with the illusion that they *must* eat animals to be healthy. Now we know that's not true. Second, because of humankind's lack of moral — or even just plain — imagination, we activists have to tell people exactly what they *should* do. Then we must make it easier for them to do it. If we put a moral stepladder in front of people, a lot of them will walk up it. But most people feel powerless as individuals and ask, "Who am I? I'm only one person. What can I do?" We must show them.

HITT: Roger, I'm wondering whether your moral center has shifted since we began. Originally you weren't offended by my using 2,000 rabbits to test a new shampoo. Are you now?

GOLDMAN: I am still a utilitarian. But if the test is unnecessary or just repetitive, clearly, I'm persuaded that it should be stopped.

NEWKIRK: Precisely Gary's point. Armed with the facts, Roger opts not to hurt animals.

ENFRANCHISING ALL CREATURES

HITT: Art, what makes human beings have rights and animals not have rights?

CAPLAN: Some would argue a biblical distinction. God created humans in his image and did not create animals that way. That's one special property. Another philosophical basis is natural law, which holds that inalienable rights accrue to being human — that is a distinguishing feature in and of itself.

Personally I reject both those arguments. I subscribe to an entitlement view, which finds these rights grounded in certain innate properties, such as the ability to reason, the ability to suffer —

FRANCIONE: Let's take the ability to suffer and consider it more carefully. The ability to use language or to reason is irrelevant to the right to be free from suffering. Only the ability to feel pain is relevant. Logically, it doesn't follow that you should restrict those rights to humans. On this primary level, the question must be *who* can feel pain, *who* can suffer? Certainly animals must be included within the reach of this fundamental right.

If you don't, then you are basing the right not to suffer pain on "intelligence." Consider the grotesque results if you apply that idea exclusively to human beings. Would you say that a smart person has a right to suffer less pain than a stupid person? That is effectively just what we say with animals. Even though they can suffer, we conclude that their suffering is irrelevant because we think we are smarter than they are.

CAPLAN: The ability to suffer does count, but the level of thinking and consciousness also counts. What makes us human? What grants us the right to life? It is not just a single attribute that makes us human. Rather, there is a cluster of properties: a sense of place in the world, a sense of time, a sense of self-awareness, a sense that one *is* somebody, a sense that one is morally relevant. When you add up these features, you begin to get to the level of entitlement to rights.

FRANCIONE: And I am going to push you to think specifically about rights again. What must you possess in order to have a right to life? I think the most obvious answer is simply a *life!* 40

But let's play this question out in your terms. To have a right to life, you must possess a sense of self, a recollection of the past, and an anticipation of the future, to name a few. By those standards, the chimpanzee—and I would argue, the entire class of Mammalia—would be enfranchised to enjoy a right to life.

NEWKIRK: The question is, do they have an interest in living? If they do, then one has an obligation to recognize their natural rights. The most fundamental of these is a desire to live. They *are* alive, therefore they want to *be* alive, and therefore we should *let* them live.

The more profound question, though, is what distinguishes humans from other animals. Most scientists, at first, thought that what separates us from the other animals is that human beings use tools. So ethnologists went out into the field and returned with innumerable examples of tool use in animals. The scientists then concluded that it's not tool use but the *making* of tools. Ethnologists, such as Geza Teleki, came back with lots of different examples, everything from chimpanzees making fishing poles to ants making boats to cross rivers. One might think they would then elevate the criterion to making tools in *union* workshops, but they switched to "language." Then there was a discussion about what *is* language. Linguists, among them Noam Chomsky and Herbert Terrace, said language possessed certain "components." But when various ethnologists were able to satisfy each of these components, the Cartesian scientists became desperate and kept adding more components, including some pretty complicated ones, such as the ability to recite events in the distant past and to create new words based on past experiences. Eventually the number of components was up to sixteen! The final component was teaching someone else the language. But when Roger Fouts gave the signing ape, Washoe, a son, she independently taught him some seventy American hand-language signs.

CAPLAN: One of the sad facts of the literature of both animal and human rights is that everyone is eager to identify the magic property that separates humans from animals. Is it the ability to suffer? The ability to say something? The ability to say something *interesting!* I think the philosophers are all looking in the right place but are missing something. We have rights because we are *social.*

NEWKIRK: Since all animals are social, then you *would* extend rights to non-humans?   45

CAPLAN: It's not just sociability. Of course, all animals interact, but there is something about the way humans need to interact.

Suppose we were little Ayn Rands who marched about, self-sufficient, proud, and arrogant. If we were able to chop our own wood, cook our own meals, and fend off those who would assault us, then we wouldn't need any rights. You wouldn't need to have a right to free speech if there was no one to talk to!

My point is that our fundamental rights are not exclusively intellectual properties. They are the natural result of the unique way humans have come together to form societies, *dependent* on each other for survival and therefore respectful of each other's rights.

NEWKIRK: None of this differentiates humans from the other animals. You cannot find a relevant attribute in human beings that doesn't exist in animals as well. Darwin said that the only difference between humans and other animals was a difference of degree, not kind. If you ground any concept of human rights in a particular attribute, then animals will have to be included. Animals have rights.

CAPLAN: That brings up another problem I have with your entire argument.   50
Throughout this discussion, I have argued my position in terms of *ethics.* I have spoken about our moral imagination and animal *interests* and human decency. Why? Because I don't want our relationship with animals to be cast as a battle of rights. Only in America, with its obsession for attorneys, courts, judges, and lawsuits, is the entire realm of human relationships reduced to a clash of rights.

So I ask you: Is our relationship with animals best conceived of under the rubric of rights? I don't think so. When I am dispensing rights, I'm relatively chintzy about it. Do embryos have rights? In my opinion, no. Do irretrievably comatose people have rights? I doubt it. Do mentally retarded people below some level of intellectual functioning have rights? Probably not.

There is a wide range of creatures—some of them human—for whom our rights language is not the best way to deal with them. I want people to deal with them out of a sense of fairness or a sense of humanity or a sense of duty, but not out of a claim to rights.

NEWKIRK: I don't like your supremacist view of a custodial responsibility that grants you the luxury to be magnanimous to those beneath you. The rights of animals are not peripheral interests. In this case, we are talking about blood, guts, pain, and death.

FRANCIONE: Art, when you start talking about obligations without rights, you can justify violations of those obligations or intrusions more easily by spinning airy notions of utility. The reason many of our battles are played out in rights language is because our culture has evolved this notion that a right is something that stands between me and an intrusion. A right doesn't yield automatically because a stronger party might benefit.

If a scientist could cure cancer—without fail—by subjecting me against   55
my will to a painful experiment, it wouldn't matter. I have a right not to be used that way.

CAPLAN: Ironically, I agree with you. That's exactly the role that rights language plays. It defines the barriers or lines that can't be crossed. But if you hand out rights willy-nilly, you lose that function.

NEWKIRK: When should we stop?

CAPLAN: I'm not sure I know the answer, but if you cheapen the currency of rights language, you've got to worry that rights may not be taken seriously. Soon you will have people arguing that trees have rights and that embryos have rights. And the tendency would be to say, "Sure, they have rights, but they are not *important* rights."

NEWKIRK: Art, wouldn't you rather err on the side of giving out too many rights rather than too few?

CAPLAN: No.   60

NEWKIRK: So, according to your view, maybe we should take away some of the rights we've already granted. After all, granting rights to blacks and women has deprived society of very important things, such as cheap labor. That a society evolves and expands its protective shield should not daunt us. That's like saying, if I continue to be charitable, my God, where will it ever end?

CAPLAN: It may not be rights or bust. There may be other ways to get people to conduct themselves decently without hauling out the heavy artillery of rights language every time.

NEWKIRK: People have to be pushed; society has to be pushed. Those who care deeply about a particular wrong have to pressure the general population. Eventually a law is passed, and then adjustments are made to correct past injustices. You have to bring these matters to a head.

HITT: Roger, from a constitutional perspective, do you think that rights are cheapened when they are broadened?

GOLDMAN: When you put it in a constitutional context, you invite conflict.   65
That's inevitable. If you have a free press, you're going to have fair trial problems. If you start expanding rights of liberty, you run up against rights of
equality. I don't think expansion cheapens them, but by elevating animal
rights to a constitutional issue, you certainly multiply the difficulties.

HITT: You could argue that conflict strengthens rights. If you had no conflict
over free speech, would we have the solid right to free speech that we have
today?

GOLDMAN: It depends on who wins. What would happen if free speech lost?

FRANCIONE: Roger, you will have conflict and difficulties whether you cast
our relationship with animals as one of obligations *or* rights. The real question is, are those obligations enforceable by state authority? If they are, there
will be clashes and we will turn to the courts for resolution.

CAPLAN: Gary, I would like those obligations enforced by the authority, if
you like, of empathy, by the power of character. What matters is how people
view animals, how their feelings are touched by those animals, what drives
them to care about those animals, not what rights the animals have.

FRANCIONE: I agree that you don't effect massive social change exclusively   70
through law, but law can certainly help. That's a classic law school debate:
Do moral perceptions shape law or does law shape moral perceptions? It
probably goes both ways. I have no doubt that we could effect a great change
if animals were included within our constitutional framework.

NEWKIRK: Great changes often begin with the law. Remember the 1760s
case of the West Indian slave Jonathan Strong. Strong's master had abandoned him in England after beating him badly. The judge in that case
feared the consequences of emancipating a slave. But the judge freed Strong
and declared, "Let justice prevail, though the heavens may fall."

MOJO, THE TALKING CHIMPANZEE

HITT: Meet Mojo, the signing chimpanzee. Mojo is female and has learned
more words than any other chimpanzee. One day you're signing away with
Mojo, and she signs back, "I want a baby." Roger, are we under any obligation to grant her wish?

GOLDMAN: Since I am not persuaded animals have any rights, I don't believe
there is any obligation.

HITT: Doesn't it follow that if this chimpanzee can articulate a desire to have
a child—a primal desire and one that we would never forbid humans—we
have some obligation to fulfill it?

CAPLAN: You are alluding to a foundation for rights that we haven't yet dis-   75
cussed. Is the requirement for possessing a right the ability to *claim* it? That
is, in order to hold a right to life, one must be able to articulate a claim to
life, to be able to say, "I want to live."

659

There may be animals that can get to that level, and Mojo may be one of them. Nevertheless, I don't buy into that argument. Simply being able to claim a right does not necessarily entail an obligation to fulfill it.

FRANCIONE: But Mojo does have the right to be left alone to pursue her desires, the right *not* to be in that cage. Aren't we violating some right of Mojo's by confining her so that she cannot satisfy that primal desire?

HITT: Is this a fair syllogism? Mojo wants to be free; a right to freedom exists if you can claim it; ergo, Mojo has a right to be free. Does the ability to lay claim to a right automatically translate into the *possession* of such a right?

CAPLAN: You don't always generate obligations and duties from a parallel set of rights, matching one with another.

Look at the relationship that exists between family members. Some people might argue that children have certain rights to claim from their parents. But there is something wrong with that assumption. Parents have many obligations to their children, but it seems morally weird to reduce this relationship to a contractual model. It's not a free-market arrangement where you put down a rights chit, I put down an obligation chit, and we match them up.

My kid might say to me, "Dad, you have an obligation to care for my needs, and my need today is a new car." I don't enter into a negotiation based on a balancing of his rights and my duties. That is not the proper relationship.

NEWKIRK: But having a car is not a fundamental right, whereas the right not to be abused is. For example, children have a right not to be used in factories. That right had to be fought for in exactly the same way we are fighting for animal rights now.

CAPLAN: Gary, I want to press you further. A baby needs a heart, and some scientist believes the miniature swine's heart will do it.

FRANCIONE: Would I take a healthy pig, remove its heart, and put it into the child? No.

CAPLAN: I am stymied by your absolutist position that makes it impossible even to consider the pig as a donor.   85

FRANCIONE: What if the donor were a severely retarded child instead of a pig?

CAPLAN: No, because I've got to worry about the impact not only on the donor but on society as well.

FRANCIONE: Art, assume I have a three-year-old prodigy who is a mathematical wizard. The child has a bad heart. The only way to save this prodigy is to take the heart out of another child. Should we *consider* a child from a low socio-economic background who has limited mental abilities?

CAPLAN: You're wandering around a world of slopes, and I want to wander around a world of steps. I have argued strongly in my writing that it is possible for a human being—specifically an infant born with anencephaly, that is, without most of its brain—to drop below the threshold of a right to life. I think it would be ethical to use such a baby as a source for organ transplants.

I do not believe there is a slippery slope between the child born with most of its brain missing and the retarded. There are certain thresholds below which one can make these decisions. At some point along the spectrum of life—many people would say a pig, and I would go further to include the anencephalic baby—we are safely below that threshold.

FRANCIONE: You can't equate the pig with the anencephalic infant. The anencephalic child is not the subject of a life in any meaningful sense. That is to say, it does not possess that constellation of attributes—sense of self-awareness, anticipation of the future, memory of the past—that we have been discussing. The pig is clearly the subject of a meaningful life. 90

CAPLAN: But if it's a matter of saving the life of the baby, then I want a surgeon to saw out the pig's heart and put it in the baby's chest.

NEWKIRK: The pig can wish to have life, liberty and the pursuit of happiness, and the anencephalic baby cannot.

CAPLAN: But you must also consider the effect on others. I don't think it's going to matter very much what the pig's parents think about that pig. Whereas the child's parents care about the baby, and they don't care about the pig.

FRANCIONE: Then you change their reaction.

CAPLAN: I don't want to change their reaction. I want human beings to care about babies. 95

NEWKIRK: Like racism or sexism, that remark is pure speciesism.

CAPLAN: Speciesism! Mine is a legitimate distinction. The impact of this transplant is going to be different on humans than on lower animals.

NEWKIRK: "Lower animals." There comes speciesism rearing its ugly head again. Look, Art, I associate with the child; I don't associate with the pig. But we can't establish why that matters *except* that you are human and I am human.

If a building were burning and a baby baboon, a baby rat, and a baby child were inside, I'm sure I would save the child. But if the baboon mother went into the building, I'm sure she would take out the infant baboon. It's just that there is an instinct to save yourself first, then your immediate family, your countrymen, and on to your species. But we have to recognize and reject the self-interest that erects these barriers and try to recognize the rights of others who happen not to be exactly like ourselves.

CAPLAN: I think you can teach humans to care about the pig. The morally relevant factor here is that you will never get the pig to care about *me*. 100

NEWKIRK: Not true, Art. Read John Robbin's new book, *Diet for a New America*, in which he lists incidents of altruism by animals outside their own species. Everybody knows about dolphins rescuing sailors. Recently a pig rescued a child from a frozen lake and won an award!

CAPLAN: To the extent to which you can make animals drop *their* speciesism, perhaps you will be persuasive on this point.

NEWKIRK: Art, if you don't recognize my rights, that's tough for me. But that doesn't mean my rights don't exist.

FRANCIONE: If blacks, as a group, got together and said, "We're going to make a conscious decision to dislike non-blacks," would you say that black people no longer had rights?

CAPLAN: No, but I would hold them accountable for their racism. I could   105
never hold a pig accountable for its speciesism. And I am never going to see a meeting of pigs having that kind of conversation.

NEWKIRK: That happens when the Ku Klux Klan meets, and the ACLU upholds their rights.

CAPLAN: The difference is that there are certain things I expect of blacks, whites, yellows—of all human beings and maybe a few animals. But I am not going to hold the vast majority of animals to those standards.

NEWKIRK: So the punishment for their perceived deficiencies—which, incidentally, is shared by the human baby—is to beat them to death.

CAPLAN: I didn't say that. I am trying to reach for something that isn't captured by the speciesist charge. The difference between people and animals is that I can persuade people. I can *stimulate* their moral imaginations. But I can't do that with most animals, and I want that difference to count.

A WORLD WITH NO DANCING BEARS

HITT: How would you envision a society that embraced animal rights? What   110
would happen to pets?

NEWKIRK: I don't use the word "pet." I think it's speciesist language. I prefer "companion animal." For one thing, we would no longer allow breeding. People could not create different breeds. There would be no pet shops. If people had companion animals in their homes, those animals would have to be refugees from the animal shelters and the streets. You would have a protective relationship with them just as you would with an orphaned child. But as the surplus of cats and dogs (artificially engineered by centuries of forced breeding) declined, eventually companion animals would be phased out, and we would return to a more symbiotic relationship—enjoyment at a distance.

FRANCIONE: Much more than that would be phased out. For example, there would be no animals used for food, no laboratory experiments, no fur coats, and no hunting.

GOLDMAN: Would there be zoos?

FRANCIONE: No zoos.

HITT: Circuses?   115

FRANCIONE: Circuses would have to change. Look, right now we countenance the taking of an animal from the wild—a bear—dressing that bear in a *skirt* and parading it in front of thousands of people while it balances a ball on its nose. When you think about it, that is perverted.

662

HITT: Let's say that your logic prevails. People are sickened by dancing bears and are demanding a constitutional amendment. What would be the language of a Bill of Rights for animals?

NEWKIRK: It already exists. It's "life, liberty, and the pursuit of happiness." We just haven't extended it far enough.

GOLDMAN: I am assuming your amendment would restrict not only government action but private action as well. Our Constitution restricts only government action. The single exception is the Thirteenth Amendment, which prohibits both the government and the individual from the practice of slavery.

HITT: To whom would these rights apply? Would they apply among animals   120
themselves? Does the lion have to recognize the gazelle's right to life?

NEWKIRK: That's not our business. The behavior of the lion and the gazelle is a "tribal" issue, if you will. Those are the actions of other nations, and we cannot interfere.

GOLDMAN: What if we knew the lion was going to kill the gazelle—would we have an obligation to stop it?

NEWKIRK: It's not our business. This amendment restricts only our code of behavior.

HITT: But what Roger is asking is, should the amendment be so broad as to restrict both individual and government action?

FRANCIONE: It should be that broad. Of course, it would create a lot of issues   125
we would have to work out. First, to whom would we extend these rights? I have a sneaking suspicion that any moment someone in this room will say, "But what about cockroaches? Will they have these rights? Do they have the right to have credit cards?" Hard questions would have to be answered, and we would have to determine which animals would hold rights and how to translate these rights into concrete protections from interference.

NEWKIRK: The health pioneer W. K. Kellogg limited it to "all those with faces." If you can look into the eyes of another, and that other looks back, that's one measure.

So the amendment shouldn't be limited, as some animal rights advocates think, to mammals, because we know that birds, reptiles, insects, and fishes all feel pain. They are capable of wanting to be alive. As long as we know that they have these primal interests, then I think we need to explore down the line—if we think it is down.

GOLDMAN: Let me go up the line. What about humans?

NEWKIRK: They would be just another animal in the pack.

GOLDMAN: But your amendment would massively expand the reach of the   130
Constitution for humans. For example, the Constitution does not require states to provide rights for victims of crime. Under your proposal, if a state decriminalized adultery, shoplifting, or even murder, the victim's *constitutional* rights would be violated.

CAPLAN: And if we take the face test, how is that going to affect the way we treat the unborn? Must we enfranchise our fetuses? That's going to be the end of abortion.

FRANCIONE: Not necessarily. I am fairly comfortable with the notion that a fetus does not have a right to life. But that is not to say that a fetus doesn't have a right to be free from suffering. Fetuses do feel pain and they *ought* to be free from suffering. But it doesn't make sense to talk about a fetus having a sense of the past, anticipation of the future, and a sense of interaction with others.

CAPLAN: But a mouse?

FRANCIONE: Sure.

CAPLAN: I guess we can experiment on and eat all the animal fetuses we want.   135

FRANCIONE: I didn't say you had a right to inflict pain on animal fetuses. I don't think you have a right to inflict pain on human fetuses.

CAPLAN: Are you suggesting that we can't inflict pain, but we can kill them?

NEWKIRK: You are talking about the manner in which abortions are currently performed, not whether they should be performed. Our standard of lack of suffering holds up if you apply it across the board, for human and non-human fetuses.

GOLDMAN: Let me see if I can bring together those who advocate animal welfare with those who believe animals hold rights. What about a different amendment, similar to the difference between the Thirteenth Amendment, which is an absolute ban on slavery, and the Fourteenth Amendment, which bans discrimination, but not absolutely. In fact, the Fourteenth allows us to take race into account sometimes, such as affirmative action. Do the animal rights activists see a role for a limited amendment similar to the Fourteenth? It would broadly protect animals from unnecessary suffering, but allow for some medical experiments.

FRANCIONE: Does your amendment simply expand the word "persons" in the   140
Fourteenth Amendment to include animals?

GOLDMAN: No, but it is modeled on Fourteenth Amendment jurisprudence. It would not permit experimentation on animals unless necessary for a compelling need.

FRANCIONE: I would favor this approach if the experimenter had the burden to show the compelling need. I would have only one problem with adjudication under this compelling-need standard. My fear is that the balance would always favor the biomedical research community. Everyone agrees that no one should needlessly use animals in experimentation. Yet we all know that millions of animals are being used for frivolous purposes. That is because the biomedical researchers have persuaded enough people that their experiments are so important they have become "compelling" by definition.

GOLDMAN: Of course the difference with this constitutional amendment is that it wouldn't pass unless two-thirds of Congress and three-fourths of the states backed it. So if we're projecting a hundred years from now, you won't have the problem of science experts always prevailing.

FRANCIONE: Roger, I would retire tomorrow if I could get your amendment. The problem is that our society economically *benefits* from exploitation. The animal industries are so strong that they have shaped an entire *value* system that justifies and perpetuates exploitation. So I am not sure your compelling-need test would result in anything substantially different from what we have now. That's why I favor a hard rights notion, to protect the defenseless absolutely. As soon as you let in the "balancers," people such as Art Caplan, you've got trouble.

CAPLAN: The problem with your constitutional amendment is that, finally, it is irrelevant to human behavior. When the lawyers, the constitutional adjudicators, and the Supreme Court justices aren't there, when it's just me and my companion animal or my bug in the woods, where are the animal's rights then? 145

There was a time when I was a little boy running around in the woods in New England. It was just a bunch of Japanese beetles in a jar and me. The question was: How is little Art going to deal with those Japanese beetles? Pull their wings off? Never let them out of the jar? Step on them? What do I do with those bugs? What do I think of bugs? No Supreme Court justice is going to tell me what to do with them.

NEWKIRK: A lot of these conflicts of moral obligation result from the wide variety of *unnatural* relationships we have with animals in the first place — whether it's little Art with his jar of Japanese beetles, or the scientist in the lab with his chimpanzee, or any one of us at home with a cat. Just take the single issue of the sterilization of pets. We now have burdened ourselves with the custodial obligation to sterilize thousands of animals because we have screwed up their reproductive cycles so much through domestication and inbreeding that they have many more offspring than they normally would. What would happen if we just left animals alone, to possess their own dignity? You know, you mentioned earlier that there is something cruel in the lion chasing down and killing the gazelle. Well, nature *is* cruel, but man is crueler yet.

QUESTIONS

1. One of the central questions of this forum, and of all discussions of animal rights, is, What makes human beings have rights and animals not have rights? How does each of the participants in the forum seek to answer this question?

2. Newkirk asks, "What distinguishes humans from other animals?" (paragraph 43). How does each of the participants respond to this question? What assumptions underlie these various responses?

3. Francione states in paragraph 70, "That's a classic law school debate: Do moral perceptions shape law or does law shape moral perceptions?" Do you think that massive social change can be influenced by legislation protecting animal rights? How would our society change, according to some of the forum participants, if we embraced animal rights?

4. Should all animals have rights? In paragraph 125, one of the forum participants discusses the question, "But what about cockroaches?" Are you persuaded by any of the participants' positions? If animals have rights, what kind of rights should they be? How do you respond to this issue?

5. Newkirk concludes the forum with this powerful thought: "Well, nature *is* cruel, but man is crueler yet." How do you respond to this thought? Write an essay in which you develop your position on animal rights in the context of this comment.

6. Thomas Jefferson opens the Declaration of Independence (p. 640) by stating directly the "self-evident truths" upon which his argument is based. In fact, every argument depends on an appeal to certain unquestioned values, to a body of "truths" that the writer assumes the audience accepts (although not every writer states these "truths" as explicitly as Jefferson). Take two of the participants in this forum and try to determine the values these participants assume — not the views being argued, but the accepted "truths" on which their arguments depend. Write an essay in which you analyze the accepted truths that provide the basis for their positions.

MAKING CONNECTIONS

1. In "Animals in Research: The Case for Experimentation" (p. 695), Frederick A. King draws Arthur Caplan, one of the participants of this forum, into his argument, using Caplan to support his case for using animals in experiments. Do you think Caplan would agree with the case King is making? Where, if anywhere, would Caplan quarrel with King?

2. The first paragraph of this forum alludes to Thomas Jefferson's Declaration of Independence (p. 640). Imagine a "Continental Congress" of animals preparing to declare its independence from humans. Imagine further that you are a delegate, cast as one of whatever species you prefer, and you have been assigned the role Jefferson once held, to draft an animals' Declaration of Independence. What would you say? What evidence would you bring to your task? Go ahead and draft it.

3. Several selections in this collection focus on the special regard of humans for animals, at least for some species. Farley Mowat's "Observing Wolves" (p. 237), Jane van Lawick-Goodall's "First Observations" (p. 241), and Vicki Hearne's "What's Wrong with Animal Rights" (p. 667) are examples. Imagine at least two of these writers participating in this forum. Where would they break in? What would they say? Rewrite a section of this forum including two of these writers as participants.

WHAT'S WRONG WITH ANIMAL RIGHTS
Of Hounds, Horses, and Jeffersonian Happiness

Vicki Hearne

Vicki Hearne (b. 1946) is an animal trainer, a poet (The Parts of Light: Poems, 1994), and a writer of fiction (Adam's Task: Calling the Animals by Name, 1987) and nonfiction (Bandit: Dossier of a Dangerous Dog, 1991). She is also a teacher and a contributing editor at Harper's magazine, where this essay first appeared with the subtitle, "Of Hounds, Horses, and Jeffersonian Happiness" (1991).

Not all happy animals are alike. A Doberman going over a hurdle after a small wooden dumbbell is sleek, all arcs of harmonious power. A basset hound cheerfully performing the same exercise exhibits harmonies of a more lugubrious nature. There are chimpanzees who love precision the way musicians or fanatical housekeepers or accomplished hypochondriacs do; others for whom happiness is a matter of invention and variation—chimp vaudevillians. There is a rhinoceros whose happiness, as near as I can make out, is in needing to be trained every morning, all over again, or else he "forgets" his circus routine, and in this you find a clue to the slow, deep, quiet chuckle of his happiness and to the glory of the beast. Happiness for Secretariat is in his ebullient bound, that joyful length of stride. For the draft horse or the weight-pull dog, happiness is of a different shape, more awesome and less obviously intelligent. When the pulling horse is at its most intense, the animal goes into himself, allocating all of the educated power that organizes his desire to dwell in fierce and delicate intimacy with that power, leans into the harness, and MAKES THAT SUCKER MOVE.

If we speaking of human beings and use the phrase "animal happiness," we tend to mean something like "creature comforts." The emblems of this are the golden retriever rolling in the grass, the horse with his nose deep in the oats, the kitty by the fire. Creature comforts are important to animals—"Grub first, then ethics" is a motto that would describe many a wise Labrador retriever, and I have a pit bull named Annie whose continual quest for the perfect pillow inspires her to awesome feats. But there is something more to animals, a capacity for satisfactions that come from work in the fullest sense—what is known in philosophy and in this country's Declaration of Independence as "happiness." This is a sense of personal achievement, like the satisfaction felt by a good wood-carver or a dancer or a poet or an accomplished dressage horse. It is a

667

happiness that, like the artist's, must come from something within the animal, something trainers call "talent." Hence, it cannot be imposed on the animal. But it is also something that does not come *ex nihilo*. If it had not been a fairly ordinary thing, in one part of the world, to teach young children to play the pianoforte, it is doubtful that Mozart's music would exist.

Happiness is often misunderstood as a synonym for pleasure or as an antonym for suffering. But Aristotle associated happiness with ethics—codes of behavior that urge us toward the sensation of getting it right, a kind of work that yields the "click" of satisfaction upon solving a problem or surmounting an obstacle. In his *Ethics*, Aristotle wrote, "If happiness is activity in accordance with excellence, it is reasonable that it should be in accordance with the highest excellence." Thomas Jefferson identified the capacity for happiness as one of the three fundamental rights on which all others are based: "life, liberty, and the pursuit of happiness."

I bring up this idea of happiness as a form of work because I am an animal trainer, and work is the foundation of the happiness a trainer and an animal discover together. I bring up these words also because they cannot be found in the lexicon of the animal-rights movement. This absence accounts for the uneasiness toward the movement of most people, who sense that rights advocates have a point but take it too far when they liberate snails or charge that goldfish at the county fair are suffering. But the problem with the animal-rights advocates is not that they take it too far; it's that they've got it all wrong.

Animal rights are built upon a misconceived premise that rights were created to prevent us from unnecessary suffering. You can't find an animal-rights book, video, pamphlet, or rock concert in which someone doesn't mention the Great Sentence, written by Jeremy Bentham in 1789. Arguing in favor of such rights, Bentham wrote: "The question is not, Can they *reason*? nor, can they *talk*? but, can they suffer?" 5

The logic of the animal-rights movement places suffering at the iconographic center of a skewed value system. The thinking of its proponents—given eerie expression in a virtually sado-pornographic sculpture of a tortured monkey that won a prize for its compassionate vision—has collapsed into a perverse conundrum. Today the loudest voices calling for—demanding—the destruction of animals are the humane organizations. This is an inevitable consequence of the apotheosis of the drive to relieve suffering: Death is the ultimate release. To compensate for their contradictions, the humane movement has demonized, in this century and the last, those who made animal happiness their business: veterinarians, trainers, and the like. We think of Louis Pasteur as the man whose work saved you and me and your dog and cat from rabies, but antivivisectionists of the time claimed that rabies increased in areas where there were Pasteur Institutes.

An anti-rabies public-relations campaign mounted in England in the 1880s by the Royal Society for the Prevention of Cruelty to Animals and other organizations led to orders being issued to club any dog found not wearing a muzzle. England still has her cruel and unnecessary law that requires an animal to spend six months in quarantine before being allowed loose in the country. Most of the recent propaganda about pit bulls—the crazy claim that they "take hold with their front teeth while they chew away with their rear teeth" (which would imply, incorrectly, that they have double jaws)—can be traced to literature published by the Humane Society of the United States during the fall of 1987 and earlier. If your neighbors want your dog or horse impounded and destroyed because he is a nuisance—say the dog barks, or the horse attracts flies—it will be the local Humane Society to whom your neighbors turn for action.

In a way, everyone has the opportunity to know that the history of the humane movement is largely a history of miseries, arrests, prosecutions, and death. The Humane Society is the pound, the place with the decompression chamber or the lethal injections. You occasionally find worried letters about this in Ann Landers's column.

Animal-rights publications are illustrated largely with photographs of two kinds of animals—"Helpless Fluff" and "Agonized Fluff," the two conditions in which some people seem to prefer their animals, because any other version of an animal is too complicated for propaganda. In the introduction to his book *Animal Liberation*, Peter Singer says somewhat smugly that he and his wife have no animals and, in fact, don't much care for them. This is offered as evidence of his objectivity and ethical probity. But it strikes me as an odd, perhaps obscene, underpinning for an ethical project that encourages university and high school students to cherish their ignorance of, say, great bird dogs as proof of their devotion to animals.

I would like to leave these philosophers behind, for they are inept connoisseurs of suffering who might revere my Airedale for his capacity to scream when subjected to a blowtorch but not for his wit and courage, not for his natural good manners that are a gentle rebuke to ours. I want to celebrate the moment not long ago when, at his first dog show, my Airedale, Drummer, learned that there can be a public place where his work is respected. I want to celebrate his meticulousness, his happiness upon realizing at the dog show that no one would swoop down upon him and swamp him with the goo-goo excesses, known as the "teddy-bear complex" but that people actually got out of his way, gave him room to work. I want to say, "There can be a six-and-half-month-old puppy who can care about accuracy, who can be fastidious, and whose fastidiousness will be a foundation for courage later." I want to say, "Leave my puppy alone!"

I want to leave the philosophers behind, but I cannot, in part because the philosophical problems that plague academicians of the animal-rights movement are illuminating. They wonder, do animals have rights or do they have interests? Or, if these rightists lead particularly unexamined lives, they dismiss

10

that question as obvious (yes, of course, animals have rights, prima facie) and proceed to enumerate them, James Madison style. This leads to the issuance of bills of rights—the right to an environment, the right not to be used in medical experiments—and other forms of trivialization.

The calculus of suffering can be turned against the philosophers of festering flesh, even in the case of food animals, or exotic animals who perform in movies and circuses. It is true that it hurts to be slaughtered by man, but it doesn't hurt nearly as much as some of the cunningly cruel arrangements meted out by "Mother Nature." In Africa, 75 percent of the lions cubbed do not survive to the age of two. For those who make it to two, the average age at death is ten years. Asali, the movie and TV lioness, was still working at age twenty-one. There are fates worse than death, but twenty-one years of a close working relationship with Hubert Wells, Asali's trainer, is not one of them. Dorset sheep and polled Herefords would not exist at all were they not in a symbiotic relationship with human beings.

A human being living in the "wild"—somewhere, say, without the benefits of medicine and advanced social organization—would probably have a life expectancy of from thirty to thirty-five years. A human being living in "captivity"—in, say, a middle-class neighborhood of what the Centers for Disease Control call a Metropolitan Statistical Area—has a life expectancy of seventy or more years. For orangutans in the wild in Borneo and Malaysia, the life expectancy is thirty-five years; in captivity, fifty years. The wild is not a suffering-free zone or all that frolicsome a location.

The questions asked by animal-rights activists are flawed, because they are built on the concept that the origin of rights is in the avoidance of suffering rather than in the pursuit of happiness. The question that needs to be asked—and that will put us in closer proximity to the truth—is not, do they have rights? or, what are those rights? but rather, what is a right?

Rights originate in committed relationships and can be found, both intact and violated, wherever one finds such relationships—in social compacts, within families, between animals, and between people and nonhuman animals. This is as true when the nonhuman animals in question are lions or parakeets as when they are dogs. It is my Airedale whose excellencies have my attention at the moment, so it is with reference to him that I will consider the question, what is a right?

When I imagine situations in which it naturally arises that A defends or honors or respects B's rights, I imagine situations in which the relationship between A and B can be indicated with a possessive pronoun. I might say, "Leave her alone, she's my daughter" or, "That's what she wants, and she is my daughter. I think I am bound to honor her wants." Similarly, "Leave her alone, she's my mother." I am more tender of the happiness of my mother, my father, my child, than I am of other people's family members; more tender of my friends' happinesses than your friends' happinesses, unless you and I have a mutual friend.

Possession of a being by another has come into more and more disrepute, so that the common understanding of one person possessing another is slavery. But the important detail about the kind of possessive pronoun that I have in mind is reciprocity: If I have a friend, she has a friend. If I have a daughter, she has a mother. The possessive does not bind one of us while freeing the other; it cannot do that. Moreover, should the mother reject the daughter, the word that applies is "disown." The form of disowning that most often appears in the news is domestic violence. Parents abuse children; husbands batter wives.

Some cases of reciprocal possessives have built-in limitations, such as "my patient/my doctor" or "my student/my teacher" or "my agent/my client." Other possessive relations are extremely limited but still remarkably binding: "my neighbor" and "my country" and "my president."

The responsibilities and the ties signaled by reciprocal possession typically are hard to dissolve. It can be as difficult to give up an enemy as to give up a friend, and often the one becomes the other, as though the logic of the possessive pronoun outlasts the forms it chanced to take at a given moment, as though we were stuck with one another. In these bindings, nearly inextricable, are found the origin of our rights. They imply a possessiveness but also recognize an acknowledgment by each side of the other's existence.

The idea of democracy is dependent on the citizens' having knowledge of the government; that is, realizing that the government exists and knowing how to claim rights against it. I know this much because I get mail from the government and see its "representatives" running about in uniforms. Whether I actually have any rights in relationship to the government is less clear, but the idea that I do is symbolized by the right to vote. I obey the government, and, in theory, it obeys me, by counting my ballot, reading the *Miranda* warning to me, agreeing to be bound by the Constitution. My friend obeys me as I obey her; the government "obeys" me to some extent, and, to a different extent, I obey it.

What kind of thing can my Airedale, Drummer, have knowledge of? He can know that I exist and through that knowledge can claim his happiness, with varying degrees of success, both with me and against me. Drummer can also know about larger human or dog communities than the one that consists only of him and me. There is my household—the other dogs, the cats, my husband. I have had enough dogs on campuses to know that he can learn that Yale exists as a neighborhood or village. My older dog, Annie, not only knows that Yale exists but can tell Yalies from townies, as I learned while teaching there during labor troubles.

Dogs can have elaborate conceptions of human social structures, and even of something like their rights and responsibilities within them, but these conceptions are never elaborate enough to construct a rights relationship between a dog and the state, or a dog and the Humane Society. Both of these are concepts that depend on writing and memoranda, officers in uniform, plaques and seals of authority. All of these are literary constructs, and all of them are be-

671

yond a dog's ken, which is why the mail carrier who doesn't also happen to be a dog's friend is forever an intruder—this is why dogs bark at mailmen.

It is clear enough that natural rights relations can arise between people and animals. Drummer, for example, can insist, "Hey, let's go outside and do something!" if I have been at my computer several days on end. He can both refuse to accept various of my suggestions and tell me when he fears for his life—such as the time when the huge, white flapping flag appeared out of nowhere, as it seemed to him, on the town green one evening when we were working. I can (and do) say to him either, "Oh, you don't have to worry about that" or, "Uh oh, you're right, Drum, that guy looks dangerous." Just as the government and I—two different species of organism—have developed improvised ways of communicating, such as the vote, so Drummer and I have worked out a number of ways to make our expressions known. Largely through obedience, I have taught him a fair amount about how to get responses from me. Obedience is reciprocal; you cannot get responses from a dog to whom you do not respond accurately. I have enfranchised him in a relationship to me by educating him, creating the conditions by which he can achieve a certain happiness specific to a dog, maybe even specific to an Airedale, inasmuch as this same relationship has allowed me to plumb the happiness of being a trainer and writing this article.

Instructions in this happiness are given terms that are alien to a culture in which liver treats, fluffy windup toys, and miniature sweaters are confused with respect and work. Jack Knox, a sheepdog trainer originally from Scotland, will shake his crook at a novice handler who makes a promiscuous move to praise a dog, and will call out in his Scottish accent, "Eh! Eh! Get back, get BACK! Ye'll no be abusin' the dogs like that in my clinic." America is a nation of abused animals, Knox says, because we are always swooping at them with praise, "no gi'ing them their freedom." I am reminded of Rainer Maria Rilke's[1] account in which the Prodigal Son leaves—has to leave—because everyone loves him, even the dogs love him, and he has no path to the delicate and fierce truth of himself. Unconditional praise and love, in Rilke's story, disenfranchise us, distract us from what truly excites our interest.

In the minds of some trainers and handlers, praise is dishonesty. Paradoxically, it is a kind of contempt for animals that masquerades as a reverence for helplessness and suffering. The idea of freedom means that you do not, at least not while Jack Knox is nearby, helpfully guide your dog through the motions of, say, herding over and over—what one trainer calls "explainy-wainy." This is rote learning. It works tolerably well on some handlers, because people have vast unconscious minds and can store complex pre-programmed behaviors. Dogs, on the other hand, have almost no unconscious minds, so they can learn only by thinking. Many children are like this until educated out of it.

25

---

[1]*Rainer Maria Rilke* (1875–1926): German-Austrian poet. [Eds.]

If I tell my Airedale to sit and stay on the town green, and someone comes up and burbles, "What a pretty thing you are," he may break his stay to go for a caress. I pull him back and correct him for breaking. Now he holds his stay because I have blocked his way to movement but not because I have punished him. (A correction blocks one path as it opens another for desire to work; punishment blocks desire and opens nothing.) He holds his stay now, and—because the stay opens this possibility of work, new to a heedless young dog—he watches. If the person goes on talking, and isn't going to gush with praise, I may heel Drummer out of his stay and give him an "Okay" to make friends. Sometimes something about the person makes Drummer feel that reserve is in order. He responds to an insincere approach by sitting still, going down into himself, and thinking, "This person has no business pawing me. I'll sit very still, and he will go away." If the person doesn't take the hint from Drummer, I'll give the pup a little backup by saying, "Please don't pet him, he's working," even though he was not under any command.

The pup reads this, and there is a flicker of a working trust now stirring in the dog. Is the pup grateful? When the stranger leaves, does he lick my hand, full of submissive blandishments? This one doesn't. This one says nothing at all, and I say nothing much to him. This is a working trust we are developing, not a mutual-congratulation society. My backup is praise enough for him; the use he makes of my support is praise enough for me.

Listening to a dog is often praise enough. Suppose it is just after dark and we are outside. Suddenly there is a shout from the house. The pup and I both look toward the shout and then toward each other: "What do you think?" I don't so much as cock my head, because Drummer is growing up, and I want to know what he thinks. He takes a few steps toward the house, and I follow. He listens again and comprehends that it's just Holly, who at fourteen is much given to alarming cries and shouts. He shrugs at me and goes about his business. I say nothing. To praise him for this performance would make about as much sense as praising a human being for the same thing. Thus:

A. What's that?
B. I don't know. [Listens] Oh, it's just Holly.
A. What a goooooood human being!
B. Huh?

This is one small moment in a series of like moments that will culminate in an Airedale who on a Friday will have the discrimination and confidence required to take down a man who is attacking me with a knife and on Saturday clown and play with the children at the annual Orange Empire Dog Club Christmas party.

People who claim to speak for animal rights are increasingly devoted to the idea that the very keeping of a dog or a horse or a gerbil or a lion is in and of itself an offense. The more loudly they speak, the less likely they are to be in a rights relation to any given animal, because they are spending so much time in airplanes or transmitting fax announcements of the latest Sylvester Stallone anti-fur rally. In a 1988 *Harper's* forum, for example, Ingrid Newkirk, the national director of People for the Ethical Treatment of Animals, urged that domestic pets be spayed and neutered and ultimately phased out. She prefers, it appears, wolves—and wolves someplace else—to Airedales and, by a logic whose interior structure is both emotionally and intellectually forever closed to Drummer, claims thereby to be speaking for "animal rights."

She is wrong. I am the only one who can own up to my Airedale's inalien-   35 able rights. Whether or not I do it perfectly at any given moment is no more refutation of this point than whether I am perfectly my husband's mate at any given moment refutes the fact of marriage. Only people who know Drummer, and whom he can know, are capable of this relationship. PETA and the Humane Society and the ASPCA and the Congress and NOW—as institutions— do have the power to affect my ability to grant rights to Drummer but are otherwise incapable of creating conditions or laws or rights that would increase his happiness. Only Drummer's owner has the power to obey him—to obey who he is and what he is capable of—deeply enough to grant him his rights and open up the possibility of happiness.

QUESTIONS

1. In making her argument, Hearne is careful to define her terms, the most crucial of which is *happiness*. How does she go about defining this term?

2. How does Hearne use paradox to strengthen her argument? (See paragraph 6, for example.)

3. What are Hearne's major disagreements with animal rights groups? Why does she refer to them as "connoisseurs of suffering" (paragraph 10)?

4. Hearne turns the argument in a particular direction when she claims that animal rights groups are asking flawed questions. Hearne considers them flawed "because they are built on the concept that the origin of rights is in the avoidance of suffering rather than in the pursuit of happiness" (paragraph 14). How do you think she answers the question, "What is a right?"

5. Another important term for Hearne is *reciprocity* (paragraph 17). How does she define this term for humans? For dogs?

6. Consider Hearne's concept of training a dog. How does she use her Airedale, Drummer, to make her case?

MAKING CONNECTIONS

Hearne refers to Ingrid Newkirk, a participant in the forum on animal rights. Review Newkirk's position in "Just like Us: A Forum on Animal Rights" (p. 652) to see if Hearne is fairly representing Newkirk's view. Compare Hearne's and Newkirk's definitions of *animal rights.*

SIFTING THE ASHES

Jonathan Franzen

Jonathan Franzen's (b. 1959) first novel, The Twenty-Seventh City *(1988), was a detective novel. He has since written novels dealing with such contemporary issues as environmental pollution, abortion, and religious fundamentalism. This article first appeared in the* New Yorker *with the subtitle, "Confessions of a Conscientious Objector in the Cigarette Wars" (1996).*

Cigarettes are the last thing in the world I want to think about. I don't consider myself a smoker, don't identify with the forty-six million Americans who have the habit. I dislike the smell of smoke and the invasion of nasal privacy it represents. Bars and restaurants with a stylish profile—with a clientele whose exclusivity depends in part on the toxic clouds with which it shields itself—have started to disgust me. I've been gassed in hotel rooms where smokers stayed the night before and in public bathrooms where men use the nasty, body-odorish Winston as a laxative. ("Winston tastes bad / Like the one I just had" runs the grammatically unimpeachable parody from my childhood.) Some days in New York it seems as if two-thirds of the people on the sidewalk, in the swirls of car exhaust, are carrying lighted cigarettes; I maneuver constantly to stay upwind. The first casino I ever went to, in Nevada, was a vision of damnation: row upon row of middle-aged women with foot-long faces puffing on foot-long Kents and compulsively feeding silver dollars to the slots. When someone tells me that cigarettes are sexy, I think of Nevada. When I see an actress or an actor drag deeply in a movie, I imagine the pyrenes and phenols ravaging the tender epithelial cells and hardworking cilia of their bronchi, the carbon monoxide and cyanide binding to their hemoglobin, the heaving and straining of their chemically panicked hearts. Cigarettes are a distillation of a more general paranoia that besets our culture, the awful knowledge of our bodies' fragility in a world of molecular hazards. They scare the hell out of me.

Because I'm capable of hating almost every attribute of cigarettes (let's not even talk about cigars), and because I smoked what I believed was my last cigarette five years ago and have never owned an ashtray, it's easy for me to think of myself as nicotine-free. But if the man who bears my name is not a smoker, then why is there again a box fan for exhaust purposes in his living-room window? Why at the end of every workday is there a small collection of cigarette butts in the saucer on the table by this fan?

Cigarettes were the ultimate taboo in the culturally conservative household I grew up in—more fraught, even, than sex or drugs. The year before I was born, my mother's father died of lung cancer. He'd taken up cigarettes as a soldier in the First World War and smoked heavily all his life. Everyone who met my grandfather seems to have loved him, and, much as I may sneer at our country's obsession with health—at the elevation of fitness to godliness and of sheer longevity to a mark of divine favor—the fact remains that if my grandfather hadn't smoked I might have had the chance to know him.

My mother still speaks of cigarettes with loathing. I secretly started smoking them myself in college, perhaps in part because she hated them, and as the years went by I developed a fear of exposure very similar, I'm convinced, to a gay man's fear of coming out to his parents. My mother had created my body out of hers, after all. What rejection of parentage could be more extreme than deliberately poisoning that body? To come out is to announce: this is who I am, this is my identity. The curious thing about "smoker" as a label of identity, though, is its mutability. I could decide tomorrow not to be one anymore. So why not pretend not to be one today? To take control of their lives, people tell themselves stories about the person they want to be. It's the special privilege of the smoker, who at times feels so strongly the resolve to quit that it's as if he'd quit already, to be given irrefutable evidence that these stories aren't necessarily true: here are the butts in the ashtray, here is the smell in the hair.

As a smoker, then, I've come to distrust not only my stories about myself but *all* narratives that pretend to unambiguous moral significance. And it happens that ... Americans have been subjected to just such a narrative in the daily press, as "secret" documents shed light on the machinations of Big Tobacco, industry scientists step forward to indict their former employers, nine states and a consortium of sixty law firms launch massive liability suits, and the Food and Drug Administration undertakes to regulate cigarettes as nicotine-delivery devices. The prevailing liberal view that Big Tobacco is Evil with a capital "E" is summed up in the *Times'* review of Richard Kluger's excellent new history of the tobacco industry, "Ashes to Ashes." Chiding Kluger for (of all things) his "objectivity" and "impartiality," Christopher Lehmann-Haupt suggests that the cigarette business is on a moral par with slavery and the Holocaust. Kluger himself, impartial or not, repeatedly links the word "angels" with anti-smoking activists. In the introduction to his book he offers a stark pair of options: either cigarette manufacturers are "businessmen basically like any other" or they're "moral lepers preying on the ignorant, the miserable, the emotionally vulnerable, and the genetically susceptible."

My discomfort with these dichotomies may reflect the fact that, unlike Lehmann-Haupt, I have yet to kick the habit. But in no national debate do I feel more out of synch with the mainstream. For all that I distrust American industry, and especially an industry that is vigorously engaged in buying congressmen, some part of me insists on rooting for tobacco. I flinch as I force myself to read the latest health news: SMOKERS MORE LIKELY TO BEAR RETARDED BABIES, STUDY SAYS. I pounce on particularly choice collisions of metaphor and melodrama, such as this one from the *Times*: "The affidavits are the latest in a string of blows that have undermined the air of invincibility that once cloaked the $45 billion tobacco industry, which faces a deluge of lawsuits." My sympathy with cohorts who smoke disproportionately—blue-collar workers, African-Americans, writers and artists, alienated teens, the mentally ill—expands to include the companies that supply them with cigarettes. I think, We're all underdogs now. Wartime is a time of lies, I tell myself, and the biggest lie of the cigarette wars is that the moral equation can be reduced to ones and zeroes. Or have I, too, been corrupted by the weed?

I took up smoking as a student in Germany in the dark years of the early eighties. Ronald Reagan had recently made his "evil empire" speech, and Jonathan Schell was publishing "The Fate of the Earth." The word in Berlin was that if you woke up to an undestroyed world on Saturday morning you were safe for another week; the assumption was that NATO was at its sleepiest late on Friday nights, that Warsaw Pact forces would choose those hours to come pouring through the Fulda Gap, and that NATO would have to go ballistic to repel them. Since I rated my chances of surviving the decade at fifty-fifty, the additional risk posed by smoking seemed negligible. Indeed, there was something invitingly apocalyptic about cigarettes. The nightmare of nuclear proliferation had a counterpart in the way cigarettes—anonymous, death-bearing, missilelike cylinders—proliferated in my life. Cigarettes are a fixture of modern warfare, the soldier's best friend, and, at a time when a likely theater of war was my own living room, smoking became a symbol of my helpless civilian participation in the Cold War.

Among the anxieties best suited to containment by cigarettes is, paradoxically, the fear of dying. What serious smoker hasn't felt the surge of panic at the thought of lung cancer and immediately lighted up to beat the panic down? (It's a Cold War logic: we're afraid of nuclear weapons, so let's build even more of them.) Death is a severing of the connection between self and world, and, since the self can't imagine not existing, perhaps what's really scary about the prospect of dying is not the extinguishment of my consciousness but the extinguishment of the world. The potential deadliness of cigarettes was comforting because it allowed me, in effect, to become familiar with apocalypse, to acquaint myself with the contours of its terrors, to make the world's potential death less strange and so a little less threatening. Time stops for the duration of a cigarette: when you're smoking, you're acutely present to yourself; you step outside the unconscious forward rush of life. This is why the condemned are allowed a final cigarette, this is why (or so the story goes) gentlemen in evening dress stood puffing at the rail as the Titanic went down: it's a lot easier to leave the world if you're certain you've really been in it. As Goethe[1] writes in "Faust," "Presence is our duty, be it only a moment."

The cigarette is famously the herald of the modern, the boon companion of industrial capitalism and high-density urbanism. Crowds, hyperkinesis, mass production, numbingly boring labor, and social upheaval all have correlatives in the cigarette. The sheer number of individual units consumed surely dwarfs that of any other manufactured consumer product. "Short, snappy, easily attempted, easily completed or just as easily discarded before completion," the *Times* wrote in a 1925 editorial that Richard Kluger quotes, "the cigarette is the symbol of a machine age in which the ultimate cogs and wheels and levers are human nerves." Itself the product of a mechanical roller called the Bonsack machine, the cigarette served as an opiate for assembly-line workers, breaking up into manageable units long days of grinding sameness. For women, the *Atlantic Monthly* noted in 1916, the cigarette was "the symbol of emancipation, the temporary substitute for the ballot." Altogether, it's impossible to imagine the twentieth century without cigarettes. They show up with Zelig-like[2] ubiquity in old photographs and newsreels, so devoid of individuality as to be hardly noticeable and yet, once noticed, utterly strange.

Kluger's history of the cigarette business reads like a history of American business in general. An industry that in the early eighteen-eighties was splintered into hundreds of small, family-owned concerns had by the turn of the century come under the control of one man, James Buchanan Duke, who by pioneering the use of the Bonsack roller and reinvesting a huge portion of his revenues in advertising, and then by alternately employing the stick of price wars and the carrot of attractive buyout offers, built his American Tobacco Company into the equivalent of Standard Oil or Carnegie Steel. Like his fellow-monopolists, Duke eventually ran afoul of the trust-busters, and in 1911 the Supreme Court ordered the breakup of American. The resulting oligopoly immediately brought out new brands—Camel, Lucky Strike, and Chesterfield—that have vied for market share ever since. To American retailers, the cigarette was the perfect commodity, a staple that generated large profits on a small investment in shelf space and inventory; cigarettes, Kluger notes, "were lightweight and durably packed, rarely spoiled, were hard to steal since they were usually sold from behind the counter, underwent few price changes, and required almost no selling effort."

Since every brand tasted pretty much the same, tobacco companies learned early to situate themselves at the cutting edge of advertising. In the twenties, American Tobacco offered five free cartons of Lucky Strike ("it's toasted") to

---

[1] *Johann Wolfgang Goethe* (1749–1832): German author and scientist, author of the dramatic poem *Faust*. [Eds.]

[2] *Zelig*: A 1984 film, written and directed by Woody Allen, in which the protagonist appears in a number of historical newsreels. [Eds.]

678

any doctor who would endorse it, and then launched a campaign that claimed, "20,679 Physicians Say Luckies Are Less Irritating"; American was also the first company to target weight-conscious women ("When tempted to over-indulge, reach for a Lucky instead"). The industry pioneered the celebrity endorsement (the tennis star Bill Tilden: "I've smoked Camels for years, and I never tire of their smooth, rich taste"), radio sponsorship (Arthur Godfrey: "I smoked two or three packs of these things [Chesterfields] every day—I feel pretty good"), as-saultive outdoor advertising (the most famous was the "I'd Walk a Mile for a Camel" billboard in Times Square, which for twenty-five years blew giant smoke rings), and, finally, the sponsorship of television shows like "Candid Camera" and "I Love Lucy." The brilliant TV commercials made for Philip Morris—Benson & Hedges smokers whose hundred-millimeter cigarettes were crushed by elevator doors; faux-hand-cranked footage of chambermaids sneak-ing smokes to the tune of "You've got your own cigarette now, baby"—were vital entertainments of my childhood. I remember, too, the chanted words "Silva Thins, Silva Thins," the mantra for a short-lived American Tobacco product that wooed the female demographic with such appalling copy as "Cig-arettes are like girls, the best ones are thin and rich."

The most successful campaign of all, of course, was for Marlboro, an up-scale cigarette for ladies which Philip Morris reintroduced in 1954 in a filtered version for the mainstream. Like all modern products, the new Marlboro was designed with great care. The tobacco blend was strengthened so as to survive the muting of a filter, the "flip-top" box was introduced to the national vocabu-lary, the color red was chosen to signal strong flavor, and the graphics under-went endless tinkering before the final look, including a fake heraldic crest with the motto "*Veni, vidi, vici*," was settled on; there was even market-testing in four cities to decide the color of the filter. It was in Leo Burnett's ad cam-paign for Marlboro, however, that the real genius lay. The key to its success was its transparency. Place a lone ranch hand against a backdrop of buttes at sunset, and just about every positive association a cigarette can carry is in the picture: rugged individualism, masculine sexuality, escape from an urban modernity, strong flavors, the living of life intensely. The Marlboro marks our commercial culture's passage from an age of promises to an age of pleasant empty dreams.

It's no great surprise that a company smart enough to advertise as well as this ascended, in just three decades, to a position of hegemony in the industry. Kluger's account of the triumph of Philip Morris is the kind of thing that busi-ness schools have their students read for edification and inspiration: to succeed as an American corporation, the lesson might be, do exactly what Philip Morris did. Concentrate on products with the highest profit margin. Design new prod-ucts carefully, then get behind them and push *hard*. Use your excess cash to di-versify into businesses that are structurally similar to your own. Be a meritoc-racy. Avoid crippling debt. Patiently build your overseas markets. Never scruple to gouge your customers when you see the opportunity. Let your lawyers attack your critics. Be classy—sponsor "The Mahabharata." Defy conventional morality. Never forget that your primary fealty is to your stockholders.

While its chief competitor, R. J. Reynolds, was growing logy and inbred down in Winston-Salem—sinking into the low-margin discount-cigarette business, diversifying disastrously, and nearly drowning in debt after its leveraged buyout by Kohlberg Kravis Roberts & Company—Philip Morris was becoming the global leader in the cigarette industry and one of the most profitable corporations in the world. By the early nineties, its share of the domestic nondiscount-cigarette market had risen to eighty percent. One share of Philip Morris stock bought in 1966 was worth a hundred and ninety-two shares in 1989 dollars. Healthy, wealthy, and wise the man who quite smoking in '64 and put his cigarette money into Philip Morris common.

The company's spectacular success is all the more remarkable for having oc- 15 curred in the decades when the scientific case against cigarettes was becoming overwhelming. With the possible exception of the hydrogen bomb, nothing in modernity is more generative of paradox than cigarettes. Thus, in 1955, when the Federal Trade Commission sought to curb misleading advertising by banning the publication of tar and nicotine levels, the ruling proved to be a boon to the industry, by enabling it to advertise filter cigarettes for their implicit safety even as it raised the toxic yields to compensate for the filters. So it went with the 1965 law requiring warning labels on cigarette packs, which preempted potentially more stringent state and local regulations and provided a priceless shield against future liability suits. So it went, too, with the 1971 congressional ban on broadcast cigarette advertising, which saved the industry millions of dollars, effectively froze out potential new competitors by denying them the broadcast platform, and put an end to the devastating anti-smoking ads then being broadcast under the fairness doctrine. Even such left-handed regulation as the 1982 increase in the federal excise tax benefited the industry, which used the tax as a screen for a series of price increases, doubling the price per pack in a decade, and invested the windfall in diversification. Every forward step taken by government to regulate smoking—the broadcast ban, the ban on in-flight smoking, the welter of local bans on smoking in public places—has moved cigarettes a step further back from the consciousness of nonsmoking voters. The result, given the political power of tobacco-growing states, has been the specific exemption of cigarettes from the Fair Labeling and Packaging Act of 1966, the Controlled Substances Act of 1970, the Consumer Product Safety Act of 1972, and the Toxic Substances Act of 1976. In the industry's defense in liability suits, the paradox can be seen in its purest form: because no plaintiff can claim ignorance of tobacco's hazards—i.e., precisely *because* the cigarette is the most notoriously lethal product in America—its manufacturers cannot be held negligent for selling it. Small wonder that until the Liggett Group broke ranks ... no cigarette maker had ever paid a penny in civil damages.

Now, however, the age of paradox may be coming to an end. As the nation dismantles its missiles, its attention turns to cigarettes. The wall of secrecy that protected the industry is coming down as surely as the Berlin Wall did. The Third Wave is upon us, threatening to extinguish all that is quintessentially modern. It hardly seems an accident that the United States, which is leading the way into the information age, is also in the forefront of the war on cigarettes. Unlike the nations of Europe, which have taken a more pragmatic approach to the smoking problem, taxing cigarettes at rates as high as five dollars a pack, the anti-smoking forces in this country bring to the battle a puritanical zeal. We need a new Evil Empire, and Big Tobacco fills the bill.

The argument for equating the tobacco industry with slave traders and the Third Reich goes like this: because nearly half a million Americans a year die prematurely as a direct consequence of smoking, the makers of cigarettes are guilty of mass murder. The obvious difficulty with the argument is that the tobacco industry has never physically forced anyone to smoke a cigarette. To speak of its "killing" people, therefore, one has to posit more subtle forms of coercion. These fall into three categories. First, by publicly denying a truth well known to its scientists, which was that smokers were in mortal peril, the industry conspired to perpetrate a vast and deadly fraud. Second, by luring impressionable children into a habit very difficult to break, the industry effectively "forced" its products on people before they had developed full adult powers of resistance. Finally, by making available and attractive a product that it knew to be addictive, and by manipulating nicotine levels, the industry willfully exposed the public to a force (addiction) with the power to kill.

A "shocking" collection of "secret" industry documents which was express-mailed by a disgruntled employee of Brown & Williamson to the anti-smoking crusader Stanton A. Glantz, and has now been published by the University of California Press as "The Cigarette Papers," makes it clear that Big Tobacco has known for decades that cigarettes are lethal and addictive and has done everything in its power to suppress and deny that knowledge. "The Cigarette Papers" and other recent disclosures have prompted the Justice Department to pursue perjury charges against various industry executives, and may provide the plaintiffs now suing the industry with positive proof of tortious fraud. In no way, though, are the disclosures shocking. How could anyone who noticed that different cigarette brands have different (but consistent) nicotine levels fail to conclude that the industry can and does control the dosage? What reasonable person could have believed that the industry's public avowals of "doubt" about the deadliness of its products were anything but obligatory, ceremonial lies? If researchers unearthed a secret document proving that Bill Clinton inhaled, would we be shocked? When industry spokesmen impugn the integrity of the Surgeon General and persist in denying the undeniable, they're guilty not so much of fraud as of sounding (to borrow the word of one executive quoted by Kluger) "Neanderthal."

"The simple truth," Kluger writes, "was that the cigarette makers were getting richer and richer as the scientific findings against them piled higher and higher, and before anyone fully grasped the situation, the choice seemed to have narrowed to abject confession and surrender to the health advocates or steadfast denial and rationalization." In the early fifties, when epidemiological studies first demonstrated the link between smoking and lung cancer, cigarette executives did indeed have the option of simply liquidating their businesses and finding other work. But many of these executives came from families that had been respectably trading in tobacco for decades, and most of them appear to have been heavy smokers themselves: unlike the typical heroin wholesaler, they willingly ran the same risks they imposed on their customers. Because they were corporate officers, moreover, their ultimate allegiance was to their stockholders. If having simply stayed in business constitutes guilt, then the circle of those who share this guilt must be expanded to include every individual who held stock in a tobacco company after 1964, either directly or through a pension fund, a mutual fund, or a university endowment. We might also toss in every drugstore and supermarket that sold cigarettes and every publication that carried ads for them, since the Surgeon General's warning, after all, was there for everyone to see.

Once the companies made the decision to stay in business, it was only a matter of time before the lawyers took over. Nothing emerges from "Ashes to Ashes" more clearly than the deforming influence of legal counsel on the actions of the industry. Many industry scientists and some executives appear to have genuinely wished both to produce a safer cigarette and to acknowledge frankly the known risks of smoking. But the industry's attempts to do good were no less paradoxically self-defeating than the government's attempts at regulation. When executives in R. & D. proposed that filtered cigarettes and reduced tar and nicotine yields be marketed as a potential benefit to public health, in-house lawyers objected that calling one brand "safe" or "safer" constituted an admission that other brands were hazardous and thus exposed the maker to liability claims. Likewise, after Liggett had spent millions of dollars developing a substantially less carcinogenic "palladium cigarette" in the seventies, it was treated like contagion by the company's lawyers. Marketing it was bad from a liability standpoint, and developing it and then not marketing it was even worse, because in that case the company could be sued for negligently failing to introduce it. Epic, as the new cigarette was called, was ultimately smothered in legal paper.

Kluger describes an industry in which lawyerly paranoia quickly metastasized into every vital organ. Lawyers coached the executives appearing before congressional committees, oversaw the woefully self-serving "independent" research that the industry sponsored, and made sure that all paperwork connected with studies of addiction or cancer was funneled through outside counsel so that it could be protected under the attorney-client privilege. The result

20

was a weird replication of the dual contradictory narratives with which I, as a smoker, explain my life: a true story submerged beneath a utilitarian fiction. One longtime Philip Morris executive quoted by Kluger sums it up like this:

> There was a conflict in the company between science and the law that's never been resolved . . . and so we go through this ritual dance— what's "proven" and what isn't, what's causal and what's just an association—and the lawyers' answer is, "Let's stonewall." . . . If Helmut Wakeham [head of R. & D.] had run things, I think there would have been some admissions. But he was outflanked by the lawyers . . . who . . . were saying, in effect, "My God, you can't make that admission" without risking liability actions against the company. So there was no cohesive plan—when critics of the industry speak of a "conspiracy," they give the companies far too much credit.

In the inverted moral universe of a tobacco-liability trial, every honest or anguished statement by an executive is used to prove the defendants' guilt, while every calculated dodge is used to support their innocence. There's something very wrong here; but absent a demonstration that Americans actually swallowed the industry's lies it's far from clear that this something qualifies as murder.

More damning are recent reports of the industry's recruitment of underage smokers. Lorillard representatives have been observed handing out free Newports to kids in Washington, D.C.; Philip J. Hilts, in his new book, "Smokescreen," presents evidence that R. J. Reynolds deliberately placed special promotional displays in stores and kiosks known to be high-school hangouts; and the cuddly, penis-faced Joe Camel must rank as one of the most disgusting apparitions ever to appear in our cultural landscape. Tobacco companies claim that they are merely vying for market share in the vital eighteen-to-twenty-four age group, but internal industry documents described by Hilts suggest that at least one Canadian company has in fact studied how to target entry-level smokers as young as twelve. (According to Hilts, studies have shown that eighty-nine percent of today's adult smokers picked up the habit before the age of nineteen.) In the opinion of anti-tobacco activists, cigarette advertising hooks young customers by proffering images of carefree, attractive adult smokers while failing to hint at the havoc that smoking wreaks. By the time young smokers are old enough to appreciate the fact of mortality, they're hopelessly addicted.

Although the idea that a manufacturer might willingly stress the downside of its products is absurd, I have no doubt that the industry aims its ads at young Americans. I do doubt, though, whether these ads cause an appreciable number of children to start smoking. The insecure or alienated teen who lights up for the first time is responding to peer pressure or to the example of grownup role models—movie villains, rock stars, supermodels. At most, the industry's ads function as an assurance that smoking is a socially acceptable grownup activity. For that reason alone, they should probably be banned or more tightly controlled, just as cigarette-vending machines should be outlawed. Most people who start smoking end up regretting it, so any policy that reduces the number of starters is laudable.

That cigarettes innately appeal to teen-agers, however, is hardly the fault of 25 the manufacturers. In recent weeks, I've noticed several anti-tobacco newspaper ads that offer, evidently for its shock value, the image of a preadolescent girl holding a cigarette. The models are obviously not real smokers, yet, despite their phoniness, they're utterly sexualized by their cigarettes. The horror of underage smoking veils a horror of teen and preteen sexuality, and one of the biggest pleasant empty dreams being pushed these days by Madison Avenue is that a child is innocent until his or her eighteenth birthday. The truth is that without firm parental guidance teen-agers make all sorts of irrevocable decisions before they're old enough to appreciate the consequences—they drop out of school, they get pregnant, they major in sociology. What they want most of all is to sample the pleasures of adulthood, like sex or booze or cigarettes. To impute to cigarette advertising a "predatory" power is to admit that parents now have less control over the moral education of their children than the commercial culture has. Here, again, I suspect that the tobacco industry is being scapegoated—made to bear the brunt of a more general societal rage at the displacement of the family by the corporation.

The final argument for the moral culpability of Big Tobacco is that addiction is a form of coercion. Nicotine is a toxin whose ingestion causes the smoker's brain to change its chemistry in defense. Once those changes have occurred, the smoker must continue to consume nicotine on a regular schedule in order to maintain the new chemical balance. Tobacco companies are well aware of this, and an attorney cited by Kluger summarizes the legal case for coercion as follows: "You addicted me, and you knew it was addicting, and now you say it's my fault." As Kluger goes on to point out, though, the argument has many flaws. Older even than the common knowledge that smoking causes cancer, for example, is the knowledge that smoking is a tough habit to break. Human tolerance of nicotine varies widely, moreover, and the industry has long offered an array of brands with ultra-low doses. Finally, no addiction is unconquerable: millions of Americans quit every year. When a smoker says he wants to quit but can't, what he's really saying is "I want to quit, but I want even more not to suffer the agony of withdrawal." To argue otherwise is to jettison any lingering notion of personal responsibility.

If nicotine addiction were purely physical, quitting would be relatively easy, because the acute withdrawal symptoms, the physical cravings, rarely last more than a few weeks. At the time I myself quit, six years ago, I was able to stay nicotine-free for weeks at a time, and even when I was working I seldom smoked more than a few ultralights a day. But on the day I decided that the cigarette I'd had the day before was my last, I was absolutely flattened. A month passed in which I was too agitated to read a book, too fuzzy-headed even to focus on a newspaper. If I'd had a job at the time, or a family to take care of, I might have hardly noticed the psychological withdrawal. But as it happened nothing much was going on in my life. "Do you smoke?" Lady Bracknell asks Jack Worthing in "The Importance of Being Earnest," and when he admits that he does she replies, "I am glad to hear it. A man should always have an occupation of some kind."

There's no simple, universal reason that people smoke, but of one thing I'm convinced: they don't do it because they're slaves to nicotine. My best guess about my own attraction to the habit is that I belong to a class of people whose lives are insufficiently structured. The mentally ill and the indigent are also members of this class. We embrace a toxin as deadly as nicotine, suspended in an aerosol of hydrocarbons and nitrosamines, because we have not yet found pleasures or routines that can replace the comforting, structure-bringing rhythm of need and gratification that the cigarette habit offers. One word for this structuring might be "self-medication"; another might be "coping." But there are very few serious smokers over thirty, perhaps none at all, who don't feel guilty about the harm they inflict on themselves. Even Rose Cipollone, the New Jersey woman whose heirs in the early eighties nearly sustained a liability judgment against the industry, had to be recruited by an activist. The sixty law firms that have pooled their assets for a class-action suit on behalf of all American smokers do not seem to me substantially less predatory than the suit's corporate defendants. I've never met a smoker who blamed the habit on someone else.

The United States as a whole resembles an addicted individual, with the corporated id going about its dirty business while the conflicted political ego frets and dithers. What's clear is that the tobacco industry would not still be flourishing, thirty years after the first Surgeon General's report, if our legislatures weren't purchasable, if the concepts of honor and personal responsibility hadn't largely given way to the power of litigation and the dollar, and if the country didn't generally endorse the idea of corporations whose ultimate responsibility is not to society but to the bottom line. There's no doubt that some tobacco executives have behaved despicably, and for public-health advocates to hate these executives, as the nicotine addict comes eventually to hate his cigarettes, is natural. But to cast them as moral monsters—a point source of evil—is just another form of prime-time entertainment.

By selling its soul to its legal advisers, Big Tobacco long ago made clear its expectation that the country's smoking problem would eventually be resolved in court. The industry may soon suffer such a devastating loss in a liability suit that thereafter only foreign cigarette makers will be able to afford to do business here. Or perhaps a federal court will undertake to legislate a solution to a problem that the political process has clearly proved itself unequal to, and the Supreme Court will issue an opinion that does for the smoking issue what

685

Brown v. Board of Education did for racial segregation and Roe v. Wade for abortion. "Businessmen are combatants, not healers," Kluger writes in "Ashes to Ashes," "and when they press against or exceed the bounds of decency in their quest for gain, unhesitant to profit from the folly of others, should the exploited clientele and victimized society expect the perpetrators to restrain themselves out of some sudden divine visitation of conscience? Or must human nature be forcibly corrected when it goes awry?"

Liggett's recent defection notwithstanding, the Medicare suits filed by nine states seem unlikely to succeed as a forcible correction. Kluger notes that these cases arguably amount to "personal injury claims in disguise," and that the Supreme Court has ruled that federal cigarette-labeling laws are an effective shield against such claims. Logically, in other words, the states ought to be suing smokers, not cigarette makers. And perhaps smokers, in turn, ought to be suing Social Security and private pension funds for all the money they'll save by dying early. The best estimates of the nationwide dollar "cost" of smoking, including savings from premature death and income from excise taxes, are negative numbers. If the country's health is to be measured fiscally, an economist quoted by Kluger jokes, "cigarette smoking should be subsidized rather than taxed."

The giant class-action suit filed in New Orleans in March of 1994 represents a more serious threat to Big Tobacco. If a judge concludes that smoking constitutes a social ill on a par with racial segregation, he or she is unlikely to deny standing to the forty-six-million-member "class" represented by the consortium of law firms, and once plaintiffs in a class-action suit are granted standing they almost never lose. The case for regulation of tobacco by the F.D.A is likewise excellent. The modern cigarette is a heavily engineered product, bolstered with a long list of additives, and its nicotine content is manipulable at will. Tobacco companies insist that cigarettes, because no health claims are made for them by the companies, should not be considered a drug. But if nicotine is universally understood to be habit-forming—a central tenet of the industry's liability defense—then the absence of explicit health claims is meaningless. Whether Congress, in its various wafflings, intended cigarettes to be immune from F.D.A. regulation in the first place is, again, a matter that will be decided in court, but a demonstrable history of lies and distortion is sure to weaken the industry's defense.

Ultimately, the belief that the country's century-long love affair with the cigarette can be ended rationally and amicably seems as fond as the belief that there's a painless way to kick nicotine. The first time I quit, I stayed clean for nearly three years. I found I was able to work *more* productively without the distraction and cumulative unpleasantness of cigarettes, and I was happy finally to be the nonsmoker that my family had always taken me to be. Eventually, though, in a season of great personal loss, I came to resent having quit for other people rather than for myself. I was hanging out with smokers, and I drifted back into the habit. Smoking may not look sexy to me anymore, but it still *feels* sexy. The pleasure of carrying the drug, of surrendering to its imperatives and relaxing behind a veil of smoke, is thoroughly licentious. If longevity were the highest good that I could imagine, I might succeed now in scaring myself into quitting. But to the fatalist who values the present more than the future the nagging voice of conscience—of society, of family—becomes just another factor in the mental equilibrium that sustains the habit. "Perhaps," Richard Klein writes in "Cigarettes Are Sublime," "one stops smoking only when one starts to love cigarettes, becoming so enamored of their charms and so grateful for their benefits that one at last begins to grasp how much is lost by giving them up, how urgent it is to find substitutes for some of the seductions and powers that cigarettes so magnificently combine." To live with uncontaminated lungs and an unracing heart is a pleasure that I hope someday soon to prefer to the pleasure of a cigarette. For myself, then, I'm cautiously optimistic. For the body politic, rhetorically torn between shrill condemnation and Neanderthal denial, and habituated to the poison of tobacco money in its legal system, its legislatures, its financial markets, and its balance of foreign trade, I'm considerably less so.

A few weeks ago in Tribeca, in a Magritte-like twilight,[3] I saw a woman in a lighted window on a high floor of a loft apartment building. She was standing on a chair and lowering the window's upper sash. She tossed her hair and did something complicated with her arms which I recognized as the lighting of a cigarette. Then she leaned her elbow and her chin on the sash and blew smoke into the humid air outside. I fell in love at first sight as she stood there, both inside and outside, inhaling contradiction and breathing out ambivalence.

QUESTIONS

1. In publishing this essay with the subtitle "Confessions of a Conscientious Objector in the Cigarette Wars," the *New Yorker* sets it up as confessional, yet we have placed it in the arguing section of this book. How would you categorize this essay? Is Franzen confessing or arguing or both?

2. How does Franzen answer the questions of why he started smoking, why he gave it up, and why he started again? Note how he uses the first question as a frame, returning to it in paragraph 28 to link his own addiction to a national addiction.

3. Consider the symbolic values given the cigarette and cigarette smoking. If giving up cigarettes means, as Richard Klein says, finding "substitutes for some of the seductions and powers that cigarettes so magnificently combine" (paragraph 33), what would you suggest as some possible substitutes?

4. The central section of Franzen's essay presents some of the evidence that has been gathered against "Big Tobacco" and its attempts to squelch evidence of how harm-

---

[3]*René Magritte* (1898–1967): French surrealist artist whose twilight skies were sometimes full of hats or umbrellas. [Eds.]

ful cigarette smoking is. "The argument for equating the tobacco industry with slave traders and the Third Reich" starts in paragraph 17. What does Franzen mean by this comparison?

5. How strong is the evidence Franzen presents for his argument? In what order does he place his evidence? Why do you think he organizes his evidence in this way?

6. Since this article was published, the Federal Drug Administration has decided to regulate tobacco. Do some research on this issue, and report on the implications of such regulation, as well as the issues Franzen raises in paragraph 32.

MAKING CONNECTIONS

Compare Franzen's argument with Allan Gurganus's in "A Letter to Granddad, the Tobacco Farmer" (p. 689). In what ways do they each use personal experience?

A LETTER TO GRANDDAD, THE TOBACCO FARMER
Allan Gurganus

Allan Gurganus (b. 1947) was born in North Carolina into a tobacco family. He served on an aircraft carrier in the Vietnam War; while he was in the navy he began research on the historical background for his best-known novel, Oldest Living Confederate Widow Tells All *(1992). His novel* Plays Well With Others *(1997) deals with the gay art scene in New York City in the 1980s just as AIDS is appearing. The essay reprinted here first appeared on the op-ed page of the* New York Times *(1995).*

Dear Granddad,

I remember being 8 years old, bound for church, wearing a little seersucker monkey suit and—as we walked toward your Packard—you turned and chuckled from pure pleasure. You'd seen your fields spread below us, 40 acres, still varnished with dew. You said, "Is that tobacco not *happy* tobacco?" This occurred in '59 in North Carolina, mid-July and the heat was already a standing presence, the horizon seemed jellied. But those green plants stood tent-high, sure and promising as food.

"Isn't it a beautiful *looking* plant?" you asked. My smile died. The way you said that, I knew you knew. I would've preferred you innocent or dumb.

At the local service station, I'd heard other farmers call cigarettes "cancer sticks" and "coffin nails." Now, tentative, over-polite, I nodded toward your neighbor's cotton field, "Why not grow that?"

"Son, this one acre is worth nine of those. My great-grandfather grew this same thing, just here. It's all our people know." 5

If you are born into a rice paddy, I guess you just farm rice? With a kid's nose for hypocrisy, I told myself that if a man as famously decent and tender as you, Granddad, could grow cancer-stick fillings, then the world was going to be lots tougher to figure.

You said: "Young man, you'd best remember two things. The history of America is the history of tobacco. Our Founding Fathers grew it, smoked it, too. Why, they put tobacco leaves on that first $5 bill and . . ."

"You *al*-ways say that. What's the other thing?"

You squatted, your face large before mine, you held my shoulders in hard hands: "Don't you ever smoke. You hear me? Promise. Mustn't even try it. They get you hooked."

They! 10

Just behind your head, our family's own perfect tobacco stretched money-green as far as I could see.

- In London, in the 1590s, a pound of the best cost the equivalent of $125.

- From the very start, a healthy confusion. Sir Walter Raleigh received the first seeds from North Carolina (six acres per teaspoonful). He grew a crop on his Irish estate, then settled down to smoke some. A servant, bringing Master a tankard of ale, noticed that Master's head was wreathed in fumes. He dumped the drink all over Master's pate. Wasn't that his duty, to protect? Human heads didn't seemed designed to accept the sustained smoke that, say, hams need.

- An estimated 100,000 carved cigar-store Indians stood before late 19th century tobacco shops; that was roughly half the population of living Native Americans.

- My hometown movie theater was named "The Golden Leaf." The local radio station's call letters spelled W-E-E-D. During market days, our tar streets were paved with gold leaf—tattered cured tobacco blown from farm trucks. And the smell! If the stuff tasted as good as it smelled before burning, we'd all choose it as a form of suicide. A scent autumnal, healthy, luxurious—like living safe inside the Lord's own humidor.

- From the beginning, tobacco has demanded the best talent of American advertising. People will buy bread, whatever the brand or motto. But a toxic product needs to be made attractive long enough to lure, soothe, addict. Any child who has ever kept treasures in a gilded, opulent cigar box knows the allure of such no-expenses-spared come-ons. The names of plug and smoking tobaccos from the early days still charm, cajole and deny: Climax, Gay Bloomers, Fat Gal, World for a Dime. There was a Brooklyn plug called Daddy Wouldn't Buy Me a Bow Wow.

One friend, my address book's oldest living impenitent smoker, just returned from a trip to China's more obscure outposts. Leaving, she'd worried most about bad Diet Coke withdrawal. She'd heard that cigarettes were everywhere—a nation of one billion, many already utterly hooked.

In China, she discovered a whole new reason to quit. At first she made do with picturesquely packaged if harsh-tasting Chinese brands. Finally, she broke down and bought some costly Marlboros, her home brand. She ripped open the pack and found the cigarettes water-stained in wavy black. They seemed rolled of the stems and sticks judged unsuitable for anything but export. Chinese Marlboros were like her usuals in two ways only: their packet and addictiveness.

"I must say I felt betrayed," she later admitted, holding her "works"—the gold lighter and red pack, clasped with the meditative succor usually accorded rosary beads. "I mean, I've been faithful to them for so long." That's one word for it. Consumption as addiction, as monogamy, as faith. But, her surprise was so touching.

To be an American is to live within such push-pull battles of profit, promise ₁₅ and jeopardy. Now that our adults are finally admitting that cigarettes cause painful lingering deaths, only the young are still fair game. And so, it's just good business to go after them.

President Clinton takes political risks in even mentioning an epidemic of smoking among children. He adds greatly to his luster—as a father of a young Joe Camel target, and as a genuine leader. He is saying a word so rarely uttered since the Reagan Revolution. He is saying, "Enough."

"Behind every great fortune, there's a crime," Balzac[1] tells us. Is the history of America just the history of tobacco? No, Granddad.

Columbus and his scurvy crew waded ashore expecting to find mounds of spices, gold; instead, awed native people held out exotic fruit, wooden spears and, the captain's record tells us, in a strange and oddly chilling phrase, "certain dried leaves."

Sailors, their teeth loose from beriberi, gobbled the fruit; the weapons got saved as souvenirs, but those first leaves were dropped on the mud of that beach. Their true use seemed "savage," odd. You inhaled the leaves' smoke after wrapping leaves with maize "in the manner of a musket."

This new Eden offered produce from the Tree of the Knowledge of Good ₂₀ and Evil. Here, you *smoked* it.

Tobacco is the quintessential American product. It fulfills no appetite but the one it creates. Predicting a throwaway culture, it is rendered useful only by being destroyed. Along with autos, movies, jazz and striptease, it remains our abiding gift to world culture.

Since many of my childhood friends had fathers in the industry, cigarettes were often scattered around their homes as decorative "accents." I remember a brandy snifter big as a goldfish bowl and full of loose packs—Winstons and Salems and other brands named for Carolina cities. Since I wanted to look exactly like James Dean, and since these freebies seemed placed here for guests, I was just fishing out a pack of Winstons when my buddy's pretty mom chanced by. She gave me such a look.

"Darling, you do *know* about them, don't you?" She was living in a semi-mansion bought with their proceeds. Her husband spent the hottest part of each summer in stifling Georgia warehouses, grading tobacco. He was breathing pure snuff; and every year he'd come home hacking and, under the pretense of "a pesky summer cold," would check directly into the hospital. He would ask for his favorite room. His pals were nearby in theirs, just back from the same market; a party. He would be dead at 54.

"I know," I replied. "Grand told me early. But these are just to, like, roll in my sleeve."

---

[1]*Honoré de Balzac* (1799–1850): French author. [Ed.]

"Well, so long as they're for show. We love you too much to let you get   25
started doing all that to yourself."

I nodded but glanced back, with wonder, at the 60 packs, all red and blue,
stuffed into a crystal bowl—like kept pets—looking out.

Finally, at 14, I decided to "work tobacco." This job was undertaken only by
strong black people or desperate white ones. Granddad, I thought it'd please
you, my laboring in your fields. You just shook your head, laughed, "Go ahead,
but don't do it for me. I warn you, it's *work*."

I felt insulted. Hadn't I spent a summer as country club lifeguard? Hadn't I
trimmed my parents' acre of lawn, even before we got the riding mower?

I turned up at the farm at 5 A.M. wearing old madras shorts and a French
sailor shirt. I was amazed to see elderly black women wound in long sleeves,
hidden under kerchiefs and huge straw hats.

The sun was just getting serious and the plants stood tall as good-sized men.   30
Each looked complete as a Christmas tree and it seemed a sort of a shame to
pick at them. One of the veteran black women showed me harvesting techniques used since the 17th century: tie leaves to sticks, hang sticks in smoking
barns. I acted frisky and polite and quizzed her about her grandchildren in Detroit, two becoming dentists.

"Yeah," I answered a question she'd not asked. "I wanted to see how all this
was done. Figured I'd snag me some spending money *and* work on my tan."

She gave a snort, "By evening, that tan might could be working on you." It
was not just a sunburn I received; it was how nicotine, when touched, goes direct through your skin into your bloodstream. My hands were soon coated with
a dark essence that caked like opium, and I was so near hallucinating that
when I touched a massive tobacco worm, a white thing of surpassing ugliness
whose sting took me beyond pain, I knew I had met a caterpillar literally
hooked on tobacco, and not a bit interested in quitting.

At this job, I lasted four days. And if you think I'm apologizing, you're
wrong. Bragging.

Living with the lie of tobacco, North Carolina has prospered, has been deformed. If you know that your major crop kills, you need big-time spin control.
You need a pit-bull single-issue politician who will make a militant merit of his
state's lowest-common-denominator xenophobia. You need somebody smart
who's still willing to yuk it up with the good old boys at tobacco warehouses. A
man of preternatural energy willing—in a familiar Southern mode—to play
the fool to disarm any enemy. Meet Jesse Helms.

I am sometimes asked how a state as progressive as North Carolina can   35
choose this man to represent it. I have a one-word answer: Tobacco.

Now, restaurants and airplanes forbid smoking. The fashion has turned
against it. From the start the industry has seen this crisis coming. Every time a
shameless spokesman told another Congressional hearing, "We deny the addictive properties of nicotine and feel further studies are needed," that tobacco

consortium went right out and bought a computer factory, a cookie conglomerate. Diversifying, getting ready.

Granddad, though you died in 1964 of "natural causes," I'm writing you this letter. Wanted you to know how the Tobacco Interest is treating its small farmers (most North Carolina farms are still family ones). The growers must now be counted among this industry's many victims. "We deny the addictive qualities of both smoking and *growing* tobacco, for however many generations." These farmers need help in finding some new crop; it's the sort of help now being offered former coca growers in Peru.

Dear Granddad, it hasn't turned out quite the way we thought, has it? Cultivating beautiful plants was not enough. I keep a garden of my own now, perennials. My main joy is concentrating on old roses, lilies, foxglove and beautiful domesticated specimens of a plant you'd know, "Nicotiniana affinis." Gardening is sort of addictive, actually.

I end by sending, across the barricades of time, through all the terrible filters that separate those still breathing from those not,

Love,
Allan

P.S. "They" haven't hooked me yet.   40

QUESTIONS

1. What is the argument in Gurganus's op-ed piece? Is this a grandson's argument for not being a tobacco farmer, an argument against Big Tobacco, or something else?

2. What is Gurganus's attitude toward his grandfather?

3. What are the grandfather's arguments for growing tobacco? How does Gurganus refute them in this essay?

4. Why does Gurganus's friend who visited China feel "betrayed" when she opens the pack of Marlboros? What purpose does this anecdote serve for Gurganus's larger message?

5. How does Gurganus arrange his argument? In what ways does he use autobiographical material?

MAKING CONNECTIONS

There is some overlap between Gurganus's essay and Jonathan Franzen's (p. 675). That is, they criticize similar aspects of Big Tobacco. Compare some of these similarities and the ways in which they are presented.

Sciences and Technologies

ANIMALS IN RESEARCH
The Case for Experimentation

Frederick A. King

Frederick A. King (b. 1925) is a neuroscientist and an edu-cator. He is director of Emory University's primate research center and has served on many committees on animal re-search and experimentation. He has edited books on pri-mate biology and primate social dynamics. In this essay, King argues that while humans have a moral responsibility to animals, animals do not share the same rights as hu-mans.

The Mobilization for Animals Coalition (MFA) is an international network of more than 400 animal-protectionist organizations that address themselves to a variety of issues, including hunting, trapping, livestock protection, vegetarian-ism, and pets. Their primary concern, however, is an adamant opposition to animal research. Some groups within the movement want to severely curtail re-search with animals, but the most visible and outspoken faction wants to elimi-nate it.

The astonishing growth of this activist movement during the past three years has culminated this year in an intense attack on the use of animals in psycho-logical research. This past spring, John McArdle of the Humane Society of the United States charged that torture is the founding principle and fundamental characteristic of experimental psychology, and that psychological experimenta-tion on animals among all the scientific disciplines is "the ideal candidate for elimination. No major scientific endeavor would suffer by such an act." A re-cent pamphlet published by the MFA stated, "Of all these experiments, those conducted in psychology are the most painful, pointless, and repulsive."

The following specific allegations have been made by the MFA: Animals are given intense, repeated electric shocks until they lose the ability even to scream in pain; animals are deprived of food and water and allowed to suffer and die from hunger and thirst; animals are put in isolation until they are driven insane or die from despair and terror; animals are subjected to crushing forces that smash their bones and rupture their internal organs; the limbs of animals are mutilated or amputated to produce behavioral changes; animals are the victims of extreme pain and stress, inflicted out of idle curiosity, in nightmarish experiments designed to make healthy animals psychotic.

Such irresponsible accusations of research cruelty have consistently characterized the publications of the MFA. However, a recent study by psychologists D. Caroline Coile and Neal E. Miller of Rockefeller University counters these charges. Coile and Miller looked at every article (a total of 608) appearing in the past five years in journals of the American Psychological Association that report animal research. They concluded that none of the extreme allegations made by the MFA could be supported.

Coile and Miller admit that charges of cruelty may have gone unreported or   5
been reported elsewhere but, they say, if such studies did occur, "they certainly were infrequent, and it is extremely misleading to imply that they are typical of experimental psychology."

Furthermore, there are standards and mechanisms to ensure that research animals are treated in a humane and scientifically sensible way. These mechanisms include the Federal Animal Welfare Act of 1966 (amended in Congress in 1970, 1976, and 1979); periodic inspection of all animal-research facilities by the Department of Agriculture; visits by federal agencies that fund animal research and are increasingly attentive to the conditions of animal care and experimental procedures that could cause pain or distress; and a comprehensive document, "Guide for the Care and Use of Laboratory Animals," prepared by the National Academy of Sciences. In addition, virtually every major scientific society whose members conduct animal research distributes guidelines for such research. Above and beyond all of this, most universities and research institutes have animal-care committees that monitor animal research and care.

The United States Public Health Service is revising its guidelines to require institutions that do research with animals to designate even clearer lines of authority and responsibility for animal care. This will include detailed information about how each institution complies with the new regulations as well as a requirement that animal-research committees include not only the supervising laboratory veterinarian and scientists but also a nonscientist and a person not affiliated with the institution. These committees will review programs for animal care, inspect all animal facilities, and review and monitor all research proposals before they are submitted to agencies of the United States Public Health Service. The committees will also have the power to disapprove or terminate any research proposal.

This is not to say that research scientists are perfect. There will be occasional errors, cases of neglect, and instances of abuse—as is the case with any human endeavor, whether it be the rearing of children, the practicing of a trade or profession, or the governing of a nation. But a high standard of humane treatment is maintained.

The choice of psychological research for special attack almost certainly stems from the fact that such research is viewed as more vulnerable than are studies of anatomy, physiology, or microbiology. In the minds of many, psychology is a less well-developed science than the biological sciences and the benefits that have accrued from psychological research with animals are less well known. Hence, it is more difficult to grasp the necessity for animal research in behavioral studies than it is in biomedical studies.

Anyone who has looked into the matter can scarcely deny that major advances in medicine have been achieved through basic research with animals. Among these are the development of virtually all modern vaccines against infectious diseases, the invention of surgical approaches to eye disorders, bone and joint injuries and heart disease, the discovery of insulin and other hormones, and the testing of all new drugs and antibiotics.

The benefits to humans of psychological research with animals may be less well known than those of medical research but are just as real. Historically, the application of psychological research to human problems has lagged considerably behind the applied use of medical research. Mental events and overt behavior, although controlled by the nervous system and biology of an organism, are much more difficult to describe and study than are the actions of tissues or organ systems. To describe the complex interplay of perceptions, memories, cognitive and emotional processes with a physical and social environment that changes from moment to moment, elaborate research designs had to be developed. Since even a single type of behavior, such as vocalization, has so many different forms, a wide variety of ways of measuring the differences had to be developed. Finally, because much psychological research makes inferences from behavioral observations about internal states of an organism, methods were needed to insure that the interpretations were valid. Such complexities do not make the study of animal or human behavior less scientific or important than other kinds of research, but they do make it more difficult and slow its readiness for clinical applications.

Basic psychological research with animals has led to important achievements in the interest of human welfare. Examples include the use of biofeedback, which had its origin in studies of behavioral conditioning of neuromuscular activities in rats and other animals. Today, biofeedback can be used to control blood pressure and hypertension and help prevent heart attacks. In the case of paralyzed patients, it can be used to elevate blood pressure, enabling those who would otherwise have to spend their lives lying down to sit upright. Biofeedback techniques also are used in the reduction and control of severe pain and as a method of neuromuscular control to help reverse the process of scoliosis, a disabling and disfiguring curvature of the spine. Biofeedback can

697

also be a cost-effective alternative to certain medical treatments and can help avoid many of the complications associated with long-term drug use.

Language studies with apes have led to practical methods of teaching language skills to severely retarded children who, prior to this work, had little or no language ability. Patients who have undergone radiation therapy for cancer can now take an interest in nutritious foods and avoid foods that have little nutritional value, thanks to studies of conditioned taste aversion done with animals. Neural and behavioral studies of early development of vision in cats and primates—studies that could not have been carried out with children—have led to advances in pediatric ophthalmology that can prevent irreversible brain damage and loss of vision in children who have cataracts and various other serious eye problems.

Behavioral modification and behavioral therapy, widely accepted techniques for treating alcohol, drug, and tobacco addiction, have a long history of animal studies investigating learning theory and reward systems. Programmed instruction, the application of learning principles to educational tasks, is based on an array of learning studies in animals. These are but a few examples of the effectiveness and usefulness for humans of psychological research with animals.

Those opposed to animal research have proposed that alternatives to animal research, such as mathematical and computer models and tissue cultures, be used. In some cases, these alternatives are both feasible and valuable. Tissue cultures, for example, have been very effective in certain toxicological studies that formerly required live animals. For psychological studies, however, it is often necessary to study the whole animal and its relationship to the environment. Visual problems, abnormal sexual behavior, depression, and aggression, for example, are not seen in tissue cultures and do not lend themselves to computer models. When human subjects cannot be used for such studies, animals are necessary if the research is to be done at all.

Extremists within the animal-rights movement take the position that animals have rights equal to or greater than those of humans. It follows from this that even if humans might benefit from animal research, the cost to animals is too high. It is ironic that despite this moral position, the same organizations condone—and indeed sponsor—activities that appear to violate the basic rights of animals to live and reproduce. Each year 10,000,000 dogs are destroyed by public pounds, animal shelters, and humane societies. Many of these programs are supported and even operated by animal-protectionist groups. Surely there is a strong contradiction when those who profess to believe in animal rights deny animals their right to life. A similar situation exists with regard to programs of pet sterilization, programs that deny animals the right to breed and to bear offspring and are sponsored in many cases by antivivisectionists and animal-rights groups. Evidently, animal-rights advocates sometimes recognize and subscribe to the position that animals do not have the same rights as humans. However,

15

their public posture leaves little room for examining these subtleties or apply-ing similar standards to animal research.

Within the animal-protectionist movement there are moderates who have confidence in scientists as compassionate human beings and in the value of re-search. Their primary aims are to insure that animals are treated humanely and that discomfort in animal experimentation is kept to a minimum. It is to this group that scientists and scientific organizations have the responsibility to ex-plain what they do, why and how they do it and what benefits occur.

I believe that the values guiding contemporary animal research represent prevailing sentiment within the scientific community and, indeed, within soci-ety at large. And I believe that these values are congruent with those of the moderates within the animal-protectionist movement. As articulated by ethicist Arthur Caplan, rights, in the most realistic sense, are granted by one group to another based on perceived similarities between the groups. Plainly, animals lack those characteristics that would allow them to share in the rights we grant to humans. We do not grant domestic animals the right to go where they wish or do what they want because they are obviously unable to comprehend the re-sponsibilities and demands of human society. In fact, we do not as a society even grant all domestic animals and pets the right to live.

This does not mean, however, that we do not have a moral responsibility to animals. I believe, along with Caplan and the scientific research community at large, that we hold a moral stewardship for animals and that we are obliged to treat them with humane compassion and concern for their sentience. Many animal forms can and do feel pain and are highly aware of their environment. This awareness makes them worthy of our respect and serious concern. Caplan is certainly correct when he says that this moral obligation ought to be part of what it means to be a scientist today.

Science must proceed. The objective quest for knowledge is a treasured en-terprise of our heritage and culture. Scientific inquiry into the nature of our living world has freed us from ignorance and superstition. Scientific under-standing is an expression of our highest capacities—those of objective obser-vation, interpretive reasoning, imagination, and creativity. Founded on the results of basic research, often conducted with no goal other than that of in-creased understanding, the eventual practical use of this knowledge has led to a vastly improved well-being for humankind. 20

Extremists in the animal-rights movement probably will never accept such justifications for research or assurances of humane treatments. They may reject any actions, no matter how conscientious, that scientists take in realistically and morally reconciling the advance of human welfare with the use of ani-mals. But, fortunately, there are many who, while deeply and appropriately concerned for the compassionate treatment of animals, recognize that human welfare is and should be our primary concern.

QUESTIONS

1. King begins his argument by presenting the opposition's position. In paragraph 2, he offers the charge from a member of the Humane Society of the United States that "torture is the founding principle and fundamental characteristic of experimental psychology." Why does King begin by presenting the opposition's case? How does he characterize their claims? How does he use this information to strengthen his own argument?

2. King argues that "it is more difficult to grasp the necessity for animal research in behavioral studies than it is in biomedical studies" (paragraph 9). What examples does he offer to make his case that animal research in behavioral studies has had important human benefits? Do you find these examples convincing?

3. Summarize King's position. What is the case for animals in research?

4. What values does King appeal to? What assumptions underlie his position?

5. Compose a position in response to King. You might begin by deciding whether you want to present yourself as a moderate or an extremist, or whether you would reject from the outset those labels.

6. Spend some time in a psychology lab at your school where animals are used for research. What do you observe about the conditions and treatment of these animals? Interview the researchers in the lab to learn about the kind of research conducted and the projected benefits for behavioral studies. Using this information as evidence and your own responses to the various readings on animal rights, write an essay supporting your position.

MAKING CONNECTIONS

King writes, "Many animal forms can and do feel pain and are highly aware of their environment. This awareness makes them worthy of our respect and serious concern" (paragraph 19). How would Alice Walker respond to this claim and to King's argument? Read her essay, "Am I Blue?" (p. 567). Would King call Walker an "extremist" as he uses that term in paragraph 16? Imagine a conversation between King and Walker, and compose a dialogue for them.

THE EGG AND THE SPERM
How Science Has Constructed a Romance Based on Stereotypical Male-Female Roles
Emily Martin

Emily Martin (b. 1944) is a professor of anthropology at Johns Hopkins University. She has written The Woman in the Body: A Cultural Analysis of Reproduction *(1987) and* Flexible Bodies: Tracking Immunity in American Culture—From the Days of Polio to the Age of AIDS *(1994). In the following article, which originally appeared in the journal* Signs *(1991), Martin's intent is to expose the cultural stereotypes operative in the so-called scientific language surrounding human reproduction.*

The theory of the human body is always a part of a world-picture. . . . The theory of the human body is always a part of a fantasy.

[James Hillman, *The Myth of Analysis*][1]

As an anthropologist, I am intrigued by the possibility that culture shapes how biological scientists describe what they discover about the natural world. If this were so, we would be learning about more than the natural world in high school biology class; we would be learning about cultural beliefs and practices as if they were part of nature. In the course of my research I realized that the picture of egg and sperm drawn in popular as well as scientific accounts of reproductive biology relies on stereotypes central to our cultural definitions of male and female. The stereotypes imply not only that female biological processes are less worthy than their male counterparts but also that women are less worthy than men. Part of my goal in writing this article is to shine a bright light on the gender stereotypes hidden within the scientific language of biology. Exposed in such a light, I hope they will lose much of their power to harm us.

Portions of this article were presented as the 1987 Becker Lecture, Cornell University. I am grateful for the many suggestions and ideas I received on this occasion. For especially pertinent help with my arguments and data I thank Richard Cone, Kevin Whaley, Sharon Stephens, Barbara Duden, Susanne Kuechler, Lorna Rhodes, and Scott Gilbert. The article was strengthened and clarified by the comments of the anonymous *Signs* reviewers as well as the superb editorial skills of Amy Gage.
    [1]James Hillman, *The Myth of Analysis* (Evanston, Ill.: Northwestern University Press, 1972), 220.

EMILY MARTIN

EGG AND SPERM: A SCIENTIFIC FAIRY TALE

At a fundamental level, all major scientific textbooks depict male and female reproductive organs as systems for the production of valuable substances,
such as eggs and sperm.[2] In the case of women, the monthly cycle is described
as being designed to produce eggs and prepare a suitable place for them to be
fertilized and grown—all to the end of making babies. But the enthusiasm
ends there. By extolling the female cycle as a productive enterprise, menstruation must necessarily be viewed as a failure. Medical texts describe menstruation as the "debris" of the uterine lining, the result of necrosis, or death of tissue. The descriptions imply that a system has gone awry, making products of
no use, not to specification, unsalable, wasted, scrap. An illustration in a widely
used medical text shows menstruation as a chaotic disintegration of form, com-
plementing the many texts that describe it as "ceasing," "dying," "losing," "de-
nuding," "expelling."[3]

Male reproductive physiology is evaluated quite differently. One of the texts
that sees menstruation as failed production employs a sort of breathless prose
when it describes the maturation of sperm: "The mechanisms which guide the
remarkable cellular transformation from spermatid to mature sperm remain
uncertain. . . . Perhaps the most amazing characteristic of spermatogenesis is its
sheer magnitude: the normal human male may manufacture several hundred
million sperm per day."[4] In the classic text *Medical Physiology*, edited by Ver-
non Mountcastle, the male/female, productive/destructive comparison is more
explicit: "Whereas the female *sheds* only a single gamete each month, the seminiferous tubules *produce* hundreds of millions of sperm each day" (emphasis
mine).[5] The female author of another text marvels at the length of the microscopic seminiferous tubules, which, if uncoiled and placed end to end, "would
span almost one-third of a mile!" She writes, "In an adult male these structures
produce millions of sperm cells each day." Later she asks, "How is this feat accomplished?"[6] None of these texts expresses such intense enthusiasm for any
female processes. It is surely no accident that the "remarkable" process of making sperm involves precisely what, in the medical view, menstruation does not:
production of something deemed valuable.[7]

---

[2]The textbooks I consulted are the main ones used in classes for undergraduate premedical students or medical students (or those held on reserve in the library for these classes) during the past
few years at Johns Hopkins University. These texts are widely used at other universities in the country as well.

[3]Arthur C. Guyton, *Physiology of the Human Body*, 6th ed. (Philadelphia: Saunders College
Publishing, 1984), 624.

[4]Arthur J. Vander, James H. Sherman, and Dorothy S. Luciano, *Human Physiology: The Mechanisms of Body Function*, 3d ed. (New York: McGraw Hill, 1980), 483–84.

[5]Vernon B. Mountcastle, *Medical Physiology*, 14th ed. (London: Mosby, 1980), 2:1624.

[6]Eldra Pearl Solomon, *Human Anatomy and Physiology* (New York: CBS College Publishing,
1983), 678.

[7]For elaboration, see Emily Martin, *The Woman in the Body: A Cultural Analysis of Reproduction* (Boston: Beacon, 1987), 27–53.

One could argue that menstruation and spermatogenesis are not analogous processes and, therefore, should not be expected to elicit the same kind of response. The proper female analogy to spermatogenesis, biologically, is ovulation. Yet ovulation does not merit enthusiasm in these texts either. Textbook descriptions stress that all of the ovarian follicles containing ova are already present at birth. Far from being *produced*, as sperm are, they merely sit on the shelf, slowly degenerating and aging like overstocked inventory: "At birth, normal human ovaries contain an estimated one million follicles [each], and no new ones appear after birth. Thus, in marked contrast to the male, the newborn female already has all the germ cells she will ever have. Only a few, perhaps 400, are destined to reach full maturity during her active productive life. All the others degenerate at some point in their development so that few, if any, remain by the time she reaches menopause at approximately 50 years of age."[8] Note the "marked contrast" that this description sets up between male and female: the male, who continuously produces fresh germ cells, and the female, who has stockpiled germ cells by birth and is faced with their degeneration.

Nor are the female organs spared such vivid descriptions. One scientist writes in a newspaper article that a woman's ovaries become old and worn out from ripening eggs every month, even though the woman herself is still relatively young: "When you look through a laparoscope . . . at an ovary that has been through hundreds of cycles, even in a superbly healthy American female, you see a scarred, battered organ."[9]

To avoid the negative connotations that some people associate with the female reproductive system, scientists could begin to describe male and female processes as homologous. They might credit females with "producing" mature ova one at a time, as they're needed each month, and describe males as having to face problems of degenerating germ cells. This degeneration would occur throughout life among spermatogonia, the undifferentiated germ cells in the testes that are the long-lived, dormant precursors of sperm.

But the texts have an almost dogged insistence on casting female processes in a negative light. The texts celebrate sperm production because it is continuous from puberty to senescence, while they portray egg production as inferior because it is finished at birth. This makes the female seem unproductive, but some texts will also insist that it is she who is wasteful.[10] In a section heading for *Molecular Biol-*

---

[8]Vander, Sherman, and Luciano, 568.

[9]Melvin Konner, "Childbearing and Age," *New York Times Magazine* (December 27, 1987), 22–23, esp. 22.

[10]I have found but one exception to the opinion that the female is wasteful: "Smallpox being the nasty disease it is, one might expect nature to have designed antibody molecules with combining sites that specifically recognize the epitopes on smallpox virus. Nature differs from technology, however: it thinks nothing of wastefulness. (For example, rather than improving the chance that a spermatozoon will meet an egg cell, nature finds it easier to produce millions of spermatozoa.)" (Niels Kaj Jerne, "The Immune System," *Scientific American* 229, no. 1 [July 1973]: 53). Thanks to a *Signs* reviewer for bringing this reference to my attention.

ogy of the Cell, a best-selling text, we are told that "Oogenesis is wasteful." The text goes on to emphasize that of the seven million oogonia, or egg germ cells, in the female embryo, most degenerate in the ovary. Of those that do go on to become oocytes, or eggs, many also degenerate, so that at birth only two million eggs remain in the ovaries. Degeneration continues throughout a woman's life: by puberty 300,000 eggs remain, and only a few are present by menopause. "During the 40 or so years of a woman's reproductive life, only 400 to 500 eggs will have been released," the authors write. "All the rest will have degenerated. It is still a mystery why so many eggs are formed only to die in the ovaries."[11]

The real mystery is why the male's vast production of sperm is not seen as wasteful.[12] Assuming that a man "produces" 100 million (10^8) sperm per day (a conservative estimate) during an average reproductive life of sixty years, he would produce well over two trillion sperm in his lifetime. Assuming that a woman "ripens" one egg per lunar month, or thirteen per year, over the course of her forty-year reproductive life, she would total five hundred eggs in her lifetime. But the word "waste" implies an excess, too much produced. Assuming two or three offspring, for every baby a woman produces, she wastes only around two hundred eggs. For every baby a man produces, he wastes more than one trillion (10^{12}) sperm.

How is it that positive images are denied to the bodies of women? A look at language—in this case, scientific language—provides the first clue. Take the egg and the sperm.[13] It is remarkable how "femininely" the egg behaves and how "masculinely" the sperm.[14] The egg is seen as large and passive.[15] It does

---

[11]Bruce Alberts et al., *Molecular Biology of the Cell* (New York: Garland, 1983), 795.

[12]In her essay "Have Only Men Evolved?" (in *Discovering Reality: Feminist Perspectives on Epistemology, Metaphysics, Methodology, and Philosophy of Science*, ed. Sandra Harding and Merrill B. Hintikka [Dordrecht, The Netherlands: Reidel, 1983], 45–69, esp. 60–61), Ruth Hubbard points out that sociobiologists have said the female invests more energy than the male in the production of her large gametes, claiming that this explains why the female provides parental care. Hubbard questions whether it "really takes more 'energy' to generate the one or relatively few eggs than the large excess of sperms required to achieve fertilization." For further critique of how the greater size of eggs is interpreted in sociobiology, see Donna Haraway, "Investment Strategies for the Evolving Portfolio of Primate Females," in *Body/Politics*, ed. Mary Jacobus, Evelyn Fox Keller, and Sally Shuttleworth (New York: Routledge, 1990), 155–56.

[13]The sources I used for this article provide compelling information on interactions among sperm. Lack of space prevents me from taking up this theme here, but the elements include competition, hierarchy, and sacrifice. For a newspaper report, see Malcolm W. Browne, "Some Thoughts on Self Sacrifice," *New York Times* (July 5, 1988), C6. For a literary rendition, see John Barth, "Night-Sea Journey," in his *Lost in the Funhouse* (Garden City, N.Y.: Doubleday, 1968), 3–13.

[14]See Carol Delaney, "The Meaning of Paternity and the Virgin Birth Debate," *Man* 21, no. 3 (September 1986): 494–513. She discusses the difference between this scientific view that women contribute genetic material to the fetus and the claim of long-standing Western folk theories that the origin and identity of the fetus comes from the male, as in the metaphor of planting a seed in soil.

[15]For a suggested direct link between human behavior and purportedly passive eggs and active sperm, see Erik H. Erikson, "Inner and Outer Space: Reflections on Womanhood," *Daedalus* 93, no. 2 (Spring 1964): 582–606, esp. 591.

not *move* or *journey*, but passively "is transported," "is swept,"[16] or even "drifts"[17] along the fallopian tube. In utter contrast, sperm are small, "streamlined,"[18] and invariably active. They "deliver" their genes to the egg, "activate the developmental program of the egg,"[19] and have a "velocity" that is often remarked upon.[20] Their tails are "strong" and efficiently powered.[21] Together with the forces of ejaculation, they can "propel the semen into the deepest recesses of the vagina."[22] For this they need "energy," "fuel,"[23] so that with a "whiplashlike motion and strong lurches"[24] they can "burrow through the egg coat"[25] and "penetrate" it.[26]

At its extreme, the age-old relationship of the egg and the sperm takes on a royal or religious patina. The egg coat, its protective barrier, is sometimes called its "vestments," a term usually reserved for sacred, religious dress. The egg is said to have a "corona,"[27] a crown, and to be accompanied by "attendant cells."[28] It is holy, set apart and above, the queen to the sperm's king. The egg is also passive, which means it must depend on sperm for rescue. Gerald Schatten and Helen Schatten liken the egg's role to that of Sleeping Beauty: "a dormant bride awaiting her mate's magic kiss, which instills the spirit that brings her to life."[29] Sperm, by contrast, have a "mission,"[30] which is to "move through the female genital tract in quest of the ovum."[31] One popular account has it that the sperm carry out a "perilous journey" into the "warm darkness," where some fall away "exhausted." "Survivors" "assault" the egg, the successful candidates "surrounding the prize."[32] Part of the urgency of this journey, in more scientific terms, is that "once released from the supportive environment of the ovary, an egg will die within hours unless rescued by a sperm."[33] The wording stresses the fragility and dependency of the egg, even though the same text acknowledges elsewhere that sperm also live for only a few hours.[34]

---

[16]Guyton (n. 3), 619; and Mountcastle (n. 5), 1609.

[17]Jonathan Miller and David Pelham, *The Facts of Life* (New York: Viking Penguin, 1984), 5.

[18]Alberts et al., 796.

[19]Ibid., 796.

[20]See, e.g., William F. Ganong, *Review of Medical Physiology*, 7th ed. (Los Altos, Calif.: Lange Medical Publications, 1975), 322.

[21]Alberts et al. (n. 11), 796.

[22]Guyton, 615.

[23]Solomon (n. 6), 683.

[24]Vander, Sherman, and Luciano (n. 4), 4th ed. (1985), 580.

[25]Alberts et al., 796.

[26]All biology texts quoted use the word "penetrate."

[27]Solomon, 700.

[28]A. Beldecos et al., "The Importance of Feminist Critique for Contemporary Cell Biology," *Hypatia* 3, no. 1 (Spring 1988): 61–76.

[29]Gerald Schatten and Helen Schatten, "The Energetic Egg," *Medical World News* 23 (January 23, 1984): 51–53, esp. 51.

[30]Alberts et al., 796.

[31]Guyton (n. 3), 613.

[32]Miller and Pelham (n. 17), 7.

[33]Alberts et al. (n. 11), 804.

[34]Ibid., 801.

In 1948, in a book remarkable for its early insights into these matters, Ruth Herschberger argued that female reproductive organs are seen as biologically interdependent, while male organs are viewed as autonomous, operating independently and in isolation:

> At present the functional is stressed only in connection with women: it is in them that ovaries, tubes, uterus, and vagina have endless interdependence. In the male, reproduction would seem to involve "organs" only.
>
> Yet the sperm, just as much as the egg, is dependent on a great many related processes. There are secretions which mitigate the urine in the urethra before ejaculation, to protect the sperm. There is the reflex shutting off of the bladder connection, the provision of prostatic secretions, and various types of muscular propulsion. The sperm is no more independent of its milieu than the egg, and yet from a wish that it were, biologists have lent their support to the notion that the human female, beginning with the egg, is congenitally more dependent than the male.[35]

Bringing out another aspect of the sperm's autonomy, an article in the journal *Cell* has the sperm making an "existential decision" to penetrate the egg: "Sperm are cells with a limited behavioral repertoire, one that is directed toward fertilizing eggs. To execute the decision to abandon the haploid state, sperm swim to an egg and there acquire the ability to effect membrane fusion."[36] Is this a corporate manager's version of the sperm's activities—"executing decisions" while fraught with dismay over difficult options that bring with them very high risk?

There is another way that sperm, despite their small size, can be made to loom in importance over the egg. In a collection of scientific papers, an electron micrograph of an enormous egg and tiny sperm is titled "A Portrait of the Sperm."[37] This is a little like showing a photo of a dog and calling it a picture of the fleas. Granted, microscopic sperm are harder to photograph than eggs, which are just large enough to see with the naked eye. But surely the use of the term "portrait," a word associated with the powerful and wealthy, is significant. Eggs have only micrographs or pictures, not portraits.

One depiction of sperm as weak and timid, instead of strong and powerful—the only such representation in western civilization, so far as I know—occurs in Woody Allen's movie *Everything You Always Wanted to Know about*

---

[35]Ruth Herschberger, *Adam's Rib* (New York: Pelligrini & Cudaby, 1948), esp. 84. I am indebted to Ruth Hubbard for telling me about Herschberger's work, although at a point when this paper was already in draft form.

[36]Bennett M. Shapiro. "The Existential Decision of a Sperm," *Cell* 49, no. 3 (May 1987): 293–94, esp. 293.

[37]Lennart Nilsson, "A Portrait of the Sperm," in *The Functional Anatomy of the Spermatozoan*, ed. Bjorn A. Afzelius (New York: Pergamon, 1975), 79–82.

Sex* *But Were Afraid to Ask. Allen, playing the part of an apprehensive sperm inside a man's testicles, is scared of the man's approaching orgasm. He is reluctant to launch himself into the darkness, afraid of contraceptive devices, afraid of winding up on the ceiling if the man masturbates.

The more common picture—egg as damsel in distress, shielded only by her sacred garments; sperm as heroic warrior to the rescue—cannot be proved to be dictated by the biology of these events. While the "facts" of biology may not *always* be constructed in cultural terms, I would argue that in this case they are. The degree of metaphorical content in these descriptions, the extent to which differences between egg and sperm are emphasized, and the parallels between cultural stereotypes of male and female behavior and the character of egg and sperm all point to this conclusion.

NEW RESEARCH, OLD IMAGERY

As new understandings of egg and sperm emerge, textbook gender imagery is being revised. But the new research, far from escaping the stereotypical representations of egg and sperm, simply replicates elements of textbook gender imagery in a different form. The persistence of this imagery calls to mind what Ludwik Fleck termed "the self-contained" nature of scientific thought. As he described it, "the interaction between what is already known, what remains to be learned, and those who are to apprehend it, go to ensure harmony within the system. But at the same time they also preserve the harmony of illusions, which is quite secure within the confines of a given thought style."[38] We need to understand the way in which the cultural content in scientific descriptions changes as biological discoveries unfold, and whether that cultural content is solidly entrenched or easily changed.

In all of the texts quoted above, sperm are described as penetrating the egg, and specific substances on a sperm's head are described as binding to the egg. Recently, this description of events was rewritten in a biophysics lab at Johns Hopkins University—transforming the egg from the passive to the active party.[39]

Prior to this research, it was thought that the zona, the inner vestments of the egg, formed an impenetrable barrier. Sperm overcame the barrier by mechanically burrowing through, thrashing their tails and slowly working their way along. Later research showed that the sperm released digestive enzymes that chemically broke down the zona; thus, scientists presumed that the sperm used mechanical *and* chemical means to get through to the egg.

---

[38]Ludwik Fleck, *Genesis and Development of a Scientific Fact*, ed. Thaddeus J. Trenn and Robert K. Merton (Chicago: University of Chicago Press, 1979), 38.

[39]Jay M. Baltz carried out the research I describe when he was a graduate student in the Thomas C. Jenkins Department of Biophysics at Johns Hopkins University.

In this recent investigation, the researchers began to ask questions about the mechanical force of the sperm's tail. (The lab's goal was to develop a contraceptive that worked topically on sperm.) They discovered, to their great surprise, that the forward thrust of sperm is extremely weak, which contradicts the assumption that sperm are forceful penetrators.[40] Rather than thrusting forward, the sperm's head was now seen to move mostly back and forth. The sideways motion of the sperm's tail makes the head move sideways with a force that is ten times stronger than its forward movement. So even if the overall force of the sperm were strong enough to mechanically break the zona, most of its force would be directed sideways rather than forward. In fact, its strongest tendency, by tenfold, is to escape by attempting to pry itself off the egg. Sperm, then, must be exceptionally efficient at *escaping* from any cell surface they contact. And the surface of the egg must be designed to trap the sperm and prevent their escape. Otherwise, few if any sperm would reach the egg.

The researchers at Johns Hopkins concluded that the sperm and egg stick together because of adhesive molecules on the surfaces of each. The egg traps the sperm and adheres to it so tightly that the sperm's head is forced to lie flat against the surface of the zona, a little bit, they told me, "like Br'er Rabbit getting more and more stuck to tar baby the more he wriggles." The trapped sperm continues to wiggle ineffectually side to side. The mechanical force of its tail is so weak that a sperm cannot break even one chemical bond. This is where the digestive enzymes released by the sperm come in. If they start to soften the zona just at the tip of the sperm and the sides remain stuck, then the weak, flailing sperm can get oriented in the right direction and make it through the zona—provided that its bonds to the zona dissolve as it moves in.

Although this new version of the saga of the egg and the sperm broke through cultural expectations, the researchers who made the discovery continued to write papers and abstracts as if the sperm were the active party who attacks, binds, penetrates, and enters the egg. The only difference was that sperm were now seen as performing these actions weakly.[41] Not until August 1987, more than three years after the findings described above, did these researchers reconceptualize the process to give the egg a more active role. They began to describe the zona as an aggressive sperm catcher, covered with adhesive molecules that can capture a sperm with a single bond and clasp it to the zona's sur-

[40]Far less is known about the physiology of sperm than comparable female substances, which some feminists claim is no accident. Greater scientific scrutiny of female reproduction has long enabled the burden of birth control to be placed on women. In this case, the researchers' discovery did not depend on development of any new technology. The experiments made use of glass pipettes, a manometer, and a simple microscope, all of which have been available for more than one hundred years.

[41]Jay Baltz and Richard A. Cone, "What Force Is Needed to Tether a Sperm?" (abstract for Society for the Study of Reproduction, 1985), and "Flagellar Torque on the Head Determines the Force Needed to Tether a Sperm" (abstract for Biophysical Society, 1986).

face.[42] In the words of their published account: "The innermost vestment, the *zona pellucida*, is a glyco-protein shell, which captures and tethers the sperm before they penetrate it.... The sperm is captured at the initial contact between the sperm tip and the *zona*.... Since the thrust [of the sperm] is much smaller than the force needed to break a single affinity bond, the first bond made upon the tip-first meeting of the sperm and *zona* can result in the capture of the sperm."[43]

Experiments in another lab reveal similar patterns of data interpretation. Gerald Schatten and Helen Schatten set out to show that, contrary to conventional wisdom, the "egg is not merely a large, yolk-filled sphere into which the sperm burrows to endow new life. Rather, recent research suggests the almost heretical view that sperm and egg are mutually active partners."[44] This sounds like a departure from the stereotypical textbook view, but further reading reveals Schatten and Schatten's conformity to the aggressive-sperm metaphor. They describe how "the sperm and egg first touch when, from the tip of the sperm's triangular head, a long, thin filament shoots out and harpoons the egg." Then we learn that "remarkably, the harpoon is not so much fired as assembled at great speed, molecule by molecule, from a pool of protein stored in a specialized region called the acrosome. The filament may grow as much as twenty times longer than the sperm head itself before its tip reaches the egg and sticks."[45] Why not call this "making a bridge" or "throwing out a line" rather than firing a harpoon? Harpoons pierce prey and injure or kill them, while this filament only sticks. And why not focus, as the Hopkins lab did, on the stickiness of the egg, rather than the stickiness of the sperm?[46] Later in the article, the Schattens replicate the common view of the sperm's perilous journey into the warm darkness of the vagina, this time for the purpose of explaining its journey into the egg itself: "[The sperm] still has an arduous journey ahead. It must penetrate farther into the egg's huge sphere of cytoplasm and somehow locate the nucleus, so that the two cells' chromosomes can fuse. The sperm dives down into the cytoplasm, its tail beating. But it is soon interrupted

---

[42]Jay M. Baltz, David F. Katz, and Richard A. Cone, "The Mechanics of the Sperm-Egg Interaction at the Zona Pellucida," *Biophysical Journal* 54, no. 4 (October 1988): 643–54. Lab members were somewhat familiar with work on metaphors in the biology of female reproduction. Richard Cone, who runs the lab, is my husband, and he talked with them about my earlier research on the subject from time to time. Even though my current research focuses on biological imagery and I heard about the lab's work from my husband every day, I myself did not recognize the role of imagery in the sperm research until many weeks after the period of research and writing I describe. Therefore, I assume that any awareness the lab members may have had about how underlying metaphor might be guiding this particular research was fairly inchoate.

[43]Ibid., 643, 650.

[44]Schatten and Schatten (n. 29), 51.

[45]Ibid., 52.

[46]Surprisingly, in an article intended for a general audience, the authors do not point out that these are sea urchin sperm and note that human sperm do not shoot out filaments at all.

by the sudden and swift migration of the egg nucleus, which rushes toward the sperm with a velocity triple that of the movement of chromosomes during cell division, crossing the entire egg in about a minute."[47]

Like Schatten and Schatten and the biophysicists at Johns Hopkins, another researcher has recently made discoveries that seem to point to a more interactive view of the relationship of egg and sperm. This work, which Paul Wassarman conducted on the sperm and eggs of mice, focuses on identifying the specific molecules in the egg coat (the zona pellucida) that are involved in egg-sperm interaction. At first glance, his descriptions seem to fit the model of an egalitarian relationship. Male and female gametes "recognize one another," and "interactions . . . take place between sperm and egg."[48] But the article in *Scientific American* in which those descriptions appear begins with a vignette that presages the dominant motif of their presentation: "It has been more than a century since Hermann Fol, a Swiss zoologist, peered into his microscope and became the first person to see a sperm penetrate an egg, fertilize it and form the first cell of a new embryo."[49] This portrayal of the sperm as the active party—the one that *penetrates* and *fertilizes* the egg and *produces* the embryo—is not cited as an example of an earlier, now outmoded view. In fact, the author reiterates the point later in the article: "Many sperm can bind to and penetrate the zona pellucida, or outer coat, of an unfertilized mouse egg, but only one sperm will eventually fuse with the thin plasma membrane surrounding the egg proper (*inner sphere*), fertilizing the egg and giving rise to a new embryo."[50]

The imagery of sperm as aggressor is particularly startling in this case: the main discovery being reported is isolation of a particular molecule *on the egg coat* that plays an important role in fertilization! Wassarman's choice of language sustains the picture. He calls the molecule that has been isolated, ZP3, a "sperm receptor." By allocating the passive, waiting role to the egg, Wassarman can continue to describe the sperm as the actor, the one that makes it all happen: "The basic process begins when many sperm first attach loosely and then bind tenaciously to receptors on the surface of the egg's thick outer coat, the zona pellucida. Each sperm, which has a large number of egg-binding proteins on its surface, binds to many sperm receptors on the egg. More specifically, a site on each of the egg-binding proteins fits a complementary site on a sperm receptor, much as a key fits a lock."[51] With the sperm designated as the "key" and the egg the "lock," it is obvious which one acts and which one is acted upon. Could this imagery not be reversed, letting the sperm (the lock) wait

---

[47]Schatten and Schatten, 53.
[48]Paul M. Wassarman, "Fertilization in Mammals," *Scientific American* 259, no. 6 (December 1988): 78–84, esp. 78, 84.
[49]Ibid., 78.
[50]Ibid., 79.
[51]Ibid., 78.

until the egg produces the key? Or could we speak of two halves of a locket matching, and regard the matching itself as the action that initiates the fertilization?

It is as if Wassarman were determined to make the egg the receiving partner. Usually in biological research, the *protein* member of the pair of binding molecules is called the receptor, and physically it has a pocket in it rather like a lock. As the diagrams that illustrate Wassarman's article show, the molecules on the sperm are proteins and have "pockets." The small, mobile molecules that fit into these pockets are called ligands. As shown in the diagrams, ZP3 on the egg is a polymer of "keys"; many small knobs stick out. Typically, molecules on the sperm would be called receptors and molecules on the egg would be called ligands. But Wassarman chose to name ZP3 on the egg the receptor and to create a new term, "the egg-binding protein," for the molecule on the sperm that otherwise would have been called the receptor.[52]

Wassarman does credit the egg coat with having more functions than those of a sperm receptor. While he notes that "the zona pellucida has at times been viewed by investigators as a nuisance, a barrier to sperm and hence an impediment to fertilization," his new research reveals that the egg coat "serves as a sophisticated biological security system that screens incoming sperm, selects only those compatible with fertilization and development, prepares sperm for fusion with the egg and later protects the resulting embryo from polyspermy [a lethal condition caused by fusion of more than one sperm with a single egg]."[53] Although this description gives the egg an active role, that role is drawn in stereotypically feminine terms. The egg *selects* an appropriate mate, *prepares* him for fusion, and then *protects* the resulting offspring from harm. This is courtship and mating behavior as seen through the eyes of a sociobiologist: woman as the hard-to-get prize, who, following union with the chosen one, becomes woman as servant and mother.

And Wassarman does not quit there. In a review article for *Science*, he outlines the "chronology of fertilization."[54] Near the end of the article are two subject headings. One is "Sperm Penetration," in which Wassarman describes how the chemical dissolving of the zona pellucida combines with the "substantial propulsive force generated by sperm." The next heading is "Sperm-Egg Fusion." This section details what happens inside the zona after a sperm "penetrates" it. Sperm "can make contact with, adhere to, and fuse with (that is, fertilize) an egg."[55] Wassarman's word choice, again, is astonishingly skewed in

---

[52]Since receptor molecules are relatively *immotile* and the ligands that bind to them relatively *motile*, one might imagine the egg being called the receptor and the sperm the ligand. But the molecules in question on egg and sperm are immotile molecules. It is the sperm as a *cell* that has motility, and the egg as a cell that has relative immotility.

[53]Wassarman, 78–79.

[54]Paul M. Wassarman, "The Biology and Chemistry of Fertilization," *Science* 235, no. 4788 (January 30, 1987): 553–60, esp. 554.

[55]Ibid., 557.

favor of the sperm's activity, for in the next breath he says that sperm *lose* all motility upon fusion with the egg's surface. In mouse and sea urchin eggs, the sperm enters at the *egg's* volition, according to Wassarman's description: "Once fused with egg plasma membrane [the surface of the egg], how does a sperm enter the egg? The surface of both mouse and sea urchin eggs is covered with thousands of plasma membrane-bound projections, called microvilli [tiny "hairs"]. Evidence in sea urchins suggests that, after membrane fusion, a group of elongated microvilli cluster tightly around and interdigitate over the sperm head. As these microvilli are resorbed, the sperm is drawn into the egg. There- fore, sperm motility, which ceases at the time of fusion in both sea urchins and mice, is not required for sperm entry."[56] The section called "Sperm Penetra- tion" more logically would be followed by a section called "The Egg En- velops," rather than "Sperm-Egg Fusion." This would give a parallel—and more accurate—sense that both the egg and the sperm initiate action.

Another way that Wassarman makes less of the egg's activity is by describing components of the egg but referring to the sperm as a whole entity. Deborah Gordon has described such an approach as "atomism" ("the part is indepen- dent of and primordial to the whole") and identified it as one of the "tenacious assumptions" of Western science and medicine.[57] Wassarman employs atom- ism to his advantage. When he refers to processing going on within sperm, he consistently returns to descriptions that remind us from whence these activities came: they are part of sperm that penetrate an egg or generate propulsive force. When he refers to processes going on within eggs, he stops there. As a result, any active role he grants them appears to be assigned to the parts of the egg, and not to the egg itself. In the quote above, it is the microvilli that actively cluster around the sperm. In another example, "the driving force for engulf- ment of a fused sperm comes from a region of cytoplasm just beneath an egg's plasma membrane."[58]

SOCIAL IMPLICATIONS: THINKING BEYOND

All three of these revisionist accounts of egg and sperm cannot seem to es- cape the hierarchical imagery of older accounts. Even though each new ac- count gives the egg a larger and more active role, taken together they bring into play another cultural stereotype: woman as a dangerous and aggressive threat. In the Johns Hopkins lab's revised model, the egg ends up as the female

---

[56]Ibid., 557–58. This finding throws into question Schatten and Schatten's description (n. 29 above) of the sperm, its tail beating, diving down into the egg.

[57]Deborah R. Gordon, "Tenacious Assumptions in Western Medicine," in *Biomedicine Exam- ined*, ed. Margaret Lock and Deborah Gordon (Dordrecht, The Netherlands: Kluwer, 1988), 19–56, esp. 26.

[58]Wassarman, "The Biology and Chemistry of Fertilization," 558.

aggressor who "captures and tethers" the sperm with her sticky zona, rather like a spider lying in wait in her web.[59] The Schatten lab has the egg's nucleus "interrupt" the sperm's dive with a "sudden and swift" rush by which she "clasps the sperm and guides its nucleus to the center."[60] Wassarman's description of the surface of the egg "covered with thousands of plasma membrane-bound projections, called microvilli" that reach out and clasp the sperm adds to the spiderlike imagery.[61]

These images grant the egg an active role but at the cost of appearing disturbingly aggressive. Images of woman as dangerous and aggressive, the femme fatale who victimizes men, are widespread in Western literature and culture.[62] More specific is the connection of spider imagery with the idea of an engulfing, devouring mother.[63] New data did not lead scientists to eliminate gender stereotypes in their descriptions of egg and sperm. Instead, scientists simply began to describe egg and sperm in different, but no less damaging, terms.

Can we envision a less stereotypical view? Biology itself provides another model that could be applied to the egg and the sperm. The cybernetic model—with its feedback loops, flexible adaptation to change, coordination of the parts within a whole, evolution over time, and changing response to the environment—is common in genetics, endocrinology, and ecology and has a growing influence in medicine in general.[64] This model has the potential to shift our imagery from the negative, in which the female reproductive system is castigated both for not producing eggs after birth and for producing (and thus wasting) too many eggs overall, to something more positive. The female reproductive system could be seen as responding to the environment (pregnancy or menopause), adjusting to monthly changes (menstruation), and flexibly changing from reproductivity after puberty to nonreproductivity later in life. The sperm and egg's interaction could also be described in cybernetic terms. J. F. Hartman's research in reproductive biology demonstrated fifteen years ago that if an egg is killed by being pricked with a needle, live sperm cannot get through the zona.[65] Clearly, this evidence shows that the egg and sperm *do* interact on more mutual terms, making biology's refusal to portray them that way all the more disturbing.

[59]Baltz, Katz, and Cone (n. 42 above), 643, 650.

[60]Schatten and Schatten, 53.

[61]Wassarman, "The Biology and Chemistry of Fertilization," 557.

[62]Mary Ellman, *Thinking about Women* (New York: Harcourt Brace Jovanovich, 1968), 140; Nina Auerbach, *Woman and the Demon* (Cambridge, Mass.: Harvard University Press, 1982), esp. 186.

[63]Kenneth Alan Adams, "Arachnophobia: Love American Style," *Journal of Psychoanalytic Anthropology* 4, no. 2 (1981): 157–97.

[64]William Ray Arney and Bernard Bergen, *Medicine and the Management of Living* (Chicago: University of Chicago Press, 1984).

[65]J. F. Hartman, R. B. Gwatkin, and C. F. Hutchison, "Early Contact Interactions between Mammalian Gametes In Vitro," *Proceedings of the National Academy of Sciences (U.S.)* 69, no. 10 (1972): 2767–69.

We would do well to be aware, however, that cybernetic imagery is hardly neutral. In the past, cybernetic models have played an important part in the imposition of social control. These models inherently provide a way of thinking about a "field" of interacting components. Once the field can be seen, it can become the object of new forms of knowledge, which in turn can allow new forms of social control to be exerted over the components of the field. During the 1950s, for example, medicine began to recognize the psychosocial *environment* of the patient: the patient's family and its psychodynamics. Professions such as social work began to focus on this new environment, and the resulting knowledge became one way to further control the patient. Patients began to be seen not as isolated, individual bodies, but as psychosocial entities located in an "ecological" system: management of "the patient's psychology was a new entrée to patient control."[66]

The models that biologists use to describe their data can have important social effects. During the nineteenth century, the social and natural sciences strongly influenced each other: the social ideas of Malthus about how to avoid the natural increase of the poor inspired Darwin's *Origin of Species*.[67] Once the *Origin* stood as a description of the natural world, complete with competition and market struggles, it could be reimported into social science as social Darwinism, in order to justify the social order of the time. What we are seeing now is similar: the importation of cultural ideas about passive females and heroic males into the "personalities" of gametes. This amounts to the "implanting of social imagery on representations of nature so as to lay a firm basis for reimporting exactly that same imagery as natural explanations of social phenomena."[68]

Further research would show us exactly what social effects are being wrought from the biological imagery of egg and sperm. At the very least, the imagery keeps alive some of the hoariest old stereotypes about weak damsels in distress and their strong male rescuers. That these stereotypes are now being written in at the level of the *cell* constitutes a powerful move to make them seem so natural as to be beyond alteration.

The stereotypical imagery might also encourage people to imagine that what results from the interaction of egg and sperm—a fertilized egg—is the result of deliberate "human" action at the cellular level. Whatever the intentions of the human couple, in this microscope "culture" a cellular "bride" (or femme fatale) and a cellular "groom" (her victim) make a cellular baby. Rosalind Petchesky points out that through visual representations such as sonograms, we are given "*images* of younger and younger, and tinier and tinier, fetuses being 'saved.'" This leads to "the point of viability being 'pushed back'

---

[66]Arney and Bergen, 68.
[67]Ruth Hubbard, "Have Only Men Evolved?" (n. 12 above), 51–52.
[68]David Harvey, personal communication, November 1989.

indefinitely."[69] Endowing egg and sperm with intentional action, a key aspect of personhood in our culture, lays the foundation for the point of viability being pushed back to the moment of fertilization. This will likely lead to greater acceptance of technological developments and new forms of scrutiny and manipulation, for the benefit of these inner "persons": court-ordered restrictions on a pregnant woman's activities in order to protect her fetus, fetal surgery, amniocentesis, and rescinding of abortion rights, to name but a few examples.[70]

Even if we succeed in substituting more egalitarian, interactive metaphors to describe the activities of egg and sperm, and manage to avoid the pitfalls of cybernetic models, we would still be guilty of endowing cellular entities with personhood. More crucial, then, than what *kinds* of personalities we bestow on cells is the very fact that we are doing it at all. This process could ultimately have the most disturbing social consequences.

One clear feminist challenge is to wake up sleeping metaphors in science, particularly those involved in descriptions of the egg and the sperm. Although the literary convention is to call such metaphors "dead," they are not so much dead as sleeping, hidden within the scientific content of texts—and all the more powerful for it.[71] Waking up such metaphors, by becoming aware of when we are projecting cultural imagery onto what we study, will improve our ability to investigate and understand nature. Waking up such metaphors, by becoming aware of their implications, will rob them of their power to naturalize our social conventions about gender.

QUESTIONS

1. Summarize Martin's argument. How has she structured it?

2. The first subhead of the essay is "Egg and Sperm: A Scientific Fairy Tale." The implications are that the actions of the egg and sperm constitute a story written by scientists. Why does Martin call it a fairy tale? What fairy tales does it resemble? In the process of your sexual education, what stories were you told?

3. Martin's argument raises the issue of scientific objectivity. Do you think there can be such a thing as a "pure" fact? Or can we only say that one fact is less encumbered by cultural baggage than another fact? What does Martin suggest as the best approach in presenting reproductive facts?

---

[69]Rosalind Petchesky, "Fetal Images: The Power of Visual Culture in the Politics of Reproduction," *Feminist Studies* 13, no. 2 (Summer 1987): 263–92, esp. 272.

[70]Rita Arditti, Renate Klein, and Shelley Minden, *Test-Tube Women* (London: Pandora, 1984); Ellen Goodman, "Whose Right to Life?" *Baltimore Sun* (November 17, 1987); Tamar Lewin, "Courts Acting to Force Care of the Unborn," *New York Times* (November 23, 1987), A1 and B10; Susan Irwin and Brigitte Jordan, "Knowledge, Practice, and Power: Court Ordered Cesarean Sections," *Medical Anthropology Quarterly* 1, no. 3 (September 1987): 319–34.

[71]Thanks to Elizabeth Fee and David Spain, who in February 1989 and April 1989, respectively, made points related to this.

4. Look at some biology textbooks. How is reproduction presented? Are the same or similar "sleeping metaphors" that Martin discusses present in the discussion? What about other bodily processes and functions? Is the male body used as the sole example in discussions of the heart, blood pressure, digestion, or AIDS, for instance?

5. Using the biological information in Martin's essay, write a nonsexist description of the reproductive functions. In your conclusion, reflect on any difficulties you encountered in keeping your cellular entities free of personhood. Switch papers with a classmate to check one another for "sleeping metaphors."

6. Look at a sampling of sex education texts and materials designed for elementary or secondary school students to see if the cultural stereotypes Martin warns against are present. What analogies and metaphors do you find being used? Write up your discussion as an argument either for or against the revision of those texts.

MAKING CONNECTIONS

1. Martin's research is an important addition to the argument and issues surrounding stereotyping of the sexes. How does her essay augment the argument in Margaret Atwood's "The Female Body" (p. 343)? What might a Madonna rock video version of a reproductive story be like?

2. Martin warns us to be on the alert for manipulative "sleeping metaphors." Carol Gilligan discusses the metaphors used by adolescent girls (p. 409), and James Jeans relies on analogy to tell his scientific story (p. 489). Are there "sleeping metaphors" lurking in other essays in this text?

WOMEN'S BRAINS
Stephen Jay Gould

*Stephen Jay Gould (b. 1941) is a professor of biology, geol-
ogy, and the history of science at Harvard University. He is
also a baseball fan and a prolific essayist. In 1974, he
began writing "This View of Life," a monthly column for*
Natural History, *where he has not only explained and defended Darwinian ideas of evolution, but also exposed
abuses and misunderstandings of scientific concepts and
methods. The latest of his many publications is* Questioning the Millennium: A Rationalist's Guide to Time and Its
Passage *(1997). The following essay appeared in* Natural
History *in 1992.*

In the prelude to *Middlemarch*, George Eliot lamented the unfulfilled lives
of talented women:

> Some have felt that these blundering lives are due to the inconvenient
> indefiniteness with which the Supreme Power has fashioned the na-
> tures of women: if there were one level of feminine incompetence as
> strict as the ability to count three and no more, the social lot of women
> might be treated with scientific certitude.

Eliot goes on to discount the idea of innate limitation, but while she wrote
in 1872, the leaders of European anthropometry were trying to measure "with
scientific certitude" the inferiority of women. Anthropometry, or measurement
of the human body, is not so fashionable a field these days, but it dominated
the human sciences for much of the nineteenth century and remained popular
until intelligence testing replaced skull measurement as a favored device for
making invidious comparisons among races, classes, and sexes. Craniometry, or
measurement of the skull, commanded the most attention and respect. Its unquestioned leader, Paul Broca (1824–80), professor of clinical surgery at the
Faculty of Medicine in Paris, gathered a school of disciples and imitators
around himself. Their work, so meticulous and apparently irrefutable, exerted
great influence and won high esteem as a jewel of nineteenth-century science.

Broca's work seemed particularly invulnerable to refutation. Had he not
measured with the most scrupulous care and accuracy? (Indeed, he had. I have
the greatest respect for Broca's meticulous procedure. His numbers are sound.
But science is an inferential exercise, not a catalog of facts. Numbers, by themselves, specify nothing. All depends upon what you do with them.) Broca depicted himself as an apostle of objectivity, a man who bowed before facts and

cast aside superstition and sentimentality. He declared that "there is no faith, however respectable, no interest, however legitimate, which must not accommodate itself to the progress of human knowledge and bend before truth." Women, like it or not, had smaller brains than men and, therefore, could not equal them in intelligence. This fact, Broca argued, may reinforce a common prejudice in male society, but it is also a scientific truth. L. Manouvrier, a black sheep in Broca's fold, rejected the inferiority of women and wrote with feeling about the burden imposed upon them by Broca's numbers:

> Women displayed their talents and their diplomas. They also invoked philosophical authorities. But they were opposed by *numbers* unknown to Condorcet[1] or to John Stuart Mill.[2] These numbers fell upon poor women like a sledge hammer, and they were accompanied by commentaries and sarcasms more ferocious than the most misogynist imprecations of certain church fathers. The theologians had asked if women had a soul. Several centuries later, some scientists were ready to refuse them a human intelligence.

Broca's argument rested upon two sets of data: the larger brains of men in modern societies, and a supposed increase in male superiority through time. His most extensive data came from autopsies performed personally in four Parisian hospitals. For 292 male brains, he calculated an average weight of 1,325 grams; 140 female brains averaged 1,144 grams for a difference of 181 grams, or 14 percent of the male weight. Broca understood, of course, that part of this difference could be attributed to the greater height of males. Yet he made no attempt to measure the effect of size alone and actually stated that it cannot account for the entire difference because we know, a priori, that women are not as intelligent as men (a premise that the data were supposed to test, not rest upon):

> We might ask if the small size of the female brain depends exclusively upon the small size of her body. Tiedemann has proposed this explanation. But we must not forget that women are, on the average, a little less intelligent than men, a difference which we should not exaggerate but which is, nonetheless, real. We are therefore permitted to suppose that the relatively small size of the female brain depends in part upon her physical inferiority and in part upon her intellectual inferiority.

In 1873, the year after Eliot published *Middlemarch*, Broca measured the cranial capacities of prehistoric skulls from L'Homme Mort cave. Here he found a difference of only 99.5 cubic centimeters between males and females, while modern populations range from 129.5 to 220.7. Topinard, Broca's chief

---

[1]*Marquis de Condorcet* (1743–1794): French mathematician and revolutionary. [Eds.]
[2]*John Stuart Mill* (1806–1873): British economist and philosopher. [Eds.]

disciple, explained the increasing discrepancy through time as a result of differing evolutionary pressures upon dominant men and passive women:

> The man who fights for two or more in the struggle for existence, who has all the responsibility and the cares of tomorrow, who is constantly active in combating the environment and human rivals, needs more brain than the woman whom he must protect and nourish, the sedentary woman, lacking any interior occupations, whose role is to raise children, love, and be passive.

In 1879, Gustave Le Bon, chief misogynist of Broca's school, used these data to publish what must be the most vicious attack upon women in modern scientific literature (no one can top Aristotle). I do not claim his views were representative of Broca's school, but they were published in France's most respected anthropological journal. Le Bon concluded:

> In the most intelligent races, as among the Parisians, there are a large number of women whose brains are closer in size to those of gorillas than to the most developed male brains. This inferiority is so obvious that no one can contest it for a moment; only its degree is worth discussion. All psychologists who have studied the intelligence of women, as well as poets and novelists, recognize today that they represent the most inferior forms of human evolution and that they are closer to children and savages than to an adult, civilized man. They excel in fickleness, inconstancy, absence of thought and logic, and incapacity to reason. Without doubt there exist some distinguished women, very superior to the average man, but they are as exceptional as the birth of any monstrosity, as, for example, of a gorilla with two heads; consequently, we may neglect them entirely.

Nor did Le Bon shrink from the social implications of his views. He was horrified by the proposal of some American reformers to grant women higher education on the same basis as men:

> A desire to give them the same education, and, as a consequence, to propose the same goals for them, is a dangerous chimera. . . . The day when, misunderstanding the inferior occupations which nature has given her, women leave the home and take part in our battles; on this day a social revolution will begin, and everything that maintains the sacred ties of the family will disappear.

Sound familiar?[3]

---

[3]When I wrote this essay, I assumed that Le Bon was a marginal, if colorful, figure. I have since learned that he was a leading scientist, one of the founders of social psychology, and best known for a seminal study on crowd behavior, still cited today (*La psychologie des foules*, 1895), and for his work on unconscious motivation.

I have reexamined Broca's data, the basis for all this derivative pronouncement, and I find his numbers sound but his interpretation ill-founded, to say the least. The data supporting his claim for increased difference through time can be easily dismissed. Broca based his contention on the samples from L'Homme Mort alone—only seven male and six female skulls in all. Never have so little data yielded such far ranging conclusions.

In 1988, Topinard published Broca's more extensive data on the Parisian hospitals. Since Broca recorded height and age as well as brain size, we may use modern statistics to remove their effect. Brain weight decreases with age, and Broca's women were, on average, considerably older than his men. Brain weight increases with height, and his average man was almost half a foot taller than his average woman. I used multiple regression, a technique that allowed me to assess simultaneously the influence of height and age upon brain size. In an analysis of the data for women, I found that, at average male height and age, a woman's brain would weigh 1,212 grams. Correction for height and age reduces Broca's measured difference of 181 grams by more than a third, to 113 grams.

I don't know what to make of this remaining difference because I cannot assess other factors known to influence brain size in a major way. Cause of death has an important effect: degenerative disease often entails a substantial diminution of brain size. (This effect is separate from the decrease attributed to age alone.) Eugene Schreider, also working with Broca's data, found that men killed in accidents had brains weighing, on average, 60 grams more than men dying of infectious diseases. The best modern data I can find (from American hospitals) records a full 100-gram difference between death by degenerative arteriosclerosis and by violence or accident. Since so many of Broca's subjects were elderly women, we may assume that lengthy degenerative disease was more common among them than among the men.

More importantly, modern students of brain size still have not agreed on a proper measure for eliminating the powerful effect of body size. Height is partly adequate, but men and women of the same height do not share the same body build. Weight is even worse than height, because most of its variation reflects nutrition rather than intrinsic size—fat versus skinny exerts little influence upon the brain. Manouvrier took up this subject in the 1880s and argued that muscular mass and force should be used. He tried to measure this elusive property in various ways and found a marked difference in favor of men, even in men and women of the same height. When he corrected for what he called "sexual mass," women actually came out slightly ahead in brain size.

Thus, the corrected 113-gram difference is surely too large; the true figure is probably close to zero and may as well favor women as men. And 113 grams, by the way, is exactly the average difference between a 5 foot 4 inch and a 6 foot 4 inch male in Broca's data. We would not (especially us short folks) want to ascribe greater intelligence to tall men. In short, who knows what to do with Broca's data? They certainly don't permit any confident claim that men have bigger brains than women.

To appreciate the social role of Broca and his school, we must recognize that his statements about the brains of women do not reflect an isolated prejudice toward a single disadvantaged group. They must be weighed in the context of a general theory that supported contemporary social distinctions as biologically ordained. Women, blacks, and poor people suffered the same disparagement, but women bore the brunt of Broca's argument because he had easier access to data on women's brains. Women were singularly denigrated but they also stood as surrogates for other disenfranchised groups. As one of Broca's disciples wrote in 1881: "Men of the black races have a brain scarcely heavier than that of white women." This juxtaposition extended into many other realms of anthropological argument, particularly to claims that, anatomically and emotionally, both women and blacks were like white children—and that white children, by the theory of recapitulation, represented an ancestral (primitive) adult stage of human evolution. I do not regard as empty rhetoric the claim that women's battles are for all of us.

Maria Montessori did not confine her activities to educational reform for young children. She lectured on anthropology for several years at the University of Rome, and wrote an influential book entitled *Pedagogical Anthropology* (English edition, 1913). Montessori was no egalitarian. She supported most of Broca's work and the theory of innate criminality proposed by her compatriot Cesare Lombroso. She measured the circumference of children's heads in her schools and inferred that the best prospects had bigger brains. But she had no use for Broca's conclusions about women. She discussed Manouvrier's work at length and made much of his tentative claim that women, after proper correction of the data, had slightly larger brains than men. Women, she concluded, were intellectually superior, but men had prevailed heretofore by dint of physical force. Since technology has abolished force as an instrument of power, the era of women may soon be upon us: "In such an epoch there will really be superior human beings, there will really be men strong in morality and in sentiment. Perhaps in this way the reign of women is approaching, when the enigma of her anthropological superiority will be deciphered. Woman was always the custodian of human sentiment, morality and honor."

This represents one possible antidote to "scientific" claims for the constitutional inferiority of certain groups. One may affirm the validity of biological distinctions but argue that the data have been misinterpreted by prejudiced men with a stake in the outcome, and that disadvantaged groups are truly superior. In recent years, Elaine Morgan has followed this strategy in her *Descent of Woman*, a speculative reconstruction of human prehistory from the woman's point of view—and as farcical as more famous tall tales by and for men.

I prefer another strategy. Montessori and Morgan followed Broca's philosophy to reach a more congenial conclusion. I would rather label the whole en-

15

721

terprise of setting a biological value upon groups for what it is: irrelevant and highly injurious. George Eliot well appreciated the special tragedy that biological labeling imposed upon members of disadvantaged groups. She expressed it for people like herself—women of extraordinary talent. I would apply it more widely—not only to those whose dreams are flouted but also to those who never realize that they may dream—but I cannot match her prose. In conclusion, then, the rest of Eliot's prelude to *Middlemarch*:

> The limits of variation are really much wider than anyone would imagine from the sameness of women's coiffure and the favorite love stories in prose and verse. Here and there a cygnet is reared uneasily among the ducklings in the brown pond, and never finds the living stream in fellowship with its own oary-footed kind. Here and there is born a Saint Theresa, foundress of nothing, whose loving heartbeats and sobs after an unattained goodness tremble off and are dispersed among hindrances instead of centering in some long-recognizable deed.

QUESTIONS

1. In paragraph 3, Gould claims, "Numbers, by themselves, specify nothing. All depends upon what you do with them." What exactly does Gould do with numbers?

2. How does Gould's use of numbers differ from what Broca and his followers did with numbers? Specifically, what distinguishes Gould's and Broca's methods of calculating and interpreting the facts about women's brains?

3. It might also be said, "Quotations, by themselves, specify nothing. All depends upon what you do with them." What does Gould do with quotations in this essay?

4. Why do you suppose Gould begins and ends his piece with passages by George Eliot?

5. Why does Gould quote so extensively from Broca and his followers, particularly from Le Bon? What purpose do all of these quotations serve in connection with the points that Gould is trying to make about women's brains and "biological labeling"?

6. Using Gould's essay as a model, write an essay on a subject with which you are familiar, showing how different ways of gathering, calculating, and interpreting numbers have produced significantly different understandings of the subject in question.

7. Write an essay on a subject with which you are familiar, showing how different ways of gathering, citing, and interpreting quotations have produced significantly different understandings of the subject in question.

MAKING CONNECTIONS

Compare the stereotyping of women's reproductive functions, as presented by Emily Martin in "The Egg and the Sperm" (p. 701), with the stereotyping Gould presents in this essay. What similarities do you find?

THE HISTORICAL STRUCTURE OF SCIENTIFIC DISCOVERY

Thomas Kuhn

Thomas Kuhn (1922–1996) was a professor of philosophy at the Massachusetts Institute of Technology. His best-known book is The Structure of Scientific Revolutions *(2nd edition, 1970). The following essay was abstracted, as his first note says, from its third chapter; the essay appeared originally in* Science *magazine in 1962. Other books of his include* The Essential Tension: Selected Studies in Scientific Tradition and Change *(1977) and* Black-Body Theory and the Quantum Discontinuity, 1894–1912 *(1978). He made the process of scientific investigation his special subject; historians and philosophers of science are his chief audience.*

My object in this article is to isolate and illuminate one small part of what I take to be a continuing historiographic revolution in the study of science.[1] The structure of scientific discovery is my particular topic, and I can best approach it by pointing out that the subject itself may well seem extraordinarily odd. Both scientists and, until quite recently, historians have ordinarily viewed discovery as the sort of event which, though it may have preconditions and surely has consequences, is itself without internal structure. Rather than being seen as a complex development extended both in space and time, discovering something has usually seemed to be a unitary event, one which, like seeing something, happens to an individual at a specifiable time and place.

This view of the nature of discovery has, I suspect, deep roots in the nature of the scientific community. One of the few historical elements recurrent in the textbooks from which the prospective scientist learns his field is the attribution of particular natural phenomena to the historical personages who first discovered them. As a result of this and other aspects of their training, discovery becomes for many scientists an important goal. To make a discovery is to achieve one of the closest approximations to a property right that the scientific career affords. Professional prestige is often closely associated with these acqui-

---

[1]The larger revolution will be discussed in my forthcoming book, *The Structure of Scientific Revolutions*, to be published in the fall by the University of Chicago Press. The central ideas in this paper have been abstracted from that source, particularly from its third chapter, "Anomaly and the Emergence of Scientific Discoveries" [2nd ed., 1970].

sitions.[2] Small wonder, then, that acrimonious disputes about priority and independence in discovery have often marred the normally placid tenor of scientific communication. Even less wonder that many historians of science have seen the individual discovery as an appropriate unit with which to measure scientific progress and have devoted much time and skill to determining what man made which discovery at what point in time. If the study of discovery has a surprise to offer, it is only that, despite the immense energy and ingenuity expended upon it, neither polemic nor painstaking scholarship has often succeeded in pinpointing the time and place at which a given discovery could properly be said to have "been made."

That failure, both of argument and of research, suggests the thesis that I now wish to develop. Many scientific discoveries, particularly the most interesting and important, are not the sort of event about which the questions "Where?" and, more particularly, "When?" can appropriately be asked. Even if all conceivable data were at hand, those questions would not regularly possess answers. That we are persistently driven to ask them nonetheless is symptomatic of a fundamental inappropriateness in our image of discovery. That inappropriateness is here my main concern, but I approach it by considering first the historical problem presented by the attempt to date and to place a major class of fundamental discoveries.

The troublesome class consists of those discoveries—including oxygen, the electric current, X rays, and the electron—which could not be predicted from accepted theory in advance and which therefore caught the assembled profession by surprise. That kind of discovery will shortly be my exclusive concern, but it will help first to note that there is another sort and one which presents very few of the same problems. Into this second class of discoveries fall the neutrino, radio waves, and the elements which filled empty places in the periodic table. The existence of all these objects had been predicted from theory before they were discovered, and the men who made the discoveries therefore knew from the start what to look for. That foreknowledge did not make their task less demanding or less interesting, but it did provide criteria which told them when their goal had been reached.[3] As a result, there have been few pri-

---

[2]For a brilliant discussion of these points, see R. K. Merton, "Priorities in Scientific Discovery: A Chapter in the Sociology of Science," *American Sociological Review* 22 (1957): 635. Also very relevant, though it did not appear until this article had been prepared, is F. Reif, "The Competitive World of the Pure Scientist," *Science* 134 (1961): 1957.

[3]Not all discoveries fall so neatly as the preceding into one or the other of my two classes. For example, Anderson's work on the positron was done in complete ignorance of Dirac's electron theory from which the new particle's existence had already been very nearly predicted. On the other hand, the immediately succeeding work by Blackett and Occhialini made full use of Dirac's theory and therefore exploited experiment more fully and constructed a more forceful case for the positron's existence than Anderson had been able to do. On this subject see N. R. Hanson, "Discovering the Positron," *British Journal for the Philosophy of Science* 12 (1961): 194; 12 (1962): 299. Hanson suggests several of the points developed here. I am much indebted to Professor Hanson for a preprint of this material.

ority debates over discoveries of this second sort, and only a paucity of data can prevent the historian from ascribing them to a particular time and place. Those facts help to isolate the difficulties we encounter as we return to the troublesome discoveries of the first class. In the cases that most concern us here there are no benchmarks to inform either the scientist or the historian when the job of discovery has been done.

As an illustration of this fundamental problem and its consequences, consider first the discovery of oxygen. Because it has repeatedly been studied, often with exemplary care and skill, that discovery is unlikely to offer any purely factual surprises. Therefore it is particularly well suited to clarify points of principle.[4] At least three scientists—Carl Scheele, Joseph Priestley, and Antoine Lavoisier[5]—have a legitimate claim to this discovery, and polemicists have occasionally entered the same claim for Pierre Bayen.[6] Scheele's work, though it was almost certainly completed before the relevant researches of Priestley and Lavoisier, was not made public until their work was well known.[7] Therefore it had no apparent causal role, and I shall simplify my story by omitting it.[8] Instead, I pick up the main route to the discovery of oxygen with the work of Bayen, who, sometime before March 1774, discovered that red precipitate of

5

---

[4]I have developed a less familiar example from the same viewpoint in "The Caloric Theory of Adiabatic Compression," *Isis* 49 (1958): 132. A closely similar analysis of the emergence of a new theory is included in the early pages of my essay "Energy Conservation as an Example of Simultaneous Discovery," in *Critical Problems in the History of Science*, ed. M. Clagett (Madison: University of Wisconsin Press, 1959), pp. 321–56. Reference to these papers may add depth and detail to the following discussion.

[5]*Carl Wilhelm Scheele* (1742–1786): Swedish chemist; *Joseph Priestley* (1733–1804): British chemist and clergyman; *Antoine-Laurent Lavoisier* (1743–1794): French chemist. *Pierre Bayen* (1725–1798), mentioned at the end of the sentence, was a French chemist. [Eds.]

[6]The still classic discussion of the discovery of oxygen is A. N. Meldrum, *The Eighteenth Century Revolution in Science: The First Phase* (Calcutta, 1930), chap. 5. A more convenient and generally quite reliable discussion is included in J. B. Conant, *The Overthrow of the Phlogiston Theory: The Chemical Revolution of 1775–1789*. Harvard Case Histories in Experimental Science, case 2 (Cambridge: Harvard University Press, 1950). A recent and indispensable review, which includes an account of the development of the priority controversy, is M. Daumas, *Lavoisier, théoricien et expérimentateur* (Paris, 1955), chaps. 2 and 3. H. Guerlac has added much significant detail to our knowledge of the early relations between Priestley and Lavoisier in his "Joseph Priestley's First Papers on Gases and Their Reception in France," *Journal of the History of Medicine* 12 (1957): 1 and in his very recent monograph, *Lavoisier: The Crucial Year* (Ithaca: Cornell University Press, 1961). For Scheele see J. R. Partington, *A Short History of Chemistry*, 2d ed. (London, 1951), pp. 104–9.

[7]For the dating of Scheele's work, see A. E. Nordenskjöld, *Carl Wilhelm Scheele, Nachgelassene Briefe und Aufzeichnungen* (Stockholm, 1892).

[8]U. Bocklund ("A Lost Letter from Scheele to Lavoisier," *Lychnos*, 1957–58, pp. 39–62) argues that Scheele communicated his discovery of oxygen to Lavoisier in a letter of 30 Sept. 1774. Certainly the letter is important, and it clearly demonstrates that Scheele was ahead of both Priestley and Lavoisier at the time it was written. But I think the letter is not quite so candid as Bocklund supposes, and I fail to see how Lavoisier could have drawn the discovery of oxygen from it. Scheele describes a procedure for reconstituting common air, not for producing a new gas, and that, as we shall see, is almost the same information that Lavoisier received from Priestley at about the same time. In any case, there is no evidence that Lavoisier performed the sort of experiment that Scheele suggested.

mercury (HgO) could, by heating, be made to yield a gas. That aeriform product Bayen identified as fixed air (CO_2), a substance made familiar to most pneumatic chemists by the earlier work of Joseph Black.[9] A variety of other substances were known to yield the same gas.

At the beginning of August 1774, a few months after Bayen's work had appeared, Joseph Priestley repeated the experiment, though probably independently. Priestley, however, observed that the gaseous product would support combustion and therefore changed the identification. For him the gas obtained on heating red precipitate was nitrous air (N_2O), a substance that he had himself discovered more than two years before.[10] Later in the same month Priestley made a trip to Paris and there informed Lavoisier of the new reaction. The latter repeated the experiment once more, both in November 1774 and in February 1775. But, because he used tests somewhat more elaborate than Priestley's, Lavoisier again changed the identification. For him, as of May 1775, the gas released by red precipitate was neither fixed air nor nitrous air. Instead, it was "[atmospheric] air itself entire without alteration . . . even to the point that . . . it comes out more pure."[11] Meanwhile, however, Priestley had also been at work, and, before the beginning of March 1775, he, too, had concluded that the gas must be "common air." Until this point all of the men who had produced a gas from red precipitate of mercury had identified it with some previously known species.[12]

The remainder of this story of discovery is briefly told. During March 1775 Priestley discovered that his gas was in several respects very much "better" than common air, and he therefore reidentified the gas once more, this time calling it "dephlogisticated air," that is, atmospheric air deprived of its normal complement of phlogiston.[13] This conclusion Priestley published in the *Philosophical Transactions*, and it was apparently that publication which led Lavoisier to reexamine his own results.[14] The reexamination began during February 1776 and within a year had led Lavoisier to the conclusion that the gas was actually a separable component of the atmospheric air which both he and Priestley had

---

[9]P. Bayen, "Essai d'expériences chymiques, faites sur quelques précipités de mercure, dans la vue de découvrir leur nature, Seconde partie," *Observations sur la physique* 3 (1774): 280–95, particularly pp. 289–91. (*Joseph Black* [1728–1799]: Scottish physician and chemist. [Eds.])

[10]J. B. Conant, *The Overthrow of the Phlogiston Theory*, pp. 34–40.

[11]Ibid., p. 23. A useful translation of the full text is available in Conant.

[12]For simplicity I use the term *red precipitate* throughout. Actually, Bayen used the precipitate: Priestley used both the precipitate and the oxide produced by direct calcination of mercury: and Lavoisier used only the latter. The difference is not without importance, for it was not unequivocally clear to chemists that the two substances were identical.

[13]*phlogiston*, a New Latin coinage from the Greek word for inflammable, naming a substance formerly thought to escape when a material burns. Though a faulty theory, its investigation contributed to the discovery of oxygen. [Eds.]

[14]There has been some doubt about Priestley's having influenced Lavoisier's thinking at this point, but, when the latter returned to experimenting with the gas in February 1776, he recorded in his notebooks that he had obtained "l'air dephlogistique de M. Priestley" (M. Daumas, *Lavoisier*, p. 36).

previously thought of as homogeneous. With this point reached, with the gas recognized as an irreducibly distinct species, we may conclude that the discovery of oxygen had been completed.

But to return to my initial question, when shall we say that oxygen was discovered and what criteria shall be used in answering that question? If discovering oxygen is simply holding an impure sample in one's hands, then the gas had been "discovered" in antiquity by the first man who ever bottled atmospheric air. Undoubtedly, for an experimental criterion, we must at least require a relatively pure sample like that obtained by Priestley in August 1774. But during 1774 Priestley was unaware that he had discovered anything except a new way to produce a relatively familiar species. Throughout that year his "discovery" is scarcely distinguishable from the one made earlier by Bayen, and neither case is quite distinct from that of the Reverend Stephen Hales, who had obtained the same gas more than forty years before.[15] Apparently to discover something one must also be aware of the discovery and know as well what it is that one has discovered.

But, that being the case, how much must one know? Had Priestley come close enough when he identified the gas as nitrous air? If not, was either he or Lavoisier significantly closer when he changed the identification to common air? And what are we to say about Priestley's next identification, the one made in March 1775? Dephlogisticated air is still not oxygen or even, for the phlogistic chemist, a quite unexpected sort of gas. Rather it is a particularly pure atmospheric air. Presumably, then, we wait for Lavoisier's work in 1776 and 1777, work which led him not merely to isolate the gas but to see what it was. Yet even that decision can be questioned, for in 1777 and to the end of his life Lavoisier insisted that oxygen was an atomic "principle of acidity" and that oxygen *gas* was formed only when that "principle" united with caloric, the matter of heat.[16] Shall we therefore say that oxygen had not yet been discovered in 1777? Some may be tempted to do so. But the principle of acidity was not banished from chemistry until after 1810 and caloric lingered on until the 1860s. Oxygen had, however, become a standard chemical substance long before either of those dates. Furthermore, what is perhaps the key point, it would probably have gained that status on the basis of Priestley's work alone without benefit of Lavoisier's still partial reinterpretation.

I conclude that we need a new vocabulary and new concepts for analyzing events like the discovery of oxygen. Though undoubtedly correct, the sentence "Oxygen was discovered" misleads by suggesting that discovering something is a single simple act unequivocally attributable, if only we knew enough, to an

10

---

[15]J. R. Partington, *A Short History of Chemistry*, p. 91. (*Reverend Stephen Hales* [1677–1761]: British botanist and physiologist. [Eds.])

[16]For the traditional elements in Lavoisier's interpretations of chemical reactions, see H. Metzger, *La philosophie de la matière chez Lavoisier* (Paris, 1935), and Daumas, *Lavoisier*, chap. 7.

individual and an instant in time. When the discovery is unexpected, however, the latter attribution is always impossible and the former often is as well. Ignoring Scheele, we can, for example, safely say that oxygen had not been discovered before 1774; probably we would also insist that it had been discovered by 1774; probably we would also insist that it had been discovered by 1777 or shortly thereafter. But within those limits any attempt to date the discovery or to attribute it to an individual must inevitably be arbitrary. Furthermore, it must be arbitrary just because discovering a new sort of phenomenon is necessarily a complex process which involves recognizing both *that* something is and *what* it is. Observation and conceptualization, fact and the assimilation of fact to theory, are inseparably linked in the discovery of scientific novelty. Inevitably, that process extends over time and may often involve a number of people. Only for discoveries in my second category—those whose nature is known in advance—can discovering *that* and discovering *what* occur together and in an instant.

Two last, simpler, and far briefer examples will simultaneously show how typical the case of oxygen is and also prepare the way for a somewhat more precise conclusion. On the night of 13 March 1781, the astronomer William Herschel made the following entry in his journal: "In the quartile near Zeta Tauri ... is a curious either nebulous star or perhaps a comet."[17] That entry is generally said to record the discovery of the planet Uranus, but it cannot quite have done that. Between 1690 and Herschel's observation in 1781 the same object had been seen and recorded at least seventeen times by men who took it to be a star. Herschel differed from them only in supposing that, because in his telescope it appeared especially large, it might actually be a *comet!* Two additional observations on 17 and 19 March confirmed that suspicion by showing that the object he had observed moved among the stars. As a result, astronomers throughout Europe were informed of the discovery, and the mathematicians among them began to compute the new comet's orbit. Only several months later, after all those attempts had repeatedly failed to square with observation, did the astronomer Lexell suggest that the object observed by Herschel might be a planet.[18] And only when additional computations, using a planet's rather than a comet's orbit, proved reconcilable with observation was that suggestion generally accepted. At what point during 1781 do we want to say that the planet Uranus was discovered? And are we entirely and unequivocally clear that it was Herschel rather than Lexell who discovered it?

Or consider still more briefly the story of the discovery of X rays, a story which opens on the day in 1895 when the physicist Roentgen interrupted a well-precedented investigation of cathode rays because he noticed that a bar-

---

[17]P. Doig, *A Concise History of Astronomy* (London: Chapman, 1950), pp. 115–16. (*William Herschel* [1738–1822]: German-born English astronomer. [Eds.])

[18]*Anders Johan Lexell* (1740–1784): Swedish astronomer. [Eds.]

ium platinocyanide screen far from his shielded apparatus glowed when the discharge was in process.[19] Additional investigations—they required seven hectic weeks during which Roentgen rarely left the laboratory—indicated that the cause of the glow traveled in straight lines from the cathode ray tube, that the radiation cast shadows, that it could not be deflected by a magnet, and much else besides. Before announcing his discovery Roentgen had convinced himself that his effect was not due to cathode rays themselves but to a new form of radiation with at least some similarity to light. Once again the question suggests itself: When shall we say that X rays were actually discovered? Not, in any case, at the first instant, when all that had been noted was a glowing screen. At least one other investigator had seen that glow and, to his subsequent chagrin, discovered nothing at all. Nor, it is almost as clear, can the moment of discovery be pushed back to a point during the last week of investigation. By that time Roentgen was exploring the properties of the new radiation he had *already* discovered. We may have to settle for the remark that X rays emerged in Würzburg between 8 November and 28 December 1895.

The characteristics shared by these examples are, I think, common to all the episodes by which unanticipated novelties become subjects for scientific attention. I therefore conclude these brief remarks by discussing three such common characteristics, ones which may help to provide a framework for the further study of the extended episodes we customarily call "discoveries."

In the first place, notice that all three of our discoveries—oxygen, Uranus, and X rays—began with the experimental or observational isolation of an anomaly, that is, with nature's failure to conform entirely to expectation. Notice, further, that the process by which that anomaly was educed displays simultaneously the apparently incompatible characteristics of the inevitable and the accidental. In the case of X rays, the anomalous glow which provided Roentgen's first clue was clearly the result of an accidental disposition of his apparatus. But by 1895 cathode rays were a normal subject for research all over Europe; that research quite regularly juxtaposed cathode-ray tubes with sensitive screens and films; as a result, Roentgen's accident was almost certain to occur elsewhere, as in fact it had. Those remarks, however, should make Roentgen's case look very much like those of Herschel and Priestley. Herschel first observed his oversized and thus anomalous star in the course of a prolonged survey of the northern heavens. That survey was, except for the magnification provided by Herschel's instruments, precisely of the sort that had repeatedly been carried through before and that had occasionally resulted in prior observations of Uranus. And Priestley, too—when he isolated the gas that behaved almost but not quite like nitrous air and then almost but not quite like common air—was seeing something unintended and wrong in the outcome of

---

[19]L. W. Taylor, *Physics, the Pioneer Science* (Boston: Houghton Mifflin Co., 1941), p. 790. (*Wilhelm Konrad Roentgen* [1845–1923]: German physicist. [Eds.])

a sort of experiment for which there was much European precedent and which had more than once before led to the production of the new gas.

These features suggest the existence of two normal requisites for the begin- [15] ning of an episode of discovery. The first, which throughout this paper I have largely taken for granted, is the individual skill, wit, or genius to recognize that something has gone wrong in ways that may prove consequential. Not any and every scientist would have noted that no unrecorded star should be so large, that the screen ought not to have glowed, that nitrous air should not have supported life. But that requisite presupposes another which is less frequently taken for granted. Whatever the level of genius available to observe them, anomalies do not emerge from the normal course of scientific research until both instruments and concepts have developed sufficiently to make their emergence likely and to make the anomaly which results recognizable as a violation of expectation.[20] To say that an unexpected discovery begins only when something goes wrong is to say that it begins only when scientists know well both how their instruments and how nature should behave. What distinguished Priestley, who saw an anomaly, from Hales, who did not, is largely the considerable articulation of pneumatic techniques and expectations that had come into being during the four decades which separate their two isolations of oxygen.[21] The very number of claimants indicates that after 1770 the discovery could not have been postponed for long.

The role of anomaly is the first of the characteristics shared by our three examples. A second can be considered more briefly, for it has provided the main theme for the body of my text. Though awareness of anomaly marks the beginning of a discovery, it marks only the beginning. What necessarily follows, if anything at all is to be discovered, is a more or less extended period during which the individual and often many members of his group struggle to make the anomaly lawlike. Invariably that period demands additional observation or experimentation as well as repeated cogitation. While it continues, scientists repeatedly revise their expectations, usually their instrumental standards, and sometimes their most fundamental theories as well. In this sense discoveries have a proper internal history as well as prehistory and a posthistory. Furthermore, within the rather vaguely delimited interval of internal history, there is no single moment or day which the historian, however complete his data, can identify as the point at which the discovery was made. Often, when several individuals are involved, it is even impossible unequivocally to identify any one of them as the discoverer.

---

[20] Though the point cannot be argued here, the conditions which make the emergence of anomaly likely and those which make anomaly recognizable are to a very great extent the same. That fact may help us understand the extraordinarily large amount of simultaneous discovery in the sciences.

[21] A useful sketch of the development of pneumatic chemistry is included in Partington, *A Short History of Chemistry*, chap. 6

Finally, turning to the third of these selected common characteristics, note briefly what happens as the period of discovery draws to a close. A full discussion of that question would require additional evidence and a separate paper, for I have had little to say about the aftermath of discovery in the body of my text. Nevertheless, the topic must not be entirely neglected, for it is in part a corollary of what has already been said.

Discoveries are often described as mere additions or increments to the growing stockpile of scientific knowledge, and that description has helped make the unit discovery seem a significant measure of progress. I suggest, however, that it is fully appropriate only to those discoveries which, like the elements that filled missing places in the periodic table, were anticipated and sought in advance and which therefore demanded no adjustment, adaptation, and assimilation from the profession. Though the sorts of discoveries we have here been examining are undoubtedly additions to scientific knowledge, they are also something more. In a sense that I can now develop only in part, they also react back upon what has previously been known, providing a new view of some previously familiar objects and simultaneously changing the way in which even some traditional parts of science are practiced. Those in whose area of special competence the new phenomenon falls often see both the world and their work differently as they emerge from the extended struggle with anomaly which constitutes the discovery of that phenomenon.

William Herschel, for example, when he increased by one the time-honored number of planetary bodies, taught astronomers to see new things when they looked at the familiar heavens even with instruments more traditional than his own. That change in the vision of astronomers must be a principal reason why, in the half century after the discovery of Uranus, twenty additional circumsolar bodies were added to the traditional seven.[22] A similar transformation is even clearer in the aftermath of Roentgen's work. In the first place, established techniques for cathode-ray research had to be changed, for scientists found they had failed to control a relevant variable. Those changes included both the redesign of old apparatus and revised ways of asking old questions. In addition, those scientists most concerned experienced the same transformation of vision that we have just noted in the aftermath of the discovery of Uranus. X rays were the first new sort of radiation discovered since infrared and ultraviolet at the beginning of the century. But within less than a

---

[22]R. Wolf, *Geschichte der Astronomie* (Munich, 1877), pp. 513–15, 683–93. The prephotographic discoveries of the asteroids [are] often seen as an effect of the invention of Bode's law. But that law cannot be the full explanation and may not even have played a large part. Piazzi's discovery of Ceres, in 1801, was made in ignorance of the current speculation about a missing planet in the "hole" between Mars and Jupiter. Instead, like Herschel, Piazzi was engaged on a star survey. More important, Bode's law was old by 1800 (ibid., p. 683), but only one man before that date seems to have thought it worthwhile to look for another planet. Finally, Bode's law, by itself, could only suggest the utility of looking for additional planets; it did not tell astronomers where to look. Clearly, however, the drive to look for additional planets dates from Herschel's work on Uranus.

decade after Roentgen's work, four more were disclosed by the new scientific sensitivity (for example, to fogged photographic plates) and by some of the new instrumental techniques that had resulted from Roentgen's work and its assimilation.[23]

Very often these transformations in the established techniques of scientific 20 practice prove even more important than the incremental knowledge provided by the discovery itself. That could at least be argued in the cases of Uranus and of X rays; in the case of my third example, oxygen, it is categorically clear. Like the work of Herschel and Roentgen, that of Priestley and Lavoisier taught scientists to view old situations in new ways. Therefore, as we might anticipate, oxygen was not the only new chemical species to be identified in the aftermath of their work. But, in the case of oxygen, the readjustments demanded by assimilation were so profound that they played an integral and essential role— though they were not by themselves the cause—in the gigantic upheaval of chemical theory and practice which has since been known as the chemical revolution. I do not suggest that every unanticipated discovery has consequences for science so deep and so far-reaching as those which followed the discovery of oxygen. But I do suggest that every such discovery demands, from those most concerned, the sorts of readjustment that, when they are more obvious, we equate with scientific revolution. It is, I believe, just because they demand readjustments like these that the process of discovery is necessarily and inevitably one that shows structure and that therefore extends in time.

QUESTIONS

1. State in your own words the principle Kuhn identifies at the end of paragraph 2.

2. Distinguish the two kinds of scientific discoveries Kuhn outlines in paragraphs 3 and 4. Which is the subject of this article?

3. Summarize the three characteristics of scientific discovery that Kuhn reviews in paragraphs 14 through 20.

4. Why does Kuhn spend so much more time on the discovery of oxygen than on the comet or X rays? Would that first example have been sufficient in itself? Do all three examples contribute substantially to "the characteristics of scientific discovery" that Kuhn goes on to outline?

5. If a single word were to distinguish the scientific discoveries that most interest Kuhn, that word might be *process* (as paragraph 10 suggests). Describe an event you know well—a class, a game, a meeting, an accident—as if it were a process rather than

---

[23]For α-, β-, and γ-radiation, discovery of which dates from 1896, see Taylor, *Physics*, pp. 800–804. For the fourth new form of radiation, N rays, see D. J. S. Price, *Science Since Babylon* (New Haven: Yale University Press, 1961), pp. 84–89. That N rays were ultimately the source of a scientific scandal does not make them less revealing of the scientific community's state of mind.

a single event. How does your description of that process allow you to understand the event in a way you had not understood it before?

6. Seen from one point of view, the papers you write are events. You hand them in when due and get them back, graded, later. But in another sense, they are part of a process, as well. Describe the process of the last paper you wrote. When did that process begin? What pattern did it take? What were the crucial moments, perhaps the turning points? And when can you say the process came to an end?

MAKING CONNECTIONS

The process of scientific discovery, with its three stages as reviewed by Kuhn in paragraphs 14 through 20, might apply to other developments in our lives. Consider, for example, the several articles in this collection that report, reflect on, and argue about the atom bomb: Zoë Tracy Hardy's "What Did You Do in the War, Grandma?" (p. 111) in "Reflecting"; William L. Laurence's "Atomic Bombing of Nagasaki Told by Flight Member" (p. 230) and John Hersey's "Hatsuyo Nakamura" (p. 181), both in "Reporting"; and John Berger's "Hiroshima" (p. 559) in this section. What kind of discovery is made in the course of those investigations? What are the stages of its process? When can you say a discovery was made? What was it? Do you agree with it? Do you foresee more stages of discovery to come?

A PROPOSAL TO DEVELOP MEANINGFUL LABELING FOR CIGARETTES

Jack E. Henningfield, Lynn T. Kozlowski, and Neal L. Benowitz

Jack E. Henningfield, Ph.D., is with the Clinical Pharmacology Branch, Addiction Research Center, National Institute on Drug Abuse, in Baltimore, Maryland. Lynn T. Kozlowski, Ph.D., is with the Program in Biobehavioral Health, College of Health and Human Development at Pennsylvania State University. Neal L. Benowitz, M.D., is with the Division of Clinical Pharmacology and Experimental Therapeutics and the Departments of Medicine and Psychiatry at the University of California—San Francisco. This article first appeared in the Journal of the American Medical Association.

Since the 1980s, tobacco researchers have understood that the advertised nicotine-yield ratings of cigarettes do not accurately predict nicotine intake by individual cigarette smokers.[1-5] Cigarette smokers obtain an average of 1 mg of nicotine from each cigarette they smoke, whether the nicotine yield is 0.1 mg or 2 mg.[4,6] However, smokers with whom we have spoken believe that their "light" or "ultralight" cigarettes are providing them with substantially lower doses of nicotine and other constituents of tobacco smoke. These smokers seem to assume that nicotine-yield ratings are equivalent to the content ratings provided on food products, and they are often distressed to learn that nicotine-yield ratings are not indicative of how much nicotine they can obtain.

We propose a new strategy for testing and labeling cigarettes that would provide consumers with improved information about how much nicotine they will absorb by smoking a particular brand of cigarette. Our proposal is roughly parallel to the approach of the Food and Drug Administration (FDA) for labeling food products with respect to constituents such as sodium and fat.[7]

PROBLEMS WITH THE PRESENT RATING SYSTEM

A variety of terms are commonly misused in discussions of nicotine ratings. Most fundamentally, cigarette nicotine *content* is confused with cigarette nicotine *yield*. The nicotine content is the total amount of nicotine present in the tobacco cigarette. Nicotine yields are derived from tests using smoking machines that were originally developed to provide standardized comparisons of the characteristics of tobacco smoke from different strains of tobacco.[8] Unfortunately, neither content nor yield ratings accurately predict how much nicotine the individual is likely to absorb from a cigarette.[2,4]

The present testing method entails inserting cigarettes into the ports of automated systems, which then draw in smoke according to a set of parameters generally referred to as the Federal Trade Commission method.[9,10] According to this method of determining yields, one 35-mL puff of 2 seconds' duration is taken every minute until a specified cigarette butt length is reached; if there is a filter overwrap, approximately 10% of the tobacco might be left unburned. However, people smoke more intensively than the smoking machines. For example, data accumulated from 18 studies indicate that on average, smokers take 43-mL puffs at 34-second intervals.[4] Furthermore, when faced with a nominally low-yield cigarette or when faced with limited availability of cigarettes (owing, for example, to smoking restrictions, restricted access to cigarettes, or economic constraints), people smoke cigarettes more intensively to consume an adequate level of nicotine.[4,5,11-13] For example, smokers may take more frequent or deeper puffs or block the ventilation holes with their fingers or lips.[1-5,14]

The discrepancy between cigarette yield ratings and how much nicotine people obtain from cigarettes is explained by the differences between the testing-machine method and how people actually smoke cigarettes. Cigarettes have been designed to reduce machine-testing yields by diluting the mainstream smoke via the use of porous paper and filter ventilation.[15,16] Additional design features include placing less tobacco in each cigarette by using expanded tobacco and/or smaller diameters of cigarettes, shortening the cigarette length, increasing the burn rate of the paper, and increasing the length of the filter overwrap so that the machine is able to take fewer puffs before the cigarette is burned to its specified length.[1-5] However, regardless of their machine-yield rating, all marketed tobacco cigarettes contain approximately 6 to 11 mg of nicotine and enable cigarette smokers to readily extract sufficient levels to produce and sustain dependence.[4,15,16]

PROPOSED NEW RATING AND LABELING SYSTEM

We propose a new system of rating and labeling cigarettes. The food-labeling regulations implemented by the FDA in 1994[7] could provide a model for this reformation. Our strategy is summarized in Table 1. An additional strategy that could be used to assist consumers in making informed decisions would be to fully disclose the tobacco smoke constituents of potential health significance, analogous to harmful constituent disclosure for foods.[7]

Our proposal involves categorizing cigarettes based on the amount of nicotine delivered (Table 2). These ratings would be included as part of a new label for cigarettes (Table 3). Developing meaningful categories for cigarettes is somewhat more complicated than for foods because a cigarette is a complex

Table 1. Strategies to Provide Meaningful Cigarette Labeling

- Use biologically meaningful categories that have plausible significance with respect to total daily nicotine intake and level of addiction.
- Develop machine-testing parameters based on data relevant to how people smoke and base yield ratings on maximal yields.
- Verify yield ratings with bioavailability testing of cigarette smokers to determine if humans can readily extract more nicotine than predicted by the machine tests.
- Limit the nicotine content of cigarettes in each category to limit maximal nicotine extraction and provide actual content values in the cigarette labeling.
- Link nicotine-rating categories to other factors of toxicological importance, eg, a low nicotine rating would only be permitted if there was also low tar and carbon monoxide deivery.
- Ban the use of terms such as "light" and "ultralight."

drug-delivery system,[5,17] but the principle is the same. We propose broad categories that should both serve consumer interests[18] and have plausible biological significance. The categories are based on nicotine delivery for two reasons. First, nicotine intake by smokers can be accurately measured. Second, nicotine delivery from cigarettes can be controlled to a maximum limit by controlling the nicotine content of the tobacco. It should be noted, however, that tar and other combustion products of cigarette smoke are believed to be the primary cause of human disease rather than nicotine per se. Unfortunately, it is more difficult to quantitate human tar exposure or to predict tar delivery based on the composition of the cigarette.

Accurate categorization of cigarettes based on their nicotine delivery would also be useful if cigarette manufacturers are ever required to gradually eliminate nicotine from their cigarettes. Cigarettes meeting our criteria of very low nicotine or no nicotine are unlikely to be generally addicting.[14]

We suggest that cigarette descriptors such as "ultralight" and "light" not be allowed. In terms of the food-labeling model introduced earlier, the FDA has limited use of these designations for foods where there is an adequate level of consensus as to the general meaning of the terms and a consensus that prod-

Table 2. Proposed New Nicotine-Delivery Categories for Cigarette Labeling, Based on Revised Machine-Testing Procedures and Validated by Bioavailability Testing

Cigarette Label	Maximum Nicotine Yield, mg
Nicotine free	0.01
Very low nicotine	0.17
Low nicotine	1.0
Regular	>1.0

Table 3. Content of the New Cigarette Label

- Warning statement
- Nicotine-yield category
- Nicotine, tar, and carbon monoxide yields (average and maximal)
- Nicotine content
- Harmful additives
- Information about factors affecting nicotine delivery

ucts so designated might actually represent generally healthier choices for consumers than the standard products.[7] A similar level of consensus would need to be developed with respect to cigarettes. This may not be possible because terms such as "light" provide connotations that may be interpreted as "beneficial," when, in fact, even exposure to the smoke of a few cigarettes per day has well-documented adverse health effects.[19]

In the reform of food labeling by the FDA, one of the basic issues addressed was to insist that estimates of intake be based on meaningful serving sizes and the number of typical servings taken per day.[7] To this end, machines used to provide estimates of nicotine yield should be programmed with puffing parameters that are representative of the behavior of cigarette smokers. We believe that the actual nicotine content of cigarettes should be included on the label, just as fat content is for food, but such information should not constitute the basis of nicotine-yield categorization. Nicotine content, while providing information on the maximal possible yield, is not reliably predictive of yield when cigarettes are smoked.[2]

Smoking-machine tests should be modified to include the testing of each cigarette under an average smoking condition as well as a heavy smoking condition; in this way, consumers could be informed of the usual and maximal yields of a particular cigarette. The average smoking condition would be a closer approximation to typical smoking than the model currently used. The machines would be programmed to continue puffing until all the consumable tobacco is smoked in filtered cigarettes and until the smallest plausible smokable butt length is reached in nonfiltered cigarettes (e.g., 10 mm).

For cigarettes in which ventilation holes are incorporated, if it is possible for vents to be blocked with the smoker's lips or fingers, then the vents would be occluded in the heavy smoking condition. Ventilation would be incorporated in the test condition only if the ventilation holes were (1) clearly visible, (2) far enough out (perhaps 15 mm) on the filter to discourage easy blocking by the smoker's lips, and (3) described on the package label with a warning to the smoker that blocking the holes would defeat the intent of the product and result in higher levels of exposure to nicotine and other tobacco smoke toxins. Labeling should similarly disclose the sources of nicotine yield variation (e.g., puff size and number) and advise how individuals might minimize their intake of nicotine per cigarette.

Cigarettes are, in essence, sophisticated drug-delivery systems,[5,7,15,17] and therefore nicotine bioavailability should be evaluated to verify that human absorption does not exceed levels predicted by the new delivery ratings. Bioavailability testing of smoked drugs is more complex than with conventional drug-delivery systems. The bioavailability of smoked drugs can be affected by parameters both within and outside the control of the user.[1,4,5] However, when factors are known to affect the bioavailability of a drug in a medication, such factors are often noted in labeling and similarly should be noted on cigarette package labels. Bioavailability could be estimated by measuring levels of nicotine, or its metabolite cotinine, in the blood, urine, or saliva of cigarette smokers.[4] Such testing would be important to determine whether alterations in cigarette design affect bioavailability in ways that could affect the categorization of the cigarette.

Although our proposal focuses on nicotine delivery, the model could be applied to other smoke constituents such as tar and carbon monoxide. A precedent for this exists in the reformation of food labeling by the FDA, in which special categories are permitted based primarily on the level of one constituent when another constituent also remains within certain boundaries. Thus, a product high in fat cannot be labeled "cholesterol free," regardless of its cholesterol level.[7] Similarly, we recommend that a cigarette be accorded one of the reduced-nicotine labels only if its tar and carbon monoxide yields are below certain levels. For example, the designation of a cigarette as low nicotine might require that the maximum bioavailability be less than 1 mg of nicotine, 5 mg of tar, and 5 mg of carbon monoxide. Of course, the tar content and carbon monoxide content of cigarettes are not meaningful concepts, because these substances are products of tobacco combustion. However, the ratio of tar or carbon monoxide yield to nicotine yield can be controlled by the design of cigarettes[16,17,20] and may also be useful to include on the label as information to consumers who wish to minimize their exposure to tar and carbon monoxide.

An implication of the present proposal is that few, if any, currently marketed tobacco cigarettes would meet the criteria for a designation other than "regular." To achieve a rating such as "low nicotine," the cigarette would need to be lower in nicotine content, and other design changes involving the use of filters and ventilation holes might be necessitated. It is possible that the proposed rating system would encourage the development of cigarettes useful in helping smokers to lessen their intake of nicotine and other constituents.

15

HEALTH BENEFITS

The enhanced labeling system should inform smokers that smoking cigarettes with reduced nicotine yield may facilitate their efforts to quit smoking but may provide little if any general health benefit compared with regular cigarettes. Ultimately, and of greater public health importance, the proposed labeling changes could lessen the prevalence of tobacco smoking. This could come about in several ways. Many consumers are already highly motivated to smoke cigarettes with lower nicotine yield for their presumed health benefits;[21] cigarettes currently labeled "lower yield" (less than 16 mg of tar) account for approximately 60% of the market.[18] If such misleading labeling is prohibited and replaced with an accurate depiction of nicotine yield, health-conscious smokers may be more motivated to attempt to quit. In addition, if manufacturers were to develop and market cigarettes reflecting a broad range of nicotine yields, these products might facilitate the efforts of motivated smokers to effect a gradual nicotine-weaning process. The major goal of improved labeling, however, would be to provide the basic information that can now be obtained with most other consumable products, including alcoholic beverages.

NOTES

1. Kozlowski LT. Tar and nicotine delivery: what a difference a puff makes. *JAMA.* 1981;245:158–159.

2. Benowitz NL, Hall SM, Herning RI, Jacob P III, Jones RT, Osman AL. Smokers of low-yield cigarettes do not consume less nicotine. *N Engl J Med.* 1983;309:139–142.

3. Kozlowski LT, Rickert W, Robinson J, Grunberg NE. Have tar and nicotine yields of cigarettes changed? *Science.* 1980;209:1550–1551.

4. *The Health Consequences of Smoking: Nicotine Addiction: A Report of the Surgeon General.* Washington, DC: US Dept of Health and Human Services; 1988. DHHS CDC publication 88-8406.

5. Henningfield JE. Behavioral pharmacology of cigarette smoking. In: Thompson T, Dews PB, Barrett JE, eds. *Advances in Behavioral Pharmacology.* Orlando, Fla: Academic Press; 1984;4:131–210.

6. Benowitz NL, Jacob P III. Daily intake of nicotine during cigarette smoking. *Clin Pharmacol Ther.* 1984;35:499–504.

7. US Dept of Health and Human Services, Food and Drug Administration. 21 CFR §1, et al. Food labeling; general provisions; nutrition labeling; label format; nutrient content claims; health claims; ingredient labeling; state and local requirements and exemptions; final rules. *Federal Register.* Washington, DC: US Government Printing Office; January 6, 1993;pt 4.

8. Kozlowski LT. Physical indicators of actual tar and nicotine yields of cigarettes. In: Grabowski J, Bell CS, eds. *Measurement in the Analysis and Treatment of Smoking Behavior.* Washington, DC: Dept of Health and Human Services; 1983:50–61. National Institute on Drug Abuse Research monograph 48; DHHS publication ADM83-1285.

9. *Tar, Nicotine, and Carbon Monoxide of the Smoke of 475 Varieties of Domestic Cigarettes.* Washington, DC: US Federal Trade Commission; 1991.

10. Pillsbury HC, Bright CC, O'Conner KJ, Irish FW. Tar and nicotine in cigarette smokers. *J Assoc Off Anal Chem.* 1969;52:458–462.

11. Kozlowski LT, Heatherton TF, Frecker RC, Nolte HE. Self-selected blocking of vents on low-yield cigarettes. *Pharmacol Biochem Behav.* 1989;33:815–819.

12. Benowitz NL, Jacob P III, Yu L, Talcott R, Hall S, Jones RT. Reduced tar, nicotine, and carbon monoxide exposure while smoking ultralow- but not low-yield cigarettes. *JAMA.* 1986;256:241–246.

13. Benowitz NL, Jacob P III, Kozlowski LT, Yu L. Influence of smoking fewer cigarettes on exposure to tar, nicotine and carbon monoxide. *N Engl J Med.* 1986;315: 1310–1313.

14. Kozlowski LT, Pope MA, Lux JE. Prevalence of the misuse of ultra-low-tar cigarettes by blocking filter vents. *Am J Public Health.* 1988;78:694–695.

15. Benowitz NL, Henningfield JE. Nicotine threshold for addiction: implications for tobacco regulation. *N Engl J Med.* In press.

16. *Hearings Before the Subcommittee on Health and the Environment of the US House of Representatives, 103rd Cong, 1st Sess* (March 25, 1994) (testimony of David A. Kessler, MD, JD, on behalf of the Food and Drug Administration).

17. Browne CL. *The Design of Cigarettes.* New York, NY: Hoechst Celanese Corp; 1990.

18. Shapiro E. FTC confronts 'healthier' cigarette ads. *Wall Street Journal.* April 21, 1994:B7.

19. *The Health Consequences of Involuntary Smoking: A Report of the Surgeon General.* Washington, DC: US Dept of Health and Human Services; 1986, DHHS CDC publication 87-8398.

20. Young JC, Robinson JC, Rickert WS. How good are the numbers for cigarette tar at predicting deliveries of carbon monoxide, hydrogen cyanide, and acrolein? *J Toxicol Environ Health.* 1981;7:801–808.

21. Cohen JB. Research and policy issues in Ringold and Calfee's treatment of cigarette health claims. *J Public Policy Marketing.* Spring 1992;11:82–86.

QUESTIONS

1. In describing cigarettes as "sophisticated drug-delivery systems" (paragraph 13), the writers might be accused of a lapse from scientific objectivity. What other assumptions about cigarette smoking lie behind this proposal?

2. The writers recommend banning the use of the terms *light* and *ultralight* for cigarettes. Why? What connotations do these terms have? Consider their use (and misuse) with respect to other consumer products.

3. What's wrong with the testing being done with smoking machines? Tobacco companies use them in their research, but the writers suggest that such testing has aided in developing cigarettes "designed to reduce machine-testing yields" (paragraph 5).

4. Take a poll of smokers you know. Ask them to tell you—without looking—what labeling is on the pack of cigarettes they smoke. Also ask whether they pay any attention to ratings of tar and nicotine or to health hazard warnings.

5. Do some research in news or medical journals on the labeling issue. Now that the Federal Drug Administration will be regulating tobacco, new information should be available.

MAKING CONNECTIONS

How would Jonathan Franzen (p. 675) respond to this proposal for more accurate, or "meaningful," labeling of cigarette packages? Do you think such labeling would be likely to deter him from smoking? What would you suggest as effective deterrent labeling?

Thomas Kuhn. "The Historical Structure of Scientific Discovery." From *Science*, vol. 136, June 1, 1962, pp. 760–764. Copyright © 1962 American Association for the Advancement of Science. Reprinted by permission.

William L. Laurence. "Atomic Bombing of Nagasaki Told by Flight Member." From *The New York Times*, September 9, 1945. Copyright © 1945 by The New York Times. Reprinted by permission.

William Least Heat-Moon. "Pancakes and Scripture Cake." From *Blue Highways* by William Least Heat-Moon. Copyright © 1982 by William Least Heat-Moon. By permission of Little, Brown & Company.

Robert J. Lifton. "What Made This Man? Mengele." From *The New York Times*, July 21, 1985. Copyright © 1985 by The New York Times Company. Adapted from *The Nazi Doctors* by Robert J. Lifton. Copyright © 1986 by Robert Jay Lifton. Reprinted by permission of Basic Books, a division of HarperCollins Publishers and The New York Times.

Emily Martin. "The Egg and the Sperm: How Science Has Constructed a Romance Based on Stereotypical Male-Female Roles." From *Signs: Journal of Women in Culture and Society*, vol. 16, no. 3, pp. 485–501. Copyright © 1991 The University of Chicago Press. Reprinted by permission of the publisher and the author.

Stanley Milgram. "Some Conditions of Obedience and Disobedience to Authority." From *Human Relations*, Vol. 18, No. 1, 1965, pp. 57–76. Copyright © 1972 by Stanley Milgram. Reprinted by permission. All rights controlled by Alexandra Milgram, Literary Executor.

N. Scott Momaday. "The Way to Rainy Mountain." From *The Way to Rainy Mountain*. Copyright © 1969 N. Scott Momaday. First published in *The Reporter*, January 26, 1967. Reprinted by permission of The University of New Mexico Press.

Monica M. Moore. "Nonverbal Courtship Patterns in Women: Context and Consequences." Previously published in *Ethology and Sociobiology*, Volume 6, #4, 1995 by Elsevier Science Publishing Co., Inc. Copyright © 1995 by Monica M. Moore. Reprinted by permission of the author.

Farley Mowat. "Observing Wolves." From *Never Cry Wolf* by Farley Mowat. Copyright © 1963 by Farley Mowat Limited. © renewed. By permission of Little, Brown and Company.

George Orwell. "Politics and the English Language," and "Shooting an Elephant." Reprinted from his volume *Shooting an Elephant and Other Stories*. Copyright © 1950 by Sonia Brownell Orwell and renewed 1978 by Sonia Pitt-Rivers. Copyright © Mark Hamilton as the literary executor of the estate of the late Sonia Brownell Orwell and Martin Secker & Warburg Limited. Reprinted by permission of Harcourt Brace & Company and A. M. Heath & Co., Ltd.

Oliver Sacks. "The Man Who Mistook His Wife for a Hat." Pages 8–22, from *The Man Who Mistook His Wife for a Hat* by Oliver Sacks. Copyright © 1970, 1981, 1983, 1984, 1985 by Oliver Sacks. Reprinted with permission of Simon & Schuster.

Carl Sagan. "Can We Know the Universe? Reflections on a Grain of Salt." From *Broca's Brain*. Copyright © 1979 by Carl Sagan. Reprinted by permission of the Estate of Carl Sagan.

Roy C. Selby Jr. "A Delicate Operation." Copyright © 1975 by *Harper's Magazine*. Reproduced from the December issue by special permission. All rights reserved.

Richard Selzer. "A Mask on the Face of Death." First published in *Life* magazine.

Rhetorical Index

749

POINT OF VIEW

PROCESS ANALYSIS

PURPOSE

REFLECTING

REPORTING

Author and Title Index